DATE DUE

APR 3 0 2002		
DEC 1 3 2005		

Demco, Inc. 38-293

An Index to Short and Feature Film Reviews in the *Moving Picture World*

THE
Moving Picture World
AND VIEW PHOTOGRAPHER

The only Independent Weekly Journal published in the interests of Manufacturers
and Operators of Animated Photographs and Cinematograph Projection,
Illustrated Songs, Lantern Lectures and Lantern Slide Makers

PUBLISHED BY

THE WORLD PHOTOGRAPHIC PUBLISHING COMPANY, 361 BROADWAY, NEW YORK

Vol. 1., No. 1.　　　　　March 9, 1907　　　　　Price, 5 Cents

This is the first number of this paper.
Do not miss its regular weekly visitations.
Send $2.00 for a year's subscription to-day.
Valuable articles every week and all the
news of the Lantern Lecture Field and
Moving Picture World.

A copy of the front cover of the first issue of the *Moving Picture World*, March 9, 1907.

An Index to Short and Feature Film Reviews in the *Moving Picture World*

The Early Years, 1907–1915

Compiled by
ANNETTE M. D'AGOSTINO

Bibliographies and Indexes in the Performing Arts,
Number 20

GREENWOOD PRESS
Westport, Connecticut • London

Library of Congress Cataloging-in-Publication Data

D'Agostino, Annette M.
    An index to short and feature film reviews in the moving picture
world : the early years, 1907–1915 / compiled by Annette M.
D'Agostino.
        p.   cm. — (Bibliographies and indexes in the performing arts,
ISSN 0742–6933 ; no. 20)
    Includes bibliographical references.
    ISBN 0–313–29381–3 (alk. paper)
    1. Moving picture world—Indexes.   2. Motion pictures—Reviews—
Indexes.   I. Moving picture world.   II. Title.   III. Series.
Z5784.M9D33   1995
[PN1995]
016.79143'75—dc20   95–9907

British Library Cataloguing in Publication Data is available.

Library of Congress Catalog Card Number: 95–9907
ISBN: 0–313–29381–3
ISSN: 0742–6933

First published in 1995

Greenwood Press, 88 Post Road West, Westport, CT 06881
An imprint of Greenwood Publishing Group, Inc.

Printed in the United States of America

The paper used in this book complies with the
Permanent Paper Standard issued by the National
Information Standards Organization (Z39.48–1984).

10 9 8 7 6 5 4 3 2 1

Dedicated
to the Vision and Memory
of the Founding Publisher of the
Moving Picture World
James Petrie Chalmers
(8 Feb 1866 - 27 Mar 1912)

CONTENTS

PREFACE

The *Moving Picture World* magazine began publication as a weekly journal on **March 9, 1907**, published by The World Photographic Publishing Company, 361 Broadway, New York. In 1909, branch offices were moved to 125 East 23 Street, in the Beach Building, in New York. As of November 25, 1912, offices were headquartered in the Pullman Building, 17 Madison Avenue, 7th Floor, New York. At the beginning, a year's subscription cost $2. In 1912, the distribution of the magazine was taken over by Chalmers Publishing Company of New York. (Just a bit of news from the time: the founding publisher of the *World,* James Petrie Chalmers, died on March 27, 1912, at the age of 46. At the time of his death, he was attending a convention in Dayton, Ohio: he tragically fell down an elevator shaft, thinking he was walking through sliding doors.) Through **December 31, 1927**, 89 volumes of the *Moving Picture World* provided varied information about the new medium of film: technical innovations, musical scores, exhibitor news, film synopses, and film reviews. This was one of the most widely used, and most popular, of the film trade publications, whose competitors included *Motion Picture News, Motography, The New York Dramatic Mirror,* and *Exhibitors Herald,* which merged with the *Moving Picture World* in 1928 to form *Exhibitors Herald and Moving Picture World*; its name was eventually condensed to *Exhibitors Herald World.*

This index is designed to assist the researcher in the location of reviews of films that were available for evaluation between **March 9, 1907** and **December 25, 1915**, (v.1-v.26), inclusive. Beginning with the **January 1, 1916** issue (n.1 of v.27), an "Index to Reviews, Comments and Stories of the Films" was provided for each volume; the magazine began indexing all reviews and synopses in alphabetical order. These indexes include all films reviewed or commented on during the time span of the volume. However, prior to 1916, there was no helpful guide to such reviews -- until now. This index does not include every film released between 1907 and 1915, for not every film released was necessarily reviewed. In addition, no text from the reviews is included, as this index is designed to encourage research through the *Moving Picture World:* it does not want to take away from the source. However, the index does provide the researcher with the opportunity to glean insight into contemporary thought regarding the early films, many of which have not survived, and cannot be reappraised. These reviews contain valuable information about the standards and tastes of film in its infancy, and shed light on story content in those early days. What was funny then may not be funny now. What was decidedly dramatic then, may *be* funny now...

A note on page numbering: pages ascended cumulatively within volumes. With the first issue of each new volume, the page numbering will revert to page 1; the first page of the second issue of each volume will build from the last page of the first issue, and will continue to build from there, until the end of the volume.

A note on the earliest citations: with the premiere **March 9, 1907** issue, commentary can be found under the heading "Film Reviews." With the **September 19, 1908** issue, this title was changed to "Stories of the Films." Beginning with the **October 3, 1908** issue, a new feature was headlined "Comments on Film Subjects." It is at this point that the "reviews" took on a new look. In the first year and a half, the content of each review was primarily a synopsis, with perhaps a paragraph of true review, as we know it. However, it was all we had. Starting with the October 3 issue, the commentary became pure evaluation, with very little story synopsis.

Consequently, beginning with the **January 2, 1909** issue (the beginning of v.4), citations no longer reflect those films listed under "Stories of the Films." Note that, at the beginning of each volume of the *Moving Picture World*, there is an index provided to the "Stories of the Films," which provide synopses to the valuable films of yesteryear. These indexes do not deal with reviews until 1916, thus the further need for this index.

OTHER CHANGES, AS THEY HAPPENED...

Beginning with the **April 17, 1909** issue, citations also include films reviewed under the title "Notable Films of the Week."

Beginning with the **July 17, 1909** issue, the heading of "Comments on Film Subjects" is changed to "Comments on the Week's Films."

Beginning with the **September 4, 1909** issue, citations also include films reviewed under the title "Coming Headliners."

Beginning with the **December 18, 1909** issue, citations also include films reviewed under the title "Coming Feature Films."

Beginning with the **March 26, 1910** issue, citations for "Independent Films" are listed separately from citations for "Licensed Films" under the heading "Comments on the Films" (note that, now, the word "Week's" is gone from the title, broadening the time span for review of released films).

Beginning the the **July 15, 1911** issue, citations also include films reviewed under the title "Reviews of Notable Films."

Beginning with the **September 2, 1911** issue, most reviews listed under "Comments on the Films" include the release date of the film.

Beginning with the **September 30, 1911** issue, citations also include films reviewed under the title "Superior Plays."

Beginning with the **January 6, 1912** issue, limited citations also include films noted in "Manufacturer's Advance Notes," but only when they are cross-referenced in "Comments on the Films." This is due to the fact that most of these Advance Notes are studio-generated announcements of coming films, and are pure synopsis, not reviews.

Beginning with the **September 6, 1913** issue, Licensed and Independent "Specials" are listed separately from the Licensed and Independent films within the "Comments on the Films."

Beginning with the **January 2, 1915** issue, the *Moving Picture World* begins printing the date of the issue on each page.

Beginning with the **April 3, 1915** issue, the "Comments on the Films" are listed separately by exchanges and manufacturing companies, with films and specials continuing to be separated. This individualizes the exchanges, and aids in identification of the large number of companies within companies. In addition, with this issue, citations also include films reviewed under the title "Reviews of Current Productions."

Beginning with **Volume 27** of the *Moving Picture World,* a new feature is added to ease in research: "Index to Reviews, Comments and Stories of the Films." Such indexes are now provided for each subsequent volume.

* * * * *

This index has been compiled alphabetically by **film title**, in a two-column format. The following is a sample entry with notes:

LONESOME LUKE (Pa)/Jun 12, 1915; p. 1778
(1)   *(2)*   *(3)*

(1)   **Title of film**. This is in ALL CAPS and **boldface** for ease in identification. These will appear alphabetically (except by The, A, and An). In many cases, film titles were used over and over by different companies: the name of such films will be listed once, with the individual companies and review citations following underneath (see **NEVER AGAIN** for a prolific example). Spelling of film titles will be corrected only when it is certain that the magazine entry is incorrectly spelled.

(2)   **Manufacturer/Distributor**. At this time, there were distribution companies that circulated films for independent production companies, and there were production companies that handled their own distribution. This classification is provided because the films reviewed in the *Moving Picture World* were identified by the name of the film, and the manufacturer. The key to the abbreviations of the manufacturer names can be found later in the Preface. The manufacturer code is set apart in parentheses. In many cases, there will be no such company listed: this reflects either films released anonymously, or films for which the manufacturer was not able to be located in the issue. The company name will always reflect the heading in the magazine, in order to keep ease of review location at a premium.

(3)   The **date of the issue** in which the review can be found, with the each month abbreviated by its first three letters (Jan, Feb, Mar, Apr, May, Jun, Jul, Aug, Sep, Oct, Nov, Dec). After the semi-colon is the **page location** of the review. In cases where the review wraps onto another page, it will be reflected either with a dash (pp 351-52), or a comma (pp 351, 353). Many films were reviewed more than once: the dates will be listed chronologically, separated by a slash (/). In some cases, the cited dates for a given film might be months, or as much as years, apart. This reflects the common practice of re-release of films. In the cases where it is impossible to guarantee that two reviewed films of the same name and distributor are, indeed, the same film re-issued, the two films will be listed separately, and chronologically.

Dates of Volumes of the *Moving Picture World*
For Reference With This Index

v. 1	Mar 9, 1907	-	Dec 28, 1907	v.14	Oct 5, 1912	-	Dec 28, 1912
v. 2	Jan 4, 1908	-	Jun 27, 1908	v.15	Jan 4, 1913	-	Mar 29, 1913
v. 3	Jul 4, 1908	-	Dec 26, 1908	v.16	Apr 5, 1913	-	Jun 28, 1913
v. 4	Jan 2, 1909	-	Jun 26, 1909	v.17	Jul 5, 1913	-	Sep 27, 1913
v. 5	Jul 3, 1909	-	Dec 31, 1909	v.18	Oct 4, 1913	-	Dec 27, 1913
v. 6	Jan 8, 1910	-	Jun 25, 1910	v.19	Jan 3, 1914	-	Mar 28, 1914
v. 7	Jul 2, 1910	-	Dec 31, 1910	v.20	Apr 4, 1914	-	Jun 27, 1914
v. 8	Jan 7, 1911	-	Jul 8, 1911	v.21	Jul 4, 1914	-	Sep 26, 1914
v. 9	Jul 15, 1911	-	Sep 30, 1911	v.22	Oct 3, 1914	-	Dec 26, 1914
v.10	Oct 7, 1911	-	Dec 30, 1911	v.23	Jan 2, 1915	-	Mar 27, 1915
v.11	Jan 6, 1912	-	Mar 30, 1912	v.24	Apr 3, 1915	-	Jun 26, 1915
v.12	Apr 6, 1912	-	Jun 29, 1912	v.25	Jul 3, 1915	-	Sep 25, 1915
v.13	Jul 6, 1912	-	Sep 28, 1912	v.26	Oct 2, 1915	-	Dec 25, 1915

* * * * *

Key to Distributor/Manufacturer Abbreviations

Aa	Alhambra/Associated Film Sales
AA	Anglo-American Film Corp.
Abo	Abo
AC	All-Celtic Film Co.
Aca	A.C.A.D./United Film Service
ACF	American Correspondence Film Co.
Act	Actophone
AKC	A.K.C.
Alb	Albuquerque Film Co.
Alc	Alco
AlD	Al Dia Feature Film Co.
All	Alliance Films Corp.
Am	American Film Mfg. Co.
Amb	Film Ambrosio
Amm	Ammex Film Co.
Ap	Apollo
Ape	Apex Film Co.
Aq	Aquila
Ar	Arrow Film Corp.
Arc	Arctic Film Co.
Ari	Arias Film Co.
AS	All Star Feature Corp.
Asc	Associated Film Sales Corp.
AsC	Associated Service
ASF	Austro-Serb Film Co.
At	Atlas Film Co.

Ata	Atlas/Associated Film Sales
Aur	Aurora Film Plays Corp.
Ayl	Aylesworth's Wild Life and Big Game Pictures
Ba	Banner/Associated Film Sales
Bal	Balboa Amusement Producing Co./Pathé
Be	Beauty Films/American
Bel	Belmont Feature Film Co.
BFF	Blaché Feature Film Co.
Bi	Bison
Bio	American Mutoscope & Biograph Co. (until Spring 1909); Biograph Co.
Bla	Blackstone Films
Bli	Albert Blinkhorn Feature Co.
Bos	Bosworth Co., Inc.
Box	Box Office Attraction Film Co.
Br	Broadway Film Co.
Bra	Brady/World Film Corp.
Bri	British-American Co. (Briam)
Bro	Broncho
Bsf	Broadway Star Features
Buc	F.M. Buckland
Bz	Blazon Film Co./Paramount
Cal	California Motion Picture Co.
Cam	Cameo/United Film Service

Can	Canadian Bioscope Co.	Elc	Electric
Cap	Capitol Films	Ele	Electragraff Co.
Cas	Casino	Elu	Exclusive Features Co.
Cen	Centaur Film Mfg. Co.	Emp	Empress/United Film Service
CGP	Compagnie Générale Pathé Cinématographique (C.G.P.C.)	Eq	Equitable Film Corp.
		Exc	Excelsior Co.
		Fa	Federal/Associated Film Sales
Ch	Champion Film Co.	FA	Film d'Art
Cha	Challenge	Fal	Falstaff
Chi	Children Photoplayers	FaP	Favorite Players Film Co.
Chn	Chandler	Fl	Features Ideal
Cin	Societa Italiana Cines; Cines Co.	FiA	Fine Arts Co.
CK	Celio/Celio-Kline	Fic	Fiction Pictures, Inc./Paramount
CKC	Continental Kunstfilm Co.	Fid	Fidelity Film Co.
Cla	Clarendon	FIT	Film Import & Trading Co.
Cli	Clipper Star Features	Fla	Flamingo Film Company
CM	Cricks & Martin	Fox	Fox Film Corp.
CMP	Colorado Motion Picture Co.	FP	Famous Players Co.
Co	Cosmofotofilm	Fr	Frontier Film Co.
Cob	Columbus	FRA	Film Releases of America Co.
Col	Columbia Film Co.	Fro	Frohman Amusement Co.
Com	Comet Co.	Gau	Gaumont Co.
CoM	Columbia/Metro Pictures Corp.	GB	Great Britain
Cor	Cort Film Corp.	Gem	Gem
Cos	Cosmos Film Co.	Gen	General Film Co.
CR	Carlo Rossi	GFP	Green's Feature Photoplays
Cre	Crescent Film Co.	GG	Gene Gauntier Feature Players
Cry	Crystal Film Co.	GK	George Kleine
Cub	Cub Comedies	Gl	Globe/Pathé
Cur	Curtis	GL	Good Luck Film Co.
Cy	Century Film Co.	Glo	Gloria American Film Co.
Da	Deer/Associated Film Sales	GN	Great Northern Co.
Dai	Daisy Feature Film Co.	Go	Goodfellow
DB	Dania Biofilm	Got	Gotham Film Co.
De	Defender Film Co.	Gov	Governor Boss Photoplay Co.
DeL	DeLuxe Attraction Film Co.	GP	Great Players Feature Film Corp.
Deu	Deutsche	GR	Gold Rooster Plays/Pathé
Dia	Diamond Film Co.	Gra	Grandin/United Film Service
Dil	Dilmars	Gri	D.W. Griffith Feature Film Co.
Dom	Domino Motion Picture Corp.	GS	Gold Seal
Dor	Dormet Film Co.	Ha	Hagy's Features
Dr	Dramascope	Har	Harstn & Co.
Dra	Dragon	HaW	Harris/World Film Corp.
Ea	Empire/Associated Film Sales	He	Hepworth Mfg. Co.
Ec	Eclair	Hec	Hecla Films
Ecl	Eclectic Film Co./Pathé	Hef	Hefco
Ed	Edison Film Mfg. Co.	Hel	Helen Gardner Co. (Helgar)
EFE	Exhibitor's Film Exchange	Hep	Hepwix
Eik	Eiko Film Co.	HLE	Holy Land Exhibition Co.

HUC	Hochstetter Utility Co.	Llo	Lloyds Films, Inc.
IA	Italian-American Film Corp.	Lon	London Film Co.
Id	Ideal/United Film Service	LP	Leading Players' Film Corp.
IFF	Interstate Feature Film Co.	Lu	Lubin Film Mfg. Co.
IFT	International Film Traders	Lun	Luna/United Film Service
Imp	Independent Moving Picture Co.	Lux	Lux Film Co.
Ind	Independent Film Co.	Ma	Monte/Associated Film Sales
InP	Industrial Moving Picture Co.	Mac	MacNamara Feature Film Co.,
ISP	I.S. Plaut Co.		Inc.
It	Itala Film Co.	Mag	Magnet Film Co.
Iv	Ivan Film Productions Co.	Maj	Majestic Motion Picture Co.
Jo	Joker Comedy Co.	Mao	Magneto Film Corp.
Ka	Kalem Film Mfg. Co.	Mar	Marion Leonard Films
Kai	Kaiser Film Co.	Mas	Masko Film Co.
KB	Kay-Bee	McE	James McEnnery Syndicate
Ke	United Keanograph Co.	Me	Méliès Co.
KE	Klaw & Erlanger/Biograph	Mec	Mecca Feature Film Co.
Kec	Katherine E. Carter, Inc.	Mel	Melee Society
KEd	Kleine-Edison Feature Service	Mes	Messter and Co.
Key	Keystone Film Co.	MES	Motherhood Educational Society
Ki	Kinograph	Met	Metropolitan
Kin	Kinemacolor	MFA	Manufacturers' Film Agency
Kio	Kineto	MFC	Masterpiece Film Co.
Kip	Kinetophote Corp.	Mi	Miles Bros.
Kis	Kismet Feature Film Co.	Mid	Midgar Features
Kni	Knickerbocker Star Features	Mil	Milano Films Co.
Ko	Komic Film Co.	Mir	Mirograph Corp.
KO	Kleine Optical Co.	MiR	Miller Brothers 101 Ranch
KR	K&R Film Co.	MnA	MinA Films
KrA	Alhambra/Kriterion	Moh	Mohawk Feature
KrC	C.K./Kriterion	Mom	Momus Producing Co.
Kri	Kriterion	Mon	Monopol Film Co.
KrM	Monty/Kriterion	Mor	Oliver Morosco Photoplay Co.
Krn	Nolege/Kriterion	Mos	B.S. Moss Corp.
KrN	Navajo/Kriterion	Mot	Motograff Co.
Krp	Punchinello/Kriterion	MP	Master Producers' Film Co.
KrP	Paragon/Kriterion	MPS	Motion Picture Specialty Corp.
KrS	Santa Barbara/Kriterion	Mto	Metro Pictures Corp.
Krt	Trump/Kriterion	Mus	Mustang
KrT	Thistle/Kriterion	Mut	Mutual Film Corp.
La	Liberty/Associated Film Sales	Na	Nafcor
Lae	Laemmle/Universal	NA	Navajo/Associated Film Sales
LaM	Lady Mackensie	NAm	North American Feature Film Co.
Lar	Lariat/United Film Service	Nas	Nash Moving Picture Co.
Las	Lasky Feature Play Co.	Ne	Nestor Co.
LeL	LeLion	Neu	Neutral Co.
LeP	Lewis Pennant	NFF	Nonpareil Feature Film Co.
LF	Life Photo Film Corp.	Nor	Nordisk Films
Lko	Lehrman-Knock Out (L-KO)	Nov	Novelty

NyC	New York Central Lines	Rol	B.A. Rolfe Photo-Play Co./Metro Pictures Corp.
NYM	New York Motion Picture Co.		
Oc	Ocean Film Corp.	RoU	Rollin/United Film Service
101	Bison 101/Universal	Roy	Royal
Oz	Oz Film Corp./Paramount	RR	Raleigh & Roberts
Pa	Pathé Frères/Pathé Exchange, Inc.	Ryn	Ryno
PA	Pan-American	SA	Essanay Film Mfg. Co.
Pal	Pallas Pictures	Sal	Sales Co.
Pan	Pantograph Co.	Sav	Savoia Film Co./Central Features
Par	Paramount Pictures Corp.	Saw	Sawyer Film Corp.
Pas	Pasquali Co.	SBa	Santa Barbara/Associated Film Sales
PD	Photo-Drama Motion Picture Co.		
PF	Panama Films/Pathé	SEF	Special Event Film Co.
PFP	Progressive Film Producers of America	Sel	Selig Film Mfg. Co.
		SFF	Superior Feature Film Co.
Phc	Photocolor/Pathé	Sha	Shamrock
Pho	Phoenix Co.	SHF	Sacred and Historic Film Co.
Phu	Phunphilms/Pathé	Shu	Shubert/World Film Corp.
Pi	Pilot Film Corp.	Sig	Signal Film Corp.
Pik	Pike's Peak/United Film Service	Sma	Smallwood/United Film Service
Pla	Playgoers Film Co.	Sol	Solax Co.
PMP	Penn Motion Picture Co.	Spp	Select Photoplay Producing Co.
Po	Powers Co.	St	Sterling Co.
Pop	Popular Plays and Players	Ste	Stellar Photoplay Co.
PP	Picture Playhouse Film Co.	StP	Starlight/Pathé
Pr	Princess Co.	StU	Starlight/United Film Service
Pre	Premier/United Film Service	Su	Supreme Features Corp.
Pri	Primagraph Co.	Sun	Sun Photoplay Co., Inc.
Pro	Prohibition Film Corp.	Sup	Superba/United Film Service
PSF	Puritan Special Feature Co.	Ter	Terriss Feature Film Co.
Pun	Punch Comedies	TFA	Triangle/Fine Arts
Py	Photoplay Co.	TFC	Tournament Film
Pyr	Pyramid/Kriterion	U	Big "U"/Universal
PyR	Photoplay Releasing Co.	UB	Universal-Bison
Qua	Quality/Metro Pictures Corp.	UBO	U.B.O. of N.Y.
QV	Quo Vadis Film Co.	UE	Urban-Eclipse/Eclipse
Ra	Ramona/Associated Film Sales	UF	Union Features Film Co.
Rad	Radios	UFC	Unique Film Co.
Ram	Ramo Features Inc.	Ufs	United Film Service
Ray	Ray/United Booking Offices	UI	Universal Ike
Re	Reliance Pictures	UnF	Universal Features
Reg	Regent/United Film Service	Uni	Universal Film Mfg. Co.
Rep	Republic Film Co.	Ur	Urbanore
Rev	Revier Motion Picture Co.	USF	U.S. Film Co.
Rex	Rex Co.	Th	Thanhouser Film Corp.
Ria	Rialto	Tif	Tiffany Corp.
RMF	Raising the Maine Film Co.	Tiu	Triumph Co./Equitable
Ro	Roma	TK	Triangle/Keystone
Rod	Rodeo/Mutual Film Corp.	TKB	Triangle/Kay-Bee

Tor	Toronto Moving Picture Machine	War	Warwick
	Operators' Local Union No.	Wat	Waterloo Film Co.
	173, I.A.T.S.E.	WBE	Williams, Brown & Earle
TP	Theophile Pathé	WBF	World's Best Film Co.
Tri	Triangle Film Corp.	WF	Warner's/Warner's Features
Tru	True Feature Co.	WFF	Western Feature Film Co.
Tur	Turner Films, Ltd.	Wil	Williamson
20C	20th Century Feature Film Co.	WL	World's Leader Features
Uy	University Film Co.	Wor	World Film Mfg. Co.
VF	Venus Feature Co.	Wre	Wrench
VFC	Victory Film Co./Pathé	Wrr	Warrick
Vi	Vitagraph Film Mfg. Co.	WS	World Special Films Corp.
Vic	Victor Film Co.	Ya	Yankee Film Co.
Vim	Vim		

* * * * *

A note on serials and continuing series: this index provides a single citation which represents the names of the numerous serials that followed cinema's first series, **WHAT HAPPENED TO MARY?** (Edison, 1912). After the name and manufacturer will follow the number of the episode reviewed, and its issue and page location. This will be the formula for all serials, for most were known by their balloon name, followed by a number. Some of the reviews provide a title for each individual episode; however, many do not, so these titles will not be delineated in this index -- only the general title, and the episode numbers. In addition, please note that not every episode of every serial was necessarily reviewed, thus many series will not have each number represented. In many of the reviews of these individual episodes of series and serials, the number of the episode was not mentioned: in these cases, verifications were made against the published release charts, which are found in the back of each issue of the *Moving Picture World* (as, it will be remembered, release dates for reviewed films started being provided within the reviews in September, 1911). All reviewed episodes will be listed in order of their release, not necessarily in the order of their review.

The serials and series will be listed by their proper title, and not the shortened form that was common in the *Moving Picture World* entries -- for example, the Edison series **THE ACTIVE LIFE OF DOLLY OF THE DAILIES** was often referred to as the "Dolly" series.

A few serials and series have characteristics that need clarification:

1. ZUDORA/THE 20 MILLION DOLLAR MYSTERY: This 20 part serial was known as **ZUDORA** for its first eleven (11) episodes, and the remaining nine assumed the title of **THE 20 MILLION DOLLAR MYSTERY.**
2. ELAINE: This 36 part serial was known as **THE EXPLOITS OF ELAINE** for its first fourteen (14) episodes; **THE NEW EXPLOITS OF ELAINE** for its next ten (10), and **THE ROMANCE OF ELAINE** for its final twelve (12) episodes.
3. Incomplete citations: As this index ends with the December 25, 1915 issue, there are a few series that are not fully represented, such as **GRAFT** (20 episodes), **THE GIRL AND THE GAME** (15 episodes), and the mother of them all, **THE HAZARDS OF HELEN** (119 episodes). All of the above mentioned serials, as well as all other such serials, end in 1916.

4. News pictorials and similar series: In the albeit infrequent case that an offering of a pictorial is listed within the "Comments on the Films" section, yet is accompanied by "Not yet seen by our reviewer," that episode will not be included in this index (for there is no review to access).

* * * * *

The *Moving Picture World* is available for purchase on microfilm through the Library of Congress Photo Duplication Service, Washington, D.C. 20540. The journal's "shelf number" is 02762, and purchase is on a per-reel basis. Price will be quoted. 59 reels cover the 89 volumes comprising 1907-1927.

* * * * *

There has long been a need for an index such as this, and it is hoped that this will be a helpful assistant in the furtherance of study in areas of silent cinema. This index, as well, will be a unique correspondent of popular culture and taste, both in terms of language and in contemporary happenings. Many of the titles of the films in this index will shock you; many will make you laugh, and many will amaze you by their brilliance. The films, their titles and their reviews are all part of a time that is gone, but not unworthy of remembrance. The importance of these reviews cannot be overstated: they remain our only link to many films of the early cinema, and are a key to understanding the origins of film study. In a sense, the criticism in these evaluations can be seen as a precursor to "Film 101." Actually, in some cases, it was on the basis of these reviews that theatres booked, or did not book, certain films. While the index will be extremely valuable for its purpose -- finding film reviews in the *Moving Picture World* from 1907-1915 -- it does not pretend to be a one-stop shopping source of data on cinema in its infancy. It is hoped that this index will complement the wealth of excellent resources available, and the researcher is encouraged to always **keep digging**. *Happy Hunting!*

ACKNOWLEDGMENTS

A project of this magnitude cannot be attempted without realizing a need: I needed this book, it had not been done already, and so I did it. However, such an index, its research and its typing, requires both fortitude and determination, both from within and from others. I would like to thank the following people for their valued opinions, suggestions and assistance: Rosemary C. Hanes and Brian Taves (Library of Congress, Motion Picture, Broadcasting and Recorded Sound Division), Kevin Brownlow (Photoplay Productions, Ltd.), Brigitte Kueppers (U.C.L.A. Arts Library, Special Collections), Lorraine Palmer and Domenica Barbuto (Hofstra University Library), Alan Gevinson (American Film Institute, Catalog Department), Leonard Maltin ("Entertainment Tonight"), the staff of the New York Public Library for the Performing Arts at Lincoln Center, and researchers Philip Liebfried and John Cocchi. A note of special thanks to Gene Vazzana (Editor, *The Silent Film Newsletter)* for his help in making sense of a most complex time in cinema. A very special thank you to James Robert Parish and Richard E. Braff for their guidance and example. A heartfelt thank you to Joe Franklin for his encouragement and belief in me. My unending gratitude to the entire staff of the Island Trees Public Library for their assistance in the researching endeavors. To my students at Hofstra University and South Side High School, thank you for continuing to inspire me daily. To my loving parents and family, God Bless You for your presence in my life. To my wonderful friends -- know that your support and patience mean the world to me: thanks ever so much for putting up with me. To my production editor, Emily Okenquist -- your "eye" and thoroughness are enviable. To my editor, Alicia Merritt -- your trust and your faith are most appreciated. To Harold Lloyd -- thank you for always being my finest inspiration. Finally, to the men and women whose pioneering cinematic efforts made the films in this index possible, I say thanks, and I'm hoping that research in the *Moving Picture World* will contribute to the preservation of your names, and your worthy art form. Here's hoping we never forget the many stars -- with names like Florence Lawrence, King Baggott, J. Warren Kerrigan, Kathlyn Williams, Arthur Johnson, and Mary Fuller -- who all did such wonderful work, and who are deserving of study and remembrance. I am so grateful to have had the opportunity to offer this index to film scholarship.

THE INDEX

A LA FRANCAISE
(CGP)/May 11, 1912; p. 528

ABACA, ITS CULTURE AND
USE IN THE PHILIPPINES
(CGP)/May 11, 1912; p. 528

ABALONE INDUSTRY, THE
(Key)/Oct 18, 1913; p. 265

ABANDONED WELL, THE
(Bio)/Jan 17, 1914; p. 288

ABBEY OF PAVIA, ITALY, THE
(UE)/Apr 29, 1911; p. 957

ABDUCTION OF PARSON JONES, THE
(Ya)/Mar 18, 1911; p. 604

ABDUCTION OF PINKIE, THE
(Sel)/Nov 1, 1913; p. 495

ABE GETS EVEN WITH FATHER
(Bio)/Dec 16, 1911; p. 904

ABERNATHY KIDS' RESCUE, THE
(Pa)/May 27, 1911; p. 1200

ABIDE WITH ME (Pa)/Mar 28, 1914; p.1680

ABOVE THE ABYSS (SA)/Jun 12, 1915; p.1777

ABOVE THE LAW (Lu)/Apr 11, 1914; p. 213

ABRAHAM LINCOLN'S CLEMENCY (Pa)/
Oct 29, 1910; p. 993/Nov 19, 1910;
pp 1176, 1178

ABRAHAM'S SACRIFICE
(CGP)/Apr 27, 1912; p. 328

ABSENT MINDED ARTHUR (Po)/Dec 3,
1910; p. 1299/Dec 10, 1910; p. 1359

ABSENT-MINDED BURGLAR, AN
(Bio)/Dec 14, 1912; p. 1080

ABSENT-MINDED CUPID, AN
(Ed)/Jul 17, 1909; p. 89
(Ed)/Sep 19, 1914; p. 1645

ABSENT MINDED DOCTOR, THE
(Ec)/Nov 5, 1910; p. 1060

ABSENT MINDED MOTHER, AN
(Ed)/Mar 21, 1914; p. 1524

ABSENT-MINDED MR. BOOB, THE
(Sel)/May 17, 1913; p. 704

ABSENT-MINDED VALET, THE
(Vi)/Dec 14, 1912; p. 1082

ABSENTEE, THE
(Maj)/May 15, 1915; pp 1090-91

ABSINTHE (Gem)/Jan 18, 1913; p. 265
(Uni)/Dec 20, 1913; p. 1391

ABUNDANT CANDLE, AN
(It)/Jan 27, 1912; p. 305

ABYSS, THE (Sel)/Dec 26, 1914; p. 1840

ACADEMY GIRL, THE
(Gau)/Aug 26, 1911; pp 541-42

ACADEMY ROMANCE, AN
(Po)/Feb 7, 1914; p. 678

ACADIAN ELOPEMENT, AN
(Bio)/Sep 14, 1907; p. 441

ACCIDENT, THE (Lux)/Jul 29, 1911; p. 212

ACCIDENT INSURANCE
(Cry)/Feb 15, 1913; p. 680

ACCIDENT POLICY, AN
(Lu)/Nov 27, 1915; p. 1663

ACCIDENTAL ALIBI, AN (Ed)/Apr 26,
1913; p. 361/May 24, 1913; p. 812

ACCIDENTAL BANDIT, THE
(SA)/Sep 6, 1913; p. 1067

ACCIDENTAL DENTIST, AN
(Lu)/Jan 25, 1913; p. 364

ACCIDENTAL MILLIONAIRE, AN
(Lu)/Nov 23, 1912; p. 767

ACCIDENTAL OUTLAW, AN
(Lu)/Aug 12, 1911; p. 377

ACCIDENTAL SERVANT, AN
(Ec)/Jan 18, 1913; p. 265

ACCIDENTAL SHOT, AN
(Pa)/Sep 27, 1913; p. 1391

ACCIDENTS WILL HAPPEN
(Ed)/May 28, 1910; p. 888
(Ka)/Feb 3, 1912; p. 393

ACCOMPLICE, THE
(Pa)/May 27, 1911; p. 1200
(Ka)/Jun 26, 1915; p. 2108

ACCOMPLISHED MRS. THOMPSON, THE
(Vi)/Jun 27, 1914; p. 1828

ACCORDING TO ADVICE
(Vi)/Mar 29, 1913; p. 1337

ACCORDING TO THEIR LIGHTS
(Ed)/Jun 12, 1915; p. 1777

ACCORDING TO VALUE
(Lae)/Jul 24, 1915; p. 651

ACCORDION, THE (KO)/Apr 18,1908;p.353

ACCUSATION, THE (Vic)/Dec 26,1914;p.1842

ACCUSATION OF BRONCHO BILLY, THE
(SA)/Apr 26, 1913; p. 381

ACCUSED (Ka)/Aug 1, 1914; p. 704

ACCUSER, THE (Pa)/Jul 11, 1908; p. 33

ACCUSING EYE, THE
(Pa)/May 16, 1914; p. 969

ACCUSING HAND, THE
(Lu)/Jun 21, 1913; p. 1253

ACCUSING PEN, THE
(Lu)/May 1, 1915; p. 727

ACCUSING VISION, THE
(KO)/May 9, 1908; p. 423

ACE OF CLUBS, THE
(Po)/Mar 27, 1915; p. 1933

ACE OF DEATH, THE
(Ria)/Dec 18, 1915; p. 2203

ACE OF DIAMONDS, THE
(Bio)/Sep 4, 1915; p. 1643

ACE OF HEARTS, THE
(Gau)/Aug 20, 1910; p. 406
(Dra)/Jun 21, 1913; p. 1255
(Dom)/Jul 10, 1915; p. 309

ACE OF SPADES, THE
(Sel)/Mar 16, 1912; p. 962

ACH LOUIE (StU)/Feb 6,1915;p.829

ACHING VOID, AN (Vi)/Apr 1, 1911; p. 718

ACID TEST, THE (Sel)/Aug 9, 1913; p. 636
        (Vi)/May 30, 1914; p.1261
        (Bal)/Feb 17, 1915; p.1290
ACRES OF ALFALFA
    (Key)/May 30, 1914; p. 1261
ACROBATIC EXERCISES BY CALIBRI'S
    DWARFS (Pa)/Feb 5, 1910; p. 169
ACROBATIC FLY, THE
    (UE)/Feb 26, 1910; p. 299
ACROBATIC MAID, THE (Pa)/Dec 12,
    1908; p. 476/Dec 26, 1908; p. 526
ACROSS RUSSIAN POLAND
    (Gau)/Aug 27, 1910; p. 463
ACROSS SWIFTCURRENT PASS
    (Ed)/Nov 8, 1913; p. 612
ACROSS THE ALLEY
    (Key)/Oct 18, 1913; p. 265
ACROSS THE ATLANTIC (Imp)/Jun 13,
    1914; p. 1542/Jun 20, 1914; p. 1668
ACROSS THE BORDER
    (Gau)/Apr 3, 1909; p. 403
    (WF)/Aug 15, 1914; p. 970
ACROSS THE BROAD PACIFIC
    (SA)/Oct 5, 1912; p. 41
ACROSS THE BURNING TRESTLE
    (Ed)/Jun 27, 1914;p.1803/Aug 1, 1914;p.704
ACROSS THE CAUCASUS
    (Ec)/Jul 27, 1912; p. 344
ACROSS THE CHASM
    (Pa)/Sep 27, 1913; p. 1391
ACROSS THE COURT
    (Jo)/Oct 17, 1914; p. 337
ACROSS THE DESERT
    (Sel)/Jun 5, 1915; p. 1604
ACROSS THE DIVIDE
    (Sel)/Oct 9, 1909; p. 489
    (Ne)/Sep 30, 1911; p. 974
ACROSS THE FOOTLIGHTS
    (U)/Jun 12, 1915; p. 1779
ACROSS THE GREAT DIVIDE
    (SA)/Mar 1, 1913; p. 887
    (Ed)/Sep 18, 1915; p. 1995
ACROSS THE ISTHMUS
    (Sel)/Nov 20, 1909; p. 720
ACROSS THE ISTHMUS IN 1912
    (Sel)/Mar 16, 1912; pp 952-53
ACROSS THE MEXICAN BORDER
    (Po)/Mar 11, 1911; p. 543
ACROSS THE MEXICAN LINE (Sol)/
    May 13, 1911; p. 1083/May 27, 1911; p.1201
ACROSS THE MOUNTAIN PASSES OF
    NEW ZEALAND (Pa)/Sep 9, 1911; p. 716
ACROSS THE PLAINS
    (Sel)/Mar 26, 1910; p. 466
    (SA)/Apr 15, 1911; p. 842
ACROSS THE POLAR SEAS
    (Pa)/Oct 14, 1911; p. 129
ACROSS THE RIO GRANDE

    (SA)/Jul 5, 1913; p. 49
ACROSS THE ROCKY MOUNTAINS IN
    THE SNOW (Sol)/Feb 3, 1912; p. 395
ACROSS THE SIERRAS
    (Ne)/Apr 6, 1912; p. 43
ACROSS THE VELDT
    (101)/Apr 4, 1914; p. 74
ACROSS THE WAY (Pr)/Feb 20, 1915; p. 1140
ACTIVE LIFE OF DOLLY OF THE
    DAILIES, THE (Ed)
    No.1/Feb 14, 1914; p. 808
    No.2/Mar 14, 1914; p. 1384
    No.3/Mar 28, 1914; p. 1680
    No.4/Apr 11, 1914; p. 212
    No.5/Apr 25, 1914; p. 517
    No.6/May 9, 1914; p. 820
    No.7/May 23, 1914; p. 1116
    No.8/Jun 6, 1914; p. 1409
    No.9/Jun 27, 1914; p. 1828
    No.10/Jul 11, 1914; p. 255
    No.11/Jul 25, 1914; p. 571
    No.12/Aug 8, 1914; p. 836
ACTOR, THE (Rex)/Jul 26, 1913; p. 430
ACTOR AND THE RUBE, THE
    (Fal)/Apr 24, 1915; p. 556
ACTOR AS A SOLDIER, THE
    (GN)/Nov 11, 1911; p. 473
ACTOR BOOK AGENT, THE
    (Ko)/Dec 13, 1913; p. 1280
ACTOR FINNEY'S FINISH
    (SA)/Jun 6, 1914; p. 1408
ACTOR IN A NEW ROLE, AN
    (Lu)/Dec 16, 1911; p. 903
ACTORS' BOARDING HOUSE, THE
    (Lu)/Jun 19, 1915; p. 1939
ACTOR'S CHILD, THE (Sel)/Nov 7, 1908;
    pp 358, 367-68/Nov 14, 1908; p. 379
ACTOR'S CHILDREN, THE (Th)/Mar 19,
    1910; p. 427/Mar 26, 1910; p. 468
ACTOR'S CHRISTMAS, THE
    (Imp)/Jan 10, 1914; p. 173
ACTORS FROM THE JUNGLE
    (Vic)/Nov 13, 1915; p. 1313
ACTOR'S FUND FAIR (Vi)/Oct 22,1910;p.938
ACTOR'S MOTHER, THE
    (Gau)/May 22, 1909; p. 671
ACTOR'S ROMANCE, AN
    (Sel)/Dec 6, 1913; p. 1150
ACTOR'S STRATEGY, THE
    (Lu)/Aug 2, 1913; pp 536-37
ACTRESS, THE (Po)/Apr 23, 1910; p. 642
        (Maj)/Dec 16, 1911; p. 886
        (Rex)/Jan 18, 1913; p. 265
        (Ed)/Jan 3, 1914; p. 48
        (Po)/Sep 26, 1914; p. 1777
ACTRESS AND CHILD
    (Pho)/Nov 20, 1909; p. 722
ACTRESS AND HER JEWELS, THE

ALIEN, THE (Ka)/May 24, 1913; p. 811
            (KB)/Jun 12, 1915; p. 1789
ALIXE (Vi)/Apr 19, 1913; p. 279
"ALKALI" BESTS BRONCHO BILLY
   (SA)/Apr 6, 1912; p. 42
ALKALI IKE AND THE HYPNOTIST
   (SA)/Jul 5, 1913; p. 48
ALKALI IKE AND THE WILDMAN
   (SA)/Nov 1, 1913; p. 496
ALKALI IKE IN JAYVILLE
   (SA)/Jan 25, 1913; p. 363
ALKALI IKE PLAYS THE DEVIL (Ed)/
   Aug 24, 1912; pp 754-55/Sep 7, 1912; p. 976
ALKALI IKE STUNG
   (SA)/Oct 19, 1912; p. 243
ALKALI IKE'S AUTO (SA)/Jun 3, 1911; p.
   1259/Jun 17,1911;p.1362/Nov 29,1913;p.1007
ALKALI IKE'S BOARDING HOUSE
   (SA)/May 4, 1912; p. 427
ALKALI IKE'S CLOSE SHAVE
   (SA)/Nov 30, 1912; p. 877
ALKALI IKE'S GAL (SA)/Aug 30, 1913; p.960
ALKALI IKE'S HOMECOMING
   (SA)/May 3, 1913; p. 487
ALKALI IKE'S LOVE AFFAIR
   (SA)/Feb 17, 1912; 582
ALKALI IKE'S MISFORTUNES (SA)/
   May 24, 1913; p. 800/Jun 14, 1913; p. 1136
ALKALI IKE'S MOTHER-IN-LAW
   (SA)/May 24, 1913; p. 813
ALKALI IKE'S PANTS
   (SA)/Oct 5, 1912; p. 40
ALL A MISTAKE (Imp)/Feb 10, 1912; p. 482
ALL ABOARD (Ne)/Feb 13, 1915; p. 986
            (Th)/Nov 27, 1915; p. 1664
ALL ABOARD FOR RENO
   (Sol)/Aug 5, 1911; p. 294
ALL ABOUT A BABY
   (Sup)/May 22, 1915; p. 1261
ALL ALONE (Re)/Jul 1, 1911;p.1521
ALL-AROUND MISTAKE, AN
   (Imp)/Oct 9, 1915; p. 254
ALL AT SEA (Ne)/Aug 8, 1914; p. 838
            (Key)/Sep 19, 1914; p. 1646
            (WF)/Dec 5, 1914; p. 1386
ALL COOKED UP (Ed)/Jun 12, 1915; p. 1776
ALL FOR A BIG ORDER
   (Imp)/Jul 1, 1911; p. 1522
ALL FOR A BIRD (Pa)/May 23, 1908;
   p. 464/May 1, 1909; p. 554
ALL FOR A GIRL (Vi)/Dec 28, 1912; p. 1292
            (Mir)/Jul 10, 1915; p. 318
ALL FOR A NICKEL (Gau)/Oct 9, 1909; p.490
ALL FOR A TOOTH (Ed)/Aug 22,1914; p.1100
ALL FOR BUSINESS
   (Bio)/Nov 14, 1914; p. 932
ALL FOR HER (Imp)/May 11, 1912; p. 529
ALL FOR HIS SAKE

(Ed)/Mar 7, 1914; p. 1237
ALL FOR JIM (Maj)/Oct 26, 1912; pp 343-44
ALL FOR LOVE (Lu)/Aug 1, 1914; p. 704
ALL FOR LOVE OF A GIRL
   (Po)/Dec 4, 1909; p. 800
ALL FOR MONEY (Pa)/Jun 10, 1911;
   p. 1316/Jun 24, 1911; p. 1427
ALL FOR OLD IRELAND
   (Lu)/Jul 24, 1915; pp 667-68
ALL FOR PEGGY (Rex)/Mar 20,1915;p.1765
ALL FOR SCIENCE (Bio)/Dec 6, 1913; p. 1151
ALL FOR THE BOY (Bio)/Jan 16, 1915; p. 368
ALL FOR THE LOVE OF A GIRL
   (Vi)/Dec 4, 1915; p. 1852
ALL FOR THE LOVE OF A LADY
   (Ed)/Mar 25, 1911; p. 657
ALL HAIL TO THE KING
   (Bio)/Apr 12, 1913; p. 163
ALL IN THE AIR (Lu)/Apr 25, 1914; p. 516
ALL IN THE FAMILY
   (SA)/Apr 27, 1912; p. 329
ALL IN THE SAME BOAT
   (Ne)/Apr 17, 1915; p. 394
ALL IN THE WASH (Lu)/Jun 1, 1912; p. 829
ALL IS FAIR IN LOVE AND WAR
   (SA)/Feb 29, 1908; p. 168/Jan 9, 1909;
        p. 37/Jan 16, 1909; p. 70
   (Vi)/Jan 14, 1911; p. 90
ALL LOVE EXCELLING
   (Ecl)/Aug 22, 1914; p. 1101
ALL ON ACCOUNT OF A BANANA
   (Maj)/Dec 28, 1912; p. 1294
ALL ON ACCOUNT OF A BUTTERFLY
   (Lu)/Oct 30, 1908; p. 338
ALL ON ACCOUNT OF A JUG
   (Am)/Aug 15, 1914; p. 960
ALL ON ACCOUNT OF A LAUNDRY MARK
   (Ed)/Jun 4, 1910; p. 942
ALL ON ACCOUNT OF A LETTER
   (Lu)/Oct 2, 1909; p. 451
ALL ON ACCOUNT OF A LIE
   (SA)/Nov 5, 1910; p. 1059
ALL ON ACCOUNT OF A PHOTO
   (Lko)/Aug 28, 1915; p. 1481
ALL ON ACCOUNT OF A PORTRAIT
   (Ed)/Jul 19, 1913; p. 319
ALL ON ACCOUNT OF A RING
   (Ec)/Oct 19, 1912; p. 243
ALL ON ACCOUNT OF A TRANSFER
   (Ed)/Mar 15, 1913; p.1103
ALL ON ACCOUNT OF A WIDOW
   (Po)/Sep 28, 1912; p. 1277
ALL ON ACCOUNT OF AN EGG
   (Ec)/Jun 7, 1913; p. 1033
ALL ON ACCOUNT OF CHECKERS
   (Sel)/Apr 13, 1912; p. 137
ALL ON ACCOUNT OF DAISY
   (Lu)/Nov 1, 1913; p. 496

ALL ON ACCOUNT OF POLLY
(Pa)/Feb 28, 1914; p. 1087
ALL ON ACCOUNT OF THE CHEESE
(Bio)/Dec 5, 1914; p. 1384
ALL ON ACCOUNT OF THE MILK
(Bio)/Jan 29, 1910; p. 127
ALL ON ACCOUNT OF THE PORTER
(SA)/Oct 7, 1911; p. 39
ALL ON ACCOUNT OF TOWSER
(Vi)/Aug 7, 1915; p. 996
ALL RIVERS MEET AT SEA
(Bro)/Jul 5, 1913; p. 50
ALL THAT TROUBLE FOR A DRINK
Dec 19, 1908; p. 501
ALL THE WORLD'S A STAGE
(Imp)/Oct 15, 1910; p. 876
ALL THROUGH A BANK NOTE
(Lux)/Nov 2, 1912; p. 451
ALL THROUGH A RAT
(Lux)/Jun 3, 1911; p. 1261
ALL WOOL GARMENT, AN (SA)/Nov 21,
1908; p. 406/Dec 5, 1908; p. 448
ALLAH-3311 (Ec)/Jul 25,1914;p.573
ALLIGATOR FARM, THE
(Lu)/Apr 27, 1912; p. 329
ALL'S WELL THAT ENDS WELL
(Sel)/Oct 12, 1907; p. 505
(Pa)/Mar 13, 1909; p. 303
(Pr)/Mar 7, 1914; p. 1237
ALMA'S CHAMPION (Vi)/Jan 27,1912;p.302
ALMIGHTY DOLLAR, THE
(Lu)/Jul 23, 1910; p. 192
ALMOND EYED MAID, AN
(Ed)/Jun 14, 1913; p. 1136
ALMOST A BRIDEGROOM
(Cry)/Apr 25, 1914; p. 518
ALMOST A HERO (Ed)/Oct 8, 1910; p. 813
(Po)/Jan 18, 1913; p. 265
(UI)/May 2, 1914; p. 674
(Vi)/Jun 5, 1915; p. 1604
ALMOST A KING (Ne)/May 8, 1915; p. 901
(Ka)/Dec 25, 1915; p. 2388
ALMOST A KNOCKOUT
(Ne)/Oct 23, 1915; p. 621
ALMOST A MAN (SA)/Dec 21, 1912; p. 1183
ALMOST A PAPA (Imp)/Dec 11,1915; p.2033
ALMOST A RESCUE (Ne)/Aug 9, 1913; p. 638
ALMOST A SUICIDE
(Ne)/Dec 14, 1912; p. 1082
ALMOST A WHITE HOPE
(Po)/Feb 21, 1914; p. 947
ALMOST A WIDOW (Be)/Nov 13,1915; p.1312
ALMOST A WILD MAN
(Bio)/Jul 5, 1913; p. 48
ALMOST A WINNER
(Cry)/Apr 12, 1913; p. 166
ALMOST AN ACTRESS
(Imp)/Nov 1, 1913; p. 497

ALMOST AN OUTRAGE
(Bio)/May 30, 1914; p. 1260
ALMOST LUCKY (Sup)/Jun 12, 1915; p.1778
ALMOST MARRIED (St)/Jul 25, 1914; p. 572
ALOHA OE (KB)/Nov 13, 1915; pp 1313, 1322
ALONE AT NIGHT (Gau)/Jun 10, 1911; p 1313
ALONE IN LONDON
(Id)/Oct 30, 1915; pp 794, 811
ALONE IN THE JUNGLE (Sel)/Jun 7,
1913; p. 1006/Jun 28, 1913; p. 1358
ALONE IN THE WORLD
(Amb)/Aug 19, 1911; p. 465
ALONE WITH THE DEVIL
(GN)/Apr 4, 1914; p. 59
ALONG CAME A CITY CHAP
(Bio)/May 9, 1914; p. 820
ALONG THE BANKS OF THE RIVER EURE
(Pa)/May 31, 1913;p.920
ALONG THE COAST OF DALMATIA
(UE)/Jan 25, 1913; p. 363
ALONG THE COLUMBIA RIVER
(Pa)/Feb 15, 1913; p. 678
ALONG THE DANUBE RIVER
(Pa)/Jul 22, 1911; p. 124
ALONG THE MEDITERRANEAN
(Ka)/May 18, 1912; p. 628
ALONG THE NILE (Ed)/Jun 28, 1913; p. 1359
ALONG THE PADAS RIVER IN BORNEO
(Pa)/Oct 18, 1913; p. 264
ALONG THE RIVER NILE
(Ka)/Oct 12, 1912; p. 142
ALONG THE RIVIERA
(CGP)/Feb 1, 1913; p. 464
ALPHONSE, THE DEAD SHOT
(Gau)/Oct 30, 1909; p. 604
ALPHONSE GETS IN WRONG
(Pa)/Jun 5, 1909; p. 754
ALPINE ECHO, AN (Vi)/Sep 25, 1909; p. 414
ALPINE LEASE, THE (Ka)/Sep 30,1911; p.971
ALPINE RETREAT: GERSAW AND THE
LAKE OF URI, SWITZERLAND, AN
(UE)/Nov 26, 1910; p. 1238
ALPINE TRAGEDY, AN
(Mil)/Oct 12, 1912; p. 143
ALSTER CASE, THE (SA)/Dec 4, 1915; p.1845
ALTAR OF AMBITION, THE
(Am)/May 22, 1915; p. 1260
ALTAR OF DEATH, THE
(KB)/Nov 23, 1912; p. 769
ALTAR OF HEAVEN, THE
(Gl)/Oct 23, 1915; p. 621
ALTAR OF LOVE, THE
(Vi)/Jun 25, 1910; p. 1101
ALTAR OF THE AZTECS, THE
(Sel)/Feb 15, 1913; p. 679
ALTERED MESSAGE, THE
(Sol)/Oct 7, 1911; p. 41
ALWAYS A WAY (Lu)/Jul 22, 1911; p. 124

ALWAYS IN THE WAY
(Mto)/Jul 10, 1915; pp 318-19
ALWAYS TOGETHER (Maj)/Nov 1,1913;p.498
AMATEUR ACROBAT, AN (Pa)/Apr 4,
1908; p. 298/Mar 27, 1909; p. 368
AMATEUR ANIMAL TRAINER, AN
(Th)/Jan 10, 1914; p. 174
AMATEUR BILLIARDS
(Gau)/Apr 16, 1910; p. 597
AMATEUR BURGLAR, THE
(Ka)/Aug 30, 1913; p. 960
AMATEUR CAMERA MAN, THE (Nov)/
Oct 2, 1915; p. 79/Oct 9, 1915; p. 253
AMATEUR DETECTIVE, THE
(Pa)/Sep 25, 1909; p. 415
AMATEUR DETECTIVES, THE
(Th)/Dec 19, 1914; p. 1680
AMATEUR HIGHWAYMAN, THE
(Sol)/Jun 28, 1913; p. 1361
AMATEUR HOLD-UP, THE
(SA)/Dec 25, 1909; p. 922
AMATEUR HYPNOTIST, THE
(Po)/Jun 11, 1910; p. 999
AMATEUR ICEMAN, THE
(Lu)/Oct 12, 1912; pp 136, 143
AMATEUR LION TAMER, THE
(Vi)/Jun 7, 1913; p. 1031
AMATEUR NIGHT
(Ed)/Dec 17, 1910; p. 1418
(StU)/Jun 5, 1915; p. 1606/
Aug 21, 1915; p. 1318
AMATEUR NURSE, THE (MnA)/Apr 3,
1915; p. 84/May 8, 1915; p. 899
AMATEUR PRODIGAL, AN
(SA)/Mar 6, 1915; p. 1448
AMATEUR RIDER, THE
(KO)/Jun 22, 1907; pp 252-53
AMATEUR SKATER, AN
(UE)/Aug 5, 1911; p. 294
AMATEUR SLEUTH, THE
(Gau)/Mar 22, 1913; p. 1221
AMATEUR WILLIAM TELL, AN
(Ed)/Sep 25, 1909; p. 415
AMAZON, THE (Gau)/Nov 5, 1910; p. 1058
AMBASSADOR FROM THE DEAD, AN
(Lu)/Dec 4, 1915; p. 1852
AMBASSADOR'S DAUGHTER, THE
(Ed)/Feb 1, 1913; p. 465
AMBASSADOR'S DISAPPEARANCE, THE
(Vi)/Jan 25, 1913; p. 364
AMBITION
(Rex)/Dec 12, 1914; p. 1537/
Dec 19, 1914; p. 1681
(Th)/Dec 25, 1915; p. 2390
AMBITION OF THE BARON, THE
(SA)/Feb 13, 1915; p. 985
AMBITIOUS BOOTBLACK, AN
(Gau)/Mar 18, 1911; p. 603

AMBITIOUS PA, AN
(Bio)/May 2, 1914; p. 673
AMBLYSTOMA (Ec)/Nov 15, 1913; p. 736
AMBROSE'S FURY (Key)/Apr 10, 1915; p. 236
AMBROSE'S LOFTY PERCH
(Key)/Apr 24, 1915; p. 556
AMBROSE'S NASTY TEMPER
(Key)/May 15, 1915; p. 1072
AMBROSE'S SOUR GRAPES
(Key)/Mar 6, 1915; p. 1449
AMBULANCE DOGS (Pa)/Oct 30,1908;p.346
AMBULANCE VENTILATORS
(Gau)/Nov 6, 1909; p. 643
AMERICA (AS)/Mar 21,1914;p.1510
AMERICAN BEAUTIES
(Pa)/Jun 3, 1911; p. 1258
AMERICAN BORN (Am)/Dec 13, 1913; p.1280
AMERICAN CITIZEN, AN
(Uni)/Jan 17, 1914; p. 292
AMERICAN COUNT, AN
(Lu)/Jan 7, 1911; p. 32
AMERICAN FIELD ARTILLERY
MANEUVERS (Pa)/Aug 19, 1911; p.463
AMERICAN FLEET IN FRENCH
WATERS, THE (Pa)/Jan 14, 1911; p. 88
AMERICAN GAME TRAILS
(Buc)/Aug 14, 1915; p. 1176
AMERICAN IN THE MAKING, AN
(Th)/May 3, 1913; p. 489
AMERICAN INSURRECTO, THE
(Ka)/Dec 9, 1911; p. 817
AMERICAN INVASION, AN
(Ka)/Feb 24, 1912; p. 690
AMERICAN KING, AN (Ed)/Jan 31, 1914;
p. 525/Feb 21, 1914; p. 947
AMERICAN LUMBER CO.
(Ne)/May 4, 1912; p. 428
AMERICAN NIECE, THE
(Ec)/Feb 8, 1913; p. 573
AMERICAN OLYMPIC TRYOUTS
(Po)/Aug 3, 1912; p. 447
AMERICAN PRINCESS, AN (Ka)/Mar 22,
1913; p. 1227/Apr 12, 1913; p. 164
AMERICAN QUEEN, THE
(Th)/Nov 19, 1910; p. 1178
AMERICAN RHINE, THE
(Ka)/Nov 16, 1912; p. 658
AMERICAN TOURISTS ABROAD
(Ka)/May 25, 1912; p. 728
AMERICANO, THE (Bio)/Apr 17,1915; p.392
(Re)/Jul 31, 1915; p.817
AMONG BEDOUINS (Ec)/Jun 29, 1912; p.1228
AMONG CLUB FELLOWS
(Bio)/Sep 13, 1913; p. 1176
AMONG MANY LOVES
(CGP)/Oct 19, 1912; p. 243
AMONG THE IRISH FISHERFOLK
(Ka)/Dec 16, 1911; p. 904

AMONG THE JAPANESE
(Sel)/Sep 9, 1911; p. 715
AMONG THE MOURNERS
(Key)/Dec 12, 1914; p. 1524
AMONG THE ROSES (Imp)/Aug 27,1910;p.464
AMONG THOSE KILLED
(Bio)/Aug 28, 1915; p. 1492
AMOROUS SOLDIER, THE
Nov 28, 1908; p. 423
AMULET, THE (Gem)/Jan 4, 1913; p. 52
ANALYSIS OF MOTION, THE
(Pa)/Apr 26, 1913; p. 380
ANARADHAPURA, THE BIRTHPLACE OF
BUDDHISM (Ec)/May 31, 1913; p. 921
ANARCHIST, THE (Imp)/Oct 18,1913; p.265
ANARCHISTIC GRIP, THE
(Lu)/Sep 17, 1910; p. 630
ANARCHISTS ON BOARD
(GN)/Jan 29, 1910; p. 128
ANARCHIST'S SWEETHEART, THE
(He)/May 1, 1909; p. 555
ANCESTRY (Am)/Apr 3, 1915; p. 65
ANCIENT AND MODERN LONDON
(Ur)/Jul 22, 1911; p. 123
ANCIENT BOW, THE (Vi)/Sep 7, 1912; p. 975
ANCIENT CASTLES OF AUSTRIA
(Gau)/Sep 10, 1910; p. 575
ANCIENT GREECE (Pa)/May 3, 1913; p.487
ANCIENT MARINER, AN
(Gau)/Aug 20, 1910; p. 406
ANCIENT ORDER OF GOOD FELLOWS,
THE (Vi)/Dec 20, 1913; p. 1418/
Jan 3, 1914; p. 49
ANCIENT PORT OF JAFFA, THE
(Ka)/Sep 28, 1912; p. 1276
ANCIENT ROME (KO)/Jul 4, 1908; p. 14
ANCIENT RUINS AT THEBES, EGYPT
(Pa)/Apr 25, 1914; p. 516
ANCIENT TEMPLES OF EGYPT
(Ka)/Oct 19, 1912; p. 242
ANCIENT TEMPLES OF KARNAK
(Vi)/Nov 22, 1913; p. 867
AND A LITTLE CHILD SHALL LEAD
THEM (Lu)/Mar 21, 1908; p.242
AND BY THESE DEEDS
(Bio)/Sep 11, 1915; p. 1846
AND HE CAME BACK
(SA)/May 2, 1914; p. 672
AND HE CAME STRAIGHT HOME
(At)/Nov 6, 1915; p. 1141
AND HE NEVER KNEW
(Pr)/Mar 13, 1915; p. 1608
AND HIS COAT CAME BACK
(Vi)/Mar 6, 1909; p. 270
AND HIS WIFE CAME BACK
(Vi)/Feb 15, 1913; p. 679
AND PERCY MADE GOOD
(Kri)/Jan 9, 1915; p. 223

AND SHE CAME BACK
(Lux)/Dec 24, 1910; p. 1479
AND SHE NEVER KNEW
(Bio)/Dec 26, 1914; p. 1840
AND THE BEST MAN WON
(Ne)/Oct 16, 1915; pp 441-42
AND THE CAT CAME BACK
(SA)/Jul 8, 1911; p. 1584
AND THE DANCE WENT ON
(Ka)/Jun 13, 1914; p. 1540
AND THE DOG CAME BACK
(Lu)/Jun 22, 1907; p. 252
AND THE PARROT SAID - ?
(Lu)/Dec 11, 1915; p. 2031
AND THE VILLAIN STILL PURSUED HER
(Ne)/Jan 3, 1914; p. 50
(Ka)/Apr 11, 1914; p. 212
AND THE WATCH CAME BACK
(Ka)/Oct 18, 1913; p. 263
AND THEN IT HAPPENED
(Sel)/Mar 27, 1915; p. 1932
ANDREU, THE (Pa)/Oct 12, 1912; p. 142
ANDREW CARNEGIE'S GIFT TO THE
WORLD (Ka)/Dec 20, 1913; p. 1412
ANDREW JACKSON (Am)/Feb 15, 1913; p.681
ANDROCLUS AND THE LION
(Gau)/Aug 31, 1912; p. 882
ANDROMACHE (FA)/Aug 6, 1910; p. 298
ANDY, THE ACTOR
(Ed)/Mar 28, 1914; p. 1680
ANDY AND THE HYPNOTIST
(Ed)/Apr 25, 1914; p. 516
ANDY AND THE REDSKINS
(Ed)/Oct 31, 1914; p. 640
ANDY FALLS IN LOVE
(Ed)/Nov 28, 1914; p. 1231
ANDY GETS A JOB (Ed)/Jan 17, 1914; p. 288
ANDY GOES A-PIRATING
(Ed)/Jun 27, 1914; p. 1828
ANDY GOES ON THE STAGE
(Ed)/Feb 28, 1914; p. 1087
ANDY HAS THE TOOTHACHE
(Ed)/Jul 25, 1914; p. 571
ANDY LEARNS TO SWIM
(Ed)/Aug 29, 1914; p. 1240
ANDY OF THE ROYAL MOUNTED
(SA)/Apr 24, 1915; p. 555
ANDY PLAYS CUPID
(Ed)/May 30, 1914; p. 1260
ANDY PLAYS HERO (Ed)/Jan 31, 1914; p. 543
ANGEL, THE (Re)/Jul 29, 1911; p. 213
ANGEL AND THE STRANDED TROUPE,
THE (Ed)/Jun 29, 1912; p.1226
ANGEL CAKE AND AXEL GREASE
(Lu)/Apr 26, 1913; p. 379
ANGEL CHILD, THE (Ed)/Dec 19, 1908; p.500
ANGEL IN THE MASK, THE
(Th)/Jun 5, 1915; p. 1605

.NIMATION POWDERS
(At)/Oct 1, 1910; p. 749
.NN (Ed)/Mar 15, 1913; p. 1105
.NN, THE BLACKSMITH
(Vi)/Nov 28, 1914; p. 1232
.NN OF THE TRAILS
(Vi)/Oct 25, 1913; p. 379

ANNA KARENINA (Fox)/Apr 10, 1915; p. 245
ANNE BOLEYN
(CGP)/Nov 16, 1912; p. 659
(UE)/May 16, 1914; pp 943-44
ANNE OF THE GOLDEN HEART
(Vi)/Feb 7, 1914; p. 676
ANNE OF THE MINES
(Vi)/Nov 7, 1914; p. 788
ANNETTE KELLERMAN
Nov 28, 1908; p. 422
ANNIE (Imp)/Oct 15, 1910; p.878
ANNIE CRAWLS UPSTAIRS
(Ed)/Dec 21, 1912; p. 1185
ANNIE LAURIE
(SA)/Jun 5, 1909; p. 754
(Re)/Jun 21, 1913; p. 1254
ANNIE ROWLEY'S FORTUNE
(Lu)/Mar 8, 1913; p. 996
**ANNUAL HORSE SHOW AT LONG
BRANCH, N.J., THE**
(Po)/Aug 24, 1912; p. 772
ANONA'S BAPTISM (Pa)/Aug 17, 1912; p. 669
ANONYMOUS LETTER, THE
(Pa)/Feb 13, 1909; p. 172
(Re)/Oct 14, 1911; p. 131
(CGP)/Apr 27, 1912; p. 329
ANONYMOUS LOVE (SA)/Jun 28,1913; p.1360
ANOTHER CHANCE (Maj)/Dec 5,1914; p.1384
ANOTHER SHADE OF GREEN
(Lu)/Feb 13, 1915; p. 984
ANOTHER TALE (Lu)/May 16, 1914; p. 968
ANOTHER'S GHOST (Pa)/Nov 5, 1910; p.1056
ANSELO LEE (Vi)/Nov 13, 1915; p. 1312
ANSWER, THE (Ec)/Feb 27, 1915; p. 1290
ANSWER OF THE ROSES
(Vi)/Oct 28, 1911; pp 290-91
ANSWERED PRAYER, THE
(Ka)/Apr 5, 1913; p. 47
ANT-LION, THE (Pa)/May 17, 1913; p. 703
ANTI-FAT SANITARIUM
(Pa)/Oct 23, 1909; p. 568
ANTI-HAIR POWDER
(Pa)/May 30, 1908; p. 480
ANTIBES AND ITS ENVIRONS
(Pa)/Jul 5, 1913; p. 47
ANTICS IN INK (Imp)/Sep 20, 1913; p. 1285
ANTICS OF TWO SPIRITED CITIZENS
(KO)/Apr 11, 1908; p. 328
ANTIDOTES FOR SUICIDE
(Lu)/Feb 28, 1914; p. 1087
ANTIQUE ENGAGEMENT RING, THE
(Vi)/May 23, 1914; p. 1117
ANTIQUE RING, AN
(Lu)/Feb 24, 1912; p. 689
ANTONY AND CLEOPATRA
(Vi)/Nov 14, 1908; pp 379-80
(Cin)/Jan 10, 1914; pp 150-51
(Pa)/Jun 6, 1914; p. 1409

ARIZONA ROMANCE, AN
(Pa)/Oct 1, 1910; p. 748
(Am)/Jan 21, 1911; p. 145
ARIZONA - THE NEW STATE
(Ne)/Mar 23, 1912; p. 1064
ARIZONA WOOING, AN
(Sel)/May 22, 1915; p. 1259
ARLINE'S CHAUFFEUR
(Bio)/Nov 6, 1915; p. 1139
ARM OF THE LAW, THE
(At)/Dec 31, 1910; p. 1539
ARM OF VENGEANCE, THE
(SA)/Mar 14, 1914; p. 1384
ARMADILLO, THE (UE)/Jun 21, 1913; p. 1251
ARMED INTERVENTION (Am)/Nov 29,
1913; p. 993/Dec 13, 1913; p. 1280
ARMS AND THE GRINGO
(Maj)/Jul 11, 1914; p. 257
ARMS AND THE WOMAN (Ed)/Dec 10,
1910; p. 1358/Dec 17, 1910; p. 1416
ARMSTRONG'S WIFE
(Las)/Dec 4, 1915; pp 1846-47
ARMY AVIATION PRACTICE
(Lu)/Mar 2, 1912; p. 780
ARMY DOGS (Pa)/Aug 15, 1908; p. 129
ARMY MANEUVERS AT GOVERNOR'S
ISLAND (Maj)/Jul 26, 1913; p. 429
ARMY MANOEVERS IN CUBA
(Imp)/Mar 18, 1911; p. 603
ARMY-NAVY FOOTBALL GAME
(Nov)/Dec 18, 1915; p. 2203
ARMY OF TWO, THE
(Ed)/Oct 30, 1908; pp 338, 344
ARMY SURGEON, THE
(KB)/Dec 7, 1912; pp 977-78
ARMY TARGET PRACTICE
(Lu)/Mar 22, 1913; p. 1220
ARNOLD HAS A GOOD TRY
(Lux)/Jun 17, 1911; p. 1389
AROUND CONSTANTIN, ALGERIA
(Pa)/Mar 18, 1911; p. 602
AROUND CONSTANTINOPLE
(Ec)/Sep 28, 1912; p. 1278
AROUND PEKIN (Pa)/Oct 29, 1910; p. 997
AROUND THE BATTLE TREE
(Sel)/Sep 27, 1913; p. 1391
AROUND THE COAST OF BRITTANY
(KO)/Jun 6, 1908; p. 496
AROUND THE CORNER
(Po)/Aug 7, 1915; p. 998
AROUND THE WORLD IN EIGHTY DAYS
(LeP)/Jun 13, 1914; p.1542
ARRAH-NA-POGUE
(Ka)/Nov 18, 1911; p. 536
ARRANGEMENT WITH FATE, AN
(Lae)/Mar 27, 1915; p. 1933
'ARRIET'S BABY (Vi)/Jul 5, 1913; p. 48
ARRIVAL OF JOSIE, THE

(Vi)/Aug 1, 1914; p. 704
ARRIVAL OF PERPETUA, THE
(Wor)/Apr 3, 1915; p. 71
ARRIVAL OF THE AMERICAN FLEET AT
SYDNEY (UE)/Feb 20, 1909; p. 203
ARROW HEAD, THE
(Lu)/Aug 26, 1911; p. 541
ARROW MAIDEN, THE
(Re)/Jul 24, 1915; p. 650
ARROW MAKER'S DAUGHTER, THE
(Pa)/Aug 24, 1912; p. 770
(KB)/Feb 14, 1914; p. 810
ARROW OF DEFIANCE, THE
(Pa)/Mar 30, 1912; p. 1165
ARROWHEAD ROMANCE, AN
(Rex)/Jan 10, 1914; p. 173
ARROW'S TONGUE, THE
(WF)/Sep 19, 1914; p. 1647
ART AND HONOR (Lu)/Mar 8, 1913; p. 997
ART AND THE LEGACY (Lu)/Jan 14, 1911;
p. 90/Jan 21, 1911; p. 146
ART FOR A HEART
(Vi)/Mar 28, 1914; p. 1680
ART INDUSTRIES IN KABYLIE
(Pa)/Sep 30, 1911; p. 970
ART LOVER'S STRATEGY, THE
(UE)/Aug 6, 1910; p. 297
ART OF MAKING SILVER PLATE, THE
(Imp)/Jun 15, 1912; p. 1028
ART OF THE FURRIER, THE
(Pa)/Aug 22, 1914; p. 1100
ART OF PRINTING, THE
(CGP)/May 4, 1912; p. 426
ART VERSUS MUSIC
(Lu)/Dec 30, 1911; p. 1072
ARTFUL ART (Aq)/Apr 24, 1909; p. 516
ARTFUL ARTIST, AN
(Lu)/Sep 18, 1915; p. 1995
ARTFUL CONTRAN (Ec)/Jul 27, 1912; p.344
ARTFUL KATE (Imp)/Mar 11, 1911; p. 542
ARTFUL LOVERS, THE
(WBE)/Jan 18, 1908; p. 45
ARTFUL TWEEDLEDUM
(Amb)/Aug 12, 1911; p. 377
ARTHUR TRUMAN'S WARD
(Vi)/Jan 2, 1915; p. 76
ARTIE THE ARTIST
(Th)/Sep 12, 1914; p. 1513
ARTIFICIAL BROODING
(KO)/Jul 11, 1908; p. 36
ARTIFICIAL PREPARATION OF THE
DIAMOND (KO)/Jun 6, 1908; p. 496
ARTILLERY AND LOVE
(Nov)/Oct 30a, 1915; p. 968
ARTILLERY PRACTICE AT MONTAUK
POINT (Maj)/Aug 30, 1913; p. 962
ARTISAN, THE (UE)/Oct 1, 1910; p. 747
ARTIST AND THE BRAIN SPECIALIST,

THE (Ed)/Jun 8, 1912; p. 942
ARTIST AND THE BRUTE, THE
(Sel)/Feb 22, 1913; p. 780
ARTIST AND THE VENGEFUL ONE, THE
(Vic)/Apr 24, 1915; p. 558
ARTIST FINANCIER, THE (Rex)/Aug 5,
1911; p. 289/Aug 19, 1911; p. 466
ARTISTIC EARTHENWARE IN THE
MAKING (Lux)/Jan 13, 1912; p. 127
ARTISTIC PAPER CUTTING AND
DESIGNING (Jo)/Feb 13, 1915; p. 985
ARTISTIC RAGPICKERS
(Pa)/Feb 8, 1908; p. 104
ARTISTIC VENICE (Cin)/Feb 3, 1912; p.393
ARTIST'S CHILD, THE
(Lux)/May 14, 1910; p. 786
ARTIST'S DREAM, THE
(GN)/Apr 17, 1909; p. 476
(Pa)/Jun 28, 1913; p. 1359
ARTIST'S GREAT MADONNA, THE
(Vi)/Mar 1, 1913; p. 870
ARTIST'S INHERITANCE
(Pa)/May 16, 1908; p. 445
ARTIST'S JOKE, THE
(Ed)/Jul 27, 1912; p. 343
ARTIST'S LUCK, THE
(GN)/Nov 5, 1910; p. 1060
ARTIST'S MODEL, THE
Dec 12, 1908; p. 476
(CK)/Mar 7, 1914; p. 1237
(Dom)/Apr 24, 1915; p. 557
ARTIST'S PAY DAY, THE (Gau)/Jan 14,
1911; p. 90/Jan 21, 1911; p. 142
ARTIST'S REVENGE, THE
(Vi)/Aug 7, 1909; p. 196
ARTIST'S ROMANCE, THE
(Lu)/Jan 25, 1913; p. 364
ARTIST'S SACRIFICE, THE
(Ka)/May 31, 1913; p. 919
ARTIST'S SONS, THE
(Sel)/Oct 21, 1911; p. 209
ARTIST'S TRICK, THE
(Pa)/Mar 1, 1913; p. 887
ARTIST'S WIFE, THE
(Maj)/Apr 17, 1915; p. 393
AS A BOY DREAMS (Imp)/Aug 12, 1911;
p. 360/Sep 2, 1911; p. 630
AS A FATHER SPARETH HIS SON
(Sel)/Nov 1, 1913; p. 495
AS A MAN CHOOSES
(WF)/Nov 7, 1914; p. 789
AS A MAN SOWETH
(GN)/Jul 22, 1911; p. 126
AS A MAN SOWS (Saw)/Dec 26,1914; p.1847
AS A MAN THINKS
(Be)/Dec 5, 1914; p. 1384
AS FATE DECREED
(Pa)/Aug 12, 1911; p. 376

AS FATE WILLED (Vic)/May 9, 1914; p.822
AS FATE WILLS (Fr)/Apr 19, 1913; p. 281
AS IN A LOOKING GLASS
(Bio)/Dec 30, 1911; p. 1071
(Mon)/Feb 22, 1913; p. 783
AS IN DAYS OF OLD
(Re)/Oct 16, 1915; pp 440-41
AS IT HAPPENED (Bio)/Jul 31, 1915; p. 816
AS IT IS IN LIFE
(Bio)/Apr 16, 1910; p. 597
AS IT MIGHT HAVE BEEN
(Bio)/Feb 28, 1914; p. 1087
AS IT WAS IN THE BEGINNING
(Th)/Feb 10, 1912; p. 483
AS OTHERS SEE US
(Th)/Aug 24, 1912; p. 773
AS THE BELL RINGS
(Sol)/Jul 19, 1913; p. 322
AS THE BELLS RANG OUT
(Bio)/Aug 6, 1910; p. 296
AS THE DOCTOR ORDERED
(Imp)/Jan 4, 1913; p. 52
AS THE FATES DECREE
(Sel)/Sep 14, 1912; p. 1074
AS THE MASTER ORDERS
(Re) Jan 21, 1911; p. 145
AS THE TOOTH CAME OUT
(Ed)/Aug 23, 1913; p. 842
AS THE TWIG IS BENT
(Lu)/Dec 4, 1915; p. 1850
AS THE WIND BLOWS
(Po)/Aug 17, 1912; p. 676
(Rex)/Oct 3, 1914; p. 65
AS TIME ROLLED ON
(Sel)/Jun 6, 1914; p. 1408
AS WE FORGIVE THOSE
(Lu)/Sep 26, 1914; p. 1776
AS WE SOW (Sol)/Aug 9, 1913; p. 638
AS WE TRAVEL THROUGH LIFE
(Ne)/Nov 28, 1914; p. 1233
AS YE SOW (Rex)/Apr 15, 1911; p. 844
          (Wor)/Jan 2, 1915; p. 58
AS YOU LIKE IT
(Ka)/Oct 3, 1908; p. 253
(Vi)/Aug 10, 1912; pp 528-29
AS YOUR HAIR GROWS WHITE
(Po)/May 27, 1911; p. 1202
ASCENDING MOUNT BLANC
(Gau)/Aug 23, 1913; p. 845
ASCENDING MT. PILATUS IN
SWITZERLAND/Nov 7, 1908; p. 358
ASCENDING THE JURA MOUNTAINS
(Gau)/Feb 12, 1910; p. 216
ASCENDING THE SEA OF ICE
(Ec)/Apr 30, 1910; p. 690
ASCOLI PICENO, SOUTH ITALY
(Cin)/Nov 2, 1912; p. 450
ASHES

(Ed)/Jan 22, 1910; p.91
(Re)/Jul 19, 1913; p. 321/Jul 26, 1913; p. 406
ASHES OF GOLD (Sel)/Apr 17, 1915; p. 392
ASHES OF HOPE (SA)/May 30, 1914; p.1261
ASHES OF INSPIRATION
(Bio)/Jul 24, 1915; p. 671
ASHES OF THREE (Am)/May 31, 1913; p. 921
ASPIRANTS TO THE HAND OF HELEN
(Ec)/Mar 26, 1910; p. 468
ASPIRATIONS OF GERALD AND PERCY
(Imp)/Dec 17, 1910; p. 1419
**ASSASSINATION OF PRESIDENT
LINCOLN** (PMP)/Jan 30, 1909; p. 121
**ASSASSINATION OF THE DUKE de
GUISE** (Pa)/Feb 27, 1909; p. 236
ASSAYER OF LONE GAP, THE
(Am)/Aug 28, 1915; p. 1480
ASSISI (Cin)/Apr 13, 1912; p. 136
ASSISTED ELOPEMENT, AN
(Th)/Sep 10, 1910; p. 575
(Am)/Mar 9, 1912; p. 867
(Sel)/Oct 19, 1912; p. 242
ASSORTMENT OF AEROPLANES, AN
(Pa)/Jul 3, 1909; p. 13
ASTIS, THE (Pa)/Nov 25, 1911; p. 637
ASTRAKHAN FISHERIES
(Pa)/Jun 20, 1908; p. 532
ASTRAKHAN FISHERMAN
(Pa)/Jan 23, 1909; p. 93
ASTROLOGER, THE (KO)/Apr 11,1908; p.327
AT BAY (Pa)/Nov 27, 1915; pp 1676-77
AT BREAK OF DAWN
(SA)/Jul 22, 1911; p. 124
AT CAIRN, NORTH QUEENSLAND
(Me)/May 31, 1913; p. 920
AT CEDAR RIDGE (Ne)/Feb 11, 1911; p.319
AT CONEY ISLAND
(Key)/Nov 9, 1912; p. 554
AT CRIPPLE CREEK
(Re)/Jul 13, 1912; p. 148
AT CROSS PURPOSES
(Cin)/Jan 10, 1914; p. 173
AT DAWN (Maj)/Dec 26,1914;p.1841
AT DOUBLE CROSS RANCH
(Ne)/Apr 23, 1910; p. 642
AT DOUBLE TROUBLE RANCH
(Ch)/Feb 25, 1911; p. 431
AT EVENTIDE (Gau)/Feb 11, 1911; p. 316
AT HIS EXPENSE
(Lu)/Apr 25, 1914; p. 517
AT HIS OWN TERMS
(U)/Mar 20, 1915; p. 1765
AT HOME IN THE WATER
(Ed)/Nov 9, 1912; p. 552
AT HOME WITH THE HERON
(Pa)/Feb 7, 1914; p. 676
AT IT AGAIN (Key)/Nov 16, 1912; p. 660
AT JONES' FERRY

(Ed)/Sep 23, 1911; p. 891
AT LAST THEY EAT
(Ka)/Feb 7, 1914; p. 676
AT LAST WE ARE ALONE
(Sel)/May 30, 1914; p. 1260
AT LIBERTY - GOOD PRESS AGENT
(Th)/Dec 21, 1912; p. 1185
AT MAD MULE CANYON
(Bi)/Mar 15, 1913; p. 1105
AT MEXICO'S MERCY
(Vic)/Jul 11, 1914; p. 257
AT MIDNIGHT
(Rex)/Feb 15, 1913; p. 681
(Ed)/Aug 9, 1913; p. 635
AT NAPOLEON'S COMMAND (Cin)/
Nov 23, 1912; p. 753/Dec 14, 1912; p. 1082
AT NIGHT/Nov 28, 1908; p.423
AT OLD FORT DEARBORN
(UB)/Sep 28, 1912; pp 1267-68
AT PANTHER CREEK
(Ne)/Jun 10, 1911; p. 1317
AT PERRY'S RANCH
(Ne)/Sep 30, 1911; p. 976
AT PHNOM PENH, CAMBODIA
(Me)/Dec 27, 1913; p. 1543
AT ROLLING FORKS
(Ne)/Mar 9, 1912; p. 867
AT SCROGGINSES CORNER
(Vi)/Apr 27, 1912; p. 328
AT SEA UNDER NAVAL COLORS
(GN)/Jul 29, 1911; p. 212
AT SHILOH (Bi)/Jun 28, 1913; p. 1360
AT SUNSET RANCH
(Ne)/Jul 8, 1911; p. 1586
AT SWORD'S POINTS
(Rel)/Apr 1, 1911; p. 720
AT THE ALTAR (Bio)/Mar 6, 1909; p. 268
AT THE BANQUET TABLE (Imp)/Apr 3,
1915; pp 69-70/May 1, 1915; p. 730
AT THE BAR OF JUSTICE
(UE)/Mar 19, 1910; p. 426
AT THE BASKET PICNIC
(Bio)/Nov 9, 1912; p. 553
AT THE BEACH, INCOGNITO
(Jo)/Sep 11, 1915; p. 1834
AT THE BINGVILLE BARBECUE
(Jo)/Jun 19, 1915; p. 1941
AT THE BOTTOM OF THINGS
(Re)/Feb 13, 1915; p. 985
AT THE BURGLAR'S COMMAND
(Pa)/Oct 19, 1912; p. 242
**AT THE COURT OF PRINCE MAKE
BELIEVE** (Ec)/Mar 14, 1914; p. 1386
AT THE CROSSING
(Ec)/Jan 31, 1914; p. 545
AT THE CROSSROADS OF LIFE
(Bio)/Jul 4, 1908; p. 11
AT THE CRUCIAL MOMENT

(Ec)/Nov 14, 1914; p. 933
AT THE DAWNING
(Gau)/Jun 25, 1910; p. 1101
AT THE DOG SHOW
(Vi)/Jan 4, 1913; p. 50
AT THE DUKE'S COMMAND
(Imp)/Feb 18, 1911; p. 372
AT THE EDGE OF THINGS
(Am)/May 29, 1915; p. 1432
AT THE ELEVENTH HOUR
(Vi)/Aug 17, 1912; p. 672
(Bi)/Jan 10, 1914; p. 174
(Sel)/Feb 21, 1914; p. 946
AT THE END OF A PERFECT DAY
(Am)/Aug 15, 1914; p. 961
(SA)/Feb 13, 1915; p. 984
AT THE END OF THE ROAD
(Gau)/Mar 4, 1911; p. 482
AT THE END OF THE ROPE
(Ka)/Aug 29, 1914; p. 1241
AT THE END OF THE TRAIL
(SA)/Apr 13, 1912; p. 136
(Vi)/Jul 13, 1912; p. 148
AT THE FARM (It)/Apr 23, 1910; p. 642
**AT THE FLAME THE BUTTERFLY
BURNT ITS WINGS** (Ec)/Dec 7,1912; p.976
AT THE FLOOD TIDE
(Sel)/Aug 7, 1915; p. 996
AT THE FOOT OF THE HILL
(SA)/Aug 1, 1914; p. 704
AT THE FOOT OF THE LADDER
(Th)/Sep 28, 1912; p. 1277
AT THE FOOT OF THE SCAFFOLD (Kio)/
Aug 2, 1913; p. 519/Aug 9, 1913; p. 638
AT THE FOOT OF THE STAIRS
(Rex)/Jul 25, 1914; p. 573
AT THE FRENCH BALL
(Bio)/Jul 4, 1908; p. 11
AT THE GRINGO MINE
(SA)/Aug 19, 1911; p. 462
AT THE HALF BREED'S MERCY
(Am)/Jul 19, 1913; p. 321
AT THE HOUR OF DAWN
(Gau)/Apr 18, 1914; p. 339
AT THE HOUR OF ELEVEN
(Re)/May 22, 1915; p. 1260
AT THE LARIAT'S END
(SA)/Jul 19, 1913; p. 320
AT THE MASK BALL
(Sel)/May 15, 1915; p. 1071
AT THE MASQUERADE BALL
(Ed)/Nov 9, 1912; p. 552
AT THE OLD CROSS ROADS
(Spp)/Oct 17, 1914; p. 351
AT THE OLD MAID'S CALL
(SA)/Jan 10, 1914; p. 172
AT THE OLD MILL
(UE)/Apr 22, 1911; p. 900

AT THE PATRICIAN CLUB
(Th)/Oct 30, 1915; p. 792
AT THE 'PHONE (Sol)/Nov 9, 1912; p. 555
AT THE POINT OF THE SWORD
(Ed)/Mar 2, 1912; p. 780
AT THE POSTERN GATE
(Re)/Jul 17, 1915; p. 486
AT THE POTTER'S WHEEL
(Am)/Feb 7, 1914; p. 677
AT THE RAINBOW'S END
(Lu)/Nov 30, 1912; p. 876
AT THE RISK OF HER LIFE
(Ape)/May 3, 1913; p. 467
AT THE RISK OF HIS LIFE
(Sel)/Oct 3, 1914; p. 64
AT THE ROAD'S END
(Bio)/Oct 2, 1915; p. 78
AT THE SIGN OF THE LOST ANGEL
(Vi)/Nov 8, 1913; p. 612
AT THE STAGE DOOR
(Vi)/Mar 14, 1908; p. 219
AT THE STROKE OF THE ANGELUS
(Maj)/May 29, 1915; p. 1432
AT THE STROKE OF TWELVE
(SA)/Dec 9, 1911; p. 817
AT THE TELEPHONE
(Lu)/Jul 5, 1913; p. 48
AT THE THRESHOLD OF LIFE
(Ed)/Oct 28, 1911; p. 291
AT THE TRANSFER CORNER
(Sel)/Nov 14, 1914; p. 932
AT THE WHEEL (GN)/Oct 18, 1913; p. 266
AT THE WHITE MAN'S DOOR
(Vi)/Feb 25, 1911; p. 430
AT THE WINDOW (Po)/Apr 29, 1911; p.961
AT THREE O'CLOCK
(St)/Aug 15, 1914; p. 961
AT TWELVE O'CLOCK
(Key)/Apr 5, 1913; p. 49
ATHALIAN (Pa)/Apr 15, 1911; p. 842
ATHEIST, THE (Ka)/Oct 11, 1913; p. 156
ATHENS (Pa)/Jul 12, 1913; p. 204
ATHLETIC AMBITIONS
(Sel)/Nov 13, 1915; p. 1311
ATHLETIC CARNIVAL
(Lu)/Jun 24, 1911; p. 1454
**ATHLETIC CARNIVAL OF THE
UNIVERSITY OF PENNSYLVANIA,
THE** (Lu)/Jul 15, 1911; p. 39
**ATHLETIC EXERCISES AND TESTS OF
STRENGTH IN THE FRENCH ARMY**
(Pa)/May 1, 1915; p. 729
ATHLETIC FAMILY, THE
(Vi)/Dec 26, 1914; p. 1840
ATHLETIC INSTRUCTOR, AN
(De)/Sep 24, 1910; p. 689
ATHLETIC SPORTS IN INDIA
(Pa)/Apr 16, 1910; p. 597

ATHLETIC WOMAN (Pa)/May 30, 1908; p.480
ATHLETICS IN FRANCE
(Pa)/Jun 28, 1913; p. 1359
ATLANTIS (GN)/Jun 13, 1914; p. 1520
ATONEMENT, THE
(Pa)/Jan 7, 1911; p. 34
(SA)/Jun 3, 1911; p. 1259
(Maj)/Apr 4, 1914; p. 59
(SA)/Apr 11, 1914; p. 212
ATONEMENT OF THAIS, THE
(Gau)/Apr 22, 1911; p. 900
ATTACK AT ROCKY PASS, THE
(Ka)/Apr 5, 1913; p. 48
ATTACK ON FORT RIDGELY, THE
(Ka)/Nov 26, 1910; p. 1236
ATTACK ON THE MILL, THE
(Ed)/Aug 27, 1910; pp 462-63
ATTACK UPON THE TRAIN, THE
(Lux)/Apr 23, 1910; p. 643
ATTACKED BY A LION
(Gau)/May 25, 1912; p. 730
ATTACKED BY THE ARAPAHOES
(Ka)/Jul 23, 1910; p. 192
ATTEMPTED ELOPEMENT, AN
(De)/Oct 1, 1910; p. 749
ATTIC ABOVE, THE
(Sel)/Mar 14, 1914; p. 1384
ATTORNEY FOR THE DEFENSE, THE
(Ka)/Jul 5, 1913; p. 47
(Lu)/Feb 13, 1915; p. 985
ATTORNEY'S DECISION, THE
(Lu)/Sep 12, 1914; p. 1512
AUCTION SALE OF RUN-DOWN RANCH,
THE (Sel)/Oct 9, 1915; p. 252
AULD LANG SYNE (Vi)/Nov 4, 1911; p. 366
AULD ROBIN GRAY (Vi)/Oct 29,1910; p.996
AUNT AURORA (Gau)/Apr 13, 1912; p. 138
AUNT BETTY'S REVENGE
(Ne)/Feb 22, 1913; p. 781
AUNT BRIDGET (Ec)/Nov 16, 1912; p. 660
AUNT DINAH'S PLOT
(Imp)/Dec 21, 1912; p. 1186
AUNT ELSA'S VISIT
(Ed)/Mar 29, 1913; p. 1335
AUNT EMMY'S SCRAP BOOK
(Lu)/Feb 6, 1909; p. 144
AUNT HANNAH (Po)/Oct 1, 1910; p. 750
AUNT HETTY'S GOLDFISH
(Ec)/Aug 17, 1912; p. 676
AUNT HILDA, THE MATCHMAKER
(Vi)/Nov 11, 1911; p. 468
AUNT JANE'S LEGACY
(Lu)/Nov 18, 1911; p. 550
AUNT JULIA'S PORTRAIT
(Lux)/Jan 14, 1911; p. 91
AUNT KATE'S MISTAKE
(Imp)/Apr 12, 1913; p. 166
AUNT LENA'S VISIT

(Lu)/Nov 6, 1909; p. 644
AUNT MARIA'S SUBSTITUTE
(Imp)/May 21, 1910; p. 834
AUNT MARY (Sel)/Apr 24, 1915; p. 555
AUNT MATILDA OUT-WITTED (Lun)/
Jun 5, 1915; p. 1606/Aug 14, 1915; p. 1161
AUNT MIRANDA'S CAT
(Ed)/May 25, 1912; p. 728
AUNT TABITHA'S MONKEY
(Lux)/Sep 17, 1910; p. 995
AUNTIE (Vi)/Mar 28, 1914; p. 1681
AUNTIE AND THE COWBOYS
(Am)/Sep 9, 1911; p. 717
AUNTIE AT THE BOAT RACE
(Vi)/Jun 11, 1910; p. 995
AUNTIE TAKES THE CHILDREN TO THE
COUNTRY (Lu)/Oct 30, 1908; p. 345
AUNTIE'S MONEY BAG
(Ec)/Jun 20, 1914; p. 1690
AUNTIE'S PORTRAIT
(Vi)/Jan 16, 1915; p. 368
AUNTIE'S ROMANTIC ADVENTURE
(Cry)/Mar 28, 1914; p. 1682
AUNTS TOO MANY (Bio)/Nov 1, 1913; p. 495
AUNTY AND THE GIRLS
(Ed)/May 24, 1913; p. 812
AUNTY'S AFFINITY
(Lu)/Mar 15, 1913; p. 1104
AUNTY'S ROMANCE
(Vi)/Jul 27, 1912; pp 337, 344
AURORA FLOYD
(Th)/Dec 14, 1912; p. 1063/
Dec 21, 1912; p. 1185
(Bio)/Feb 27, 1915; p. 1267/
Mar 27, 1915; p. 1932
AURORA OF THE NORTH
(Rex)/May 23, 1914; p. 1118
AUSABLE FALLS AND CHASM
(Sol)/Mar 9, 1912; p. 867
AUSTRALIAN SPORTS AND PASTIMES
(KO)/Jul 11, 1908; p. 36
AUSTRIAN MOUNTAIN TORRENT, AN
(Gau)/Sep 30, 1911; p. 971
AUTHOR! AUTHOR!
(Mus)/Dec 25, 1915; p. 2390
AUTO BUG, THE (Lu)/Sep 2, 1911; p. 628
AUTO BUNGALOW FRACAS, AN
(Be)/Oct 30a, 1915; p. 968
AUTO HEROINE, AN
(Vi)/Oct 17, 1908; pp 298, 307-8
AUTO SMASH-UP, THE
(Gau)/Jun 29, 1912; p. 1228
AUTO SUGGESTION
(Sol)/May 25, 1912; p.729
AUTOCRAT OF FLAPJACK JUNCTION, AN
(Vi)/Oct 18, 1913; p. 263
AUTOMATIC LAUNDRY, THE
(Lu)/May 9, 1908; p. 423

AUTOMATIC LIGHTER, AN
(Ec)/Dec 2, 1911; p. 727
AUTOMATIC MONKEY, THE
(Gau)/May 1, 1909; p. 554
AUTOMATIC MOVING COMPANY
(CGP)/May 18, 1912; p. 629
AUTOMATIC SERVANT
(KO)/Jul 18, 1908; p. 52
AUTOMOBILE RACES AT SANTA
MONICA, CAL. (Vi)/Jul 6, 1912; p. 43
AUTUMN LEAVES (Gau)/Feb 25,1911; p.430
AUTUMN LOVE (SA)/Dec 20, 1913; p. 1411
AUTUMN SUNSET DREAM, AN
(Amb)/Jan 20, 1912; p. 205
AVAILING PRAYER, THE
(Re)/Nov 7, 1914; p. 788
AVALANCHE, THE (LF)/Jan 30, 1915; p.676
AVARICE (Id)/May 8, 1915; p. 901
AVARICIOUS FATHER
(Pa)/Mar 28, 1908; p. 269
AVENGED (Th)/Oct 22, 1910; p. 938
(UE)/Jul 8, 1911; p. 1584
AVENGED BY A FISH
(Lko)/Oct 2, 1915; p. 80
AVENGING BILL (Lu)/Sep 18, 1915; p. 1995
AVENGING CONSCIENCE
(Re)/Aug 15, 1914; p. 936
AVENGING DENTIST, THE
(Gau)/Jan 15, 1910; p. 57
(Lko)/Mar 6, 1915; p. 1449
AVENGING SEA, THE
(Bio)/Jun 12, 1915; p. 1776
AVENGING SHOT, THE
(Bio)/Dec 25, 1915; p. 2380
AVERTED STEP, THE
(Rep)/May 4, 1912; p. 427
AVIATION AT LOS ANGELES, CAL.
(SA)/Feb 26, 1910; p. 299
AVIATION AT MONTREAL
(Cen)/Jul 23, 1910; p. 193
AVIATION AT RHEIMS
(FIT)/Sep 18, 1909; p. 378
AVIATION CRAZE, THE
(Pa)/Oct 29, 1910; p. 994
AVIATOR AND THE AUTOIST RACE FOR
A BRIDE, THE (Ch)/Feb 17, 1912; p. 583
AVIATOR'S SUCCESS, THE
(Ch)/Jan 20, 1912; p. 203
AWAITED HOUR, THE
(Imp)/Feb 6, 1915; pp 829-30
AWAKENED CONSCIENCE, AN
(Gau)/Sep 11, 1909; p. 345
AWAKENED MEMORIES
(UE)/Nov 6, 1909; p. 643
AWAKENING, THE
(Bio)/Oct 9, 1909; p. 490
(Ec)/Feb 10, 1912; p. 483
(Sel)/Nov 9, 1912; p. 552

(Am)/Jan 25, 1913; p. 365
(Po)/Jul 26, 1913; p. 430
(Rex)/May 30, 1914; p. 1262
(Vi)/Jun 5, 1915; p. 1604-5
AWAKENING AT SNAKEVILLE, THE
(SA)/Dec 20, 1913; p. 1390
AWAKENING HOUR, THE
(SA)/May 29, 1915; p. 1432
AWAKENING OF A MAN, THE
(Ed)/Sep 20, 1913; p. 1284
AWAKENING OF BARBARA DARE, THE
(Vi)/May 9, 1914; p. 820
AWAKENING OF BIANCA, THE
(Vi)/Dec 21, 1912; p. 1184
AWAKENING OF GALATEA, THE
(Po)/May 20, 1911; p. 1142
AWAKENING OF JACK CLARK, THE
(Po)/Oct 28, 1911; p. 293
AWAKENING OF JOHN BOND, THE
(Ed)/Nov 18, 1911; pp 535-36
AWAKENING OF JOHN BRIDD, THE
(Gem)/Dec 21, 1912; p. 1186
AWAKENING OF JONES, THE
(Vi)/Aug 17, 1912; p. 669
AWAKENING OF PAPITA, THE
(Ne)/May 10, 1913; p. 597
AWARD OF JUSTICE, THE
(Ka)/Apr 4, 1914; p. 58
AWAY OUT WEST (SA)/Jun 18,1910; p.1048
AWFUL ADVENTURES OF AN AVIATOR,
THE (Sel)/Sep 18, 1915; p.1995
AWFUL MOMENT, AN
(Bio)/Dec 19, 1908; p. 507
AWFUL SCARE, AN
(Cry)/Feb 22, 1913; p. 781
AWFUL SKATE, AN
(SA)/Aug 3, 1907; pp 346-47
AWFUL SYMPHONY (Pa)/Jul 30,1910; p.245
AWKWARD CINDERELLA, AN
(Rex)/Aug 1, 1914; p. 706
AWKWARD ORDERLY
(KO)/May 16, 1908; p. 445
AXOLOTL, THE (Pa)/Mar 4, 1911; p. 482
AYAH'S REVENGE, THE
(FIT)/Oct 3, 1908; p. 263
AYLESWORTH ANIMAL PICTURES, THE
(Ayl)/Apr 10, 1915; p. 243
AZTEC TREASURER, THE
(Ec)/Sep 26, 1914; p. 1778

BABES IN THE WOOD, THE
(Po)/Aug 26, 1911; p. 545
BABES IN THE WOODS
(Mi)/Oct 5, 1907; p. 491
BABES IN THE WOODS, THE
(Pa)/Apr 5, 1913; p. 49
BABE'S SCHOOL DAYS
(Lu)/Oct 2, 1915; p. 78

BABETTE (Gem)/Aug 24,1912;p.772
BABIES' DOLL, THE
(Rex)/Apr 11, 1914; p. 214
BABIES PROHIBITED
(Th)/Mar 22, 1913; p. 1222
BABIES' STRIKE, THE
(It)/Sep 4, 1909; p. 314
BABIES THREE (Po)/Jun 15, 1912; p. 1028
BABIES WILL PLAY
(SA)/Feb 1, 1908; p. 82
BABY (Vic)/May 22, 1915; p. 1262
BABY, THE (Ed)/Mar 23, 1912; p. 1062
(Maj)/Jan 10, 1914; p. 174
(Re)/May 15, 1915; p. 1072
BABY AND LEOPARD, THE
(Sel)/Dec 18, 1915; p. 2202
BABY AND THE COP, THE
(Pun)/Dec 14, 1912; p. 1083
BABY AND THE STORK, THE
(Bio)/Jan 13, 1912; p. 126
BABY BELMONT WINS A PRIZE
(Cry)/Nov 1, 1913; p. 498
BABY BENEFACTOR, THE
(Th)/Jun 5, 1915; p. 1606
BABY BET (UE)/Mar 12, 1910; p. 384
BABY BETTY (Sel)/Jul 20, 1912; p. 244
BABY BRIDE, THE (Th)/Apr 13, 1912;
p. 143/Apr 27, 1912; p. 330
BABY DAY (Key)/Sep 6, 1913; p. 1069
BABY DID IT, A (Ne)/Sep 5, 1914; p. 1373
BABY ELEPHANT, THE
(Vi)/Sep 20, 1913; p. 1283
BABY FINGERS (Gem)/Sep 7, 1912; p. 977
BABY FORTUNE HUNTERS, THE
(Gau)/Feb 11, 1911; p. 315
BABY HANDS (Th)/Aug 10, 1912; p. 547
BABY IS KING (UE)/Aug 21, 1909; p. 256
BABY NEEDS MEDICINE
(Sol)/Nov 25, 1911; p. 638
BABY OF THE BOARDING HOUSE, THE
(Ed)/May 27, 1911; p. 1200
(SA)/Mar 23, 1912; p. 1062
BABY QUESTION, THE
(Cry)/Dec 20, 1913; p. 1413
BABY SHERLOCK (Po)/Aug 3, 1912; p. 447
BABY SHOW, THE
(Pa)/Mar 14, 1908; pp 217-18
BABY SPY, THE (Sel)/Jun 13, 1914; p. 1541
BABY STRIKE, THE (KO)/May 9,1908;p.422
BABY SWALLOWS A NICKEL
(SA)/Dec 11, 1909; p. 842
BABY TRAMP, THE (Lu)/Mar 16,1912;p.961
BABY'S ADVENTURES
(Ch)/Apr 27, 1912; p. 330
BABY'S CHOICE (Sol)/Dec 16, 1911; p. 906
BABY'S FALL (Ed)/Apr 1, 1911; p. 718
BABY'S FAULT, THE
(Ne)/Apr 10, 1915; p. 237

BABY'S FIRST TOOTH
(SA)/Feb 26, 1910; p. 299
BABY'S GHOST (Lux)/Feb 24, 1912; p. 690
BABY'S NEW PIN (Lu)/May 3, 1913; p. 488
BABY'S RATTLE (Sol)/Jul 22, 1911; p. 127
BABY'S REVENGE (EFE)/Sep 4, 1909; p.315
BABY'S RIDE (Maj)/Jan 9, 1915; p. 221
BABY'S SHOE, A (Bio)/May 15, 1909; p. 634
(Ed)/Nov 16, 1912; p. 658
BABY'S TRUMPET (Pa)/May 29,1915;p.1433
BACHELOR AND MAID
(SA)/Dec 18, 1909; p. 882
BACHELOR AND THE BABY, THE
(Vi)/Oct 15, 1910; p. 876
(Ne)/Apr 6, 1912; p. 42
BACHELOR BILL'S BIRTHDAY PRESENT
(Po)/Apr 5, 1913; p. 49
BACHELOR GIRLS' CLUB, THE
(Gem)/Sep 27, 1913; p. 1393
BACHELOR'S BABY, THE
(Vi)/Jun 21, 1913; p. 1252
(SA)/Jul 31, 1915; p. 816
BACHELOR'S BRIDE, THE
(Ka)/Nov 30, 1912; p. 877
BACHELOR'S BURGLAR, THE
(SA)/Jun 12, 1915; p. 1776
BACHELOR'S CHRISTMAS, THE
(Rex)/Dec 18, 1915; p. 2204
BACHELOR'S CLUB, THE
(Sol)/Mar 30, 1912; p. 1167
BACHELOR'S FINISH, THE
(Po)/Dec 31, 1910; p. 1539
(Cry)/Sep 20, 1913; p. 1286
BACHELOR'S HOUSEKEEPER, THE
(Cry)/Sep 12, 1914; p. 1513
BACHELOR'S LOVE AFFAIR, A
(SA)/Nov 20, 1909; p. 721
BACHELOR'S OLD MAID, THE
(Ch)/Apr 15, 1911; p. 843
BACHELOR'S PERSISTENCE, A
(UE)/Apr 24, 1909; p. 516
BACHELOR'S ROMANCE, A
(Com)/Aug 10, 1912; p. 547
BACHELOR'S ROMANCE, THE
(FP)/Feb 27, 1915; p. 1295
BACHELOR'S VISIT, THE
(Sel)/Oct 2, 1909; p. 451
BACHELOR'S WATERLOO, A
(Lu)/Jun 8, 1912; p. 942
BACHELOR'S WATERLOO, THE
(Ed)/Jan 27, 1912; p. 303
BACK AMONG THE OLD FOLKS
(Sel)/Mar 12, 1910; p. 383
BACK IN THE MOUNTAINS
(Ne)/Jul 30, 1910; p. 246
BACK OF THE SHADOWS
(Kri)/Mar 6, 1915; p. 1456
BACK TO BOARDING

BALDY BELMONT AND THE OLD MAID
(Cry)/Sep 6, 1913; p. 1069
BALDY BELMONT AS A ROMAN
GLADIATOR (Cry)/Sep 27, 1913; p. 1393
BALDY BELMONT BREAKS OUT
(Cry)/Mar 14, 1914; p. 1386
BALDY BELMONT LANDS A SOCIETY
JOB (Cry)/Nov 29, 1913; p. 1008
BALDY BELMONT NEARLY A HERO
(Cry)/Mar 21, 1914; p. 1526
BALDY BELMONT PICKS A PEACH
(Cry)/Feb 7, 1914; p. 677
BALDY BELMONT WANTED A WIFE
(Cry)/Oct 11, 1913; p. 157
BALDY BELMONT'S BUMPS
(Cry)/Jan 10, 1914; p. 173
BALDY IS A WISE OLD BIRD
(Cry)/Dec 6, 1913; p. 1152
BALKAN CRISIS, THE
(Gau)/Nov 9, 1912; p. 555
BALKAN WAR, THE
(Kin)/Dec 28, 1912; p. 1294
BALKED AT THE ALTAR
(Bio)/Aug 29, 1908; p. 160
BALL PLAYER AND THE BANDIT, THE
(Bro)/Dec 7, 1912; p. 977
BALLAD OF THE SOUTH SEAS, A
(Me)/Jan 18, 1913; pp 248-49
BALLYHOO'S STORY, THE
(Vi)/Oct 25, 1913; p. 380
BALTIC SEA, THE (Jo)/Feb 13, 1915; p. 985
BAMBOO AND ITS USES
(Pa)/Nov 20, 1915; p. 1501
BAMBOO POLE EQUALIBRISTS, INDIA
(UE)/May 15, 1909; p. 634
BANAKIE MAIDEN, A
(Re)/Jan 16, 1915; p. 369
BANANA PLANTER'S PERIL, THE
(Ya)/Jun 3, 1911; p. 1261
BAND LEADER, THE
(Vi)/Sep 26, 1914; p. 1775
BANDIT, THE (Pa)/Feb 19, 1910; p. 257
(Key)/Jun 28, 1913; p. 1361
BANDIT AND THE BABY, THE
(Bio)/Mar 27, 1915; p. 1932
BANDIT OF DEVIL'S GAP, THE
(WF)/Oct 31, 1914; p. 642
BANDIT OF PORT AVON, THE
(Co)/Aug 29, 1914; p. 1215
BANDIT OF TROPICO, THE
(Ne)/Jun 29, 1912; p. 1228
BANDITS, THE/Dec 12, 1908;p.476
BANDIT'S BRIDE, THE
(Pa)/Nov 25, 1911; p. 637
BANDIT'S CHILD, THE
(SA)/Mar 2, 1912; p. 768
(Ka)/Jun 14, 1913; p. 1136
BANDIT'S MASK, THE

(Sel)/Feb 3, 1912; p. 393
BANDITS OF THE ATLAS GORGES
(Ec)/Nov 20, 1909; p. 721
BANDIT'S REDEMPTION, THE
(Fr)/Apr 12, 1913; p. 165
BANDIT'S SPUR, THE
(Pa)/Oct 5, 1912; p. 40
BANDIT'S SURPRISE, THE
(Po)/Mar 18, 1911; p. 604
BANDIT'S WATERLOO, THE
(Bio)/Aug 8, 1908; p. 108
BANDIT'S WIFE, THE
(SA)/Jul 2, 1910; p. 24
BANGS' BURGLAR ALARM
(Po)/May 4, 1912; p. 427
BANGS BURGLAR ALARM
(WF)/Dec 26, 1914; p. 1842
BANGVILLE POLICE, THE
(Key)/Apr 26, 1913; p. 381
BANK, THE (SA)/Sep 4, 1915; p. 1643
BANK BURGLAR'S FATE, THE
(Re)/Aug 22, 1914; p. 1101
BANK MESSENGER, THE
(Lu)/Mar 6, 1909; p. 270
BANK PRESIDENT'S SON, THE
(Ed)/May 4,1912;p.418/May 25,1912;p.729
BANKER AND THE THIEF, THE
(Bio)/Oct 30a, 1915; p. 967
BANKER'S DAUGHTER, THE
(Bio)/Nov 5, 1910; p. 1058
(Ka)/Apr 13, 1912; p. 137
(Ec)/Sep 20, 1913; p. 1286
(LF)/Apr 25, 1914; p. 519
BANKER'S DOUBLE, THE
(Ed)/Jan 30, 1915; p. 671
BANKER'S SONS, THE
(Maj)/Jun 28, 1913; p. 1361
BANKHURST MYSTERY, THE
(Re)/Dec 25, 1915; p. 2389
BANKRUPT, THE (Gau)/May 27, 1911; p.1201
BANKS OF THE DANUBE, THE (Gau)/
May 14, 1910; p. 784/May 11, 1912; p. 529
BANKS OF THE GANGES, THE
(Pa)/Apr 9, 1910; p. 553
BANSHEE, THE (KB)/Jul 12, 1913;
p. 205/Jul 26, 1913; p. 408
BANZAI (KB)/Aug 2, 1913; p. 538
BAPTISM OF FIRE, THE
(GN)/Dec 6, 1913; p. 1154
BAR CROSS LIAR, THE
(Ec)/May 30, 1914; p. 1262
BAR K FOREMAN (Lu)/Dec 28, 1912; p. 1292
BAR Z'S NEW COOK
(Bi)/Dec 23, 1911; p. 990
BARBARA FREITCHE
(Vi)/Nov 14, 1908; p. 380
(Ch)/Oct 14, 1911; p. 131
(Mto)/Dec 4, 1915; pp 1846, 1853

BARBARY COAST, THE
(PFP)/Nov 1, 1913; p. 474
BARBER CURE, THE
(Bio)/Nov 15, 1913; p. 735
BARBER OF SEVILLE, THE
(Amb)/Apr 11, 1914; p. 213
BARBER SHOP FRAUD, A
(Cry)/Dec 5, 1914; p. 1385
BARBERINE (Ec)/May 7, 1910; p. 738
BARBER'S DAUGHTER, THE
(Gau)/Mar 18, 1911; p. 603
BARBER'S REVENGE, THE
(Pa)/Aug 7, 1909; p. 194
BARCELONA, THE LARGEST SEAPORT
IN SPAIN (Pa)/Aug 2, 1913; p. 536
BAREFOOT BOY, THE
(Ka)/Aug 17, 1912; p. 672
(Ka)/Aug 29, 1914; p. 1220
BARGAIN, THE
(Rex)/Feb 10, 1912; p. 492/
Feb 24, 1912;p.671/Mar 9, 1912;p.868
(Par)/Dec 5, 1914; p. 1390
BARGAIN AUTOMOBILE, A
(Lu)/Jun 27, 1914; p. 1828
BARGAIN HUNTERS, THE
(SA)/Apr 25, 1914; p. 516
BARGAIN IN BRIDES, A
(Ka)/Nov 27, 1915; p. 1663
BARGAIN TABLE CLOTH, A
(Lu)/Nov 28, 1914; p. 1231
BARGAIN WITH SATAN, A
(Ape)/Nov 29, 1913; p. 989
BARGEE'S DAUGHTER, THE
(Pa)/May 9, 1908; pp 423-24
BARGEMAN OF OLD HOLLAND, THE
(Sel)/Jun 18, 1910; p. 1048
BARGEMAN'S SON, THE
(KO)/May 9, 1908; p. 423
BARNABY RUDGE (He)/Feb 13, 1915; p.996
BARNEY OLDFIELD'S RACE FOR LIFE
(Key)/Jun 7, 1913; p. 1033
BARNSTORMERS, THE
(Po)/Aug 15, 1914; p. 961
(Ka)/Aug 21, 1915; p. 1322
BARNYARD FLIRTATIONS
(Key)/Apr 4, 1914; p. 58
BARNYARD MIXUP, A
(Lu)/Aug 7, 1915; p. 996
BARON, THE (Bio)/Sep 16, 1911; p. 789
BARON BINKS' BRIDE
(Imp)/Jul 26, 1913; p. 430
BARON'S BEAR ESCAPE, THE
(Lko)/Dec 19, 1914; p. 1681
BARRED FROM THE MAILS
(Th)/May 17, 1913; p. 705
BARREL ORGAN, THE
(Vi)/Sep 19, 1914; p. 1644
BARRELED (Cry)/Aug 29, 1914; p. 1242

BARRELS TO SELL/Nov 21, 1908; p. 398
BARREN GAIN, THE
(Am)/Oct 2, 1915; p. 80
BARRIER, THE (Bro)/Mar 8, 1913; p. 998
BARRIER BETWEEN, THE
(Bio)/Jan 23, 1915; p. 515
BARRIER OF BARS, THE
(Vic)/Dec 6, 1913; p. 1152
BARRIER OF BLOOD, THE
(Amm)/Nov 8, 1913; p. 613
BARRIER OF FAITH, THE
(Vi)/Feb 13, 1915; p. 984
BARRIER OF FLAMES, THE
(Th)/Dec 26, 1914; pp 1842, 1851
BARRIER OF IGNORANCE, THE
(Ka)/May 23, 1914; p. 1098
BARRIER ROYAL, A
(Bro)/Feb 28, 1914; p. 1090
BARRIER THAT WAS BURNED, THE
(Vi)/Aug 10, 1912; p. 546
BARRIERS BURNED AWAY
(Vi)/Jul 8, 1911; p. 1585
BARRIERS OF PREJUDICE
(Vi)/Oct 23, 1915; p. 620
BARRIERS SWEPT ASIDE
(Ka)/Feb 27, 1915; p. 1292
BARROW RACE, A (Gau)/Nov 13, 1909; p.684
BARRY SISTERS, THE
(Pa)/Jun 25, 1910; p. 1101
BARRY'S BREAKING IN
(Ed)/Feb 22, 1913; p. 781
BARTERED CROWN, THE
(Bio)/Jan 24, 1914; p. 412
BASEBALL, A GRAND OLD GAME
(Bio)/Sep 12, 1914; p. 1512
BASEBALL, THAT'S ALL
(Me)/Sep 24, 1910; p. 688
BASEBALL AND TROUBLE
(Lu)/Jan 30, 1915; p. 671
BASEBALL BUG, THE
(Th)/Dec 2, 1911; p. 726
BASEBALL FAN, THE
(Vic)/Jun 13, 1914; p. 1543
BASEBALL FANS OF FANVILLE, THE
(Jo)/Oct 10, 1914; p. 189
BASEBALL INDUSTRY
(Lu)/Aug 31, 1912; p. 880
BASEBALL STAR FROM BINGVILLE,
THE (SA)/Jul 8, 1911; p. 1585
BASEBALL STARS (Vi)/Jan 31, 1914; p. 543
BASEBALL'S PEERLESS LEADER
(Pa)/Dec 20, 1913; p. 1412
BASHFUL BACHELOR BILL
(Maj)/Aug 30, 1913; p. 962
BASHFUL BEN (Cry)/Aug 29, 1914; p. 1242
BASHFUL BILLIE (Lu)/Dec 18,1915; p.2202
BASHFUL GLEN (Imp)/Oct 16, 1915; p. 441
BASHFUL SON, THE

(Re)/Jul 1, 1911; p. 1520
BASHFUL YOUNG MAN, A
(Pa)/Jul 18, 1908; p. 50
BASKET HABIT, THE
(Ed)/Jul 11, 1914; p. 255
BASKET MAKER'S DAUGHTER, THE
(KO)/May 16, 1908; p. 444
BASKET PARTY, A (Pa)/Oct 3, 1908;
p. 264/Oct 24, 1908; p. 318
BASQUE WEDDING (Pa)/Aug 15, 1914; p. 960
BATH HOUSE TRAGEDY, A
(Lko)/Oct 16, 1915; p. 442
BATHERS IN CEYLON
(Ec)/Feb 8, 1913; p. 573
BATHHOUSE BEAUTY, A
(Key)/Apr 18, 1914; p. 361
BATHING CAVALRY HORSES
(CGP)/May 4, 1912; p. 426
BATTERED BRIDEGROOMS, THE
(Am)/Jan 28, 1911; p. 197
BATTLE, THE
(Bio)/Nov 4,1911; p.367/May 22,1915;p.1273
(St)/Oct 3, 1914; p. 65
BATTLE AT REDWOOD, THE
(Pa)/Jan 28, 1911; p. 194
**BATTLE FIELDS AROUND
CHATTANOOGA** (Ed)/Aug 30, 1913; p.960
BATTLE FOR FREEDOM, THE
(Ka)/Apr 26, 1913; p. 360
BATTLE FOR LIFE
(WF)/Aug 22, 1914; p. 1101
BATTLE GROUND, THE
(Am)/Aug 3, 1912; p. 430
BATTLE IN THE CLOUDS, THE
(UE)/Jan 15, 1910; p. 56
(Ape)/Mar 14, 1914; p. 1364
BATTLE IN THE VIRGINIA HILLS
(Ka)/Nov 30, 1912; p. 876
**BATTLE OF AMBROSE AND WALRUS,
THE** (Key)/Sep 4, 1915; p. 1644
BATTLE OF BALLOTS, THE
(GL)/Jul 31, 1915; p. 832
BATTLE OF BLOODY FORD, THE
(Ka)/Mar 8, 1913; p. 977
BATTLE OF BULL CON, THE
(Ne)/Sep 20, 1913; p. 1285
BATTLE OF BULL RUN, THE (101)/
Mar 15, 1913;p.1107/Mar 29, 1913;p.1337
BATTLE OF BUNKER HILL
(Ed)/Aug 26, 1911; p. 542
BATTLE OF CHILI AND BEANS, THE
(Ap)/Apr 11, 1914; p. 213
BATTLE OF ELDERBUSH GULCH, THE
(Bio)/Jun 26, 1915; p. 2110
BATTLE OF FLOWERS AT NICE
(KO)/Jun 6, 1908; p. 496
BATTLE OF FORT LARAMIE, THE
(Ka)/Oct 18, 1913; p. 264

BATTLE OF FRENCHMAN'S RUN, THE
(Vi)/Apr 3, 1915; p. 63
BATTLE OF LITTLE TIN HORN, THE
(UI)/Mar 28, 1914; p. 1681
BATTLE OF LONG SAULT, THE
(Bri)/Apr 26, 1913; p. 381
BATTLE OF MANILA, THE
(Bi)/Jun 28, 1913; p. 1361
BATTLE OF MONMOUTH, JUNE 28, 1778
(Lu)/Jul 18, 1908; p. 50
BATTLE OF POTTSBURG BRIDGE, THE
(Ka)/Feb 17, 1912; p. 581
BATTLE OF PRZEMYSL, THE
(ACF)/Aug 14, 1915; p. 1175
BATTLE OF RUNNING BILL, THE
(St)/May 22, 1915; p. 1262
BATTLE OF SAN JUAN HILL
(Bi)/Jun 7, 1913; p. 1032
BATTLE OF SHILOH, THE
(Lu)/Nov 22, 1913; p. 877
BATTLE OF THE NATIONS, THE
(Jo)/Nov 21, 1914; p. 1077
BATTLE OF THE REDMEN
(101)/Mar 23, 1912; p. 1063
BATTLE OF THE ROSES, THE
(Ne)/Mar 9, 1912; p. 867
BATTLE OF SNAKEVILLE, THE
(SA)/Jan 23, 1915; p. 515
BATTLE OF THE WEAK, THE
(Vi)/Apr 25, 1914; p. 517
BATTLE OF THE WILLS, THE
(Imp)/Sep 2, 1911; p. 630
BATTLE OF TRAFALGAR, THE (Ed)/
Sep 9, 1911; p. 695/Oct 7, 1911; p. 40
BATTLE OF TWO PALMS, THE
(Mil)/Aug 17, 1912; p. 674
BATTLE OF WATERLOO, THE
(Wat)/Sep 20, 1913; p. 1265
BATTLE OF WHO RUN, THE
(Key)/Jan 25, 1913; p. 365
BATTLE OF WITS, A
(Ka)/Sep 11, 1915; p. 1832
BATTLE ROYAL, A/Dec 19, 1908; p. 500
BATTLES OF A NATION, THE
(ACF)/Nov 20, 1915; p. 1502
BATTY BILL, MONKEY AND PELICAN
(Me)/May 16, 1914; p. 968
BATTY BILL ALMOST MARRIED
(Me)/May 30, 1914; p. 1260
BATTY BILL AND THE SUICIDE CLUB
(Me)/May 23, 1914; p. 1116
BATTY BILL WINS A BABY
(Me)/Apr 25, 1914; p. 516
BATTY BILL'S HONEYMOON
(Me)/Feb 14, 1914; p. 808
BATTY BILL'S LOVE AFFAIR
(Me)/Apr 18, 1914; p. 360
BATTY BILL'S PERTINACITY

(Me)/May 2, 1914; p. 672
BATTY BILL'S ROUGH HOUSE
(Me)/Apr 11, 1914; p. 212
BATTY BILLY AND HIS PAL'S LEGACY
(Me)/Mar 14, 1914; p. 1384
BAWLEROUT, THE
(Re)/May 3, 1913; pp 468, 489
BAXTER'S BUSY DAY
(Po)/Jan 18, 1913; p. 265
BAY OF HA-LONG (Pa)/May 15, 1915; p. 1073
BAY OF THE SEVEN ISLES, THE
(Lae)/Apr 3, 1915; p. 66
BE IT EVER SO HUMBLE
(Ne)/May 31, 1913; p. 921
BE NEUTRAL (Po)/Sep 26, 1914; p. 1777
BEACH BIRDS (Lko)/Sep 25, 1915; p. 2177
BEACH COMBERS, THE
(Pa)/Jan 11, 1913; p. 158
BEACH ROMANCE, A
(St)/Jul 25, 1914; p. 572
BEACHCOMBERS, THE
(Me)/Oct 12, 1912; p. 142
BEACHED AND BLEACHED
(MnA)/Oct 30a, 1915; p. 967
BEADED BUCKSKIN BAG, THE
(Sel)/Jul 12, 1913; p. 205
BEANS (SA)/Jun 20, 1914; p. 1688
BEAR AFFAIR, A (Key)/May 22,1915;p.1260
BEAR ESCAPE (St)/Nov 21, 1914; p. 1077
BEAR ESCAPE, A (Key)/Dec 7, 1912; p. 977
(Pa)/Dec 20, 1913; p.1412
(Box)/Nov 7, 1914; p. 789
"BEAR" FACTS, THE
(Vi)/Jul 11, 1914; p. 255
BEAR HUNT IN CANADA
(Pa)/Oct 30, 1908; p. 346
BEAR HUNT IN RUSSIA
(GN)/Oct 24, 1908; p. 319
(Pa)/Dec 25, 1909; p. 920
BEAR HUNT IN THE ROCKIES
(Ed)/Jan 22, 1910; p. 92
BEAR HUNTER, THE
(Pa)/Feb 22, 1913; p. 780
BEAR HUNTING (GN)/Jan 14, 1911; p. 93
BEAR IN THE FLAT, A
(KO)/Apr 18, 1908; p. 353
BEAR YE ONE ANOTHER'S BURDENS
(Imp)/Aug 13, 1910; p. 351
BEARDED BANDIT, THE
(SA)/Oct 22, 1910; p. 936
BEARDED YOUTH (Bio)/Jul 1, 1911; p. 1520
BEARER OF BURDENS, THE
(Imp)/Jan 11, 1913; p. 159
BEAST, THE (Ka)/Aug 8, 1914; p. 836
(Lu)/Jul 24, 1915; p. 650
BEAST AT BAY, A (Bio)/Jun 8, 1912; p. 944
BEASTS OF THE JUNGLE
(Su)/Sep 26, 1914; p. 1761

BEAT AT HIS OWN GAME
(Imp)/Mar 16, 1912; p. 963
BEAT OF THE YEAR, THE
(Re)/Jan 2, 1915; pp 54, 77
BEATEN PATH, THE
(Ec)/Aug 23, 1913; p. 845
BEATING HE NEEDED, THE
(Key)/Oct 26, 1912; p. 344
BEATING MOTHER TO IT
(Lu)/May 3, 1913; p. 488
BEATING THE BURGLAR
(Lu)/Nov 28, 1914; p. 1231
BEATING THEIR BOARD BILL
(Bio)/Feb 21, 1914; p. 946
BEATRICE CENCI (Pa)/Jun 20, 1908;
p. 532/Oct 10, 1908; p. 279
BEATRIX D'ESTE
(CGP)/Sep 14, 1912; p. 1075
BEAU AND HOBO (Jo)/Sep 19, 1914; p. 1646
BEAU BRUMMEL (Vi)/Jul 27, 1912;
pp 332-34/Mar 8, 1913; p. 995
BEAU BRUMMEL AND HIS BRIDE
(Ed)/Jun 28, 1913; p. 1359
BEAUT FROM BUTTE, THE
(Lu)/Jul 12, 1913; p. 204
BEAUTIES OF PORTUGAL, THE
(CGP)/Nov 30, 1912; p. 877
BEAUTIES OF SAN SOUCI
(UE)/Mar 18, 1911; p. 602
BEAUTIFUL BELINDA
(Sel)/Jun 19, 1915; p. 1939
BEAUTIFUL BISMARK
(Maj)/Jun 21, 1913; p. 1255
BEAUTIFUL BUTTERFLIES
(Kin)/Mar 29, 1913; p. 1338
BEAUTIFUL CATALONIA
(Pa)/Aug 2, 1913; p. 536
BEAUTIFUL CHRISTIANA
(Po)/Feb 10, 1912; p. 483
BEAUTIFUL LADY, THE
(Bio)/Mar 27, 1915; p. 1931
BEAUTIFUL LOVE (Ko)/Jul 10, 1915; p.308
BEAUTIFUL MARGARET, THE
(Gau)/Aug 6, 1910; p. 297
BEAUTIFUL PALO DURO
(Rep)/Jun 22, 1912; p. 1128
BEAUTIFUL SNOW (Vi)/Mar 19, 1910;p.425
(Pr)/Apr 11, 1914; p.213
BEAUTIFUL THOUGHTS
(Vi)/Nov 13, 1915; p. 1311
BEAUTIFUL UNKNOWN, THE (Vic)/
Dec 26, 1914; p. 1844/Jan 2, 1915; p. 77
BEAUTIFUL VINTAGE TIME, THE
(Ec)/Aug 17, 1912; p. 674
BEAUTIFUL VOICE, THE
(Bio)/Aug 19, 1911; p. 464
BEAUTIFUL WINDERMERE
(Vi)/Mar 5, 1910; p. 338

BEHIND THE TIMES
(Imp)/Aug 26, 1911; p. 544
BEHIND THE VEIL
(Rex)/Aug 8, 1914; p. 837
BELATED BRIDEGROOM
(Lu)/May 20, 1911; p. 1141
BELATED MEAL, THE
(Vi)/May 1, 1909; p. 554
BELATED WEDDING, THE
(Pa)/Oct 30, 1909; p. 604
BELGIAN ARMY, THE
(Pa)/Sep 24, 1910; p. 688
BELIEVE ME IF ALL THOSE
ENDEARING YOUNG CHARMS
(Ed)/Sep 21, 1912; p. 1176
BELIEVER IN DREAMS, A
(Lu)/Dec 19, 1914; p. 1679
BELINDA, THE SLAVEY
(Vi)/Apr 5, 1913; p. 48
BELL HOP, THE (SA)/Aug 28, 1915; p.1479
BELL OF JUSTICE, THE
(Vi)/Sep 2, 1911; p. 628
BELL OF PENANCE, THE
(Ka)/Jun 19, 1915; p. 1939
BELL RINGER OF THE ABBEY, THE
(Pa)/Oct 14, 1911; p. 129
BELLA DONNA (FP)/Nov 20,1915;pp1510-11
BELLA'S BEAUS (Cry)/Nov 2, 1912; p. 451
BELLA'S ELOPEMENT
(Vi)/Sep 26, 1914; p. 1775
BELLBOY'S REVENGE, THE
(Roy)/Apr 11, 1914; p. 213
BELLE BOYDE, A CONFEDERATE SPY
(Sel)/May 24, 1913; p. 811
BELLE OF BALD-HEAD ROW
(Go)/Oct 26, 1907; p. 542
BELLE OF BAR Z RANCH, THE
(Ne)/Jun 22, 1912; p. 1128
BELLE OF BARNEGAT
(Lu)/Oct 30, 1915; p. 791
BELLE OF BREWERYVILLE, THE
(Lu)/Sep 26, 1914; p. 1775
BELLE OF NEW ORLEANS, THE
(Ka)/Mar 30, 1912; p. 1166
BELLE OF NORTH WALES, THE
(Ka)/Mar 1, 1913; p. 887
BELLE OF SISKYOU, THE
(SA)/Oct 18, 1913; p. 263
BELLE OF THE BEACH, THE
(Ka)/Oct 26, 1912; p. 342
BELLE OF THE HARVEST
(UE)/Dec 11, 1909; p. 841
BELLE OF THE SCHOOL, THE
(Pr)/Sep 5, 1914; p. 1372
BELLE OF YORKTOWN, THE
(Dom)/Nov 29, 1913; p. 1009
BELLIGERENT BENJAMIN
(Maj)/Oct 12, 1912; p. 143

BELLS, THE (Re)/Mar 1, 1913; p. 889
(Ed)/Aug 9, 1913; p. 637
BELLS OF AUSTI, THE
(Dom)/Mar 21, 1914; p. 1526
BELLS OF DEATH, THE
(Amb)/Dec 20, 1913; p. 1415
BELMONT BUTTS IN (Cry)/Oct 3,1914;p.65
BELMONT STUNG (Cry)/Jul 26, 1913; p.429
BELOVED ADVENTURER, THE (Lu)/
No.1/Aug 29, 1914; p. 1218
No.2/Oct 3, 1914; p. 64
No.3/Oct 10, 1914; p. 173
BELOVED VAGABOND, THE
(Pa)/Dec 18, 1915; pp 2196, 2204
BELOW STAIRS (Rex)/Mar 1, 1913; p. 889
BELOW THE DEADLINE
(Re)/Aug 2, 1913; p. 537
BEN, THE STOWAWAY
(Imp)/Feb 22, 1913; p. 782
BEN BOLT (Sol)/Dec 27, 1913; p. 1512
BENARES (Pa)/Jul 29, 1911;p.210
BENEATH SOUTHERN SKIES
(Po)/Mar 4, 1911; p. 484
BENEATH THE COAT OF A BUTLER
(Th)/Nov 20, 1915; p. 1500
BENEATH THE CZAR
(Sol)/Feb 21, 1914; p. 952
BENEATH THE MASK
(Imp)/May 23, 1914; p. 1118
BENEATH THE SEA (Lu)/Mar 13,1915; p.1607
BENEATH THE TOWER RUINS
(UE)/Apr 29, 1911; p. 957
BENEATH THE VEIL
(Th)/Dec 9, 1911; p. 818
BENEATH THE WALLS OF NOTRE DAME
(Gau)/Jun 18, 1910; p. 1048
BENEDICT ARNOLD (Vi)/Nov 27, 1909; p.757
BENEDICTION OF THE SEA, THE
(WBE)/Sep 28, 1907; p. 473
BENEFACTOR, THE
(Lu)/Aug 2, 1913; p. 536
BENEVOLENCE OF CONDUCTOR 786,
THE (Th)/Oct 24, 1914; p. 492
BENEVOLENT EMPLOYER, A
(UE)/Apr 3, 1909; p. 402
BEN-HUR (Ka)/Dec 7, 1907; p. 651
BENJAMIN BUNTER, BOOK-AGENT
(Vi)/Dec 25, 1915; p. 2388
BENOIT'S FORTUNE
(GN)/Sep 28, 1912; p. 1277
BEN'S KID (Sel)/Jul 10, 1909; p. 50
BENVENUTO CELLINI
(Pa)/Nov 7, 1908; pp 358, 366
BEPPO (Am)/Nov 28, 1914; pp 1232-33
BEPPO, THE BARBER
(Ko)/Jul 24, 1915; p. 650
BERGEN, NORWAY (UE)/Jul 6, 1912; p. 42
BERLIN (Pa)/May 28, 1910;p.888

BERNARD PALISSY
(Gau)/Feb 27, 1909; pp 236-37
BERNE, SWITZERLAND
(GN)/Jun 3, 1911; p. 1261
BERNESE OBERLAND, SWITZERLAND,
THE (Kin)/Apr 26, 1913; p. 381
BERTHA, THE BUTTONHOLE MAKER
(Bio)/Dec 19, 1914; p. 1679
BERTHA'S BIRTHDAY
(RR)/Nov 27, 1909; p. 758
BERTHA'S MISSION
(Vi)/Mar 18, 1911; p. 602
BERTIE AND HIS RIVALS
(Lux)/Nov 4, 1911; p. 381
BERTIE'S BANDIT
(Am)/Feb 11, 1911; pp 316, 318
BERTIE'S BRAINSTORM
(Th)/Jan 28, 1911; p. 197
BERTIE'S ELOPEMENT
(Sel)/Oct 1, 1910; p. 748
BERTIE'S LOVE LETTER
(WBE)/Jun 29, 1907; p. 269
BERTIE'S REFORMATION
(Ka)/Jun 17, 1911; pp 1362, 1386
BERTIE'S STRATAGEM
(Vi)/Jul 24, 1915; p. 649
BESS OF THE FOREST
(Lu)/Sep 9, 1911; p. 716
BESSIE HAS THREE AUNTS
(Cin)/Feb 10, 1912; p. 482
BESSIE THE DETECTRESS, IN THE DOG
WATCH (Jo)/Jul 11, 1914; p. 257
BESSIE THE DETECTRESS, IN TICK,
TICK, TICK! (Jo)/Jul 4, 1914; p. 66
BESSIE THE DETECTRESS, or THE OLD
MILL AT MIDNIGHT
(Jo)/Jun 13, 1914; p. 1541
BESSIE'S BACHELOR BOOBS
(Fal)/Sep 25, 1915; p. 2177
BESSIE'S DREAM (Sel)/May 4, 1912; p. 426
BESSIE'S RIDE (Me)/Aug 5, 1911; p. 292
BEST GLUE, THE (KO)/May 2, 1908; p. 401
BEST MAN, THE (Lu)/Mar 21, 1914; p. 1524
                (Ed)/Nov 28, 1914; p.1242
                (Fr)/Dec 12, 1914; p. 1524
BEST MAN WINS (Th)/May 28, 1910; p. 889
BEST MAN WINS, THE
(SA)/Dec 4, 1909; p. 798
(Ne)/Jan 6, 1912; p. 42
(Maj)/Mar 16, 1912; p. 963
(Am)/Oct 26, 1912; p. 345
(Bio)/Jan 25, 1913; p. 363
BEST OF ENEMIES, THE
(TK)/Nov 13, 1915; p. 1313
BEST POLICY, THE
(Sol)/Sep 23, 1911; p. 893
(Am)/Jan 13, 1912; p. 130
BEST REMEDY, THE

(KO)/Jul 18, 1908; p. 52
BETRAYED BY A HANDPRINT
(Bio)/Sep 5, 1908; p. 181
BETRAYED BY ONE'S FEET
(Pa)/Mar 7, 1908; p. 193
BETRAYING MARK, THE
(Pa)/Feb 13, 1915; p. 986
BETRAYING MIRROR, THE
(It)/Apr 2, 1910; p. 510
BETROTHED, THE (Amb)/Aug 30, 1913;
p. 964/Sep 6, 1913; p. 1047
BETROTHED'S NIGHTMARE, THE
Aug 21, 1909; p. 255
BETROTHED'S SECRET, THE
(Amb)/Oct 22, 1910; p. 939
BETTER DAYS (Vi)/Aug 2, 1913;
p. 514/Sep 6, 1913; p. 1067
BETTER FATHER, THE
(Ec)/Aug 30, 1913; p. 961
BETTER MAN, THE
(Me)/Dec 30, 1911; p. 1071
(Re)/Feb 24,1912; p.684/Mar 16,1912; p.963
(Gau)/Mar 7, 1914; p. 1241
(FP)/Aug 22, 1914; p. 1085
(Lu)/Sep 12, 1914; p. 1511
(Maj)/Feb 6, 1915; p. 829
BETTER PART, THE
(Gem)/Nov 16, 1912; p. 660
BETTER THAN GOLD
(Gau)/Mar 5, 1910; p. 339
(Imp)/Mar 30, 1912; p. 1166
BETTER TO HAVE REMAINED BLIND
(Ec)/Oct 21, 1911; p. 211
BETTER UNDERSTANDING, A
(Bio)/Nov 21, 1914; p. 1076
BETTER WAY, THE
(Bio)/Aug 21, 1909; p. 253
(Imp)/Oct 21, 1911; p. 211
(Ram)/Mar 8, 1913; p. 998
(Sel)/Mar 28, 1914; p. 1681
(Maj)/Jan 2, 1915; p. 77
BETTER WOMAN, THE
(Tiu)/Oct 30a, 1915; pp 970, 983-84
BETTY AND THE DOCTOR
(Lu)/Mar 16, 1912; p. 961
BETTY AND THE ROSES
(Lu)/Sep 28, 1912; p. 1276
BETTY AS AN ERRAND GIRL
(Pa)/Aug 13, 1910; p. 351
BETTY BECOMES A MAID
(Vi)/Mar 25, 1911; p. 657
BETTY BURTON, M.D.
(Nov)/Dec 4, 1915; p. 1853
BETTY BUTTIN AND THE BAD MAN
(Ka)/Nov 8, 1913; p. 611
BETTY FOOLS DEAR OLD DAD
(Sel)/Sep 7, 1912; p. 975
BETTY IN SEARCH OF A THRILL

(Bos)/Jun 5, 1915; p. 1622

BETTY IN THE LION'S DEN
(Vi)/Dec 13, 1913; p. 1279

BETTY IS PUNISHED
(Pa)/Oct 22, 1910; p. 936

BETTY IS STILL AT HER OLD TRICKS
(Pa)/Oct 15, 1910; p. 876

BETTY IS WORSE THAN EVER
(CGP)/May 11, 1912; p. 528

BETTY ROLLS ALONG
(Pa)/Feb 11, 1911; p. 315

BETTY'S APPRENTICESHIP
(Pa)/Feb 25, 1911; p. 431

BETTY'S BABY (Vi)/Feb 1, 1913; p. 465

BETTY'S BANDIT (Ne)/Nov 2, 1912; p. 451
(Fr)/May 17, 1913; p. 705

BETTY'S BOAT (Pa)/Oct 21, 1911; p. 208

BETTY'S BONDAGE
(Rex)/Aug 14, 1915; p. 1162

BETTY'S BUTTONS
(Ed)/Sep 16, 1911; p. 789

BETTY'S CHOICE (Vi)/Oct 16, 1909; p. 531

BETTY'S DREAM HERO
(Lae)/Jul 10, 1915; p. 309

BETTY'S FIREWORKS (Pa)/Jan 7,1911;p.32

BETTY'S FIRST SPONGE CAKE
(Be)/Aug 7, 1915; p. 997

BETTY'S NIGHTMARE
(Vic)/Oct 19, 1912; p. 244

BETWEEN DANCES (Lu)/Jan 10, 1914;p.172

BETWEEN DUTY AND HONOR
(Ec)/Sep 24, 1910; p. 690

BETWEEN FATHER AND SON
(Bio)/Nov 13, 1915; p. 1312

BETWEEN HOME AND COUNTRY
(Re)/Sep 6, 1913; p. 1069

BETWEEN LAKES AND MOUNTAINS
(Nov)/Dec 25, 1915; p. 2389

BETWEEN LOVE AND DUTY
(Ka)/May 28, 1910; p. 888
(GN)/Apr 1, 1911; p. 720

BETWEEN LOVE AND HONOR
(Pa)/May 8, 1909; p. 594
(Vi)/Jul 23, 1910; p. 192

BETWEEN LOVE AND THE LAW
(Sel)/Nov 30, 1912; p. 876

BETWEEN MATINEE AND NIGHT
(Sel)/Feb 6, 1915; p. 827

BETWEEN MEN (TKB)/Dec 4, 1915; p. 1848

BETWEEN ONE AND TWO
(Lu)/Oct 10, 1914; p. 188

**BETWEEN ORTON JUNCTION AND
FALLONVILLE** (Ed)/Apr 12, 1913; p. 164

BETWEEN THE TWO OF THEM
(Vi)/Apr 17, 1915; p. 398

BETWEEN TWO FIRES
(Ed)/Apr 15, 1911; p. 843
(Sol)/Jul 13, 1912; p. 148

(Lu)/Jan 24, 1914; p. 413
(Vi)/Nov 13, 1915; p. 1311

BETWEEN TWO GIRLS
(CGP)/Jan 18, 1913; p. 264

BETWIXT LOVE AND FIRE
(Key)/May 17, 1913; p. 706

BEULAH (Bal)/May 1, 1915; p. 737

BEWARE THE BOMB
(Ec)/Mar 11, 1911; p. 543

BEWILDERED BAKER, THE
(Ka)/Aug 12, 1911; p. 376

BEWILDERED PROFESSOR, THE (KO)/
Nov 28, 1908; p. 432/Dec 5, 1908; p. 448

BEWILDERING CABINET, THE
(Me)/Sep 7, 1907; p. 426

BEWITCHED (Lux)/Nov 12,1910; pp 1118-19

BEWITCHED BANDBOX, THE
(Mil)/Nov 23, 1912; p. 769

BEWITCHED MANOR HOUSE
(Pa)/Jul 31, 1909; p. 160

BEWITCHED MATCHES
(Ec)/May 10, 1913; p. 597

BEWITCHED TRICYCLE, THE
(KO)/Aug 29, 1908; p. 161

BEWITCHING BRETON (KO)/Jan 9, 1909;
p. 36/Jan 30, 1909; p. 120

BEYOND ALL IS LOVE
(Lu)/Dec 25, 1915; p. 2383

BEYOND ALL LAW (Bio)/Jan 3, 1914; p. 48

BEYOND THE CITY
(Am)/May 23, 1914; p. 1117

BEYOND THE LAW
(Ne)/Sep 27, 1913; p. 1393

BEYOND THE ROCKIES
(Cen)/Dec 31, 1909; p. 961

BEYOND YOUTH'S PARADISE
(SA)/Dec 12, 1914; p. 1523

BIANCA (Vi)/Nov 15, 1913; p. 735

BIANCA FORGETS (Th)/May 1, 1915; p.729

BIARRITZ (KO)/May 2, 1908; p. 401

BICYCLE BUG'S DREAM, THE
(Imp)/Oct 7, 1911; p. 42

BICYCLE POLO (Pa)/Nov 21,1908;pp398,409

BICYCLE ROBBERS/Dec 26, 1908; p. 525

BIDDY BRADY'S BIRTHDAY
(Fal)/Sep 11, 1915; p. 1833

BIG BOB (Ne)/Mar 8, 1913; p. 997

BIG BOSS, THE (Re)/May 24, 1913; p. 813

BIG BROTHER, THE
(Re)/Aug 28, 1915; p. 1480

BIG BROTHER BILL
(Th)/Apr 24, 1915; p. 556

BIG DAM, THE (Ed)/Oct 7, 1911; p. 40

BIG DRUM, THE (It)/Dec 17, 1910; p. 1419

BIG GAME AT THE LONDON ZOO
(UE)/Jun 7, 1913; p. 1031

BIG HEARTED JIM
(Ec)/Oct 25, 1913; p. 382

BILL No. 1 (Ko)/Jul 18, 1914; p. 433
BILL ORGANIZES A UNION
  (Ko)/Sep 12, 1914; p. 1513
BILL PAYS HIS DEBTS
  (Lux)/Oct 28, 1911; p. 292
BILL PLAYS BOWLS
  (Lux)/Jan 7, 1911; p. 35
BILL POSTER'S TRIALS, A
  (Pa)/Sep 11, 1909; p. 346
BILL SAVES THE DAY
  (Ko)/Aug 29, 1914; p. 1242
BILL SPOILS A VACATION
  (Ko)/Oct 24, 1914; p. 492
BILL SQUARES IT WITH THE BOSS
  (Ko)/Aug 8, 1914; p. 837
BILL TAKES A LADY TO LUNCH
  (Ko)/Aug 15, 1914; p. 960
BILL TELL, PAWNBROKER
  (Bio)/Apr 18, 1914; p. 360
BILL THE CYCLIST
  (Lux)/Oct 21, 1911; p. 210
BILL TRIES TO MAKE BREAD
  (Lux)/Aug 26, 1911; p. 543
BILL TUNES THE PIANO
  (Lux)/Feb 24, 1912; p. 690
BILL WILSON'S GAL
  (Vi)/Oct 5, 1912; p.42
BILLIE (Ed)/May 18, 1912; p. 629
BILLIE - THE HILL BILLIE
  (Be)/Oct 16, 1915; p. 440
BILLIE GOAT (Maj)/Aug 14, 1915; p. 1161
BILLIE JOINS THE NAVY
  (Lu)/Sep 11, 1915; p. 1832
BILLIE'S DEBUT (Lu)/Aug 21, 1915; p.1316
BILLIE'S HEIRESS (Lu)/Aug 14,1915;p.1160
BILLIE'S RESCUE (Re)/Aug 7, 1915; p. 997
BILLIKEN (Lu)/Oct 16, 1909; p. 530
BILLIONAIRE, THE
  (Gen)/Mar 14, 1914; p. 1366
BILL'S AND GERTIE'S WEDDING DAY
  (Lux)/Dec 2, 1911; p. 726
BILL'S BIRTHDAY PRESENT
  (Sel)/Mar 1, 1913; p. 888
BILL'S BLIGHTED CAREER
  (Lko)/Jun 12, 1915; p. 1779
BILL'S BOARD BILL
  (Ka)/Jan 17, 1914; p. 288
BILL'S BOOTS (Lu)/Feb 12, 1910; p. 215
BILL'S BOY (SA)/Sep 26, 1914; p. 1775
BILL'S CAREER AS A BUTLER
  (Ed)/Nov 1, 1913; p. 495
BILL'S DAY OUT (Lux)/Jul 8, 1911; p. 1587
BILL'S GARDEN
  (Lux)/May 13, 1911; pp 1082-83
BILL'S LITTLE PLAN
  (Lux)/Apr 22, 1911; p. 901
BILL'S MOTOR (Lux)/Mar 2, 1912; p. 781
BILL'S NEW PAL (Lko)/Mar 6, 1915; p.1449

BILL'S PLUMBER AND PLUMBER'S BILL
  (Imp)/Nov 13, 1915; p. 1313
BILL'S SERENADE (Lux)/Jul 30,1910; p.245
BILL'S SWEETHEART
  (Ed)/May 17, 1913; p. 703
BILL'S WIDOW (Ch)/Jan 21, 1911; p. 145
BILLY, THE BEAR TAMER
  (Vi)/Jul 31, 1915; p. 816
BILLY, THE WISE GUY
  (Gem)/Jul 19, 1913; p. 321
BILLY AND HIS PAL
  (Me)/Mar 4, 1911; p. 482
BILLY AND THE BUTLER
  (SA)/Jul 6, 1912; p. 43
BILLY BUNKS THE BANDITS
  (Fal)/Dec 18, 1915; p. 2203
BILLY CHANGES HIS MIND
  (SA)/Jun 22, 1912; pp 1126-27
BILLY DODGES BILLS
  (Key)/Oct 11, 1913; p. 157
BILLY FOOLS DAD (Gem)/Feb 22,1913; p.782
BILLY GETS ARRESTED
  (Gem)/Apr 12, 1913; p. 166
BILLY IN ARMOR (Gem)/Jun 14, 1913; p.1138
BILLY IN TROUBLE
  (Pa)/Jun 3, 1911; p. 1258
BILLY IS ON FIRE
  (Pa)/Mar 14, 1908; p. 218
BILLY JOINS THE BAND
  (Gem)/Mar 1, 1913; p. 890
BILLY JONES OF NEW YORK
  (Ch)/Dec 14, 1912; p. 1083
BILLY McGRATH'S ART CAREER
  (SA)/Dec 7, 1912; p. 976
BILLY McGRATH'S LOVE LETTER
  (SA)/Sep 28, 1912; p. 1277
BILLY PLAYS POKER
  (Gem)/May 31, 1913; p. 921
BILLY THE DETECTIVE
  (Sol)/Apr 27, 1912; p. 330
BILLY TURNS BURGLAR
  (Gem)/Apr 26, 1913; p. 382
BILLY TURNS VALET
  (Ko)/Feb 20, 1915; p. 1140
BILLY VAN DEUSEN AND THE MERRY
  WIDOW (Be)/Nov 27, 1915; p. 1664
BILLY VAN DEUSEN'S CAMPAIGN
  (Be)/Nov 6, 1915; p. 1140
BILLY WAS A RIGHT SMART BOY
  (St)/Feb 13, 1915; p. 985
BILLY WINS (Gem)/Mar 22, 1913; p. 1221
BILLY'S ADVENTURE
  (Gem)/May 31, 1913; p. 921
BILLY'S BABY (Lae)/Jul 10, 1915; p. 309
BILLY'S BOARD BILL
  (Gem)/Feb 15, 1913; p. 680
BILLY'S BURGLAR (Vi)/Nov 16,
  1912; p. 640/Dec 7, 1912; p. 975

BILLY'S CHARGE (St)/Dec 12, 1914; p.1524
BILLY'S COLLEGE JOB
(Imp)/Oct 2, 1915; p. 80
BILLY'S DOUBLE (Gem)/Apr 5, 1913; p. 49
BILLY'S DOUBLE CAPTURE
(Rex)/Feb 22, 1913; p. 782
BILLY'S FIRST QUARREL
(Gem)/May 17, 1913; p. 705
BILLY'S HONEYMOON
(Gem)/Jun 7, 1913; p. 1032
BILLY'S INSOMNIA
(Sol)/May 11, 1912; p. 529
BILLY'S LETTERS
(Com)/Dec 16, 1911; p. 905
BILLY'S MARRIAGE
(Pa)/Aug 26, 1911; p. 542
BILLY'S MISTAKEN OVERCOAT
(Gem)/Apr 5, 1913; p. 49
BILLY'S NEW WATCH
(Maj)/May 17, 1913; p. 705
BILLY'S NIGHTMARE
(UE)/Aug 10, 1912; p. 545
BILLY'S NURSE (MnA)/Aug 28,1915;p.1479
BILLY'S RIOT (St)/Jul 11, 1914; p. 256
BILLY'S RIVAL (Am)/Oct 17, 1914; p. 337
BILLY'S RUSE (Pr)/Mar 28, 1914; p. 1681
BILLY'S SEANCE (Imp)/Dec 23, 1911; p.990
BILLY'S SHOES (Sol)/Apr 6, 1912; p. 43
BILLY'S SISTER (Me)/Oct 22, 1910; p. 934
BILLY'S STRATEGEM (Bio)/Feb 24, 1912;
p. 690/Oct 23, 1915; p. 619
BILLY'S STRATEGY
(Gem)/Feb 22, 1913; p. 782
BILLY'S STUPIDITY
(Lae)/Jun 19, 1915; p. 1941
BILLY'S SURRENDER
(Po)/Feb 10, 1912; p. 483
BILLY'S TROUBLES
(Gem)/Mar 22, 1913; p. 1221
BILLY'S TROUBLESOME GRIP
(Sol)/Apr 13, 1912; p. 138
BILLY'S VALENTINE
(Vi)/Apr 15, 1911; p. 842
BILLY'S WAGER (Vi)/Jan 23, 1915; p. 515
BILTMORE DIAMOND, THE
(Me)/Aug 29, 1914; p. 1241
BIMBERG'S LOVE AFFAIR
(Cry)/Mar 14, 1914; p. 1386
BINDING SHOT, THE
(Am)/Dec 31, 1910; p. 1539
BING, BANG, BIFF
(Pa)/Jul 3, 1915; p. 65
BING BANG BROTHERS
(Fal)/Oct 23, 1915; p. 620
BINGLES AND THE CABARET
(Vi)/Jul 12, 1913; p. 205
BINGLES MENDS THE CLOCK
(Vi)/May 17, 1913; p. 703

BINGLES' NIGHTMARE
(Vi)/Aug 23, 1913; p. 844
BINGVILLE FIRE DEPARTMENT, THE
(Ka)/Aug 8, 1914; p. 836
BINKS, THE HAWKSHAW
(Imp)/Sep 13, 1913; p. 1177
BINKS, THE TIGHTWAD
(Imp)/Mar 8, 1913; p. 997
BINKS ADVERTISES FOR A WIFE
(Imp)/Aug 30, 1913; p. 962
BINKS AND THE BATHING GIRLS
(Imp)/Sep 20, 1913; p. 1285
BINKS AND THE BLACK HAND
(Imp)/Mar 15, 1913; p. 1105
BINKS DID IT (Imp)/Feb 22, 1913; p. 782
BINKS ELEVATES A STAGE
(Imp)/Sep 13, 1913; p. 1177
BINKS ENDS THE WAR
(Imp)/Jul 26, 1913; p. 430
BINKS PLAYS CUPID
(Imp)/Sep 27, 1913; p. 1393
BINKS' VACATION (Bio)/Dec 13,1913; p.1279
BIRD IN THE HAND, A
(SA)/Jan 13, 1912; p. 125
BIRD OF PREY (UE)/Jul 4, 1914; p. 66
BIRD'S A BIRD, A
(Key)/Feb 20, 1915; p. 1140
BIRDS AND ANIMALS OF BRAZIL
(Pa)/Jun 21, 1913; p. 1252
BIRD'S EYE VIEW OF ROTTERDAM, A
(UE)/Feb 24, 1912;p.689
BIRDS OF A FEATHER
(Vi)/Sep 2, 1911; pp 628-29
BIRDS OF PASSAGE
(Ec)/Mar 14, 1914; p. 1386
BIRDS OF PREY (Ka)/Aug 23, 1913; p. 842
(Pa)/Oct 11, 1913; p. 155
BIRDS OF THE INLAND MARSH
(Pa)/Dec 27, 1913; p. 1543
BIRDS OF THE SOUTHERN SEA COAST
(Ed)/Oct 18, 1913; p. 264
BIRTH AND ADVENTURES OF A
FOUNTAIN PEN (Vi)/Jul 24, 1909; p. 124
BIRTH MARK, THE
(Ya)/Jun 10, 1911; p. 1317
(Lu)/May 10, 1913; p. 596
BIRTH OF A DRAGON FLY, THE
(CGP)/Feb 1, 1913; p. 465
BIRTH OF A FLOWER, THE
(CGP)/Nov 25, 1911; p. 638
BIRTH OF A NATION, THE
(Gri)/Mar 13, 1915; pp 1586-87
BIRTH OF EMOTION, THE
(Nas)/Jan 9, 1915; p. 224
BIRTH OF JESUS, THE
(Pa)/Jan 8, 1910; p. 16
BIRTH OF LOTUS BLOSSOM, THE
(Th)/Sep 21, 1912; p. 1177

BLACK PRINCESS (Pa)/Apr 4, 1908; p. 299
BLACK RING, THE
(Ka)/May 15, 1915; p. 1092
BLACK RODERICK
(Ecl)/Sep 19, 1914; p. 1626
BLACK SHEEP (Sol)/Jan 20, 1912; p. 204
(Bio)/Aug 10, 1912; p. 546
(Bio)/May 22, 1915; p. 1260
BLACK SHEEP, A
(Sel)/Oct 9, 1915; pp 285-86
BLACK SHEEP, THE
(SA)/Jul 10, 1909; p. 49
(Vi)/Aug 3, 1912; p. 445
(Ec)/Dec 21, 1912; p. 1186
(UF)/Aug 23, 1913; p. 828
(Bro)/Oct 18, 1913; p. 265
(Ka)/Jan 9, 1915; p. 221
(Re)/Apr 3, 1915; p. 65
BLACK SIGNAL, THE
(SA)/Sep 5, 1914; p. 1371
BLACK SMALLBOX SCARE, THE
(Po)/May 10, 1913; p. 597
BLACK SNAKE, THE
(Ape)/Aug 23, 1913; p. 823
BLACK SPOT, THE (Co)/Jan 2, 1915; p. 87
BLACK THIRTEEN, THE
(Ape)/Jan 10, 1914; p. 181
BLACK TRAILERS, THE
(Me)/May 31, 1913; p. 920
BLACK TRIANGLE, THE
(Llo)/May 2, 1914; p. 655
BLACK VIPER, THE
(Bio)/Jul 25, 1908; p. 67
BLACK WALL, THE
(Vi)/Mar 30, 1912; p. 1165
BLACK WALLET, THE
(Vi)/Mar 27, 1915; p. 1932
BLACKBEARD (Sel)/Dec 9, 1911; p. 816
BLACKBIRDS (Las)/Oct 30, 1915; p. 810
BLACKENED HILLS
(Am)/Jan 11, 1913; p. 159
BLACKFOOT CONSPIRACY, THE
(101)/Nov 23, 1912; pp 768, 769
BLACKFOOT HALF-BREED, THE
(Ka)/Oct 14, 1911; p. 129
BLACKMAILER, THE
(Mi)/Oct 5, 1907; pp 490-91
(Pa)/Jul 4, 1908; p.11/Dec 26, 1908; p.525
(Ne)/Jan 18, 1913; p. 265
BLACKSMITH, THE
(Lu)/Jan 27, 1912; p. 302
BLACKSMITH BEN (Bio)/Dec 5,1914;p.1383
BLACKSMITH'S BRIDE, THE
(Gau)/Mar 13, 1909; p. 303
BLACKSMITH'S DAUGHTER, THE
(FIT)/Sep 18, 1909; p. 379
(Fr)/Oct 31, 1914; p. 642
BLACKSMITH'S LOVE, THE

(Sel)/Sep 2, 1911; p. 626
BLACKSMITH'S STORY, THE (Pi)/Feb 8,
1913; p. 557/Mar 1, 1913; p. 889
BLACKSNAKE'S TREACHERY
(Bi)/Jul 22, 1911; p. 126
BLADE O' GRASS (Ed)/Dec 25, 1915; p. 2387
BLAME THE TAYLOR
(Bio)/Mar 28, 1914; p. 1680
BLAME THE WIFE (Bio)/May 10, 1913; p. 596
BLAMING THE DUCK OR DUCKING THE
BLAME (Lu)/Dec 4, 1915; p. 1852
BLANK PAGE, THE (Imp)/May 8, 1915; p.901
BLASTED HOPES (Sel)/Nov 12, 1910;p.1116
BLAZED TRAIL, THE
(Ne)/Sep 10, 1910; p. 576
BLAZING A NEW TRAIL IN GLACIER
NATIONAL PARK (Pa)/Oct 11, 1913; p.156
BLAZING THE TRAIL
(Pre)/Apr 10, 1915; p. 237
BLEEDING HEARTS (Imp)/Oct 4, 1913; p.50
BLESSED MIRACLE, THE
(Lu)/Apr 10, 1915; p. 236
BLESSING THE BOATS IN ARCACHON
(KO)/Jul 11, 1908; p. 36
BLESSINGS SOMETIMES COME IN
DISGUISE (Pa)/May 29, 1909; p.714
BLESSINGTON'S BONNY BABIES
(Pa)/Oct 30, 1909; p. 604
BLIGHT, THE (Pa)/Dec 20, 1913; p. 1411
BLIGHT OF WEALTH, THE
(Th)/Dec 6, 1913; p. 1153
BLIGHTED LIVES (Sol)/Mar 16, 1912; p.963
BLIGHTED SPANIARD, A
(Lko)/Dec 5, 1914; p. 1385
BLIND AGAINST HIS WILL
(Lux)/Sep 18, 1909; p. 379
BLIND BASKET WEAVER, THE
(Ka)/Sep 6, 1913; p. 1068
BLIND BOY, THE (Lu)/Feb 1, 1908; p. 83
BLIND BUSINESS, A
(Lu)/May 23, 1914; p. 1116
BLIND CATTLE KING, THE
(Lu)/Jan 11, 1913; p. 158
BLIND COMPOSER'S DILEMNA, THE
(Ka)/Mar 22, 1913; p. 1219
BLIND FIDDLER, THE
(Ed)/Sep 26, 1914; p. 1775
BLIND GIRL OF CASTLE GUILLE, THE
(Pa)/Sep 13, 1913; p. 1176
BLIND GYPSY, THE (Pa)/Oct 4, 1913; p. 48
BLIND JUSTICE
(SA)/Dec 18, 1915; pp 2196-97, 2203
BLIND LOVE (Bio)/Sep 28, 1912; p. 1276
BLIND MAN OF JERUSALEM, THE
(Gau)/May 29, 1909; p. 713
BLIND MAN'S BUFF
(Ne)/Mar 2, 1912; p. 782
(SA)/Jun 13, 1914; p. 1540

BLIND MAN'S DOG, THE
  (Ec)/Oct 1, 1910; p. 750
  (Mil)/Oct 26, 1912; p. 345
BLIND MAN'S SACRIFICE, THE
  (Mil)/Aug 10, 1912; p. 547
BLIND MINER, THE (Vi)/Jan 20,
  1912; p. 194/Feb 3, 1912; p. 392
BLIND MUSIC MASTER, THE
  (SBa)/Oct 23, 1915; p. 622
BLIND MUSICIAN (Imp)/Sep 28,1912;p.1278
BLIND PRINCESS AND THE POET, THE
  (Bio)/Aug 12, 1911; p. 358
BLIND RECEPTION, A
  (Lu)/Dec 9, 1911; p. 816
BLIND WOMAN'S STORY (Pa)/May 23,
  1908; pp 464-65/May 1, 1909; p. 554
BLINDED HEART, THE
  (Lu)/Feb 7, 1914; p. 677
BLINDFOLDED (SA)/May 15, 1915; p. 1071
BLINDNESS OF COURAGE, or BETWEEN
  TWO LOVES (Dra)/Sep 6, 1913; p. 1070
BLINDNESS OF DEVOTION, THE
  (Fox)/Nov 20, 1915; pp 1500, 1505
BLINDNESS OF VIRTUE, THE
  (SA)/Jul 17, 1915; pp 505-6
BLINKHORN NATURAL HISTORY
  TRAVELS (Bli)/May 2, 1914; p. 675
"BLINKS AND JINKS," ATTORNEYS-AT-
  LAW (Ed)/May 18, 1912; p. 628
BLISSVILLE, THE BEAUTIFUL
  (Lu)/Jan 8, 1910; p. 17
BLOOD AND WATER (Sol)/Jun 28, 1913;
  p. 1361/Oct 25, 1913; p. 382
BLOOD BROTHERHOOD, THE
  (Rex)/Nov 15, 1913; p. 737
BLOOD HERITAGE
  (Imp)/Nov 13, 1915; p. 1314
BLOOD IS THICKER THAN WATER
  (Imp)/Aug 17, 1912; p. 676
BLOOD OF HIS BROTHER, THE
  (Bi)/May 15, 1915; pp 1073-74
BLOOD OF OUR BROTHERS, THE
  (Cen)/Oct 30a, 1915; p. 968
BLOOD OF THE POOR, THE
  (Ch)/Jan 13, 1912; p. 127
BLOOD RED TAPE OF CHARITY, THE
  (Po)/Sep 13, 1913; p. 1177
BLOOD RUBY, THE (Vi)/Oct 10, 1914;p.188
BLOOD SEEDLING, THE
  (Sel)/Oct 9, 1915; p. 253
BLOOD TEST, THE
  (Imp)/Apr 11, 1914; p. 213
BLOOD VENGEANCE, THE
  (Amb)/Jan 13, 1912; p. 126
BLOOD WILL TELL
  (Pa)/Nov 14, 1908; p.385/Nov 21, 1908;p.398
  (KB)/Nov 23,1912;p.754/Dec 21,1912;p.1185
  (Imp)/Apr 19, 1913; p. 281

BLOOD YOKE, THE
  (Sel)/Jun 19, 1915; p. 1940
BLOODHOUNDS OF THE NORTH
  (GS)/Dec 27, 1913; p. 1545
BLOODLESS DUEL (KO)/May 9, 1908;p.423
BLOODSTONE, THE/Oct 30, 1908; p. 338
BLOPPS IN SEARCH OF THE BLACK
  HAND (Lux)/Dec 3, 1910; p. 1298
BLOT ON THE ESCUTCHEON, A
  (Bio)/Feb 17, 1912; pp 581-82
BLOT ON THE SHIELD, THE
  (Am)/Oct 23, 1915; p. 621
BLOTTED BRAND, THE
  (Am)/Sep 2, 1911; p. 631
BLOTTED OUT (Lu)/Jun 20, 1914; p. 1688
BLOTTED PAGE, A (Re)/Nov 7,1914; p.789
BLOW FOR BLOW (Bio)/Oct 30,1915;p.791
BLOWN INTO CUSTODY
  (Bio)/Mar 20, 1915; p. 1764
BLOWN UP (Kri)/Jan 23, 1915; p. 517
BLOWOUT AT SANTA BANANA, A
  (Am)/Feb 7, 1914; p. 678
BLUDGEON, THE (Eq)/Oct 23, 1915;
  p. 627/Oct 30, 1915; p. 793
BLUDSOE'S DILEMNA
  (Am)/Dec 7, 1912; p. 978
BLUE AND THE GREY, THE
  (Ed)/Jun 6, 1908; p. 498
BLUE BIRD, THE (Pa)/Aug 22, 1908; p. 143
BLUE BLOOD AND RED
  (Sel)/Jan 31, 1914; p. 543
BLUE BLOOD AND YELLOW BACKS
  (Lko)/Jun 19, 1915; p. 1941
BLUE BONNET, THE
  (Sel)/May 2, 1908; p. 403
BLUE COYOTE CHERRY CROP, THE
  (Ed)/Sep 12, 1914; p. 1516
BLUE FISHING NETS
  (Gau)/Mar 12, 1910; p. 382
BLUE FLAME, THE
  (Sel)/Oct 31, 1914; p. 641
BLUE GARTER, THE (Lu)/Nov 20,
  1909; p. 719/Nov 27, 1909; p. 758
BLUE GRASS (Eq)/Oct 16, 1915; p. 462
BLUE HORSE MINE, THE
  (Lu)/Jan 14, 1911; p. 88
BLUE JACKETS' MANEOUVERS
  (Amb)/May 28, 1910; p. 891
BLUE KNOT, KING OF POLO
  (Am)/Jul 4, 1914; p. 65
BLUE LEGEND, THE
  (Pa)/Jun 26, 1909; p. 874
BLUE MOUNTAIN BUFFALOES
  (Ch)/Apr 20, 1912; p. 230
BLUE MOUSE, THE (DeL)/Apr 11,1914; p.190
BLUE NILE, THE (Ec)/May 13, 1911; p.1083
BLUE OR GRAY (Bio)/Dec 20, 1913; p. 1411
BLUE PETE'S ESCAPE

(Re)/Jul 25, 1914; p. 573
BLUE RIDGE FOLKS
(Ch)/Nov 30, 1912; p. 878
BLUE RIDGE ROMANCE, A
(Rep)/Feb 3, 1912; p. 395
BLUE WING AND THE VIOLINIST
(Pa)/Aug 19, 1911; p. 463
BLUEBIRD THE SECOND
(Bio)/Sep 19, 1914; p. 1645
BLUFFERS, THE (Am)/Nov 27, 1915; p.1664
BLUNDERER, THE (Lu)/Mar 26,1910; p.467
BLUNDERER'S MARK, THE
(Ec)/Jun 27, 1914; p. 1830
BLUNTED SWORD, THE
(It)/Aug 26, 1911; p. 544
BOARDERS AND BOMBS
(Bio)/Nov 15, 1913; p. 735
BOARDING HOUSE ACQUAINTANCE, A
(Pa)/Aug 1, 1908;p.91
BOARDING HOUSE FEUD, THE
(Vi)/May 15, 1915; p. 1071
BOARDING HOUSE HEIRESS, A
(Sol)/Mar 23, 1912; p. 1064
BOARDING HOUSE MYSTERY, THE
(Rex)/Jan 20, 1912; p. 205
BOARDING HOUSE ROMANCE, A
(Ed)/Apr 4, 1914; p. 57
BOARDING-HOUSE ROMANCE, A
(Lu)/Feb 3, 1912; p. 393
BOARDING-SCHOOL ROMANCE, A
(Vi)/Jul 16, 1910; p. 143
BOARDING HOUSE SCRAMBLE, A
(SA)/Jul 25, 1914; p. 571
BOB AND ROWDY (Ed)/Aug 5, 1911; p. 294
BOB BUILDS A BOAT
(Lu)/Jun 28, 1913; p. 1358
BOB BUILDS A CHICKEN HOUSE
(Lu)/Jun 21, 1913; p. 1251
BOB BUYS AN AUTO
(Lu)/Jul 12, 1913; p. 204
BOBBIE THE COWARD
(Bio)/Jul 29, 1911; p. 209
BOBBY, SOME SPIRITUALIST
(Me)/Apr 18, 1914; p 360-61
BOBBY HAS A PIPE DREAM
Jan 16, 1909; p. 70
BOBBY THE BANKER
(Me)/May 9, 1914; p. 820
BOBBY WHITE IN WONDERLAND
(Sel)/Jul 25, 1908; p. 71
BOBBY'S BABY (Rex)/Apr 5, 1913;
p. 49/Apr 12, 1913; p. 166
BOBBY'S BANDIT (Maj)/Mar 20,1915;p.1765
BOBBY'S BARGAIN
(Bio)/May 15, 1915; p. 1091
BOBBY'S BUM BOMB
(Pun)/Mar 8, 1913; p. 998
BOBBY'S DREAM (Ed)/Nov 16, 1912; p. 659

BOBBY'S DREAM, THE
(Lux)/Sep 24, 1910; p. 690
BOBBY'S KODAK (Bio)/Feb 8, 1908; p. 102
BOBBY'S MEDAL (Re)/Jan 9, 1915; p. 221
BOBBY'S PLOT (Re)/Jul 25, 1914; p. 573
BOBBY'S SKETCHES
(Pa)/Feb 6, 1909; p. 145
BOB'S BABY (Gem)/Aug 9, 1913; p. 638
BOB'S DECEPTION (Rex)/Oct 12, 1912; p. 144
BOB'S LOVE AFFAIRS
(Bio)/Oct 23, 1915; p. 619
BOB'S MICROSCOPE
(Pa)/Jun 10, 1911; p. 1316
BOB'S ELECTRIC THEATER
(Pa)/Oct 30, 1909; p. 604
BOB'S NEW SCHEME
(Lu)/Aug 26, 1911; p. 540
BOB-SLEDDING (Vi)/Apr 22, 1911; p. 900
BODY AND SOUL (Wor)/Nov 27,1915;p.1677
BODY IN THE TRUNK, THE
(Maj)/May 9, 1914; p. 822
BOER WAR, THE (Ka)/Mar 7, 1914; p. 1216
BOGEY WOMAN, THE (Pa)/Jul 10, 1909; p.51
BOGGS' PREDICAMENT
(Ka)/Sep 20, 1913; p. 1283
BOGUS BARON, A (St)/Sep 12, 1914; p. 1513
BOGUS GOVERNESS, THE
(GN)/Jun 17, 1911; p. 1389
BOGUS HEIR (Pa)/Nov 6, 1909; p. 644
BOGUS HERO, A (GN)/Nov 15, 1913; p. 737
BOGUS LORD, THE (Lu)/Aug 8, 1908; p. 108
BOGUS MAGIC POWDER
(KO)/May 9, 1908; p. 423
BOGUS NAPOLEON, THE
(Vi)/Aug 31, 1912; p. 880
BOGUS PROFESSOR, THE
(Cin)/Jun 15, 1912; p. 1027
BOIL YOUR WATER
(Pa)/May 6, 1911; p. 1019
BOIS DE BOULOGNE, THE
(Pa)/Aug 28, 1915; p. 1481
BOLD, BAD BOYS
(StP)/Aug 7, 1915; p. 998
BOLD, BAD BURGLAR, A
(Ka)/Jan 30, 1915; p. 671
**BOLD BANDITTI AND THE RAH RAH
BOYS, THE** (Ka)/Dec 26, 1914; p. 1840
BOLD EMMETT, IRELAND'S MARTYR
(Lu)/Aug 28, 1915; p. 1479
BOLD GAME, A (CGP)/Aug 10, 1912; p. 545
BOLD IMPERSONATION, A
(Re)/Sep 11, 1915; p. 1833
BOLT FROM THE SKY, A
(Ka)/Aug 2, 1913; p. 537
(Bal)/Nov 20, 1915; p. 1501
BOLTED DOOR, THE
(Ka)/Jan 14, 1911; p. 90
(Vic)/Apr 18, 1914; p. 362

BOMB, THE (Lu)/Jan 2, 1915; p. 76
BOMB THROWER, THE
  (Pa)/Jan 30, 1915; p. 674
BOMBARDED (Sel)/Jun 27, 1914; p. 1828
BOMBARDMENT OF ALEXANDRIA, THE
  (Vi)/Jan 17, 1914; p. 269
BOMBAY BUDDHA, THE (Imp)/Mar 27,
  1915; p. 1914f/Apr 17, 1915; p. 394
BOMBS AND BANGS
  (Key)/Sep 19, 1914; p. 1646
BOMBSKY AND THE BOMB
  (Roy)/Jun 13, 1914; p. 1541
BONAFACIO AS A BLACKMOOR
  (Mil)/Nov 30, 1912; p. 878
BONANZA KING, THE
  (Am)/Feb 4, 1911; p. 249
BOND ETERNAL, THE
  (Ka)/Sep 5, 1914; p. 1372
BOND OF BROTHERHOOD, THE
  (Gau)/Mar 1, 1913; pp 874, 889
BOND OF FRIENDSHIP, THE
  (Aa)/Mar 27, 1915; p. 1942
BOND OF LOVE, THE
  (Sel)/Apr 18, 1914; p. 360
  (Ecl)/Sep 12, 1914; p. 1494
BOND OF MUSIC (Vi)/Sep 14, 1912; p. 1074
BOND OF WOMANHOOD, THE
  (Lu)/Oct 31, 1914; p. 641
BOND SINISTER, THE
  (Bio)/Jan 2, 1915; p. 75
BOND THAT BINDS, THE
  (Fr)/Nov 29, 1913; p. 1008
BONDAGE OF FEAR, THE
  (Bio)/Apr 25, 1914; p. 517
BONDMAN'S FATE, THE
  (Pa)/May 29, 1909; p. 713
BONDSMAN, THE
  (Dom)/Sep 20, 1913; p. 1286
BONDWOMAN, THE
  (Ka)/Jul 17, 1915; p. 485
BONDWOMEN (KEd)/Dec 25, 1915; p. 2382
BONESETTER'S DAUGHTER, THE
  (Pa)/Jun 25, 1910; p. 1101
BONIFACE IS BASHFUL
  (Mil)/Dec 7, 1912; p. 976
BONITA OF EL CAJON
  (Am)/Jan 6, 1912; p. 42
BONNIE OF THE HILLS
  (Ch)/Jan 6, 1912; p. 42
  (SA)/Sep 27, 1913; p. 1391
BOOB, THE (Sel)/Aug 24, 1912; p. 771
          (Rex)/May 31, 1913; p. 922
BOOB AND THE BAKER, THE
  (Bio)/Jan 23, 1915; p. 496
BOOB AND THE MAGICIAN, THE
  (Bio)/Mar 20, 1915; p. 1763
BOOB FOR LUCK, A
  (Ka)/Jan 30, 1915; p. 671

BOOB INCOGNITO, THE
  (Rex)/Apr 18, 1914; p. 362
BOOB THERE WAS, A
  (Rex)/May 16, 1914; p. 970
BOOBLEY'S BABY (Vi)/May 15,1915;p.1071
BOOBS AND BRICKS
  (Am)/Apr 26, 1913; p. 382
BOOB'S DREAM GIRL, THE
  (Rex)/Nov 1, 1913; p. 497
BOOB'S HONEYMOON, THE
  (Rex)/Feb 21, 1914; p. 948
BOOB'S INHERITANCE, THE
  (Imp)/Jan 25, 1913; p. 365
BOOB'S LEGACY, THE
  (Rex)/Oct 10, 1914; p. 189
BOOB'S NEMESIS, THE
  (Rex)/Aug 29, 1914; p. 1242
BOOB'S RACING CAREER, THE
  (Kri)/Jan 23, 1915; p. 517
BOOB'S ROMANCE, A
  (Lae)/Jun 26, 1915; p. 2097
BOOB'S VICTORY, THE
  (Pa)/Dec 25, 1915; p. 2384
BOOL DETECTIVE, THE
  (Rex)/Jun 27, 1914; p. 1830
BOOK AGENT, THE
  (Po)/Nov 11, 1911; p. 472
  (Nov)/Dec 18, 1915; p. 2203
BOOK OF NATURE, THE
  (Dil)/Nov 7, 1914; p. 769
BOOK OF VERSES, A
  (Rex)/Apr 19, 1913; p. 281
BOOKWORM, THE
  (Sel)/Jul 6, 1907; pp 284-85
BOOMERANG, THE
  (Ne)/Oct 12, 1912; p. 144
  (Ka)/Feb 8, 1913; p. 572
  (KB)/May 31, 1913; p. 921
  (Bro)/Jun 7, 1913; p. 1013
  (SA)/Oct 25,1913; p.359/Nov 29,1913;p.1008
BOOMERANG SWINDLE, A
  (Lu)/Nov 21, 1914; p. 1075
BOOMING BUSINESS
  (Th)/Jul 16, 1910; p. 144
BOOSTING BUSINESS
  (SA)/May 31, 1913; p. 920
BOOTLEGGER, THE
  (Sel)/Nov 25, 1911; p. 636
BOOTLES' BABY (Ed)/Jul 2, 1910; p. 25/
  Oct 3, 1914; p. 39
BORDER DETECTIVE, THE
  (Am)/Oct 26, 1912; p. 344
BORDER PARSON, THE
  (Ne)/Nov 2, 1912; pp 451-52
BORDER RANGER, THE
  (SA)/Feb 4, 1911; p. 244
BORDER TALE, A
  (Pa)/Dec 10, 1910; p. 1356

BORN WARRIOR, A
(WF)/Jun 13, 1914; pp 1548-49
BORNEO POTTERY (CGP)/Mar 1, 1913; p.888
BORROWED BABY, THE
(Ka)/Aug 27, 1910; p. 462
BORROWED BOOK, THE
(Bio)/Oct 17, 1914; p. 336
BORROWED CLOTHES
(Vi)/Sep 4, 1909; p. 316
BORROWED FINERY
(Ed)/Apr 11, 1914; p. 212
BORROWED FLAT, THE
(Am)/Jan 28, 1911; p. 196
BORROWED GOLD (KB)/Nov 1, 1913; p. 498
BORROWED IDENTITY, A
(SA)/Nov 1, 1913; p. 495
BORROWED LADDER, THE
(Lu)/Apr 13, 1907; p. 90
BORROWED NECKLACE, THE
(Bio)/Feb 20, 1915; p. 1139
BORROWED PLUMAGE
(Cin)/Jun 14, 1913; p. 1135
BORROWING TROUBLE
(Sel)/Aug 9, 1913; p. 637
BOSS, THE (Wor)/May 29, 1915; p. 1442
BOSS OF LUCKY RANCH, THE
(Am)/May 13, 1911; p. 1082
BOSS OF LUMBER CAMP No.4, THE
(Ed)/May 4, 1912; p. 425
BOSS OF THE CIRCLE E RANCH, THE
(Ne)/Jul 2, 1910; p. 25
BOSS OF THE 8th, THE
(Bro)/Oct 3, 1914; p. 66
BOSS OF THE KATY MINE, THE
(SA)/Dec 14, 1912; p. 1080
BOSS OF THE LUMBER CAMP, THE
(Ed)/Apr 13, 1912; p. 118
BOSTON FLOATING HOSPITAL, THE
(Ka)/Nov 1, 1913; p. 495
BOSTON TEA PARTY, THE (Ed)/Jul 11,
1908; p. 32/Nov 28, 1908; p. 423/
Mar 20, 1915; p. 1773
BOSUN'S MATE, THE
(Co)/Aug 15, 1914; p. 937
BO'SUN'S WATCH, THE
(Ed)/Dec 2, 1911; p. 725
BOTH SIDES OF LIFE
(Lae)/Sep 11, 1915; p. 1834
BOTH WERE STUNG
(Gau)/Nov 12, 1910; p. 1118
BOTHERSOME HUSBAND
(Pa)/Jul 11, 1908; p. 51
BOTTLE OF MILK, A
(It)/May 13, 1911; p. 1082
BOTTLE OF MUSK, A
(SA)/Mar 22, 1913; p. 1220
BOTTLED ROMANCE, A
(Ka)/Mar 7, 1914; p. 1236

BOTTLED SPIDER, THE
(Ka)/Jun 13, 1914; p. 1541
BOTTLED UP (Pa)/Jun 5, 1909; p. 753
BOTTLES (Sol)/Aug 10,1912;p.547
BOTTOM OF THE SEA, THE
(Lu)/Apr 11, 1914; p. 212
BOTTOMLESS PIT, THE
(KB)/Jan 30, 1915; p. 673
BOUGHT (Wor)/Oct 30a, 1915; p. 985/
Nov 6, 1915; p. 1141
BOUND BY THE LEOPARD'S LOVE
(Sel)/Jul 24, 1915; p. 649
BOUND ON THE WHEEL
(Rex)/Jul 31, 1915; p. 818
BOUND TO OCCUR (SA)/Mar 8, 1913; p. 995
BOUNDARY, THE (Pa)/Aug 8, 1908; p. 110
BOUNDARY RIDER, THE
(Ecl)/Aug 8, 1914; p. 841
BOUNDER (Sel)/Mar 23,1912;p.1062
BOUQUET, THE (SA)/Nov 5, 1910; p. 1059
(SA)/May 1, 1915; p. 727
BOWL-BEARER, THE
(Th)/Sep 18, 1915; p. 1996
BOWL OF ROSES, A
(Rex)/Aug 22, 1914; p. 1101
BOWLING CRAZE, THE
(Ec)/Dec 24, 1910; p. 1480
BOWLING FIEND, THE
(Pa)/Jan 7, 1911; p. 34
BOWLING MATCH, THE
(Key)/Sep 27, 1913; p. 1394
BOX AND COX (Cry)/Feb 8, 1913; p. 574
BOX CAR BABY, THE
(Sel)/Aug 31, 1912; p. 881
BOX CAR BRIDE, THE
(Ka)/Jun 27, 1914; p. 1828
BOX COUCH, THE (Imp)/Feb 21,1914;p.947
BOX OF BANDITS, THE
(Vic)/Aug 28, 1915; p. 1481
BOX OF CHOCOLATES, THE
(Bio)/Mar 6, 1915; p. 1447
BOXES AND BOXERS
(Cry)/Jun 20, 1914; p. 1690
BOXING ENGLISHMAN, THE
(KO)/May 9, 1908; p. 423
BOXING UNDER DIFFICULTIES
(Lux)/Nov 23, 1912; p. 768
BOY (Ec)/Sep 5, 1914; p. 1385/
Sep 12, 1914; p. 1513
BOY AND THE GIRL, THE
(Ed)/Sep 14, 1912; p. 1074
BOY DETECTIVE, THE
(Bio)/Mar 14, 1908; p. 216
BOY FOR A DAY, A
(Roy)/May 30, 1914; p. 1261
BOY MAYOR, THE (Ne)/Nov 14, 1914; p. 932
BOY OF THE REVOLUTION, A
(Pa)/Sep 9, 1911; p. 716

BOY RANGERS, THE
(Ed)/Nov 9, 1912; p. 552
BOY SCOUTS, THE
(Ch)/Jul 8, 1911; p. 1588
BOY SCOUTS OF AMERICA
(Ed)/Nov 12, 1910; p. 1118
BOY SCOUTS TO THE RESCUE, THE
(Ne)/May 17, 1913; p. 705
BOY WANTED (Ed)/Oct 25, 1913; p. 379
BOYS AGAIN (Ec)/Aug 17, 1912; p. 674
BOYS AND THE COALMAN
(KO)/Apr 11, 1908; p. 327
BOY'S BEST FRIEND, A
(Imp)/Aug 26, 1911; p. 544
BOYS OF THE I.O.U., THE
(Vi)/Jun 13, 1914; p. 1540
BOYS OF TOPSY-TURVY RANCH, THE
(Ne)/Oct 29, 1910; p.999
BOY'S VEST (Pa)/Mar 4, 1911; p. 482
BOYS WILL BE BOYS
(Lu)/May 8, 1909; p. 594
(UE)/Jul 22, 1911; p. 123
(SA)/Aug 14, 1915; p. 1160
BOZO ARRIVES (Po)/May 10, 1913; p. 597
BRACELET, THE
(GN)/Nov 6, 1909; p. 645
(Box)/Nov 21, 1914; p. 1078
BRADFORD'S CLAIM
(Ed)/Apr 9, 1910; p. 554
BRADHURST FIELD CLUB
(Imp)/Apr 20, 1912; p. 231
BRAGGART, THE (Vi)/Jul 4, 1908; p. 14
BRAGG'S NEW SUIT
(Ed)/Jun 7, 1913; p. 1030
BRAHMIN'S MIRACLE, THE
(Pa)/Sep 26, 1908; p. 243
BRAID, THE (Com)/Jan 27, 1912; pp 304-5
BRAINS AND BRAWN
(Sel)/Jun 1, 1912; p. 830
BRAINS VS BRAWN
(Th)/Dec 28, 1912; pp 1292-93
BRAND, THE (Am)/Jun 8, 1912; p. 946
(Ka)/Sep 12, 1914; p. 1512
BRAND BLOTTER, THE
(Sel)/Oct 5, 1912; p. 40
BRAND BLOTTERS (Id)/Jun 19,1915;p.1941
BRAND FROM THE BURNING, A
(Fr)/Aug 9, 1913; p. 637
BRAND-NEW HERO, A
(Key)/Sep 26, 1914; p. 1776
BRAND OF BARS, THE
(WF)/Aug 22, 1914; p. 1101
BRAND OF CAIN, THE
(Po)/Jun 20, 1914; p. 1690
BRAND OF EVIL, THE (SA)/Nov 22, 1913;
p. 846/Dec 13, 1913; p. 1280
BRAND OF FEAR, THE
(Am)/Aug 26, 1911; p. 544

BRAND OF HIS TRIBE, THE (101)/Nov 21,
1914; p. 1088/Nov 28, 1914; p. 1233
BRANDED ARM, THE
(Pa)/Nov 30, 1912; p. 876
BRANDED BY HIS BROTHER'S CRIME
(Fr)/Mar 29, 1913; p. 1337
BRANDED FOR LIFE
(It)/Jul 12, 1913; p. 206
BRANDED INDIAN, THE
(Po)/Oct 14, 1911; p. 131
BRANDED MAN, THE
(Bi)/Nov 19, 1910; p. 1179
BRANDED SHOULDER, THE
(Ka)/Sep 16, 1911; p. 788
BRANDED SIX SHOOTER, THE
(Fr)/Feb 15, 1913; p. 680
BRANDING A BAD MAN
(Am)/Jun 3, 1911; p. 1260
BRANNIGAN'S BAND
(Lu)/Jan 9, 1915; p. 220
BRANSFORD IN ARCADIA
(Ec)/Aug 22, 1914; p. 1101
BRASS BOWL, THE (Ed)/Apr 11, 1914; p. 213
BRASS BUTTON, A (Re)/Feb 18, 1911; p. 372
BRASS BUTTONS (Maj)/Mar 15, 1913; p. 1105
(Be)/Jan 2, 1915; p. 77
BRAVE, BRAVER, BRAVEST
(Lu)/May 25, 1912; p. 729
BRAVE AND BOLD (Bio)/Jan 27, 1912; p. 303
(Ko)/Jun 19, 1915; p. 1940
BRAVE DESERVE THE FAIR, THE
(Lu)/Jun 11, 1910; p. 995
(Cin)/Feb 3, 1912; p. 393
(Sel)/Oct 30a, 1915; p. 967
BRAVE HEARTS (Ka)/Aug 6, 1910; p. 296
BRAVE HUNTER, THE
(Bio)/May 4, 1912; p. 426
BRAVE LITTLE GIRL, A
(Pa)/Jun 4, 1910; p. 941
BRAVE LITTLE INDIAN, THE
(Pa)/Aug 3, 1912; p. 446
BRAVE LITTLE WOMAN, A
(Ne)/Jan 27, 1912; p. 304
BRAVE OLD BILL (Ka)/Jan 11, 1913; p. 158
BRAVE POLICEMAN, A
(Imp)/Nov 27, 1909; p. 760
BRAVE SWIFT EAGLE'S PERIL
(Bi)/Jun 10, 1911; p. 1317
BRAVE WESTERN GIRL, A
(Bi)/Dec 24, 1910; p. 1479
BRAVERY OF DORA, THE
(Lu)/Jan 18, 1913; p. 263
BRAVEST GIRL IN CALIFORNIA, THE
(Ka)/May 3, 1913; p. 488
BRAVEST GIRL IN THE SOUTH, THE
(Ka)/May 7, 1910; p. 737
BRAVEST MAN, THE
(Maj)/Nov 15, 1913; p. 738

BRAVEST OF THE BRAVE, THE
(Jo)/Aug 28, 1915; p. 1481
BRAVING DEATH TO SAVE A CHILD
Jan 16, 1909; p. 70
BRAZIL - THE CASCADES
(Pa)/Jun 13, 1908; p. 516
BREACH OF FAITH, THE
(Rex)/Nov 4, 1911; p. 381
BREACH OF PROMISE
(UE)/Oct 9, 1909; p. 489
(Imp)/May 18, 1912; p. 630
BREAD CAST UPON THE WATERS
(Gem)/Aug 3, 1912; p. 446
(Bro)/Apr 26, 1913; p. 382
BREAD LINE, THE (Re)/Oct 30, 1915; p. 792
BREAD ON THE WATERS
(Ed)/Apr 5, 1913; p. 48
BREAD UPON THE WATERS
(Sel)/Oct 12, 1912; p. 143
(SA)/Aug 23, 1913; p. 842
(Pr)/Nov 29, 1913; p. 1009
(Vi)/Aug 8, 1914; p. 837
BREADWINNERS, THE
(Lu)/Oct 10, 1908; p. 279
BREAK, BREAK, BREAK
(Am)/Sep 19, 1914; p. 1645
BREAK FOR FREEDOM, A
(Pa)/Dec 20, 1913; p. 1411
BREAKERS IN THE CLOUDS
(Gau)/Mar 25, 1911; p. 657
BREAKING EVEN (Pa)/May 9, 1914; p. 821
BREAKING HOME TIES
(Col)/Nov 5, 1910; p. 1060
BREAKING IN (Vi)/Feb 27, 1915; p. 1287
BREAKING INTO JAIL
(Sel)/Sep 12, 1914; p. 1511
BREAKING INTO SOCIETY
(SBa)/Oct 30a, 1915; p. 970
BREAKING INTO THE BIG LEAGUE
(Ka)/Aug 9, 1913; p. 620
BREAKING THE SEVENTH
COMMANDMENT (Imp)/Nov 18, 1911;
p. 554/Nov 25, 1911; p. 638
BREAKING THE SHACKLES (Ed)/Sep 4,
1915; p. 1665/Sep 25, 1915; p. 2176
BREAKING UP ICE IN FINLAND
(Pa)/Aug 6, 1910; p. 297
BREAKS OF THE GAME, THE
(Ed)/Jul 10, 1915; p. 307
BREAKUP, THE (Box)/Feb 13, 1915; p. 986
BREATH OF ARABY, THE
(Vi)/Apr 10, 1915; p. 241
BREATH OF SCANDAL, THE
(Ka)/Oct 4, 1913; p. 47
BREATH OF SUMMER, A
(Re)/Jul 24, 1915; p. 650
BRED IN THE BONE
(Bi)/Apr 26, 1913; p. 382

(Re)/Oct 9, 1915; p. 254
BREED O' THE MOUNTAINS
(Vic)/Mar 21, 1914; p. 1525
BREED OF THE NORTH
(Lu)/Oct 25, 1913; p. 380
BREEDING TROUT BY THE MILLION
(Pa)/Nov 8, 1913; p. 612
BREEZY BILL - OUTCAST
(Mus)/Oct 23, 1915; p. 620
BREEZY MORNING, A
(Sol)/Oct 14, 1911; p. 130
BRENNAN OF THE MOOR
(Sol)/Sep 6, 1913; p. 1070
BREST, A FORTIFIED HARBOR OF
FRANCE (Gau)/Apr 29, 1911; p.958
BRETHREN OF THE SACRED FISH
(Th)/Jul 26, 1913; p. 429
BREWERYTOWN ROMANCE, A
(Lu)/Jun 20, 1914; p. 1688
BREWSTER'S MILLIONS
(Las)/Apr 18, 1914; p. 336
BRIBE, THE (Ka)/Sep 20, 1913; p. 1284
(Vic)/May 23, 1914; p. 1118
(Vic)/Feb 6, 1915; p. 828
BRIDAL BOUQUET, THE
(Th)/Jan 16, 1915; p. 369
BRIDAL COUPLE DODGING THE
CAMERAS (Ed)/May 9, 1908; p. 422
BRIDAL ROOM, THE (Imp)/Oct 12,
1912; p. 151/Oct 19, 1912; p. 244
BRIDAL TRAIL, THE
(Ne)/Feb 11, 1911; p. 318
BRIDE FROM THE SEA, A
(Vic)/Sep 13, 1913; p. 1178
BRIDE OF GUADALOUPE, THE
(Dom)/Feb 13, 1915; p. 986
BRIDE OF LAMMERMOOR, THE
Jan 9, 1909; pp 36, 46
(Cin)/Sep 14, 1912; p. 1074
BRIDE OF MYSTERY, THE
(GS)/Feb 7, 1914; p. 678
BRIDE OF THE NANCY LEE, THE
(Lae)/Dec 11, 1915; p. 2033
BRIDE OF THE SEA, THE
(Dra)/Aug 9, 1913; p. 638
(Re)/Aug 14, 1915; p. 1161
BRIDE WON BY BRAVERY
(Lu)/Jun 5, 1909; p. 754
BRIDEGROOM'S DILEMNA, THE
(Ed)/Jul 31, 1909; p. 161
(Vi)/Mar 25, 1911; pp 656-57
BRIDEGROOM'S JOKE, THE
(Vi)/Dec 11, 1909; p. 841
BRIDEGROOM'S TROUBLES, THE
(Po)/May 18, 1912; p. 630
BRIDES AND BRIDLES
(Ne)/Dec 14, 1912; p. 1082
BRIDE'S DREAM, THE

(Lu)/May 2, 1908; p. 403
BRIDGE (Ec)/Mar 23,1912;p.1064
BRIDGE ACROSS, THE
(Bio)/Apr 24, 1915; p. 555
BRIDGE BUILDING AND RAILWAY
TRACK LAYING BY THE FRENCH
ARMY (Pa)/Apr 24, 1915; p. 557
BRIDGE OF SHADOWS, THE
(Sel)/Oct 4, 1913; p. 26
BRIDGE OF SIGHS, THE
(Ed)/Oct 10, 1908; pp 285-86/Oct 17,
1908; p. 298/Oct 24, 1908; p. 318
(Br)/Mar 20, 1915; p. 1775
(Lu)/Jul 3, 1915; p. 64
BRIDGE OF SORROW, THE
(Gau)/Dec 21, 1912; p. 1174
BRIDGE OF TIME, THE
(SA)/Oct 23, 1915; p. 620
BRIDGET, THE FLIRT
(Sol)/Jun 17, 1911; p. 1388
BRIDGET AND THE EGG
(Lu)/Apr 8, 1911; p. 780
BRIDGET BRIDGES IT
(SA)/Apr 11, 1914; p. 212
BRIDGET ON STRIKE
(Vi)/May 22, 1909; p. 676
BRIDGET'S DREAM/Dec 12, 1908; p. 478
BRIDGET'S SUDDEN WEALTH
(Ed)/Sep 21, 1912; p. 1175
BRIGAND, THE (Cin)/Apr 20, 1912; p. 230
(Ne)/Oct 18, 1913; p. 265
BRIGHTENED SUNSETS
(Lu)/Jun 7, 1913; p. 1031
BRING ME SOME ICE
(SA)/Feb 27, 1909; p. 238
BRINGING A HUSBAND TO TIME
(Com)/Dec 28, 1912; p. 1294
BRINGING FATHER AROUND
(SA)/Nov 9, 1912; p. 552
BRINGING HOME THE PUP
(Ed)/Nov 9, 1912; pp 553-54
BRINGING IN THE LAW
(CMP)/Jun 13, 1914; p. 1548
BRINGING UP HUBBY
(Sel)/Feb 14, 1914; p. 808
BRINK, THE (Am)/Oct 23, 1915; p. 620
BRITON AND BOER (Sel)/Oct 23,
1909; pp 569-70/Nov 6, 1909; p. 644
BRITON'S PROMISE, A
(Pa)/Mar 14, 1908; pp 216-17
BRITTANY LASSIES
(Pa)/Mar 19, 1910; p. 425
BROADCLOTH AND BUCKSKIN
(Mus)/Dec 11, 1915; p. 2032
BROCKTON FAIR AND HORSE SHOW
(Ed)/Dec 30, 1911; p. 1071
BROKE, or HOW TIMOTHY ESCAPED
(Imp)/Jan 6, 1912; p. 42

BROKEN BARRIER, THE
(Fr)/Jul 11, 1914; p. 256
(Am)/Aug 1, 1914; p. 709
BROKEN BOTTLE, THE
(Re)/May 16, 1914; p. 969
BROKEN CHAIN, THE
(Cin)/May 23, 1914; p. 1117
BROKEN CLOUD, A
(Am)/Dec 11, 1915; p. 2032
BROKEN COIN, THE
(Re)/Jun 24, 1911; p. 1455
BROKEN COIN, THE (Uni)
No.1/Jun 19, 1915; p.1946/Jul 3, 1915; p.66
No.2/Jun 19, 1915; p.1946/Jul 3, 1915; p.66
No.3/Jun 19, 1915;p.1946/Jul 10, 1915;p.309
No.4/Jul 17, 1915; p. 487
No.5/Jul 24, 1915; p. 651
No.6/Jul 31, 1915; p. 818
No.7/Aug 7, 1915; p. 998
No.8/Aug 14, 1915; p. 1162
No.9/Aug 28, 1915; p. 1481
No.10/Sep 4, 1915; p. 1645
No.11/Sep 11, 1915; p. 1834
No.12/Sep 18, 1915; p. 1997
No.13/Sep 18, 1915; p. 1997
No.14/Oct 2, 1915; p. 80
No.15/Oct 9, 1915; p. 254
No.16/Oct 9, 1915; p. 254
No.17/Oct 23, 1915; p. 621
No.18/Oct 30, 1915; p. 793
No.19/Oct 30a, 1915; p. 969
No.20/Oct 30a, 1915; p. 969
No.21/Nov 13, 1915; p. 1314
No.22/Nov 20, 1915; p. 1501
BROKEN CROSS, THE
(Bio)/Apr 22, 1911; p. 898
BROKEN DOLL, THE
(Bio)/Oct 29, 1910; p. 994
(St)/Sep 19, 1914; p. 1645
BROKEN FRIENDSHIP, THE
(Ec)/May 7, 1910; p. 738
BROKEN GLASS, THE
(KrS)/Mar 27, 1915; p. 1934
BROKEN HEART, A
(Lu)/Feb 27, 1909; p. 238
BROKEN HEART, THE (SA)/Feb 1, 1913;
pp 445-46/Feb 22, 1913; p. 779
BROKEN HEARTS
(Pa)/Nov 23, 1912; p. 766
BROKEN HEARTS AND PLEDGES
(Lko)/May 29, 1915; p. 1433
BROKEN IDOL, THE
(Gau)/Nov 23, 1912; p. 768
BROKEN IDYLL, THE
(Pa)/Apr 19, 1913; p. 280
BROKEN LAW, THE
(Fox)/Dec 4, 1915; pp 1845-46, 1853
BROKEN LEASE, THE

(Imp)/Mar 2, 1912; p. 781
BROKEN LIFE, A
(Ro)/Nov 13, 1909; p. 684
(Pa)/Jun 24, 1911; p.1452/Jul 8, 1911; p.1567
BROKEN LIVES (Pa)/Feb 28, 1914; p. 1088
BROKEN LOCKET, THE (Bio)/Sep 25,
1909; p. 414/Oct 2, 1909; p. 451
BROKEN LULLABY, THE
(Maj)/Feb 6, 1915; pp 807, 828
BROKEN MELODY, A
(Vi)/Nov 22, 1913; p. 867
BROKEN NOSE BAILEY
(Re)/Sep 26, 1914; pp 1759, 1777
BROKEN OATH (Sol)/Jul 27, 1912; p. 344
BROKEN OATH, THE
(Imp)/Mar 26, 1910; pp 467-68
BROKEN PAROLE, THE
(SA)/Oct 4, 1913; p. 48
BROKEN PATHS (Pa)/Feb 21, 1914; p. 947
BROKEN PLEDGE, THE
(SA)/Jul 3, 1915; p. 64
BROKEN PROMISE, THE
(Pa)/Oct 24, 1914; p. 494
BROKEN ROSE, THE
(Bio)/Nov 7, 1914; p. 787
BROKEN SPELL, A (Vi)/Apr 16, 1910; p.597
BROKEN SPELL, THE
(Cry)/Jul 26, 1913; p. 430
BROKEN SPUR, A (Sel)/Feb 24, 1912; p. 690
BROKEN SYMPHONY, A
(Vi)/Jul 30, 1910; p. 244
BROKEN THREADS UNITED
(SA)/Sep 13, 1913; p. 1176
BROKEN TIES (Gau)/Sep 11, 1909; p. 347
                    (Am)/Mar 2, 1912; p. 775
BROKEN TOY, THE (Imp)/Mar 20, 1915;
p. 1778/Apr 10, 1915; p. 238
BROKEN TRAIL, THE
(Ka)/Feb 25, 1911; p. 430
BROKEN TRAP, THE
(Bi)/Dec 2, 1911; p. 726
BROKEN VASE, THE
(Gau)/Dec 11, 1909; p. 841
(Sel)/Aug 23, 1913; p. 844
BROKEN VIOLIN, THE
(Gau)/Oct 30, 1909; p. 604
BROKEN VOW, THE
(Cin)/May 17, 1913; p. 703
BROKEN VOWS (Vic)/May 9,1914;pp 821-22
BROKEN WAYS (Bio)/Mar 22, 1913;
p.1220/Jul 10,1915;p.323/Jul 31,1915;p.816
BROKEN WINDOW, THE
(Am)/May 22, 1915; p. 1260
BROKEN WORD, THE
(Ed)/Oct 30a, 1915; p. 967
BROKEN WRIST, THE
(Bio)/Sep 25, 1915; p. 2176
BROKEN "X," THE

(Sel)/Dec 5, 1914; p. 1383
BROKER'S DAUGHTER, THE
(Ya)/Aug 27, 1910; p. 464
BRONCHO AND THE LAND GRABBER
(SA)/Jul 3, 1915; p. 64
BRONCHO BESS (Ch)/May 25, 1912; p. 730
BRONCHO BILL, THE BRAVE COWBOY
(Lux)/Mar 4, 1911; p. 484
BRONCHO BILL'S MEXICAN WIFE
(SA)/Nov 30, 1912; p. 867
BRONCHO BILL'S REDEMPTION
(SA)/Aug 13,1910;p.350
BRONCHO BILLY, A FRIEND IN NEED
(SA)/Sep 26, 1914; p. 1775
BRONCHO BILLY - FAVORITE
(SA)/Nov 7, 1914; p. 787
BRONCHO BILLY, GUARDIAN
(SA)/Jan 31, 1914; p. 544
BRONCHO BILLY - GUNMAN
(SA)/May 9, 1914; p. 820
BRONCHO BILLY - OUTLAW
(SA)/Jul 4, 1914; p. 64
BRONCHO BILLY, SHEEPMAN
(SA)/Oct 23, 1915; p. 619
BRONCHO BILLY, THE VAGABOND
(SA)/Sep 19, 1914; p. 1644
BRONCHO BILLY AND THE BABY
(SA)/Feb 6, 1915; pp 827-28
BRONCHO BILLY AND THE BAD MAN
(SA)/Feb 7, 1914; p. 676
BRONCHO BILLY AND THE BANDITS
(SA)/May 18, 1912; p. 629
BRONCHO BILLY AND THE CARD SHARK
(SA)/Oct 2, 1915; p. 78
**BRONCHO BILLY AND THE CLAIM
JUMPERS** (SA)/Jan 23, 1915; p. 515
**BRONCHO BILLY AND THE ESCAPED
BANDIT** (SA)/Jan 16, 1915; p. 368
**BRONCHO BILLY AND THE EXPRESS
RIDER** (SA)/Jun 7, 1913; p. 1031
BRONCHO BILLY AND THE FALSE NOTE
(SA)/Feb 13, 1915; p. 984
BRONCHO BILLY AND THE GAMBLER
(SA)/Aug 8, 1914; p. 836
BRONCHO BILLY AND THE GIRL
(SA)/Apr 20, 1912; p. 230
BRONCHO BILLY AND THE GREASER
(SA)/Oct 24, 1914; p. 492
BRONCHO BILLY AND THE INDIAN MAID
(SA)/Jul 13, 1912; p. 148
BRONCHO BILLY AND THE MINE SHARK
(SA)/Jun 27, 1914; p. 1828
**BRONCHO BILLY AND THE NAVAJO
MAID** (SA)/Aug 23, 1913; p. 844
**BRONCHO BILLY AND THE OUTLAW'S
MOTHER** (SA)/Feb 1, 1913; p. 465
BRONCHO BILLY AND THE POSSE
(SA)/Aug 7, 1915; p. 996

BULL FIGHT IN MEXICO
(Pa)/Mar 26, 1910; p. 467
BULL FIGHT IN NUEVO, LAREDO, TEXAS
(Imp)/Jun 22, 1912; pp 1127-28
BULL TRAINER'S REVENGE, THE
(Me)/Sep 5, 1914; p. 1372
BULLDOGS OF THE TRAIL, THE
(PP)/May 8, 1915; p. 922
BULLY, THE (Pa)/Apr 30, 1910; p. 689
(KB)/Oct 18, 1913; p. 265
BULLY AFFAIR, A
(Be)/Sep 18, 1915; p. 1996
BULLY AND THE SHRIMP, THE
(Re)/Sep 21, 1912; p. 1177
BULLY OF BINGO GULCH, THE
(Sel)/Jan 6, 1912; p. 41
BULLY'S DOOM, THE
(Lu)/Apr 25, 1914; p. 516
BULLY'S WATERLOO, A
(At)/Sep 3, 1910; p. 521
BUM AND A BOMB, A
(Sol)/Aug 26, 1911; p. 543
BUM AND THE BOMB, THE
(Vi)/Dec 3, 1910; p. 1296
(Ch)/Aug 31, 1912; p. 882
BUM MISTAKE, A (Pr)/Dec 5, 1914; p. 1384
BUMPED FOR FAIR
(Sup)/May 29, 1915; p. 1433
BUMPS (Vi)/Sep 14,1912;p.1074
BUMPS AND WILLIE
(Sel)/Oct 4, 1913; p. 48
BUMPTIOUS AS A FIREMAN
(Ed)/Oct 1, 1910; p. 747
BUMPTIOUS AS AN AVIATOR
(Ed)/Aug 13, 1910; p. 350
BUMPTIOUS AS ROMEO
(Ed)/Feb 18, 1911; p. 370
BUMPTIOUS PLAYS BASEBALL
(Ed)/Oct 22, 1910; p. 934
BUMPTIOUS TAKES UP AUTOMOBILING
(Ed)/Sep 3, 1910; p. 518
BUM'S HALLOWE'EN, A
(Ch)/Mar 15, 1913; p. 1105
BUNCH OF FLOWERS, A
(Bio)/Mar 14, 1914; p. 1385
BUNCH OF KEYS, A
(SA)/Aug 7, 1915; p. 1014
BUNCH OF LILACS, A
(Pa)/Dec 11, 1909; pp 840-41
BUNCH OF MATCHES, A
(SA)/Jun 12, 1915; p. 1776
BUNCH OF VIOLETS, A
(Vi)/Jul 27, 1912; p. 344
BUNCO BILL'S VISIT
(Vi)/May 16, 1914; p. 968
BUNCO GAME AT LIZARD HEAD, THE
(SA)/May 20, 1911; p.1141
BUNCOED STAGE JOHNNIE

(Me)/Sep 26, 1908; p. 242
BUNGALOW BURGLARS
(Imp)/Dec 23, 1911; p. 990
BUNGALOW CRAZE, THE
(Am)/Apr 29, 1911; p. 960
BUNGLING BUNK'S BUNKO
(Ecl)/Sep 26, 1914; p. 1778
BUNKIE (Sel)/Feb 17, 1912; p.582
BUNKS BUNKED (MnA)/May 15, 1915; p.1071
BUNNY ALL AT SEA (Vi)/Nov 2, 1912; p. 450
BUNNY AND THE DOGS
(Vi)/Aug 24, 1912; p. 770
BUNNY AND THE TWINS
(Vi)/Mar 2, 1912; p. 780
BUNNY AS A REPORTER
(Vi)/Jun 21, 1913; p. 1251
BUNNY AT THE DERBY
(Vi)/Nov 9, 1912; p. 553
BUNNY BACKSLIDES
(Vi)/Nov 14, 1914; p. 931
BUNNY BLARNEYED
(Vi)/Apr 12, 1913; p. 163
BUNNY BUYS A HAREM
(Vi)/May 30, 1914; p. 1260
BUNNY BUYS A HAT FOR HIS BRIDE
(Vi)/Jun 13, 1914; p. 1540
BUNNY FOR THE CAUSE
(Vi)/Oct 11, 1913; p. 155
BUNNY IN BUNNYLAND
(Vi)/Jun 19, 1915; p. 1939
BUNNY IN DISGUISE
(Vi)/May 23, 1914; p. 1116
BUNNY VERSUS CUTEY
(Vi)/May 17, 1913; p. 704
BUNNY'S BIRTHDAY
(Vi)/Feb 28, 1914; p. 1087
BUNNY'S BIRTHDAY SURPRISE
(Vi)/May 31, 1913; p. 919
BUNNY'S DILEMNA (Vi)/Jul 5, 1913; p. 48
BUNNY'S HONEYMOON
(Vi)/Apr 19, 1913; p. 281
BUNNY'S LITTLE BROTHER
(Vi)/Dec 19, 1914; p. 1680
BUNNY'S MISTAKE (Vi)/Jan 24,1914;p.412
BUNNY'S SCHEME (Vi)/Apr 18, 1914;p.360
BUNNY'S SUICIDE (Vi)/Sep 21,1912;p.1175
BUNNY'S SWELL AFFAIR
(Vi)/Jun 13, 1914; p. 1540
BURDEN, THE (Maj)/Jul 4, 1914; p. 65
BURDEN BEARER, THE
(Lu)/Apr 19, 1913; pp 269, 280
(U)/Jul 24, 1915; p. 651
BURDEN OF SHAME, THE
(Amb)/Jan 27, 1912; p. 304
BURGLAR ALARM, THE
(Me)/Aug 29, 1914; p. 1240
BURGLAR ALARM MAT, THE
(Maj)/Jul 6, 1912; p. 44

BURGLAR AND THE BABY, THE
(Po)/Jul 23, 1910; p. 193
(Ka)/Oct 4, 1913; p. 47
BURGLAR AND THE GIRL, THE
(GN)/Aug 19, 1911; p. 466
BURGLAR AND THE LADY, THE
(WF)/Nov 14, 1914; p. 936
(Sun)/Dec 18, 1915; pp 2198, 2205
BURGLAR AND THE MOUSE, THE
(WF)/Jan 16, 1915; p. 370
BURGLAR AND THE ROSE, THE
(Po)/Aug 17, 1912; p. 676
BURGLAR CUPID, A
(Ed)/Jan 30, 1909; p. 120
BURGLAR GODFATHER, THE
(SA)/Dec 11, 1915; p. 2031
BURGLAR IN A BASKET, THE
Jan 16, 1909; p. 70
BURGLAR IN A PIANO, THE
(KO)/Jan 9, 1909; p. 38
BURGLAR IN THE TRUNK
(Pa)/Nov 13, 1909; p. 684
BURGLAR WHO ROBBED DEATH, THE
(Sel)/May 17, 1913; p. 704
BURGLARIZING BILLY
(Gem)/Apr 26, 1913; p. 381
BURGLAR'S BABY, THE
(Dom)/Jul 17, 1915; p. 486
BURGLARS BY REQUEST
(Roy)/Apr 24, 1915; p. 556
BURGLAR'S DILEMNA, THE
(Bio)/Dec 28, 1912; p. 1292
BURGLAR'S FEE, THE
(Pa)/Apr 29, 1911; p. 958
BURGLAR'S LOVE, THE (GN)/Feb 10,
1912; p. 472/Feb 17, 1912; pp 583-84
BURGLAR'S MISTAKE, A
(Bio)/Apr 3, 1909; p. 404
BURGLARS' NEW TRICK
(Pa)/May 30, 1908; p. 480
BURGLAR'S REFORMATION, THE
(Re)/May 4, 1912; p. 427
BURGLAR'S SACRIFICE, THE
(Bio)/Apr 18, 1914; p. 360
BURGLAR'S WEIRD RECEPTION, A
(CGP)/Aug 24, 1912; p. 771
BURGLARY IN THE YEAR 200
(RR)/Apr 24, 1909; p. 516
**BURIAL OF A RICH CHINAMAN AT
SUMATRA** (Pa)/Jul 5, 1913; p. 47
BURIAL OF THE MAINE, THE
(Sel)/Apr 20, 1912; p. 229
BURIED ALIVE (Vi)/Aug 15, 1908; p. 130
(Sel)/Jan 8, 1910; p. 16
BURIED MAN OF TEBESSA, THE
(Ec)/Aug 20, 1910; p. 408
BURIED PAST, A (Ed)/Apr 29, 1911; p. 958
BURIED PAST, THE

(Bro)/Nov 29, 1913; p. 1008
BURIED SECRET, A
(It)/Mar 7, 1914; p. 1238
BURIED TREASURE
(Me)/May 17, 1913; p. 704
BURIED TREASURE, THE
(Re)/May 8, 1915; p. 900
BURLESQUE BULL FIGHT
(CGP)/Nov 11, 1911; p. 469
BURLESQUE QUEEN, THE
(Po)/Sep 10, 1910; p. 575
BURLY BILL (SA)/Jun 18, 1910; p. 1049
BURMA, RANGOON
(Ed)/Nov 9, 1912; p. 553
BURNED HAND, THE
(Maj)/Jun 26, 1915; p. 2096
BURNING BRAND, THE
(Bro)/Jan 4, 1913; pp 51-52
BURNING LARIAT, THE
(Fr)/Apr 19, 1913; p. 282
**BURNING OF THE MATCH FACTORY,
THE** (Vi)/Oct 5, 1912; p. 41
BURNING TRAIN, THE
(It)/Jan 10, 1914; p. 173
BURNT CORK (Vi)/Apr 20, 1912; p. 230
BURSTUP HOMES' MURDER CASE
(Sol)/Apr 5, 1913; p. 49
BUSHLEAGUER'S DREAM, THE
(Th)/Dec 27, 1913; p. 1545
BUSINESS AND LOVE
(Lu)/May 2, 1914; p. 672
BUSINESS BUCCANEER, A (Ka)/Jan 11,
1913; p. 158/Aug 14, 1915; p. 1160
BUSINESS IS BUSINESS
(Id)/Jun 5, 1915; p. 1606
BUSINESS MAN'S WIFE, A
(Rex)/Jan 4, 1913; p. 52
BUSINESS MUST NOT INTERFERE
(Ec)/Mar 29, 1913; p. 1337
BUSINESS RIVALS
(SA)/Aug 21, 1915; p. 1316
BUSINESS WOMAN, A
(Th)/May 31, 1913; p. 922
BUSTED BUT BENEVOLENT
(Fal)/Oct 23, 1915; p. 620
BUSTER AND HIS GOAT
(Ed)/Sep 12, 1914; p. 1511
BUSTER AND THE CANNIBALS
(Lu)/Dec 28, 1912; p. 1291
BUSTER AND THE GYPSIES
(Lu)/Oct 5, 1912; p. 41
BUSTER AND THE PIRATES
(Lu)/Sep 28, 1912; p. 1276
**BUSTER BROWN, TIGE AND THEIR
CREATOR, R.F. OUTCAULT**
(SA)/Jun 7, 1913; p. 1031
**BUSTER BROWN AND THE GERMAN
BAND** (Ed)/Dec 5, 1914; p. 1383

CALAMITY ANNE'S LOVE AFFAIR
(Am)/May 9, 1914; p. 822
CALAMITY ANNE'S PARCEL POST
(Am)/May 24, 1913; p. 813
CALAMITY ANNE'S TRUST
(Am)/Apr 26, 1913; p. 382
CALAMITY ANNE'S VANITY
(Am)/Feb 15, 1913; p. 681
CALEB WEST (Re)/Sep 21, 1912; p. 1178
CALIFORNIA OIL CROOKS, THE
(Ka)/Apr 26, 1913; p. 380
CALIFORNIA OSTRICH AND PIGEON
FARM (Lu)/Apr 27, 1912; p. 329
CALIFORNIA POULTRY
(Am)/Jun 14, 1913; p. 1138
CALIFORNIA REVOLUTION OF 1846,
THE (Ka)/Oct 21, 1911; p.207
CALINO AS A STATION MASTER
(Gau)/Nov 30, 1912; p. 877
CALINO AS MASON
(Gau)/Apr 13, 1912; p. 138
CALINO TAKES NEW LODGINGS
(Gau)/Sep 17, 1910; p. 631
CALINO TRAVELS AS A PRINCE
(Gau)/Dec 10, 1910; p. 1356
CALL, THE
(Bio)/Feb 5, 1910; p. 168
(Rex)/Aug 30, 1913; p. 961
(Vi)/Sep 6,1913; p.1046/Sep 13,1913; p.1176
CALL BOY'S VENGEANCE, THE
(Vi)/Jan 22, 1910; p. 92
CALL FROM HOME, A
(Cry)/Jun 21, 1913; p. 1254
CALL HIM WHISKERS
(Gem)/May 17, 1913; p. 705
CALL OF A CHILD, THE
(Pa)/Jan 30, 1915; p. 674
CALL OF HER CHILD, THE
(Bio)/Mar 13, 1915; p. 1607
CALL OF MOTHER LOVE, THE
(Mec)/Mar 1, 1913; p. 889
CALL OF MOTHERHOOD, THE
(Lu)/Aug 14, 1915; p. 1160
CALL OF THE ANGELUS, THE
(Fr)/Jun 21, 1913; p. 1254
CALL OF THE BLOOD
(Kin)/Feb 1, 1913; p. 466
CALL OF THE BLOOD, THE
(Ka)/Aug 27, 1910; p. 463
(Maj)/Oct 5, 1912; p.34/Oct 12, 1912; p.144
(Pa)/Aug 23, 1913; p. 842
CALL OF THE CIRCUS, THE
(Imp)/Jul 23, 1910; p. 193
CALL OF THE DANCE, THE
(Ka)/Sep 11, 1915; p. 1843
CALL OF THE DESERT
(Ne)/Nov 9, 1912; p. 554
CALL OF THE DRUM

(Imp)/Mar 16, 1912; p. 963
CALL OF THE FOOT LIGHTS, THE
(Ed)/Feb 14, 1914; p. 808
CALL OF THE FOREST
(Gau)/May 21, 1910; p. 832
CALL OF THE GREAT, THE
(Po)/Mar 11, 1911; p. 543
CALL OF THE HEART, THE
(Lu)/Sep 18, 1909; p. 379
(Lu)/Aug 9, 1913; p. 637
(Bal)/Jul 11, 1914; p. 257
CALL OF THE HILLS, THE
(Po)/Oct 14, 1911; p. 130
CALL OF THE NORTH, THE (Las)/Jul 25,
1914; p. 582/Aug 22, 1914; p. 1080
CALL OF THE PLAINS, THE
(SA)/Aug 9, 1913; p. 637
CALL OF THE ROAD, THE
(Ram)/Jun 21, 1913; p. 1255
CALL OF THE SEA, THE
(SA)/Oct 9, 1915; p. 253
CALL OF THE SONG, THE (Imp)/Jul 22,
1911; p. 112/Aug 19, 1911; pp 465-66
CALL OF THE TRAUMEREI, THE
(Am)/Mar 7, 1914; p. 1214
CALL OF THE TRIBE, THE
(Ka)/Jun 20, 1914; p. 1689
CALL OF THE WAVES, THE
(GS)/Dec 26, 1914; p. 1842
CALL OF THE WEST, THE
(Ne)/Jul 23, 1910; p. 194
CALL OF THE WILD, THE
(Bio)/Oct 30, 1908; p. 344
CALL OF THE WILDERNESS, THE
(Me)/Sep 16, 1911; p. 789
CALL OF YESTERDAY, THE
(SA)/Aug 14, 1915; p. 1160
CALL TO ARMS, THE
(Bio)/Aug 6, 1910; pp 296-97
CALLED BACK
(Rex)/Jun 10, 1911; pp 1317, 1319
(Th)/Jun 15, 1912; p. 1020
(GS)/Nov 28, 1914; p. 1241
(Co)/Dec 5, 1914; p. 1395
CALLED BACK ON THE RIGHT PATH
(Amb)/Feb 17, 1912; p. 583
CALLED TO SEA (UE)/May 21, 1910; p. 834
CALLING DAY (Pa)/Feb 6, 1909; p. 145
CALLING OF JIM BARTON, THE
(SA)/Feb 28, 1914; p. 1088
CALLING OF LOUIS MONA, THE
(Po)/Mar 29, 1913; p. 1338
CALLY'S COMET (Th)/Apr 29, 1911; p. 961
CALUCOWANI (Cry)/Mar 22, 1913; p. 1221
CAMBODIAN IDYLL, A
(Me)/Oct 11, 1913; pp 155-56
CAMBRIDGESHIRE RACE MEET
(Ka)/Jan 17, 1914; p. 288

CAMBYSES, KING OF PERSIA
(Gau)/Dec 31, 1909; p. 960
CAMEL AND HORSE RACING IN EGYPT
(UE)/Aug 27, 1910; p. 462
CAMEO KIRBY (Las)/Jan 9, 1915; p. 200
CAMEO RING, THE (U)/Apr 3, 1915; p. 66
CAMERA'S TESTIMONY, THE
(Lu)/Aug 23, 1913; p. 843
CAMERON GIRLS (Po)/Jul 3, 1915; p. 66
CAMILLE (Pa)/Jan 22, 1910; p. 93
(Ch)/May 18, 1912; pp 606-10/
Jun 15, 1912; p. 1028
CAMILLE, AS SHE NEVER WAS
(WF)/Dec 5, 1914; p. 1385
CAMOENS (Gau)/Dec 23, 1911; p. 988
CAMPAIGN MANAGERESS, THE
(Th)/Nov 15, 1913; p. 738
CAMPBELLS ARE COMING, THE (Br)/
May 29, 1915; p. 1439/Oct 23, 1915; p. 621
CAMPING OUT (Rex)/Nov 23, 1912; p. 769
CAMPING WITH CUSTER
(Bi)/Aug 16, 1913; p. 745
CAMPING WITH THE BLACKFEET
(Ed)/Nov 22, 1913; p. 868
CAN A JEALOUS WIFE BE CURED
(Cam)/May 29, 1915; p. 1433
CAN A MAN FOOL HIS WIFE
(Cam)/May 1, 1915; p. 729
CAN HE SAVE HER (Ec)/Jul 15, 1911; p. 41
CAN LOVE GROW COLD
(Cam)/May 15, 1915; p. 1073
CAN OF BAKED BEANS, A
(Th)/Feb 28, 1914; p. 1089
CANADIAN IRON CENTER, PORT ARTHUR
(UE)/Feb 25, 1911; p. 430
CANADIAN MOONSHINERS, THE
(Ka)/Sep 10, 1910; pp 574-75
CANADIAN NATIONAL EXHIBITION AT
TORONTO (Kin)/Nov 23, 1912; p. 769
CANADIAN WINTER CARNIVAL AT
MONTREAL (Ed)/Mar 27, 1909; p. 369
CANALS OF VENICE
(Vi)/Nov 22, 1913; p. 868
CANCELLED (Ec)/Jan 30, 1915; p. 673
CANCELLED MORTGAGE, THE
(Bio)/Jun 5, 1915; p. 1604
CANDIDATE, THE (Pa)/Jul 11, 1908;
p. 34/Nov 14, 1908; p. 379
CANDIDATE FOR MAYOR, THE
(Lu)/Jul 11, 1914; p. 256
CANDIDATE'S PAST, THE
(Bio)/Jun 12, 1915; p. 1776
CANDLE OF LIFE, THE
(Amb)/Sep 2, 1911; p. 630
CANDY GIRL, THE
(Imp)/Nov 30, 1912; p. 878
CANIMATED NOOZ PICTORIAL (SA)/
No.1/Oct 30, 1915; p. 791

No.2/Nov 27, 1915; p. 1663
CANINE MATCHMAKER, A
(Sel)/Feb 15, 1913; p. 678
CANINE RIVALS (Sol)/Jan 11, 1913; p. 160
CANINE SAGACITY
(KO)/May 16, 1908; p. 444
CANNED CURIOSITY
(Pyr)/Jun 12, 1915; p. 1778
CANNED HARMONY
(Sol)/Oct 26, 1912; p. 344
CANNIBAL KING, THE
(Lu)/Jul 24, 1915; p. 649
CANNING INDUSTRY IN CALIFORNIA
(SA)/Apr 18, 1914; p. 360
CANNON BALL, THE
(Key)/Jun 19, 1915; p. 1940
CANTON, CHINA (Sel)/May 3, 1913; p. 487
CANYON DWELLERS, THE
(Am)/Aug 3, 1912; p. 446
CAP OF DESTINY, THE
(Rex)/May 31, 1913; p. 921
CAP OF FORTUNE, THE
(Ed)/Jan 8, 1910; p. 17
CAPERS OF COLLEGE CHAPS
(Fal)/Oct 23, 1915; p. 620
CAPERS OF CUPID
(Vi)/Jun 28, 1913; p. 1360
CAPITAL OF THE MALAY STATES
(Pa)/Dec 13, 1913; p. 1279
CAPITAL PUNISHMENT
(Kni)/Aug 28, 1915; pp 1490-91
CAPITAL vs. LABOR
(Vi)/Apr 2, 1910; p. 509
CAPITULATION OF THE MAJOR, THE
(Vi)/Apr 3, 1915; p. 63
CAPRICE (FP)/Nov 15, 1913; p. 718
CAPRICE OF A DAME, THE
(Amb)/Sep 17, 1910; p. 632
CAPRICES OF A KING, THE
(CGP)/Jan 11, 1913; p. 159
CAPRICES OF FORTUNE
(Ec)/Oct 26, 1912; p. 344
CAPRICES OF KITTY, THE
(Bos)/Feb 27, 1915; p. 1299
CAPT. BARNACLE'S CHAPERONE
(Vi)/Nov 12, 1910;p.1116
CAPT. BARNACLE'S COURTSHIP
(Vi)/Mar 11, 1911; p. 542
CAPT. F.E. KLEINSCHMIDT'S ARCTIC
HUNT (Arc)/Feb 21, 1914; p. 956
CAPTAIN ALVAREZ
(Vi)/May 9, 1914; p. 799
CAPTAIN BARNACLE, DIPLOMAT
(Vi)/Nov 11, 1911; p. 469
CAPTAIN BARNACLE, REFORMER
(Vi)/Nov 23, 1912; p. 767
CAPTAIN BARNACLE'S BABY
(Vi)/Aug 26, 1911; p. 540

(Pa)/Apr 8, 1911; p. 780
(Sel)/Oct 5, 1912; p. 41

CATTLE RUSTLER'S DAUGHTER, THE
(Bi)/Oct 8, 1910; p. 816

CATTLE RUSTLER'S END, THE
(Am)/Aug 19, 1911; p. 465

CATTLE RUSTLER'S FATHER, THE
(SA)/Dec 2, 1911; p. 725

CATTLE THIEF'S BRAND, THE
(Am)/Aug 12, 1911; p. 377

CATTLE THIEF'S ESCAPE, THE
(Sel)/Oct 18, 1913; p. 263

CATTLE THIEF'S REVENGE, THE
(De)/Oct 8, 1910; p. 816

CATTLE THIEVES, THE (Ka)/Oct 30, 1909;
p. 604/Nov 20, 1909; p. 721

CATTLEMEN'S FEUD, THE (Col)/Dec 17,
1910; p. 1419/Dec 31, 1910; p. 1539

CATTLEMEN'S WAR, THE
(Bi)/Nov 11, 1911; p. 473

CAUCASIAN CUSTOMS
(Pa)/Oct 9, 1909; p. 490

CAUGHT (Vi)/Feb 1, 1908; p. 83
(SA)/Sep 25, 1915; p. 2176

CAUGHT AT HIS OWN GAME
(Fr)/Nov 15, 1913; p. 738

CAUGHT AT LAST
(Vi)/Jun 19, 1909; p. 835

CAUGHT BLUFFING
(Lu)/Nov 2, 1912; p. 450

CAUGHT BY A THREAD
(Ne)/May 8, 1915; p. 901

CAUGHT BY CINEMATOGRAPHY
(Lux)/Jan 6, 1912; p. 42

CAUGHT BY COWBOYS
(Ch)/Dec 3, 1910; p. 1298

CAUGHT BY THE CAMERA
(Lu)/Dec 3, 1910; p. 1296

CAUGHT BY THE HANDLE
(Ko)/Mar 27, 1915; p. 1933

CAUGHT BY WIRELESS
(Bio)/Mar 21, 1908; p. 241

CAUGHT IN A CABARET
(Key)/May 9, 1914; p. 821

CAUGHT IN A FLASH
(Imp)/Jul 20, 1912; p. 245

CAUGHT IN A PARK
(Key)/Feb 27, 1915; p. 1288

CAUGHT IN A TIGHT PINCH
(Be)/Oct 3, 1914; p. 65

CAUGHT IN HIS OWN NET
(GN)/Oct 7, 1911; p. 43
(Ko)/Nov 15, 1913; p. 737

CAUGHT IN HIS OWN TRAP
(Pa)/Oct 2, 1909; p. 451
(Vi)/Feb 12, 1910; p. 216

CAUGHT IN THE ACT
(Sel)/Aug 12, 1911; p. 376

(Cry)/Aug 23, 1913; p. 845

CAUGHT IN THE TOILS
(Ka)/Mar 2, 1912; p. 781

CAUGHT IN THE WEB
Oct 17, 1908; p. 298

CAUGHT IN TIGHTS
(Key)/Jul 11, 1914; p. 256

CAUGHT ON THE CLIFFS
(UE)/May 29, 1909; p. 714

CAUGHT WITH THE GOODS
(Pa)/Oct 24, 1908; p. 327/Oct 30, 1908;
p. 339/Dec 19, 1908; p. 501
(SA)/Apr 22, 1911; p. 898
(Bio)/Jan 6, 1912; p. 41
(Vi)/Feb 21, 1914; p. 947
(Lko)/Jan 23, 1915; p. 516
(Lu)/Jul 3, 1915; p. 64

CAUSE, THE (Ne)/Mar 8, 1913; p. 998

CAUSE FOR THANKFULNESS, A
(Ed)/Dec 6, 1913; p. 1150

CAUSE FOR THANKSGIVING
(Vi)/Dec 12, 1914; p. 1523

CAUSE FOR THANKSGIVING, A
(Ed)/Nov 8, 1913; p. 591

CAUSE OF ALL THE TROUBLE, THE
(Lu)/May 9, 1908; p. 423

CAUSE OF IT ALL (Ka)/Feb 13,1915; p.984

CAUSED BY A CLOCK
(Ko)/Nov 22, 1913; p. 869

CAVE DWELLERS, THE
(Bi)/Aug 2, 1913; p. 538
(Vi)/Nov 7, 1914; p. 788

CAVE HOMES IN THE CANARY ISLES
(Gau)/Dec 9, 1911; p. 816

CAVE MAN, THE
(Vi)/May 4, 1912; p. 425
(Vi)/Dec 4, 1915; pp 1844-45/
Dec 11, 1915; p. 2033

CAVE MAN WOOING, A
(Imp)/Jun 1, 1912; p. 831

CAVE MEN'S WAR, THE (Ka)/Nov 22,
1913; p. 878/Dec 20, 1913; p. 1412

CAVE OF DEATH, THE
(Ka)/Sep 12, 1914; p. 1512

CAVE OF THE SPOOKS (Pa)/Nov 21, 1908;
p.410/Nov 28,1908; p.422/Dec 5,1908; p.449

CAVE ON THUNDER CLOUD, THE
(SA)/Aug 28, 1915; p. 1480

CAVES OF LA JOLLA, THE
(Am)/Oct 28, 1911; p. 292

CEDARVILLE SCANDAL, THE
(Ec)/Jul 20, 1912; p. 245

CELEBRATED CASE, A
(Gem)/Sep 7, 1912; pp 961-62/
Sep 14, 1912; p. 1075
(Ka)/Feb 14,1914; p.814/Apr 17,1915; p.400
(Bio)/Apr 17, 1915; p. 400

CELERY INDUSTRY IN FLORIDA, THE

CHARACTER WOMAN, THE
(Ec)/Aug 29, 1914; p. 1243
CHARCOAL INDUSTRY IN CUBA, THE
(Pa)/May 11, 1912; p. 528
CHARGE OF THE LIGHT BRIGADE, THE
(Ed)/Oct 12,1912; p.134/Oct 26,1912; p.342
CHARITABLE LITTLE LADY, THE
(It)/Aug 5, 1911; p. 295
CHARITY BEGINS AT HOME
(Vi)/Dec 5, 1908; p. 448
(Pa)/Aug 14, 1909; p. 225
CHARITY OF THE POOR
(Th)/Apr 22, 1911; p. 901
CHARLES LE TREMERAIRE
(FA)/Aug 27, 1910; p. 464
CHARLES THE FIFTH
(Lux)/Jul 16, 1910; p. 143
CHARLIE, THE COMEDIAN, WANTS A
CONGENIAL SON-IN-LAW
(Ec)/Feb 24, 1912; p. 691
CHARLIE AND A DOG
(Cry)/May 2, 1914; p. 674
CHARLIE AND KITTIE IN BRUSSELS
(Pa)/Dec 24, 1910; p. 1478
CHARLIE FORCED TO FIND A JOB
(Gau)/Apr 17, 1909; p. 476
CHARLIE HAS A MANUSCRIPT TO SELL
(Ec)/Jul 29, 1911; p. 212
CHARLIE TAKES HIS HOLIDAYS
(Ec)/Jan 13, 1912; p. 127
CHARLIE WOOES VIVIAN
(Cry)/Dec 5, 1914; p. 1385
CHARLIE'S BUTTIE
(Ch)/Sep 23, 1911; p. 893
CHARLIE'S LITTLE JOKE
(Cry)/Sep 27, 1913; p. 1393
CHARLIE'S MA-IN-LAW
(Lu)/Jan 2, 1909; p. 11
CHARLIE'S NEW SUIT
(Cry)/May 16, 1914; p. 969
CHARLIE'S REFORM
(Ed)/Apr 20, 1912; p. 229
CHARLIE'S RIVAL (Cry)/Apr 25,1914;p.518
CHARLIE'S SMOKER (Cry)/Oct 3,1914;p.65
CHARLIE'S TOOTHACHE
(Cry)/Aug 1, 1914; p. 706
CHARLIE'S TWIN SISTER
(Nov)/Dec 4, 1915; p. 1853
CHARLIE'S WATERLOO
(Cry)/May 16, 1914; p. 970
CHARLOTTE CORDAY
(Pa)/Mar 13, 1909; pp 302-3
CHARMED ARROW, THE
(Sel)/Feb 7, 1914; p. 676
CHARMED SWORD (Pa)/Feb 1, 1908; p. 82
CHASE ACROSS THE CONTINENT, A
(Ed)/Dec 7, 1912; p. 975
CHASE BY MOONLIGHT, A

(Ko)/Jul 31, 1915; p. 817
CHASE OF CHERRY PURCELLE, THE
(Ec)/Jan 3, 1914; p. 50
CHASED BY BLOODHOUNDS
(Vi)/Jul 6, 1912; p. 42
CHASER, THE (WF)/Dec 19, 1914; p. 1681
CHASING A SEA LION IN THE ARCTICS
(Pa)/Oct 2, 1909; p. 452
CHASING GLOOM (Ko)/Jan 31, 1914; p. 545
CHASING THE BALL
(UE)/Oct 16, 1909; p. 528
CHASING THE LIMITED
(Bi)/Aug 14, 1915; p. 1162
CHASING THE RAINBOW
(Rex)/Oct 21, 1911; p. 210
CHASING THE SMUGGLERS
(Ka)/Mar 7, 1914; p. 1237
CHASM, THE (SA)/Jul 11, 1914; p. 256
           (Th)/Nov 21, 1914; p. 1076
CHATEAU OF BLOIS, FRANCE, THE
(Pa)/May 17, 1913; p. 703
CHATEAU OF CHAMBORD, THE
(Pa)/Apr 12, 1913; p. 163
CHATEAU OF CHENONCEAU, THE
(Pa)/Jun 21, 1913; p. 1252
CHAUFFEUR, THE (Cin)/Mar 16,1912;p.962
CHAUFFEUR, THE GIRL AND THE COP,
THE (SA)/May 18, 1912; p. 628
CHAUFFEUR'S DREAM, THE
(Ka)/Jul 6, 1912; pp 42, 43
CHAUNCEY PROVES A GOOD
DETECTIVE (Cre)/Oct 30, 1908; p. 338
CHEAP TRANSPORTATION
(Lu)/Dec 5, 1914; p. 1383
CHEAPEST WAY, THE
(Pa)/Mar 15, 1913; p. 1104
CHEAT, THE (Gau)/Nov 5, 1910; p. 1056
             (Las)/Dec 25, 1915; p. 2384
CHEATERS CHEATED, THE
(WBE)/Sep 14, 1907; p. 442
CHEATING (Po)/May 31, 1913; p. 921
CHECK No. 130 (Pr)/Jan 23, 1914; p. 516
CHECKED THROUGH
(Roy)/Mar 6, 1915; p. 1449
CHECKERS (AS)/Nov 29, 1913; p. 992
CHECKING CHARLIE'S CHILD
(Fal)/Dec 4, 1915; p. 1853
CHECKMATE
(Th)/Mar 4, 1911; p.484/Mar 11, 1911; p.542
(Am)/Apr 20, 1912; p. 231
(Maj)/May 8, 1915; p. 900
CHECKMATED (Vi)/Apr 12, 1913; p. 165
CHEEKIEST MAN ON EARTH
(Mi)/Sep 28, 1907; p. 473
CHEESE MINING (Ed)/Mar 14, 1914; p.1384
CHEESE OF POLICE, THE
(Ap)/May 16, 1914; p. 969
CHEESE RACE, THE

(KO)/Aug 15, 1908; p. 128
CHEESE SPECIAL, THE
(Jo)/Nov 15, 1913; p. 737
CHEESEVILLE COPS, THE
(Bio)/Aug 8, 1914; p. 836
CHEF AT CIRCLE G, THE
(Sel)/Nov 20, 1915; p. 1499
CHEF'S REDEMPTION, THE
(Bla)/Jan 16, 1915; p. 389
CHEF'S REVENGE, THE
(St)/Jan 2, 1915; p. 76
CHERRIES, THE (Pa)/May 21, 1910; p. 832
CHERRY (Vi)/Apr 18, 1914; p. 361
CHERRY BLOSSOMS (Vi)/Sep 23, 1911; p.891
CHERRY PICKERS, THE
(Sel)/Apr 25, 1914; p. 517
CHEST OF FORTUNE, THE
(Ka)/Mar 14, 1914; p. 1385
CHEVAL MYSTERY, THE
(Uni)/Jun 26, 1915; p. 2106
CHEW-CHEW LAND (Vi)/Sep 17,1910;p.631
CHEYENNE BRAVE, A
(Pa)/Sep 3, 1910; p. 518
CHEYENNE DAYS (Po)/Aug 26, 1911; p.545
CHEYENNE MASSACRE, THE
(Ka)/Apr 19, 1913; p. 283
CHEYENNE MEDICINE MAN, THE
(Bi)/Jun 3, 1911; p. 1260
CHEYENNE RAIDERS, THE
(Ka)/Jul 9, 1910; p. 84
CHEYENNE'S BRIDE, THE
(Pa)/Sep 9, 1911; p. 716
CHEYENNE'S COURTSHIP, THE
(Bi)/Aug 5, 1911; p. 295
CHICAGO STOCKYARDS FIRE, THE
(Imp)/Jun 3,1911;p.1239/Jun 24,1911;p.1455
CHICKEN (Sel)/May 28, 1910; p. 888
(Sel)/Jul 4, 1914; p. 64
C-H-I-C-K-E-N SPELLS CHICKEN
(SA)/Jul 9, 1910; p. 85
CHICKEN CHASERS, THE
(Jo)/Feb 14, 1914; p. 810
**CHICKEN INDUSTRY, CAUTANCES,
FRANCE** (UE)/Jun 7, 1913; p. 1031
CHICKEN INSPECTOR, THE
(Vi)/May 2, 1914; p. 672
CHIEF BLACKFOOT'S VINDICATION
(Ka)/May 21,1910;p.834
CHIEF INSPECTOR, THE
(Bio)/Nov 27, 1915; p. 1663
CHIEF OF POLICE, THE
(Ka)/Aug 22, 1914; p. 1099
CHIEF WHITE EAGLE
(Lu)/Nov 30, 1912; p. 877
CHIEFLY CONCERNING MALES
(Vi)/Jan 30, 1915; p. 671
CHIEF'S BLANKET, THE
(Bio)/Oct 26, 1912; p. 342

CHIEF'S DAUGHTER, THE
(Bio)/Apr 22, 1911; p. 900
(Sel)/Dec 23, 1911; p. 988
CHIEF'S GOAT, THE
(Vi)/Feb 13, 1915; p. 984
CHIEF'S LOVE AFFAIR, THE
(Bio)/Sep 19, 1914; p. 1644
CHIEF'S PREDICAMENT, THE
(Key)/Mar 15, 1913; p. 1166
CHIEF'S TALISMAN, THE
(Pa)/May 6, 1911; p. 1020
CHIEFTAIN'S SONS, THE
(Bio)/Oct 28, 1913; p. 264
**CHILD, THE DOG, AND THE VILLAIN,
THE** (Sel)/Aug 14, 1915; p. 1160
CHILD ACCUSER, THE
(KO)/Jun 8, 1907; p. 221
CHILD AND THE TRAMP, THE
(Ed)/May 13, 1911; p. 1081
CHILD DETECTIVE, THE
(Bel)/Nov 22, 1913; p. 848
CHILD IN JUDGMENT, A (Ed)/Oct 2, 1915;
p. 91/Nov 27, 1915; p. 1664
CHILD NEEDS A MOTHER, THE
(Lko)/Jul 10, 1915; p. 309
CHILD OF GENIUS, A
(GN)/Oct 5, 1912; p. 43
CHILD OF GOD, A (Mut)/May 8, 1915;
p. 918/May 15, 1915; p. 1072
CHILD OF THE DESERT, A
(Am)/Mar 7, 1914; p. 1238
CHILD OF THE FOREST
(Ed)/Sep 4, 1909; p. 313
CHILD OF THE GHETTO, A
(Bio)/Jun 18, 1910; p. 1048
CHILD OF THE NORTH, A
(Vi)/May 22, 1915; p. 1260
CHILD OF THE PURPLE SAGE, A
(SA)/Jun 22, 1912; p. 1126
CHILD OF THE RANCH, A
(Bi)/Jun 24, 1911; p. 1455
CHILD OF THE REGIMENT
(Pa)/Apr 3, 1909; p. 403
CHILD OF THE SEA, A
(Ka)/Jun 5, 1909; p. 753
(Lu)/May 7, 1910; p. 736
(Sel)/Aug 9, 1913; pp 623-24/
Aug 30, 1913; p. 961
CHILD OF THE SQUADRON, A
(UE)/Jul 2, 1910; p. 25
CHILD OF THE SURF, A
(Maj)/Sep 11, 1915; p. 1833
CHILD OF THE TENEMENTS, A
(Sol)/Mar 30, 1912; pp 1166-67
CHILD OF THE WEST, A
(Bi)/Dec 17, 1910; p. 1419
(SA)/Jan 20, 1912; p. 202
CHILD OF THE WILDERNESS, A

(Sel)/Jun 8, 1912; p. 944
CHILD OF TWO MOTHERS, THE
(Ec)/Dec 31, 1910; p. 1539
CHILD OF WAR, A
(Bro)/May 10, 1913; pp 576, 598
CHILD STEALERS OF PARIS, THE
(Imp)/Nov 15,1913;p.721/Nov 22,1913;p.869
CHILD THOU GAVEST ME, THE
(Bio)/Nov 28, 1914; p. 1232
CHILD TO THE RESCUE, A
(Ec)/Aug 31, 1912; p. 882
CHILDHOOD OF JACK HARKAWAY,
THE (Th)/Jan 7, 1911; pp 34-35
CHILDREN OF DESTINY
(Bio)/Mar 21, 1914; p. 1524
CHILDREN OF EDWARD IV, THE
(Sa)/Jun 25, 1910; p. 1102
CHILDREN OF JAPAN, THE
(CGP)/Mar 15, 1913; p. 1104
CHILDREN OF ST. ANNE, THE
(Maj)/May 10, 1913; p. 598
CHILDREN OF THE FEUD
(Vi)/Feb 28, 1914; p. 1088
CHILDREN OF THE FOREST
(SA)/Dec 27, 1913; p. 1543
CHILDREN OF THE GHETTO, THE
(Box)/Feb 27, 1915; p. 1290
CHILDREN OF THE NETHERLANDS
(Phc)/Nov 13, 1915; p. 1313
CHILDREN OF THE PLAINS
(Vi)/Apr 3, 1909; pp 403-4
CHILDREN OF THE SEA
(Lu)/Nov 27, 1909; pp 758-59
(Maj)/Jul 10, 1915; p. 308
CHILDREN WHO LABOR
(Ed)/Mar 9, 1912; p. 866
CHILDREN'S CONSPIRACY, THE
(Th)/May 3, 1913; p. 489
CHILDREN'S FRIEND, THE
(Bio)/Sep 25, 1909; p. 415
CHILDREN'S HOUR, THE
(Th)/Nov 22, 1913; p. 869
CHILDREN'S HOUSE, THE
(Bio)/Apr 17, 1915; p. 397
CHILDREN'S PARADISE, A
(Ya)/Aug 26, 1911; p. 543
CHILDREN'S REVOLT, THE
(Vi)/Nov 19, 1910; p. 1176
CHILD'S CAPTIVE, THE
(Lu)/Jul 16, 1910; p. 142
CHILD'S DEBT, A (KO)/Nov 7, 1908; p. 364
CHILD'S DEVOTION, A
(KO)/Nov 28, 1908; p. 432
(Lu)/Oct 5, 1912; p. 41
CHILD'S FAITH, A
(Bio)/Jul 30, 1910; p. 244
CHILD'S FIRST LOVE, A
(Re)/Mar 2, 1912; p. 782

CHILD'S HEROIC ACT, A
(Lux)/Aug 26, 1911; p. 543
CHILD'S HEROISM, A
(Ec)/Jul 22, 1911; p. 127
CHILD'S IMPULSE, A
(Bio)/Jul 9, 1910; p. 84
CHILD'S INFLUENCE, A
(Imp)/Jul 6, 1912; p. 44
(Cry)/Aug 9, 1913; p. 637
CHILD'S INTUITION, A
(Sol)/Sep 13, 1913; p. 1177
CHILD'S JUDGMENT, A
(Imp)/Dec 24, 1910; p. 1479
CHILD'S LOVE, A
(Pa)/Jul 10, 1909; p. 50
CHILD'S PLEA, A
(Pho)/Oct 23, 1909; p. 568
(Gau)/Jan 21, 1911; p. 144
(Ec)/Mar 16, 1912; p. 963
CHILD'S PRAYER, A
(Vi)/Mar 14, 1908; p.219/Dec 12, 1908;p.478
(Lux)/Mar 11, 1911; p. 542
(Lu)/Jul 20, 1912; p. 243
CHILD'S PRAYER, THE
(Pa)/Sep 25, 1909; p. 415
CHILD'S REMORSE, A
(Bio)/Aug 24, 1912; p. 771
CHILD'S SACRIFICE, A
(Sol)/Nov 5, 1910; p. 1060
CHILD'S STRATEGEM, A
(Bio)/Dec 17, 1910; p. 1416
CHILLS AND CHICKEN
(Jo)/Nov 13, 1915; p. 1314
CHIMES, THE (He)/Aug 22, 1914; p. 1076
(Wor)/Sep 19, 1914; p. 1624
CHIMMIE FADDEN
(Las)/Jul 10, 1915; p. 322
CHIMMIE FADDEN OUT WEST
(Las)/Nov 27, 1915; p. 1680
CHIMNEY SWEEPS, THE
(Pas)/Jul 4, 1914; p. 72
CHIMNEY'S SECRET, THE
(Vic)/Sep 11, 1915; p. 1834
CHINA AND THE CHINESE
(SA)/Feb 1, 1913; p. 465
CHINAMAN, THE (Gau)/Feb 27, 1909; p.236
CHINATOWN SLAVERY
(Sel)/May 8, 1909; p. 593
CHINESE AMUSEMENTS
(Pa)/Dec 11, 1909; p. 840
CHINESE CRUISER HAI CHI
(Imp)/Dec 30, 1911; p. 1072
CHINESE DEATH THORN, THE (Ka)/
Dec 6, 1913; p. 1134/Dec 27, 1913; p. 1544
CHINESE FUNERAL, A
(Me)/Aug 2, 1913; p. 535
CHINESE LOTTERY, THE
(Re)/Feb 20, 1915; p. 1140

No.10/Sep 12, 1914; p. 1511
No.11/Oct 17, 1914; p. 335
No.12/Nov 14, 1914; p. 931
No.13/Nov 28, 1914; p. 1231
CHRYSANTHEMUMS
(Gau)/Jun 24, 1911; p. 1453
(Pa)/Sep 2, 1911; p. 626
CHUMS (Pa)/Oct 30, 1909; p. 604
(UE)/May 18, 1912; p. 628
CHUMPS (Vi)/Jan 27, 1912;p.303
CHUNCHO INDIANS, THE
(Ed)/Oct 29, 1910; p. 994
CHURCH ACROSS THE WAY, THE
(Vi)/Jul 20, 1912; p. 243
CHURCH AND COUNTRY
(Ed)/Apr 27, 1912; p. 328
CIDER INDUSTRY (Pa)/Apr 18,
1908; p. 353/Jan 2, 1909; p. 11
CIGAR BUTT PICKERS OF PARIS
(Pa)/Aug 28, 1909; p. 283
CIGAR BUTTS (Maj)/May 9, 1914; p. 821
CIGARETTE MAKER OF SEVILLE, THE
(Ed)/May 14, 1910; p. 784
CIGARETTE MAKING
(Vi)/May 29, 1909; p. 713
CIGARETTE - THAT'S ALL, A
(GS)/Aug 14, 1915; p. 1162
CINDER ELFRED (He)/Oct 24, 1914; p. 493
CINDERELLA
Nov 21, 1908; p. 398
(Sel)/Dec 2, 1911; p.704/Jan 27, 1912; p.288
(Th)/Dec 30, 1911; p. 1073
(FP)/Jan 9, 1915; p. 224
CINDERELLA AND THE BOOB
(Bio)/Jun 7, 1913; p. 1030
CINDERELLA UP-TO-DATE
(Me)/Nov 6, 1909; p. 644
CINDERELLA'S GLOVES
(SA)/Jun 28, 1913; p. 1359
CINDERELLA'S SLIPPER
(Vi)/Mar 8, 1913; p. 995
CINDERS (Vi)/May 17, 1913; p. 704
CINEMATOGRAPH FIEND, THE
(Gau)/Sep 30, 1911; p. 971
CINTRA, A PICTURESQUE TOWN OF
PORTUGAL (Gau)/Oct 21, 1911; p. 207
CIRCLE C RANCH WEDDING PRESENT
(SA)/Dec 17, 1910; p. 1416
CIRCLE C's NEW BOSS
(Ch)/May 27, 1911; p. 1202
CIRCLE OF FATE, THE
(Ka)/Jun 7, 1913; p. 1030
(KB)/Jan 17, 1914; p. 290
CIRCLE OF GOLD, THE
(Fr)/Dec 5, 1914; p. 1385
CIRCLE 17 (Rex)/Aug 1, 1914; p. 706
CIRCLE'S END, THE
(Lu)/Jan 17, 1914; p. 288

CIRCULAR FENCE, THE
(Am)/Oct 7, 1911; p. 43
CIRCULAR PATH, THE
(SA)/Oct 9, 1915; p. 252
CIRCULAR STAIRCASE, THE
(Sel)/Sep 18, 1915; p. 2007
CIRCUMSTANCES MAKE HEROES
(Ed)/Jul 12, 1913; p. 205
CIRCUMSTANTIAL EVIDENCE
(Vi)/Jun 13, 1908; pp 516-17
(Cen)/Nov 28, 1908; p. 435
(Ch)/Oct 28, 1911; p. 292
(Sel)/Sep 21, 1912; p. 1175
CIRCUMSTANTIAL HERO, A
(Bio)/Dec 13, 1913; p. 1279
CIRCUMSTANTIAL NURSE, A
(Pri)/Jan 24, 1914; p. 414
CIRCUMSTANTIAL SCANDAL, A
(Ne)/Oct 30a, 1915; p. 969
CIRCUS, THE (St)/Aug 1, 1914; p. 705
(Rex)/Nov 13, 1915; p. 1313
CIRCUS AND THE BOY, THE
(Vi)/Jul 18, 1914; p. 432
CIRCUS BOY, THE
(KO)/May 23, 1908; p. 463
CIRCUS IN AUSTRALIA
(Pa)/Oct 14, 1911; p. 130
CIRCUS MAN, THE
(Las)/Dec 5, 1914; p. 1394
CIRCUS MARY (Vic)/Jun 26, 1915; p. 2097
CIRCUS ROMANCE, A
(Mil)/Sep 7, 1912; p. 976
(Pr)/May 30, 1914; p. 1261
(Me)/Sep 19, 1914; p. 1623
CIRCUS STOWAWAY, A
(Th)/Jun 17, 1911; p. 1388
CISSY'S INNOCENT WINK
(Cas)/Dec 18, 1915; p. 2203
CITIES OF JAPAN
(Me)/Jan 3, 1914; p. 48
CITIZEN IN THE MAKING, A
(Sel)/Jun 1, 1912; p. 830
CITY, THE (Re)/Aug 26, 1911; p. 543
(KB)/Jul 18, 1914; p. 434
CITY BOARDER, THE
(Ch)/Jan 11, 1913; p. 160
CITY FELLER, THE
(Sel)/Aug 5, 1911; p. 293
CITY FELLOW, THE
(Maj)/Mar 22, 1913; p. 1222
CITY OF A HUNDRED MOSQUES,
BROUSSA, ASIA MINOR
(UE)/Nov 5, 1910; p. 1059
CITY OF AMALFI, ITALY, THE
(Gau)/Apr 22, 1911; p. 898
CITY OF BORDEAUX (Gau)/Oct 7,1911;p.40
CITY OF DARKNESS, THE (Bro)/Dec 5,
1914; p. 1396/Dec 12, 1914; p. 1525

CITY OF DENVER, THE
(Ed)/Feb 24, 1912; p. 689
CITY OF FLORENCE, ITALY, THE
(Gau)/Jul 1, 1911; p. 1519
CITY OF GOLD, THE
(Sel)/Jul 12, 1913; p. 204
CITY OF HER DREAMS, THE
(Th)/Dec 3, 1910; p. 1298
CITY OF MEXICO, THE
(SA)/May 10, 1913; p. 595
CITY OF MOSQUES, THE
(Ec)/Mar 2, 1912; p. 781
CITY OF NAPLES, THE
(Pa)/Sep 25, 1909; p. 414
CITY OF PROMISE, THE
(WF)/Jul 4, 1914; p. 66
CITY OF RAUEN, FRANCE, THE
(Pa)/Jun 7, 1913; p. 1031
CITY OF SAN FRANCISCO, THE
(Ed)/Mar 1, 1913; p. 887
CITY OF SINGAPORE, THE
(Pa)/Aug 26, 1911; p. 541
CITY OF TERRIBLE NIGHT
(Imp)/Apr 3, 1915; p. 66
CITY OF WASHINGTON, THE
(Ed)/Aug 24, 1912; p. 770
CITY RUBE, A (Vi)/Sep 11, 1915; p. 1832
CITY WOLF, A (At)/Feb 4, 1911; p. 249
CIVIC PARADE (Ed)/Jul 5, 1913; p. 47
CIVIL WAR (Gau)/Feb 19, 1910; p. 257
CIVILIAN, THE (Bro)/Dec 7, 1912; p. 978
CIVILIZATION (Po)/May 20, 1911;
p. 1143/Jun 10, 1911; p. 1319
CIVILIZED AND SAVAGE
(Rex)/Aug 9, 1913; p. 638
CLAIM JUMPERS, THE
(Am)/Oct 7, 1911; p. 41
(KB)/Nov 29, 1913; p. 1008
CLAIM NUMBER THREE
(Lu)/Jun 27, 1914; p. 1828
CLAIM OF HONOR, THE
(Bio)/Jul 24, 1915; p. 649
CLAM SHELL SUFFRAGETTE, THE
(Sel)/Apr 10, 1915; p. 235
CLANCY (Vi)/Jan 7, 1911; p. 32
CLANCY, THE MODEL
(Cry)/Jun 7, 1913; p. 1032
CLARA'S MYSTERIOUS TOYS
(Ec)/Aug 16, 1913; p. 744
CLARENCE, THE COWBOY
(Pa)/Jul 12, 1913; p. 204
CLARENCE AND PERCY
(Ed)/Apr 18, 1914; p. 361
CLARENCE AT THE THEATER
(Lu)/May 17, 1913; p. 703
CLARENCE CHEATS AT CROQUET
(Fal)/Dec 4, 1915; p. 1853
CLARIONET SOLO (KO)/Jun 27,1908; p.549

CLARISSA'S CHARMING CALF
(Fal)/Oct 30a, 1915; p. 968
CLARK'S CAPTURE OF KASKASKIA
(Ch)/May 13, 1911;p.1083
CLASH OF VIRTUES, A
(SA)/Aug 15, 1914; p. 959
CLASS REUNION, THE
(Imp)/Jul 29, 1911; p. 213
CLASSIC DANCES BY COUNTESS de
SWINSKY (Imp)/Mar 30, 1912; p. 1166
CLASSMATES (Bio)/Feb 1, 1908; pp 81-82
CLASSMATES' FROLIC
(Vi)/Feb 22, 1913; p. 779
CLASSY GATHERING, A
(Tor)/Jan 28, 1911; p. 196
CLAUSE IN THE CONSTITUTION, THE
(Sel)/Sep 4, 1915; p. 1644
CLAUSE IN THE WILL, A
(De)/Nov 12, 1910; p. 1118
CLAY INDUSTRY, THE
(Sel)/Feb 1, 1913; p. 464
CLEAN SLATE, A (Lu)/Jan 16, 1915; p. 368
CLEAN SWEEP, A (Ed)/Apr 24, 1915; p. 555
CLEAN UP, THE
(Am)/Dec 25, 1915; pp 2389-90
CLEANING TIME (Lu)/May 1, 1915; p. 727
CLEANLINESS IS NEXT TO GODLINESS,
BUT -- (Lux)/Dec 28, 1912; p. 1293
CLEMENCEAU CASE, THE
(Fox)/Apr 24, 1915; p. 567
CLEMENCY OF ISABEAU, THE
(CGP)/Apr 13, 1912; p. 137
CLEO AND PHYLETES
(It)/Sep 16, 1911; p. 778
CLEOPATRA (Pa)/May 21, 1910; pp 833-34
(Hel)/Nov 30, 1912; pp 859-60
CLEOPATRA'S LOVERS
(Vi)/Feb 6, 1909; p. 144
CLERK, THE (Maj)/Feb 28, 1914; p. 1089
CLEVER BEYOND HER YEARS
(UE)/Sep 23, 1911; p. 891
CLEVER DOMESTIC, A
(Pa)/Dec 17, 1910; p. 1418
CLEVER FRAUD, A
(Vi)/Jun 17, 1911; pp 1362, 1387
CLEVER RUSE, A (Imp)/Dec 24,1910;p.1480
CLEVER SLEUTH, A
(Gau)/Jan 8, 1910; p. 17
CLEVER STORY, THE
(Pa)/Oct 18, 1913; p. 263
CLIFF DWELLERS, THE
(Ka)/Jun 4, 1910; p. 942
CLIFF GIRL, THE (Re)/Jun 5, 1915; p. 1605
CLIMAX, THE (Sol)/Apr 5, 1913; p. 50
(Pa)/Sep 20, 1913; p. 1283
CLIMBERS, THE (Lu)/May 29,1915; p.1443
CLINK OF GOLD, THE
(Gau)/Jul 16, 1910; p. 143

CLOAK OF GUILT, THE
(Ka)/Jul 12, 1913; p. 204
CLOCK-MAKER'S SECRET, THE
(Pa)/Nov 30, 1907; p. 636
CLOCK WENT WRONG, THE
(Sel)/Jun 13, 1914; p. 1540
CLOD, THE (Lu)/Oct 4, 1913; p. 49
CLOG MAKING IN BRITTANY
(Pa)/May 2, 1908;p.402/Jan 2, 1909;p.10
CLOISONNE WARE (Vi)/Jul 12, 1913; p.205
CLOISTER, THE (UE)/Jun 12, 1909; p. 834
CLOISTER AND THE HEARTH, THE
(Bli)/Mar 7, 1914; p. 1222
CLOISTER'S TOUCH, THE
(Bio)/Feb 12, 1910; p. 215
CLOSE CALL, A
(Ya)/Apr 29, 1911; pp 960-61
(Pa)/Jun 3, 1911; p. 1259
(GN)/May 18, 1912; p. 636
(Bio)/Jun 8, 1912; p. 942
(Vi)/Oct 10, 1914; p. 187
(St)/Oct 17, 1914; p. 337
CLOSE CROPPED CLIPPINGS
(Ecl)/Jan 23, 1915; p. 517
**CLOSE OF THE AMERICAN
REVOLUTION, THE**
(Ed)/Jul 20, 1912; p. 243
CLOSE SHAVE, A (Pun)/Feb 15, 1913; p.681
CLOSED DOOR, THE
(Vi)/May 28, 1910; p. 888
(Vic)/Oct 4, 1913; p. 28
CLOSED GATES (Rex)/Jun 13, 1914; p. 1541
CLOSING CHAPTER, THE
(U)/Jul 17, 1915; p. 487
CLOSING HOUR, THE
(KO)/Jul 11, 1908; p. 34
CLOSING NET, THE
(Pa)/Oct 9, 1915; p. 284
CLOSING OF THE CIRCUIT, THE
(Vi)/May 8, 1915; p. 900
CLOSING WEB, THE
(Bio)/Dec 19, 1914; p. 1680
CLOTHES (FP)/Mar 21, 1914; p. 1527
CLOTHES COUNT (Lu)/Apr 24,1915; p.555
CLOTHES LINE QUARREL, A
(Th)/Nov 29, 1913; p. 1009
CLOTHES MAKE THE MAN
(Vi)/Nov 5, 1910; p. 1056
(Ed)/Sep 11, 1915; p. 1832
CLOUDS AND ICE FIELDS
(Amb)/Feb 25, 1911; p. 432
CLOUDS AND SUNSHINE
(Re)/Sep 16, 1911; p. 790
CLOWN AND THE BEGGAR, THE
(Imp)/Oct 11, 1913; p. 157
CLOWN AND THE MINISTER, THE
(Lu)/Oct 22, 1910; p. 936
CLOWN AND THE PRIMA DONNA, THE

(Vi)/Sep 13, 1913; p. 1175
CLOWN DOCTOR, THE/Nov 28, 1908;p.422
CLOWN HERO, THE
(Ch)/May 10, 1913; p. 597
CLOWNLAND (Imp)/Jul 13, 1912; p. 149
CLOWN'S BABY, THE
(SA)/Aug 12, 1911; p. 377
CLOWN'S BEST PERFORMANCE, THE
(Vi)/Aug 19, 1911; p. 464
CLOWN'S CHRISTMAS EVE, THE
(Vi)/Sep 5, 1908; pp 183-84
CLOWN'S DAUGHTER, THE
(Pa)/Dec 12, 1908; pp 476, 477, 486
(Re)/Sep 20, 1913; p. 1286
CLOWN'S REVENGE, THE
(GN)/Mar 29, 1913; p. 1317
CLOWN'S TRIUMPH, THE
(Imp)/Jun 1, 1912; p. 831
CLUB CURE, THE (Bio)/Jan 10,1914; p.173
CLUB MAN AND THE CROOK, THE
(Bio)/Nov 23, 1912; p. 767
CLUB OF THE CORPULENT, THE
(GN)/May 28, 1910; p. 891
CLUB PEST, THE (Bio)/Feb 20,1915; p.1139
CLUBMAN, THE (Lu)/Jun 5, 1915; p. 1604
CLUBMAN'S WAGER, THE
(Am)/Jan 30, 1915; p. 672
CLUE, THE (SA)/Apr 27, 1912; p. 329
(Sel)/Feb 1, 1913; p. 465
(Rex)/Oct 11, 1913; p. 158
(Las)/Jul 24, 1915; p. 670
CLUE IN THE DUST, THE
(Maj)/Dec 28, 1912; p. 1293
CLUE OF THE PORTRAIT, THE
(Ec)/Jan 30, 1915; p. 672
CLUTCH OF CIRCUMSTANCE, THE
(SA)/Jun 19, 1915; p. 1940
CLUTCH OF CONSCIENCE, THE
(Pa)/Mar 1, 1913; p. 888
CLUTCH OF THE EMPEROR, THE
(Rex)/Apr 10, 1915; p. 237
**COACHING TRIP IN DEVONSHIRE,
ENGLAND, A** (UE)/Jan 14, 1911; p. 88
COACHMAN OF THE VILLAGE, THE
(It)/Feb 18, 1911;p.372
COAL INDUSTRY, THE
(Vi)/Feb 8, 1913; p. 572
COAL MAN'S SAVINGS, THE
(KO)/Apr 18, 1908; p. 353
COALING SHIPS BY MODERN METHODS
(Po)/May 4, 1912; p. 427
COALS OF FIRE (UE)/Feb 19, 1910; p. 258
(At)/Mar 4, 1911; p. 483
(Sel)/Nov 4, 1911; p. 380
(Th)/Jan 24, 1914; p. 414
(Am)/Feb 6, 1915; p. 828
COAST GUARD, THE
(UE)/Jan 29, 1910; p. 128

COLLEEN BAWN (Ya)/Aug 5, 1911; p. 289
COLLEEN BAWN, THE (Ka)/Sep 30, 1911;
pp 954, 956/Mar 28, 1914; p. 1681
COLLEGE CHAPERONE, THE
(Sel)/Mar 8, 1913; p. 996
COLLEGE CHICKEN, A
(SA)/Aug 20, 1910; p. 407
COLLEGE CHUMS
(Ed)/Dec 14, 1907; pp 670-71
(Am)/Mar 18, 1911; p. 603
(Cry)/Jul 26, 1913; p. 429
COLLEGE CUPID, A
(Lu)/Jan 10, 1914; p. 172
COLLEGE DAYS (KB)/Feb 6, 1915; p. 830
COLLEGE GIRL, A (Lu)/Apr 6, 1912; p. 40
COLLEGE ORPHAN, THE
(Uni)/Oct 23, 1915; p. 628
COLLEGE SPENDTHRIFT, THE
(Am)/Mar 4, 1911; p. 484
COLLEGE SWEETHEARTS
(Pa)/Sep 30, 1911; p. 970
COLLEGE WIDOW, THE
(Lu)/Apr 3, 1915; p. 69
COLLINGSBY PEARLS, THE
(Ec)/Jan 9, 1915; p. 223
COLOMBA (Bio)/Feb 27, 1915; p. 1267/
Mar 20, 1915; p. 1764
COLOMBO (Ec)/Feb 28, 1914; p. 1089
COLONEL AND THE KING, THE
(Th)/May 27, 1911; p. 1202
COLONEL CARTER OF CARTERSVILLE
(Wor)/Jul 10, 1915; p. 320
COLONEL CUSTARD'S LAST STAND
(Fr)/Mar 21, 1914; p. 1526
COLONEL HEEZA LIAR
(Pa)/Feb 27, 1915; p. 1289
COLONEL HEEZA LIAR, GHOST
BREAKER (Pa)/Feb 13, 1915; p. 986
COLONEL HEEZA LIAR, WAR DOG
(Pa)/Aug 21, 1915; p. 1318
COLONEL HEEZA LIAR AS EXPLORER
(Ecl)/Aug 15, 1914; p. 962
COLONEL HEEZA LIAR AT THE BAT
(Pa)/Sep 4, 1915; p. 1645
COLONEL HEEZA LIAR IN THE
WILDERNESS (Ecl)/Oct 17, 1914; p. 337
COLONEL OF THE NUTTS, THE
(Fr)/Mar 14, 1914; p. 1386
COLONEL OF THE RED HUSSARS, THE
(Ed)/Nov 21, 1914; p. 1085
COLONEL STEELE, MASTER GAMBLER
(U)/Dec 11, 1915; p. 2033
COLONEL'S ADOPTED DAUGHTER, THE
(KB)/Feb 7, 1914; p. 677
COLONEL'S BOOT, THE
(Ec)/Aug 27, 1910; p. 464
COLONEL'S DAUGHTER, THE
(Rex)/Aug 26, 1911; p. 545

COLONEL'S ERRAND, THE
(Ka)/Jul 16, 1910; p. 142
COLONEL'S ORDERLY, THE
(Dom)/Apr 18, 1914; p. 362
COLONEL'S PERIL, THE
(101)/Jul 13, 1912; p. 149
COLONEL'S WIFE, THE
(Ecl)/Sep 26, 1914; p. 1780
COLONIAL BELLE, A
(Ka)/Aug 20, 1910; p. 407
COLONIAL ROMANCE, A
(Vi)/Feb 6, 1909; p. 144
COLONIAL VIRGINIA (Ed)/Nov 21, 1908;
pp 398, 405/Nov 28, 1908; p. 422
COLOR SERGEANT'S HORSE, THE
(Vi)/Dec 24, 1910; p. 1478
COLORADO (Uni)/Nov 6, 1915; p. 1154
COLORED GIRL'S LOVE, A
(Key)/Jan 2, 1915; p. 77
COLORED STENOGRAPHER, THE
(Ed)/Mar 13, 1909; p. 304
COLORED VILLAINY
(Key)/Feb 6, 1915; p. 828
COLUMBO, CAPITAL OF CEYLON
(Pa)/Aug 16, 1913; p. 743
COLUMBO, CEYLON
(Pa)/Nov 28, 1914; p. 1233
COLUMBO AND ITS ENVIRONS
(Pa)/Oct 8, 1910; p. 814
COLUMBUS DAY CONSPIRACY, A
(Th)/Jan 13, 1912; p. 126
COMATA, THE SIOUX
(Bio)/Oct 2, 1909; pp 450-51
COMBINATION, THE
(Vi)/Feb 20, 1915; p. 1139
COMBINATION OF THE SAFE, THE
(Ka)/Oct 26, 1912; p. 343
COME BACK, THE
(Pre)/Apr 10, 1915; p. 237
COME BACK TO ERIN
(Po)/Mar 25, 1911; p. 658
COME 'ROUND AND TAKE THAT
ELEPHANT AWAY
(Sel)/Mar 27, 1914; p. 1932
COME SEBEN LEBEN
(Bio)/Aug 30, 1913; p. 960
COMEBACK, THE
(Maj)/May 15, 1915; p. 1072
COMEDIAN FOR LOVE, A
(Ec)/Mar 8, 1913; p. 997
COMEDIAN'S DOWNFALL, THE
(Ed)/Oct 4, 1913; p. 47
COMEDIAN'S MASK, THE
(Imp)/Jun 21, 1913; p. 1254
COMEDIENNE'S STRATEGY, THE
(Lu)/Jan 2, 1915; p. 75
COMEDY AND TRAGEDY (Ed)/Dec 4,
1909; p. 797/Feb 14, 1914; p. 788/

(Ka)/Apr 18, 1914; p. 360
CONFLICT, THE (Re)/May 27, 1911; p.1202
　　　　　　　(SA)/Apr 3, 1915; p. 64
CONFLICT'S END, THE
　(Rex)/Oct 5, 1912; p. 42
CONFUSION (Cin)/May 11, 1912; p. 528
CONJURERS, THE
　(Cin)/Mar 8, 1913; p. 995
CONJUROR, THE (GN)/May 7, 1910; p. 738
CONNECTING LINK, THE
　(Ec)/Aug 5, 1911; p. 274
　(Bi)/Nov 27, 1915; p. 1666
CONQUERED AGAIN
　(It)/Jun 4, 1910; pp 942-43
CONQUERED, or THE MADCAP
　PRINCESS (GN)/Jan 4, 1913; p. 31
CONQUERING CARRIE
　(Ka)/Aug 12, 1911; p. 377
CONQUERING HERO, THE
　(Lu)/Oct 9, 1909; p. 491
　(Ne)/Dec 17, 1910; p. 1418
CONQUEROR, THE (Vi)/Apr 23, 1910;p.641
　　　　　　　(SA)/Feb 7, 1914; p.676
CONQUEST, A (Pa)/Apr 16, 1910; p. 597
CONQUEST OF CONSTANTIA, THE
　(Vi)/Dec 11, 1915; p. 2031
CONQUEST OF MAN, THE
　(SA)/Mar 21, 1914; p. 1524
CONSCIENCE (Vi)/Mar 26, 1910; p.466
　　　　　(Bio)/Mar 25, 1911; p.657
　　　　　(Gem)/Mar 8, 1913; p. 998
　　　　　(Bro)/Jan 10, 1914; p. 174
　　　　　(Th)/Sep 5, 1914; p. 1373
　　　　　(Imp)/Jun 12, 1915; p. 1784
　　　　　(Uni)/Jun 12, 1915; p. 1784
CONSCIENCE, or THE CHAMBER OF
　HORRORS (Vi)/Jul 27, 1912; p. 344
CONSCIENCE AND THE TEMPTRESS
　(Sel)/Jan 31, 1914; p. 543
CONSCIENCE FUND, THE
　(Sel)/Oct 18, 1913; p. 264
CONSCIENCE OF A CHILD, THE
　(FA)/Sep 24, 1910; p. 690
CONSCIENCE OF HASSAN BEY, THE
　(Bio)/Jan 3, 1914; p. 48
CONSCIENCE OF JUROR No. 10, THE
　(Th)/Oct 30, 1915; p. 793
CONSCIENTIOUS CAROLINE
　(Ed)/Jun 13, 1914; p. 1540
CONSEQUENCES, THE
　(Vic)/Dec 28, 1912; p. 1293
CONSEQUENCES OF A NIGHT OUT, THE
　(KO)/Apr 18, 1908; p. 354
CONSIDERABLE MILK
　(StP)/Oct 2, 1915; p. 80
CONSPIRACY, THE
　Dec 4, 1909; p. 799
　(Sel)/Feb 14, 1914; p. 808

(WS)/Feb 21, 1914; p. 948
(FP)/Dec 19, 1914; p. 1700
CONSPIRACY AGAINST THE KING, A
　(Ed)/Nov 4, 1911; p. 379
CONSPIRACY AT THE CHATEAU, THE
　(SA)/May 8, 1915; p. 900
CONSPIRACY OF CATILINE, THE
　(Cin)/Sep 28, 1912; p. 1276
CONSPIRATORS, THE
　(Ka)/Sep 11, 1909; p. 346
　(GN)/Sep 30, 1911; p. 976
CONSTABLE'S DAUGHTER, THE
　(Lu)/Oct 18, 1913; p. 263
　(Be)/Mar 6, 1915; p. 1448
CONSTANCY OF JEANNE, THE
　(Pa)/Apr 11, 1914; p. 213
CONSTANTINOPLE (KO)/Jul 4, 1908; p. 13
　　　　　　(Ec)/Nov 23,1912;p.768
CONSTRUCTION OF BALLOONS
　(Pa)/Oct 2, 1909; p. 451
CONSTRUCTION OF THE PIANO
　(Lux)/Jan 6, 1912; p. 42
CONSUL CROSSES THE ATLANTIC
　(UE)/Dec 11, 1909; p. 841
CONSUMING LOVE (Vi)/Feb 25, 1911;p.431
CONTAGION (Po)/May 20, 1911; p. 1143
CONTAGIOUS NERVOUS TWITCHING
　(Pa)/Jul 18, 1908; p. 51
CONTAGIOUS NERVOUSNESS, A
　(KO)/Apr 11, 1908; pp 327-28
CONTENTS OF THE SUITCASE, THE
　(Ed)/Oct 18, 1913; p. 264
CONTEST AND NO PRIZE, A
　(Cin)/May 18, 1912; p. 629
CONTEST FOR A HANDKERCHIEF
　(Pa)/Jan 8, 1910; p. 17
CONVENIENT BURGLAR, A
　(Bio)/Oct 7, 1911; p. 39
CONVERSION OF FROSTY BLAKE, THE
　(Bro)/Jun 5, 1915; p. 1606
CONVERSION OF MR. ANTI, THE
　(Sel)/Nov 22, 1913; p. 867
CONVERSION OF SMILING TOM, THE
　(Sel)/May 8, 1915; p. 899
CONVERT, THE (Imp)/Mar 4, 1911; p. 484
CONVERT OF SAN CLEMENTE, THE
　(Sel)/Dec 9, 1911; p. 816
CONVERTABLE AUTO, THE
　(CGP)/Nov 2, 1912; p. 449
CONVERTED (Gau)/Mar 13, 1909; p. 302
CONVERTED DEACON, THE
　(Th)/Jul 30, 1910; p. 245
CONVERTS, THE (Bio)/Mar 26, 1910; p. 466
CONVICT, THE (Th)/Oct 8, 1910; p. 816
CONVICT, COSTUMES AND CONFUSION
　(Vi)/Dec 12, 1914; p. 1524
CONVICT B-75 (Amb)/Mar 30, 1912; p. 1166
CONVICT No. 796 (Vi)/Jun 4, 1910; p. 941

COUNTESS' WEDDING DAY, THE
(GN)/Oct 10, 1908; p. 286
COUNTING HOUSE MYSTERY, THE
(Ya)/Feb 18, 1911; p. 372
COUNTING OF TIME, THE
(Ne)/May 25, 1912; p. 730
COUNTING OUT THE COUNT
(St)/May 8, 1915; p. 901
COUNTLESS COUNT, A
(SA)/Jul 17, 1915; p. 485
COUNTLESS COUNT, THE
(Jo)/Oct 3, 1914; p. 65
COUNTRY ABOUT ROME
(KO)/May 9, 1908; p. 423
COUNTRY BLOOD (Lu)/Aug 21,1915;p.1317
COUNTRY BOARDER, THE
(Imp)/Dec 10, 1910; p. 1358
COUNTRY BOY, THE
(Pa)/Dec 7, 1912; p. 976
(Las)/Feb 27, 1915; p. 1297
COUNTRY CIRCUS, A
(Vic)/Sep 11, 1915; p. 1834
COUNTRY COUSIN, THE
(Ne)/May 10, 1913; p. 597
COUNTRY CUPID, A
(Bio)/Aug 12, 1911; p. 375
COUNTRY DOCTOR, THE
(Bio)/Jul 10, 1909; p. 49
COUNTRY GIRL, A
(Imp)/Oct 12, 1912; p. 143
COUNTRY GIRL, THE
(Th)/Jun 26, 1915; pp 2096-97
(Imp)/Aug 21, 1915; p. 1318
COUNTRY GIRL'S PERIL, A
(Sel)/Jul 3, 1909; p. 13
COUNTRY GIRL'S ROMANCE, A
(Maj)/May 17, 1913; p. 705
COUNTRY GIRL'S SEMINARY LIFE AND
EXPERIENCES, A (Ed)/Mar 28, 1908;p.269
COUNTRY INNOCENCE
(Imp)/Oct 17, 1914; p. 338
COUNTRY LAD, A (Pa)/Aug 29,1908; p.163
(Id)/May 15,1915; p.1073
COUNTRY LIFE IN A FLAT
(Gau)/Nov 6, 1909; p. 643
COUNTRY LOVERS (Bio)/Jun 3,1911;p.1258
COUNTRY MOUSE, THE
(Bos)/Nov 21, 1914; p. 1084
COUNTRY OF THE "BOGOUDENS," THE
(Pa)/Jul 4, 1908; p. 12
COUNTRY PARSON, THE
(Bio)/Sep 25, 1915; p. 2195
COUNTRY SCANDAL, A
(Gau)/Nov 2, 1912; p. 451
COUNTRY SCHOOL TEACHER, THE
(Lu)/Nov 30, 1912; p. 876
COUNTS, THE (Vi)/Oct 12, 1912; p. 142
COUNT'S WILL, THE

(Pa)/May 10, 1913; p. 596
COUNT'S WOOING, THE
(Me)/Nov 27, 1909; pp 757-58
COUNTY CHAIRMAN, THE (FP)/Oct 17,
1914; p. 348/Oct 31, 1914; p. 649
COUNTY FAIR, THE
(Sel)/Dec 31, 1910; p. 1538
(Ka)/Nov 9, 1912; p. 552
COUNTY SEAT WAR, THE
(Ka)/Feb 28, 1914; p. 1088
COUNTY'S PRIZE BABY, THE
(Th)/Nov 23, 1912; p. 768
COUPLE NEXT DOOR, THE
(Pa)/Jan 3, 1914; p. 48
COUPLE OF SIDE-ORDER FABLES, A
(SA)/Mar 20, 1915; p. 1763
COUPON COLLECTORS
(Lu)/Dec 19, 1914; p. 1679
COUPON COURTSHIP, A
(Ka)/May 17, 1913; p. 704
COURAGE (U)/May 1, 1915; p. 729
COURAGE AND THE MAN
(Lu)/Jun 26, 1915; p. 2096
COURAGE OF FEAR, THE
(Mil)/Aug 31, 1912; p. 881
COURAGE OF SORTS
(Vi)/Jul 15, 1911; p. 38
(Am)/Oct 18, 1913; p. 265
COURAGE OF THE COMMONPLACE,
THE (Vi)/Aug 16, 1913; p. 743
COURAGEOUS BLOOD
(Lu)/Jan 18, 1913; p. 264
COURSE OF TRUE LOVE, THE
(Bio)/Feb 19, 1910; p. 257
(Vi)/Jan 20, 1912; p. 203
COURT JESTER (Ka)/Mar 12, 1910; p. 384
COURT MARSHALL, THE
(Gau)/Apr 29, 1911; p. 957
COURT MARTIALED
(Imp)/May 22, 1915; p. 1262
COURTHOUSE CROOKS
(Key)/Jul 10, 1915; p. 321
COURTING ACROSS THE COURT
(Th)/Jul 8, 1911; p. 1587
COURTING BETTY'S BEAU
(Ed)/Mar 7, 1914; p. 1236
COURTING OF MARY, THE (Maj)/Nov 25,
1911; p. 619/Dec 2, 1911; p. 727
COURTING OF PRUDENCE, THE
(Be)/May 30, 1914; p. 1261
COURTING THE WIDOW
(Vi)/Apr 2, 1910; p. 508
COURTING TROUBLE
(Emp)/Mar 27, 1915; p. 1933
COURT'S DECREE, THE
(Th)/Jul 22, 1911; p. 126
COURTSHIP OF MILES STANDISH, THE
(Sel)/Feb 5, 1910; p. 168

CRICKET ON THE HEARTH, THE
(Am)/Feb 21, 1914; p. 948
CRIME OF CAIN, THE
(Vi)/Jun 27, 1914; p. 1829
CRIME OF THOUGHT, THE
(Po)/Jan 30, 1915; p. 673
CRIME ON THE COAST, THE
(FA)/Aug 23, 1913; p. 824
CRIME'S TRIANGLE
(Imp)/Sep 18, 1915; p. 1997
CRIMINAL, THE (Vi)/Jun 26, 1915; p. 2109
CRIMINAL CHIEF'S CAPTURE
(GN)/Feb 18, 1911; pp 371-72
CRIMINAL HYPNOTIST, THE
(Bio)/Jan 23, 1909; p. 94
CRIMINAL IN SPITE OF HIMSELF, A
(Ec)/Nov 30, 1912; p. 878
CRIMINAL PATH, THE
(Ram)/Mar 21, 1914; p. 1509
CRIMINALS (Rex)/Oct 11, 1913; p. 158
CRIMINALS, THE (Mec)/Apr 5, 1913; p. 49
CRIMINAL'S DAUGHTER, THE
Oct 17, 1908; p. 298
CRIMINOLOGIST, THE
(Ne)/Oct 5, 1912; p. 42
CRIMINOLOGY AND REFORM
(Bio)/Mar 7, 1914; p. 1236
CRIMSON HEART, THE
(Lux)/May 4, 1912; p. 427
CRIMSON CROSS, THE (Ec)/Mar 8, 1913;
p. 1002/Mar 15, 1913; p. 1105
CRIMSON MOTH, THE
(Bio)/Dec 26, 1914; p. 1850
CRIMSON SABRE, THE
(Th)/Nov 27, 1915; p. 1665
CRIMSON SCARS, THE
(Me)/Jan 28, 1911; p. 194
CRIMSON STAIN, THE
(KB)/Jul 5, 1913; p. 50
CRIMSON WING, THE
(SA)/Nov 6, 1915; pp 1141, 1154-55
CRINGER, THE (Lu)/Oct 26, 1912; p. 343
CRIPPLE, THE (Lux)/Aug 26, 1911; p. 543
(Th)/Oct 17, 1914; p. 337
CRIPPLED TEDDY BEAR, A
(Imp)/Dec 31, 1910; p. 1539
CRIPPLE'S MARRIAGE, THE
(Gau)/Jun 5, 1909; p. 753
CRIPPLE'S TALLY, THE
(Lux)/Sep 14, 1912; p. 1076
CRISIS, THE (Th)/Sep 2, 1911; p. 629
(Po)/May 20, 1911; p. 1142
CROCODILE HUNT, THE (Pa)/Oct 17,
1908; p. 306/Dec 4, 1909; pp 797-98
CROCODILE TURNS THIEF
(Pa)/Jul 25, 1908; p. 70
CROGMERE RUBY, THE
(Th)/Aug 28, 1915; p. 1480

CROOK AND THE GIRL, THE
(Bio)/Sep 6, 1913; p. 1068
CROOKED BANKERS, THE
(Pa)/May 24, 1913; p. 811
CROOKED PATH, THE
(Lu)/Dec 28, 1912; p. 1292
(Ka)/Jul 10, 1915; pp 319-20
CROOKED ROAD, THE
(Bio)/Jun 3, 1911; pp 1239, 1259
CROOKED TO THE END
(TK)/Dec 4, 1915; p. 1848
CROOKED TRAIL, THE
(Ne)/Jul 9, 1910; p. 85
CROOKS, THE (Lu)/Nov 7, 1914; pp 787-78
CROOKS AND CREDULOUS
(Am)/Oct 18, 1913; p. 265
CROOK'S SWEETHEART, A
(KB)/Nov 28, 1914; p. 1234
CROOKY SCRUGGS (Vi)/Jul 3, 1915; p. 82
CROSS, THE (Rex)/Sep 26, 1914; p. 1777
CROSS CURRENTS
(TFA)/Dec 4, 1915; p. 1848
CROSS IN THE CACTI, THE
(Ec)/Feb 21, 1914; p. 956
CROSS IN THE DESERT, THE
(Bro)/Nov 28, 1914; p. 1234
CROSS OF CRIME, THE
(Lu)/Aug 1, 1914; p. 705
CROSS OF FIRE, THE
(KB)/Jan 16, 1915; p. 371
CROSS OF PEARLS, THE
(Me)/Nov 4, 1911; p. 379
CROSS PURPOSES (Po)/Nov 1, 1913; p. 497
CROSS ROADS (Fr)/Jan 10, 1914; p. 174
CROSS ROADS, THE (Lu)/Nov 7, 1908;
p. 366/Nov 14, 1908; p. 379
'CROSS THE MEXICAN LINE
(Ne)/Jun 20, 1914; p. 1690
CROSS YOUR HEART
(Th)/Dec 7, 1912; p. 977
CROSSED LOVE AND SWORDS
(Key)/May 29, 1915; p. 1432
CROSSED SWORDS
(GN)/May 10, 1913; p. 598
CROSSED WIRES (Emp)/Feb 13,1915; p.986
(Th)/Jul 10, 1915; p. 308
CROSSING POLICEMAN, THE
(SA)/May 3, 1913; p. 488
CROSSING THE ALPS
(Gau)/Sep 30, 1911; p. 972
CROSSING THE ANDES
(UE)/Nov 12, 1910; p. 1118
CROSSROADS, THE
(Vi)/Aug 24, 1912; p. 771
CROWDED HOTEL (Sel)/Mar 26, 1910; p. 467
CROWN OF RICHARD III, THE
(Pa)/Nov 14, 1914; p. 937
CROWN PRINCE OF GERMANY

(Vi)/Dec 26, 1914; p. 1851
DAUGHTER OF ITALY, A
(Re)/Dec 2, 1911; p. 726
DAUGHTER OF ROMANY, A
(Ed)/Oct 18, 1913; p. 263
DAUGHTER OF THE CLOWN, THE
(CGP)/Dec 2, 1911; p. 725
DAUGHTER OF THE CONFEDERACY, A
(GG)/Mar 1, 1913; p. 892
(Sel)/May 31, 1913; p. 920
DAUGHTER OF THE EARTH, A
(Bio)/Jul 10, 1915; p. 317
DAUGHTER OF THE GYPSY, THE
(FIT)/Sep 12, 1908; p. 200
DAUGHTER OF THE HILLS, A
(FP)/Dec 27, 1913; p. 1528
DAUGHTER OF THE JUNGLE, A
(Bi)/Jul 17, 1915; p. 506
DAUGHTER OF THE MINES, A
(Ed)/Dec 10, 1910; p. 1356
DAUGHTER OF THE RED SKINS, A
(UB)/Nov 2, 1912; p. 451
DAUGHTER OF THE REGIMENT
(Cin)/Mar 9, 1912; p. 866
DAUGHTER OF THE REVOLUTION, A
(Rex)/May 6, 1911; p. 1021
DAUGHTER OF THE SEA, A
(Eq)/Nov 20, 1915; p. 1507
DAUGHTER OF THE SHEEP RANCH,
THE (Fr)/May 3, 1913; p. 488
DAUGHTER OF THE SHERIFF, THE
(Ka)/Aug 31, 1912; p. 881
(SA)/Jul 19, 1913; p. 320
DAUGHTER OF THE SIOUX, A
(Sel)/Jan 15, 1910; p. 56
DAUGHTER OF THE SOUTH, A
(Pa)/Sep 23, 1911; p. 889
DAUGHTER OF THE SPY, THE
(Ka)/Sep 7, 1912; pp 954-56
DAUGHTER OF THE UNDERWORLD, A
(Ka)/Nov 8, 1913; p. 612
DAUGHTER OF THE WATCH, THE
(Pa)/Jul 29, 1911; p. 210
DAUGHTER OF THE WEST, A
(Rep)/Jun 1, 1912; p. 831
DAUGHTER OF THE WILDERNESS, A
(Ed)/Nov 8, 1913; p. 612
DAUGHTER OF VIRGINIA, A
(Po)/Jan 14, 1911; p. 92
(Ch)/Feb 22, 1913; p. 781
DAUGHTER'S CHOICE, THE
(Lu)/Apr 16, 1910; p. 597
DAUGHTER'S DEVOTION, A (Ne)/
Feb 26, 1910; p.300/Mar 26, 1910; p.467
DAUGHTER'S DIPLOMACY, A
(Cin)/Aug 3, 1912; p. 446
DAUGHTER'S HONESTY, A
(Pa)/Aug 29, 1908; p. 162

DAUGHTERS OF KINGS
(Th)/May 29, 1915; p. 1432
DAUGHTERS OF POVERTY
(Gau)/Dec 25, 1909; p. 920
DAUGHTERS OF SENOR LOPEZ, THE
(Am)/Dec 21, 1912; p. 1186
DAUGHTER'S SACRIFICE, A (Ka)/Dec 21,
1912; p. 1184/Oct 9, 1915; p. 252
DAUGHTER'S STRANGE INHERITANCE, A
(Vi)/Mar 20, 1915; p. 1764
DAVE'S LOVE AFFAIR
(Bio)/Jun 24, 1911; p. 1452
DAVID AND GOLIATH
(Ka)/Nov 21, 1908; p. 406
DAVID COPPERFIELD
(Th)/Sep 30, 1911; pp 952-53
(He)/Oct 4, 1913; p. 29
DAVID GARRICK
(SA)/Nov 7,1908; p.358/Nov 14,1908; p.380
(Vi)/Aug 29, 1914; p. 1241
DAVID GRAY'S ESTATE
(Am)/Apr 25, 1914; p. 518
DAVID HARUM (FP)/Mar 6, 1915; p. 1453
DAVY CROCKETT (Sel)/May 7, 1910; p.737
DAVY CROCKETT (who was some hero)
(Sup)/May 22, 1915; p. 1261
DAVY JONES AND CAPT. BRAGG
(Vi)/Aug 6, 1910; p. 296
DAVY JONES' DOMESTIC TROUBLES
(Vi)/Nov 5, 1910; p. 1056
DAVY JONES/HIS WIFE'S HUSBAND
(Vi)/Apr 1, 1911; p. 718
DAVY JONES IN THE SOUTH SEAS
(Vi)/Feb 11, 1911; p. 315
DAVY JONES' LANDLADIES
(Vi)/Jul 2, 1910; p. 24
DAWN (Sel)/Jun 13, 1914; p. 1540
DAWN AND TWILIGHT
(SA)/Feb 21, 1914; p. 946
DAWN OF A TO-MORROW, THE
(FP)/Jun 19, 1915; p. 1948
DAWN OF COURAGE, THE
(Bio)/Oct 30, 1915; p. 791
DAWN OF FREEDOM, THE
(Sel)/Mar 26, 1910; pp 466-67
(Pa)/Aug 7, 1915; p. 1016
DAWN OF NETTA (Ne)/Jul 6, 1912; p. 44
DAWN OF PASSION, THE
(Am)/Sep 14, 1912; p. 1076
DAWN OF ROMANCE, THE
(Imp)/May 9, 1914; p. 821
DAWN OF THE NEW DAY, THE
(Imp)/Jun 6, 1914; p. 1409
DAWN OF UNDERSTANDING, THE
(Vi)/Sep 4, 1915; p. 1644
DAWNING, THE (Vi)/Dec 21, 1912; p. 1183
DAY AFTER, THE (Bio)/Jan 15, 1910; p. 56
DAY AFTER THE SPREE, THE

(LeL)/Sep 11, 1909; pp 346-47
DAY AT MIDLAND BEACH, A
(Jo)/Nov 6, 1915; p. 1140
DAY AT THE SAN DIEGO FAIR, A
(Jo)/May 22, 1915; p. 1261
DAY AT THE ZOOLOGICAL GARDENS,
N.Y., A (Re)/Jun 22, 1912; p. 1128
DAY AT WEST POINT MILITARY
ACADEMY, A (Ed)/Nov 4, 1911; p. 380
DAY BY DAY (SA)/Nov 8, 1913; p. 611
DAY IN AN INFANT ASYLUM, A
(Imp)/Oct 12, 1912; p. 143
DAY IN SINGAPORE, A
(Me)/Sep 20, 1913; p. 1283
DAY IN THE LIFE OF A SUFFRAGETTE, A
(Pa)/May 2, 1908; p. 401/May 8, 1909; p. 596
DAY IN WASHINGTON, A
(Vi)/Mar 13, 1909; pp 303-4
DAY OF DAYS, THE
(FP)/Jan 31, 1914; p. 529
DAY OF HASTE, A
(Amb)/Apr 27, 1912; p. 330
DAY OF HAVOC, A (Lu)/Aug 21, 1915; p.1316
DAY OF HIS OWN, A
(WBE)/Oct 12, 1907; p. 509
DAY OF JUDGMENT, THE
(UF)/Jul 19, 1913; p. 311
DAY OF PLEASURE, A
(Po)/Sep 24, 1910; p. 690
DAY OF RECKONING, THE
(USF)/Jul 25, 1914; p. 574
(Am)/May 8, 1915; p. 900
DAY OF STORMS, A
(Ec)/Mar 25, 1911; p. 658
DAY OF THE DOG (Lu)/Mar 27, 1909; p. 368
DAY OF THE DOG, THE
(Sel)/Aug 29, 1914; p. 1240
DAY OFF, A (GN)/May 7, 1910; p. 738
(Sel)/Aug 3, 1912; p. 446
DAY ON A BUFFALO RANCH, A
(Imp)/Feb 10, 1912; p. 482
DAY ON THE BATTLESHIP FLORIDA, A
(Maj)/Nov 16, 1912; p. 660
DAY ON THE FARM WITH THE BOY
SCOUTS, A (Pa)/Jan 30, 1915; p. 673
DAY ON THE FORCE, A
(Lu)/Jul 17, 1915; p. 485
DAY ON THE FRENCH BATTLESHIP
JUSTICE, A (Vi)/Nov 12, 1910; p. 1116
DAY THAT IS DEAD, A
(Ed)/Feb 15, 1913; p. 678
(Maj)/Mar 20, 1915; p. 1766
DAY WITH A CIRCUS, A
(Sel)/Dec 23, 1911; p. 988
DAY WITH A HINDU FAMILY, A
(Pa)/Sep 13, 1913; p. 1175
DAY WITH AN ENGLISH BARGEMAN, A
(Po)/May 13, 1911; p. 1081

DAY WITH OUR SOLDIER BOYS
(Vi)/Dec 18, 1909; p. 881
DAYBREAK (Re)/Jan 10, 1914; p. 174
DAYLIGHT (Am)/Oct 31, 1914; p. 642
DAYLIGHT BURGLAR, THE
(Bio)/May 10, 1913; p. 596
DAY'S ADVENTURE, A
(Bio)/May 22, 1915; p. 1259
DAYS OF '49 (Ka)/Nov 23, 1912; p. 767
DAYS OF '49, THE
(Ne)/May 7, 1910; p. 739
(KB)/Nov 22, 1913; p. 868
DAYS OF '61, THE (Ka)/Jan 4, 1908; p. 11
DAYS OF TERROR, THE
(Vi)/Jun 29, 1912; p. 1227
DAYS OF THE PONY EXPRESS
(SA)/Oct 11, 1913; p. 155
DAYS OF THE EARLY WEST
(Ch)/Jan 14, 1911; p. 92
DAY'S OUTING, A
(UE)/Feb 27, 1909; p. 236
(Bio)/Jan 11, 1913; p. 158
DAZZLE'S BLACK EYE
(Cry)/Mar 21, 1914; p. 1526
DEACON BILLINGTON'S DOWNFALL
(Ed)/Jan 31, 1914; p. 544
DEACON DEBBS (Th)/Dec 23, 1911; p. 990
DEACON'S DILEMNA, THE
(SA)/May 10, 1913; p. 595
DEACON'S LOVE LETTER, THE
(Vi)/Feb 6, 1909; p. 144
DEACON'S REWARD, THE
(SA)/Oct 28, 1911; p. 290
DEACON'S SHOES, THE
(Maj)/Nov 23, 1912; p. 768
DEACON'S SON, THE
(Bio)/Dec 19, 1914; p. 1679
DEACON'S TROUBLES, THE
(Key)/Nov 23, 1912; p. 769
DEACON'S WHISKERS, THE
(Ko)/Aug 14, 1915; p. 1161
DEAD ALIVE, THE
(Gau)/Apr 26, 1913; pp 363, 382
DEAD BROKE (Cry)/May 30, 1914; p. 1261
DEAD CANARY, THE
(Com)/Dec 16, 1911; p. 905
DEAD LETTER, THE
(Lu)/Dec 31, 1910; p. 1538
DEAD LINE, THE (Pr)/Nov 14, 1914; p. 932
DEAD MAN'S CLAIM, THE
(SA)/May 25, 1912; pp 728-29
DEAD MAN'S HONOR, A
(Vi)/Jun 3, 1911; p. 1259
DEAD MAN'S KEY'S, THE
(Th)/Oct 2, 1915; p. 80
DEAD MAN'S SHOES
(Am)/Jun 28, 1913; p. 1361
DEAD MEN'S TALES

(SA)/May 18, 1912; p. 615
DETECTIVE DOT (Lu)/Jun 7, 1913; p. 1031
DETECTIVE FINN
(MFA)/Mar 14, 1914; p. 1394
DETECTIVE KELLY
(Pa)/Apr 25, 1914; p. 517
DETECTIVE KNOWALL ON THE TRAIL
(Lux)/Feb 8, 1913; p. 573
DETECTIVE SHORT (Lu)/Apr 11,1914;p.212
DETECTIVE SWIFT
(Ecl)/Sep 5, 1914; p. 1380
DETECTIVES, THE (Ka)/Jan 30, 1909; p. 120
DETECTIVE'S CONSCIENCE, THE
(Lu)/Aug 17, 1912; p. 669
DETECTIVE'S DOG, THE
(Sol)/Apr 20, 1912; p. 231
(Ec)/Jun 29, 1912; p. 1228
DETECTIVE'S DREAM, THE
(Pa)/Aug 6, 1910; p. 297
DETECTIVES OF THE INDIAN BUREAU
(Ka)/Feb 13, 1909; p. 173
DETECTIVE'S SANTA CLAUS, THE
(Ec)/Jan 25, 1913; p. 365
DETECTIVE'S SISTER, THE
(Ka)/May 23, 1914; p. 1117
DETECTIVE'S STRATAGEM, THE
(Bio)/Dec 6, 1913; p. 1150
DETECTIVE'S STRATEGY, A
(Sel)/Oct 5, 1912; p. 41
DETECTIVE'S TRAP, THE
(Ka)/Jul 5, 1913; p. 48
DETERMINED LOVERS, THE
(Vi)/Jun 27, 1908; p. 549
DETERMINED WOMAN, A
(Imp)/Jun 25, 1910; p. 1101
DETERMINED WOOER (Pa)/Jul 10,1909; p.51
DEUCE AND TWO PAIR, A
(Po)/Jan 24, 1914; p. 414
DEVIL, THE
(Bio)/Oct 3, 1908; pp 253, 262
(Ed)/Sep 12, 1908; p. 200
(Po)/Oct 29, 1910; p. 999
(NYM)/Mar 20,1915;p.1767/Apr 3,1915;p.68
DEVIL, THE SERPENT AND THE MAN,
THE (SA)/May 4, 1912; p. 425
DEVIL, THE SERVANT AND THE MAN,
THE (Sel)/Feb 12, 1910; p. 216
DEVIL AND MRS. WALKER, THE
(Ka)/Dec 19, 1914; p. 1679
DEVIL AND TOM WALKER, THE
(Sel)/Aug 16, 1913; p. 744
DEVIL FOX OF THE NORTH, THE
(Ec)/Feb 28, 1914; p. 1090
DEVIL IN IDLE HANDS, THE
(Lae)/Nov 27, 1915; pp 1665-66
DEVIL OF A TIME, A
(Pun)/Dec 14, 1912; p. 1083
DEVIL ON TWO STICKS, THE

(Amb)/May 28, 1910; p. 891
DEVIL WITHIN, THE
(Ram)/Dec 20, 1913; p. 1414
DEVILISH DOCTOR, THE
(Maj)/Aug 23, 1913; p. 845
DEVIL'S ASSISTANT, THE (Pa)/Mar 7,
1914; p. 1237/Mar 14, 1914; p. 1385
DEVIL'S BARGAIN, THE
(WBE)/Nov 21, 1908; p. 398
DEVIL'S BILLIARD TABLE, THE
(Ec)/Nov 26, 1910; p. 1239
DEVIL'S DANSANT, THE
(Ka)/Sep 5, 1914; p. 1354
DEVIL'S DARLING, THE (Ria)/Nov 6,
1915; pp 1140, 1157/Nov 13, 1915; p. 1312
DEVIL'S EYE, THE (Ape)/Jul 18, 1914; p. 418
DEVIL'S FIDDLE, THE
(Ape)/Aug 22, 1914; p. 1075
DEVIL'S SIGNATURE, THE
(SA)/Sep 26, 1914; p. 1776
DEVIL'S THREE SONS, THE
(Pa)/Mar 21, 1908; p. 243
DEVIL'S WAND, THE
(Lux)/Jul 2, 1910; p. 25
DEVOTED LITTLE BROTHER, A
(Lux)/Aug 6, 1910; p. 298
DEVOTION (Dom)/Dec 13, 1913; p. 1280
DEWEY (Ch)/Aug 19, 1911;
p. 466/Aug 26, 1911; p. 543
DIABOLO, THE JAPANESE TOP
SPINNER (KO)/Jul 6, 1907; p. 284
DIAMOND BROOCH, THE
(Vi)/Mar 16, 1912; p. 962
DIAMOND CROWN, THE
(Ed)/Jul 26, 1913; p. 428
DIAMOND CUT DIAMOND
(Pa)/May 21, 1910; p. 834
(Vi)/Jun 8, 1912; p. 942
(Mil)/Dec 14, 1912; p. 1083
(Lu)/May 10, 1913; p. 595
(Bi)/Nov 1, 1913; p. 498
DIAMOND FROM THE SKY, THE (Am)
No.1/May 1,1915; p.738/May 8,1915; p.900
No.2/May 1,1915; p.738/May 15,1915;p.1072
No.3/May 1,1915; p.738/May 22,1915;p.1261
No.4/May 29, 1915; p. 1440
No.5/May 29, 1915; p. 1440
No.6/Jul 3, 1915; p. 65
No.7/Jun 26, 1915; p. 2097
No.8/Jul 3, 1915; p. 65
No.9/Jul 10, 1915; p. 309
No.10/Jul 17, 1915; p. 486
No.11/Jul 24, 1915; p. 651
No.12/Jul 31, 1915; p. 817
No.13/Aug 7, 1915; p. 997
No.14/Aug 14, 1915; p. 1161
No.15/Aug 21, 1915; p. 1317
No.16/Aug 28, 1915; p. 1480

No.17/Sep 4, 1915; p. 1644
No.18/Sep 11, 1915; p. 1833
No.19/Sep 18, 1915; pp 1996-97
No.20/Sep 25, 1915; p. 2177
No.21/Oct 2, 1915; p. 80
No.22/Oct 9, 1915; p. 254
No.23/Oct 16, 1915; p. 441
No.24/Oct 23, 1915; p. 621
No.25/Oct 30, 1915; p. 793
No.26/Oct 30a, 1915; p. 968
No.27/Oct 30a, 1915; p. 968
No.28/Nov 13, 1915; p. 1313
No.29/Nov 20, 1915; p. 1501
No.30/Nov 27, 1915; p. 1665
DIAMOND GANG, THE
(SA)/Sep 23, 1911; p. 890
DIAMOND IN THE ROUGH, A
(Sel)/Dec 16, 1911; p. 904
(Maj)/May 2, 1914; p. 674
(Ka)/Jul 25, 1914; p. 572
DIAMOND LOCKET, THE
(Com)/Dec 2, 1911; p. 727
DIAMOND MAKER, THE
(Vi)/Jun 26, 1909; p. 873
(Cin)/Mar 21, 1914; p. 1525
DIAMOND MAKERS, THE (Rex)/Aug 16,
1913; p. 726/Sep 13, 1913; p. 1178
DIAMOND MINIATURE, THE
(Pa)/May 3, 1913; p. 469
DIAMOND MYSTERY, THE
(Vi)/Jul 26, 1913; p. 428
DIAMOND NIPPERS, THE
(Jo)/Aug 22, 1914; p. 1101
DIAMOND OF DISASTER, THE
(Th)/Oct 24, 1914; p. 505
DIAMOND S RANCH, THE
(Sel)/Mar 16, 1912; p. 961
DIAMOND STAR, THE
(Bio)/Mar 4, 1911; p. 483
DIAMOND SWINDLER, THE
(GN)/Dec 3, 1910; p. 1299
DIAMONDS OF DESTINY, THE
(Mid)/Mar 14, 1914; p. 1365
DIAMONDS OF FATE
(Po)/May 22, 1915; p. 1261
DIANA OF EAGLE MOUNTAIN
(Bi)/Mar 13, 1915; p. 1609
DIANA OF THE FARM
(Ka)/Nov 13, 1915; p. 1311
DIANA'S DRESS REFORM
(Vi)/Jan 24, 1914; p. 412
DIARY OF A BAD BOY, THE
(Lux)/Dec 7, 1912; p. 977
DIARY OF A NURSE
(Gau)/Apr 9, 1910; p. 554
DICK, THE DEAD SHOT
(Vi)/Apr 5, 1913; p. 48
DICK POTTER'S WIFE

(Ed)/Sep 26, 1914; p. 1775
DICK TURPIN (WBE)/Jul 20, 1907; p. 315
DICK WHITTINGTON AND HIS CAT (Sol)/
Mar 1, 1913; pp 873-74/Apr 12, 1913; p. 145
DICKEY'S COURTSHIP
(GN)/Dec 31, 1910; p. 1540
DICK'S A WINNER (Pa)/Feb 12, 1910; p.215
DICK'S AUNT (Lu)/Jan 2, 1909; p. 11
DICK'S TURNING (Re)/Jul 12, 1913; p. 206
DICKSON'S DIAMONDS
(Ed)/Dec 5, 1914; p. 1383
DICKY'S DEMON DACHSHUND
(Fal)/Oct 16, 1915; p. 440
DICTATOR, THE (FP)/Jul 3, 1915; p. 81
DID HE SAVE HER? (Lu)/Oct 10,1914;p.188
DID MOTHER GET HER WISH?
(Bio)/Jan 27, 1912; p. 303
DID SHE CURE HIM?
(Sel)/Jul 25, 1914; p. 571
DID SHE RUN? (Roy)/Jul 18, 1914; p. 433
DIEPPE CIRCUIT, 1908
(Pa)/Aug 15, 1908; p. 128
DIFFERENCE OF OPINION, A
(Bio)/Aug 21, 1915; p. 1324
DIFFERENCES BETWEEN TANGOS
(Me)/May 16, 1914; p. 968
DIFFERENT MAN, THE
(Maj)/May 16, 1914; p. 969
DIFFERENT TRADES IN BOMBAY
(Pa)/Nov 5, 1910; p. 1059
DIFFERENT WAYS OF SMUGGLING
(Pa)/Mar 28, 1908; p.270
DIFFICULT CAPTURE, A
(Ec)/Dec 10, 1910; p. 1359
DIGNIFIED FAMILY, A
(SA)/Jul 10, 1915; p. 308
DILEMNA, THE (GN)/Nov 15, 1913; p. 737
(Bio)/Feb 21, 1914; p. 946
DIME NOVEL DAN (Vi)/May 22, 1909; p. 676
DIME NOVEL DETECTIVE, THE
(Lu)/Mar 6, 1909; p. 269
DIMITRI DOUSKOJ
(Pa)/Jun 25, 1910; p. 1100
DIMPLES, THE AUTO SALESGIRL
(Vi)/Jun 5, 1915; p. 1604
DIMPLES AND THE RING
(Vi)/Aug 21, 1915; p. 1316
DINAN, FRANCE (Pa)/Nov 23, 1912; p. 766
DING DONG BELL (Ch)/Feb 10, 1912; p.482
DINKA CHIEF'S RECEPTION, THE
(CGP)/Nov 23, 1912; p. 767
DINKELSPIEL'S BABY
(Ed)/Apr 4, 1914; p. 58
DINNER BELL ROMANCE, A
(Ne)/Feb 8, 1913; p. 574
DIOGENES' WEEKLY (Bio)
No.13/Dec 12, 1914; p. 1530/
Dec 26, 1914; p. 1840

DOZEN OF FRESH EGGS, A
(Pa)/Sep 12, 1908; p. 202
DR. BILL'S PATIENT
(SA)/Nov 4, 1911; p. 379
DR. BROMPTON WATT'S AGE ADJUSTER
(Ed)/Apr 20, 1912; p. 230
DR. BUNION (Imp)/Feb 8, 1913; p. 573
DR. CATHERN'S EXPERIMENT
(Vi)/Aug 9, 1913; p. 636
DR. CHARCOT'S TRIP TOWARD THE
SOUTH POLE (UE)/Apr 15, 1911; p. 843
DR. COOK (GN)/Oct 2, 1909; p. 450
DR. CUPID (Vi)/Jan 21, 1911; p. 144
DR. CUREM'S PATIENTS
(Lu)/Jul 18, 1908; p. 50
DR. FENTON'S ORDEAL
(He)/Sep 26, 1914; p. 1789
DR. GRANT'S WONDERFUL DISCOVERY
(Lux)/May 6, 1911;p.1021
DR. JEKYLL AND MR. HYDE
(Sel)/Mar 7, 1908; pp 194-95
(GN)/Sep 24, 1910; p. 685
(Th)/Jan 27, 1912; p. 305
(Imp)/Mar 8, 1913; p. 997
DR. JEKYLL AND MR. HYDE DONE TO
A FRAZZLE (WF)/Nov 21, 1914; p. 1077
DR. JIM (Maj)/Apr 17, 1915; p. 393
DR. KILLEM'S DOPE
(WF)/Dec 19, 1914; p. 1681
DR. LAFLEUR'S THEORY
(Vi)/May 18, 1912; p. 629
DR. MASON'S TEMPTATION
(Lae)/Sep 4, 1915; p. 1645
DR. MAXWELL'S EXPERIMENT
(Lu)/Mar 15, 1913; p. 1104
DR. NICHOLSON AND THE BLUE
DIAMOND (FRA)/Aug 16, 1913; pp 724-25
DR. RAMEAU (Fox)/Jul 31, 1915; p. 834
DR. SKINNEM'S WONDERFUL INVENTION
(Ka)/Sep 28, 1912; p. 1276
DR. SKINUM (Bio)/Dec 14, 1907; p. 670
DR. TURNER TURNS THE TABLES
(Pa)/Oct 4, 1913; p. 47
DRAB SISTER, THE
(Bio)/Aug 21, 1915; p. 1316
DRAGON'S BREATH, THE
(Rex)/Apr 26, 1913; p. 381
DRAGON'S CLAW, THE (Kni)/Oct 23, 1915;
p. 631/Oct 30, 1915; p. 792
DRAMA IN A SPANISH INN
(KO)/Jul 20, 1907; pp 314-15
DRAMA IN HEYVILLE, THE
(Ed)/Mar 14, 1914; p. 1385
DRAMA IN THE AIR, A
(Pa)/Mar 1, 1913; p. 887
DRAMA IN THE TYROL
(Pa)/Jun 13, 1908; pp 515-16
DRAMA OF HEYVILLE, THE

(Ed)/Feb 7, 1914; p. 656
DRAMA OF THE DESERT, A
(Ec)/Apr 25, 1914; p. 518
DRAMA OF THE ENGINEER
(Amb)/Jan 14, 1911; p. 91
DRAMA OF THE MOUNTAIN PASS, A
(Gau)/Apr 16, 1910; p. 598
DRAMA ON A ROOF, THE
(KO)/Apr 18, 1908; p. 354
DRAMA ON THE REEF, A
(Lux)/Apr 9, 1910; p. 554
DRAMATIC MISTAKE, A
(St)/Aug 15, 1914; p. 961
DRAMATIC REHEARSAL, THE
(Ka)/Nov 16, 1907; p. 599
DRAMATIST'S DREAM, THE
(Vi)/Jul 10, 1909; p. 50
DRASTIC REMEDY, A
(Me)/May 23, 1914; p. 1116
DRAWING THE COLOR LINE
(Ed)/Jan 23, 1909; pp 93-94
DRAWING THE LINE
(Am)/Sep 4, 1915; p. 1644
DRAWN CURTAIN, THE
(Gau)/Jun 24, 1911; p. 1452
DREAD OF DOOM, THE
(It)/May 24, 1913; p. 792
DREAD OF MICROBES, THE
(Amb)/Sep 2, 1911; p. 630
DREADFUL DILEMNA, A
(Lux)/Feb 4, 1911; p. 249
DREAM, THE (Imp)/Jan 28, 1911; p. 182/
Feb 4, 1911; p. 251
DREAM CHILD, THE
(Am)/Feb 28, 1914; p. 1090
DREAM DANCE, THE
(Lu)/Jul 10, 1915; p. 308
DREAM DANCES (Ed)/May 4, 1912; p. 426
DREAM FAIRY, THE (Ed)/Aug 2,1913;p.535
DREAM GIRL, THE (Sel)/Oct 24,1914;p.492
DREAM HOME, THE
(Re)/Jun 21, 1913; p. 1255
DREAM OF A FISHERMAN
Nov 27, 1909; p. 760
DREAM OF A MOVING PICTURE
DIRECTOR (Lu)/Jun 22, 1912; p. 1126
DREAM OF A PAINTING, A
(Jo)/Dec 5, 1914; p. 1385
DREAM OF AN OPIUM FIEND, THE
(Me)/Mar 21, 1908; p. 244
DREAM OF DAN McGUIRE, THE
(Sel)/Oct 25, 1913; p. 380
DREAM OF THE CIRCUS, A
(Lu)/May 9, 1914; p. 820
DREAM OF THE WILD, A
(Ka)/Jan 17, 1914; p. 288
DREAM PILL, THE (Lu)/Sep 17,1910; p.630
DREAM SEEKERS, THE (Ka)/Oct 30, 1915;

p. 809/Nov 20, 1915; p. 1500
DREAM SHIP, THE
(Be)/Jun 27, 1914; p. 1829
DREAM SPECTERS
(Gau)/May 8, 1909; p. 595
DREAM WITH A LESSON, A
(GN)/Sep 23, 1911; p. 893
DREAM WOMAN, THE
(Box)/Mar 21, 1914; p. 1508
DREAMER, THE (Gau)/Apr 16, 1910; p. 597
(Lu)/Sep 5, 1914; p. 1372
DREAMERS, THE (Ec)/Jul 27, 1912; p. 344
DREAMLAND TRAGEDY, A
(Po)/Nov 9, 1912; p. 555
DREAMS AND REALITIES
(KO)/May 9, 1908; p. 423
DREAMY DUD (SA)/Jun 12, 1915; p. 1776
DREAMY DUD AT THE "OLD SWIMMIN"
HOLE (SA)/Oct 16, 1915; p. 439
DREAMY DUD GOES BEAR HUNTING
(SA)/Aug 14, 1915; p. 1160
DREAMY DUD IN A VISIT TO UNCLE
DUDLEY'S FARM
(SA)/Aug 21, 1915; p. 1316
DREAMY DUD IN KING KOO KOO'S
KINGDOM (SA)/Jul 24, 1915; p. 649
DREAMY DUD IN LOVE
(SA)/Dec 18, 1915; p. 2202
DREAMY DUD RESOLVES NOT TO SMOKE
(SA)/Jul 17, 1915; p. 485
DREAMY DUD SEES CHARLIE CHAPLIN
(SA)/Sep 5, 1915; p. 1643
DREAMY DUD UP IN THE AIR
(SA)/Nov 6, 1915; p. 1139
DREAMY DUD'S COWBOY
(SA)/Oct 2, 1915; p. 78
DREDGES AND FARM IMPLEMENTS IN
THE WEST (Pa)/Jun 14, 1913; p. 1137
DREGS (Lu)/Sep 6, 1913; p. 1067
DRESS OF LOLITA, THE
(Re)/Nov 15, 1913; p. 738
DRESS REFORM (Cry)/Oct 11, 1913; p. 157
DRESSMAKER'S SURPRISE, THE
(KO)/Jul 11, 1908; p. 34
DREYFUS AFFAIR, THE
(Pa)/Jul 4, 1908; p. 11
DRIFTING (Lu)/Jun 3, 1911;
p. 1259/Jun 10, 1911; p. 1301
DRIFTING HEARTS (Be)/Jun 13,1914;p.1541
DRIFTS OF SNOW IN THE CHAMOUNIX
VALLEY (Gau)/Aug 27, 1910; p. 462
DRIFTWOOD (Sel)/Apr 20, 1912; p. 231
(Am)/May 4, 1912; p. 427
DRILLS ON BOARD U.S. CALIFORNIA
(Ka)/Sep 27, 1913; p. 1391
DRINK (Me)/Sep 7, 1907; p.426
(WBE)/Oct 12, 1907; p.506
(Pa)/Oct 16, 1909; p.531

DRINK CURE, A (WBE)/Nov 16,1907; p.600
DRINK'S LURE (Bio)/Mar 1, 1913; p. 888
DRIVEN BY FATE
(Imp)/Jul 31, 1915; pp 831-32
DRIVEN FROM HOME
(Lu)/Jul 17, 1909; p. 88
DRIVEN FROM THE RANCH
(Gau)/Apr 27, 1912; p. 330
DRIVEN TO STEAL (Pa)/Apr 9, 1910; p. 554
DRIVER OF THE DEADWOOD COACH,
THE (Ka)/Dec 21, 1912; p. 1184
DRIVING HOME THE COWS
(Ka)/Jan 13, 1912; p. 126
DROP OF BLOOD, A
(Sol)/Aug 23, 1913; p. 846
DROP OF BLOOD, THE (Vi)/Jul 5, 1913; p.47
DROPPED FROM THE CLOUDS
(Gau)/Oct 2, 1909; p. 452
DROPPINGTON'S DEVILISH DEED
(Key)/Apr 24, 1915; p. 556
DROPPINGTON'S FAMILY TREE
(Key)/Apr 17, 1915; p. 393
DROWSY DICK, OFFICER No. 73
(Ed)/May 14, 1910; p. 784
DRUDGE, THE (Vi)/Mar 14, 1914; p. 1385
DRUG CLERK, THE
(SA)/Sep 11, 1915; p. 1832
DRUG TRAFFIC, THE
(Ec)/Apr 11, 1914; p. 214
DRUID REMAINS IN BRITTANY
(Pa)/Feb 26, 1910; p. 299
DRUMMER BOY OF SHILOH, THE
(Ya)/Nov 4, 1911; p. 382
DRUMMER GIRL OF VICKSBURG, THE
(Ka)/Jun 22, 1912; p. 1126
DRUMMER OF THE EIGHTH, THE
(Bro)/May 17, 1913; pp 705-6
DRUMMER'S DAY OFF, THE
(Vi)/May 2, 1908; p. 404
DRUMMER'S NOTEBOOK, THE
(Cry)/Apr 5, 1913; p. 49
DRUMMER'S TRUNK, THE
(Be)/Nov 27, 1915; p. 1664
DRUMMER'S UMBRELLA, THE
(SA)/Jul 12, 1913; p. 205
DRUMMER'S VACATION, THE
(Key)/Dec 28, 1912; p. 1293
DRUMSTICKS (Vi)/Oct 29, 1910;
p. 1002/Dec 3, 1910; p. 1296
DRUNKARD'S CHILD, THE
(Lu)/Aug 21, 1909; p. 256
DRY TOWN, A (Ec)/Jan 4, 1913; p. 52
DUAL LIFE, A (Sel)/Dec 5, 1908;
pp 450, 462/Dec 12, 1908; p. 478
DuBARRY (Ecl)/Mar 8, 1913; pp 980-81
(GK)/Jan 30, 1915; pp 653-54
DUBLIN (Gem)/Jul 19, 1913; p. 321
DUBLIN DAN (Sol)/Sep 7, 1912; pp 956-57

DUBLIN HORSE SHOW, THE
 (Ka)/Dec 6, 1913; p. 1151
DUBUQUE REGATTA, THE
 (Ch)/Aug 19, 1911; p. 465
DUCHESS, THE (GS)/Apr 3, 1915; p. 66
DUCHESS de LANGEAIS
 (Pa)/Apr 16, 1910; p. 598
DUCK FARM, THE (Lu)/Aug 27, 1910; p. 463
DUCK HUNTING (Ch)/May 25, 1912; p. 730
DUCK RAISING INDUSTRY
 (SA)/Oct 4, 1913; p. 478
DUCK'S FINISH, THE
 (KO)/Aug 29, 1908; p. 161
DUDE COWBOY, THE
 (Bi)/Jul 1, 1911; p. 1523
 (Ka)/Jan 20, 1912; p. 202
DUEL, THE (Re)/Mar 16, 1912; p. 963
         (Key)/Jan 4, 1913; p. 52
DUEL AT DAWN, THE
 (Jo)/Jul 24, 1915; p. 651
DUEL IN MIDAIR, A
 (Ed)/Nov 20, 1909; p. 721
DUEL IN THE DARK, THE
 (Th)/Mar 27, 1915; p. 1934
DUEL UNDER RICHELIEU, THE
 (Pa)/Jan 16, 1909; p. 68
DUKE AND THE ACTOR, THE
 (Ch)/Mar 1, 1913; p. 890
DUKE de RIBBON COUNTER
 (Lu)/Jul 1, 1911; p. 1519
DUKE FOR A DAY, A
 (Jo)/Jun 19, 1915; p. 1941
DUKE'S DILEMNA, THE
 (Ed)/Apr 19, 1913; p. 279
DUKE'S GOOD JOKE, THE (Me)/Oct 24,
 1908; p. 326/Oct 30, 1908; p. 338
DUKE'S JESTER, THE
 (Vi)/Jun 26, 1909; p. 871
DUKE'S MOTTO, THE
 (Sel)/Dec 5, 1908; p. 533
DUKE'S TALISMAN, THE
 (Gau)/Jan 24, 1914; p. 394
DULL KNIFE, THE (Vi)/Oct 30, 1909; p. 604
DULL RAZOR, THE (Sel)/Dec 3, 1910; p. 1296
DUMB HERO, A (Ed)/Aug 1, 1908;
 p. 87/Nov 7, 1908; p. 358
DUMB MESSENGER, THE
 (Imp)/Dec 16, 1911; p. 905
 (Ka)/Nov 1, 1913; p. 496
DUMB SAGACITY (He)/Nov 16, 1907;
 p. 602/Dec 7, 1907; p. 652
DUMB WITNESS, THE (Vi)/Sep 5, 1908;
 p. 183/Dec 12, 1908; p. 477
DUMB WOOING, THE
 (Ed)/Apr 6, 1912; p. 28/May 4, 1912; p. 425
 (Ed)/Jun 12, 1915; p. 1776
DUMMIES ON THE SPREE
 (GN)/Dec 12, 1908; p. 476

DUMMY DIRECTOR, THE
 (Ch)/Sep 28, 1912; p. 1278
DUMMY HUSBAND, THE
 (Ec)/Jan 16, 1915; p. 369
DUMMY IN DISGUISE, A
 (Gau)/Oct 1, 1910; p. 747
DUPE, THE (Ec)/Aug 1, 1914; p. 706
DURING CHERRY TIME
 (Lu)/Aug 12, 1911; p. 375
DURING THE CARNIVAL
 (GN)/Apr 13, 1912; p. 137
DURING THE PLAGUE
 (GN)/Sep 20, 1913; p. 1286
DURING THE ROUND-UP
 (Bio)/Aug 2, 1913; p. 536
DUST OF EGYPT, THE
 (Vi)/Oct 2, 1915; p. 94
DUSTY RHODES TAKES A FLIGHT
 (Pa)/Jan 21, 1911; p. 144
DUTCH GOLD MINE
 (Bio)/Jun 17, 1911; pp 1362, 1386
DUTCH KIDS (Pa)/Jan 14, 1911; p. 90
DUTCH TYPES (Pa)/Nov 26, 1910; p. 1236
DUTCHESS' LADY COMPANION, THE
 (Amb)/Mar 16, 1912; p. 963
DUTY
 (Imp)/Sep 23, 1911; p. 893
 (Ec)/Jun 27,1914; p. 1833/Jul 11,1914; p. 257
DUTY AND CONSCIENCE
 (Ec)/Mar 5, 1910; p. 340
DUTY AND THE MAN
 (Re)/Jan 11, 1913; p. 137
DUTY VERSUS REVENGE
 (Vi)/Oct 3, 1908; p. 267
DWELLERS IN GLASS HOUSES
 (Bio)/Mar 6, 1915; p. 1448
DYED, BUT NOT DEAD
 (Bio)/Oct 11, 1913; p. 156
DYNAMITE, THE NEW FARM HAND
 (Pa)/Jul 26, 1913; p. 428
DYNAMITE DUEL (Pa)/Jun 13, 1908; p. 516
DYNAMITED DOG (Sol)/Jul 5, 1913; p. 49
DYNAMITERS (Pa)/Apr 11, 1908; pp 326-7
DYNAMITERS, THE
 (Imp)/Mar 18, 1911; p. 603
 (Sel)/Nov 23, 1912; p. 766
DYSPEPTIC'S DOUBLE, THE
 (Ka)/Sep 11, 1909; p. 346

EACH IN HIS TURN
 (Pa)/May 9, 1908; p. 424
EAGLE, THE (Lae)/Sep 4, 1915; p. 1645
EAGLE AND THE EAGLET, THE
 (FA)/Aug 20, 1910; p. 408
EAGLE AND THE SPARROW, THE
 (Sel)/Mar 27, 1915; p. 1931
EAGLE'S EGG, THE
 (GN)/Jun 11, 1910; p. 999

(Re)/Sep 4, 1915; p. 1644
EDITOR, THE (Ch)/Mar 23, 1912; p. 1064
EDMUNDS' KLAMM RAVINE, THE
(CGP)/Oct 5, 1912; p. 41
EDNA'S IMPRISONMENT
(Ed)/May 20, 1911; p. 1141
EDUCATING HIS DAUGHTERS
(Maj)/Jan 10, 1914; p. 174
EDUCATION (SA)/Jul 24, 1915; p. 649
**EDUCATION OF AUNT GEORGIANNA,
THE** (Vi)/Jan 17, 1914; p. 288
EDUCATION OF MARY JANE, THE
(De)/Dec 3, 1910; p. 1298
EDUCATION OF THE BLIND
(Ec)/Feb 10, 1912; p. 483
EDWIN MASQUERADES
(Bio)/Apr 12, 1913; p. 164
EDWIN'S BADGE OF HONOR
(Bio)/Sep 13, 1913; p. 1176
EFFECT OF A SHAVE, THE
(SA)/Oct 17, 1908; p. 304
EFFECTING A CURE
(Bio)/Dec 24, 1910; p. 1476
EFFECTIVE HAIR GROWER, THE
(KO)/Jun 27, 1908; p. 549
EFFECTS OF A ROCKET, THE
(It)/Nov 18, 1911; p. 552
EFFICACY OF PRAYER, THE
(KB)/Nov 15, 1913; p. 737
EFFICIENCY SQUAD, THE
(Bio)/Jan 16, 1915; p. 368
EGG TRUST, THE
(SA)/Mar 12, 1910; p. 384
EGRET HUNTER, THE
(Ka)/May 21, 1910; p. 832
EGYPT, THE MYSTERIOUS
(Ka)/Jun 1, 1912; p. 829
EGYPT AS IT WAS IN THE TIME OF
MOSES (Ka)/Apr 27, 1912; pp 311-12/
Jun 1, 1912; p. 830
EGYPTIAN MUMMY, THE
(Ka)/Jun 7, 1913; p. 1031
(Vi)/Jan 2, 1915; p. 75
EGYPTIAN MYSTERY, THE
(Ed)/Jul 24, 1909; p. 124
EGYPTIAN PRINCESS, AN
(Sel)/Aug 1, 1914; p. 704
EGYPTIAN SPORTS (Ka)/Aug 3,1912; p.445
EGYPTIAN TEMPLES
(Pa)/Nov 22, 1913; p. 867
1861 (Sel)/Apr 15, 1911; p.842
EIGHTH NOTCH, THE
(Ka)/May 17, 1913; p. 704
EIGHTH WONDER OF THE WORLD, THE
(Com)/Oct 12, 1912; p. 144
EIGHTY MILLION WOMEN WANT--?
(UFC)/Nov 15, 1913; p. 741
EILEEN OF ERIN

(Dom)/Dec 27, 1913; p. 1545
EL CAPITAN AND THE LAND GRABBERS
(Bi)/Jan 4, 1913; p. 52
ELASTIC TRANSFORMATIONS
(Pa)/Sep 4, 1909; p. 315
ELDA OF THE MOUNTAINS
(Ne)/Jan 14, 1911; p. 92
ELDER ALDEN'S INDIAN WARD
(Ka)/Dec 17, 1910; p. 1416
ELDER BROTHER, THE
(Ed)/Apr 12, 1913; p. 164
ELDER SISTER, THE (Gau)/Jul 9, 1910; p. 85
ELDORA, THE FRUIT GIRL
(Ed)/Jan 7, 1911; p. 34
ELDORADO LODE, THE
(Ed)/Jan 25, 1913; p. 363
ELEANOR CUYLER (Ed)/Jan 13, 1912; p. 125
ELECTION BET, AN
(Imp)/Dec 14, 1912; p. 1083
ELECTION DAY IN CALIFORNIA
(Ka)/Oct 26, 1912; p. 342
ELECTRIC ALARM, THE
(Maj)/May 29, 1915; p. 1432
ELECTRIC BATHTUB, THE
(Pan)/Mar 19, 1910; p. 425
ELECTRIC BELT, THE
(Pa)/Mar 27, 1909; p. 367
ELECTRIC BOOTS (Pa)/Oct 7, 1911; p. 39
ELECTRIC GIRL, THE
(Ec)/Feb 28, 1914; p. 1089
ELECTRIC HOTEL (Pa)/Dec 19, 1908;
p.510/Dec 26, 1908; p.525/Jan 9, 1909; p.37
ELECTRIC INSOLES
(SA)/Jan 22, 1910; p. 93
ELECTRIC LAUNDRY, THE
(CGP)/Dec 21, 1912; p. 1183
ELECTRIC PILE (Cin)/Sep 21, 1907; p. 456
ELECTRIC SWORD (KO)/Mar 14,1908;p.218
ELECTRICIAN'S HAZARD, THE
(Ka)/Jan 3, 1914; p. 48
ELECTRIFIED HUMPBACK
(Lux)/Dec 4, 1909; p. 799
ELECTROTYPING PROCESS, THE
(CGP)/Mar 1, 1913; p. 887
ELEKTRA (Vi)/Apr 23, 1910; p. 634
ELEPHANT BUTTE DAM AT
ALBUQUERQUE (Sel)/Jul 13, 1912; p. 147
ELEPHANT CIRCUS, THE
(Po)/Aug 14, 1915; p. 1162
ELEPHANT HUNTING IN THE CAMBOGE
(LeL)/Nov 20, 1909; p. 722
ELEPHANT HUNTING IN VICTORIA
NYANZA (Pa)/Aug 12, 1911; p. 376
ELEPHANT ON HIS HANDS, AN
(Ne)/Nov 22, 1913; p. 869
ELEPHANT ON THEIR HANDS, AN
(Vi)/Nov 2, 1912; p. 449
ELEPHANTS AT WORK (Vi)/Jan 3,1914; p.48

ELEPHANTS IN INDIA
(Pa)/Dec 14, 1907; p. 672
(GN)/Nov 23, 1912; p. 769
ELEVATOR MAN, THE
(Th)/Feb 7, 1914; p. 678
ELEVATOR ROMANCE, AN
(Th)/May 13, 1911; p. 1083
ELEVEN-THIRTY P.M.
(Maj)/Jun 5, 1915; pp 1606, 1623
ELEVENTH DIMENSION, THE
(Imp)/Jul 17, 1915; p. 487
ELEVENTH HOUR, THE
(Ed)/Mar 19, 1910; p. 425
(Mil)/Oct 30,1915; p.812/Oct 30a,1915; p.969
ELEVENTH HOUR REDEMPTION, AN
(Pa)/Dec 10, 1910; p. 1356
ELEVENTH HOUR REFORMATION, AN
(KB)/Aug 15, 1914; p. 961
ELITE BALL, THE (Key)/Feb 8, 1913; p.573
ELIXIR OF BRAVERY, THE
(Ec)/Feb 25, 1911; p. 432
ELIXIR OF DREAMS, THE
(Pa)/Mar 27, 1909; p. 368
ELIXIR OF LIFE, THE
(Pa)/Nov 9, 1907; p. 584
ELIXIR OF LOVE, THE
(Imp)/Feb 14, 1914; p. 810
ELIXIR OF YOUTH, THE
(Po)/Apr 19, 1913; p. 281
ELIZABETH'S PRAYER
(Sel)/Mar 28, 1914; p. 1680
ELOPEMENT, THE
(Bio)/Dec 7, 1907; pp 650-51
(GN)/Aug 6, 1910; p. 298
(Cry)/Jan 4, 1913; p. 52
ELOPEMENT AT HOME, AN
(Vi)/Nov 29, 1913; p. 1007
ELOPEMENT BY AEROPLANE, AN
(Lux)/Aug 19, 1911; p. 466
ELOPEMENT IN ROME, AN
(Ka)/Jul 11, 1914; p. 255
ELOPEMENT OF ELIZA, THE
(Me)/Sep 12, 1914; p. 1511
ELOPEMENT ON DOUBLE L RANCH,
THE (Am)/Jun 17, 1911; p. 1389
ELOPING WITH AUNTY
(Bio)/May 29, 1909; p. 713
ELSA'S BROTHER (Vi)/May 1, 1915; p. 728
ELSIE'S AUNT (Po)/Jun 28, 1913; p. 1360
ELSIE'S UNCLE (Vic)/Sep 26, 1914; p. 1778
ELUSIVE DIAMOND, THE
(Th)/Jan 31, 1914; pp 544-45
ELUSIVE KISS, THE
(Pa)/Feb 8, 1913; p. 572
ELUSIVE TURKEY, THE
(Pa)/Dec 13, 1913; p. 1279
EMANCIPATED WOMEN
(Ka)/Jan 10, 1914; p. 172

EMBARRASSED BRIDEGROOM, AN
(Sel)/Jun 21, 1913; p. 1253
EMBARRASSING GIFT, AN
(KO)/Aug 1, 1908; p. 88
EMBARRASSING PREDICAMENT, AN
(Sel)/Oct 17, 1914; p. 335
EMBARRASSING PURCHASE, AN
(Lux)/Apr 27, 1912; p. 330
EMBARRASSMENT OF RICHES, THE
(Ed)/Oct 11, 1913; p. 155
EMBEZZLER, THE
(GS)/Apr 4, 1914; p. 59
(KB)/May 30, 1914; p. 1262
EMERALD BROOCH, THE
(Maj)/Mar 27, 1915; p. 1933
EMERALD GOD, THE
(Lu)/Oct 30, 1915; p. 791
EMERGENCY WAITER, AN
(GN)/Jan 4, 1913; p. 51
EMIGRANT, THE
(Sel)/Sep 10, 1910; pp 570, 574
EMMA JANE MAKES GOOD
(KrA)/Mar 20, 1915; p. 1765
EMMY OF STORK'S NEST
(Mto)/Oct 16, 1915; pp 461-62
EMPEROR NERO ON THE WARPATH
(GN)/May 16, 1908; p. 443
EMPEROR'S DEBT, THE
(Amb)/Jul 22, 1911; pp 125-26
EMPEROR'S GENEROSITY, AN
(Gau)/Sep 11, 1909; p. 346
EMPEROR'S MESSAGE, THE
(Amb)/Jun 25, 1910; p. 1102
(Gau)/Nov 9, 1912; p. 554
EMPEROR'S RETURN, THE
(Gau)/Jun 3, 1911; p. 1259
EMPEROR'S SPY, THE
(Th)/Sep 26, 1914; p. 1776
EMPLOYER'S LIABILITY
(Ne)/Oct 19, 1912; p. 243
EMPTY BOX, THE
(Rex)/Mar 15, 1913; p. 1105
EMPTY CRADLE, THE
(Pa)/Jun 18, 1910; p. 1049
EMPTY CRIB, THE (Re)/Nov 4, 1911; p. 381
EMPTY GRAVE, THE (Pa)/May 25,1912;p.728
EMPTY HOLSTER, THE
(Lux)/Jul 20, 1912; p. 245
EMPTY SADDLE, THE
(SA)/Nov 25, 1911; p. 637
EMPTY SHELL, THE
(Imp)/Jan 28, 1911; p. 196
EMPTY SLEEVE, THE
(Vi)/Jun 5, 1909; p. 753
(Sel)/Jul 18, 1914; p. 432
EMPTY STUDIO, THE
(Sel)/Feb 15, 1913; p. 678
EMPTY TEPEE, THE

(Bi)/Dec 16, 1911; p. 905
EMPTY WATER KEG, THE
  (Bi)/Feb 10, 1912; p. 483
ENCHANTED BOOTS, THE
  (KO)/Apr 11, 1908; p. 328
ENCHANTED CASTLE, THE
  (Ka)/Apr 2, 1910; p. 508
ENCHANTED FIFER, THE
  (CGP)/Jun 22, 1912; p. 1126
ENCHANTED GUITAR, THE
  (KO)/Apr 18, 1908; p. 354
ENCHANTED LEG, THE
  (Kin)/Mar 15, 1913; p. 1106
ENCHANTED MANTLE, THE
  (KO)/Aug 29, 1908; pp 160-61
ENCHANTED UMBRELLA, THE
  (Mil)/Dec 7, 1912; p. 976
ENCHANTED VOICE, AN (Ec)/Jan 24,
  1914; p. 414/Jan 31, 1914; p. 528
END OF A DREAM
  (Pa)/May 23, 1908; pp 463-64
END OF BLACK BART, THE
  (Am)/Oct 18, 1913; p. 265
END OF ROBESPIERRE, THE
  (CGP)/Aug 3, 1912; p. 445
END OF THE ALLEY, THE
  (Bro)/Oct 10, 1914; p. 189
END OF THE BRIDGE, THE
  (Box)/Nov 21, 1914; p. 1090
END OF THE CIRCLE, THE
  (SA)/Dec 6, 1913; p. 1151
END OF THE FEUD, THE
  (Am)/May 11, 1912; p. 529
  (SA)/Oct 26, 1912; p. 342
  (Rex)/Apr 11, 1914; p. 214
END OF THE PLAY, THE
  (Bio)/Apr 24, 1915; p. 555
END OF THE QUEST, THE
  (Lu)/May 10, 1913; p. 595
END OF THE ROAD, THE
  (Gem)/Nov 8, 1913; p. 613
  (Mut)/Nov 13, 1915; pp 1312-13, 1320
END OF THE RUN, THE
  (Ka)/Oct 18, 1913; p. 264
END OF THE TRAIL, THE
  (Ne)/Aug 19, 1911; p. 465
END OF THE WORLD, THE
  (Bio)/Oct 11, 1913; p. 156
ENDS OF THE EARTH, THE
  (Vi)/Jun 17, 1911; p. 1386
ENEMIES (Pa)/May 13, 1911; p. 1081
ENEMIES, THE (Bsf)/Mar 6, 1915; p. 1464
ENEMY TO SOCIETY, AN
  (Mto)/Oct 2, 1915; p. 79
ENEMY'S AID, AN
  (Lu)/Dec 27, 1913; p. 1543
ENEMY'S BABY, THE
  (Bio)/Jul 26, 1913; p. 427

ENERGETIC ADVERTISER, THE
  (SA)/Jun 26, 1909; p. 872
ENERGETIC MEMBER, AN
  (Po)/Dec 14, 1912; p. 1082
ENERGETIC STREET CLEANER, THE
  (SA)/Mar 27, 1909; p. 368
ENERGIZER (Bio)/Jan 18, 1908; p. 44
ENGAGED, IN SPITE OF THEMSELVES
  (Ec)/May 27, 1911; p. 1201
ENGAGED AGAINST HIS WILL
  (Pa)/Apr 18, 1908; p. 352
ENGAGEMENT, THE
  (Bio)/Mar 23, 1912; p. 1063
ENGAGEMENT RING, THE
  (GN)/Aug 12, 1911; p. 378
ENGAGING KID, THE
  (Lu)/Sep 13, 1913; p. 1176
ENGINE OF DEATH, THE
  (Ape)/Dec 13, 1913; p. 1261
ENGINE OF DESTRUCTION, AN
  (Gau)/Jun 21, 1913; pp 1254-55
ENGINEER, THE (Lu)/Nov 21, 1908; p. 408
ENGINEER'S DAUGHTER, THE
  (Sel)/Dec 18, 1909; p. 880
  (Ka)/Nov 25, 1911; p. 637
  (Pa)/Apr 19, 1913; p. 279
ENGINEER'S REVENGE, THE
  (Lu)/Jan 24, 1914; p. 412
ENGINEER'S ROMANCE, THE
  (Ed)/Jan 22, 1910; p. 91
ENGINEER'S SWEETHEART, THE
  (Ka)/Sep 24, 1910; p. 685
ENGLAND EXPECTS --
  (He)/Oct 17, 1914; p. 347
ENGLAND'S KING AT LIVERPOOL
  (Ka)/Dec 13, 1913; p. 1279
ENGLAND'S MENACE
  (Co)/Sep 5, 1914; p. 1347
ENGLISH BOXING BOUT, AN
  (Pa)/Jan 22, 1910; p. 91
ENGLISH STAG HUNT, AN
  (Imp)/Jun 1, 1912; p. 832
ENGLISH WALNUT INDUSTRY, THE
  (Am)/Jan 25, 1913; p. 365
ENGLISHMAN AND THE GIRL, THE
  (Bio)/Mar 5, 1910; p. 338
ENGLISHMAN'S HONOR, AN
  (Sel)/Feb 4, 1911; p. 243
ENGRAVER, THE (Lu)/Mar 8, 1913; p. 995
ENGULFED IN QUICKSANDS
  (Pa)/Mar 21, 1908; p. 243
ENLISTED MAN'S HONOR, AN
  (Sol)/Aug 26, 1911; pp 543-44
ENMESHED BY FATE
  (Vic)/Jun 20, 1914; p. 1690
ENOCH AND EZERA'S FIRST SMOKE
  (Ed)/Dec 6, 1913; p. 1151
ENOCH ARDEN

(Bio)/Jun 17, 1911; pp 1358-59/
    Jun 24, 1911; p. 1454
(Maj)/Apr 24, 1915; pp 557, 568
ENOCH ARDEN II (Bio)/Jul 1, 1911; p. 1519
ENTERTAINING AUNTIE
    (Kin)/Feb 1, 1913; p. 466
ENTERTAINING UNCLE
    (Ka)/Jul 26, 1913; p. 427
ENTOMBED ALIVE (Vi)/Nov 13,1909; p.683
ENVIRONMENT (Maj)/Oct 31, 1914; p. 641
ENVIRONS OF NAPLES
    (KO)/May 9, 1908; p. 423
ENVIRONS OF SILKEBORG, JUTLAND,
    DENMARK (GN)/Mar 22, 1913; p. 1222
EPH'S DREAM (Po)/Mar 8, 1913 p. 998
EPIDEMIC, THE (SA)/Jul 11, 1914; p. 255
EPIDEMIC IN PARADISE GULCH, THE
    (Sel)/Mar 30, 1912; p. 1165
EPISODE, AN (Rex)/May 2, 1914; p. 674
EPISODE AT CLOUDY CANYON, AN
    (SA)/Sep 13, 1913; p. 1175
EPISODE OF NAPOLEON'S WAR WITH
    SPAIN, AN (It)/Jan 22, 1910; p. 93
EPISODE OF THE HUNDRED YEARS'
    WAR, AN (CGP)/Mar 23, 1912; p. 1063
EPISODE UNDER HENRY III, THE
    (CGP)/Nov 18, 1911; p. 551
EQUAL CHANCE, AN
    (Sel)/Dec 27, 1913; p. 1543
EQUAL TO THE EMERGENCY
    (Ed)/Jul 16, 1910; p. 143
EQUINE HERO, AN
    (Ed)/Feb 26, 1910; p. 298
    (Sel)/Sep 14, 1912; p. 1075
    (Pa)/Mar 22, 1913; p. 1220
EQUINE SPY, THE
    (Sol)/Jul 20, 1912; pp 231-32
EQUITABLE BUILDING FIRE, THE
    (Po)/Feb 3, 1912; p. 394
ERIC, THE RED'S WOOING
    (Dom)/Oct 31, 1914; p. 643
ERIKS, THE (Pa)/Sep 3, 1910; p. 518
ERNEST MALTRAVERS
    (Bio)/Dec 5, 1914; p. 1384
ERRAND OF MERCY, AN
    (Th)/Jul 19, 1913; p. 321
ERRING BROTHER, THE
    (Pa)/Aug 30, 1913; p. 960
ERRING SON, THE
    (Gau)/May 6, 1911; p. 1020
ERRING SON'S AWAKENING, AN
    (Ya)/Jan 21, 1911; p. 145
ERROR IN KIDNAPPING, AN
    (Vi)/Aug 9, 1913; p. 635
ERROR OF OMISSION, THE (SA)/Dec 14,
    1912; p. 1086/Dec 28, 1912; p. 1291
ESCAPE, THE (Pa)/Apr 5, 1913; p. 47
    (Ka)/Sep 6, 1913; p. 1067

(Re)/Jun 13, 1914; p. 1515
ESCAPE FROM ANDERSONVILLE, THE
    (Ka)/Jul 24, 1909; p. 124
ESCAPE FROM THE DUNGEON, THE
    (Gau)/Dec 9, 1911; p. 816
ESCAPE FROM THE TUILLERIES, THE
    (Pa)/Feb 11, 1911; p. 316
ESCAPE OF BRONCHO BILLY, THE
    (SA)/Dec 18, 1915; p. 2202
ESCAPE OF GAS, AN
    (Pa)/Mar 11, 1911; p. 542
    (CGP)/Dec 7,1912;p.984/Dec 21,1912;p.1184
ESCAPE OF JIM DOLAN, THE
    (Sel)/Nov 29, 1913; p. 1008
ESCAPED FROM SIBERIA
    (GP)/May 9, 1914; p. 795
ESCAPED FROM THE ASYLUM
    (Imp)/Oct 4, 1913; p. 50
ESCAPED LUNATIC, THE
    (Ed)/Sep 30, 1911; p. 970
ESCORT, THE (Roy)/Feb 13, 1915; p. 985
ESCORT OF THE VICEROY OF
    CAUCASUS (Amb)/Mar 18, 1911; p. 603
ESKIMOS IN LABRADOR
    (Ed)/Dec 23, 1911; p. 989
ESMERALDA (FP)/Sep 18, 1915; p. 2010
ESTERBROOK CASE, THE
    (Vi)/May 22, 1915; p. 1274
ESTHER AND MORDECAI
    (Gau)/Jul 2, 1910; p. 24
ESTHETIC MATCH, AN
    (Maj)/Oct 4, 1913; p. 49
ESTRANGEMENT, THE
    (Gau)/Aug 27, 1910; p. 463
    (Sel)/Jun 6, 1914; p. 1408
ESTUDILLO HOUSE, CALIFORNIA
    (Ne)/May 25, 1912; p. 730
ETERNAL CITY, THE
    (FP)/Jan 9, 1915; p. 194
ETERNAL DUEL, THE
    (Lu)/Jan 31, 1914; p. 544
ETERNAL FEMININE, THE
    (Sel)/Oct 9, 1915; pp 252-53
ETERNAL MASCULINE, THE
    (Maj)/Apr 6, 1912; p. 43
ETERNAL MOTHER, THE
    (Bio)/Jan 27, 1912; p. 302
ETERNAL ROMANCE, THE
    (Pa)/Sep 4, 1909; p. 316
ETERNAL SACRIFICE, THE
    (Re)/May 24, 1913; p. 813
ETERNAL TRIANGLE, THE
    (Imp)/Jun 4, 1910; p. 943
ETHEL GAINS CONSENT
    (Ko)/Mar 6, 1915; p. 1448
ETHEL GETS THE EVIDENCE
    (Ko)/Jan 16, 1915; p. 369
ETHEL HAS A STEADY

(Ko)/Dec 5, 1914; p. 1384
ETHEL'S BURGLAR
(U)/Aug 21, 1915; p. 1318
ETHEL'S DEADLY ALARM CLOCK
(Ko)/Apr 17, 1915; p. 393
ETHEL'S DISGUISE
(Ko)/May 15, 1915; p. 1072
ETHEL'S DOG-GONE LUCK
(Ko)/Apr 3, 1915; p. 64
ETHEL'S LUNCHEON
(Ed)/Sep 18, 1909; p. 377
ETHEL'S NEW DRESS
(Ko)/May 1, 1915; p. 728
ETHEL'S ROOF PARTY
(Ko)/Nov 21, 1914; p. 1076
ETHEL'S ROMANCE
(Ko)/May 29, 1915; p. 1432
ETHEL'S ROMEOS (Cas)/Oct 30, 1915; p. 792
ETHEL'S TEACHER
(Ko)/Aug 22, 1914; p. 1100
ETHICS OF THE PROFESSION, THE
(Bio)/Jun 20, 1914; p. 1689
ETIENNE OF THE GLAD HEART
(Sel)/Aug 15, 1914; p. 960
ETTA OF THE FOOTLIGHTS
(Vi)/Jun 6, 1914; p. 1409
EUCHRED (Sel)/Oct 26, 1912; p. 342
EUGENE ARAM (Ed)/Jul 3, 1915; p. 81
EUGENE WRAYBURN
(Ed)/Oct 14, 1911; p. 128
EUGENIC BOY, THE
(Th)/Mar 21, 1914; p. 1526
EUGENIC GIRL, THE
(Sel)/Oct 3, 1914; p. 63
EUGENICS AT BAR "U" RANCH
(Sel)/Jun 27, 1914; p. 1828
EUGENICS VERSUS LOVE
(Be)/May 23, 1914; p. 1117
EUREKA (Imp)/May 17, 1913; p. 705
EUROPEAN ARMIES IN ACTION
(GK)/Aug 22, 1914; p. 1079
EVA (Mec)/Feb 15, 1913; p. 681
EVA, THE CIGARETTE GIRL
(Bio)/Jul 18, 1914; p. 433
EVA IS TIRED OF LIFE
(Pa)/Sep 23, 1911; p. 891
EVA MOVES IN (Pa)/Nov 4, 1911; p. 379
EVADING JUSTICE (Lux)/Oct 19,1912;p.244
EVANGELINE (Sel)/Dec 30, 1911; p. 1071
(Can)/Feb 7, 1914; p. 662
EVANGELIST, THE
(Lu)/Mar 27, 1915; p. 1914e
EVAN'S LUCKY DAY
(Be)/Feb 6, 1915; p. 828
EVELYN'S STRATEGY
(Re)/Mar 8, 1913; p. 998
EVEN A WORM WILL TURN
(WBE)/Nov 16, 1907; p. 600

EVEN BREAK, AN (Bi)/Aug 10, 1912; p. 547
EVEN EXCHANGE, AN
(Am)/Aug 16, 1913; p. 745
EVEN UNTO DEATH
(Alb)/Oct 17, 1914; p. 342
EVENING BELLS, THE
(It)/Aug 19, 1911; p. 466
EVENING STORY, AN
(Ec)/Jan 27, 1912; p. 304
EVENING WITH WILDER SPENDER, AN
(Bio)/Nov 8, 1913; p. 612
EVENTFUL BARGAIN DAY, THE
(Imp)/Oct 26, 1912
EVENTFUL ELOPEMENT, AN
(Vi)/Jun 15, 1912; p. 1027
EVENTFUL EVENING, AN
(Ed)/Feb 4, 1911; p. 244
EVENTFUL TRIP, AN
(Pa)/Oct 16, 1909; p. 530
EVER-GALLANT MARQUIS, THE
(Ed)/Aug 1, 1914; p. 704
EVER-LIVING ISLES, THE
(Re)/Oct 30, 1915; p. 793
EVER THE ACCUSER
(Rel)/Mar 11, 1911; p. 542
EVERLASTING JUDY, THE
(Ne)/May 11, 1912; p. 529
EVERLASTING TRIANGLE, THE
(Ed)/Oct 31, 1914; p. 651
EVERY DOUBLE CAUSES TROUBLE
(Pa)/Aug 23, 1913; p. 844
EVERY INCH A HERO
(Gem)/Jul 5, 1913; p. 49
(Lko)/Jan 23, 1915; p. 517
EVERY INCH A KING
(SA)/Dec 26, 1914; p. 1841
EVERY INCH A MAN
(Vi)/Oct 26, 1912; p. 343
EVERY MAN HAS HIS PRICE
(Maj)/Oct 3, 1914; pp 64-65
EVERY MAN'S MONEY
(Po)/Sep 25, 1915; p. 2177
EVERY ROSE HAS ITS STEM (Ed)/May 4,
1912; p. 418/May 25, 1912; p. 728
EVERY THIEF LEAVES A CLUE
(SA)/Aug 2, 1913; p. 535
EVERYBODY LOVES FATHER
(Th)/Jan 21, 1911; p. 145
EVERYBODY'S DOING IT
(Vi)/Feb 8, 1913; p. 572
(Me)/Jul 4, 1914; p. 64
EVERYBODY'S TROUBLES
(SA)/Oct 7, 1911; p. 39
EVERYBODY'S WEARING THEM
(Po)/Aug 30, 1913; p. 962
EVERYDAY LIFE IN MALACCA
(Pa)/Sep 30, 1911; p. 971
EVERYGIRL (Vic)/Feb 13, 1915; p. 986

FABLE OF THE STRUGGLE BETWEEN
PERSONAL LIBERTY AND REFORM
WAVE, THE (SA)/Apr 10, 1915; p. 235
FABLE OF THE THROUGH TRAIN, THE
(SA)/Oct 9, 1915; p. 252
FABLE OF THE TIP AND THE TREASURE,
THE (SA)/Aug 28, 1914; p. 1479
FABLE OF THE TWO MANDOLIN
PLAYERS AND THE WILLING
PERFORMER, THE
(SA)/Sep 5, 1914; p. 1371
FABLE OF THE TWO SENSATIONAL
FAILURES, THE (SA)/Jun 5, 1915; p. 1604
FABLE OF THE UNFETTERED BIRDS,
THE (SA)/May 8, 1915; p. 899
FACE AT THE WINDOW, A
Dec 19, 1908; p. 501
FACE AT THE WINDOW, THE
(Bio)/Jul 2, 1910; p. 24
(Ka)/Apr 12, 1913; p. 164
(Sel)/May 8, 1915; p. 899
FACE FROM THE PAST, A
(Ed)/Nov 22, 1913; p. 868
FACE IN THE CROWD, THE
(Lu)/Sep 19, 1914; p. 1645
FACE IN THE MIRROR, THE
(Sel)/Aug 28, 1915; p. 1479
FACE IN THE MOONLIGHT, THE
(Wor)/Jul 3, 1915; p. 80
FACE OF FEAR, THE (Vi)/Jan 3,1914; p. 48
FACE OF THE MADONNA, THE
(Ka)/Apr 17, 1915; pp 395-96
FACE ON THE BARROOM FLOOR, THE
(Ed)/Jul 25, 1908; p. 67
(Key)/Aug 29, 1914; pp 1241-42
FACE ON THE CEILING, THE
(Bro)/Jan 2, 1915; p. 78
FACE ON THE CURTAIN, THE
(SA)/May 1, 1915; p. 727
FACE OR THE VOICE, THE
(Vi)/Nov 16, 1912; p. 659
FACE TO FACE (Ec)/Mar 5, 1910; p. 340
FACE TO FACE WITH A LEOPARD
(Lux)/Jan 25, 1913; p. 365
FACE VALUE (Ed)/Sep 26, 1914; p. 1776
FACES IN THE NIGHT
(Rex)/May 1, 1915; p. 729
FACING THE GATTLING GUNS
(WF)/Jul 4, 1914; p. 66
FACORI FAMILY (Pa)/Nov 12, 1910; p.1118
FACTORY GIRL, THE
(Ka)/Aug 14, 1909; p. 225
(UE)/Mar 23, 1912; p. 1062
FADDISTS, THE (Bio)/Feb 21, 1914; p. 946
FADED BEAUTIES (GN)/Sep 6,1913; p.1070
FADED LILLIES (Bio)/Jun 26, 1909; p. 872
FADED ROSES (Ya)/Sep 23, 1911; p. 893
FAILURE, THE (Bio)/Dec 23, 1911; p. 989

(Re)/Jun 5, 1915; p. 1605
(Dom)/Jul 3, 1915; p. 65
FAILURE OF SUCCESS, THE
(Gau)/Jul 30, 1910; p. 245
(KB)/Jun 14, 1913; p. 1138
FAINT HEART NE'ER WON FAIR LADY
(Cin)/Apr 19, 1913; p. 280
(Ed)/Aug 22, 1914; p. 1099
FAINT HEART NEVER WON FAIR LADY
(Lux)/Feb 8, 1913; p. 574
FAIR DENTIST, THE
(Imp)/May 20, 1911; p. 1143
FAIR EXCHANGE, A
(Bio)/Oct 9, 1909; p. 491
(SA)/Aug 6, 1910; p. 297
(Sel)/Aug 19, 1911; p. 464
(Vic)/May 10, 1913; p. 597
FAIR EXCHANGE IS NO ROBBERY
(UE)/Jan 6, 1912; p. 41
FAIR GOD OF SUN ISLAND, THE
(GS)/Oct 23, 1915; p. 621
FAIR REBEL, THE (KE)/Sep 5, 1914; p. 1377
FAIRIES' HALLOWE'EN, THE
(Th)/Nov 12, 1910; p. 1119
FAIRY AND THE WAIF, THE
(Wor)/Mar 6, 1915; p. 1453
FAIRY FALLS OF OSWEGO, THE
(Sol)/Feb 10, 1912; p. 483
FAIRY FERN SEED (Th)/Jun 5, 1915; p. 1606
FAIRYLAND BRIDE, THE
(Re)/Dec 21, 1912; p. 1186
FAIRYLAND OF FROST AND SNOW, A
(Gau)/Nov 4, 1911; p. 378
FAIRY'S PRESENTS, THE
(Pa)/May 1, 1909; p. 556
FAITH (Rex)/Sep 30, 1911; p.974
FAITH AND FORTUNE (Ed)/Dec 11, 1915;
p. 2029/Dec 18, 1915; p. 2203
FAITH HEALER, THE
(Re)/Nov 9,1912; p.533/Nov 23,1912; p.769
(Ec)/Jun 7, 1913; p. 1032
FAITH LOST AND WON
(Lu)/Jul 16, 1910; p. 142
FAITH OF A GIRL, THE
(Lu)/Jun 21, 1913; p. 1253
FAITH OF HER FATHERS, THE
(Re)/Jan 24, 1914; p. 414
(GS)/May 8, 1915; p. 901
FAITH OF SONNY JIM, THE
(Vi)/Dec 25, 1915; p. 2388
FAITH OF TWO, THE
(Po)/Mar 14, 1914; p. 1386
FAITHFUL (Bio)/Apr 2, 1910; p. 509
FAITHFUL DOG, THE
(KO)/Jun 8, 1907; p. 220
FAITHFUL FOOL, A
(Vi)/May 1, 1909; p. 556
FAITHFUL GOVERNESS REWARDED

(KO)/Jun 27, 1908; p. 548
FAITHFUL INDIAN, THE
  (SA)/Apr 1, 1911; p. 718
FAITHFUL LITTLE DOGGY, A
  (Pa)/Dec 26, 1908;p.525/Jan 9, 1909;p.38
FAITHFUL MAX (Imp)/Dec 24, 1910; p.1480
FAITHFUL OLD HORSE, THE
  (Pa)/May 22, 1909; p. 676
FAITHFUL SERVANT, A
  (Vi)/Aug 16, 1913; p. 744
FAITHFUL SERVITOR, A
  (Gau)/Oct 4, 1913; p. 50
FAITHFUL SHEP (Re)/Jun 7, 1913; p. 1032
FAITHFUL TO THE FINISH
  (Ko)/Sep 4, 1915; p. 1644
FAITHFUL TO THE TEST
  Dec 19, 1908; p. 500
FAITHFUL UNTO DEATH
  (Ecl)/Jun 6, 1914; p. 1387
FAITHLESS FRIEND, THE
  (Pa)/Dec 13, 1913; pp 1279-80
FAITHLESS LOVER, THE
  (Pa)/Jul 23, 1910; p. 193
FAITHLESS MAN, A
  (Imp)/Apr 22, 1911; p. 902
FAKE ALARM, THE (Cry)/Feb 1,1913;p.466
FAKE DIAMOND SWINDLER, A
  (Me)/May 23, 1908; p. 463
FAKE DOCTOR, THE
  (Pa)/Oct 10, 1908; p. 287
FAKE GAS MAN, THE
  (Cry)/Jan 25, 1913; p. 365
FAKE SOLDIERS, THE
  (Lu)/Apr 12, 1913; p. 165
FAKIR, THE (Dom)/Apr 3, 1915; p. 65
FAKIR'S DREAM, THE (Pa)/Oct 24, 1908;
  p. 326/Oct 30, 1908; p. 339
FAKIR'S NEW SERVANT, THE
  (GN)/Apr 8, 1911; p. 782
FALL OF A KNIGHT, THE
  (Rex)/Mar 25, 1911; p. 658
FALL OF BABYLON, THE (Gau)/Mar 26,
  1910; p. 468/Apr 16, 1910; p. 597
FALL OF BLACK HAWK, THE (Am)/
  Jun 15, 1912; p. 1018/Jul 6, 1912;
  pp 31-34/Aug 17, 1912; pp 672-73
FALL OF CONSTANTINOPLE, THE
  (Gau)/Oct 18, 1913; p. 246
FALL OF FRANCE, THE
  (Ape)/Jan 3, 1914; p. 36
FALL OF MONTEZUMA, THE
  (SA)/May 18, 1912; p. 634
FALL OF MUSCLE-BOUND HICKS, THE
  (Bio)/Oct 10, 1914; p. 187
FALL OF TROY, THE
  (It)/Apr 29, 1911; p. 935
FALLEN ANGEL, THE
  (Rex)/Jul 26, 1913; p. 430

(Bio)/Feb 14, 1914; p. 808
FALLEN HERO, A (Bio)/Nov 8, 1913; p. 611
  (Ka)/Mar 28,1914; p.1680
FALLEN IDOL, THE
  (Ed)/Jan 8, 1910; p. 17
  (Imp)/Jul 16, 1910; p. 144
  (GN)/Jun 6, 1914; p. 1410
FALLEN STANDARD, THE
  (Bal)/Sep 11, 1915; p. 1834
FALLING ARROW, THE
  (Lu)/May 8, 1909; p. 594
FALLING IN LOVE WITH INEZ
  (Ed)/Jan 3, 1914; p. 48
FALLING LEAVES
  (Sol)/Mar 23, 1912; p. 1063
FALLING OUT, THE
  (Imp)/Nov 25, 1911; p. 638
FALLS AND RAPIDS OF SIVASAMUDRAM
  (Pa)/Jun 5, 1915; p. 1606
FALLS OF THE IMATRA, FINLAND (Pa)/
  Dec 10, 1910; p. 1358/Dec 17, 1910; p. 1416
FALLS OF THE RHINE, THE
  (Ec)/Oct 1, 1910; p. 750
FALSE ACCUSATION, A
  (Vi)/May 22, 1909; p. 676
  (Pa)/Aug 9, 1913; p. 635
FALSE ACCUSATION, THE
  (It)/Dec 31, 1910; p. 1539
FALSE ALARM, A (KO)/Aug 29,1908; p.161
  (GN)/Sep 11, 1909; p.346
FALSE ALARM, THE
  (GN)/Mar 4, 1911; p. 484
FALSE AND THE TRUE, THE
  (Vi)/Jul 18, 1914; p. 433
FALSE COIN (Pa)/May 9, 1908; p. 425
FALSE COLORS (Bos)/Jan 2, 1915; p. 85
FALSE FRIAR, THE
  (It)/May 14, 1910; p. 785
FALSE FRIEND, A (Lu)/Apr 19, 1913; p.279
FALSE FRIEND, THE
  (Sel)/Oct 18, 1913; p. 263
FALSE GODS (Am)/Aug 15, 1914; p. 938/
  Aug 29, 1914; p. 1242
FALSE GUARDIAN, THE (Ka)/Oct 17, 1914;
  p. 345/Nov 7, 1914; p. 788
FALSE HEIR, THE
  (MnA)/Nov 13, 1915; p. 1311
FALSE LOVE AND TRUE
  (Lu)/Nov 12, 1910; p. 1116
  (Cry)/Jun 14, 1913; p. 1138
FALSE MONEY (KO)/Apr 18, 1908; p. 354
FALSE MOVE, A (Vi)/Jun 20, 1914; p. 1688
FALSE ORDER, A (Sel)/Jan 25, 1913; p. 363
FALSE PRIDE (Maj)/Nov 14, 1914; p. 932
FALSE PRIDE HAS A FALL
  (Alb)/Oct 17, 1914; p. 344
FALSE SHADOW, THE
  (Lu)/Aug 8, 1914; p. 837

FALSE SUSPICION, A
(SA)/Oct 28, 1911; pp 291-92
FALSE TO BOTH (Imp)/Apr 20, 1912; p.231
FALSELY ACCUSED
(Bio)/Jan 18, 1908; p. 44
(Bi)/Jan 27, 1912; p. 305
(Sol)/Aug 23, 1913; p. 846
FAMILY BIBLE, THE
(Ed)/Mar 27, 1915; p. 1932
FAMILY CUPBOARD, THE
(Wor)/Oct 16, 1915; p. 465
FAMILY DOCTOR, THE
(Re)/Sep 18, 1915; p. 1996
FAMILY FEUD, A (Vi)/Jul 2, 1910; p. 84
(Lux)/Apr 2, 1910; p. 509
FAMILY MIX UP, A
(Key)/Dec 21, 1912; p. 1185
FAMILY NEXT DOOR, THE
(Lu)/Nov 16, 1912; pp 658-59
FAMILY OF CATS (Pa)/Jun 6, 1908; p. 498
FAMILY OF VEGETARIANS, A (Ed)/
Jan 14, 1911; p. 88/Jan 21, 1911; p. 146
FAMILY OUTING, A
(UE)/Mar 5, 1910; p. 339
FAMILY OUTING, THE
(Me)/Aug 22, 1914; p. 1099
FAMILY PET'S REVENGE, THE
(SA)/Nov 4, 1911; p. 380
FAMILY PICNIC, A
(Vi)/Nov 13, 1915; p. 1311
FAMILY RECORD, THE
(Sel)/Aug 29, 1914; p. 1240
FAMILY QUARREL, A
(SA)/Apr 23, 1910; p. 641
FAMILY SKELETON, THE
(Ka)/Apr 4, 1914; p. 57
FAMILY STAIN, THE
(Fox)/Nov 6, 1915; pp 1141, 1153
FAMILY TROUBLES
(Gau)/Apr 15, 1911; p. 842
FAMILY TYRANT, THE
(Ka)/Aug 10, 1912; p. 546
FAMILY'S HONOR, THE
(Ed)/Oct 25, 1913; p. 380
FAMINE, THE (KB)/Jan 30, 1915; p. 673
FAMINE IN THE FOREST
(Ka)/Jul 3, 1909; p. 13
FAMOUS BATTLES OF NAPOLEON
(Cos)/Feb 7, 1914; p. 657
FAMOUS DUEL, A (Ed)/Aug 5, 1911; p. 292
FAMOUS ESCAPE, A
(Bio)/Apr 4, 1908; p. 297
FAMOUS GERMAN RESORT, WIESBADEN,
A (Pa)/Apr 3, 1915; p. 65
FAN, THE (Pa)/Jul 17, 1909; p. 89
FANCHON, THE CRICKET
(FP)/May 22, 1915; p. 1276
FANCHON THE CRICKET

(Imp)/Jun 22, 1912; p. 1127
FANCY FOWLS (Sel)/Aug 2, 1913; p. 535
FANCY POULTRY (Sel)/Jul 5, 1913; p. 47
FANCY SKATING (Sel)/Apr 18, 1914; p. 360
FANCY SOLDIER/Sep 18, 1909; pp 378-79
FANGS OF FATE, THE
(Ram)/Dec 6, 1913; p. 1154
FANNY'S CONSPIRACY
(Vi)/Nov 29, 1913; p. 1007
FANNY'S MELODRAMA
(Vi)/May 9, 1914; p. 820
FANTASCA, THE GYPSY
(Ka)/Aug 10, 1912; p. 546
FANTASTIC FURNITURE
(Ec)/Sep 10, 1910; p. 575
FANTASTIC HEADS
(Pa)/Aug 7, 1909; p. 196
FANTINE (Bio)/Oct 9, 1909; pp 490-91
FANTOMAS (Gau)
No.1/Jun 28, 1913; p. 1361
No.2/Oct 25, 1913; p. 381/Nov 8, 1913; p. 594
No.3/Dec 27, 1913; p. 1531
No.4/Mar 14, 1914; p. 1367
No.5/Jul 11, 1914; p. 271
FAR AWAY FIELDS
(Rex)/Sep 28, 1912; p. 1278
FAR FROM ERIN'S ISLE
(Ka)/Feb 3, 1912; p. 401
FAR FROM THE BEATEN TRACK
(Imp)/Mar 16, 1912; p. 963
FAR FROM THE MADDENING CROWD
(Ed)/Aug 28, 1909; p. 282
FARES, PLEASE (Jo)/Apr 10, 1915; p. 237
FAREWELL DINNER, A
(Maj)/Feb 13, 1915; pp 986, 997
FAREWELL TO THEE
(Re)/Sep 4, 1915; p. 1644
FARM HOUSE ROMANCE, A
(CGP)/Jan 4, 1913; p. 51
FARMAN AEROPLANE
(Pa)/Feb 15, 1908; p. 123
FARMER ALLEN'S DAUGHTER
(Maj)/Aug 10, 1912; pp 546-47
FARMER RODNEY'S DAUGHTER
(Ed)/Aug 15, 1914; p. 959
FARMER'S DAUGHTER, THE
(Vi)/Mar 7, 1908; pp 195-96
(Ed)/Oct 22, 1910; p. 934
(SA)/Feb 8, 1913; p. 573
FARMER'S DAUGHTERS, THE
(Th)/Oct 11, 1913; p. 157
FARMER'S GRANDSON, THE
(GN)/May 29, 1909; p. 713
FARMER'S SON, A (Lu)/Aug 10, 1912; p. 545
FARMER'S TREASURE, THE
(UE)/Oct 2, 1909; p. 451
FARMING IN ANCIENT THEBES
(Vi)/Dec 6, 1913; p. 1150

FARMING OLD AND NEW
(Gau)/Sep 23, 1911; p. 891
FARMING WITH DYNAMITE
(InP)/Nov 11, 1911; p. 474
FASCINATING BACHELOR, A
(Lu)/May 13, 1911; p. 1081
FASCINATING EYE, THE
(Jo)/May 16, 1914; p. 970
FASCINATING FLUFFY DIMPLES
(Lu)/Sep 5, 1908; p. 182
FASCINATING WIDOW, A
(Sol)/Jul 15, 1911; p. 40
FASCINATION OF THE FLEUR-de-LIS,
THE (Uni)/Sep 25, 1915; p. 2195
FASHION AND ITS CONSEQUENCES
(Lux)/May 20, 1911; p. 1142
FASHION SHOP, A (Bio)/Jan 23, 1915; p. 515
FASHION SHOP, THE
(GK)/Oct 23, 1915; p. 619
FASHIONABLE HAT (Pa)/May 23, 1908; p.464
FASHIONABLE SPORT, THE
(It)/May 14, 1910; p. 785
FASHIONS AND THE SIMPLE LIFE
(Th)/May 1, 1915; p. 728
FASHION'S LAW IN SWISS CANTONS
(Pa)/Dec 13, 1913; p. 1279
FASHION'S TOY (Lu)/Sep 27,1913; p.1392
FAST FREIGHT 3205
(Ka)/Apr 18, 1914; p. 360
FAT, FAIR AND SAUCY
(Vi)/Jun 26, 1915; p. 2095
FAT AND THIN OF IT, THE
(Cry)/Mar 28, 1914; p. 1681
FAT BABY, THE (Pa)/Jun 27, 1908; p. 547
FAT BILL'S WOOING
(Ka)/Oct 5, 1912; p. 40
FAT GIRL'S ROMANCE, THE
(Cry)/Jan 2, 1915; p. 76
FAT MAN'S BURDEN, THE
(Pa)/Feb 21, 1914; p. 946
FATAL BALL, THE (Me)/Dec 18, 1909; p. 881
FATAL BELL, THE (Gau)/Sep 6, 1913; p. 1069
FATAL BLACK BEAN, THE
(Maj)/Mar 6, 1915; p. 1448
FATAL CARD, A (Lu)/Aug 22, 1914; p. 1099
FATAL CARD, THE
(Lu)/Apr 18, 1908; p. 351
(Fr)/Feb 21, 1914; p. 948
(FP)/Oct 16, 1915; pp 462-63
FATAL CHOCOLATE, THE
(Bio)/Mar 2, 1912; p. 781
FATAL CLUES, THE
(Ka)/Feb 28, 1914; p. 1088
FATAL DRESS SUIT, THE
(Ko)/Apr 18, 1914; p. 361
FATAL FASCINATION
(Gau)/Jan 29, 1910; p. 128
FATAL FINGER PRINTS, THE

(Ko)/Aug 28, 1915; p. 1480
FATAL FLIRTATION, A
(Key)/Jun 6, 1914; p. 1409
FATAL GLASS, THE
(Ch)/Mar 23, 1912; p. 1064
FATAL GOLD, THE
(Bi)/Nov 12, 1910; p. 1119
FATAL GROTTO, THE (It)/Jun 14, 1913;
p. 1140/Jun 21, 1913; p. 1254
FATAL HANSOM, THE
(St)/Dec 19, 1914; p. 1681
FATAL HOUR, THE
(Bio)/Aug 22, 1908; p. 142
(Maj)/Sep 4, 1915; p. 1644
FATAL IMPRUDENCE
(Amb)/Mar 26, 1910; p. 467
FATAL KISS, THE (Jo)/Apr 24, 1915; p. 557
FATAL LEGACY, THE
(Ka)/Sep 27, 1913; p. 1392
FATAL LETTER, THE
(Jo)/Jun 20, 1914; p. 1690
FATAL LIKENESS, A
(Lu)/Jul 25, 1908; p. 67
FATAL LOVE, THE (UE)/Sep 25, 1909; p. 414
FATAL MALLET, THE
(Key)/Jun 13, 1914; p. 1541
FATAL MARRIAGE, THE
(Lko)/Nov 14, 1914; p. 933
FATAL NOTE, THE
(Sel)/Nov 28, 1914; p. 1231
(Lko)/Apr 10, 1915; p. 238
FATAL OPAL, THE (Ka)/Jan 9, 1915; p. 221
FATAL PICNIC, A (GN)/Nov 19, 1910; p. 1179
FATAL PLUNGE, THE
(Ecl)/Nov 22, 1913; p. 870
FATAL PORTRAIT, THE
(Ka)/Jul 18, 1914; p. 433
FATAL RESEMBLANCE, A
(Pa)/Apr 15, 1911; p. 843
FATAL SCAR, THE (Lu)/Aug 23,1913; p.842
FATAL SHOT, THE (Ka)/Nov 15,1913;p.736
FATAL SONATA, THE
(It)/Aug 12, 1911; pp 377-78
FATAL STEP, THE (Imp)/Jun 27, 1914; p.1830
FATAL TAXICAB, THE
(Key)/Oct 4, 1913; p. 49
FATAL VENGEANCE, A
(Amb)/Sep 3, 1910; p. 521
FATAL VERDICT, THE
(Imp)/Sep 27, 1913; p. 1393
FATAL WEDDING, A (St)/May 2, 1914; p. 674
FATALITY (KO)/Jul 6, 1907; p. 284
(Uni)/Sep 7, 1912; pp 963-64
FATALITY AND MYSTERY
(Fl)/Jan 31, 1914; p. 528
FATE (Rex)/Jul 22, 1911; p. 126
(Bio)/Apr 5, 1913; p. 48/Dec 4, 1915;
p. 1844/Dec 25, 1915; p. 2388

FATHER'S GRIEF, A (GN)/Jun 4, 1910; p. 942
FATHER'S HATBAND
(Vi)/Nov 15, 1913; p. 735
FATHER'S HEART, A
(Ec)/Nov 11, 1911; pp 472-73
(Lu)/May 2, 1914; p. 673
FATHER'S HELPING HAND
(Ne)/Oct 30a, 1915; p. 969
FATHER'S LESSON (WBE)/Jun 6, 1908; p.501
FATHER'S LESSON, A
(Bio)/Mar 1, 1913; p. 887
FATHER'S LOVE, A (Po)/Jan 7, 1911; p. 35
(Lu)/Jul 5, 1913; p. 47
FATHER'S LUCKY ESCAPE
(Ne)/Nov 6, 1915; p. 1140
FATHER'S NEW MAID
(SA)/Mar 27, 1915; p. 1931
FATHER'S PATRIOTISM, A
(Lux)/Mar 19, 1910; p. 427
FATHER'S SCAPEGOAT, THE
(Bio)/May 30, 1914; p. 1261
FATHER'S STRATAGEM, A
(Mil)/Jan 11, 1913; p. 160
FATHER'S STRATEGY
(Vic)/Jan 16, 1915; p. 370
FATHER'S TEMPER (Lu)/Mar 14,1914; p.1385
FATHER'S THREE (Vic)/Jan 23, 1915; p.517
FATHER'S TIMEPIECE
(Vi)/Oct 3, 1914; p. 63
FATHER'S TOOTHACHE
(Cin)/Mar 30, 1912; p. 1165
FATHER'S WASHING DAY
(Lu)/Jun 15, 1907; p. 238
FATIMA (Cin)/May 11, 1912; p. 519
FATTY AGAIN (Key)/Oct 17, 1914; p. 337
FATTY AND THE BANDITS
(Ne)/Feb 15, 1913; p. 680
FATTY AND THE BROADWAY STARS
(Key)/Dec 11, 1915; p. 2028/
Dec 18, 1915; p. 2204
FATTY AND THE SHYSTER LAWYER
(Ka)/Dec 5, 1914; p. 1383
FATTY AT SAN DIEGO
(Key)/Nov 15, 1913; p. 737
FATTY BUYS A BATH
(Lux)/Nov 19, 1910; p. 1178
FATTY JOINS THE FORCE
(Key)/Nov 29, 1913; p. 1008
FATTY OF E.Z. RANCH
(Ne)/Aug 17, 1912; p. 674
FATTY ON THE JOB
(Vi)/Mar 7, 1914; p. 1236
FATTY'S AFFAIR OF HONOR
(Vi)/Nov 15, 1913; p. 735
FATTY'S AND MABEL'S MARRIED LIFE
(Key)/Feb 20, 1915; pp 1140, 1143
FATTY'S BIG MIX-UP
(Ne)/Nov 9, 1912; p. 554

FATTY'S BUSY DAY
(Ka)/May 17, 1913; p. 704
FATTY'S DAY OFF (Key)/Sep 6,1913;p.1069
FATTY'S DEBUT (Key)/Sep 26,1914; p.1777
FATTY'S DECEPTION
(Ka)/Apr 19, 1913; p. 280
FATTY'S ECHO (Ka)/Feb 13, 1915; p. 984
FATTY'S FATAL FUN
(StP)/Oct 23, 1915; p. 621
FATTY'S FLIRTATION
(Key)/Dec 20, 1913; p. 1413
FATTY'S FOLLIES (Pa)/Sep 26, 1908; p.243
FATTY'S INFATUATION
(Lko)/Feb 27, 1915; p. 1289
FATTY'S JONAH DAY
(Key)/Nov 28, 1914; p. 1232
FATTY'S MINNIE-HE-HAW
(Key)/Dec 12, 1914; p. 1525
FATTY'S SWEETHEART
(Vi)/Oct 31, 1914; p. 640
FATTY'S TINTYPE TANGLE
(Key)/Aug 7, 1915; p. 997
FATTY'S WINE PARTY
(Key)/Nov 28, 1914; p. 1233
FAULT OF THE GRANDMOTHER, THE
(It)/Nov 19, 1910; p. 1178
FAUN, THE (Pa)/Dec 26, 1908; pp 525, 533
FAUST (Ed)/Jan 15, 1910; p.58
(Ec)/Jul 16, 1910; p.144
(Pa)/Jun 3, 1911; p. 1236/
Jul 1, 1911; p. 1520
FAUST AND THE LILY
(Bio)/Jul 19, 1913; p. 319
FAVORING CURRENT, A
(Gau)/Aug 5, 1911; p. 294
FAVORITE FOOL, A
(Key)/Oct 16, 1915; p. 441
FAVORITE SON, THE
(KB)/Feb 15, 1915; p. 681
FEAR (SA)/Jul 5, 1913; p. 47
FEAR, THE (Po)/Apr 19, 1913; p. 281
FEAR OF FIRE, THE
(Ec)/Jan 7, 1911; p. 35
FEAST OF FOOLSHEAD, THE
(It)/Feb 18, 1911; p. 372
FEATHERTOP (Ec)/Jun 8, 1912; p. 946
(Kin)/Apr 19, 1913; p. 281
FEEDING THE KITTY
(Ne)/Sep 12, 1914; p. 1513
FEEDING TIME (Key)/Jun 14, 1913; p. 1138
FEEL MY MUSCLE
(Lu)/Jan 23, 1915; p. 515
FEENEY'S SOCIAL EXPERIMENT
(Re)/Sep 6, 1913; p. 1069
FELIX AT THE BALL
(Lu)/Nov 23, 1912; p. 767
FELIX HOLT (Bio)/Jun 5, 1915; p. 1605
FELLING A SMOKESTACK

FINAL JUSTICE, THE
(Vi)/Mar 15, 1913; p. 1103
FINAL PARDON, THE
(Rex)/Mar 9, 1912; p. 868
FINAL RECKONING, THE
(Bro)/Jul 11, 1914; p. 257
(Th)/Mar 13, 1915; p. 1609
FINAL SETTLEMENT, THE
(Bio)/Mar 12, 1910; p. 382
FINAL TEST, THE
(Pr)/Oct 10, 1914; p. 188
FINAL VERDICT, THE
(Maj)/Sep 26, 1914; p. 1777
FINANCIAL SCARE, THE
(Sel)/Jan 25, 1908; p. 64
FINDING THE LAST CHANCE MINE
(Me)/May 25, 1912 ;p. 728
FINE EASTER EGG, A
(KO)/Jul 4, 1908; p. 13
FINE FEATHERS (Wor)/Jun 19,1915; p.1947
FINE FEATHERS MAKE FINE BIRDS
(Me)/Apr 25, 1914; p. 516
(Vi)/Oct 3, 1914; p. 64
FINER THINGS, THE
(Am)/Feb 22, 1913; p. 782
FINEST GOLD, THE
(U)/Sep 11, 1915; p. 1834
FINGER OF FATE, THE
(Pa)/Jan 3, 1914; p. 49
FINGER PRINT, THE
(Sel)/Nov 1, 1913; p. 497
FINGER-PRINTS (SA)/Jul 4, 1914; p. 65
FINGER PRINTS, THE
(Sol)/Jan 4, 1913; p. 53
FINGER PRINTS OF FATE
(Th)/Feb 6, 1915; p. 829
FINN AND HADDIE
(Lu)/Sep 25, 1915; p. 2176
FINNEGAN (SA)/Apr 5, 1913; p. 47
FINNEY'S LUCK (Pun)/Jan 11, 1913; p. 160
FIRE (Ec)/Apr 26, 1913; p. 381
FIRE AND STRAW (Lu)/Jun 29,1912; p.1226
FIRE AND SWORD (Kis)/Feb 14,1914; p.815
FIRE AT SEA
(Ka)/Oct 10, 1908; p. 286
(CGP)/Aug 17, 1912; pp 644-45
FIRE BRIDE, THE (Pa)/Jan 3, 1914; p. 48
FIRE CHIEF'S BRIDE, THE
(Bio)/Oct 3, 1914; p. 64
FIRE CHIEF'S DAUGHTER, THE
(Sel)/Jul 16, 1910; p. 142
FIRE COWARD, THE
(Ka)/Mar 8, 1913; p. 996
FIRE DEPARTMENT OF NEW YORK, THE
(Ed)/Jan 21, 1911; p. 142
FIRE ESCAPE, THE
(Vi)/Sep 18, 1915; p. 1995
FIRE FIGHTER'S LOVE, THE (Sel)/Nov 9,

1912; pp 531-32/Dec 7, 1912; p. 976
FIRE-FIGHTING ZOUAVES, THE
(Ka)/May 3, 1913; p. 487
FIRE! FIRE! (Pa)/May 30, 1908; pp 479-80
(Lu)/Jun 20, 1914; p. 1688
FIRE! FIRE! FIRE!
(Me)/Jan 28, 1911; p. 194
FIRE JUGGLERS, THE
(Sel)/Apr 25, 1914; p. 516
FIRE MANEUVERS IN MADRID
(Pa)/Feb 15, 1908; p. 124
FIRE OF VENGEANCE, THE
(Pa)/Apr 26, 1913; p. 381
FIREBUGS, THE (Key)/Aug 30, 1913; p.962
FIRED COOK, THE (Ka)/Apr 12,1913; p.163
FIREFLY, THE (FRA)/Oct 11, 1913; p. 158
FIRELIGHT (Ec)/Aug 8, 1914; p. 838
FIREMAN AND THE GIRL, THE
(Pa)/Nov 14, 1914; p. 937
FIREMAN AT THE THEATER, THE
(Cin)/Aug 31, 1907; pp 409-10
FIREMAN'S SOCIAL, THE
(Bio)/Jul 18, 1914; p. 432
FIREMEN OF CAIRO, THE
(Ec)/Sep 3, 1910; p. 521
FIREMEN'S DRILL, NEW YORK FIRE
DEPARTMENT (Vi)/Mar 22, 1913; p. 1220
FIREMEN'S PARADE, THE
(Vi)/Feb 4, 1911; p. 244
FIREPROOFING CHILDREN
(Jo)/Nov 21, 1914; p. 1090
FIRES OF AFFLICTION, THE
(Pa)/Jan 16, 1915; p. 371
FIRES OF CONSCIENCE
(Re)/Dec 28, 1912; p. 1293
(Ne)/Jan 31, 1914; p. 545
FIRES OF DRIFTWOOD
(Vi)/Dec 30, 1911; p. 1072
FIRES OF FATE, THE
(Vi)/Jun 17,1911; p.1386/Jun 24,1911; p.1427
(Rex)/Nov 29, 1913; p. 1009
FIRESIDE REALIZATION, A
(Rex)/May 22, 1915; p. 1261
FIRESIDE REMINISCENCES
(Ed)/Feb 1, 1908; p. 82
FIRING LINE, THE (101)/Oct 5, 1912; p. 43
FIRING OF THE PATCHWORK QUILT,
THE (Vi)/Mar 16, 1912; p. 961
FIRST AID TO THE INJURED
(Sel)/Feb 24, 1912; 690
(Ed)/Sep 6, 1913; p. 1067
FIRST AIRSHIP CROSSING THE
ENGLISH CHANNEL (Gau)/Sep 11, 1909;
p. 344/Sep 18, 1909; pp 377-8
FIRST CHRISTMAS, THE
(Ed)/Dec 27, 1913; p. 1543
FIRST-CLASS COOK, A
(Bio)/Oct 10, 1914; p. 188

FIRST COMMANDMENT, THE
(Ka)/Mar 13, 1915; p. 1617
FIRST EDITION OF MOTHER GOOSE
RHYMES (Ch)/Dec 9, 1911; pp 818-19, 822
FIRST ENDORSEMENT, THE
(Vi)/Mar 7, 1914; p. 1236
FIRST GLASS, THE (Po)/Nov 16, 1912; p. 659
FIRST GRAY HAIR, THE
(Gau)/Nov 5, 1910; p. 1058
FIRST LAW, THE (Bio)/Oct 31, 1914; p. 640
FIRST LOVE (Cry)/Dec 6, 1913; p. 1152
FIRST LOVE IS BEST
(Lu)/Apr 16, 1910; p. 599
FIRST MAN, THE (SA)/Dec 2,
1911; p. 728/Dec 23, 1911; pp 988-89
FIRST NUGGET, THE
(Ec)/Jan 10, 1914; p. 174
FIRST PIANO IN CAMP, THE
(Bio)/Jun 5, 1915; p. 1604
FIRST PRIZE, THE
(Lu)/Mar 15, 1913; p. 1104
FIRST SETTLERS' STORY, THE (Ed)/
Dec 7, 1912; p. 958/Jan 4, 1913; p. 50
FIRST STONE, THE (Be)/Apr 10,1915; p.236
FIRST VIOLIN, THE
(Vi)/Feb 17, 1912; p. 582
FIRST WOMAN JURY IN AMERICA, THE
(Vi)/Apr 6, 1912; p. 40
FISH PERSERVING AT ASTRAKHAN
(Pa)/Jun 6, 1908; p. 498
FISH STORY, A (Maj)/Aug 23, 1913; p. 845
FISH WITH A STORAGE BATTERY IN ITS
BRAIN, THE (Pa)/Oct 11, 1913; p. 155
FISHER FOLKS (Bio)/Mar 4, 1911; p. 482
FISHER MAID, THE (Imp)/Apr 1,1911;p.721
FISHERBOY'S FAITH, THE
(Sel)/Nov 9, 1912; p. 554
FISHERMAID OF BALLYDAVID, THE
(Ka)/Dec 2, 1911; p. 724
FISHERMAID'S LOVE STORY, THE
(Pa)/May 4, 1912; p. 426
FISHERMAN KATE (Vi)/Oct 17,1914; p.336
FISHERMAN'S CRIME, THE
(Amb)/Sep 10, 1910; p. 576
FISHERMAN'S FORTUNE, THE
(Re)/Jul 19, 1913; p. 321
FISHERMAN'S GRANDDAUGHTER, THE
(Ka)/Feb 26, 1910; pp 299-300
FISHERMAN'S HONOR, THE
(Lux)/Mar 5, 1910; p. 340
FISHERMAN'S LIFE, THE
Nov 21, 1908; p. 398
FISHERMAN'S LUCK (Sol)/Nov 1,1913;p.497
FISHERMAN'S LUCK, THE
(Lu)/Apr 23, 1910; p. 641
(SA)/Nov 16, 1912; p. 658
FISHERMAN'S RIVAL, THE
(Sel)/Oct 24, 1908; pp 319, 327-28

FISHERWOMAN, THE
(Th)/Oct 30a, 1915; p. 968
FISHES OF THE TROPICS
(Ec)/Apr 20, 1912; p. 231
FISHING BOATS ON THE OCEAN
(KO)/Aug 1, 1908; p. 88
FISHING IN FLORIDA
(Lu)/Mar 16, 1912; p. 961
FISHING INDUSTRY AT GLOUCESTER,
MASS. (Ed)/Jan 15, 1910; p. 56
FISHING SMACK, THE
(Gau)/Nov 19, 1910; p. 1176
FISHING WITH CORMORANTS
(Gl)/Sep 18, 1915; p. 1997
FISHGUARD HARBOR
(UE)/Jun 3, 1911; p. 1258
FISHY AFFAIR, A (Key)/Apr 26, 1913; p.381
FITFUL PEGGY (Bio)/Sep 17, 1910; p. 630
FITS AND CHILLS (Vi)/Oct 23, 1915; p. 619
FITZHUGH'S RIDE (Lu)/Feb 28,1914;p.1088
FIUME (Cin)/May 18, 1912; p. 629
FIVE BOLD BAD MEN
(SA)/Aug 5, 1911; p. 293
FIVE COPIES (GN)/Aug 23, 1913; p. 846
FIVE DAUGHTERS OF M. DURANT, THE
(Ec)/Dec 9, 1911; p.818
FIVE HOURS (Rex)/Apr 1, 1911; p. 699/
Apr 8, 1911; p. 782
$500 REWARD (Bio)/Sep 9, 1911; p. 715
(KrP)/Feb 20, 1915; p. 1141
$5,000,000 COUNTERFEITING PLOT, THE
(Dr)/Aug 22, 1914; p. 1083
FIVE MINUTES TO TWELVE
(Vi)/Feb 5, 1910; p. 168
FIVE POUND NOTE, THE
(Imp)/Mar 13, 1915; p. 1609
FIVE ROSE SISTERS, THE
(Th)/Oct 14, 1911; p. 131
FIVE SENSES, THE
(Vi)/Mar 23, 1912; p. 1062
(Po)/May 11, 1912; p. 529
(WF)/Jan 16, 1915; p. 370
$5000 REWARD, DEAD OR ALIVE
(Am)/Jun 24, 1911; p. 1454
FIXER, THE (Lu)/Apr 5, 1913; p. 48
FIXER FIXED, THE
(Sol)/Feb 10, 1912; p. 483
FIXING A FLIRT (Lu)/Nov 16, 1912; p. 659
FIXING AUNTY UP (Lu)/May 17, 1913; p. 703
FIXING THE FAKERS
(Imp)/Apr 26, 1913; p. 382
FIXING THE FLIRTS
(Imp)/Feb 1, 1913; p. 466
FIXING THEIR DADS
(Vi)/Dec 5, 1914; p. 1383
FJORDS AND MOUNTAINS OF NORWAY,
THE (Pa)/Apr 3, 1915; p. 65
FLAG DIDN'T RISE, THE

FOOL LUCK (Ka)/Sep 6, 1913; p. 1068
FOOL THERE WAS, A
(Lu)/Sep 19, 1914; p. 1644
FOOLING FANNY'S FATHER
(Lu)/Jul 25, 1914; p. 571
FOOLING FATHER
(Lu)/Apr 20, 1912; p. 230
(Jo)/Feb 20, 1915; p. 1140
FOOLING THE SPECIALIST
(Re)/Dec 28, 1912; p. 1294
FOOLING UNCLE (Be)/Jan 31, 1914; p. 522
FOOLISH, FAT FLORA
(Fal)/Dec 25, 1915; p. 2389
FOOLISH AGREEMENT, A (Ed)/May 16,
1914; p. 946/Jul 11, 1914; p. 255
FOOLISH LOVERS (Cry)/Jun 20,1914;p.1690
FOOLISHNESS OF JEALOUSY, THE
(Vi)/Nov 4, 1911; p. 379
FOOLISHNESS OF OLIVER, THE
(Vic)/Dec 14, 1912; p. 1083
FOOLS AND PAJAMAS
(Jo)/Nov 24, 1914; p. 933
FOOL'S GOLD (Bio)/May 15, 1915; p. 1071
FOOL'S HEART, THE (Ec)/Oct 9, 1915;
p. 254/Oct 16, 1915; p. 440
FOOL'S JEST, THE (Ed)/Nov 14,1908; p.378
FOOLS OF FATE (Bio)/Oct 23, 1909; p. 567
FOOLSHEAD, A PROTECTOR OF
INNOCENCE (It)/Nov 25, 1911; p. 639
FOOLSHEAD, A SPORTMAN FOR LOVE
(It)/Aug 28, 1909; p. 283
FOOLSHEAD, A VICTIM OF HIS HONESTY
(It)/Dec 3, 1910; p. 1299
FOOLSHEAD, CHIEF OF REPORTERS
(It)/Mar 19, 1910; p. 427
FOOLSHEAD, FISHERMAN
(It)/Oct 22, 1910; p. 938
FOOLSHEAD, HYPNOTIZER
(It)/Sep 23, 1911; p. 893
FOOLSHEAD, SOMNAMBULIST
(It)/Jul 1, 1911; p. 1521
FOOLSHEAD, VOLUNTEER OF THE RED
CROSS (It)/Nov 12, 1910; p. 1118
FOOLSHEAD, WAITER (It)/Jul 15,1911;p.41
FOOLSHEAD, WRANGLE FOR LOVE
(It)/May 6, 1911; p. 1020
FOOLSHEAD A MODEL GUEST
(It)/Oct 21, 1911; p. 209
FOOLSHEAD AS A LIFE INSURANCE
AGENT (It)/May 20, 1911; p. 1142/
Jun 10, 1911; p. 1319
FOOLSHEAD AS A MANIKIN
(It)/Aug 26, 1911; p. 544
FOOLSHEAD AS A POLICEMAN
(It)/Oct 8, 1910; p. 816
FOOLSHEAD AS A PORTER
(It)/Jun 18, 1910; p. 1049
FOOLSHEAD AS A TELEGRAPH ERRAND

BOY (It)/May 13, 1911; p. 1082
FOOLSHEAD AT SOIREE
(It)/Apr 1, 1911; p. 720
FOOLSHEAD AT THE BALL
(It)/Mar 12, 1910; p. 385
FOOLSHEAD AT THE CINEMATOGRAPH
(It)/Feb 25, 1911; p. 431
FOOLSHEAD BETWEEN TWO FIRES
(It)/Nov 5, 1910; p. 1060
FOOLSHEAD EMPLOYED IN A BANK
(It)/Oct 15, 1910; p. 878
FOOLSHEAD GOES TO A COCK FIGHT
(It)/Apr 15, 1911; p. 844
FOOLSHEAD HEELS (It)/Aug 5, 1911; p.296
FOOLSHEAD IN THE LION'S CAGE
(It)/Sep 10, 1910; p. 575
FOOLSHEAD IS JEALOUS
(It)/Jul 8, 1911; p. 1587
FOOLSHEAD KNOWS ALL
(It)/Nov 26, 1910; p. 1239
FOOLSHEAD KNOWS HOW TO TAKE
PRECAUTIONS (It)/Dec 24, 1910; p. 1480
FOOLSHEAD LEARNS TO SOMERSAULT
(It)/May 28, 1910;p.891
FOOLSHEAD MARRIES AGAINST HIS
WILL (It)/Jun 11, 1910; p. 999
FOOLSHEAD MORE THAN EVER
(It)/Mar 18, 1911; p. 604
FOOLSHEAD PREACHES TEMPERANCE
(It)/Feb 26, 1910; p.300
FOOLSHEAD RECEIVES
(It)/Feb 26, 1910; p. 300
FOOLSHEAD SHOOTING
(It)/Mar 25, 1911; p. 658
FOOLSHEAD WISHES TO BREAK WITH
HIS SWEETHEART (It)/Nov 4, 1911; p.381
FOOLSHEAD WISHES TO MARRY THE
GOVERNOR'S DAUGHTER
(It)/Apr 16, 1910; p. 599
FOOLSHEAD'S CHRISTMAS
(It)/Dec 30, 1911; p. 1074
FOOLSHEAD'S HOLIDAYS
(It)/Nov 11, 1911; p. 472
FOOLSHEAD'S PRESENTS
(It)/Mar 11, 1911; p. 543
FOOT JUGGLER, THE
(Pa)/Feb 26, 1910; p. 299
FOOT OF ROMANCE, A
(SA)/Jan 24, 1914; p. 412
FOOTBALL DAYS AT CORNELL (SA)/
Dec 7, 1912; p. 968/Dec 21, 1912; p. 1183
FOOTBALL FIEND, THE (Sel)/Dec 5, 1908;
p. 462/Dec 12, 1908; p. 448
FOOTBALL GAME
(Com)/Dec 23, 1911; p. 990
FOOTBALL HERO, A
(SA)/Dec 16, 1911; p. 903
FOOTBALL WARRIOR, A

(Ed)/Oct 30, 1908; p. 344

FOOTHILL PROBLEM, A
(Bio)/Apr 10, 1915; p. 235

FOOTLIGHTS OR THE FARM
(Ed)/Oct 8, 1910; p. 814

FOOTPATH TO HAPPINESS, THE
(Ne)/Feb 8, 1913; p. 574

FOOTPRINT CLUE, THE
(Ka)/Dec 20, 1913; p. 1412

FOOTPRINTS (Sel)/Aug 8, 1914; p. 836

FOOTPRINTS OF MOZART
(Am)/May 23, 1914; p. 1118

FOOZLE AT THE TEE PARTY, A
(Phu)/Dec 18, 1915; p. 2204

FOR A KISS TO NINI
(It)/Dec 20, 1913; p. 1414

FOR A THOUSAND DOLLARS
(Pre)/Apr 3, 1915; p. 65

FOR A WESTERN GIRL
(Bi)/Oct 1, 1910; p. 749

FOR A WIDOW'S LOVE
(Lu)/Dec 19, 1914; p. 1679

FOR A WIFE'S HONOR
(Bio)/Aug 29, 1908; p. 160

FOR A WOMAN'S HONOR
(Ka)/Nov 26, 1910; p. 1236

FOR A WOMAN'S SAKE
(Mi)/Sep 14, 1907; p. 442

FOR ANOTHER'S CRIME
(Re)/Dec 20, 1913; p. 1414
(Vi)/Feb 20, 1915; p. 1140

FOR ANOTHER'S SIN
(Th)/May 3, 1913; p. 489

FOR AULD LANG SYNE
(Bio)/Mar 21, 1914; p. 1525

FOR BETTER - BUT WORSE
(Key)/Jun 5, 1915; p. 1605

FOR BETTER OR WORSE
(Rev)/Jan 28, 1911; p. 196
(Ec)/Mar 29, 1913; p. 1337

FOR CASH (Vic)/May 8, 1915; p. 901

FOR HER (Ed)/Jan 11, 1913; p. 159

FOR HER BOY'S SAKE
(Th)/Apr 5, 1913; p. 50

FOR HER BROTHER'S SAKE
(Imp)/May 27, 1911; p. 1202
(Vi)/Jun 17, 1911; p. 1387
(Ka)/Nov 11,1911; p.469/Aug 7,1915; p.996
(Lu)/Oct 18, 1913; p. 264
(KB)/Jan 31, 1914; p. 545

FOR HER CHILD (Th)/Jul 4, 1914; p. 66

FOR HER COUNTRY'S SAKE
(Vi)/May 15, 1909; p. 635
(Sel)/Oct 22, 1910; p. 934

FOR HER FATHER'S HONOR
(Bi)/Mar 5, 1910; p. 340

FOR HER FATHER'S SINS (Maj)/Oct 31,
1914; p. 642/Nov 7, 1914; p. 794

FOR HER FRIEND (Bio)/Jun 19,1915; p.1939

FOR HER HAPPINESS
(Bio)/Jun 5, 1915; p. 1604

FOR HER LORD (CGP)/Sep 28,1912; p.1277

FOR HER PEOPLE (Pa)/Dec 26,1914; p.1840
(Pa)/Feb 6, 1915; p. 834

FOR HER SAKE (Vi)/Oct 23,1909; pp 568-69
(Th)/Feb 25, 1911; p. 432
(GN)/Mar 23, 1912; p. 1063
(Ne)/Apr 26, 1913; p. 382

FOR HER SIN (Ch)/Jul 1, 1911; p. 1523

FOR HER SISTER'S SAKE
(Ka)/Aug 23, 1913; p. 844

FOR HER SON'S SAKE
(Cen)/Jul 16, 1910; p. 144

FOR HE'S A JOLLY GOOD FELLOW
(Vi)/Mar 14, 1908; p. 219/Dec 12, 1908;
p. 478/Jan 9, 1909; p. 36
(SA)/Sep 2, 1911; p. 626

FOR HIGH STAKES
(Ka)/Aug 21, 1915; p. 1317

FOR HIS BROTHER'S CRIME
(Cin)/Oct 11, 1913; p. 156
(WF)/Nov 7, 1914; p. 789

FOR HIS CHILD (Ch)/Aug 24, 1912; p. 772

FOR HIS CHILD'S SAKE
(Lu)/Apr 19, 1913; p. 281

FOR HIS FATHER'S LIFE
(Ec)/Sep 19, 1914; p. 1645

FOR HIS LOVED ONE
(Maj)/Sep 20, 1913; p. 1285

FOR HIS MASTER (Re)/Feb 21, 1914; p. 948

FOR HIS MOTHER (Ed)/Jul 31, 1915; p. 816

FOR HIS MOTHER'S SAKE
(Pa)/May 11, 1912; p. 528

FOR HIS PAL (Re)/Sep 11, 1915; p. 1833

FOR HIS PAL'S SAKE
(Sol)/Dec 30, 1911; p. 1071

FOR HIS SAKE (Vi)/Apr 22, 1911; p. 900
(Re)/Oct 7, 1911; p. 43

FOR HIS SISTER'S HONOR
(Bi)/Mar 26, 1910; p. 468

FOR HIS SISTER'S SAKE (Lu)/Oct 24,
1908; pp 318, 326/Oct 30, 1908; p. 338

FOR HIS SON (Bio)/Feb 3, 1912; p. 392

FOR HIS SUPERIOR'S HONOR
(Lae)/Jul 17, 1915; p. 487

FOR HIS WIFE'S SAKE
(NA)/Sep 25, 1915; p. 2178

FOR HOME AND HONOR
(Ch)/Mar 30, 1912; p. 1166

FOR HONOR'S SAKE
(Lux)/May 22, 1909; p. 676

FOR I HAVE FAILED
(Ne)/Dec 26, 1914; p. 1841

FOR IRELAND'S SAKE
(GG)/Jan 31, 1914; p. 526

FOR KATE'S HEALTH (Pa)/May 2, 1908;

FOR THE LOVE OF THE FLAG
(Sol)/Oct 12, 1912; p. 143
FOR THE MAN SHE LOVED
(Ec)/Jul 19, 1913; p. 321
(Th)/Jul 19, 1913; p. 321
(Ed)/Apr 3, 1915; p. 64
FOR THE MASTERY OF THE WORLD
(Ec)/Nov 14, 1914; p. 933
FOR THE MIKADO (Th)/Oct 26,1912; p.343
FOR THE PAPOOSE
(Pa)/May 11, 1912; p. 527
FOR THE PEOPLE
(Vic)/Nov 21, 1914; p. 1078
FOR THE QUEEN (Ed)/Sep 30, 1911; p. 970
FOR THE QUEEN'S HONOR
(Imp)/Jul 22, 1911; p. 126
(Amb)/Jan 17, 1914; p. 275
FOR THE SAKE OF A CHILD
(GN)/Aug 13, 1910; p. 351
FOR THE SAKE OF A CROWN
(Pa)/Jun 27, 1908; p. 546
FOR THE SAKE OF KATE
(Re)/Jun 20, 1914; p. 1689
FOR THE SAKE OF THE PAPOOSE
(Pa)/Aug 10, 1912; p. 546
FOR THE SAKE OF THE TRIBE
(Pa)/Sep 16, 1911; p. 789
FOR THE SAKE OF THE UNIFORM (Pa)/
Oct 17, 1908; p. 305/Nov 7, 1908;
p. 358/Nov 28, 1908; p.422
FOR THE SECRET SERVICE
(Rex)/Sep 5, 1914; p. 1373
FOR THE SINS OF ANOTHER
(Vic)/Sep 27, 1913; p. 1394
FOR THE SON OF THE HOUSE
(Bio)/Oct 4, 1913; p. 47
FOR THE SQUAW (Pa)/Jul 8, 1911; p. 1584
FOR THE SUNDAY EDITION
(Imp)/Sep 17, 1910; p. 632
FOR THE TRIBE (Po)/Nov 18, 1911; p. 552
FOR THEIR MOTHER
(Ec)/May 13, 1911; p. 1083
FOR THOSE UNBORN
(Maj)/Sep 19, 1914; p. 1646
FOR $200 (Me)/Oct 14, 1911;p.130
FOR TWO PINS (Gau)/Jun 7, 1913; p. 1032
(Lu)/Jun 13, 1914; p. 1540
FOR VALOUR (Ed)/Jul 27, 1912; p. 343
FOR WASHINGTON (Th)/Mar 4,1911; p.486
FOR YOUR HATS, LADIES
(Ec)/Oct 7, 1911; p. 43
FORAGING (Vi)/Sep 30, 1911;p.970
FORAGING ON THE ENEMY
(Ch)/Jul 27, 1912; p. 344
FORBIDDEN ADVENTURE, THE (Mut)/
Nov 20, 1915; p.1509/Nov 27, 1915; p.1665
FORBIDDEN CIGARETTES
(Gau)/Mar 18, 1911; p. 602

FORBIDDEN FRUIT
(Iv)/Dec 25, 1915; pp 2380, 2391
FORBIDDEN NOVEL, THE
(Gau)/Aug 13, 1910; p. 350
FORBIDDEN ROOM, THE
(101)/Jun 27, 1914; p. 1830
FORBIDDEN TRAIL, THE
(GK)/Aug 22, 1914; p 1106
FORBIDDEN WAY, THE
(SA)/Jul 19, 1913; p. 320
FORCE OF EXAMPLE, THE
(Rex)/Jun 5, 1915; p. 1606
FORCED BRAVERY (Key)/Mar 1, 1913; p. 890
FORCED INTO MARRIAGE
(Pa)/Dec 18, 1909; p. 880
FORCED LOAN, THE
(TP)/Dec 18, 1909; p. 882
FORCED TO BE STYLISH
(Pr)/May 16, 1914; p. 969
FORCES OF EVIL, THE
(LP)/Jul 18, 1914; p. 437
FORCING DAD'S CONSENT
(Vi)/Jan 16, 1915; p. 368
FORCING THE ISSUE
(Ne)/Mar 29, 1913; pp 1337-38
FORECAST, THE (Am)/Sep 18, 1915; p.1996
FORECASTLE TOM (Lu)/Apr 17, 1909; p. 477
FORECLOSURE, THE
(Am)/Sep 28, 1912; p. 1277
FOREIGN INVASION, A
(Imp)/Jul 27, 1912; p. 345
FOREIGN SPIES, THE
(Co)/Aug 29, 1914; p. 1215
FOREIGN SPY, THE
(Ne)/Jun 8, 1912; p. 944
(Imp)/Nov 9, 1912; p. 554
(Am)/Jul 12, 1913; p. 206
FOREMAN, THE (Sel)/Oct 29, 1910; p. 996
FOREMAN OF BAR Z RANCH, THE
(Sel)/Aug 7, 1915; p. 996
FOREMAN OF THE JURY, THE
(Key)/May 17, 1913; p. 706
FOREMAN'S BRIDE
(Bi)/May 27, 1911; p. 1201
FOREMAN'S CHOICE, THE
(Sel)/Oct 30, 1915; p. 791
FOREMAN'S COURAGE, THE
(Bi)/Dec 23, 1911; p. 991
FOREMAN'S COUSIN, THE
(SA)/Jul 6, 1912; p. 43
FOREMAN'S MINE, THE
(Bi)/Jul 8, 1911; p. 1586
FOREMAN'S TREACHERY, THE
(Ed)/Nov 1, 1913; p. 497
FOREST FIRE, A
(Ed)/Dec 21, 1912; p. 1183
FOREST RANGER, THE
(SA)/Jul 9, 1910; p. 84

FREAK TEMPERANCE WAVE, A
(Jo)/Jan 31, 1914; p. 545
FREAKS (Jo)/Jul 17, 1915; p. 487
FRECKLES (Dom)/Apr 4, 1914; p. 59
FRED GOES IN FOR HORSES
(Ap)/Dec 27, 1913; p. 1545
FRED SATO AND HIS DOG
(Pa)/Apr 15, 1911; p. 843
FREDDIE'S COURTSHIP
(Po)/Jan 7, 1911; p. 35
FREDDIE'S LITTLE LOVE AFFAIR
(WBE)/May 2, 1908; p. 405
FREDDIE'S SHOES (Po)/Feb 18, 1911; p.371
FREDDY, THE FAKE FISHERMAN
(Fal)/Oct 30a, 1915; p. 968
FREDERICK HOLMES' WARD
(Bio)/Aug 21, 1915; p. 1316
FREDERICK THE GREAT
(Ed)/May 16, 1914; p. 969
FRED'S TRAINED NURSE
(Ap)/Oct 11, 1913; p. 158
FRED'S WATERLOO
(Ap)/Nov 29, 1913; p. 1009
FREE ADMISSION (KO)/Apr 11, 1908; p.327
FREE CHAMPAGNE
(Gau)/May 22, 1909; p. 676
FREE LANCE, THE (UE)/Jul 22, 1911; p.125
FREEBOOTERS, THE
(Sel)/Sep 25, 1909; p. 415
FREED FROM SUSPICION
(Ka)/Aug 24, 1912; p. 771
FREEDOM FOR ALL
(Pa)/Aug 22, 1908; p. 144
FREEZING AUNTY (Ed)/Jan 20, 1912; p.203
FREIGHT CAR HONEYMOON, A
(Th)/Jun 12, 1915; p. 1777
FREIGHT TRAIN DRAMA, A
(Sel)/Dec 21, 1912; p. 1183
FRENCH ALPINE MANEUVERS
(Gau)/Feb 1, 1913; p. 466
FRENCH ARMY IN ACTION, THE
(UE)/Aug 10, 1912; p. 545
FRENCH ARMY MANEUVERS, THE
(CGP)/Feb 22, 1913; p. 780
FRENCH ARTILLERY
(CGP)/Mar 22, 1913; p. 1220
FRENCH BATTLESHIP "JUSTICE," THE
(UE)/Sep 11, 1909; p. 347
FRENCH DAIRY FARM
(KO)/Jul 11, 1908; p. 34
FRENCH FLEET MANEUVERS
(Gau)/Feb 8, 1913; p. 574
FRENCH GUARD'S BRIDE, A
(Pa)/Apr 25, 1908; p. 377
FRENCH GUINEA (Pa)/Sep 4, 1915; p. 1645
FRENCH SPY, THE
(Sel)/Mar 14, 1908; pp 218-19
FRENCH VILLAGE IN SENEGAL, WEST

AFRICA, A (Pa)/Jul 18, 1914; p. 432
FRENCHY (Maj)/Sep 12, 1914; pp 1496,1523
FRENZIED FINANCE
(Sel)/Sep 14, 1912; p. 1074
(Pa)/Nov 9, 1912; p. 553
FRENZY OF FIRE WATER, THE
(Ka)/Sep 7, 1912; p. 975
FRESH AGENT, THE
(Lu)/May 8, 1915; p. 899
FRESH AIR CURE, THE
(Lu)/Dec 26, 1914; p. 1840
FRESH-AIR FIEND, THE
(Vi)/Apr 4, 1908; p. 300
FRESH AIR ROMANCE, A
(Ed)/Oct 26, 1912; p. 342
FRESH FRESHMAN, THE
(Ap)/Jan 10, 1914; p. 174
FRESH KID, THE (Pa)/Oct 2, 1909; p. 451
FRESH START, A (Th)/Sep 17, 1910; p. 632
FRESHET, THE (Vi)/Dec 9, 1911; p. 817
FRESHWATER AQUARIUM
(Kin)/Nov 23, 1912; p. 769
FRICOT DRINKS A BOTTLE OF HORSE
EMBROCATION (Amb)/Aug 27,1910;p.464
FRICOT GETS IN A LIBERTINE MOOD
(Amb)/May 21, 1910; p. 835
FRICOT HAS LOST HIS COLLAR
BUTTON (Amb)/Sep 17, 1910; p. 632
FRICOT IN COLLEGE
(Amb)/Apr 23, 1910; p. 642
FRICOT IS LEARNING A HANDICRAFT
(Amb)/May 7, 1910; p. 739
FRICOT'S ITCHING POWDER
(Amb)/Sep 3, 1910; p. 521
FRIDAY, THE 13th
(Sel)/Mar 28, 1908; pp 270-71
(Ed)/Aug 26, 1911; p. 541
FRIDAY, THE THIRTEENTH
(Pr)/Nov 22, 1913; p. 869
FRIDOLIN (Gau)/Nov 11, 1911; p. 470
FRIEND, THE (Dom)/Nov 14, 1914; p. 933
FRIEND IN NEED, A
(Sel)/Feb 7, 1914; p. 676
(Ec)/Nov 28, 1914; p. 1233
(Be)/Oct 2, 1915; p. 79
FRIEND IN NEED IS A FRIEND INDEED,
A (Vi)/Jun 26, 1909; p. 873
FRIEND IN THE ENEMY'S CAMP, A
(Vi)/Mar 27, 1909; p. 367
FRIEND INDEED, A (Ne)/Dec 7, 1912; p.978
FRIEND JOHN (Lu)/Apr 5, 1913; p. 47
FRIEND OF THE BIRDS, A
(Pa)/Nov 28, 1914; p. 1233
FRIEND OF THE DISTRICT ATTORNEY,
A (Bio)/Apr 4, 1914; p. 57
FRIEND OF THE FAMILY, A
(Gau)/Oct 7, 1911; p. 40
(Rex)/Apr 19, 1913; p. 282

FRIEND OF THE FAMILY, THE
(Bio)/Jul 24, 1909; p. 125
FRIEND TO CHILDREN, A
(GN)/Feb 10, 1912; p. 483
FRIEND WILSON'S DAUGHTER
(Ed)/Nov 13, 1915; p. 1312
FRIENDLESS INDIAN, THE
(Pa)/Aug 2, 1913; p. 536
FRIENDLY MARRIAGE, A
(Vi)/Sep 23, 1911; p. 890
FRIENDLY NEIGHBORS
(Po)/Jun 14, 1913; p. 1138
FRIENDS (Ka)/Jun 11, 1910;p.995
(Bio)/Oct 5, 1912; p. 41
FRIENDS OF THE SEA, THE
(Re)/Nov 27, 1915; p. 1665
FRIENDSHIP OF LAMOND, THE
(Lu)/Jan 30, 1915; p. 672
FRIGHT, THE (Pa)/Sep 30, 1911; p. 972
FRIGHTENED BY BURGLARS
(KO)/Jul 11, 1908; p. 36
FRIGHTFUL BLUNDER, A
(Bio)/May 3, 1913; p. 488
FRINGE OF SIN, THE
(Imp)/Mar 15, 1913; p. 1105
FRINGE ON THE GLOVE, THE
(Ka)/May 30, 1914; p. 1261
FRITZ AND OSCAR OUT OF LUCK
(GN)/Mar 22, 1913; p. 1222
FRIVOLOUS HEART, A
(Ec)/Oct 5, 1912; p. 42
FROCK COAT, THE (Gau)/Sep 4,1909;p.316
FROG, THE (Pa)/Mar 14, 1908; p. 217
(CGP)/Jul 13, 1912; p. 148
FROG AND TOAD CELEBRITIES
(Po)/Sep 11, 1915; p. 1834
FROLIC OF THE MARIONETTES, THE
(Po)/Dec 5, 1915; p. 1854
FROLIC OF YOUTH, THE
(KO)/Jan 30, 1909; p. 120
FROLICSOME FLORRIE
(Gau)/Jul 29, 1911; p. 210
FROLICSOME POWDERS
(KO)/May 2, 1908; p. 401
FROM A LIFE OF CRIME
(Ed)/Mar 13, 1915; p. 1607
FROM BARREL TO BARREL
Nov 28, 1908; p. 422
FROM BEANERY TO BILLIONS
(Lko)/Dec 18, 1915; p. 2204
FROM BEYOND SEAS
(UE)/Mar 12, 1910; p. 384
FROM BORDEAUX TO PANILLAC
(Gau)/Sep 30, 1911; p. 972
FROM CAIRO TO KHARTOUM
(KO)/Aug 10, 1907; p.362
FROM CHAMPION TO TRAMP
(Lu)/Jul 3, 1915; p. 65

FROM DAWN TILL DARK
(Bi)/Nov 1, 1913; p. 498
FROM DEATH - LIFE
(Imp)/Mar 15, 1913; p. 1105
FROM DEATH TO LIFE
(Rex)/Jun 24, 1911; p. 1455
FROM DURBAN TO ZULULAND
(Ed)/Dec 6, 1913; p. 1151
FROM FATHER TO SON
(Rex)/Jan 31, 1914; p. 546
FROM FIREMAN TO ENGINEER
(Lu)/Jul 13, 1912; p. 147
FROM FOREST TO MILLS
(Sel)/Sep 7, 1912; p. 975
FROM GUTTER TO FOOTLIGHTS
(Ape)/Feb 14, 1914; p. 788
FROM GYPSY HANDS
(Ki)/Jul 23, 1910; p. 193
FROM HEADQUARTERS
(Vi)/Feb 20, 1915; p. 1150
FROM IGNORANCE TO LIGHT
(Lu)/Jul 5, 1913; p. 48
FROM ITALY'S SHORES
(Lae)/May 22, 1915; p. 1262
FROM JERUSALEM TO THE DEAD SEA
(Ka)/Sep 14, 1912; p. 1075
FROM LOURDES TO GARVARNIE
(Pa)/Sep 23, 1911; p. 891
FROM MILLIONAIRE TO PORTER
(LeL)/Oct 2, 1909; p. 451
FROM MINE TO MINT
(Po)/Nov 8, 1913; p. 613
FROM OESTERSUND TO STORLEIN,
SWEDEN (GN)/Aug 26, 1911; p. 524/
Dec 30, 1911; p. 1073
FROM OUT OF THE BIG SNOWS
(Vi)/Oct 9, 1915; p. 253
FROM OUT OF THE DEPTHS
(Kio)/Aug 9, 1913; p. 638
FROM OUT THE DREGS
(KB)/Jun 13, 1914; p. 1542
FROM OUT THE STORM
(Bro)/Oct 25, 1913; p. 381
FROM OXFORD TO WINDSOR, ENG.
(Pa)/May 15, 1915; p. 1073
FROM PATCHES TO PLENTY
(Key)/Mar 20, 1915; p. 1765
FROM PEN TO PICK (Pa)/Mar 1,1913;p.888
FROM PERIL TO PERIL
(Ka)/Oct 31, 1914; p. 640
FROM PITY TO LOVE
(Gau)/Jan 6, 1912; p. 40
FROM SHADOW TO SUNSHINE
(Vi)/Apr 16, 1910; p. 598
FROM SION TO CHAMPERY
(UE)/Aug 24, 1912; p. 770
FROM TENT TO MANSION
(Cin)/Apr 6, 1912; p. 40

FUNERAL THAT FLASHED IN THE PAN,
A (Ed)/Apr 13, 1912; p. 137

FUNNICUS AND HIS DOG
(GN)/Nov 23, 1912; p. 769

FUNNICUS' HUNTING EXPLOITS
(Ec)/Dec 28, 1912; p. 1292

FUNNICUS MARRIES A HUNCHBACK
(Ec)/Jan 25, 1913; p. 364

FUNNY MR. DINGLE, THE
(Vic)/Oct 17, 1914; p. 337

FUNNY SIDE OF JEALOUSY, THE
(U)/Mar 20, 1915; p. 1766

FUNNY STORY, A (Vi)/May 28, 1910; p.889

FUR AND FEATHERS
(Ne)/Jul 27, 1912; p. 344

FUR COAT, THE (Imp)/Nov 5, 1910; p. 1060

FURNACE FIRE, THE
(Vi)/Nov 9, 1912; p. 553

FURNACE MAN, THE
(Lu)/Feb 20, 1915; p. 1139

FURNISHED ROOMS TO LET
(Ed)/Aug 28, 1909; p. 282

FURS, THE (Bio)/May 25, 1912; p. 729

FURTHER ADVENTURES OF SAMMY
ORPHEUS (Sel)/Jan 23, 1915; p. 515

FURTHER ADVENTURES OF THE GIRL
SPY (Ka)/Apr 16, 1910; p. 598

FURY OF A WOMAN SCORNED, THE
(UE)/Mar 25, 1911; p. 656

FUSE OF DEATH, THE
(Ka)/Sep 26, 1914; p. 1776

FUSS AND FEATHERS
(Ed)/May 15, 1909; p. 637

FUTILITY OF REVENGE, THE
(Imp)/Oct 17, 1914; p. 338

GAAS GRUND (Lux)/Nov 25, 1911; p. 638

GAFFNEY'S GLADIATOR
(Maj)/Jul 12, 1913; p. 206

GALA DAY PARADE, YOKOHAMA
(Vi)/May 3, 1913; p. 487

GALLANT CAPT. d'ARMAYNAC
(Cin)/Apr 29, 1911; p. 961

GALLANT KNIGHT, A
(Lu)/Jun 6, 1908; p. 497

GALLANTRY OF JIMMY ROGERS, THE
(SA)/Jan 23, 1915; p. 515

GALLEGHER (Ed)/May 7, 1910; p. 736

GALLEY SLAVE, THE
(Vi)/Sep 18, 1909; p. 377
(Fox)/Dec 11, 1915; pp 2024, 2032

GALLEY SLAVE'S ROMANCE, THE
(Rex)/Nov 23, 1912; p. 768

GALLOP OF DEATH, THE
(Ec)/Feb 1, 1913; p. 466

GALLOPER, THE (GR)/Sep 4, 1915; p. 1663

GALLOPING ROMEO, THE
(Sel)/Aug 23, 1913; p. 843

GALLOWS OF THE GODS, THE
(FRA)/Nov 8, 1913; p. 613

GALVANIC FLUID (Vi)/Feb 8,1908;pp 103-4

GAMBIER'S ADVOCATE
(FP)/Jul 10, 1915; p. 321

GAMBLE FOR A WOMAN, A
(Pa)/Feb 8, 1908; p. 104

GAMBLE WITH DEATH, A
(Bio)/Jul 12, 1913; p. 205

GAMBLE WITH LOVE, A
(Po)/Mar 25, 1911; p. 658

GAMBLER, THE (Vi)/May 23, 1908; p. 465
(Pa)/Nov 6,1909;pp 643-44
(Lux)/Jun 22, 1912; p.1127
(Ne)/Jun 13, 1914; p. 1543

GAMBLER AND THE DEVIL, THE (Vi)/
Oct 3, 1908; p. 267/Oct 10, 1908; p. 279

GAMBLER OF THE WEST, A
(SA)/Jan 14, 1911; pp 88, 90

GAMBLER OF THE WEST, THE
(Bio)/Nov 27, 1915; p. 1664

GAMBLERS, THE (Vi)/Jul 6, 1912; p. 43

GAMBLER'S CHANCE, THE
(Lu)/Jun 3, 1911; p. 1259

GAMBLER'S CHARM, A
(Lu)/Nov 26, 1910; p. 1236

GAMBLER'S DAUGHTER, THE
(Re)/Feb 24, 1912; p. 691

GAMBLER'S DREAM, THE
(Pa)/Oct 28, 1911; p. 291

GAMBLER'S DOOM, THE
(Gau)/Feb 26, 1910; p. 299

GAMBLER'S END, THE
(Pa)/Nov 26, 1910; p. 1238

GAMBLER'S FATE, THE (Pa)/Sep 5, 1908;
p. 182/Jan 9, 1909; p. 36

GAMBLER'S HEART, THE
(Bi)/Jan 20, 1912; p. 203
(Me)/Mar 29, 1913; p. 1335

GAMBLER'S HONOR, A
(Bio)/Jul 26, 1913; p. 428

GAMBLER'S HONOR, THE
(Pa)/Jun 12, 1909; p. 795

GAMBLER'S I.O.U., THE
(Bio)/May 1, 1915; p. 727

GAMBLER'S INFLUENCE, THE
(Lu)/Oct 28, 1911; p. 290

GAMBLER'S LAST TRICK, A
(Bi)/Feb 1, 1913; p. 466

GAMBLER'S PAL, THE
(Bro)/Sep 6, 1913; p. 1069

GAMBLER'S PENALTY, THE
(GN)/Mar 14, 1914; p. 1386

GAMBLER'S REFORMATION, THE
(Pa)/Jul 6, 1912; p. 42
(Ka)/Sep 19, 1914; p. 1644

GAMBLER'S REVENGE, THE
(Amb)/Jan 10, 1914; p. 180

GAMBLER'S VOW, THE
(RR)/May 15, 1909; p. 636
GAMBLER'S WAY, A
(SA)/Feb 21, 1914; p. 946
GAMBLER'S WIFE, THE
(WBE)/May 9, 1908; p. 425
(Pa)/Sep 17, 1910; pp 631-32
(UE)/Mar 2, 1912; p. 780
GAMBLING DEMON, THE
(KO)/Apr 11, 1908; p. 328
GAMBLING INSIDE AND OUT
May 29, 1915; p. 1441
GAMBLING PASSION
(UE)/Oct 16, 1909; p. 528
GAMBLING RUBE, A
(Key)/Jun 27, 1914; p. 1829
GAMBLING WITH DEATH
(Vi)/Dec 25, 1909; p. 920
GAME, THE (SA)/Nov 20, 1909; p. 722
GAME FOR LIFE, A
(De)/Oct 1, 1910; p. 749
GAME FOR TWO, A
(Imp)/Jul 16, 1910; p. 144
(Maj)/Feb 10, 1912; p. 483
GAME OF BLUFF, A
(Ne)/May 18, 1912; p. 630
GAME OF BRIDGE, THE
(Com)/Dec 30, 1911; p. 1073
GAME OF CARDS, A
(Vi)/Dec 13, 1913; p. 1279
GAME OF CHESS, A
(Lu)/Mar 6, 1909; p. 271
(Pa)/Oct 16, 1909; p. 530
(Maj)/Aug 24, 1912; p. 773
GAME OF DECEPTION, A
(Lu)/Jun 17, 1911; p. 1387
GAME OF FREEZEOUT, A
(Bio)/Aug 29, 1914; p. 1241
GAME OF HEARTS, A
(Po)/Jul 30, 1910; p. 246
(Imp)/Oct 22, 1910; p. 939
GAME OF LIFE, THE
(Vi)/Feb 13, 1915; p. 985
GAME OF LOVE, A
(Lko)/Sep 11, 1915; p. 1834
GAME OF NINEPINS, A
(LeL)/Aug 7, 1909; p. 195
GAME OF PALLONE, THE
(It)/Apr 24, 1909; p. 516
GAME OF POKER, A
(Key)/Apr 19, 1913; p. 282
GAME OF POLITICS, THE
(Lu)/Apr 11, 1914; p. 213
GAME OF POOL, A
(Key)/Aug 16, 1913; p. 745
GAME OF THRILLS, A
(Re)/Apr 3, 1915; p. 64
GAME OF WITS, A

(Ec)/Dec 19, 1914; p. 1681
GAME OLD KNIGHT, A
(TK)/Oct 30, 1915; p. 793
GAME THAT FAILED, THE
(Cry)/Oct 18, 1913; p. 265
GAME WITH FAME, THE
(Ka)/Sep 10, 1910; p. 575
GAMEKEEPER'S BRIDE
Jan 16, 1909; p. 70
GAMEKEEPER'S DAUGHTER, THE
(Dom)/Oct 3, 1914; p. 65
GAMEKEEPER'S DOG, THE
(KO)/Jan 18, 1908; p. 46
Feb 27, 1909; p. 237
GAMEKEEPER'S SON, THE
(Pa)/Aug 7, 1909; p. 196
GANG FIGHTER, THE
(Re)/Jan 20, 1912; pp 204-5
GANG LEADER'S REFORM, THE
(Ya)/Sep 3, 1910; p. 521
GANG'S NEW MEMBER, THE
(Bio)/Feb 6, 1915; p. 827
GANGSTER, THE (Lu)/Sep 13, 1913; p. 1176
GANGSTERS, THE (Key)/May 31, 1913; p.922
GANGSTERS AND THE GIRL, THE
(KB)/Aug 15, 1914; p. 962
GANGSTERS OF NEW YORK, THE
(Re)/Feb 21, 1914; p. 932
GANGSTERS OF THE HILLS
(Ka)/Sep 18, 1915; p. 1996
GAP OF DEATH, THE
(LP)/Jun 6, 1914; p. 1392
GAR el HAMA (GN)/Nov 2, 1912; p. 436
GARBAGE OF PARIS, THE
(Pa)/Oct 16, 1909; p. 530
GARDEN OF FATE, THE (Imp)/Oct 8, 1910;
p. 816/Oct 29, 1910; p. 998
GARDEN OF LIES, THE
(Uni)/Jul 3, 1915; p. 76
GARDEN OF THE GODS
(Sol)/Mar 23, 1912; p. 1063
(Maj)/Jun 21, 1913; p. 1253
GARDEN PARTY IN CALIFORNIA, A
(Am)/Jul 12, 1913; p. 206
GARDENER'S LADDER, THE
(Ed)/Jan 21, 1911; p. 144
GARRISON JOKE, A
(Maj)/Oct 12, 1912; p. 143
GASOLINE ENGAGEMENT, A
(Imp)/Jul 22, 1911; p. 127
GASOLINE FOR A TONIC
(Pa)/Feb 4, 1911; p. 244
GASOLINE GUS (Ko)/Jun 5, 1915; p. 1605
GATE SHE LEFT OPEN, THE
(Pa)/Apr 12, 1913; pp 163-64
GATES OF JEALOUSY, THE
(Pa)/Dec 12, 1914; p. 1525
GATEWAY OF REGRET, THE

(Imp)/Jul 25, 1914; p. 573
GATEWAY TO AMERICA, THE
(Ch)/Dec 7, 1912; p. 978
GATHERING INDIAN FIGS
(KO)/May 9, 1908; p. 423
GAUL'S HONOR, THE
(UE)/Jun 17, 1911; p. 1387
GAUMONT WEEKLY, THE (Gau)
No.19/Jul 27, 1912; p. 344
No.20/Aug 3, 1912; p. 447
No.22/Aug 24, 1912; p. 773
No.30/Oct 19, 1912; p. 244
No.31/Oct 26, 1912; p. 344
No.32/Nov 2, 1912; p. 450
No.33/Nov 9, 1912; p. 554
No.34/Nov 9, 1912; p. 555
No.36/Nov 30, 1912; p. 877
No.39/Dec 21, 1912; p. 1185
No.41/Dec 28, 1912; p. 1294
No.42/Jan 4, 1913; p. 52
GAUNTLETS OF WASHINGTON, THE
(Ed)/Feb 22,1913; p.785/Mar 29,1913;p.1336
GAY BACHELOR, A (Sol)/Sep 9, 1911; p. 717
GAY DECEIVERS, THE
(Cin)/Jul 20, 1912; p. 244
GAY OLD BOY, THE (Lu)/Feb 1, 1908; p. 83
GAY OLD TIME IN ATLANTIC CITY, A
(Lu)/Aug 5, 1911; p. 292
GAY TIME IN JACKSONVILLE, FLA., A
(Lu)/May 4, 1912; p. 425
GAY TIME IN QUEBEC, A
(Lu)/Oct 5, 1912; p. 41
GAY TIME IN WASHINGTON, A
(Lu)/Sep 23, 1911; p. 890
GAY VAGABONDS, THE
(CR)/Jan 18, 1908; pp 46-47
GEE, I'M LATE (Pa)/Jun 4, 1910; p. 941
GEE! MY PANTS (Pa)/Sep 21, 1912; p. 1175
GEE WHIZ (SA)/Nov 25, 1911; p.636
GEISHA, THE (KB)/Apr 18, 1914; p. 362
GEISHA GIRLS OF JAPAN, THE
(Sel)/Nov 2, 1912; p. 450
GEISHA WHO SAVED JAPAN, THE
(Ka)/Dec 18, 1909; pp 880-81
GEISHA'S LOVE STORY, THE
(CGP)/Jul 27, 1912; p. 343
GEMS AND GERMS (Lko)/Jan 9,1915; p.222
GEMS OF FOSCARINA, THE
(Tru)/Feb 6, 1915; p. 836
GEN. MARION, THE SWAMP FOX
(Ch)/May 27, 1911; p. 1201
GEN. MEADE'S FIGHTING DAYS
(Ch)/May 6, 1911; p. 1020
GENDARME HAS A KEEN EYE
(Pa)/Mar 21, 1908; pp 243-44
GENDARME'S HONOR
(Pa)/May 9, 1908; p. 424
GENDARME'S HORSES

(Gau)/Feb 27, 1909; p. 236
GENDARME'S TRIBULATIONS, A
(KO)/Jul 11, 1908; p. 34
GENERAL BUNKO'S VICTORY
(Ka)/Dec 27, 1913; p. 1543
GENERAL SCOTT'S PROTEGE
(Pa)/May 17, 1913; p. 703
GENERAL STRIKE, A
(Gau)/Aug 26, 1911; p. 541
GENERAL'S BIRTHDAY PRESENT, THE
(Pa)/Nov 20, 1909; pp 720-21
GENERAL'S DAUGHTER, THE
(Vi)/Sep 16, 1911; p. 789
GENERALS OF THE FUTURE
(Ed)/Sep 26, 1914; p. 1776
GENEROUS COWBOYS
(Bi)/Jul 29, 1911; p. 212
GENEROUS CUSTOMERS
(Me)/Nov 19, 1910; p. 1176
GENEROUS POLICEMAN
(KO)/May 2, 1908; p. 401
GENESIS 4:9 (Rex)/Sep 20, 1913; p. 1285
GENET, THE (CGP)/Feb 8, 1913; p. 572
GENII AND THE VASE, THE
(Jo)/Dec 21, 1914; p. 1524
GENIUS OF FORT LAPAWAI, THE
(Bi)/Feb 1, 1913; p. 46
GENOA, ITALY (Cin)/May 11, 1912; p. 528
GENOA, PRINCIPAL PORT OF ITALY
(Pa)/Aug 23, 1913; p. 843
GENT FROM HONDURAS, THE
(Ka)/Jun 15, 1912; p. 1027
GENTLEMAN BURGLAR, THE
(Ed)/May 16, 1908; p. 443
(Sel)/Apr 24, 1915; p. 555
GENTLEMAN FIREMAN, THE
(It)/Jul 15, 1911; p. 40
GENTLEMAN FOR A DAY, A
(Th)/Jul 25, 1914; p. 572
GENTLEMAN FROM INDIANA, THE
(Pal)/Nov 27, 1915; pp 1665, 1679
GENTLEMAN FROM KENTUCKY, A
(Vic)/Sep 19, 1914; p. 1646
GENTLEMAN FROM MISSISSIPPI, A
(Wor)/Oct 3, 1914; p. 40
GENTLEMAN JOE (Lu)/Nov 2, 1912; p. 449
GENTLEMAN OF ART, A
(Imp)/Jan 16, 1915; p. 370
GENTLEMAN OF FASHION, A
(Vi)/Aug 23, 1913; p. 843
GENTLEMAN OF FORTUNE, A
(Ne)/Jul 20, 1912; p. 245
GENTLEMAN OF LEISURE, A
(SA)/Aug 29, 1914; p. 1241
(Las)/Mar 13, 1915; p. 1619
GENTLEMAN OF NERVE, A
(Key)/Nov 14, 1914; p. 932
GENTLEMAN OR THIEF

(Bio)/Mar 28, 1914; p. 1681
GENTLEMAN'S AGREEMENT, A
(Bal)/Nov 20, 1915; p. 1501
GEORGE AND MARGARET (KO)/Dec 26,
1908; p. 525/Jan 2, 1909; pp 17-18
GEORGE WARRINGTON'S ESCAPE
(Sel)/Dec 30, 1911; p. 1071
GEORGE WASHINGTON JONES
(Ed)/Oct 24, 1914; p. 492
**GEORGE WASHINGTON UNDER THE
AMERICAN FLAG** (Vi)/Jun 26, 1909;
p. 871/Jul 10, 1909; p. 51
**GEORGE WASHINGTON UNDER THE
BRITISH FLAG** (Vi)/Jun 26, 1909;
p. 871/Jul 3, 1909; pp 12-13
GEORGIA 'POSSUM HUNT, A
(Ed)/Feb 12, 1910; p. 215
GEORGIA WEDDING, A
(Vi)/Aug 7, 1909; p. 196
GERANIUM, THE (Vi)/Aug 5, 1911; p. 292
(Re)/Oct 5, 1912; p. 42
GERM IN THE KISS, THE
(Po)/Jan 31, 1914; p. 545
GERMAN BAND, THE (Lu)/Oct 3,1914; p.64
GERMANIA (LP)/Jul 11, 1914; p.275
GERMINAL (Pa)/Jan 24, 1914; p.416
GERONIMO'S LAST RAID (Am)/Sep 14,
1912; pp 1054-55/Sep 21, 1912; p. 1176
GERTIE (Box)/Jan 9, 1915; p. 222
GERTIE GETS THE CASH
(Ka)/Apr 25, 1914; p. 516
GERTIE'S JOY RIDE
(Lko)/Sep 4, 1915; p. 1645
GET-AWAY, THE (Lu)/May 16, 1914; p. 968
GET OUT AND GET UNDER
(Cry)/Apr 11, 1914; p. 214
(Ecl)/Aug 22, 1914; p. 1101
GET RICH QUICK (Pa)/Dec 31,1910; p.1538
(Th)/Jun 10,1911; p.1319
(Key)/Aug 2, 1913; p.538
GET RICH QUICK BILLINGTON
(Pa)/Jun 21, 1913; p. 1252
GET RICH QUICK HALL AND FORD
(SA)/Oct 28, 1911; p. 290
GETTING A HIRED GIRL (SA)/Feb 24,
1912; pp 683-84/Mar 23, 1912; p. 1062
GETTING A PATIENT
(Ed)/Nov 29, 1913; p. 1007
GETTING A START IN LIFE
(Sel)/Apr 24, 1915; p. 555
GETTING A SUIT PRESSED
(Ko)/Mar 7, 1914; p. 1237
GETTING ACQUAINTED
(Key)/Dec 19, 1914; p. 1680
GETTING ANDY'S GOAT
(Ed)/Sep 26, 1914; p. 1775
GETTING ATMOSPHERE
(Sel)/Nov 9, 1912; p. 552

GETTING DAD MARRIED
(Ec)/Mar 9, 1912; p. 868
GETTING EVEN (Go)/Sep 28, 1907; p. 473
(Bio)/Sep 25, 1909; p. 415
(Lu)/Mar 4, 1911; p. 482
(Ne)/Oct 7, 1911; p. 43
(Lu)/Mar 7, 1914; p. 1236
GETTING EVEN WITH EMILY
(SA)/Dec 23, 1911; p. 988
GETTING EVEN WITH THE LAWYER
(Pa)/Aug 6, 1910; p. 297
GETTING FATHER'S GOAT
(Ka)/Jan 16, 1915; p. 368
GETTING HIS GOAT
(Imp)/Nov 6, 1915; p. 1140
GETTING HIS MAN (Bi)/Jan 13, 1912; p. 127
GETTING HIS OWN BACK
(SA)/Apr 15, 1911; p. 842
GETTING INTO A SCRAPE
(Bio)/Jan 30, 1915; p. 671
GETTING MARRIED (Sel)/Dec 9, 1911; p. 816
(Lu)/Aug 16,1913; p.744
GETTING MARY MARRIED
(Imp)/Oct 5, 1912; p. 42
GETTING REUBEN BACK
(Cry)/Feb 7, 1914; p. 677
GETTING RICH QUICK
(Maj)/Jul 6, 1912; p. 44
GETTING RID OF A NEPHEW
(Bio)/Feb 27, 1915; p. 1287
GETTING RID OF ALGY
(Th)/May 9, 1914; p. 821
GETTING RID OF AUNT KATE
(Vi)/Oct 9, 1915; p. 252
GETTING RID OF TROUBLE
(Bio)/Sep 21, 1912; p. 1175
GETTING RID OF UNCLE
(Cen)/Jul 9, 1910; p. 86
GETTING SOLID WITH PA
(Lu)/Jul 4, 1914; p. 64
GETTING SQUARE WITH THE INVENTOR
(Gau)/Jan 29, 1910; p. 128
GETTING THE GARDENER'S GOAT
(Fal)/Aug 7, 1915; p. 997
GETTING THE GOODS ON FATHER
(Ea)/Oct 16, 1915; p. 442
GETTING THE GRIP
(Cry)/Oct 11, 1913; p. 157
GETTING THE MONEY
(Ka)/May 18, 1912; p. 628
GETTING THE SACK
(Bio)/Nov 21, 1914; p. 1075
GETTING TO THE BALL GAME
(Ed)/Nov 21, 1914; p. 1075
GETTING VIVIAN MARRIED
(Vic)/Jul 25, 1914; p. 573
GEYSERS OF NEW ZEALAND, THE
(Kin)/Mar 29, 1913; p. 1338

(Pa)/Dec 20, 1913; p. 1411

GHETTO SEAMSTRESS, THE
(Ya)/Jul 16, 1910; p. 144

GHOST, THE (Bio)/Aug 5, 1911; p. 292
(Vic)/Aug 23, 1913; p. 845
(Dom)/Nov 15, 1913; p. 738
(Vi)/Apr 4, 1914; p. 57
(Pa)/May 2, 1914; p. 673

GHOST BREAKER, THE
(Las)/Dec 19, 1914; p. 1692

GHOST HOLIDAY, THE
(WBE)/Sep 21, 1907; p. 458

GHOST IN UNIFORM, THE
(Th)/Mar 8, 1913; p. 997

GHOST MEETS A GHOST, A
(Th)/Apr 19, 1913; p. 281

GHOST OF A BARGAIN, THE
(Rex)/Sep 21, 1912; p. 1178

GHOST OF BINGVILLE INN, THE
(WF)/Jan 16, 1915; p. 370

GHOST OF GRANLEIGH, THE
(Ed)/Aug 30, 1913; p. 943

GHOST OF SEAVIEW MANOR, THE
(Dra)/Jun 14, 1913; p. 1137

GHOST OF SELF, THE
(SA)/Jan 17, 1914; p. 289

GHOST OF SMILING JIM, THE
(GS)/Dec 19, 1914; p. 1681

GHOST OF SULPHUR MOUNTAINS, THE
(Me)/May 4, 1912; p. 426

GHOST OF THE HACIENDA, THE (Am)/
Sep 13, 1913; p. 1154/Sep 27, 1913; p. 1394

GHOST OF THE MINE, THE
(Ec)/Dec 5, 1914; p. 1385

GHOST OF THE OVEN
(Sel)/Nov 5, 1910; p. 1058

GHOST OF THE TWISTED OAK, THE
(Lu)/Nov 20, 1915; pp 1500, 1505

GHOST OF THE VAULTS, THE
(GN)/Jul 8, 1911; p. 1587

GHOST STORY/Dec 12, 1908; p. 477

GHOST WAGON, THE (Bi)/Oct 2,1915; p.80

GHOSTS (Mut)/May 29, 1915; pp 1439-40

GHOSTS AND FLYPAPER
(Vi)/Dec 4, 1915; p. 1852

GHOSTS AT CIRCLE X CAMP
(Me)/Jun 29, 1912; p. 1226

GHOST'S WARNING, THE
(Ed)/Dec 2, 1911; p. 725

GIANT BABY, THE/Dec 19, 1908; p. 501

GIANTS OF STEEL
(Am)/Aug 10, 1912; p. 546

GIBSON AND THOSE BOYS
(Lux)/Nov 5, 1910; p. 1061

GIFT FROM SANTA CLAUS, A
(Ed)/Dec 31, 1909; p. 960

GIFT OF THE STORM, THE
(Lu)/Apr 12, 1913; p. 163

GIGANTIC WAVES (Gau)/May 21, 1910; p.832

GILDED CAGE, THE
(SA)/Jun 26, 1915; p. 2095

GILDED FOOL, THE
(Box)/Feb 20, 1915; p. 1141

GILDED KIDD, THE
(Ed)/Aug 1, 1914; pp 680-81

GILDED YOUTH (Lae)/Nov 27,1915; p.1666

GILLIAGAN'S ACCIDENT POLICY
(Bio)/May 23, 1914; p. 1116

GILT-EDGED STOCKS
(Ka)/Jan 10, 1914; p. 172

GINGER'S REIGN (Vi)/Mar 21,1914; p.1525

GINGI, SOUTHERN INDIA
(Ecl)/Jan 2, 1915; p. 77

GINHARA (Ec)/Nov 26, 1910; p.1239

GIORGIONE (Cin)/Oct 22, 1910; p. 938

GIOVANNI OF MEDICI
(Cin)/Oct 15, 1910; p. 878

GIOVANNI'S GRATITUDE
(Re)/Jan 10, 1914; p. 174

GIPSY LOVE (Cin)/Apr 4, 1914; p. 57

GIRAFFE HUNT IN AFRICA, A
(Pa)/May 15, 1915; p. 1073

GIRL, A GUARD AND A GARRET, A
(Be)/Dec 18, 1915; p. 2203

GIRL, ARTIST AND DOG
(Maj)/Feb 22, 1913; p. 781

**GIRL, THE CLOWN AND THE DONKEY,
THE** (Ed)/Sep 20, 1913; p. 1283

GIRL, THE COP AND THE BURGLAR, THE
(SA)/Mar 28, 1914; p. 1680

GIRL ACROSS THE HALL, THE
(Th)/Jun 20, 1914; p. 1690

GIRL ACROSS THE WAY, THE
(Lu)/Mar 28, 1908; p. 272
(Bio)/Nov 1, 1913; p. 496

GIRL AND A SPY, A
(Ch)/Oct 28, 1911; p. 292

GIRL AND HER MONEY, THE
(Vic)/Dec 20, 1913; p. 1413

GIRL AND HER TRUST, THE (Bio)/Apr 13,
1912; p. 136/Aug 14, 1915; p. 1176/
Oct 2, 1915; p. 78

GIRL AND THE BACHELOR, THE
(Ka)/May 1, 1915; pp 727-28

GIRL AND THE BANDIT, THE
(Ka)/Apr 2, 1910; p. 509
(Fr)/Nov 15, 1913; p. 737

GIRL AND THE BRONCHO BUSTER, THE
(Sol)/Jul 29, 1911; p.212

GIRL AND THE BURGLAR, THE
(Sol)/Feb 4, 1911; p. 249

GIRL AND THE BUTTERFLY, THE
(Pre)/Mar 20, 1915; p. 1765

GIRL AND THE CHAUFFEUR, THE
(Ya)/Oct 7, 1911; p. 42

GIRL AND THE COWBOY, THE

(Sel)/Aug 3, 1912; p. 445

GIRL AND THE EXPLORER, THE (Ka)/
Nov 21, 1914; p. 1094/Dec 12, 1914; p. 1524

GIRL AND THE FUGITIVE, THE
(SA)/Apr 2, 1910; p. 508

GIRL AND THE GAMBLER, THE
(Lu)/Feb 1, 1913; p. 464

GIRL AND THE GAME, THE (Sig)
No.1/Dec 25, 1915; pp 2383, 2390
No.2/Dec 25, 1915; p. 2383

GIRL AND THE GANGSTER, THE
(Ka)/Aug 9, 1913; p. 636

GIRL AND THE GRAFTER, THE
(Th)/Apr 26, 1913; p. 382

GIRL AND THE GREASER, THE
(Am)/Nov 8, 1913; p. 613

GIRL AND THE GUN, THE
(Am)/Aug 24, 1912; p. 773

GIRL AND THE HALF-BACK, THE
(Imp)/Dec 30, 1911; p. 1072

GIRL AND THE HOBO, THE
(Fr)/Jun 6, 1914; p. 1410

GIRL AND THE HORSESHOE, THE
(Cin)/Mar 29, 1913; p. 1336

GIRL AND THE JUDGE, THE
(Sel)/Oct 19, 1907; p. 526
(Vi)/Feb 12, 1910; p. 216
(Sel)/Jun 14, 1913; p. 1137

GIRL AND THE MAIL BAG, THE
(Sel)/Oct 23, 1915; p. 619

GIRL AND THE MATINEE IDOL, THE
(Bio)/Mar 27, 1915; p. 1943

GIRL AND THE MAYOR, THE
(Cin)/Jul 6, 1912; p. 43

GIRL AND THE MISER, THE
(Bio)/Dec 5, 1914; p. 1383

GIRL AND THE MOTOR BOAT, THE
(Ed)/Nov 18, 1911; p. 550

GIRL AND THE OATH, THE
(Ch)/Apr 29, 1911; p. 960

GIRL AND THE OUTLAW, THE
(Bio)/Sep 12, 1908; p. 200
(Ed)/Oct 25, 1913; p. 380

GIRL AND THE REPORTER, THE
(Sel)/Jul 17, 1915; pp 485-86

GIRL AND THE SHERIFF, THE
(Vi)/Nov 25, 1911; p. 638
(Ne)/Jun 29, 1912; p. 1228

GIRL AND THE SMUGGLER, THE
(Vic)/Sep 26, 1914; p. 1777

GIRL AND THE SPY, THE
(Rex)/Feb 6, 1915; p. 828

GIRL AND THE STOWAWAY, THE (Ka)/
Oct 3, 1914; p. 43/Oct 24, 1914; p. 492

GIRL AND THE TIGER, THE
(Bi)/Oct 11, 1913; p. 158

GIRL AND TWO BOYS, A
(Be)/Feb 6, 1915; p. 828

GIRL AT HIS SIDE, THE
(Sel)/Jul 4, 1914; p. 64

GIRL AT NOLAN'S, THE
(Vi)/Mar 20, 1915; p. 1763

GIRL AT THE CUPOLA, THE
(Sel)/Aug 24, 1912; pp 770-71

GIRL AT THE CURTAIN, THE
(SA)/Feb 14, 1914; p. 809

GIRL AT THE KEY, THE
(Ed)/Jul 6, 1912; p. 43

GIRL AT THE LOCK, THE
(Lu)/Oct 24, 1914; p. 492

GIRL AT THE LUNCH COUNTER, THE
(Vi)/Jan 3, 1914; pp 48-49

GIRL AT THE OLD MILL, THE (Ka)/
Jan 23, 1909; p. 93/Jan 30, 1909; p. 120

GIRL AT WAR, A (101)/Jan 18, 1913; p. 265

GIRL BACK EAST, THE
(SA)/Nov 25, 1911; p. 637
(Lu)/May 17, 1913; p. 704

GIRL BACK HOME, THE
(Am)/Jul 6, 1912; p. 44

GIRL BANDIT, THE
(Fr)/Mar 28, 1914; p. 1682

GIRL CONSCRIPT, THE
(UE)/May 28, 1910; p. 889

GIRL DEPUTY, THE (Ka)/Mar 9, 1912; p. 866

GIRL DETECTIVE, THE (Ka)
No.3/Feb 27, 1915; p. 1288
No.4/Mar 6, 1915; p. 1448
No.5/Mar 13, 1915; p. 1607
No.6/Mar 20, 1915; p. 1764
No.7/Mar 27, 1915; p. 1932
No.8/Apr 3, 1915; p. 64
No.9/Apr 10, 1915; p. 236
No.10/Apr 27, 1915; p. 392
No.11/Mar 27, 1915; p. 1941
No.12/May 1, 1915; p. 728
No.13/May 8, 1915; p. 900
No.14/May 15, 1915; p. 1072
No.15/May 22, 1915; p. 1260
No.16/May 29, 1915; p. 1432
No.17/Jun 5, 1915; p. 1605

GIRL DETECTIVE'S RUSE, THE
(Th)/May 10, 1913; p. 598

GIRL FROM ABROAD, THE
(FRA)/Nov 22, 1913; p. 869

GIRL FROM ARIZONA, THE
(Pa)/May 28, 1910; p. 889

GIRL FROM HIS TOWN, THE
(Am)/Jul 31, 1915; pp 832-33

GIRL FROM PROSPERITY, THE
(Vi)/Apr 25, 1914; p. 517

GIRL FROM TEXAS, THE
(Fr)/Nov 7, 1914; p. 789

GIRL FROM THE COUNTRY, A
(Ec)/Dec 7, 1912; p. 978

GIRL FROM THE EAST, THE

GIRL STRIKERS, THE
(Ka)/Jun 29, 1912; p. 1227
GIRL THIEF, THE (Ka)/Mar 19, 1910; p. 425
GIRL WHO DARED, THE
(De)/Jul 23, 1910; p. 193
(Be)/Apr 4, 1914; p. 58
GIRL WHO DIDN'T FORGET, THE
(Bio)/Oct 9, 1915; p. 252
GIRL WHO EARNS HER LIVING, THE (Ed)
No.1/Dec 26, 1914; p. 1840
No.2/Jan 23, 1915; p. 515
No.3/Feb 27, 1915; p. 1288
GIRL WHO HAD A SOUL, THE
(Vic)/May 15, 1915; pp 1074, 1092
GIRL WHO LIVED IN STRAIGHT STREET,
THE (He)/Sep 12, 1914; p. 1516
GIRL WHO MIGHT HAVE BEEN, THE
(KB)/Mar 13, 1915; p. 1609
(Vi)/May 8, 1915; p. 920
GIRL WITH THE CAMERA, THE
(Pre)/Apr 24, 1915; p. 557
GIRL WITH THE LANTERN, THE
(Sel)/Jun 8, 1912; p. 942
GIRL WITH THE RED FEATHER, THE
(Sel)/Sep 11, 1915; p. 1832
GIRL WORTH WHILE, A
(Th)/Oct 18, 1913; p. 265
GIRLIES (Am)/Jan 7, 1911; p.35
GIRLISH IMPULSE, A (Lu)/Dec 2, 1911;
pp 729-30/Dec 23, 1911; p. 988
GIRLS (Bi)/Jun 18, 1910; p. 1049
GIRLS AND DADDY (Bio)/Feb 6, 1909; p. 144
GIRLS AND THE CHAPERONE, THE
(Ne)/Sep 14, 1912; p. 1075
GIRL'S BRAVERY, A
(Lu)/Oct 12, 1912; p. 142
GIRL'S CROSS ROADS, A
(GN)/Dec 11, 1909; p. 842
GIRLS HE LEFT BEHIND HIM, THE
(Th)/Dec 24, 1910; p. 1479
GIRLS OF THE GHETTO, THE
(Th)/Jul 30, 1910; p. 246
GIRLS OF THE RANGE, THE
(Sel)/Mar 5, 1910; p. 338
GIRL'S STRATAGEM, A
(Bio)/Mar 22, 1913; p. 1219
GIRLS WILL BE BOYS
(SA)/Jan 7, 1911; p. 34
(Cry)/Nov 1, 1913; p. 497
GIT A HOSS (Lu)/Nov 4, 1911; p. 378
GITANA (Cin)/Sep 28, 1907; p.472
GIUSEPPE'S GOOD FORTUNE
(SA)/Jan 4, 1913; p. 51
GIVE ME A LIGHT
(FIT)/Apr 17, 1909; p. 478
GIVE ME BACK MY DUMMY
(Pa)/Apr 25, 1908; p. 377
GIVING BILL A REST

(Lu)/Nov 8, 1913; p. 612
GIVING THE BLIND THE LIGHT OF
KNOWLEDGE (Gau)/Nov 30, 1912; p. 878
GIVING THE HIGH SIGN TO WOMAN
HATERS (Gau)/Sep 9, 1911; p. 715
GIVING THEM FITS
(Phu)/Nov 13, 1915; p. 1313
GLACIER NATIONAL PARK
(Pa)/Oct 12, 1912; p. 142
GLACIER'S VICTIM, THE
Nov 14, 1908; p. 379
GLADIOLA (Ed)/Oct 23, 1915; pp 628-29/
Oct 30, 1915; p. 792
GLASS BLOWING (Ed)/Oct 23, 1909; p. 568
GLASS PISTOL, THE
(Cry)/Dec 19, 1914; p. 1681
GLIMPSE INTO THE YELLOWSTONE
NATIONAL PARK (Ka)/Dec 16, 1911; p. 904
GLIMPSE OF GENOA, ITALY, A
(Po)/Dec 23, 1911; p. 991
GLIMPSE OF NEAPOLITAN CAMORRA,
A (Amb)/Apr 15, 1911; p. 843
GLIMPSE OF SAN DIEGO, A
(Key)/Mar 6, 1915; p. 1448
GLIMPSE OF THE CITY OF LOS
ANGELES, A (Key)/Jan 10, 1914; p. 174
GLIMPSE OF TRIPOLI, A
(UE)/Mar 16, 1912; p. 961
GLIMPSES OF BELGIUM
(UE)/Jun 15, 1912; p. 1026
GLIMPSES OF BERMUDA
(Ed)/Oct 26, 1912; p. 343
GLIMPSES OF COLORADO IN WINTER
(Ed)/Jun 7, 1913; p. 1030
GLIMPSES OF ERIN
(KO)/Sep 21, 1907; p. 458
GLIMPSES OF MONTANA
(Pa)/Jan 4, 1913; p. 50
GLIMPSES OF NAPLES AND VICINITY
(Cin)/Apr 12, 1913; p. 164
GLIMPSES OF POND LIFE
(Pa)/Dec 20, 1913; p. 1412
GLIMPSES OF PROVENCE
(Pa)/Mar 15, 1913; p. 1103
GLIMPSES OF RIO DE JANEIRO
(SA)/Jan 10, 1914; p. 172
GLIMPSES OF SAN FRANCISCO
(Pa)/Dec 16, 1911; p. 903
GLIMPSES OF SOUTHERN FRANCE (GN)/
Apr 20, 1912; p. 231/May 4, 1912; p. 427
GLIMPSES OF THE ALPS OF SOUTHERN
CALIFORNIA (UI)/Jun 27, 1914; p. 1829
GLIMPSES OF THE BALKAN WAR
TERRITORY (UE)/Dec 28, 1912; p. 1291
GLIMPSES OF THE NATIONAL CAPITAL
(Pa)/May 3, 1913; p. 488
GLIMPSES OF THE YELLOWSTONE
PARK (Lu)/Oct 2, 1909; p. 452

(Nov)/Oct 16, 1915; p. 440
GOLDEN BEETLE, THE
(GK)/Oct 24, 1914; p. 477
GOLDEN CLAW, THE (TKB)/Nov 6, 1915;
p. 1157/Nov 13, 1915; p. 1313
GOLDEN CLOUD, THE
(Sel)/Nov 1, 1913; p. 495
GOLDEN CROSS, THE
(Th)/Mar 14, 1914; p. 1386
GOLDEN DROSS (Re)/Jun 13, 1914; p. 1542
GOLDEN GOOSE, THE
(Bro)/Oct 31, 1914; p. 643
GOLDEN HAIR (Ec)/Nov 23, 1912; p. 768
GOLDEN HEART, THE
(Am)/Aug 23, 1913; p. 845
(GN)/Jun 6, 1914; p. 1412
GOLDEN HOARD, THE
(Ne)/Oct 22, 1910; p. 939
(Vi)/Apr 19, 1913; pp 279-80
**GOLDEN JUBILEE OF THE NEW YORK
   CATHOLIC PROFECTORY, THE**
(Maj)/Jul 12, 1913; p. 206
GOLDEN LADDER, THE
(Vic)/Jun 6, 1914; p. 1409
GOLDEN LIE, A (Lu)/May 15, 1909; p. 634
GOLDEN OYSTER, THE
(Lu)/Oct 2, 1915; pp 78, 93
GOLDEN PATCH, THE
(Sel)/Apr 4, 1914; p. 57
GOLDEN PATHWAY, THE
(Vi)/Dec 20, 1913; p. 1412
GOLDEN PRINCESS MINE, THE
(Ne)/Nov 22, 1913; p. 869
GOLDEN RAINBOW, THE
(Am)/Jun 12, 1915; p. 1777
GOLDEN ROD (Po)/Oct 26, 1912; p. 344
GOLDEN RULE (Re)/Jul 22, 1911; p. 126
GOLDEN RULE, THE
(Po)/Aug 24, 1912; p. 772
GOLDEN SECRET, THE
(Me)/Jul 30, 1910; p. 244
GOLDEN SICKLE, THE
(UE)/Mar 4, 1911; p. 483
GOLDEN SPIDER, THE
(Vic)/Mar 20, 1915; p. 1765
GOLDEN SPURS, THE
(Sel)/Dec 25, 1915; p. 2389
GOLDEN SUPPER, THE
(Bio)/Dec 24, 1910; p. 1478
GOLDEN TRAIL, THE
(Bro)/Aug 7, 1915; p. 997
GOLDEN WEDDING (Amb)/Dec 2, 1911;
p. 726/Dec 9, 1911; p. 799
GOLDEN WEDDING, THE
(Ed)/May 24, 1913; p. 811
(Lae)/Jun 5, 1915; p. 1606
GOLF CADDY'S DOG, THE
(Th)/Apr 6, 1912; p. 42

**GOLF CHAMPION "CHICK" EVANS LINKS
   WITH SWEEDIE** (SA)/Oct 17, 1914; p. 336
GOLF FIEND, THE (Lu)/Oct 22, 1910; p. 934
GOLF GAME AND THE BONNET, THE
(Vi)/Jan 10, 1914; p. 172
GOLF MANIA, THE
(Lux)/Mar 12, 1910; p. 385
GONE TO CONEY ISLAND
(Th)/Jul 16, 1910; p. 144
GONE TO THE DOGS
(Vi)/Nov 27, 1915; pp 1663-64
GONTRAN, A KIDNAPPER
(Ec)/Jan 4, 1913; p. 52
GONTRAN IS FOND OF ANIMALS
(Ec)/Feb 24, 1912; p. 691
GONTRAN'S LOVE STRATAGEM
(Ec)/Nov 9, 1912; p. 554
GOOD BIRTHDAY PRESENT, A
(Pa)/Jun 26, 1909; pp 872-73
GOOD BOSS, THE (Pa)/Apr 16, 1910; p. 598
GOOD BOY, A (Vi)/May 23, 1908; p. 465
GOOD BUSINESS DEAL, A
(Am)/Jul 10, 1915; p. 308
GOOD CATCH, A (SA)/Jun 8, 1912; p. 942
GOOD CIDER (Lu)/Aug 4, 1914; p. 64
GOOD CIGAR, A (Imp)/Apr 22, 1911; p. 902
GOOD DAY'S WORK, A
(Po)/Jul 27, 1912; p. 345
GOOD DINNER BADLY DIGESTED, A
(Pa)/Aug 29, 1908; pp 162-63
GOOD DOCTOR, THE (Pa)/Jan 8,1910; p.17
GOOD EXCUSE, A (Me)/Jun 20,1914;p.1688
GOOD FOR EVIL
(It)/Nov 20, 1909; p. 722
(Lu)/Jul 29, 1911; p. 210
(Vic)/May 31, 1913; p. 921
(Lu)/Aug 30, 1913; p. 961
GOOD-FOR-NOTHING, THE
(SA)/May 23, 1914; pp 1092-93
GOOD FOR NOTHING, THE
(Lu)/Nov 30, 1912; p. 877
GOOD FOR NOTHING JACK
(Bi)/Oct 4, 1913; p. 50
GOOD-FOR-NOTHING NEPHEW
(It)/Jun 26, 1909; p. 873
GOOD GLUE, A (Pa)/Sep 24, 1910; p. 689
GOOD-HEARTED POLICEMAN, A
(Gau)/Jun 26, 1909; p. 870
GOOD-HEARTED SAILOR
(CR)/Mar 21, 1908; p. 244
GOOD HUNTING DOG, A
(It)/Dec 21, 1912; p. 1185
GOOD IN HIM, THE
(Lu)/Mar 20, 1915; p. 1763
GOOD IN THE WORST OF US, THE
(Ed)/Jun 7, 1913; p. 1031
(Ec)/Feb 7, 1914; p. 678
GOOD INDIAN, THE

(Sel)/Sep 6, 1913; p. 1068
GOOD JOKE, A (Pa)/Mar 21, 1908; p. 244
GOOD JOKE, BUT WHY DIDN'T HE LAUGH?, A/Nov 28, 1908; p. 422
GOOD LESSON IN CHARITY
(Pa)/Nov 27, 1909; p. 759
GOOD LITTLE DEVIL, A
(FP)/Jul 26, 1913; p. 407
GOOD LOSER, A (Pa)/Jul 30, 1910; p. 244
GOOD LUCK OF A SOUSE, THE
(Me)/Feb 8, 1908; p. 102
GOOD MEDICINE, A
(Pa)/May 23, 1908; p. 464
GOOD MORNING, JUDGE
(Th)/Feb 22, 1913; p. 781
GOOD NATURED MAN, A
(Ya)/Aug 26, 1911; p. 543
GOOD NIGHT CLOWN
(KO)/Jul 18, 1908; p. 52
GOOD NIGHT NURSE
(SA)/Aug 30, 1913; p. 960
GOOD OLD SUMMER TIME, THE
(Ka)/Dec 13, 1913; p. 1279
GOOD OMEN, THE (Gau)/Jun 5,1909; p.753
GOOD OUT OF EVIL
(SBa)/Oct 16, 1915; p. 442
GOOD PALS (Pa)/Jan 31, 1914; p. 544
GOOD PLAYTHINGS, THE
(KO)/Dec 19, 1908; p. 512
GOOD REPENTANCE
(Cin)/Oct 9, 1909; p. 490
GOOD RESOLUTIONS
Dec 12, 1908; p. 477
(Sel)/Jan 17, 1914; p. 288
GOOD SAMARITAN, THE
Sep 25, 1909; p. 416
GOOD SHEPHERD, THE
(RR)/Aug 21, 1909; p. 255
GOOD SNUFF (Po)/Oct 19, 1912; pp 243-44
GOOD SPORT, A (Ed)/Dec 6,1913;pp1151-52
GOOD THIEF, A (KO)/May 16, 1908;
p. 445/Mar 6, 1909; p. 268
GOOD TURN, A (Lu)/Jun 10, 1911; p. 1313/
Jun 24, 1911; p. 1427
GOOD WATCH DOG, A (KO)/Dec 5, 1908;
p. 459/Dec 19, 1908; p. 501
GOOD WITHIN, THE
(Re)/May 10, 1913; p. 598
GOODBYE SUMMER (Vi)/Nov 7,1914;p.788
GOODFELLOW'S CHRISTMAS EVE, THE
(SA)/Dec 16, 1911;pp 885-86
GOODY, GOODY JONES
(Sel)/Jun 29, 1912; p. 1227
GOOSE GIRL, THE
(Ya)/Oct 14, 1911; p. 131
(Las)/Feb 6, 1915; p. 809
GOPHER, THE (Bi)/Aug 21, 1915; p. 1318
GORGES OF ALBUQUERQUE

(Gau)/Nov 2, 1912; p. 452
GORGES OF THE BOURNE
(Gau)/Feb 11, 1911; p. 315
GORGES OF THE TARN, THE
(KO)/Nov 7,1908; p.358/Nov 14,1908; p.384
(Pa)/Mar 27, 1915; p. 1935
GOSSIP (Maj)/Jan 20, 1912;p.204
GOSSIP, THE (Vi)/Nov 18, 1911; p. 551
GOSSIPY YAPVILLE
(SA)/Sep 2, 1911; p. 629
GOT A MATCH (Bio)/Mar 2, 1912; p. 781
GOUNOD'S "AVE MARIA"
(Amb)/Dec 3, 1910; p. 1282
GOVERNESS, THE (Ed)/Feb 22, 1913; p.779
GOVERNMENT RATIONS
(NYM)/Feb 26, 1910; p. 300
GOVERNMENT TEST, THE
(Lu)/Sep 7, 1912; p. 976
GOVERNOR, THE (Ed)/Oct 5, 1912; p. 40
(Lu)/Aug 16, 1913; p.744
GOVERNOR JOHNSON, OF CALIFORNIA
(Ka)/Jun 28, 1913; p. 1358
GOVERNOR-MAKER, THE
(Bi)/Jan 16, 1915; p. 370
GOVERNOR (PRESIDENT) WILSON
(Vi)/Mar 15, 1913; p. 1104
GOVERNOR WHO HAD A HEART, THE
(Vi)/Apr 13, 1912; p. 136
GOVERNOR'S BOSS, THE
(Gov)/Jun 26, 1915; p. 2106
GOVERNOR'S CLEMENCY, THE
(Me)/Dec 7, 1912; p. 975
GOVERNOR'S DAUGHTER, THE
(Ka)/Dec 4, 1909; p. 798
(Th)/Jul 9, 1910; p. 86
(Sel)/Feb 15, 1913; p. 680
GOVERNOR'S DOUBLE, THE (Pa)/May 31,
1913; p. 905/Jun 28, 1913; p. 1358
GOVERNOR'S GHOST, THE
(Ram)/Feb 28, 1914; p. 1076
GOVERNOR'S LADY, THE
(Las)/Mar 27, 1915; p. 1914e
GOVERNOR'S PARDON, THE (Imp)/
Mar 12, 1910; p. 382/Mar 19, 1910; p. 427
GOVERNOR'S ROMANCE, THE
(Pi)/Jun 14, 1913; p. 1137
GRAFT (Uni)
No.1/Nov 27, 1915; pp 1680-81/
Dec 11, 1915; p. 2033
No.2/Dec 18, 1915; p. 2204
No.3/Dec 25, 1915; p. 2391
GRAFT VERSUS LOVE
(Th)/Jan 30, 1915; p. 673
GRAFTERS, THE (Re)/Apr 5, 1913; p. 50
(Pa)/Apr 25, 1914; p. 516
GRAIL, THE (Lae)/Jul 3, 1915; p. 66
GRAND CANAL AT VENICE
(KO)/Jul 18, 1908; p. 52

GRAND CANON OF ARIZONA
(Ne)/Mar 2, 1912; p. 782
GRAND CANYON, THE
(Vi)/May 24, 1913; p. 812
GRAND CANYON OF ARIZONA
(Maj)/Aug 30, 1913; p. 962
GRAND CANYON OF ARIZONA, THE
(Ed)/Aug 23, 1913; p. 842
GRAND CANYON OF NEW YORK, THE
(Pa)/Aug 23, 1913; p. 842
GRAND CHARTREUSE, THE
(UE)/Oct 14, 1911; p. 130
GRAND OLD FLAG, THE
(Bi)/Jun 14, 1913; p. 1138
GRAND OPERA IN RUBEVILLE
(Ed)/Sep 5, 1914; p. 1348
GRAND PASSION, THE
(Th)/Apr 4, 1914; p. 58
GRANDAD (Bro)/Jul 19, 1913; p. 321
GRANDDADDY AND GRANDDAUGHTER
(Vic)/Apr 11, 1914; p. 213
GRANDDADDY'S BOY
(Sel)/Dec 20, 1913; p. 1411
GRANDDAD'S EXTRAVAGANCE
(Cen)/Jul 30, 1910; p. 245
GRANDEE'S RING, THE
(IFF)/Nov 20, 1915; pp 1502, 1506-7
GRANDFATHER (Gau)/Feb 27, 1909; p. 237
(Re)/Sep 2, 1911; p. 630
(Ka)/Jan 25, 1913; p. 363
GRANDFATHER, THE
(Pa)/Jun 12, 1909; p. 833/Jul 3, 1909; p. 13
(Ed)/Aug 31, 1912; p. 847/Oct 5, 1912; p. 41
GRANDFATHER'S GIFT
(Lu)/Jun 18, 1910; p. 1048
GRANDFATHER'S PILLS (Pa)/Jun 20, 1908;
p. 532/Dec 26, 1908; p. 525
GRANDFATHER'S PIPE
(Amb)/Jan 14, 1911; p. 91
GRANDFATHER'S ROMANCE
(Ec)/Apr 18, 1914; p. 361
GRANDFATHER'S VIOLIN
(CGP)/Nov 11, 1911; p. 469
GRANDMA (SA)/Oct 14, 1911; p. 129
GRANDMA'S TOOTHACHE
(Com)/Dec 9, 1911; p. 818
GRANDMOTHER'S LAMP
(Amb)/Aug 23, 1913; p. 824
GRANDMOTHER'S PLOT
(Gau)/Oct 29, 1910; p. 996
GRANDMOTHER'S STORY (Me)/Oct 3,
1908; p. 264/Oct 10, 1908;
p. 286/Oct 30, 1908; p. 338
GRANDMOTHER'S WAR STORY
(Ka)/Mar 4, 1911; p. 482
GRANDPA (Re)/Jul 27, 1912; p. 344
GRANDPA'S DARLING
(Lux)/Apr 30, 1910; p. 690

GRANDPA'S SPECS
(Po)/May 25, 1912; pp 729-30
GRANDPA'S VACATION
(Lu)/Oct 12, 1907; p. 509
GRANITE DELLS, ARIZONA, THE
(Sel)/Aug 16, 1913; p. 744
GRANITE INDUSTRY, THE
(Ka)/Nov 15, 1913; p. 735
GRANJA, THE (CGP)/Mar 22, 1913; p. 1219
GRANNY (Lu)/May 10, 1913; p. 596
(Maj)/Sep 5, 1914; p. 1373
GRANNY'S BIRTHDAY
(Pa)/Mar 12, 1910; p. 382
GRANNY'S OLD ARMCHAIR
(Sel)/Aug 2, 1913; p. 536
GRASS COUNTY GOES DRY
(SA)/Mar 28, 1914; p. 1681
GRATEFUL HENRY
(Lux)/Dec 7, 1912; p. 977
GRATEFUL OUTCAST, A
(Cry)/Jan 31, 1914; p. 545
GRATITUDE (Vi)/Jun 13, 1908; p. 517
(SA)/Oct 2, 1909; p. 452
(Sel)/Dec 3, 1910; p. 1296
(Sol)/Sep 20, 1913; p. 1286
(Me)/Aug 22, 1914; p. 1100
(Bio)/Jun 12, 1915; p. 1776
GRATITUDE OF CONDUCTOR 786, THE
(Th)/Feb 20, 1915; p. 1140
GRATITUDE OF WANDA, THE
(Bi)/Aug 30, 1913; p. 962
GRAUSTARK (SA)/May 8, 1915; p. 918
GRAVE DISAPPOINTMENT, A
(Pa)/Sep 18, 1909; p. 379
GRAY DAME, THE (GN)/Sep 11, 1909; p. 344
GRAY HORROR, THE
(Lu)/May 29, 1915; p. 1432
GRAY MASK, THE
(Wor)/Dec 4, 1915; p. 1848
GRAY SENTINEL, THE
(Bro)/Apr 12, 1913; p. 166
GRAY WOLF'S GRIEF
(Po)/Sep 30, 1911; p. 976
GRAZIELLA, THE GYPSY
(Gau)/Aug 24, 1912; p. 773
GREASER, THE (Maj)/Apr 3, 1915; p. 64
GREASER'S REVENGE, THE
(Fr)/Oct 10, 1914; p. 189
GREAT AERIAL DISASTER, THE
(It)/Feb 8, 1913; p. 558
GREAT BANK FAILURE, THE
(It)/Jul 6, 1912; p. 43
GREAT BEYOND, THE
(SA)/Aug 2, 1913; p. 535
GREAT CENTIPEDE, THE
(CGP)/Mar 8, 1913; p. 995
GREAT CHARLESTON HURRICANE AND
FLOOD, THE (Imp)/Oct 7, 1911; p. 42

GREAT BULLION ROBBERY, THE
(Ape)/Feb 28, 1914; p. 1102

GREAT DECEIT, THE
(SA)/Oct 30, 1915; p. 792

GREAT DETECTIVE, THE
(Lu)/Dec 25, 1915; p. 2388

GREAT DIAMOND ROBBERY, THE
(Vi)/Apr 6, 1912; p. 40
(Pla)/Apr 4, 1914; p. 47

GREAT DISCOVERY, THE
(Lu)/Oct 11, 1913; p. 155

GREAT DIVIDE, THE
(Gau)/Feb 12, 1910; p. 215
(Lu)/Dec 18,1915;p.2199/Dec 25,1915;p.2391

GREAT DROUGHT, THE
(Sel)/Oct 19, 1912; p. 242

GREAT EARED BAT OF MADAGASCAR,
THE (Pa)/Feb 13, 1915; p. 986

GREAT EUROPEAN WAR, THE
(PP)/Apr 17, 1915; p. 399

GREAT EXPERIMENT, THE
(Sel)/May 8, 1915; pp 899-900

GREAT GAME, THE (SA)/Jan 10, 1914; p. 173

GREAT GANTON MYSTERY, THE
(Rex)/Mar 22, 1913; p. 1222

GREAT GEYSERS OF YELLOWSTONE
PARK, THE (Imp)/Aug 31, 1912; p. 881

GREAT GOD FEAR, THE
(Maj)/Oct 10, 1914; p. 189

GREAT HARMONY, THE
(Am)/May 17, 1913; p. 705

GREAT HEART OF THE WEST, THE
(Me)/Jul 15, 1911; p. 39

GREAT IMPEERYUL SIRKUS, THE
(Sel)/Nov 14, 1914; p. 931

GREAT ITALIAN EARTHQUAKE, THE
(Tru)/Mar 13, 1915; p. 1621

GREAT LONE LAND, THE
(Lu)/Aug 28, 1915; p. 1479

GREAT LOVE, THE
(Ed)/Dec 10, 1910; p. 1358

GREAT MARSHALL JEWELL CASE, THE
(De)/Sep 17, 1910; p. 632

GREAT MEDAL CONTEST, THE
(Ec)/Jan 14, 1911; p. 92

GREAT METROPOLITAN NEWSPAPER, A
(Ed)/Aug 2, 1913; p. 536

GREAT MINE DISASTER, THE
(Ecl)/Mar 7, 1914; p. 1215

GREAT PASADENA ROSE TOURNAMENT
THE (Ap)/Feb 14, 1914; p. 809

GREAT PEARL, THE
(Lu)/Jun 21, 1913; p. 1252

GREAT PHYSICIAN, THE
(Ed)/Oct 4, 1913; p. 47

GREAT PORTOLA FESTIVAL IN SAN
FRANCISCO, THE
(Ap)/Dec 27, 1913; p. 1545

GREAT PRAYER OF THE ARABS, THE
(Pa)/Feb 15, 1913; p. 678

GREAT QUESTION, THE
(Cli)/Oct 2, 1915; p. 79

GREAT RUBY ROBBERY, THE
(GS)/Aug 7, 1915; p. 998

GREAT SACRIFICE, THE
(KB)/Jan 4, 1913; p. 52

GREAT SANTA MONICA ROAD RACE,
THE (Maj)/Sep 13, 1913; p. 1176

GREAT SECRET, THE
(Ed)/Sep 24, 1910; p. 689
(Box)/Nov 7, 1914; p. 790

GREAT SHOCK, A/Nov 28, 1908; p. 422

GREAT SILENCE, THE
(SA)/Apr 10, 1915; p. 236

GREAT STEEPLECHASE, THE
(Pa)/Dec 14, 1912; p. 1080

GREAT STROKE, THE
(Wor)/Aug 1, 1914; p. 707

GREAT TOE MYSTERY, THE
(Key)/Aug 15, 1914; p. 960

GREAT TOWEL MYSTERY, THE
(Po)/Aug 16, 1913; pp 744-45

GREAT TRAIN HOLDUP, THE
(Pa)/Jul 9, 1910; p. 84

GREAT TRUNK MYSTERY, THE
(WBE)/May 2, 1908; p. 405

GREAT UNKNOWN, THE
(Ec)/Mar 1, 1913; p. 895

GREAT VACUUM ROBBERY, THE
(TK)/Nov 27, 1915; pp 1665, 1679

GREAT WALL OF CHINA, THE
(Sel)/Mar 29, 1913; p. 1335

GREAT WHILE IT LASTED
(Phu)/Nov 27, 1915; p. 1665

GREAT WRONG RIGHTED
(KO)/Dec 19, 1908; p. 500
(Sel)/Sep 26,1908;pp243-44/Oct 3,1908;p.253
(Lu)/Jul 10, 1909; p. 49
(Ya)/Sep 2, 1911; p. 630

GREATER CALL, THE
(SA)/Dec 31, 1910; p. 1536
(Ec)/Aug 2, 1913; p. 537

GREATER CHRISTIAN, THE
(Rex)/Aug 24, 1912; p. 771

GREATER COURAGE, THE
(SA)/Jun 26, 1915; p. 2096
(U)/Oct 23, 1915; pp 621-22

GREATER DEVOTION, THE
(Ne)/Feb 7, 1914; p. 678

GREATER INFLUENCE, A
(Cry)/Aug 23, 1913; p. 846

GREATER LOVE, THE
(Vi)/Jun 1, 1912; p. 829
(Am)/Mar 8, 1913; p. 998
(Ne)/May 3, 1913; p. 489
(It)/Aug 23, 1913; p. 846

(Pa)/Apr 25, 1914; p. 517
(SA)/May 23, 1914; p. 1116
(Lu)/Oct 17, 1914; p. 335
(Vi)/Dec 26, 1914; p. 1841
GREATER LOVE HATH NO MAN
(Sol)/Jul 15, 1911; pp 40-41
(Ed)/Oct 24, 1914; p. 491
(Mto)/Jul 10, 1915; p. 322
GREATER MOTIVE, THE
(Vi)/Aug 15, 1914; p. 959
GREATER STRENGTH, THE
(Am)/May 29, 1915; p. 1432
GREATER THAN ART
(Ed)/May 15, 1915; p. 1071
GREATER TREASURE, THE
(Lu)/Jul 11, 1914; p. 256
GREATER WEALTH (Sel)/Jan 18, 1913; p. 264
GREATER WILL, THE
(GR)/Dec 18, 1915; p. 2204
GREATEST GIFT, THE
(Cin)/Mar 28, 1914; p. 1681
GREATEST LOVE, THE
(Maj)/Aug 23, 1913; p. 845
GREATEST OF ENGINEERING FEATS,
THE (Ka)/Nov 18, 1911; p. 549
GREATEST OF THESE, THE
(Ec)/Jul 4, 1914; p. 66
GREATEST OF THESE IS CHARITY, THE
(Lux)/Jul 30, 1910; p. 245
(Ne)/Mar 8, 1913; p. 997
GREATEST THING IN THE WORLD, THE
(Vi)/May 4, 1912;p.417/May 25, 1912; p.728
GREASE PAINT INDIANS
(Ec)/Aug 9, 1913; p. 637
GREASER'S GAUNTLET, THE
(Bio)/Aug 15, 1908; p. 126
GRECIAN VASE, THE
(Ed)/Sep 13, 1913; p. 1176
GREECE (GN)/Dec 23, 1911; p.991
GREED AND GASOLINE
(Lko)/Dec 25, 1915; p. 2390
GREED FOR GOLD
(Lu)/Mar 29, 1913; p. 1336
(SA)/Nov 15, 1913; p. 735
GREED FOR GOLD, THE
(Lu)/May 30, 1908; p. 481
GREED OF GAIN, THE
(Lux)/Apr 15, 1911; p. 843
GREED OF OSMAN BEY, THE (Ed)/Jul 26,
1913; p. 416/Aug 9, 1913; p. 636
GREEDINESS PUNISHED
(KO)/May 2, 1908; p. 401
GREEDINESS SPOILS FOOLSHEAD'S
CHRISTMAS (It)/Jan 7, 1911; p. 35
GREEDY GEORGE (Ed)/Dec 27,1913;p.1544
GREEDY GIRL, THE
(WBE)/May 2, 1908; p. 405
GREEK SLAVE'S PASSION, THE

(Gau)/Jan 8, 1910; p. 17
GREEN ALARM, THE
(Lu)/Sep 19, 1914; p. 1644
GREEN APPLES (Be)/Sep 11, 1915; p. 1833
GREEN CAT, THE (Vi)/Feb 20,1915; p.1139
GREEN CLOAK, THE
(KEd)/Oct 30a, 1915; p. 986
GREEN EYE OF A YELLOW GOD, THE
(Ed)/Sep 6,1913; p.1048/Sep 27,1913; p.1391
GREEN-EYED DEVIL, THE
(Re)/Mar 7, 1914; p. 1238
GREEN-EYED MONSTER, THE
(Am)/Jun 15, 1912; p. 1028
(Ed)/Oct 12, 1912; p. 143
(Lu)/Oct 24, 1914; p. 491
(WF)/Nov 7, 1914; p. 789
GREEN-EYED MONSTER OF JEALOUSY,
THE (Pa)/Dec 6, 1913; p. 1151
GREEN GOD, THE (UF)/Aug 9, 1913; p.617
GREEN IDOL, THE
(Re)/Mar 20, 1915; p. 1766
GREEN ROSE, THE (Ka)/Oct 10,1914; p.187
GREEN SHADOW, THE
(KB)/Aug 30, 1913; p. 962
GREENBACKS AND RED SKINS
(Lu)/Feb 13, 1915; p. 984
GREENHORN, THE (Bro)/Oct 4, 1913; p. 50
GREENHORN AND THE GIRL, THE
(Lu)/Sep 24, 1910; p. 688
GREENHORNS, THE
(Pa)/Apr 30, 1910; p. 689
GREGORY'S SHADOW
(Sol)/Jun 21, 1913; p. 1254
GRETNA GREEN (FP)/Apr 3, 1915; p. 69
GREY EAGLE'S LAST STAND
(Ka)/May 9, 1914; p. 821
GREY EAGLE'S REVENGE
(Ka)/Aug 22, 1914; p. 1099
GREY SENTINEL, THE
(Bro)/Apr 19, 1913; p. 264
GREY WOLVES (Sel)/Sep 9, 1911; p. 714
GREYHOUND, THE
(LF)/Jun 13, 1914; pp 1518-19
GRIGLEY'S WIFE (Re)/May 29,1915; p.1432
GRIM TOLL OF WAR, THE
(Ka)/Mar 29, 1913; p. 1335
GRIMSOL, THE MISCHIEVOUS GOBLIN
(KO)/Dec 26, 1908; p. 525
GRIN AND WIN (Vi)/May 8, 1909; p. 594
GRIND, THE
(Imp)/Jun 17, 1911; p. 1389
(Rex)/Mar 6,1915; p.1464/Apr 17,1915;p.394
GRINGO, THE (KB)/Apr 4, 1914; p. 59
GRIP OF CIRCUMSTANCES, THE (SA)/
Jan 24, 1914; p. 393/Feb 21, 1914; p. 947
GRIP OF THE PAST, THE
(Lu)/Dec 19, 1914; p. 1680
GRIP SNATCHER, THE

(SA)/Feb 17, 1912; p. 582
GRIST TO THE MILL
(SA)/Sep 27, 1913; p. 1393
GRIT OF A GRINGO, THE
(Ne)/Jul 19, 1913; p. 320
GRIT OF THE GIRL TELEGRAPHER,
THE (Ka)/Oct 5, 1912; p. 41
GRIZZLY GULCH CHARIOT RACE, THE
(Sel)/Feb 13, 1915; p. 984
GROCER'S REVENGE, THE
(Sel)/Aug 23, 1913; p. 843
GROCERY CLERK'S ROMANCE, A
(Key)/Nov 9, 1912; p. 554
GROOM'S DOOM, THE
(Lko)/Nov 28, 1914; p. 1233
GROTESQUE MIX-UP
(Pa)/Nov 6, 1909; p. 644
GROTESQUES (Pa)/Sep 12, 1908; p. 202
GROUCH, THE (Ed)/Aug 10, 1912; p. 546
(Vic)/Jan 11, 1913; p. 159
GROUCH, THE ENGINEER
(Ka)/Oct 17, 1914; p. 335
GROUCH CURE, THE
(CGP)/Dec 2, 1911; p. 725
GROUNDLESS SUSPICION
(Ed)/May 17, 1913; p. 704
GRUBSTAKE MORTGAGE, A
(Am)/Feb 17, 1912; p. 584
GRUDGE, THE (Bro)/Feb 27, 1915; p. 1290
GUARANTEED RAINPROOF
(Lu)/May 2, 1914; p. 672
GUARDIAN ANGEL, THE
(Ec)/Mar 9, 1912; p. 867
GUARDIAN OF THE FLOCKS, THE
(Vic)/Apr 10, 1915; p. 238
GUARDIAN'S DILEMNA, THE
(Sel)/Mar 20, 1915; pp 1763-64
GUARDIAN'S LUCK, A
(SA)/Jul 13, 1912; p. 147
GUARDING OLD GLORY
Jun 12, 1915; p. 1785
GUARD'S ALARM (UE)/Feb 6, 1909; p. 144
GUARDSMAN, THE
(Rex)/May 27, 1911; p. 1202
GUERILLAS, THE (Bio)/Nov 21, 1908; p.398
GUERRILLAS OF ALGIERS, THE
(Id)/Dec 6, 1913; p. 1155
GUERRERO TROUPE
(Pa)/Oct 28, 1911; p. 291
GUEST'S PREDICAMENT, A
(Gau)/May 29, 1909; p. 713
GUIDING FATE, THE
(Bio)/Oct 24, 1914; p. 492
GUIDING HAND, THE
(Th)/Aug 15, 1914; pp 939, 961
GUIDING LIGHT, THE
(Lu)/Feb 22, 1913; p. 779
(Am)/Jun 12, 1915; p. 1777

GUILELESS COUNTRY LASSIE, THE
(KO)/May 9, 1908; p. 423
GUILT, THE (Ka)/Oct 16, 1915; p. 439
GUILTY BABY, THE
(Th)/Mar 9, 1912; p. 868
GUILTY CONSCIENCE
(Sol)/Feb 17, 1912; p. 583
GUILTY CONSCIENCE, A
Oct 10, 1908; p. 279
(Th)/Jan 11, 1913; p. 159
GUILTY OR NOT GUILTY
(TH)/Mar 21, 1914; p. 1525
GULNARA (Amb)/Sep 9, 1911; p. 717
GUM MAN, THE (SA)/Mar 15, 1913; p. 1103
GUM SHOE KID, THE
(UE)/Jun 25, 1910; p. 1101
GUN BEHIND THE MAN, THE
(SA)/Feb 28, 1914; p. 1088
GUN FIGHTER'S SON, A
(Sel)/Jan 25, 1913; p. 363
GUN MAN, THE (Am)/Sep 30,1911;pp 974, 976
GUN SMUGGLERS, THE
(Ka)/Jun 29, 1912; p. 1226
GUNBY'S SOJOURN IN THE COUNTRY,
THE (Pa)/Mar 5, 1910; p. 339
GUNFIGHTER, THE (Ne)/Jul 15, 1911; p.40
(Bro)/Jan 30,1915;p.673
GUNMAKER OF MOSCOW, THE
(Ed)/Dec 13, 1913; p. 1280
GUNMAN, THE (Re)/Aug 15, 1914; p. 961
GUNMEN OF PLUMAS, THE
(Fr)/Jun 27, 1914; p. 1830
GUNSMITH, THE (Po)/Sep 3, 1910; p. 521
GUS AND THE ANARCHISTS
(Lu)/Feb 6, 1915; p. 827
GUSHER, THE (Key)/Dec 13, 1913; p. 1280
GUSSIE, THE GRACEFUL LIFE GUARD
(Fal)/Aug 21, 1915; p. 1317
GUSSLE, THE GOLFER
(Key)/Jan 9, 1915; p. 221
GUSSLE RIVALS JONAH
(Key)/May 1, 1915; pp 728-29
GUSSLE TIED TO TROUBLE
(Key)/Jun 5, 1915; p. 1605
GUSSLE'S BACKWARD WAY
(Key)/May 22, 1915; p. 1260
GUSSLE'S DAY OF REST
(Key)/Apr 3, 1915; p. 65
GUSSLE'S WAYWARD PATH
(Key)/May 1, 1915; p. 728
GUSSY'S CONGRATULATIONS
(Ec)/Dec 9, 1911; p. 818
GUST OF WIND
(FIT)/Oct 30, 1908; pp 338, 344
GUSTAV GEBHARD'S GUTTER BAND
(Fal)/Oct 9, 1915; p. 253
GUY FAWKES (UE)/Dec 2, 1911; p. 726
GUY MANNERING (Re)/Oct 19, 1912; p.244

GWENDOLIN (Bio)/Oct 24, 1914; p. 492
GWENDOLYN, THE SEWING MACHINE GIRL (Bio)/Aug 15, 1914; p. 959
GYPSY, THE (Lu)/Aug 19, 1911; p. 462
GYPSY ARTIST, THE (NYM)/Aug 7, 1909; p. 195
GYPSY BLOOD (TFC)/Apr 13, 1912; pp 142-43
GYPSY BRIDE, A (Me)/Nov 11, 1911; p. 468
GYPSY FLIRT, THE (Cry)/Nov 23, 1912; p. 769
GYPSY GAMBLER, THE (Ka)/Jul 11, 1914; p. 255
GYPSY GIRL'S LOVE, THE (Ka)/Apr 23, 1910; p. 641
GYPSY HONOR (Pa)/Oct 14, 1911; p. 128
GYPSY LOVE (Pa)/Nov 8, 1913; p. 611
GYPSY MAIDS (Pa)/Oct 7, 1911; p. 41
GYPSY QUEEN, THE (Key)/Sep 13, 1913; p. 1176
GYPSY ROMANCE, A (Ne)/Apr 11, 1914; p. 214
GYPSY SINGER, THE (UE)/Apr 6, 1912; p. 41
GYPSY SPY, THE (Mil)/Oct 19, 1912; p. 244
GYPSY TALISMAN, THE (Bio)/Sep 5, 1914; p. 1372
GYPSY'S BRAND, THE (Ka)/Jun 28, 1913; p. 1358
GYPSY'S HEART, A (Ec)/Apr 20, 1912; p. 231
GYPSY'S KISS, THE (It)/Oct 25, 1913; pp 364, 382
GYPSY'S REVENGE, A (Pa)/Feb 1, 1908; p. 82
GYPSY'S WARNING/Nov 14, 1908; p. 378
GYPSY'S WARNING, THE (Me)/Feb 22, 1913; p. 780

HABBLE SKIRT, THE (Imp)/Nov 12, 1910; p. 1118
HABITS OF FIELD SPIDERS (Ec)/Sep 6, 1913; p. 1069
HACK AND SCHMIDT BOUT, THE (SA)/Dec 30, 1911, p. 1072
HAGENBACK'S MENAGERIE (Pa)/Nov 5, 1910; p. 1056
HAIR OF HER HEAD, THE (Vi)/Jan 30, 1915; p. 671
HAIR RESTORER (WBE)/Aug 24,1907;p.393
HAIR RESTORER AND THE INDIANS, THE (Ed)/Aug 5, 1911;p.294
HAIRDRESSING OF OTHER DAYS (CGP)/Jul 20, 1912; p. 243
HAIRY AINUS, THE (Pa)/Mar 22, 1913; p. 1220
HAKO'S SACRIFICE (Vi)/Aug 6, 1910; p. 296
HAL CHASE'S HOME RUN (Ka)/Sep 9, 1911; p. 721/Oct 7, 1911; p. 41
HALF A CHANCE (Re)/Jun 21, 1913; pp 1241, 1254
HALF A HERO (Vi)/Jun 29, 1912; p. 1226
HALF A MILLION (Lu)/Nov 20, 1915; p. 1499
HALF A PINT OF MILK (CGP)/Nov 23, 1912; p. 767
HALF BREED, A/Dec 12, 1908; p. 476/ Dec 26, 1908; p. 526
HALF BREED, THE (Pa)/Feb 8, 1913; p. 571 (Ne)/Sep 26,1914;p.1777
HALF-BREED PARSON, THE (Bi)/Apr 12, 1913; p. 165
HALF BREED SHERIFF, THE (Fr)/Jul 26, 1913; p. 429
HALF BREED'S ATONEMENT, THE (Po)/Oct 7, 1911; p. 43
HALF-BREED'S COURAGE, A (Ch)/May 6, 1911; p. 1020
HALF-BREED'S DAUGHTER, THE (Vi)/Dec 2, 1911; p. 725
HALF BREED'S PLAN, A (Bi)/Feb 25, 1911; p. 432
HALF-BREED'S SACRIFICE, THE (Lu)/Sep 21, 1912; p. 1176
HALF-BREED'S WAY, THE (Ne)/Jun 15, 1912; p. 1028
HALF-MOON TAVERN, THE (KO)/Apr 11, 1908; p. 328
HALF ORPHANS, THE (Maj)/Apr 12, 1913; pp 165-66
HALF SHOT (Imp)/Nov 16, 1912; p. 659
HALF WAY TO RENO (Th)/Mar 1, 1913; p. 889
HALF-WIT, THE (Re)/Apr 12, 1913; p. 165
HALL ROOM RIVALS, THE (Vi)/Apr 11, 1914; p. 212
HALLROOM BOYS, THE (Sel)/Jul 23, 1910; p. 193
HALLROOM GIRLS, THE (Cry)/Jul 26, 1913; p. 430
HAM, THE DETECTIVE (Ka)/Jun 12, 1915; p. 1776
HAM, THE ICEMAN (Ka)/Dec 12, 1914; p. 1523
HAM, THE LINEMAN (Ka)/Sep 26, 1914; p. 1775
HAM, THE PIANO MOVER (Ka)/Nov 28, 1914; p. 1231
HAM ACTORS, THE (Po)/Sep 25, 1915; p. 2177
HAM AMONG THE REDSKINS (Ka)/Apr 10, 1915; p. 235
HAM AND THE EXPERIMENT (Ka)/Sep 11, 1915; p. 1832
HAM AND THE JITNEY BUS (Ka)/Mar 13, 1915; p. 1607
HAM AND THE SAUSAGE FACTORY (Ka)/Feb 27, 1915; p. 1287

HAM AND THE VILLAIN FACTORY
(Ka)/Nov 14, 1914; p. 931
HAM AT THE BEACH
(Ka)/Sep 4, 1915; p. 1643
HAM AT THE FAIR
(Ka)/Jun 26, 1915; p. 2095
HAM AT THE GARBAGE GENTLEMEN'S
BALL (Ka)/Apr 3, 1915; p. 63
HAM AT THE GENTLEMAN'S BALL
(Ka)/Mar 6, 1915; p. 1452
HAM IN THE HAREM
(Ka)/Mar 6, 1915; p. 1452
HAM IN THE NUT FACTORY
(Ka)/Jun 19, 1915; p. 1939
HAMLET (Lux)/Feb 12, 1910; p. 217
(GN)/Apr 22, 1911; p. 883
(Kni)/Jul 10, 1915; pp 317-18
HAMMER, THE (KB)/Jul 10, 1915; p. 309
HAM'S EASY EATS
(Ka)/May 22, 1915; p. 1259
HAM'S HARROWING DUEL
(Ka)/Apr 24, 1915; p. 555
HAND, THE (GN)/Sep 12, 1908; p. 201
(Pa)/Feb 20, 1909; p. 202
HAND BAG, THE (Vi)/Nov 23,1912;pp767-68
HAND BELL, THE (Gau)/Jul 10, 1909; p. 51
HAND OF DESTINY, THE
(Ka)/Sep 20, 1913; p. 1284
HAND OF FATE, THE
(Lu)/Jun 6, 1908; p. 497
(Vi)/Apr 9, 1910; p. 553
(Sel)/May 4, 1912; p. 426
(SA)/Mar 22, 1913; p. 1219
(Ka)/Sep 19, 1914; p. 1644
HAND OF GOD, THE (Vi)/Jul 17, 1915; p. 486
HAND OF HORROR, THE
(Ed)/Jul 4, 1914; p. 65
HAND OF IRON, THE
(Ed)/Nov 14, 1914; p. 931
HAND OF NAHAWEE, THE
(Sel)/May 15, 1915; p. 1071
HAND OF PROVIDENCE, THE
(At)/Dec 3, 1910; p. 1298
(Cry)/Sep 13, 1913; p. 1177
HAND OF THE HEIRESS
(Lu)/Feb 26, 1910; p. 298
HAND OF THE LAW, THE
(UE)/Sep 30, 1911; p. 970
(Ed)/Dec 18, 1915; pp 2197-98/
Dec 25, 1915; p. 2389
HAND OF UNCLE SAM, THE
(SA)/Apr 2, 1910; p. 509
HAND ORGAN MAN, THE
(Ka)/Oct 23, 1909; p. 567
HAND PRINT MYSTERY, THE
(Ka)/Feb 21, 1914; p. 947
HAND THAT CONDEMNS, THE
(WF)/Nov 8, 1913; p. 613

HAND THAT ROCKS THE CRADLE, THE
(SA)/Jan 31, 1914; p. 543
HAND THAT RULES THE WORLD, THE
(Po)/Mar 7, 1914; p. 1238
HANDICAP, THE (Lu)/Mar 23, 1912; p.1063
HANDICAP OF BEAUTY, THE
(Fal)/May 1, 1915; p. 728
HANDLE WITH CARE
(Roy)/Jun 27, 1914; p. 1829
HANDS ACROSS THE CRADLE
(Ne)/Aug 26, 1911; p. 544
HANDS ACROSS THE SEA
(Ec)/Nov 25, 1911; p. 620
HANDS OF A WIZARD, THE
(UE)/Feb 20, 1909; p. 203
HANDSOME HARRY'S WOOING
(Me)/Apr 11, 1914; p. 212
HANDSOMER MAN, A
(Vi)/Sep 9, 1911; p. 716
HANGING LAMP, THE
(Pa)/May 2, 1908; p. 402
HANK AND LANK (SA)/Oct 29, 1910;
pp 996, 998/Nov 5, 1910; p. 1059/
Feb 11, 1911; p. 316
HANK AND LANK - JOY RIDING
(SA)/Oct 1, 1910; p. 747
HANK AND LANK, SANDWICH MEN
(SA)/Dec 10, 1910; p. 1356
HANK AND LANK - THEY DUDE UP SOME
(SA)/Oct 22, 1910; p. 934
HANK AND LANK AS LIFE SAVERS
(SA)/Nov 19, 1910; p. 1178
HANKOW, CHINA (Sel)/Apr 26, 1913; p.381
HANKY PANKY CARDS
(KO)/Sep 7, 1907; p. 428
HANNAH DUSTIN (Ka)/Nov 28, 1908; p. 431
HANNAH'S HENPECKED HUSBAND
(Fal)/Nov 13, 1915; p. 1312
HANNIGAN'S HAREM
(Pa)/Jul 26, 1913; p. 428
HANS AND HIS BOSS
(Ed)/Apr 10, 1915; p. 235
HAN'S MILLIONS (SA)/Apr 1, 1911; p. 720
HANSOM DRIVER, A
(Key)/Jun 14, 1913; p. 1138
HAPLESS HUBBY, THE
(Pa)/Aug 29, 1908; p. 162
HAPPIER MAN, THE
(Be)/Feb 27, 1915; p. 1288
HAPPIEST DAY OF HER LIFE, THE
(Pa)/Sep 26, 1908; p. 242
HAPPY ACCIDENT, A
(Ed)/Dec 31, 1909; p. 961
HAPPY COERCION, A
(Am)/Apr 11, 1914; p. 214
HAPPY FAMILY, A (Imp)/Sep 7, 1912; p. 977
HAPPY-GO-LUCKY (Vi)/Jul 11,1914; p.255
HAPPY HOBOES HELP, THE

(Ne)/Dec 9, 1911; p. 819
HAPPY HOME, A (GN)/Aug 12, 1911;p.378
HAPPY HOME, THE
(Pa)/Apr 26, 1913; p. 380
HAPPY HOUSE, THE
(SA)/Aug 28, 1915; p. 1479
HAPPY IN SPITE OF HIMSELF
(Cin)/Mar 16, 1912; p. 961
HAPPY JACK, A HERO
(Bio)/Dec 24, 1910; p. 1476
HAPPY MAN'S SHIRT, THE
(KO)/Aug 29, 1908; p. 160
HAPPY PAIR, A (Rex)/Jul 24, 1915; p. 651
HAPPY THANKSGIVING, A
(Re)/Dec 9, 1911; p. 818
HAPPY WIDOWER, THE
(Pa)/Jan 8, 1910; p. 17
HARA-KIRI (Ape)/Jan 17, 1914; p. 295
HARBINGER OF PEACE, THE
(Ed)/Aug 10, 1912; p. 530
HARBOR OF LOVE, THE
(Sel)/Sep 12, 1914; p. 1512
HARBOR OF MARSEILLES, FRANCE
(UE)/Dec 23, 1911; p. 989
HARBOR PIRATES (Lu)/Nov 2, 1907; p. 564
HARD CASH (Imp)/Apr 16, 1910; p. 599
(Ed)/Sep 20, 1913; p. 1263/
Oct 11, 1913; p. 156
HARD CIDER (Key)/Oct 3, 1914; p. 65
HARD LUCK BILL (Ne)/Jul 13, 1912; p. 148
(SA)/Sep 20,1913; p.1283
HARD ROAD, THE (Vic)/Feb 27,1915;p.1290
HARD TO BEAT (Ed)/Apr 3, 1909; p. 403
HARD TO GET ARRESTED
(Pa)/Jul 25, 1908; p. 71
HARDEST WAY, THE
(Ec)/Jun 15, 1912; pp 1027-28
HARDUP FAMILY'S BLUFF, THE
(Pa)/Apr 12, 1913; p. 164
**HARE SHOOTING ON THE BALTIC
ARCHIPELAGO** (Vi)/Mar 13, 1915; p. 1607
HAREM CAPTIVES (Pa)/Dec 21,1912;p.1184
HAREM SKIRT, THE
(Am)/Apr 8, 1911; p. 782
HARLEQUIN'S NIGHTMARE
(Gau)/Nov 27, 1909; p. 759
HARLOWE HANDICAP, THE
(Th)/Jul 11, 1914; p. 257
HARM THE GOSSIPS DO, THE
(Lux)/Jan 27, 1912; p. 305
HARMLESS FLIRTATION, A
(Po)/Aug 26, 1911; p. 545
(MnA)/Jul 17, 1915; p. 485
HARMLESS ONE, THE
(Lu)/Dec 6, 1913; p. 1151
HARMONY AND DISCORD
(Fr)/Oct 11, 1913; p. 157
HARNESSED FALLS OF THE NORTHWEST

(Pa)/Oct 4, 1913; p. 47
HAROLD'S BAD MAN
(Sel)/Jan 30, 1915; p. 671
HAROLD'S TOUPEE
(Roy)/Oct 24, 1914; p. 493
HARP OF TARA, THE
(Dom)/Jan 10, 1914; p. 174
HARPER MYSTERY, THE
(Tur)/Nov 29, 1913; p. 990
HARRY, THE COUNTRY POSTMAN
(Pa)/Apr 25, 1908; p. 376
HARVEST (Bio)/Nov 6, 1915; p. 1139
HARVEST, THE (Re)/May 27, 1911; p. 1202
(Ne)/Feb 22, 1913; p. 782
HARVEST IN SICILY, THE
(CGP)/May 25, 1912; p. 729
HARVEST OF FLAME, THE
(Rex)/Aug 23, 1913; p. 846
HARVEST OF REGRETS, THE
(Th)/Oct 10, 1914; p. 188
HARVEST OF SIN, THE
(KB)/Dec 27, 1913; p. 1545
HARVEST ROMANCE, A
(WF)/Nov 21, 1914; p. 1077
HARVESTING (KO)/May 9, 1908; p. 423
HARVESTING ALFALFA IN NEW MEXICO
(Sel)/Oct 12, 1912; p. 143
HARVESTING ICE (Pr)/Aug 8, 1914; p. 837
HAS BEEN, THE (Th)/Oct 16, 1915; p. 440
HASH HOUSE COUNT, THE
(Ka)/May 24, 1913; p. 811
HASHER'S DELIRIUM, THE
(Gau)/Jun 4, 1910; p. 941
HASTY EXIT, A (Roy)/Jul 11, 1914; p. 256
HASTY JILTING, A
(Fr)/Aug 9, 1913; pp 637-38
HASTY HONEYMOON, A
(CGP)/May 4, 1912; p. 426
HASTY OPERATION, A
(Pa)/Apr 23, 1910; p. 641
HAT FULL OF TROUBLE, A
(Th)/Jan 2, 1915; p. 77
HAT JUGGLER, THE
(Pa)/Sep 4, 1909; p. 315
HATCHING CHICKENS
(Sel)/May 17, 1913; p. 703
HATE THAT WITHERS, THE
(Ka)/Jan 2, 1915; p. 76
HATEFUL GOD, THE
(KB)/Nov 14, 1914; p. 933
HATERS, THE (Am)/May 25,1912; pp 730-31
HATS AND HAPPINESS
(Po)/Jun 22, 1912; p. 1128
HATS IS HATS (Vi)/Nov 20, 1915; p. 1499
HATTIE, THE HAIR HEIRESS
(Fal)/Oct 23, 1915; p. 620
HATTIE'S NEW HAT
(Lu)/May 24, 1913; p. 811

HAUNTED (Sup)/Jan 23, 1915; p. 517
HAUNTED ATTIC, THE
  (Lu)/May 8, 1915; p. 899
HAUNTED BACHELOR, THE
  (Ec)/Sep 21, 1912; p. 1177
HAUNTED BEDROOM, THE
  (Ed)/Jan 3, 1914; p. 48
HAUNTED BRIDE, THE
  (Rex)/Nov 22, 1913; p. 869
HAUNTED BY CONSCIENCE
  (Ka)/Jul 30, 1910; p. 245
HAUNTED BY THE COPS
  (Pa)/May 15, 1909; p. 637
HAUNTED CASTLE
  (Pa)/May 9, 1908; pp 424-25
HAUNTED CASTLE, THE
  (TP)/Nov 27, 1909; p. 760
HAUNTED HAT, THE
  (Lu)/Sep 11, 1909; p. 347
HAUNTED HEARTS
  (GS)/Feb 27, 1915; p. 1290
HAUNTED HOUSE, THE
  (Imp)/Sep 16, 1911; p. 790
  (Ka)/May 10, 1913; p. 596
  (Pa)/Aug 23, 1913; p. 842
  (Am)/Nov 8, 1913; p. 613
HAUNTED HOUSE OF WILD ISLE, THE
  (Ka)/May 15, 1915; p. 1071
HAUNTED ISLAND, THE
  (Po)/Jul 22, 1911; p. 127
HAUNTED ROCKER, THE
  (Vi)/Apr 13, 1912; p. 136
HAUNTED SENTINEL TOWER, THE
  (Ed)/Apr 29, 1911; p. 958
HAUNTING EYE, THE
  (Pre)/Apr 3, 1915; p. 65
HAUNTING FEAR, THE
  (Ka)/May 29, 1915; p. 1438
HAUNTING MEMORY, THE
  (Be)/Mar 13, 1915; p. 1608
HAUNTING WINDS
  (Po)/Aug 14, 1915; p. 1162
HAUNTS OF FEAR, THE
  (Pa)/Nov 1, 1913; p. 497
HAVANA, CUBA (Sol)/Jul 27, 1912; p. 344
HAVANA, ITS STREETS, BUILDINGS AND
  FORTRESSES (CGP)/Aug 17, 1912; p. 669
HAVANA CIGAR (It)/Mar 11, 1911; p. 543
HAVE YOU SEEN MY WIFE?
  (Lu)/Jan 18, 1908; p. 46
HAVEN OF REFUGE, THE
  (Sel)/Apr 29, 1911; p. 958
HAVING THEIR PICTURES TOOK
  (Po)/Mar 29, 1913; p. 1338
HAWAIIAN LOVE (Ch)/May 24, 1913; p.813
HAWKEYE AND THE CHEESE MYSTERY
  (Ne)/Jun 13, 1914; p. 1543
HAWKEYE TO THE RESCUE

  (Ne)/Aug 16, 1913; p. 744
HAWKEYE'S GREAT CAPTURE
  (Ne)/Oct 25, 1913; p. 381
HAWKINS AND HIS DOGS
  (Pa)/Jun 24, 1911; p. 1453
HAWKINS' HAT (Lu)/Nov 5, 1910; p. 1058
HAWKINS MOVES (Po)/Dec 7, 1912; p. 978
HAWKINS' ROOMER
  (Po)/Mar 15, 1913; p. 1105
HAYSEED'S BARGAIN, THE
  (KO)/Aug 29, 1908; p. 160
HAZARD FOR A HEART, A
  (Gau)/Nov 30, 1912; p. 877
HAZARD OF YOUTH, THE
  (Lu)/Dec 20, 1913; p. 1411
HAZARDOUS COURTSHIP, A
  (Ed)/Jun 5, 1915; p. 1604
HAZARDS OF HELEN, THE (Ka)
  No.1/Nov 14, 1914; p. 913
  No.2/Dec 5, 1914; p. 1383
  No.3/Dec 12, 1914; p. 1523
  No.4/Nov 28, 1914; p. 1243
  No.5/Dec 26, 1914; p. 1840
  No.6/Jan 2, 1915; p. 75
  No.7/Jan 9, 1915; p. 220
  No.8/Jan 16, 1915; p. 368
  No.9/Jan 9, 1915; p. 201
  No.10/Jan 30, 1915; p. 671
  No.12/Feb 13, 1915; p. 984
  No.13/Feb 20, 1915; p. 1139
  No.14/Feb 27, 1915; p. 1288
  No.15/Mar 6, 1915; p. 1447
  No.16/Mar 20, 1915; p. 1763
  No.17/Mar 20, 1915; p. 1764
  No.18/Mar 27, 1915; p. 1932
  No.19/Apr 3, 1915; p. 64
  No.20/Apr 10, 1915; p. 235
  No.21/Apr 17, 1915; p. 392
  No.22/Apr 24, 1915; p. 556
  No.23/May 1, 1915; p. 727
  No.24/May 8, 1915; p. 899
  No.25/May 15, 1915; p. 1071
  No.26/May 22, 1915; p. 1259
  No.27/May 29, 1915; p. 1431
  No.28/Jun 5, 1915; p. 1604
  No.29/Jun 12, 1915; p. 1776
  No.30/Jun 19, 1915; p. 1939
  No.31/Jun 26, 1915; p. 2095
  No.32/Jul 3, 1915; p. 64
  No.33/Jul 10, 1915; p. 307
  No.34/Jul 17, 1915; p. 485
  No.35/Jul 24, 1915; p. 649
  No.36/Jul 31, 1915; p. 816
  No.37/Aug 7, 1915; p. 996
  No.38/Aug 14, 1915; p. 1160
  No.39/Aug 21, 1915; p. 1316
  No.40/Aug 28, 1915; p. 1479
  No.41/Sep 4, 1915; p. 1643

No.73/Nov 21, 1914; p. 1076
No.74/Nov 28, 1914; p. 1232
No.75/Nov 28, 1914; p. 1232
No.76/Nov 28, 1914; p. 1272
No.77/Dec 5, 1914; p. 1384
No.79/Dec 12, 1914; p. 1524
No.80/Dec 19, 1914; p. 1679
No.81/Dec 19, 1914; p. 1680
No.83/Dec 26, 1914; p. 1841
No.85/Jan 2, 1915; p. 76
No.86/Jan 9, 1915; p. 220
No.3/Jan 23, 1915; p. 516
No.6/Feb 6, 1915; p. 827
No.9/Feb 13, 1915; pp 984-85
No.10/Feb 20, 1915; p. 1139
No.11/Feb 27, 1915; p. 1287
No.13/Feb 27, 1915; p. 1288
No.15/Mar 6, 1915; p. 1447
No.18/Mar 20, 1915; p. 1763
No.19/Mar 27, 1915; p. 1931
No.20/Mar 27, 1915; p. 1932
No.21/Apr 3, 1915; p. 63
No.22/Apr 3, 1915; p. 63
No.23/Apr 10, 1915; p. 235
No.24/Apr 10, 1915; p. 235
No.25/Apr 17, 1915; p. 392
No.26/Apr 17, 1915; p. 392
No.27/Apr 24, 1915; p. 555
No.29/May 1, 1915; p. 727
No.30/May 1, 1915; p. 727
No.31/May 8, 1915; p. 899
No.32/May 8, 1915; p. 899
No.33/May 15, 1915; p. 1071
No.34/May 15, 1915; p. 1071
No.35/May 22, 1915; p. 1259
No.36/May 22, 1915; p. 1259
No.37/May 29, 1915; p. 1431
No.38/May 29, 1915; p. 1431
No.39/Jun 5, 1915; p. 1604
No.40/Jun 5, 1915; p. 1604
No.41/Jun 12, 1915; p. 1776
No.42/Jun 12, 1915; p. 1776
No.44/Jun 19, 1915; p. 1939
No.45/Jun 26, 1915; p. 2095
No.46/Jun 26, 1915; p. 2095
No.47/Jul 3, 1915; p. 64
No.48/Jul 3, 1915; p. 64
No.49/Jul 10, 1915; p. 307
No.50/Jul 10, 1915; p. 307
No.51/Jul 17, 1915; p. 485
No.52/Jul 17, 1915; p. 485
No.53/Jul 24, 1915; p. 649
No.54/Jul 24, 1915; p. 649
No.55/Jul 31, 1915; p. 816
No.56/Jul 31, 1915; p. 816
No.57/Aug 7, 1915; p. 996
No.58/Aug 7, 1915; p. 996
No.59/Aug 14, 1915; p. 1160

No.60/Aug 14, 1915; p. 1160
No.61/Aug 21, 1915; p. 1316
No.62/Aug 21, 1915; p. 1316
No.63/Aug 28, 1915; p. 1479
No.64/Aug 28, 1915; p. 1479
No.65/Sep 4, 1915; p. 1643
No.66/Sep 4, 1915; p. 1643
No.67/Sep 11, 1915; p. 1832
No.68/Sep 11, 1915; p. 1832
No.69/Sep 18, 1915; p. 1995
No.70/Sep 18, 1915; p. 1995
No.71/Sep 25, 1915; p. 2176
No.72/Sep 25, 1915; p. 2176
No.74/Oct 2, 1915; p. 78
No.75/Oct 9, 1915; p. 252
No.76/Oct 9, 1915; p. 252
No.77/Oct 16, 1915; p. 439
No.79/Oct 23, 1915; p. 619
No.80/Oct 23, 1915; p. 619
No.81/Oct 30, 1915; p. 791
No.82/Oct 30, 1915; p. 791
No.84/Oct 30a, 1915; p. 967
No.85/Nov 6, 1915; p. 1139
No.87/Nov 13, 1915; p. 1311
No.88/Nov 13, 1915; p. 1311
No.89/Nov 20, 1915; p. 1499
No.91/Nov 27, 1915; p. 1663
No.92/Nov 27, 1915; p. 1663
No.93/Dec 4, 1915; p. 1852
No.97/Dec 18, 1915; p. 2202
No.98/Dec 18, 1915; p. 2202
No.99/Dec 25, 1915; p. 2388
No.100/Dec 25, 1915; p. 2388
HEART AWAKENED, A (Lu)/Oct 2,1915; p.78
HEART BEATS (Fl)/Aug 1, 1914; pp 679-80
     (Re)/Feb 20, 1915; p. 1140
HEART BEATS OF LONG AGO
   (Bio)/Feb 18, 1911; pp 370-71
HEART BOWED DOWN, A
   (Ec)/Dec 30, 1911; p. 1073
HEART BREAKER, THE
   (U)/Apr 10, 1915; p. 238
HEART BROKERS, THE
   (Lu)/Mar 29, 1913; p. 1336
HEART IN RAGS, A
   (Sel)/Nov 16, 1912; p. 658
HEART OF A BANDIT, THE
   (Bio)/Mar 6, 1915; p. 1447
HEART OF A "BOSS," THE
   (Lu)/Feb 3, 1912; p. 393
HEART OF A BRUTE, THE
   (Box)/Oct 3, 1914; p. 66
HEART OF A CLOWN
   (Ed)/Dec 11, 1909; p. 841
HEART OF A COSSACK, THE (Re)/Sep 7,
   1912; pp 959-60/Sep 14, 1912; p. 1076
HEART OF A COWBOY, THE
   (SA)/Jan 8, 1910; p. 17

(De)/Nov 5, 1910; pp 1060-61
HEART OF A CRACKSMAN, THE
(Po)/Nov 15, 1913; p. 737
HEART OF A CROOK, THE
(KB)/Jul 4, 1914; p. 66
HEART OF A DOLL, THE
(Gau)/Nov 15, 1913; p. 737
HEART OF A FOOL, THE
(Maj)/Sep 20, 1913; p. 1285
HEART OF A GAMBLER, THE
(SA)/Aug 2, 1913; p. 535
HEART OF A GYPSY, THE
(Imp)/Aug 3, 1912; p. 446
(Cin)/Jan 31, 1914; p. 544
HEART OF A GYPSY MAID (Pa)/Oct 17,
1908; p. 306/Oct 24, 1908; p. 318
HEART OF A JEWESS, THE (Uni)/Jul 19,
1913; p. 300/Aug 23, 1913; p. 845
HEART OF A MAGDALEN, A
(Po)/Dec 5, 1914; p. 1385
HEART OF A MAN, THE
(Vi)/Feb 24, 1912; p. 690
(WF)/Dec 26, 1914; p. 1842
HEART OF A PAINTED WOMAN, THE
(Mto)/May 1, 1915; p. 739
HEART OF A POLICE OFFICER, THE
(WS)/Dec 6, 1913; p. 1153
HEART OF A RACE TOUT, THE
(Sel)/Aug 7, 1909; p. 195
HEART OF A ROSE
(Ed)/Apr 16, 1910; p. 598
HEART OF A SAVAGE, THE
(Bio)/Mar 18, 1911; p. 602
HEART OF A SIOUX, THE
(Lu)/Aug 20, 1910; p. 407
HEART OF A SOLDIER, THE
(Am)/Dec 21, 1912; p. 1185
HEART OF A TIGRESS, THE
(Bi)/Nov 13, 1915; p. 1314
HEART OF A VAGABOND, THE
(Amb)/Apr 30, 1910; pp 690-91
HEART OF A VAQUERO, THE
(Ne)/Sep 27, 1913; p. 1393
HEART OF A WAIF, THE
(Ed)/May 8, 1915; p. 899
HEART OF A WARRIOR, THE
(Ec)/Mar 4, 1911; p. 484
HEART OF A WOMAN, THE
(Dom)/Jan 31, 1914; p. 545
HEART OF AN ACTRESS, THE
(Ya)/Dec 10, 1910; p. 1359
(Ka)/May 17, 1913; p. 703
(Bio)/Jun 19, 1915; p. 1939
HEART OF AN ARTIST, THE
(Cry)/Dec 20, 1913; p. 1413
HEART OF AN INDIAN MAID, THE
(Pa)/Jun 10, 1911; p. 1313
HEART OF AN INDIAN MOTHER, THE

(Ka)/Feb 4, 1911; p. 244
HEART OF CARITA, THE
(Ec)/Mar 7, 1914; p. 1238
HEART OF CERISE, THE
(Uni)/May 22, 1915; p. 1272
HEART OF ESMERALDA, THE
(Vi)/Aug 24, 1912; p. 770
HEART OF FLAME (Am)/Mar 6, 1915;
p. 1455/Mar 13, 1915; p. 1608
HEART OF HERNANDA, THE
(Po)/Jun 28, 1913; p. 1361
HEART OF INDIA, THE
(Sav)/May 29, 1915; p. 1441
HEART OF JABEZ FLINT, THE
(KB)/Aug 7, 1915; p. 997
HEART OF JENNIFER, THE
(FP)/Sep 11, 1915; p. 1844
HEART OF JIM BRICE, THE
(Vi)/Apr 17, 1915; p. 392
HEART OF JOHN BARLOW, THE
(Sel)/Sep 23, 1911; p. 891
HEART OF JOHN GRIMM, THE
(SA)/Oct 12, 1912; p. 142
HEART OF KATHLEEN, THE (Bro)/Oct 18,
1913; p. 248/Oct 25, 1913; p. 382
HEART OF LADY ALAINE, THE
(GN)/Jul 3, 1915; p. 79
HEART OF LINCOLN, THE (GS)/Jan 30,
1915; p. 686/Feb 13, 1915; p. 986
HEART OF MAGGIE MALONE, THE
(Sel)/Feb 21, 1914; p. 946
HEART OF MARYLAND, THE
(Tif)/Mar 27, 1915; p. 1945
HEART OF MIDLOTHIAN, THE
(He)/May 23, 1914; p. 1093
HEART OF MRS. ROBBINS, THE
(Vi)/Jun 21, 1913; p. 1251
HEART OF NICHETTE, THE
(Ed)/Dec 23, 1911; p. 988
HEART OF O YAMA, THE
(Bio)/Sep 19, 1908; p. 221
HEART OF PEDRO, THE
(Sel)/Aug 7, 1915; p. 996
HEART OF PRINCESS MIRSARI, THE
(Th)/May 22, 1915; p. 1260
HEART OF SMILING JOE, THE
(Fr)/Feb 14, 1914; p. 810
HEART OF SONNY JIM, THE
(Vi)/Oct 17, 1914; p. 335
HEART OF STEEL, A
(Cin)/May 10, 1913; p. 595
HEART OF TESSA, THE
(Cap)/May 28, 1910; p. 891
HEART OF THE BLUE RIDGE
(Wor)/Oct 23, 1915; p. 628
HEART OF THE FOREST, A
(Vi)/Mar 22, 1913; p. 1219
HEART OF THE HEATHEN, THE

(Po)/Aug 9, 1913; p. 638

HEART OF THE HEATHEN CHINEE, THE
(Sel)/May 28, 1910; p. 889

HEART OF THE LAW, THE
(SA)/Dec 27, 1913; p. 1543

HEART OF THE NIGHT WIND
(Vic)/Nov 28, 1914; p. 1233

HEART OF THE RED MAN, THE
(Gau)/Oct 5, 1912; p. 43

HEART OF THE ROSE, THE
(Re)/Nov 1, 1913; p. 498

HEART OF THE SHERIFF, THE
(Sel)/Jul 3, 1915; p. 64

HEART OF VALESKA, THE
(Ed)/May 24, 1913; p. 812

HEART PUNCH, THE
(Imp)/Feb 13, 1915; p. 985

HEART REBELLIOUS, THE
(Lu)/Aug 29, 1914; p. 1241

HEART RECLAIMED, A
(Rex)/Dec 7, 1912; p. 977

HEART THAT KNEW, THE
(Pa)/Jun 26, 1915; p. 2097

HEART THAT SEES, THE
(Imp)/Jun 7, 1914; p. 1032

HEART THROBS (Bro)/Jul 19, 1913; p. 321

HEART TROUBLE (Bio)/Oct 2, 1915; p. 78

HEARTACHES (Lu)/Dec 25, 1915; p. 2385

HEARTBREAKER BY TRADE, A
(Gau)/Oct 7, 1911; p. 39

HEARTBROKEN SHEP
(Vi)/Oct 25, 1913; p. 380

HEARTEASE (Vi)/Jan 10, 1914; p. 173

HEARTH LIGHTS (Re)/Jun 7,1913; p.1032

HEARTS (Re)/Oct 25, 1913; pp 381-82

HEARTS, HUNGER AND HAPPINESS
(Pa)/Feb 18, 1911; p. 370

HEARTS ABLAZE (Vi)/Sep 18, 1915; p.1995

HEARTS ADRIFT (FP)/Feb 21, 1914; p. 927

HEARTS AND CLUBS
(Jo)/Jun 5, 1915; p. 1606
(Cub)/Dec 25, 1915; p. 2389

HEARTS AND CROSSES
(Ec)/May 31, 1913; p. 921

HEARTS AND DIAMONDS
(Ed)/Oct 5, 1912; p. 40
(Vi)/Oct 10, 1914; p. 188

HEARTS AND EYES (Ec)/Oct 7, 1911; p. 43

HEARTS AND FLAGS
(Ed)/Jun 10, 1911; p. 1313

HEARTS AND FLAMES
(Lko)/Apr 3, 1915; p. 66

HEARTS AND FLOWERS
(Gem)/Jun 21, 1913; p. 1254
(SA)/Jan 24, 1914; p. 412
(Vic)/Mar 14, 1914; p. 1386
(Maj)/Sep 11, 1915; p. 1833

HEARTS AND HOOFS

(Maj)/Aug 16, 1913; p. 745

HEARTS AND HORSES
(Am)/Jun 14, 1913; p. 1138

HEARTS AND MEMORIES
(Ec)/Jul 13, 1912; p. 148

HEARTS AND PLANETS
(Key)/Mar 6, 1915; pp 1448, 1457

HEARTS AND POLITICS
(Lu)/Oct 29, 1910; p. 996

HEARTS AND ROSES
(SA)/Sep 11, 1915; p. 1832

HEARTS AND SKIRTS
(Ne)/Oct 12, 1912; p. 144

HEARTS AND SWORDS
(Bio)/Sep 23, 1911; p. 889
(St)/May 30, 1914; p. 1262
(Dom)/Jun 26, 1915; p. 2097

HEARTS AND THE HIGHWAY
(Vi)/Jan 30, 1915; p. 682

HEARTS ARE TRUMPS
(Lu)/Mar 26, 1910; p. 466
(Pa)/May 23, 1914; pp 1116-17

HEART'S BIDDING, THE
Nov 21, 1908; p. 398

HEART'S DESIRE (Sel)/Feb 13, 1915; p. 984

HEART'S DEVOTION, A
(Gau)/Dec 4, 1909; p. 799

HEARTS ENTANGLED
(Cry)/Oct 11, 1913; p. 157

HEART'S HUNGER (Bio)/Feb 6,1915; p.827

HEARTS IN EXILE
(Wor)/Apr 17, 1915; p. 401

HEARTS IN SHADOW
(Am)/Oct 9, 1915; p. 253

HEARTS OF GOLD
(Ne)/Aug 27, 1910; p. 464
(Bio)/Nov 14, 1914; p. 931

HEARTS OF ITALY
(Po)/Jan 27, 1912; p. 305

HEARTS OF MEN
(SA)/Aug 3, 1912; p. 445
(Sel)/Jul 18, 1914; p. 432
(HaW)/Nov 20, 1915; pp 1502, 1503-4

HEARTS OF OAK
(Moh)/May 23, 1914; p. 1119

HEARTS OF THE BRADYS, THE
(U)/Jan 16, 1915; p. 369

HEARTS OF THE DARK
(Re)/Oct 4, 1913; pp 49-50

HEARTS OF THE FIRST EMPIRE
(Vi)/May 10, 1913; p. 596

HEARTS OF THE FOREST
(Ed)/Sep 19, 1914; p. 1644

HEARTS OF THE JUNGLE
(Sel)/Mar 20, 1915; p. 1763

HEARTS OF THE NORTHLAND
(Imp)/Jan 18, 1913; p. 265

HEARTS OF THE WEST

HENRY'S PACKAGE
(SA)/Jun 11, 1910; p. 997
HENRY'S WATERLOO
(Th)/Aug 1, 1914; p. 705
HEN'S DUCKLING, THE
(Re)/Mar 20, 1915; p. 1765
HER ADOPTED FATHER
(SA)/Sep 7, 1912; p. 975
(Be)/Nov 13, 1915; p. 1312
HER ADOPTED FATHERS
(Sel)/Apr 8, 1911; p. 782
HER ADOPTIVE PARENTS
(Vi)/Oct 8, 1910; p. 814
HER ALIBI (Dom)/May 22, 1915; p. 1260
HER AMBITION (Po)/Oct 5, 1912; p. 42
HER ANSWER (Lu)/Jul 10, 1915; p. 307
HER ARTISTIC TEMPERAMENT
(Lu)/Apr 1, 1911; p. 718
HER ATONEMENT (Po)/Jun 3, 1911; p.1261
(Lu)/Jul 12, 1913; p. 205
(AsC)/Oct 2, 1915; p. 81
HER AWAKENING (Bio)/Oct 14,1911; p.128
(Pr)/May 2, 1914; p. 673
(Maj)/Oct 3, 1914; p. 65
HER BANDIT SWEETHEART
(WF)/Nov 7, 1914; p. 789
HER BARGAIN (U)/Feb 6, 1915; p. 829
HER BATTLE FOR EXISTENCE (Th)/
Apr 30, 1910; p.690/May 7, 1910; p.738
HER BETTER NATURE
(UE)/Jun 8, 1912; p. 942
HER "BIG" BROTHER
(Th)/Aug 29, 1914; p. 1242
HER BIG SCOOP (Bio)/May 16, 1914; p. 968
HER BIG STORY
(Am)/May 31, 1913; pp 909, 921
HER BIRTHDAY PRESENT
(Key)/Feb 15, 1913; p. 681
(WF)/Dec 19, 1914; p. 1681
HER BIRTHDAY ROSES
(Rep)/Jun 8, 1912; p. 946
HER BIRTHDAY SURPRISE (Ya)/Mar 4,
1911; p. 484/Mar 11, 1911; p. 543
HER BITTER LESSON
(Sel)/Nov 16, 1912; p. 658
(Ka)/Dec 12, 1914; p. 1524
HER BOUNTY (Rex)/Sep 19, 1914; p. 1646
HER BOY (Pa)/Aug 5, 1911; pp 292-93
(Vi)/Feb 24, 1912; p. 689
(Lu)/Jan 17, 1914; pp 288-89
HER BOYS (SA)/Feb 24, 1912; p. 689
HER BRAVE HERO
(Maj)/Dec 19, 1914; p. 1680
HER BRAVE RESCUER
(Pa)/Oct 4, 1913; p. 47
HER BROTHER (Vi)/Jul 6, 1912; p. 43
(Fr)/Jan 24, 1914; p. 413
HER BROTHER'S PARD

(Amm)/Jan 3, 1914; p. 49
HER BROTHER'S PARTNER
(Ch)/Feb 3, 1912; p. 394
HER BROTHER'S PHOTOGRAPH (Ed)/
Jul 1, 1911; p. 1520/Jul 8, 1911; pp 1567-68
HER BURGLAR (Imp)/Sep 7, 1912; p. 976
HER BURIED PAST
(Maj)/Mar 27, 1915; p. 1934
HER BUSY DAY (Gau)/Sep 25, 1909; p. 415
HER CAPTIVE (Bi)/Jul 29, 1911; p. 213
HER CAREER (Sel)/May 22, 1915; p. 1259
HER CHOICE (Vi)/Oct 12, 1912; p. 143
(Lu)/Jul 17, 1915; p. 485
HER CHUM'S BROTHER
(Ka)/Feb 4, 1911; p. 243
HER CONFESSION (Th)/Dec 11,1915;p.2032
HER CONVERT (Bio)/Jul 10, 1915; p. 307
HER CONVICT BROTHER
(Ka)/Jun 8, 1912; p. 942
HER CORNER ON HEARTS
(Ne)/May 11, 1912; p. 529
HER COUNTRY COUSIN
(Ed)/Apr 3, 1915; p. 63
HER COUSIN FRED
(Vic)/Aug 31, 1912; p. 881
HER COWBOY LOVER
(Vi)/Nov 18, 1911; p. 550
HER CROWNING GLORY
(Vi)/Sep 23, 1911; p. 889
(Kin)/Mar 8, 1913; p. 997
HER DAD, THE CONSTABLE (SA)/Jul 22,
1911; p. 106/Jul 29, 1911; p. 211
HER DAD'S PISTOL (Po)/Jul 2, 1910; p. 26
HER DARKEST HOUR
(Imp)/Feb 25, 1911; p. 432
HER DIARY (Lux)/Nov 19, 1910; p. 1178
(Vi)/Jun 29, 1912; p. 1227
(Po)/Aug 31, 1912; p. 882
HER DOLLY'S REVENGE
(Lux)/Feb 26, 1910; p. 300
HER DORMANT LOVE
(Bio)/Jun 19, 1915; p. 1939
HER DRAMATIC CAREER
(Pa)/Nov 27, 1909; p. 757
HER DREAMS OF YESTERDAY
(Exc)/Mar 29, 1913; p. 1337
HER DRESSMAKERS' BILLS
(Cry)/Oct 26, 1912; pp 344-45
HER DUPLICATE HUSBAND
(WF)/Dec 12, 1914; p. 1540
HER DUTY (Pr)/Aug 15, 1914; p. 961
HER EASTER HAT
(KB)/May 29, 1915; p. 1432
HER EDUCATION (Sel)/Nov 23, 1912; p.766
HER ESCAPE (Rex)/Dec 12, 1914; p. 1538
HER EXCLUSIVE HAT
(Lu)/Nov 4, 1911; p. 378
HER FACE (Ed)/Mar 2, 1912; pp 768-69/

(Ch)/Oct 12, 1912; p. 144
HER WINNING WAY
(Me)/Sep 3, 1910; p. 518
HER WONDERFUL DAY
(Imp)/Aug 7, 1915; p. 998
HER WOODEN LEG (Lu)/Sep 6,1913;p.1068
HER WORDS CAME TRUE
(Sel)/Apr 1, 1911; p. 720
HER YOUNGER SISTER (Am)/Dec 19,
1914; p. 1698/Dec 26, 1914; p. 1841
HERCULES AND THE BIG STICK
(Gau)/Jul 2, 1910; p. 25
HERCULES THE ATHLETE
(GN)/Dec 26, 1908; p. 525
HERDERS, THE (Sel)/Jun 3, 1911; p. 1259
HERE AND THERE IN CHINA WITH
HOMER CREY (Ne)/Dec 19, 1914; p. 1681
HERE AND THERE IN OREGON
(Pa)/Aug 24, 1912; p. 771
HERE COMES THE BRIDE
(Lu)/Apr 3, 1915; p. 63
HEREDITY (Bio)/Nov 16, 1912; p. 659
(Vi)/Nov 27, 1915; p. 1664
HERITAGE (Uni)/Jul 24, 1915; p. 666
HERITAGE, THE (Maj)/Oct 18, 1913; p. 265
HERITAGE OF EVE, THE
(Bro)/Aug 23, 1913; p. 845
HERMIT (KO)/Dec 26, 1908; p. 525
HERMIT, THE (Pa)/Sep 23, 1911; p. 890
(SA)/Sep 14, 1912; p. 1074
(Am)/Jan 31, 1914; p. 524/
Feb 7, 1914; p. 678
HERMIT CRAB, THE
(CGP)/Nov 9, 1912; p. 553
HERMIT OF BIRD ISLAND, THE
(Lu)/Mar 20, 1915; p. 1764
HERMIT OF THE ROCKIES, THE
(Ch)/Aug 20, 1910; p. 408
HERMIT'S GOLD, THE
(Am)/Jul 8, 1911; p. 1586
HERMIT'S RUSE, THE
(Ka)/Nov 1, 1913; p. 495
HERMIT'S SECRET, THE
(Ec)/Jan 9, 1915; p. 221
HERO, THE (Imp)/May 6, 1911; p. 1021
(Vi)/Mar 14, 1914; p. 1384
HERO - ALMOST, A
(Lu)/Jun 3, 1911; p. 1259
HERO AMONG MEN, A
(Lu)/Jul 26, 1913; pp 427, 436
HERO AND LEANDER
(Amb)/Feb 12, 1910; p. 217
HERO-COWARD, THE (SA)/Mar 15, 1913;
p. 1084/Apr 12, 1913; p. 163
HERO ENGINEER, THE
(Ka)/Jul 16, 1910; p. 143
HERO OF LITTLE ITALY, THE
(Bio)/Apr 19, 1913; p. 279

HERO OF THE HOUR, THE
(Imp)/Feb 1, 1913; p. 466
HERO TRACK WALKER, THE
(Ka)/Apr 15, 1911; p. 842
HEROD AND THE NEW BORN KING
(Gau)/Dec 31, 1910; pp 1519, 1536
HERODIAS (Ec)/May 6, 1911; p.1020
HEROES OF ST. BERNARD, THE
Feb 20, 1909; p. 203
HEROES OF THE BLUE AND GREY
(Ch)/Jun 8, 1912; p. 946
HEROES OF THE MUTINY
(Vi)/Dec 9, 1911; p. 816
HEROES ONE AND ALL
(Lu)/Apr 12, 1913; p. 164
HEROES THREE (Ed)/Jun 24,
1911; p. 1454/Jul 8, 1911; p. 1568
HEROIC COWARD, A
(Ya)/Aug 27, 1910; p. 464
HEROIC FATHER, AN
(Pa)/Aug 28, 1909; p. 282
HEROIC GIRL FROM DERNA
(IFT)/Jun 15, 1912; p. 1016
HEROIC HAROLD (Cry)/Jan 18, 1913; p.266
HEROIC RESCUE, A
(Ed)/Mar 1, 1913; p. 887
HEROINE OF MAFEKING, THE (Sel)/
Dec 18, 1909; p. 879/Dec 25, 1909; p. 920
HEROINE OF 101 RANCH, THE
(Col)/Nov 19, 1910; p. 1178
HEROINE OF THE REVOLUTION, A
(Sol)/Nov 11, 1911; p. 474
HEROINE OF PAWNEE JUNCTION, THE
(Ya)/Jul 9, 1910; p. 85
HEROINE OF '76, A (Rex)/Feb 18, 1911;
p. 373/Mar 4, 1911; p. 484
HEROINE OF THE FORGE, THE
(Vi)/Jan 23, 1909; p. 93
HEROINE OF THE PLAINS, THE
(Bi)/Jan 4, 1913; p. 52
HEROISM (Gau)/Dec 23, 1911; p.989
HERO'S REWARD, A (Ka)/Feb 1, 1913; p. 464
HERRING FISHING OFF BOULOGNE
(Pa)/Aug 5, 1911; p. 293
HE'S A BEAR (Lu)/Jun 26, 1915; p. 2095
HE'S A LAWYER (Bio)/Nov 29,1913; p.1007
HE'S IN AGAIN (MnA)/Aug 14,1915; p.1160
HESANUT BUYS AN AUTO
(Ka)/Oct 31, 1914; p. 641
HESANUT HUNTS WILD GAME
(Ka)/Oct 24, 1914; p. 491
HEY RUBE! (Com)/Dec 28, 1912; p. 1294
HEY THERE, LOOK OUT
(SA)/Oct 12, 1907; p. 505
HI FEATHERTOP AT THE FAIR
(SA)/Nov 18, 1911; p. 549
HIAWANDA'S CROSS
(Lu)/Nov 22, 1913; p. 867

HIGHWAYMAN, THE
 Nov 14, 1908; pp 378-79
 (Vi)/Aug 7, 1915; p. 996
HIGHWAYMAN'S HONOR, A
 (Mec)/Jun 27, 1914; p. 1802
HIGHWAYMAN'S SHOE, THE
 (Ec)/Dec 20, 1913; p. 1414
HILARY OF THE HILLS
 (SBa)/Nov 6, 1915; p. 1141
HILDA OF HERON COVE
 (Sel)/Dec 27, 1913; p. 1544
HILDA OF THE MOUNTAINS
 (Ne)/Nov 29, 1913; p. 1009
HILDA OF THE SLUMS
 (Vi)/Jun 12, 1915; p. 1776
HILDA WAKES (SA)/Jul 5, 1913; p. 47
HILLS OF CORSICA, THE
 (Gau)/Jan 21, 1911; p. 144
HILLS OF PEACE, THE
 (SA)/Jan 24, 1914; p. 412
HILLS OF STRIFE, THE
 (Lu)/Sep 27, 1913; p. 1392
HINDOO CHARM, THE
 (Vi)/Oct 4, 1913; p. 47
HINDOO CURSE, THE
 (Vi)/Sep 28, 1912; p. 1276
HINDOO DAGGER, THE
 (Bio)/Feb 27, 1909; p. 237
HINDOO'S CHARM, THE
 (Lu)/Aug 31, 1912; p. 880
HINDOO'S PRIZE, THE
 (Imp)/Aug 17, 1912; p. 674
HINDU JEWEL MYSTERY, THE
 (UE)/Nov 25, 1911; p. 638
HINDU NEMESIS, THE
 (MP)/Apr 11, 1914; p. 217
HINEMOA (Me)/Apr 12, 1913; p. 163
HIPPOPOTAMUS HUNT, A
 (Pa)/Jul 1, 1911; p. 1519
HIPPOPOTAMUS HUNTING ON THE NILE
 (Pa)/May 8, 1909; p. 595
HIRAM BUYS AN AUTO
 (Sel)/May 10, 1913; p. 597
HIRAM GREEN, DETECTIVE
 (Ed)/Nov 1, 1913; p. 496
HIRAM'S HOTEL (Ka)/Mar 21, 1914; p.1524
HIRAM'S INHERITANCE
 (Jo)/May 29, 1915; p. 1433
HIRED, TIRED, FIRED
 (SA)/Sep 19, 1908; p. 221
HIRED DRESS SUIT, THE
 (Maj)/Mar 1, 1913; p. 889
HIRED GIRL, THE
 (Maj)/Jul 17, 1915; p. 486
HIRING A GEM (SA)/Oct 29, 1910; p. 998
HIRING A GIRL (Lu)/Jul 31, 1909; p. 161
HIS AFFIANCED WIFE
 (Bro)/May 15, 1915; p. 1072

HIS AFFINITY (Ka)/Nov 9, 1907; p. 581
HIS ATHLETIC WIFE
 (SA)/Sep 13, 1913; p. 1175
HIS AUNT EMMA (Cry)/Aug 30, 1913; p.962
HIS AUTO'S MAIDEN TRIP
 (Bio)/Nov 23, 1912; p. 766
HIS AWFUL DAUGHTER
 (Cry)/May 17, 1913; p. 705
HIS BABY DOLL
 (Pa)/Jun 17, 1911; pp 1362-63, 1386
HIS BABY'S SHIRT
 (Po)/Aug 20, 1910; p. 408
HIS BACHELOR DINNER
 (Re)/Apr 24, 1915; p. 556
HIS BELOVED VIOLIN
 (U)/Aug 14, 1915; p. 1162
HIS BEST FRIEND
 (Sol)/Feb 11, 1911; p. 318
 (Lu)/Dec 27, 1913; p. 1544
HIS BEST GIRL AFTER ALL
 (Lu)/Apr 22, 1911; p. 898
HIS BEST GIRL'S LITTLE BROTHER
 (Sel)/Apr 29, 1911; p. 957
HIS BETTER SELF
 (Sel)/Nov 4, 1911; p. 379
 (Sol)/Nov 4, 1911; p. 381
 (Bro)/Oct 5, 1912; p. 43
 (Lu)/Jul 26, 1913; p. 429
 (Fr)/Dec 20, 1913; p. 1413
HIS BIG CHANCE
 (Vic)/Nov 7, 1914; p. 788
HIS BIRTHDAY (Lu)/Jul 22, 1911; p. 124
HIS BIRTHDAY GIFT
 (Bio)/Sep 11, 1915; p. 1832
HIS BODY GUARD
 (Lu)/Nov 13, 1915; p. 1311
HIS BOGUS UNCLE
 (Lu)/Feb 11, 1911; p. 316
HIS BRAND (Rex)/Sep 27, 1913; p. 1393
HIS BREACH OF DISCIPLINE
 (Ed)/Nov 5, 1910; p. 1058
HIS BROTHER BILL
 (Lu)/Oct 17, 1914; p. 336
HIS BROTHER WILLIE
 (Po)/Mar 2, 1912; p. 781
HIS BROTHER'S BLOOD
 (Lu)/Sep 5, 1914; p. 1372
HIS BROTHER'S DEBT (Am)/Apr 10, 1915;
 p. 241/Apr 17, 1915; p. 393
HIS BROTHER'S DOUBLE
 (Lu)/Dec 9, 1911; p. 816
HIS BROTHER'S KEEPER
 (Ne)/Feb 1, 1913; p. 466
 (KB)/Mar 27, 1915; p. 1934
 (Bio)/Apr 10, 1915; p. 236
HIS BROTHER'S WIFE
 (GG)/Jul 25, 1914; p. 573
HIS BROTHER'S WIVES

HIS FIGHT (Sel)/Jul 25, 1914; p. 571
HIS FIGHTING BLOOD
   (Sel)/Jan 30, 1915; p. 672
HIS FIREMAN'S CONSCIENCE
   (Bio)/Feb 7, 1914; p. 677
HIS FIRST CASE (Am)/Dec 13,1913; p.1280
                     (Lu)/Oct 17, 1914; p. 336
HIS FIRST COMMISSION
   (Ed)/Feb 25, 1911; p. 430
HIS FIRST EXPERIENCE
   (Lu)/Jun 7, 1913; p. 1031
HIS FIRST FLIGHT
   (Pa)/Feb 27, 1909; p. 238
HIS FIRST FROCK COAT (Pa)/Oct 17,
   1908; p. 305/Nov 14, 1908; p. 379
HIS FIRST GIRL
   (Vi)/May 1, 1909; pp 553, 554
HIS FIRST KODAK
   (Pun)/Mar 22, 1913; p. 1222
HIS FIRST LONG TROUSERS
   (Sel)/Nov 18, 1911; p. 550
HIS FIRST LOVE (Maj)/Mar 21,1914; p.1525
HIS FIRST MONOCLE
   (GN)/Dec 23, 1911; p. 991
HIS FIRST PATIENT
   (Imp)/Feb 4, 1911; p. 249
   (GN)/Dec 21, 1912; p. 1186
HIS FIRST PERFORMANCE
   (Ed)/Nov 8, 1913; p. 611
HIS FIRST RIDE
   (Sel)/Jun 20, 1914; p. 1688
HIS FIRST ROW/Nov 14, 1908; p. 378
HIS FIRST SKATE
   (Lu)/Dec 28, 1912; p. 1291
HIS FIRST SWEETHEART
   (Gau)/Mar 25, 1911; p. 656
HIS FIRST "TOPPER"
   (Mi)/Oct 5, 1907; p. 491
HIS FIRST TRIP
   (Ed)/Sep 2, 1911; p. 628
HIS FIRST VALENTINE
   (Ed)/Mar 26, 1910; p. 466
HIS FRIEND, THE BURGLAR
   (Lu)/Mar 25, 1911; p. 657
HIS FRIEND, THE CAPTAIN
   (Pa)/Apr 10, 1915; p. 237
HIS FRIEND, THE UNDERTAKER
   (Ne)/Aug 2, 1913; p. 538
HIS FRIEND JIMMIE
   (Ne)/Apr 26, 1913; p. 381
HIS FRIEND'S WIFE
   (SA)/Jun 17, 1911; p. 1387
HIS GIRLIE (Lu)/Sep 30, 1911; p. 970
HIS GIRL'S LAST WISH
   (KO)/Jul 18, 1908; p. 52
HIS GOLDEN CHAIN (Vi)/Oct 2, 1915; p. 79
HIS GOOD INTENTIONS
   (Ne)/Mar 9, 1912; p. 867

HIS GRANDCHILD
   (Cin)/Mar 8,1913;p.979/Mar 22,1913;p.1220
   (Ed)/Feb 28, 1914; p. 1088
HIS GREAT DUTY
   (GN)/Mar 11, 1911; p. 543
HIS GREAT SACRIFICE
   (At)/Feb 18, 1911; p. 372
   (Ya)/Jul 22, 1911; p. 126
HIS GREAT UNCLE'S SPIRIT
   (Th)/Mar 16, 1912;p. 963
HIS GREATEST VICTORY
   (Ed)/Aug 23, 1913; p. 843
HIS GUARDIAN ANGEL
   (Vic)/Jan 30, 1915; p. 673
HIS GUARDIAN AUTO
   (Fal)/Jun 19, 1915; p. 1940
HIS GUIDING ANGEL
   (Maj)/Sep 25, 1915; p. 2177
HIS GYPSY SWEETHEART
   (Po)/Dec 31, 1910; p. 1539
HIS HALTED CAREER
   (Key)/Dec 5, 1914; p. 1384
HIS HEROINE (Th)/Mar 15, 1913; p. 1106
HIS HIGHNESS, THE PRINCE (GN)/
   Apr 18, 1914; p. 367/May 30, 1914; p. 1262
HIS HOME COMING
   (Imp)/Sep 25, 1915; p. 2177
HIS HONOR, THE MAYOR
   (Vi)/Mar 29, 1913; p. 1335
HIS HOODOO (Bio)/Sep 27, 1913; p. 1392
HIS HOUR OF MANHOOD
   (Dom)/Jul 4, 1914; p. 66
HIS HOUR OF TRIUMPH
   (Imp)/Oct 18, 1913; p. 247
HIS HOUSE IN ORDER
   (Vi)/Jun 28, 1913; p. 1359
HIS I.O.U. (Th)/Jul 24, 1915; p. 650
HIS IMAGE IN THE WATER
   (Gau)/Apr 15, 1911; p. 842
HIS IMAGINARY CRIME
   (Bi)/Feb 12, 1910; p. 215
HIS IMAGINARY FAMILY
   (Pr)/Dec 27, 1913; p. 1545
HIS INDIAN BRIDE
   (Ch)/Sep 17, 1910; p. 632
HIS INDIAN NEMESIS
   (Ka)/Apr 4, 1914; p. 57
HIS INSPIRATION
   (Bio)/Nov 29, 1913; p. 1007
   (Ka)/Nov 14, 1914; p. 932
HIS JUST DESERTS
   (Ed)/Feb 19, 1910; p. 258
HIS KID SISTER (Vi)/Aug 15, 1914; p. 959
HIS LAST BET (Th)/Sep 13, 1913; p. 1177
HIS LAST BURGLARY
   (Bio)/Mar 5, 1910; p. 339
HIS LAST CALL (Vi)/May 23, 1914; p. 1116
HIS LAST CHANCE (Imp)/Jun 6,1914;p.1410

HIS LAST CROOKED DEAL
(Ch)/Jun 24, 1911; p. 1455
(Lu)/Sep 13, 1913; p. 1176
HIS LAST DEAL (Maj)/Sep 27, 1913; p. 1393
(Maj)/Feb 20, 1915; p.1140
HIS LAST DOLLAR
(Bio)/Apr 16, 1910; p. 597
HIS LAST FIGHT (Vi)/Dec 6, 1913; p. 1150
HIS LAST GAMBLE
(Cry)/Sep 27, 1913; p. 1393
HIS LAST ILLUSION GONE
(Pa)/Apr 3, 1909; pp 402-3
HIS LAST PARADE (Lu)/Jan 28, 1911; p. 194
HIS LAST RESORT
(101)/Sep 21, 1912; p. 1177
HIS LAST SERENADE
(Lae)/Mar 13, 1915; p. 1608
HIS LAST "THIRTY"
(Lae)/Sep 11, 1915; p. 1834
HIS LAST TRICK (Lae)/Apr 3, 1915; p. 66
HIS LAST WISH (Bio)/Sep 4, 1915; p. 1643
HIS LEAP FOR LIBERTY
(Gau)/Jul 1, 1911; p. 1521
HIS LESSON (Bio)/Jun 1, 1912; p. 829
(Maj)/Jan 16, 1915; p 348, 369
HIS LIFE (Lu)/Oct 19, 1912; p. 243
HIS LIFE FOR HIS EMPEROR
(Vi)/May 31, 1913; p. 919
HIS LITTLE DARLING
(Cry)/Aug 2, 1913; p. 538
HIS LITTLE GIRL (Lu)/Aug 14, 1909; p. 226
HIS LITTLE INDIAN MODEL
(Pa)/Dec 21, 1912; p. 1184
HIS LITTLE PAGE (Vi)/Mar 7,1914; p.1236
HIS LITTLE PAL (Maj)/Mar 28,1914; p.1681
HIS LITTLE PARTNER
(Ne)/Nov 16, 1912; p. 660
HIS LITTLE SISTER
(Lu)/Apr 27, 1912; p. 329
HIS LONG LOST FRIEND
(Roy)/Aug 29, 1914; p. 1242
HIS LORDSHIP (Po)/Oct 8, 1910; p. 816
HIS LORDSHIP - BILLY SMOKE
(Vi)/Sep 13, 1913; p. 1176
HIS LORDSHIP, THE VALET
(Vi)/Oct 5, 1912; p. 41
HIS LORDSHIP'S DILEMNA
(Gau)/Oct 9, 1915; p. 253
HIS LORDSHIP'S HUNT
(Bi)/Jun 17, 1911; p. 1389
HIS LORDSHIP'S ROMANCE
(Pa)/Jun 28, 1913; p. 1359
HIS LORDSHIP'S WHITE FEATHER
(Sol)/Mar 9, 1912; p. 868
HIS LOSING DAY (Bio)/Feb 27, 1915; p. 1288
HIS LOST LOVE (Bio)/Oct 30, 1909; p. 604
HIS LOVE OF CHILDREN
(Re)/May 11, 1912; p. 528

HIS LOVING SPOUSE
(Bio)/Nov 7, 1914; p. 787
HIS LUCKLESS LOVE
(Key)/Apr 24, 1915; p. 556
HIS LUCKY DAY (Cry)/Jun 13, 1914; p.1542
HIS LUCKY VACATION
(Ne)/Aug 28, 1915; p. 1481
HIS MAGIC HAND - HY MAYER
(Imp)/Jun 7, 1913; p. 1033
HIS MAJESTY, THE KING
(Th)/Dec 11, 1915; p. 2032
**HIS MANIA FOR COLLECTING THE
ANTIQUE** (Lux)/Sep 30, 1911; p. 976
HIS MASTERPIECE
(Ed)/Nov 27, 1909; p. 758
(Sel)/Jul 27, 1912; p. 343
(La)/Sep 25, 1915; p. 2178
HIS MASTER'S DOUBLE
(Gau)/Jul 12, 1913; p. 206
HIS MIND'S TRAGEDY
(Po)/Apr 1, 1911; p. 720
HIS MISJUDGMENT (Ed)/Jul 8, 1911; p. 1584
HIS MISTAKE (Lu)/Mar 2, 1912; p. 780
HIS MOTHER (Ch)/Dec 31, 1910; p. 1539
(Vi)/May 27, 1911; p. 1200
(Ka)/Feb 10, 1912; p. 481
HIS MOTHER-IN-LAW'S VISIT
(Ed)/Jul 26, 1913; p. 427
HIS MOTHER'S HOME
(Bio)/Oct 24, 1914; p. 491
HIS MOTHER'S HOPE
(Ed)/Dec 21, 1912; p. 1184
HIS MOTHER'S LETTER
(Po)/Apr 23, 1910; p. 642
HIS MOTHER'S LOVE
(Imp)/Jun 28, 1913; p. 1360
HIS MOTHER'S MELODY
(KO)/Aug 1, 1908; p. 89
HIS MOTHER'S PICTURE
(Ka)/Oct 26, 1912; p. 342
HIS MOTHER'S PORTRAIT
(KB)/Jul 3, 1915; p. 65
HIS MOTHER'S SCARE
(Bio)/May 6, 1911; p. 1019
HIS MOTHER'S SHROUD
(Vi)/Apr 13, 1912; p. 136
HIS MOTHER'S SON
(SA)/Jan 28, 1911; p. 196
(Re)/Jun 8, 1912; p. 946
(Bio)/Jun 14, 1913; p. 1136
HIS MOTHER'S SONG
(Imp)/Aug 30, 1913; p. 962
HIS MOTHER'S THANKSGIVING
(Ed)/Dec 10, 1910; p. 1356
HIS MOTHER'S TRUST
(Maj)/Oct 10, 1914; p. 189
HIS MUSICAL CAREER
(Key)/Nov 14, 1914; p. 933

(StP)/Dec 11, 1915; p. 2033
HOT REMEDY, A (KO)/Jan 30, 1909; p. 120
**HOT SPRINGS AND GEYSERS OF NEW
ZEALAND** (Pa)/Oct 4, 1913; p. 48
HOT STUFF (Bio)/Apr 6, 1912; p. 41
(StP)/Oct 2, 1915; p. 80
HOT TEMPER, THE
(Nor)/Mar 21, 1908; pp 242-43
HOT TIME IN A COLD QUARTER, A
Oct 23, 1909; p. 568
HOT TIME IN ATLANTIC CITY, A
(Lu)/Jul 31, 1909; p. 162
(Lu)/Oct 28, 1911; p. 291
HOT TIME IN PUNKVILLE, A
(Lu)/May 29, 1915; p. 1431
HOT TIME IN SNAKEVILLE, A
(SA)/Apr 4, 1914; p. 57
HOTEL de HOBO (KrC)/Mar 27,1915;p.1933
HOTEL MIX-UP, THE
(Me)/Sep 5, 1908; p. 183
HOTEL THIEVES (GN)/Jul 1, 1911; p. 1521
HOUND OF THE BASKERVILLES, THE
(Pa)/Feb 27, 1915; p 1302
HOUNDED (Rex)/Jan 2, 1915; p. 77
HOUR AND THE MAN, THE
(SA)/Jan 24, 1914; p. 413
HOUR BEFORE DAWN, AN
(FP)/Oct 25, 1913; p. 360
HOUR OF DANGER, THE
(Ka)/Jun 20, 1914; p. 1688
HOUR OF EXECUTION, THE
(Gau)/Nov 25, 1911; p. 637
HOUR OF FREEDOM, AN
(Lu)/Jul 31, 1915; p. 816
HOUR OF RECKONING, THE
(Bro)/Jun 20, 1914; p. 1690
HOUR OF TERROR, AN
(Cry)/Jul 5, 1913; p. 49
(Bio)/Apr 4, 1914; p. 58
HOUR OF YOUTH, AN
(Th)/Apr 18, 1914; p. 361
HOUSE ACROSS THE STREET, THE
(Rex)/Mar 21, 1914; p. 1525
HOUSE AT THE BRIDGE, THE
(Lu)/Mar 13, 1909; p. 305
HOUSE BREAKERS, THE
(Ko)/Dec 26, 1914; p. 1841
HOUSE BUILT BY ELECTRICITY, A
(Me)/Aug 1, 1914; p. 705
HOUSE CLEANING (Lu)/Aug 17,1912; p.669
HOUSE CLEANING DAYS
(Vi)/Oct 30, 1908; pp 338, 347
HOUSE DISCORDANT, THE
(Rex)/Jul 4, 1914; p. 66
HOUSE DIVIDED, A
(Bi)/Apr 12, 1913; p. 165
(Sol)/May 10, 1913; p. 598
HOUSE DIVIDED, THE

(Pa)/Aug 30, 1913; p. 960
(Pa)/Jul 24, 1915; p. 668
(SA)/Oct 16, 1915; p. 440
HOUSE HUNTING
(Maj)/Aug 30, 1913; pp 961-62
HOUSE IN THE TREE, THE
(Maj)/Dec 6, 1913; p. 1152
HOUSE IN THE WOODS, THE
(Lu)/Feb 15, 1913; p. 680
HOUSE OF A THOUSAND CANDLES
(Sel)/Aug 21, 1915; p. 1327
**HOUSE OF A THOUSAND RELATIONS,
THE** (Vic)/Jun 5, 1915; p. 1607
HOUSE OF A THOUSAND SCANDALS, THE
(Am)/Oct 2, 1915; p. 93/Oct 9, 1915; p. 253
HOUSE OF BENTLEY, THE
(Re)/May 15, 1915; p. 1072
HOUSE OF BONDAGE, THE
(KB)/Aug 9, 1913; pp 638, 639
(PD)/Jan 17, 1914; p. 276
HOUSE OF CARDS, A
(KO)/Nov 7, 1908; p. 364
(Lu)/Jul 31, 1915; p. 817
HOUSE OF CARDS, THE
(Ed)/Dec 25, 1909; p. 920
HOUSE OF DARKNESS, THE
(Bio)/May 24, 1913; p. 812
(Lu)/Jul 4, 1914; p. 65
HOUSE OF DISCORD, THE
(Bio)/Dec 27, 1913; p. 1543
HOUSE OF D'OR, THE
(Lu)/Dec 19, 1914; p. 1680
HOUSE OF FEAR, THE
(Lu)/Mar 7, 1914; p. 1237
(Imp)/Jan 9, 1915; p.200/Jan 23, 1915; p.517
(GR)/Dec 4, 1915; pp 1845, 1853-54
HOUSE OF HIS MASTER, THE
(Sel)/Sep 21, 1912; p. 1176
HOUSE OF HORROR, THE
(Bio)/Jan 30, 1915; p. 671
HOUSE OF MYSTERY
(Cin)/Aug 23, 1913; p. 843
HOUSE OF MYSTERY, THE
(CGP)/Jul 20, 1912; p. 243
HOUSE OF NO CHILDREN, THE
(Com)/Aug 31, 1912; p. 882
HOUSE OF PRETENSE, THE
(Re)/Jun 28, 1913; p. 1361
HOUSE OF SILENCE, THE
(Bio)/Dec 12, 1914; pp 1530-31
HOUSE OF TEARS, THE
(Rol)/Dec 11, 1915; pp 2026, 2032
HOUSE OF TEMPERLEY, THE
(Lon)/May 16, 1914; p. 974
HOUSE OF TERROR, THE
(Lu)/May 8, 1909; p. 594
HOUSE ON E' STREET, THE
(Reg)/Feb 6, 1915; p. 830

HOUSE ON THE HILL, THE
(Ed)/Jun 25, 1910; p. 1101
(Vi)/Aug 22, 1914; p. 1100
HOUSE PARTY, THE
(Cas)/Nov 27, 1915; p. 1664
HOUSE PARTY AT CARSON MANOR, THE
(Th)/Dec 4, 1915; p. 1853
HOUSE THAT JACK BUILT, THE
(Lu)/Nov 25, 1911; p. 637
HOUSE THAT JACK MOVED, THE
(Fal)/May 29, 1915; p. 1432
HOUSE THAT WENT CRAZY, THE
(Sel)/Sep 19, 1914; p. 1644
HOUSE TO LET (Vi)/Mar 7, 1908; p. 196
HOUSE WITH CLOSED SHUTTERS, THE
(Bio)/Aug 20, 1910; p. 407
HOUSE WITH NOBODY IN IT, THE
(Ria)/Oct 2, 1915; p. 80
HOUSE WITH THE DRAWN SHADES, THE
(Rex)/Sep 18, 1915; p. 1997
HOUSE WITH THE TALL PORCH, THE
(Ed)/Apr 6, 1912; p. 41
HOUSEBOAT ELOPEMENT, A
(Po)/Oct 4, 1913; p. 49
HOUSEKEEPER, THE (Po)/Jun 8, 1912; p. 946
HOUSEKEEPER OF CIRCLE C, THE
(SA)/Mar 29, 1913; p. 1337
HOUSEKEEPING UNDER COVER (Wor)/
Mar 20, 1915; p. 1770/Apr 3, 1915; p. 66
HOUSEMAID, THE (Re)/Jun 26, 1915; p. 2096
HOW A BLOSSOM OPENS
(Pa)/Jul 5, 1913; p. 49
HOW A HORSESHOE UPSET A HAPPY
FAMILY (Ed)/Jan 11, 1913; p. 159
HOW A LETTER TRAVELS FROM
CENTRAL AMERICA
(CGP)/Aug 24, 1912; p. 771
HOW A PRETTY GIRL SOLD HER HAIR
RESTORER (Lu)/Oct 30, 1908; p. 345
HOW ALGY CAPTURED A WILD MAN
(Sel)/Sep 23, 1911; p. 890
HOW ALLOPATH CONQUERED
BONEOPATH (Lun)/May 15, 1915; p. 1073
HOW AUNTY WAS FOOLED
(Po)/Jul 22, 1911; p. 127
HOW BELLA WAS WON
(Ed)/Mar 25, 1911; p. 656
HOW BETTY CAPTURED THE OUTLAW
(Ka)/Dec 16, 1911; p. 904
HOW BETTY MADE GOOD
(Sel)/Sep 13, 1913; p. 1175
HOW BETTY WON THE SCHOOL
(Vi)/Sep 9, 1911; p. 716
HOW BILLY GOT HIS RAISE
(Jo)/Jun 12, 1915; p. 1778
HOW BOBBIE CALLED HER BLUFF
(Ed)/Feb 14, 1914; p. 808
HOW BRIAR PIPES ARE MADE

(CGP)/Mar 8, 1913; p. 995
HOW BROTHER COOK WAS TAUGHT A
LESSON (GN)/Jul 2, 1910; p. 26
HOW BROWN GOT MARRIED
(Lu)/Aug 28, 1909; p. 282
HOW BROWN SAW THE BASEBALL GAME
(Lu)/Nov 23, 1907; p. 621
HOW BUILDING STONE IS QUARRIED
(Pa)/May 29, 1915; p. 1433
HOW BUMPTIOUS PAPERED THE PARLOR
(Ed)/Jul 30, 1910; p. 244
HOW BURKE AND BURKE MADE GOOD
(Vi)/Feb 21, 1914; p. 946
HOW CALLAHAN CLEANED UP LITTLE
HELL (Sel)/Jun 19, 1915; p. 1940
HOW CHAMPIONSHIPS ARE WON - AND
LOST (Vi)/Jul 2, 1910; p. 24
HOW CHIEF TE BONGA WON HIS BRIDE
(Me)/May 10, 1913; p. 595
HOW CISSY MADE GOOD (Vi)/Jan 2, 1915;
p. 51/Feb 20, 1915; p. 1140
HOW CLARENCE GOT HIS
(Me)/Oct 10, 1914; p. 187
HOW DIAMONDS ARE MADE
(Ec)/Jul 12, 1913; p. 205
HOW DID IT FINISH
(Ed)/Jul 12, 1913; p. 204
HOW DOCTOR CUPID WON
(Ne)/Feb 20, 1915; p. 1140
HOW EARLY SAVED THE FARM
(Rex)/Sep 18, 1915; p. 1997
HOW EDAM CHEESE IS MADE
(Pa)/Apr 29, 1911; p. 958
HOW EGGS ARE TESTED
(Pa)/Jul 31, 1915; p. 818
HOW FATHER ACCOMPLISHED HIS
WORK (Ed)/Jun 29, 1912; p. 1226
HOW FATHER WON OUT
(Jo)/Dec 19, 1914; p. 1681
HOW FATTY GOT EVEN
(Ne)/Apr 19, 1913; p. 282
HOW FRECKLES WON HIS BRIDE
(Po)/Dec 6, 1913; p. 1153
HOW FRENCH PERFUMES ARE MADE
(Pa)/Dec 4, 1909; p. 799
HOW GLUE IS MADE
(Pa)/Sep 19, 1908; p. 223
HOW GOD CAME TO SONNY BOY
(Vi)/Feb 14, 1914; p. 809
HOW GREEN PAID THE RENT
(Jo)/Mar 28, 1914; p. 1682
HOW GREEN SAVED HIS MOTHER-IN-
LAW (Jo)/Apr 18, 1914; p. 362
HOW GREEN SAVED HIS WIFE
(Jo)/May 16, 1914; p. 969
HOW HAZEL GOT EVEN
(Maj)/Feb 27, 1915; p. 1289
HOW HE EARNED HIS MEDAL

HOW STATES ARE MADE (Vi)/Feb 17,
1912; p. 565/Mar 23, 1912; pp 1062-63
HOW STEVE MADE GOOD
(Ne)/Aug 24, 1912; p. 772
HOW SWEDISH TROOPS CROSS A RIVER
(Pa)/May 29, 1915; p. 1433
HOW TEDDY LOST HIS BET
(Ec)/Sep 23, 1911; p. 893
HOW TEXAS GOT LEFT
(Ka)/Dec 2, 1911; p. 726
HOW THE BOYS FOUGHT THE INDIANS
(Ed)/Jul 20, 1912; p. 243
HOW THE CAUSE WAS WON (Sel)/Oct 12,
1912; pp 135-36/Oct 19, 1912; p. 243
HOW THE CINEMA PROTECTS ITSELF
AGAINST STRIKES
(Ec)/Aug 26, 1911; p. 545
HOW THE DAY WAS SAVED
(Bio)/Dec 13, 1913; p. 1279
HOW THE DOCTOR MADE GOOD
(Po)/Apr 29, 1911; p. 960
HOW THE EARTH WAS CARPETED
(Ed)/Feb 14, 1914; p. 809
HOW THE HUNGRY MAN WAS FED
(Ed)/Jun 3, 1911; p. 1258
HOW THE KIDS GOT EVEN
(Vi)/Feb 20, 1909; p. 203
HOW THE LANDLORD COLLECTED HIS
RENTS (Ed)/Oct 2, 1909; p. 452
HOW THE MASHER WAS PUNISHED
(Lu)/Jan 4, 1908; p. 11
HOW THE PAIR BUTTED IN
(Pa)/Nov 7, 1908; p. 366
HOW THE PLAY WAS ADVERTISED
(Pa)/Mar 23, 1912; p. 1063
HOW THE RANGER WAS CURED
(Ne)/Jun 1, 1912; p. 832
HOW "THE SPIRIT OF '76" WAS PAINTED
(Pi)/Mar 8, 1913; p. 1003
HOW THE SQUIRE WAS CAPTURED
(Ed)/Sep 3, 1910; p. 518
HOW THE STORY GREW
(Lu)/Jul 8, 1911; p. 1585
HOW THE TELEPHONE CAME TO TOWN
(Ed)/Nov 11, 1911; p. 468
HOW THE TENDERFOOT MADE GOOD
(Ch)/Oct 22, 1910; p. 939
HOW THEY GOT THE VOTE
(Ed)/Jan 18, 1913; p. 263
HOW THEY LOST OUT
(Cin)/Apr 27, 1912; p. 329
HOW THEY OUTWITTED FATHER
(Ed)/Feb 22, 1913; p. 780
HOW THEY PROPOSE
(Gau)/May 1, 1909; pp 553, 554
HOW THEY STOPPED THE RUN ON THE
BANK (Sel)/Nov 4, 1911; p. 379
HOW THEY STRUCK OIL

(Bio)/Jan 31, 1914; p. 543
HOW THEY TRICKED FATHER
(Lux)/Jan 21, 1911; p. 144
HOW TO CATCH A BACHELOR
(Gau)/Sep 30, 1911; p. 972
HOW TO DO IT AND WHY; or CUTEY AT
COLLEGE (Vi)/Dec 26, 1914; p. 1841
HOW TO GET A CITY JOB
(Gau)/Dec 18, 1909; p. 881
HOW TO KEEP A HUSBAND
(Cry)/Apr 25, 1914; p 517-18
HOW TO TAME A MOTHER-IN-LAW
(Pa)/Sep 25, 1909; p. 416
HOW TOMMY SAVED HIS FATHER
(Vi)/Jan 20, 1912; p. 202
HOW TOMMY'S WIT WORKED
(Pa)/Apr 1, 1911; p. 718
HOW TONY BECAME A HERO
(Ch)/Sep 9, 1911; p. 718
HOW WASHINGTON CROSSED THE
DELAWARE (Ed)/Mar 9, 1912; pp 852-53/
Apr 13, 1912; p. 137
HOW WILD ANIMALS LIVE
(Mid)/Nov 8, 1913; p. 592
HOW WILLIE RAISED TOBACCO
(Ed)/Jul 8, 1911; p. 1586
HOW WOMEN LOVE
(Po)/Nov 26, 1910; p. 1239
(Cry)/Aug 16, 1913; p. 745
HOW WOMEN WIN (Po)/Jul 1,1911; p.1522
HOWARD'S MONARCHS OF THE FOREST
(Po)/Dec 18, 1915; p. 2204
HOWLIN' JONES (Sel)/Sep 20,1913; p.1283
HOYDEN, THE (Lu)/May 6, 1911;
p. 1019/Jun 10, 1911; p. 1301
HOYDEN'S AWAKENING, THE
(Sel)/Apr 19, 1913; p. 280
HUBBY BUYS A BABY
(Vi)/Mar 15, 1913; p. 1105
HUBBY DOES THE COOKING
(UE)/Feb 15, 1913; p. 678
HUBBY DOES THE WASHING
(Sol)/Mar 2, 1912; p. 781
HUBBY MINDS THE BABY
(Re)/Jan 27, 1912; p. 304
HUBBY TO THE RESCUE
(Ko)/Jun 27, 1914; p. 1829
HUBBY'S CURE (Jo)/Jan 16, 1915; p. 370
HUBBY'S DAY AT HOME
(Ka)/Jul 29, 1911; p. 211
HUBBY'S JOB (Key)/May 17, 1913; p. 706
HUBBY'S NEW COAT
(Cry)/Nov 29, 1913; p. 1008
HUBBY'S NIGHT OFF
(Ka)/Apr 25, 1914; p. 516
HUBBY'S NIGHT OUT
(Cry)/Dec 27, 1913; p. 1544
HUBBY'S POLLY (Pa)/Feb 15, 1913; p. 678

HUBBY'S SURPRISE
(Roy)/Apr 25, 1914; p. 517
HUBBY'S TOOTHACHE
(Vi)/Aug 2, 1913; p. 535
HUBBY'S TROUBLES
(Pa)/Mar 4, 1911; p. 483
HUBBY'S VACATION (Lu)/Oct 24, 1908;
p. 326/Oct 30, 1908; p. 338
HUGHEY OF THE CIRCUS
(Vi)/Dec 18, 1915; p. 2203
HUGO, THE HUNCHBACK
(Sel)/Apr 16, 1910; p. 599
HULDA OF HOLLAND
(Ed)/May 3, 1913; p. 487
HULDA'S LOVERS (Bio)/Apr 25, 1908; p. 375
HUMAN BRIDGE, THE
(Cin)/Sep 6, 1913; p. 1069
HUMAN CLOCK, THE
(KO)/Jun 8, 1907; p. 220
HUMAN HEARTS
(Sel)/Sep 3, 1910; p. 518
(Imp)/Sep 7, 1912; p. 958/Sep 21, 1912; p.1176
(Imp)/Nov 28, 1914; p. 1233
HUMAN HOUND'S TRIUMPH, A
(Key)/May 29, 1915; p. 1432
HUMAN INVESTMENT, THE
(Lu)/Mar 13, 1915; p. 1607
HUMAN KINDNESS (Am)/May 10, 1913; p.598
HUMAN MOVEMENTS ANALYZED
(Gl)/Nov 13, 1915; p. 1313
HUMAN NATURE (Rep)/Feb 24,1912;pp690-91
HUMAN OCTOPUS, THE
(KB)/May 15, 1915; p. 1072
HUMAN SACRIFICE, THE (Re)/Oct 14,
1911; pp 109-10/Oct 21, 1911; pp 209-10
HUMAN SOUL, THE
(Box)/Aug 8, 1914; p. 838
HUMAN STATUE, THE
(Imp)/Jun 28, 1913; p. 1360
HUMAN TIGER, THE
(Amb)/Jun 17, 1911; p. 1388
HUMAN TORPEDO, THE
(Lu)/Oct 7, 1911; p. 39
HUMAN VULTURES (KO)/Aug 15,1908; p.127
HUMBLE HERO, A
(Sel)/May 18, 1912; p. 629
HUMBLE HEROES (RR)/Aug 21,1909; p.253
HUMORS OF AMETEUR GOLF PLAYERS
(KO)/Jun 29, 1907; p. 269
HUMPTY DUMPTY CIRCUS (Ka)/Oct 30,
1908; p. 339/Nov 14, 1908; p. 379
HUNCHBACK, THE
(Pa)/Jan 23, 1909; p. 94
(Ka)/Jan 3, 1914; p. 49
(Maj)/Apr 18, 1914; pp 340, 361
HUNCHBACK BRINGS LUCK (Pa)/Apr 18,
1908; p. 352/Apr 3, 1909; p. 403
HUNCHBACK FIDDLER, THE

(Pa)/Apr 23, 1910; p. 641
HUNCHBACK OF CEDAR LODGE, THE
(Box)/Aug 8, 1914; p. 838
HUNCHBACK'S ROMANCE, THE
(Imp)/Jul 31, 1915; p. 818
$100.00 BILL, THE
(KO)/May 11, 1907; p. 156
HUNDRED DOLLAR BILL, THE
(Vi)/Aug 19, 1911; p. 463
(Maj)/Jan 11, 1913; p. 159
HUNGARIAN NABOB, THE (Bio)/Nov 20,
1915; p. 1503/Dec 11, 1915; p. 2031
HUNGARY (Pa)/May 1, 1909; p. 554
HUNGER KNOWS NO LAW
(Vi)/Jun 13, 1914; p. 1540
HUNGER OF THE HEART, THE
(Pa)/Jul 12, 1913; p. 204
HUNGRY ACTOR, THE
(Lu)/Aug 28, 1909; p. 282
HUNGRY BOARDERS
(StU)/Jun 19, 1915; p. 1941
HUNGRY HANK AT THE FAIR
(Roy)/Apr 24, 1915; p. 556
HUNGRY HANK'S HALLUCINATION
(Ka)/Jul 27, 1912; p. 343
HUNGRY HEARTS (Vi)/May 20,1911;p.1141
HUNGRY PAIR, A (SA)/Jul 22, 1911; p. 123
HUNGRY SOLDIERS, THE
(Po)/May 9, 1914; p. 821
HUNTED DOWN (UB)/Nov 2, 1912; p. 451
HUNTED TO THE END
(Gau)/Jun 26, 1909; p. 873
HUNTER'S DREAM, THE
(Ka)/Apr 1, 1911; p. 718
HUNTER'S GRIEF, THE
(Pa)/May 15, 1909; p. 631
HUNTING A HUSBAND
(Vi)/Jul 17, 1915; p. 485
HUNTING ABOVE THE CLOUDS
(CR)/Dec 28, 1907; pp 708-9
HUNTING ABSURDITY, A
(Lu)/Oct 24, 1914; p. 491
HUNTING BATS IN SUMATRA
(Pa)/Aug 13, 1910; p. 351
HUNTING BIG GAME IN AFRICA
(Sel)/May 29, 1909; p. 712
HUNTING DEER (WBE)/Jun 6, 1908;
p. 501/Jun 13, 1908; p. 517
HUNTING DUCKS (It)/Feb 17, 1912; p. 583
HUNTING FOR HER BETTER HALF
(Pa)/Oct 24, 1908; p. 326
HUNTING IN CRAZYLAND
(Po)/Jan 2, 1915; p. 76
HUNTING SEA LIONS IN TASMANIA
(Pa)/Dec 31, 1910; p. 1538
HUNTING SPIDERS, THE
(Pa)/Mar 28, 1914; p. 1680
HUNTING THE DEVIL

(Cin)/Sep 21, 1907; p. 456

HUNTING THE PANTHER
(Pa)/Sep 24, 1910; p. 689

HURON CONVERTS, THE
(Re)/May 29, 1915; p. 1432

HURRAH! HURRAH! LET US MARRY
(Ec)/Apr 8, 1911; p. 782

HURRY UP, PLEASE!
(Pa)/Nov 14, 1908; pp 379, 384-85

HUSBAND WANTED (Pa)/Jul 4, 1908;
p. 11/Dec 26, 1908; p. 525

HUSBAND WON BY ELECTION, A
(Sel)/Mar 22, 1913; p. 1219

HUSBAND'S AWAKENING, A
(Lu)/Jun 22, 1912; p. 1126

HUSBAND'S EXPERIMENT, THE
(Bio)/Feb 7, 1914; p. 676

HUSBAND'S JEALOUS WIFE, A
(Th)/Oct 8, 1910; p. 816

HUSBAND'S MISTAKE, A
(Am)/Jun 28, 1913; pp 1360-61

HUSBAND'S REVENGE, A
(Vi)/Jun 6, 1908; p. 500

HUSBAND'S SACRIFICE, A
(Po)/Oct 1, 1910; p. 750

HUSBAND'S STRATEGY
(Gau)/Oct 30, 1909; p. 605

HUSBAND'S TRICK, A
(Vi)/Jun 21, 1913; pp 1252-53

HUSH MONEY (Gau)/Jan 8, 1910; p. 17

HUSKING BEE, THE
(Vi)/Dec 16, 1911; p. 904

HUSTLING MRS. BROWN, THE
(GN)/Apr 23, 1910; p. 642

HUT IN THE SYCAMORE GAP, THE
(Sel)/Feb 13, 1915; p. 984

**HUTCHINSON, KANSAS, SEMI-
CENTENNIAL CELEBRATION**
(Sel)/Jan 20, 1912; p. 203

HY MAYER (Imp)/Jun 28, 1913; p. 1360

HY MAYER'S CARTOONS
(Imp)/Jul 26, 1913; p. 430
(Imp)/Aug 30, 1913; p. 962

HY MAYER'S LIGHTNING SKETCHES
(Imp)/Jul 19, 1913; p. 321

HY MAYER'S MAGIC HAND (Imp)/May 24,
1913; p. 813/May 31, 1913; p. 921

**HYDRAULIC MINING AT THE LA GRANGE
MINES** (Vic)/Dec 20,1913;p.1413

**HYDRO-AEROPLANE FLIGHT AT PALM
BEACH, A** (Par)/Apr 10, 1915; p. 245

HYDROGEN (CGP)/Mar 22, 1913; p. 1219

HYDROPLANE, THE (It)/Jun 24, 1911; p. 1454

HYPNO AND STRANGE SUBJECTS
(Ed)/Mar 20, 1915; p. 1763

HYPNOTIC CHAIR, THE
(Maj)/Dec 14, 1912; p. 1082

HYPNOTIC DETECTIVE, THE

(Sel)/Mar 2, 1912; p. 780

HYPNOTIC MONKEY, THE
(Ka)/Aug 21, 1915; p. 1316

HYPNOTIC NELL (Ka)/May 25, 1912; p. 728

HYPNOTIC POWER (St)/Oct 10,1914; p.189

HYPNOTIC WIFE, A
(Pa)/Sep 11, 1909; p. 345

HYPNOTISM IN HICKSVILLE
(SA)/Feb 15, 1913; p. 680

HYPNOTIST'S REVENGE, THE
(Bio)/Jul 27, 1907; p. 331

HYPNOTIZED (Th)/Jan 14, 1911; p. 91
(Sel)/Mar 23, 1912; p. 1063
(Cry)/Aug 23, 1913; p. 845

HYPNOTIZING A HYPNOTIST
(Am)/Mar 18, 1911; p. 603

HYPNOTIZING HANNAH
(Gau)/Mar 22, 1913; p. 1221

HYPNOTIZING MAMIE
(Ka)/Nov 29, 1913; p. 1007

HYPNOTIZING THE HYPNOTIST
(Vi)/Dec 16, 1911; p. 904

HYPOCRITE, THE (Vic)/Jan 25, 1913; p.364

HYPOCRITES (Bos)/Feb 6, 1915; p. 832

I HAVE LOST MY LATCH KEY
(Amb)/Feb 26, 1910; p. 300

I HAVE WON A PIG
(Pa)/Mar 21, 1908; p. 244

**I HAVE WON ONE HUNDRED THOUSAND
DOLLARS** (KO)/Jul 25, 1908; p. 68/
Aug 29, 1908; p. 161

I LOVE THE NURSES
(Ecl)/Jul 25, 1914; p. 573

I LOVE YOU (Maj)/Apr 19, 1913; p. 281

I NEVER SAID A WORD
(Ne)/Feb 17, 1912; p. 583

I.O.U. $10 (Ne)/Oct 26, 1912; p. 344

I SAW HIM FIRST
(Ka)/Nov 30, 1912; p. 877

I SHOULD WORRY
(Ram)/Aug 2, 1913; p. 537
(Roy)/May 30, 1914; p. 1261

I WAS MEANT FOR YOU
(Bio)/Aug 23, 1913; p. 844

I WILL HAVE A HUSBAND
(War)/May 15, 1909; p. 636

I WISH I HAD A GIRL
(Imp)/Feb 3, 1912; p. 394

IBIS, THE (Pa)/Aug 27, 1910; p. 462

**ICE BOATING ON THE SHREWSBURY
RIVER** (Imp)/Mar 2, 1912; p. 781

ICE CREAM JACK (KO)/Apr 18, 1908; p. 354

ICE CUTTING IN SWEDEN
(Pa)/Nov 22, 1913; p. 867

ICE CUTTING ON THE ST. LAWRENCE
(Kin)/Dec 7, 1912; p. 978

ICE SCOOTERS ON LAKE RONKONKOMA

(Pa)/Apr 23, 1910; p. 642
ICEBERGS OFF THE COAST OF
LABRADOR (Ed)/Nov 25, 1911; p. 637
ICEMAN'S REVENGE, THE
(Maj)/Oct 18, 1913; p. 265
ICH GA BIBBLE (Sol)/Nov 15, 1913; p. 738
ICONOCLAST, THE
(Bio)/Oct 15, 1910; p. 876
(Bro)/Mar 29, 1913; p. 1337
IDA'S CHRISTMAS (Vi)/Jan 4, 1913; p. 51
IDEAL (Vi)/Feb 17, 1912; p. 582
IDEAL OF HER DREAMS, THE
(Cin)/Mar 22, 1913; p. 1220
IDEAL OF POWER, THE
(Po)/Feb 22, 1913; p. 781
IDEAL POLICEMEN
(Pa)/Oct 30, 1908; pp 346-47
IDENTICAL IDENTITIES
(SA)/Feb 22, 1913; p. 763
IDENTIFICATION, THE
(Ka)/Aug 15, 1914; p. 960
IDIOT, THE (Bio)/Jun 20, 1914; p. 1688
(Maj)/Aug 15, 1914; p. 961
IDLE BOAST, THE (Lu)/Oct 14, 1911; p.130
IDLE RICH, THE (Ed)/May 15, 1915; p.1071
(Lko)/Oct 30a, 1915; p.969
IDLER, THE
(Pa)/Mar 28, 1908; p.270/Apr 3, 1909; p.404
(Re)/Feb 21, 1914; p. 947
(Vi)/Apr 4, 1914; p. 57
(Box)/Jan 2, 1915; p. 84/Jan 9, 1915; p. 222
IDOL, THE (Cli)/Oct 30a, 1915; p. 968
IDOL OF BONANZA CAMP, THE
(Ne)/Jun 7, 1913; p. 1032
IDOL OF FATE, THE
(Sel)/May 8, 1915; p. 899
IDOL OF THE HOUR, THE
(Th)/Mar 22, 1913; p. 1222
IDOL WORSHIPPER, THE
(Sol)/Nov 2, 1912; p. 452
IDOL'S EYE, THE
(Imp)/Nov 12, 1910; p. 1119
IDOLS OF CLAY (GS)/Dec 4, 1915; p. 1854
IDYL OF HAWAII, AN
(Am)/Nov 30, 1912; p. 878
IDYLL OF THE HILLS, AN
(Rex)/May 15, 1915; p. 1074
IF AT FIRST YOU DON'T SUCCEED
(Sel)/Sep 5, 1914; p. 1371
IF DREAMS CAME TRUE
(Vi)/Jun 14, 1913; p. 1136
IF DREAMS COME TRUE
(Rex)/Oct 19, 1912; p. 244
IF I WERE A KING
(Amb)/Jun 29, 1912; p. 1228
IF I WERE YOUNG AGAIN
(Sel)/Nov 28, 1914; p. 1232
IF IT DON'T CONCERN YOU LET IT

ALONE (SA)/Nov 7, 1908; p. 365/
Nov 21, 1908; p. 398
IF IT WERE NOT FOR POLLY
(Bio)/Feb 14, 1914; p. 809
IF LOVE BE TRUE (Lu)/Dec 25, 1909; p.920
IF ONE COULD SEE INTO THE FUTURE
(Amb)/Aug 19, 1911; p. 465
IF WE ONLY KNEW
(Bio)/May 17, 1913; p. 704
IF YOU HAD A WIFE LIKE THIS
(Bio)/Jun 1, 1907; p. 203
IGNORANCE OF BLISS, THE
(Bal)/Mar 27, 1915; p. 1935
IL TROVATORE (Pa)/Feb 11, 1911; p. 316
I'LL ONLY MARRY A SPORT
(Lu)/Mar 13, 1909; p. 305
ILL WIND, AN (Rex)/Jan 4, 1913; p. 52
(St)/Nov 21, 1914; p. 1076
ILLUMINATION, THE (Vi)/Mar 30, 1912;
pp 1150-51/Apr 20, 1912; pp 229-30
I'M CRAZY TO BE MARRIED
(StU)/Feb 6, 1915; p. 829
I'M GLAD MY BOY GREW UP TO BE A
SOLDIER (Sel)/Nov 27, 1915; p. 1677
I'M GOING OUT FOR A SHAVE
(GN)/Oct 12, 1912; p. 144
I'M MOURNING THE LOSS OF CHLOE
(Pa)/Feb 22, 1908; p. 146
I'M NO COUNTERFEITER
(Ram)/Jun 7, 1913; p. 1032
IMA SIMP, GOAT (Pa)/May 15,1915; p.1073
IMA SIMP, DETECTIVE
(Pa)/Apr 3, 1915; p. 65
IMA SIMP HAS A DREAM
(Pa)/Mar 20, 1915; p. 1765
IMA SIMP ON THE JOB
(Pa)/Jul 31, 1915; p. 818
IMAGINARY ELOPEMENT, AN
(Imp)/Feb 18, 1911; p. 372
IMAGINATION (SA)/Apr 16, 1910; p. 598
(Sol)/Aug 10, 1912; p. 547
IMAGINATIVE WILLIE
(Po)/Oct 7, 1911; p. 43
IMAR THE SERVITOR
(Maj)/Feb 20, 1915; p. 1141
IMITATIONS (Am)/Feb 13, 1915; p. 985
IMITATOR OF BLONDIN, AN
(Pa)/Feb 18, 1911; p. 371
IMMIGRANT'S VIOLIN, THE
(Imp)/Mar 9, 1912; p. 868
IMMORTAL ALAMO, THE (Me)/Jun 10,
1911; p. 1313/Jun 24, 1911; p. 1426
IMP ABROAD, THE
(Vic)/Jan 17, 1914; p. 290
IMP OF THE BOTTLE, THE
(Ed)/Nov 27, 1909; p. 759
"IMP" ROMANCE, AN
(Imp)/Mar 1, 1913; p. 888

IN SPITE OF THE EVIDENCE
(Sel)/May 9, 1914; p. 820
IN SUNNY ITALY (Ya)/May 20,1911; p.1143
IN SWIFT WATERS (Vic)/Jul 20, 1912; p. 225
IN SWITZERLAND (Pa)/Aug 19, 1911; p.464
IN TANGLED WEB (Pa)/Apr 18,1914; p.361
IN TAXI 23 (Ne)/Nov 28, 1914; p. 1233
IN TEMPTATION'S FOILS
(GK)/Aug 8, 1914; p. 817
IN THE ABRUZZI (Pa)/Sep 20,1913; p.1283
IN THE AISLES OF THE WILD
(Bio)/Oct 26, 1912; p. 343
IN THE AMAZON JUNGLE
(Sel)/Jun 12, 1915; p. 1776
IN THE ARCTIC NIGHT
(Vi)/Jul 29, 1911; p. 211
IN THE BACKGROUND
(Lu)/Apr 17, 1915; p. 392
IN THE BAGGAGE COACH AHEAD
(Ed)/May 27, 1911; p. 1201
IN THE BARRACKS OF THE ROYAL
NORTHWEST MOUNTED POLICE OF
CANADA (Pa)/May 2, 1914; p. 673
IN THE BATTLE'S SMOKE
(Pi)/Apr 12, 1913; p. 166
IN THE BAY OF BISCAY
(Lux)/Mar 30, 1912; p. 1166
IN THE BISHOP'S CARRIAGE
(FP)/Sep 20, 1913; p. 1266
IN THE BLACK HILLS
(Ne)/Sep 3, 1910; p. 521
IN THE BLOOD (Rex)/Mar 1, 1913; p. 890
IN THE BOARDING HOUSE
(Bio)/Feb 6, 1915; p. 827
IN THE BOGIE MAN'S CAVE
(Me)/Jan 18, 1908; p. 45
IN THE BORDER STATES
(Bio)/Jun 25, 1910; p. 1101
IN THE CANDLELIGHT
(Am)/Nov 28, 1914; p. 1234
IN THE CAUCASIAN MOUNTAINS
(Pa)/Sep 13, 1913; p. 1176
IN THE CLAWS OF THE VULTURE
(Amb)/May 31, 1913; p. 924
IN THE CHORUS (Th)/Sep 30, 1911; p. 976
IN THE CLAW OF THE LAW
(Lko)/Aug 7, 1915; p. 998
IN THE CLAWS OF THE LEOPARD
(Gau)/Feb 1, 1913; p. 466
IN THE CLUTCH OF CIRCUMSTANCE
(Jo)/Apr 11, 1914; p. 214
IN THE CLUTCHES OF A GANG
(Key)/Jan 10, 1914; p. 173
IN THE CLUTCHES OF A VAPOR BATH
(Bi)/Jan 13, 1912; p.125
IN THE CLUTCHES OF THE GANGSTERS
(KB)/Nov 7, 1914; p. 790
IN THE CLUTCHES OF THE KU-KLUX

KLAN (WF)/Oct 4, 1913; p. 50
IN THE CLUTCHES OF THE VILLAIN
(Jo)/Oct 10, 1914; p. 189
IN THE COILS OF THE PYTHON (101)/
Aug 23, 1913; p. 828/Sep 20, 1913; p. 1286
IN THE COMMISSIONED RANKS
(Ne)/Mar 25, 1911; p. 658
IN THE CONSERVATORY
(Pr)/Dec 26, 1914; p. 1841
IN THE CONSOMME
(Gau)/Dec 11, 1909; p. 841
IN THE COW COUNTRY
(KB)/May 23, 1914; p. 1118
IN THE CYCLE OF LIFE
(Po)/Sep 13, 1913; p. 1177
IN THE CZAR'S NAME
(Ya)/Dec 17, 1910; p. 1419
IN THE DARK (Lu)/Jun 5, 1915; p. 1605
IN THE DARK VALLEY
(Ka)/May 21, 1910; p. 833
IN THE DAYS OF CHIVALRY
(Ed)/Jan 14, 1911; p. 90
IN THE DAYS OF FAMINE
(Vi)/May 29, 1915; p. 1440
IN THE DAYS OF '49
(Bio)/May 20, 1911; p. 1141
IN THE DAYS OF GOLD
(Sel)/Nov 25, 1911; p. 636
IN THE DAYS OF HIS YOUTH
(Rex)/Mar 28, 1914; p. 1682
IN THE DAYS OF LOUIS XVI
(Pa)/Mar 28, 1908; p. 269
IN THE DAYS OF NERO (Gau)/May 27,
1911; pp 1200-1201/Jun 10, 1911; p. 1300
IN THE DAYS OF OLIVER CROMWELL
(Pa)/Apr 17, 1909; pp 477-78
IN THE DAYS OF SLAVERY
(Ed)/Jul 4, 1914; p. 64
IN THE DAYS OF THE FIRST CHRISTMAS
(FA)/Sep 17, 1910; p. 632
IN THE DAYS OF THE PILGRIMS (Vi)/
Sep 5, 1908; p. 183/Dec 12, 1908; p. 477
IN THE DAYS OF THE SIX NATIONS
(Rep)/Jan 13, 1912; p. 127
IN THE DAYS OF THE THUNDERING
HERD (Sel)/Dec 12, 1914; p. 1506
IN THE DAYS OF TRAJAN
(Am)/Nov 1, 1913; p. 498
IN THE DAYS OF WAR
(Pa)/Apr 26, 1913; pp 380-81
IN THE DAYS OF WITCHCRAFT
(Ed)/Apr 24, 1909; p. 517
(Sel)/May 24, 1913; p. 811
IN THE DRAGON'S CLAWS
(Lu)/Mar 27, 1915; p. 1932
IN THE DREDGER'S CLAW
(Lu)/Mar 7, 1914; p. 1236
IN THE EARLY DAYS

IN THE NAME OF THE PRINCE OF PEACE (Wor)/Dec 12, 1914; p.1526
IN THE NICK OF TIME
(Sel)/May 30, 1908; pp 481-82
(Lu)/Oct 3, 1908; p. 263
(Ed)/Jan 29, 1910; p. 128
(Sol)/Jun 3, 1911; p. 1260
(Th)/Aug 9, 1913; p. 637
(Bio)/Jun 20, 1914; p. 1688
(Re)/Sep 19, 1914; pp 1618, 1646
IN THE NIGHT (Ec)/Jul 12, 1913; p. 205
IN THE NORTH WOODS
(Bio)/Sep 14, 1912; p. 1075
IN THE NORTHERN WOODS
(Imp)/Jan 20, 1912; p. 204
IN THE NORTHLAND
(Lu)/May 30, 1914; p. 1261
IN THE OLD ATTIC
(Vi)/Mar 7, 1914; p. 1237
IN THE OPEN (Am)/Oct 31, 1914; p. 641
IN THE OSSAN VALLEY, TYRENEES, FRANCE (UE)/Nov 9, 1912; p. 553
IN THE PALMY DAYS
(MnA)/Feb 20, 1915; p. 1139
IN THE PARIS SLUMS
(Pa)/Aug 26, 1911; p. 540
IN THE PARK (SA)/Apr 3, 1915; p. 63
IN THE PLACE OF THE KING
(SA)/Oct 16, 1915; pp 460-61
IN THE POWER OF BLACKLEGS
(Ka)/Feb 22, 1913; p. 780
IN THE POWER OF THE HYPNOTIST
(WF)/Nov 1, 1913; p. 499
IN THE PROVINCE OF KWANG TUNG
(UE)/May 6, 1911; p. 1019
IN THE PURPLE HILLS
(Am)/Jun 5, 1915; p. 1606
IN THE PYRANEES
(Gau)/Sep 10, 1910; p. 574
IN THE PYTHON'S DEN
(Ape)/Jan 31, 1914; p. 527
IN THE RANKS (Bro)/Jan 11, 1913; p. 159
IN THE REALM OF THE CZAR
(Gau)/Jul 23, 1910; p. 193
IN THE RED MAN'S COUNTRY
(Bi)/Feb 22, 1913; p. 781
IN THE RIGHT OF WAY
(Me)/Jul 29, 1911; p. 209
IN THE RIVIERA (KO)/Jul 11, 1908; p. 36
IN THE SAGEBUSH COUNTRY
(KB)/Dec 26, 1914; p. 1842
IN THE SAME BOAT
(Pa)/Nov 29, 1913; p. 1007
IN THE SAN FERNANDO VALLEY
(Ne)/Sep 21, 1912; p. 1177
IN THE SECRET SERVICE
(Bi)/May 10, 1913; p. 598
IN THE SERPENT'S POWER

(Sel)/Feb 19, 1910; p. 257
IN THE SERVICE OF THE STATE
(Lu)/Nov 9, 1912; p. 553
IN THE SHADOW (Vi)/Nov 8, 1913; p. 612
IN THE SHADOW OF DEATH
(Ed)/Apr 3, 1915; p. 64
IN THE SHADOW OF DISGRACE
(Ed)/Jul 25, 1914; p. 572
IN THE SHADOW OF MT. SHASTA
(Sel)/Mar 12, 1910; p. 383
IN THE SHADOW OF MT. VESUVIUS
(Gau)/Aug 5, 1911; p. 293
IN THE SHADOW OF THE CLIFFS
(Gau)/Mar 26, 1910; p. 467
IN THE SHADOW OF THE MISSION
(Me)/Oct 1, 1910; pp 748-49
IN THE SHADOW OF THE MOUNTAINS
(Ed)/Oct 25, 1913; p. 380
IN THE SHADOW OF THE NIGHT
(UE)/Oct 29, 1910; p. 998
IN THE SHADOW OF THE PINES (Sel)/
Sep 9, 1911; p. 715/Sep 16, 1911; p. 788
IN THE SHANANDOAH VALLEY
(Sel)/Dec 26, 1908; p. 532
IN THE SOUP (Ka)/Apr 18, 1914; p. 360
IN THE SOUTH SEAS
(Rex)/Mar 8, 1913; p. 997
IN THE SOUTHERN HILLS
(Dom)/Jun 20, 1914; p. 1690
IN THE SOUTHLAND
(Lu)/Sep 20, 1913; p. 1283
IN THE SOWING (Po)/Aug 10, 1912; p. 547
IN THE SPANISH PYRENEES
(Pa)/Dec 6, 1913; p. 1151
IN THE SPEEWALD
(UE)/Nov 5, 1910; p. 1059
IN THE STRETCH (Ram)/Jan 24,1914; p.395
IN THE SULTAN'S GARDEN
(Imp)/Jul 15, 1911; p. 41
IN THE SULTAN'S POWER
(Sel)/Jun 26, 1909; p. 872
IN THE SUNLIGHT (Am)/Apr 10,1915;p.236
IN THE SUNSET COUNTRY
(Bi)/Sep 11, 1915; p. 1834
(Mus)/Dec 18, 1915; p. 2203
IN THE SWIM (SA)/Jul 3, 1915; p. 64
IN THE SWITCH TOWER
(Bro)/Mar 27, 1915; p. 1934
IN THE TALL GRASS COUNTRY
(Me)/Jan 14, 1911; p. 88
IN THE TENNESSEE HILLS
(KB)/Feb 13, 1915; p. 986
IN THE TENTS OF ASRA
(Sel)/Aug 31, 1912; p. 880
IN THE TEPEE'S LIGHT
(Re)/May 6, 1911; p. 1020
IN THE TIDE (Rep)/May 18, 1912; p. 630
IN THE TIME OF REBELLION

(FIT)/Sep 19, 1908; p. 222
IN THE TOILS (Lu)/Sep 20, 1913; p. 1284
IN THE TWILIGHT
(Am)/Feb 27, 1915; p. 1289
IN THE TYROL, THE ARLBERG VALLEY
(CGP)/Nov 9, 1912; p. 553
IN THE TYROLESE ALPS
(UE)/Jun 7, 1913; p. 1031
IN THE VALE OF SORROW
(Be)/Jan 16, 1915; p. 369
IN THE VALLEY (Th)/Jun 26, 1915; p. 2096
IN THE VALLEY OF VESUBLE
(Pa)/May 24, 1913; p. 811
IN THE WARDEN'S GARDEN
(Dom)/Mar 6, 1915; p. 1449
IN THE WATCHES OF THE NIGHT
(Bio)/Nov 6, 1909; p. 644
(WF)/Oct 18, 1913; p. 266
IN THE WILD WEST
(Bi)/Aug 13, 1910; p. 351
IN THE WILDERNESS
(Sel)/Dec 24, 1910; p. 1476
IN THE WILDS OF AFRICA
(Bi)/Oct 11, 1913; p. 158
IN THE WINDOW RECESS
(Bio)/Dec 11, 1909; p. 840
IN THE WOLVES' FANGS
(Bi)/Mar 28, 1914; p. 1682
IN THE YEAR 2000
(Sol)/Jun 1, 1912; p. 832
IN THE YEAR 2014
(Jo)/Jan 31, 1914; p. 545
IN THEIR HOUR OF NEED
(Th)/May 31, 1913; p. 922
IN THREE HOURS (Am)/Nov 1, 1913; p.498
IN TRUST (Am)/Sep 18, 1915; p. 1996
IN TUNE (Am)/Dec 26, 1914; p. 1842
IN TUNE WITH THE WILD
(Sel)/Jul 18, 1914; pp 408-9
IN WIERD CRIMEA (Pa)/Aug 2, 1913; p.536
IN WILDMAN'S LAND
(Maj)/Dec 19, 1914; pp 1680-81
IN WITHERED HANDS
(Po)/Feb 7, 1914; p. 678
IN WOLF'S CLOTHING
(Ka)/Aug 1, 1914; p. 705
IN WRONG (Cin)/Jul 20, 1912; p. 243
(Po)/Jun 27, 1914; p. 1830
(Roy)/Mar 13, 1915; p. 1608
IN WRONG SIMMS
(Sel)/Dec 4, 1909; p. 799
IN ZULULAND (Lu)/Oct 16, 1915; p. 439
**INAUGURATION OF PRESIDENT TAFT,
THE** (Vi)/Mar 13, 1909; pp 303-4
**INAUGURATION OF WOODROW WILSON,
THE** (Mec)/Mar 22, 1913; p.1221
INBAD, THE COUNT
(Ne)/Feb 24, 1912; p. 690

INCENDIARY FOREMAN
(Pa)/Feb 15, 1908; pp 123-24
INCENDIARY INDIANS
(Lu)/Dec 16, 1911; p. 903
INCIDENT FROM DON QUIXOTE
(Me)/Oct 17, 1908; p. 304
INCIDENTS OF THE DURBAR AT DELHI
(Ed)/Apr 6, 1912; p. 41
INCOGNITO (Vic)/Dec 13, 1913; p. 1280
(Be)/Oct 2, 1915; p. 79
**INCOMPARABLE MISTRESS BELLAIRS,
THE** (Co)/Feb 20, 1915; p. 1152
INCOMPETENT, THE
(Lu)/Jul 25, 1914; p. 572
INCOMPETENT HERO, AN
(Key)/Nov 21, 1914; p. 1077
INCONSTANT, THE (Po)/Sep 17,1910; p.633
**INCONVENIENCE OF TAKING MOVING
PICTURES, THE** (Pa)/Aug 8, 1908; p. 109
INCORRIGIBLE DUKANE, THE
(FP)/Sep 18, 1915; pp 2009-10
INCRIMINATING EVIDENCE (Pa)/Feb 6,
1909; p. 144/Feb 27, 1909; p. 238
INCRIMINATING LETTER, THE
(SA)/Aug 23, 1913; p. 843
INDELIBLE STAIN, THE
(Sel)/Sep 28, 1912; p. 1276
INDEPENDENT WOMAN, AN
(Re)/Aug 28, 1915; p. 1480
INDESTRUCTIBLE MR. JENKS, THE
(Ka)/Apr 26, 1913; p. 380
INDIA PRINCESS, THE
(Sun)/Jul 10, 1915; pp 322-23
INDIAN, THE (Sel)/Jan 8, 1910; p. 16
INDIAN AGENT, THE
(Ka)/Aug 15, 1914; p. 960
INDIAN AMBUSCADE, THE
(Ka)/Feb 21, 1914; p. 946
INDIAN AND THE CHILD, THE
(SA)/May 11, 1912; p. 528
INDIAN AND THE COWGIRL, THE
(Bi)/Mar 19, 1910; pp 426-27
INDIAN AND THE MAID, THE
(Pa)/Nov 12, 1910; p. 1116
INDIAN ARMY EXERCISES
(Pa)/Apr 22, 1911; p. 900
INDIAN BASKET MAKING
(Vi)/Nov 27, 1909; p. 757
INDIAN BITTERS (Vi)/May 2, 1908; p. 404
INDIAN BLOOD (Lu)/May 14, 1910; p. 784
(Bi)/Mar 22, 1913; p. 1221
(Ka)/Jan 24, 1914; p. 413
INDIAN BRAVE'S CONVERSION, AN
(Ya)/May 27, 1911; p. 1201
INDIAN BROTHERS, THE
(Bio)/Jul 29, 1911; p. 210
INDIAN CHANGELING, THE
(Re)/Apr 17, 1915; p. 393

ISABELLA OF ARRAGON
(It)/May 7, 1910; p. 738
ISIS (Pa)/Dec 10, 1910; p.1356
  (He)/Dec 25, 1915; p.2381
ISLAND COMEDY, AN
(Ed)/Nov 11, 1911; p. 470
ISLAND OF CEYLON, INDIA
(Ed)/Dec 14, 1912; p. 1080
ISLAND OF ISHIA, THE
(Gau)/Sep 9, 1911; p. 716
ISLAND OF MYSTERY, THE
(Th)/Mar 20, 1915; p. 1775
ISLAND OF PERVERSITY, THE
(Ed)/Sep 27, 1913; p. 1392
ISLAND OF REGENERATION, THE
(Vi)/Feb 13, 1915; p. 993
ISLAND OF TONGA, THE
(Pa)/Aug 9, 1913; p. 635
ISLE OF CONTENT, THE
(Sel)/Aug 14, 1915; p. 1161
ISLETA, NEW MEXICO
(Ne)/May 11, 1912; p. 529
ISOLATED HOUSE, THE
(Pa)/Jul 24, 1915; p. 651
IT ALL CAME OUT IN THE WASH
(Vi)/Jan 4, 1913; p. 51
IT ALL DEPENDS (Lu)/Mar 6, 1915; p. 1448
IT ALMOST HAPPENED
(Ne)/Oct 2, 1915; p. 80
IT CAME BY FREIGHT
(Roy)/Apr 25, 1914; p. 517
IT CURED HUBBY (Lu)/Jan 2, 1915; p. 75
IT DID LOOK SUSPICIOUS
(Vi)/Feb 4, 1911; p. 244
IT HAPPENED AT THE BEACH
(Po)/Jun 21, 1913; p. 1254
IT HAPPENED IN HAVERSTRAW
(Re)/Nov 1, 1913; p. 498
IT HAPPENED IN JAVA
(Me)/Aug 23, 1913; p. 842
IT HAPPENED IN THE WEST
(Sel)/Jul 29, 1911; p. 209
IT HAPPENED ON A FRIDAY
(Ne)/Mar 27, 1915; p. 1933
IT HAPPENED ON WASHDAY
(Lu)/Apr 10, 1915; p. 235
IT HAPPENED THUS
(Vic)/Dec 7, 1912; p. 977
IT HAPPENED WHILE HE FISHED
(Ne)/Aug 7, 1915; p. 998
IT IS HARD TO PLEASE HIM
(Ec)/Aug 2, 1913; p. 538
IT IS NEVER TOO LATE TO MEND
(Ed)/Jan 18, 1913; pp 264-65
IT IS NOT THE COWL THAT MAKES THE
FRIAR (Pa)/Feb 29, 1908; p. 172
IT MAY BE YOU (Ed)/Jul 24, 1915; p. 649
IT MAY COME TO THIS

(Cry)/Jan 10, 1914; p. 173
IT MIGHT HAVE BEEN
(Lu)/Feb 19, 1910; p. 257
(Lu)/Feb 1, 1913; p. 465
IT MIGHT HAVE BEEN SERIOUS
(Ne)/Feb 20, 1915; p. 1140
IT PAYS TO ADVERTISE
(Ed)/Apr 16, 1910; p. 598
IT PAYS TO BE KIND
(Ec)/Apr 6, 1912; p. 42
IT SERVED HER RIGHT
(Ed)/Jun 10, 1911; p. 1316
IT SERVES HIM RIGHT
Dec 12, 1908; p. 478
IT SMELLS OF SMOKE
(Pa)/Aug 1, 1908; p. 90
IT STICKS EVERYTHING - EVEN IRON
(Pa)/Jul 25, 1908; p. 70
IT WAS LIKE THIS (Am)/Oct 2, 1915; p. 79
IT WAS SOME PARTY
(Bio)/Aug 1, 1914; p. 704
IT WAS TO BE (Lu)/Sep 4, 1915; p. 1643
IT WASN'T POISON, AFTER ALL
(Ed)/Mar 22, 1913; p. 1219
ITALIAN ARMY IN TRIPOLI, THE
(It)/Mar 2, 1912; p. 781
ITALIAN ARTILLERY
(Amb)/Aug 26, 1911; p. 545
ITALIAN BARBER, THE
(Bio)/Jan 21, 1911; p. 142
ITALIAN BLOOD (Bio)/Oct 21, 1911; p. 208
ITALIAN BRIDE, THE
(Pa)/May 3, 1913; p. 488
ITALIAN FRIENDSHIP
(Po)/Jun 22, 1912; p. 1128
ITALIAN GAMES AND DANCES
(Sel)/Feb 21, 1914; p. 946
ITALIAN LAKES (Amb)/Jun 29,1912; p.1228
ITALIAN LOVE (Re)/Jun 7, 1913; p. 1032
(Be)/Mar 21, 1914; p. 1525
(SA)/Mar 7, 1914; p. 1236
ITALIAN SHERLOCK HOLMES, THE
(Ya)/Nov 12, 1910; p. 1119
ITALIAN'S GRATITUDE, AN
(Sol)/Oct 7, 1911; p. 42
ITCHING FOR REVENGE
(Lko)/Sep 4, 1915; p. 1645
ITINERANT WEDDING, AN
(Pa)/May 31, 1913; p. 920
ITO, THE BEGGAR BOY
(Vi)/Jul 2, 1910; p. 24
IT'S A BEAR (Ed)/Dec 19, 1914; p. 1679
IT'S A BOY (St)/Jul 4, 1914; p. 65
IT'S A LONG, LONG WAY TO TIPERARY
(Pa)/Feb 13, 1915; p. 985
IT'S A SHAME (Lu)/Jul 18, 1914; p. 432
IT'S A SHAME TO TAKE THE MONEY
(Cry)/Nov 1, 1913; p. 497

JIM, THE BURGLAR (Lu)/Apr 5, 1913; p.47
JIM, THE MULE BOY
(Ed)/Apr 15, 1911; p. 843
JIM, THE PENMAN (FP)/Jun 19,1915;p.1949
JIM, THE RANCHMAN
(Sel)/Sep 24, 1910; p. 688
JIM AND JACK (GN)/Jul 22, 1911; p. 126
JIM AND JOE (Sel)/Jun 10, 1911; p. 1313/
Jun 24, 1911; p. 1426
JIM BENTLEY'S ADVENTURE
(Am)/Nov 23, 1912; p. 768
JIM BLUDSO (Ka)/Sep 14, 1912; p. 1074
JIM BRIDGER'S INDIAN BRIDE
(Ka)/Dec 3, 1910; p. 1296
JIM CAMERON'S WIFE
(Dom)/Aug 1, 1914; p. 706
JIM CROW - A TALE OF THE TURF
(Lux)/Aug 12, 1911; p. 377
JIM GETS A NEW JOB
(Pa)/Mar 28, 1908; p. 270
JIM IS FOND OF GARLIC
(Pa)/Aug 22, 1908; p. 144
JIM TAKES A CHANCE
(Am)/Sep 20, 1913; p. 1285
JIM WANTS TO GET PINCHED
(Pa)/May 7, 1910; p. 736
JIM WEBB, SENATOR
(Imp)/Aug 29, 1914; p. 1243
JIM WEST - GAMBLER (Lu)/Oct 16, 1915;
p. 463/Oct 23, 1915; p. 620
JIMMIE, THE BUCCANEER
(Gau)/May 18, 1912; p. 630
JIMMIE, THE DETECTIVE
(Gau)/Aug 5, 1911; p. 293
JIMMIE, THE INSURANCE AGENT
(Gau)/Jul 1, 1911; p. 1519
JIMMIE, THE PORTER
(Sel)/Oct 24, 1914; p. 491
JIMMIE AND HIS COUNTRY UNCLE
(Gau)/Nov 25, 1911; p. 636
JIMMIE AS A FOOTMAN
(Gau)/Sep 2, 1911; pp 609-10
JIMMIE AS A PHILANTHROPIST
(Gau)/Jul 29, 1911; p. 210
JIMMIE ELOPES (Gau)/Jul 15,1911;pp 18-19
JIMMIE IN LOVE (Gau)/Nov 4, 1911; p. 379
JIMMIE ON GUARD
(Gau)/Sep 30, 1911; p. 971
JIMMIE ON THE JOB
(Be)/Aug 21, 1915; p. 1317
JIMMIE TO THE RESCUE
(Gau)/Sep 16, 1911; p. 789
JIMMIE TRICKS THE LANDLADY
(Gau)/Dec 16, 1911; p.903
JIMMIE'S JOB (Vi)/Sep 23, 1911; p. 981
JIMMIE'S LUCK (Gau)/Aug 26, 1911; p. 541
JIMMIE'S REDEMPTION
(Po)/Nov 22, 1913; p. 869

JIMMIE'S TRICK (Gau)/Jul 15, 1911; p. 39
JIMMY (Sal)/Jul 23, 1910; p.193
(SA)/Jan 25, 1913; p. 364
(Dom)/Oct 10, 1914; p. 189
JIMMY, THE FISHERMAN
(Gau)/Jun 10, 1911; p. 1316
JIMMY, THE FOX
(Gau)/Apr 29, 1911; p. 958
JIMMY HAYES AND MURIEL
(Sel)/Nov 7, 1914; p. 787
JIMMY KELLY AND THE KIDNAPPERS
(Jo)/Aug 1, 1914; p. 706
JIMMY MINDS THE BABY
(Am)/Apr 29, 1911; p. 960
JIMMY ON A LARK
(Gau)/Jun 3, 1911; p. 1259
JIMMY'S FINISH (Ka)/Nov 8,1913; p.611
JIM'S ATONEMENT
(Imp)/May 25, 1912; p. 730
(Fr)/Oct 25, 1913; p. 381
JIM'S COLLEGE DAYS
(Maj)/Jan 4, 1913; p. 52
JIM'S PARTNER (Pa)/Nov 16, 1912; p. 658
JIM'S REWARD (Lu)/Aug 2, 1913; p. 536
JIM'S VINDICATION
(Sel)/Nov 9, 1912; p. 554
(Ed)/Oct 3, 1914; p.64
JIM'S WIFE (Ed)/Jun 8, 1912; p. 944
JINKS AND BARBER
(Lu)/Oct 17, 1914; p. 335
JINKS JOINS THE TEMPERANCE CLUB
(Bio)/Aug 5, 1911; p. 292
JINKS WANTS TO BE AN ACROBAT
(Pa)/Oct 29, 1910; p. 996
JINX'S BIRTHDAY PARTY
(Bio)/Dec 21, 1912; p. 1184
JITNEY ELOPEMENT, A
(SA)/Apr 17, 1915; p. 393
JIU JITSU (Pa)/Aug 2, 1913; p. 535
JOAN OF ARC (Pa)/Jul 3, 1909; p. 14
(WS)/Feb 14, 1914; p. 790
JOB AND THE GIRL, THE
(Am)/Apr 1, 1911; p. 721
JOBLOT RECRUITS, THE
(SA)/Sep 26, 1914; p. 1776
JOCKEY, THE (Pa)/Feb 26, 1910; p. 299
JOCKEY FOR LOVE, A
(Pa)/Jun 7, 1913; p. 1031
JOCKO, THE LOVESICK MONKEY
(Pa)/Sep 18, 1915; p. 1997
JOCULAR WINDS, THE
(Am)/Mar 8, 1913; p. 998
JOCULAR WINDS OF FATE, THE
(Vi)/Apr 27, 1912; p. 328
JOE BOKO SAVED BY GASOLINE
(SA)/Sep 18, 1915; p. 1995
JOE HAWKIN'S WARD
(Pr)/Mar 27, 1915; p. 1933

JOE HIBBARD'S CLAIM
(Bro)/Aug 9, 1913; p. 638
JOE MARTIN TURNS 'EM LOOSE
(Vic)/Sep 18, 1915; p. 1997
JOEL'S MARRIAGE (UE)/Mar 6,1909; p.271
JOE'S DEVOTION (NA)/Oct 23, 1915; p.622
JOE'S PARTNER, BILL
(Kri)/Jan 23, 1915; p. 518
JOE'S RETRIBUTION
(WF)/Dec 26, 1914; p. 1842
JOE'S REWARD (Re)/Dec 21, 1912; p. 1185
JOEY AND HIS TROMBONE
(Ed)/Feb 13, 1915; p. 984
JOHANNA, THE BARBARIAN
(Vi)/Jun 6, 1914; p. 1409
JOHN, THE USHER (Ec)/Jul 23, 1910; p. 193
JOHN, THE WAGONER
(Ne)/Jul 5, 1913; p. 50
JOHN ARTHUR'S TRUST
(Lu)/Jan 18, 1913; p. 263
JOHN BARLEYCORN
(Bos)/Jul 18, 1914; p. 406
JOHN BAXTER'S WARD
(Po)/Nov 4, 1911; p. 381
JOHN BONSALL OF THE U.S. SECRET
SERVICE (Sel)/Oct 18, 1913; p. 263
JOHN BROWN'S HEIR
(Ed)/Dec 16, 1911; p. 905
JOHN BURNS OF GETTYSBURG
(Ka)/Jun 14, 1913; pp 1135-36
JOHN COLTER'S ESCAPE
(Sel)/Dec 21, 1912; p. 1184
JOHN DOUGH AND THE CHERUB
(Sel)/Dec 31, 1910; p. 1538
JOHN GLAYDE'S HONOUR (Pa)/Oct 16,
1915; pp 463-64/Oct 23, 1915; p. 621
JOHN GRAHAM'S GOLD
(Lu)/Aug 6, 1910; p. 296
JOHN HALIFAX, GENTLEMAN
(Th)/Dec 17, 1910; p. 1418
JOHN HARDY'S INVENTION
(Po)/Apr 2, 1910; p. 510
JOHN IS NO MORE A CHILD
(KO)/May 2, 1908; p. 401
JOHN MANLEY'S AWAKENING
(Ed)/May 31, 1913; p. 920
JOHN MILTON (It)/Feb 25, 1911; p. 432
(UE)/May 11, 1912; p. 527
JOHN OAKHURST, GAMBLER
(Sel)/Oct 14, 1911; p. 129
JOHN RANCE, GENTLEMAN
(Vi)/Aug 15, 1914; p. 960
JOHN REDMOND, THE EVANGELIST
(GN)/Apr 10, 1915; p. 243
JOHN STERLING, ALDERMAN
(Imp)/Nov 9, 1912; p. 554
JOHN T. ROCKS AND THE "FLIVVER"
(Th)/Oct 23, 1915; p. 620

JOHN TOBIN'S SWEETHEART
(Vi)/Oct 4, 1913; p. 47
JOHNNIE FROM JONESBORO
(Fr)/May 23, 1914; p. 1117
JOHNNIE GOES DUCK HUNTING
(Ka)/Jan 25, 1913; p. 363
JOHNNY, THE BARBER
(Be)/Nov 20, 1915; p. 1500
JOHNNY'S PICTURES OF THE POLAR
REGIONS (Pa)/Apr 30, 1910; p. 689
JOHN'S NEW SUIT (Vi)/Aug 1, 1908;
p. 92/Oct 10, 1908; p. 279
JOINING THE OCEANS
(Ed)/Dec 27, 1913; p. 1544
JOKE ON HOWLING WOLF, THE
(Vi)/Feb 8, 1913; p. 571
JOKE ON JANE, A (Be)/Jul 25, 1914; p. 572
JOKE ON JANE, THE
(Ka)/Jan 24, 1914; p. 412
JOKE ON MR. HENPECK
(GN)/May 4, 1912; p. 427
JOKE ON THE JOKER, A
(Cry)/Sep 19, 1914; p. 1646
JOKE ON THE JOKER, THE
(Bio)/Jan 20, 1912; p. 202
JOKE ON THE SHERIFF, THE
(Cry)/May 3, 1913; p. 489
JOKE ON YELLENTOWN, A
(Re)/Dec 26, 1914; p. 1841
JOKE THEY PLAYED ON BUMPTIOUS,
THE (Ed)/Dec 31, 1910; p. 1536
JOKE WASN'T ON BEN BOLT, THE
(Vi)/Feb 22, 1913; p. 779
JOKER'S MISTAKE, THE
(UE)/Aug 24, 1912; p. 770
JOLIET PRISON, JOLIET, ILL.
(Abo)/Apr 11, 1914; p. 214
JOLLIER, THE (Ka)/Jul 15, 1911; p. 38
JOLLY BILL OF THE ROLLICKING R
(Am)/Dec 9, 1911; p. 818
JOLLY TRIO'S DREAM, THE
(Pa)/Mar 6, 1909; p. 269
JOLLY WHIRL, THE
(Gau)/Jul 30, 1910; p. 244
JONAH, A (Bio)/Jun 27, 1914; p. 1828
JONES AND HIS NEW NEIGHBORS
(Bio)/Apr 3, 1909; p. 403
JONES AND THE LADY BOOK AGENT
(Bio)/May 15, 1909; pp 634-35
JONES' BURGLAR TRAP
(Cry)/Jan 24, 1914; p. 414
JONES' HYPNOTIC EYE
(Vi)/Jun 19, 1915; p. 1939
JONES' JONAH DAY
(Ka)/Mar 29, 1913; p. 1336
JONES GOES SHOPPING
(Ed)/Apr 26, 1913; p. 381
JONES' REMEDY (Lux)/Mar 25, 1911; p.658

JONES RESURRECTED
(Cry)/Jan 11, 1913; p. 160
JONES' WATCH (Lu)/Apr 23, 1910; p. 641
JONES' WEDDING DAY
(Ka)/Oct 10, 1914; p. 187
JONESES HAVE AMATEUR
THEATRICALS, THE
(Bio)/Feb 27, 1909; p. 238
JORDON IS A HARD ROAD
(FiA)/Nov 20, 1915; p. 1501
JORIO'S DAUGHTER
(Amb)/Dec 16, 1911; p. 906
JOSEPH AND HIS BRETHREN
(Dor)/Dec 11, 1915; p. 2030
JOSEPH IN EGYPT (Cin)/Feb 10, 1912; p. 481
JOSEPH SOLD BY HIS BRETHREN
(Pa)/Mar 12, 1910; p. 382
JOSEPHINE (Cin)/Apr 20, 1912; p. 219/
May 25, 1912; p. 729
JOSEPH'S TRIALS IN EGYPT
(Ecl)/Feb 21, 1914; p. 933
JOSH AND CINDY'S WEDDING TRIP
(Ed)/May 20, 1911; p. 1140
JOSH'S SUICIDE (Bio)/Oct 28, 1911; p. 291
JOSIE'S CONEY ISLAND NIGHTMARE
(Vi)/Sep 12, 1914; p. 1512
JOSIE'S DECLARATION OF
INDEPENDENCE (Vi)/Sep 12, 1914; p.1511
JOSIE'S LEGACY (Vi)/Oct 24, 1914; p. 491
JOURNALS OF LORD JOHN, THE (GS)
No.1/Dec 11, 1915; p. 2033
JOURNEY OF THE WESTERN GOVERNOR
TO THE EAST, THE
(Sel)/Jan 27, 1912; p. 303
JOURNEY THROUGH CRIMEA, A
(Pa)/Oct 25, 1913; p. 379
JOURNEY TO THE ENVIRONS OF
NAPLES, A (Pa)/Dec 27, 1913; p. 1543
JOURNEY'S END (Roy)/Mar 27,1915; p.1933
JOURNEY'S END, THE
(Sel)/Jun 26, 1915; p. 2095
JOY RIDE, THE (Po)/Apr 13, 1912; p. 138
(Pa)/Jul 19, 1913; p. 319
JOYCE OF THE NORTH WOODS
(Ed)/Sep 13, 1913; p. 1176
JOYOUS SURPRISE (Pa)/Jun 13, 1908; p. 515
JOYS OF A JEALOUS WIFE, THE
(Vi)/Aug 23, 1913; p. 844
JOYS OF PERSECUTION, THE
(Po)/May 20, 1911; p. 1142
JUAN, THE PELOTA PLAYER
(Ec)/Jun 4, 1910; p. 943
JUAN AND JUANITA
(Lu)/Nov 16, 1912; p. 659
JUANITA (Ne)/Jul 5, 1913; p. 49
JUAREZ AFTER THE BATTLE
(Ka)/Jul 8, 1911; p. 1585
JUDAS (Amb)/Nov 11, 1911;p.473

JUDGE DUNN'S DECISION
(Sel)/Jun 20, 1914; p. 1689
JUDGE NOT, or THE WOMAN OF MONA
DIGGINGS (Uni)/Sep 25, 1915; pp 2194-95
JUDGE NOT, THAT YE BE NOT JUDGED
(Vi)/Sep 4, 1909; p. 316
JUDGE SIMPKINS' SUMMER COURT
(SA)/Aug 26, 1911; p. 542
JUDGE YE NOT IN HASTE
(Ya)/Nov 21, 1910; p. 633
JUDGED BY A HIGHER POWER
(Ch)/Feb 18, 1911; p. 372
JUDGE'S SON, THE
(Bro)/Sep 13, 1913; p. 1177
JUDGE'S STORY, THE (Th)/Jul 29, 1911;
p. 274/Aug 19, 1911; p. 466
JUDGE'S VINDICATION, THE
(Re)/Apr 5, 1913; pp 50, 54
JUDGE'S WHISKERS, THE
(Vi)/Aug 28, 1909; p. 282
JUDGMENT (Bio)/Dec 11, 1909; p. 840
JUDGMENT, THE (Dom)/Nov 15,1913;p.738
JUDGMENT OF BUDDHA, THE
(Me)/Nov 29, 1913; p. 1008
JUDGMENT OF MEN, THE
(Vic)/Jun 5, 1915; p. 1607
JUDGMENT OF SOLOMON
(Vi)/May 29, 1909; p. 711
JUDGMENT OF THE DEEP, THE
(Lu)/May 17, 1913; p. 703
JUDGMENT OF THE JUNGLE, THE
(Gau)/Feb 28, 1914; p. 1094
JUDGMENT OF THE MIGHTY DEEP, THE
(Ed)/Jul 9, 1910; p. 84
JUDGMENT OF THE SEA, THE
(Me)/Nov 2, 1912; p. 449
JUDITH OF BETHULIA
(Bio)/Mar 7, 1914; p. 1242
JUDY FORGOT (Uni)/Aug 14, 1915; p. 1176
JUG O'RUM (Po)/Dec 2, 1911; p. 727
JUGGERNAUT, THE
(Vi)/Mar 20, 1915; p. 1771
JUGGLER'S VENGEANCE, THE
(UE)/Jun 3, 1911; p. 1258
JUGGLING WITH FATE
(Sel)/Mar 29, 1913; p. 1335
JULIANS, THE (Pa)/Dec 24, 1910; p. 1478
JULIET WANTS TO MARRY AN ARTIST
(Ec)/Jul 9, 1910; p. 85
JULIUS CAESAR
(Vi)/Dec 5,1908;p.463/Dec 12,1908;pp476-77
(It)/Dec 4, 1909; p. 800
(GK)/Nov 21, 1914; p. 1057
JUMP TO DEATH, THE
(GN)/Jun 18, 1910; p. 1049
JUMPING CHAMPION, MacMORELAND,
THE (UE)/Jun 8, 1912; p. 942
JUNE FRIDAY (Ed)/Jul 24, 1915; p. 669

JUNGLE, THE (AS)/Jun 20, 1914; p. 1675
JUNGLE FLIRTATION, A
 (Pa)/Sep 27, 1913; p. 1391
JUNGLE LOVERS, THE
 (Sel)/Oct 2, 1915; p. 79
JUNGLE MASTER, THE (101)/Oct 31, 1914;
 p. 654/ Nov 7, 1914; p. 790
JUNGLE QUEEN, THE
 (Bi)/May 22, 1915; p. 1261
JUNGLE REVENGE, A
 (Sel)/Dec 11, 1915; p. 2031
JUNGLE SAMARITAN, THE
 (Sel)/Aug 29, 1914; p. 1240
JUNGLE STOCKADE, THE
 (Sel)/May 1, 1915; p. 727
JUNIOR OFFICER, THE
 (Sel)/Apr 6, 1912; pp 41-42
JUNIOR PARTNER, THE
 (Th)/Nov 15, 1913; p. 738
JUPITER SMITTEN
 (Gau)/Jul 30, 1910; p. 244
JUROR NUMBER SEVEN
 (Rex)/Dec 11, 1915; p. 2033
JURY'S VERDICT, THE
 (Pa)/Jul 5, 1913; p. 48
JUST A BAD KID (Th)/Jan 20, 1912; p. 205
JUST A BIT OF LIFE
 (Bio)/Oct 3, 1914; p. 64
JUST A BOY (Sol)/Jun 8, 1912; p. 940
JUST A FIRE FIGHTER
 (Imp)/Jun 14, 1913; p. 1138
JUST A KID (Bio)/Dec 19, 1914; p. 1680
JUST A LARK (Bio)/Apr 17, 1915; p. 392
JUST A NOTE (Lu)/Mar 28, 1914; p. 1681
JUST A WOMAN (Po)/Nov 2, 1912; p. 451
JUST A SONG AT TWILIGHT
 (Maj)/Feb 21, 1914; p. 947
JUST AS I AM (Sel)/Dec 11, 1915; p. 2031
JUST AS IT HAPPENED
 (Am)/Oct 9, 1915; p. 254
JUST BILL'S LUCK
 (Lux)/Jun 17, 1911; p. 1389
JUST BROWN'S LUCK
 (Key)/Feb 8, 1913; p. 573
JUST CISSY'S LITTLE WAY
 (Lu)/Dec 6, 1913; p. 1151
JUST FAME (Re)/Mar 15, 1913; p. 1106
JUST FOR GOOD LUCK
 (Pa)/Jul 23, 1910; pp 192-93
JUST FOR HER SAKE
 (Imp)/Aug 5, 1911; pp 294-95
JUST FOR LUCK (Imp)/May 31,1913; p.921
JUST GENERAL, A (Ec)/Oct 7, 1911; p. 42
JUST GOLD (Bio)/Jun 7, 1913; p. 1031
JUST HARD LUCK (Maj)/Jan 11,1913; p.159
JUST HATS (Sol)/Nov 23, 1912; p. 768
JUST HIS LUCK (Ne)/Jul 8, 1911; p. 1586
 (Sel)/Sep 14, 1912; p. 1074

JUST IN TIME (Bi)/Jul 20, 1912; p. 245
 (Rex)/Jul 26, 1913; p. 429
JUST IN TIME FOR DINNER
 (Com)/Dec 23, 1911; p. 990
JUST JIM (UnF)/Aug 21, 1915; p. 1318
JUST KIDS (Po)/Apr 1, 1911; p. 721
 (Pun)/Feb 15, 1913; p. 681
 (Bio)/Jun 21, 1913; p. 1251
 (Key)/Aug 2, 1913; p. 537
 (Pr)/Apr 24, 1915; p. 556
JUST LIKE A WOMAN
 (Bio)/May 4, 1912; pp 425-26
 (Sel)/Feb 20, 1915; p. 1139
JUST LIKE HIS WIFE
 (Mut)/Oct 16, 1915; p. 440
JUST LIKE KIDS (Lu)/Jul 10, 1915; p. 307
JUST LOOK AT JAKE
 (Lu)/May 1, 1915; p. 727
JUST MARRIED (Lu)/Jun 1, 1912; p. 829
JUST MISSED HIM (UE)/Feb 8, 1913; p.571
JUST MOTHER (Po)/Jan 10, 1914; p. 173
JUST NUTS (Pa)/Apr 24, 1915; p. 557
JUST OUT OF COLLEGE
 (Fro)/Jul 17, 1915; p. 509
JUST PLAIN FOLKS
 (Vi)/Aug 22, 1908; p. 145
JUST PRETENDING (Lu)/Aug 3, 1912; p.445
JUST PUNISHMENT, A
 (Sel)/Oct 10, 1914; p. 187
JUST RETRIBUTION
 (KO)/Apr 18, 1908; p. 354
 (Lu)/Jun 5, 1915; p. 1604
JUST REWARD, A (Lu)/Apr 3, 1909; p. 404
JUST SHOW PEOPLE
 (Vi)/Mar 8, 1913; p. 995
JUST TOO LATE (Ne)/Jan 20, 1912; p. 204
JUST TRAMPS (Pa)/May 8, 1915; p. 901
JUST TWO LITTLE GIRLS
 (Ne)/Dec 16, 1911; p. 905
JUST VERDICT, A (Lu)/Feb 3, 1912; p. 393
JUSTICE (He)/Feb 21, 1914; p.929
JUSTICE IN THE FAR NORTH (Imp)/
 Feb 19,1910; pp 258,260/Feb 26,1910; p.300
JUSTICE OF CLAUDIUS, THE
 (Pa)/Apr 22, 1911; p. 900
JUSTICE OF MANITU
 (Pa)/Jun 1, 1912; p. 830
JUSTICE OF THE DESERT, THE
 (Vi)/Mar 9, 1912; p. 867
JUSTICE OF THE REDSKIN (Pa)/Jun 6,
 1908; pp 497-98/Mar 27, 1909; p. 368
JUSTICE OF THE SAGE, THE
 (Am)/Jan 27, 1912; p. 304
JUSTICE OR MERCY
 (Gau)/May 29, 1909; p. 713
JUSTIFIED (Am)/Feb 6, 1915; p. 836/
 Feb 20, 1915; p. 1141
JUSTIFIER, THE (Ec)/Oct 2, 1909; p. 451

JUSTINIAN AND THEODORA
(Sel)/Jan 14, 1911; p. 88
JUVENILE KIDNAPPERS, THE
(Fr)/Sep 20, 1913; p. 1285
JUVENILE LOVE AFFAIR, A
(Vi)/Aug 10, 1912; p. 546

KAFFIR'S SKULL, THE
(Re)/Dec 12, 1914; p. 1525
KAINTUCKY BILL (Ka)/Jul 25, 1914; p. 571
KAISER WILLIAM II
(Kai)/Aug 22, 1914; p. 1086
KALEMITES VISIT GIBRALTA, THE
(Ka)/Mar 30, 1912; p. 1166
KANGAROO, THE (Wor)/Jun 20,1914;p.1669
KANGAROO AT HOME, THE
(Gl)/Aug 7, 1915; p. 998
KARLBERG (CGP)/Apr 6, 1912; p. 41
KASHMIR, BRITISH INDIA
(Ecl)/Sep 12, 1914; p. 1513
KATANA, THE OATH OF THE SWORD
(Saw)/Oct 10, 1914; p. 200
KATCHEM KATE (Bio)/Jun 29,1912;p.1226
KATE, THE COP (Lu)/Jun 21, 1913; p. 1251
KATE WATERS OF THE SECRET SERVICE
(Po)/Jul 25, 1914; p. 573
KATHLEEN, THE IRISH ROSE
(Th)/Mar 21, 1914; p. 1526
KATHLEEN MAVOURNEEN
(Imp)/Mar 8, 1913; p. 978
(Ed)/Mar 29, 1913; p. 1336
KATZENJAMMER KIDS, THE (Sel)
No.2/May 25, 1912; p. 729
No.3/Jun 1, 1912; p. 830
No.4/Jun 8, 1912; p. 944
No.5/Jun 15, 1912; p. 1027
No.6/Jun 22, 1912; p. 1127
No.7/Jun 29, 1912; p. 1227
No.8/Jul 6, 1912; p. 42
KEAN (GN)/Dec 10, 1910; p. 1359
KEENEST OF THE TWO
(KO)/Jul 11, 1908; p. 36
KEEP IT STRAIGHT/Oct 17, 1908; p. 298
KEEP MOVING (GK)/Nov 20, 1915; p. 1509
KEEPER OF THE LIGHT, THE
(Pr)/Sep 12, 1914; p. 1512
KEEPER OF THE FLOCK, THE
(SBa)/Feb 27, 1915; p. 1289
KEEPERS OF THE FLOCK
(Ed)/Sep 20, 1913; p. 1284
KEEPING A HUSBAND
(Th)/Nov 21, 1914; p. 1076
KEEPING AN EYE ON FATHER
(Ec)/Feb 24, 1912; p. 691
KEEPING HIS WORD
(Imp)/Nov 19, 1910; p. 1179
KEEPING HUSBANDS HOME
(Vi)/Aug 30, 1913; p. 960

KEEPING IT DARK (Ne)/Dec 4,1915; p.1854
KEEPING TAB ON SAMMY
(Cin)/Apr 26, 1913; p. 380
KEEPING UP APPEARANCES
(Lu)/Feb 22, 1913; p. 780
KEEPING UP WITH HUBBY
(Kin)/Apr 26, 1913; p. 381
KEEPING UP WITH THE JONESES (Gau)
No.1/Sep 18,1915; p.1996/Oct 2,1915; p.79
No.2/Sep 25, 1915; p. 2177
No.3/Oct 9, 1915; p. 253
No.4/Oct 16, 1915; p. 440
No.5/Oct 30, 1915; p. 792
No.7/Oct 30a, 1915; p. 968
No.8/Nov 6, 1915; p. 1140
No.9/Nov 13, 1915; p 1312
No.10/Nov 20, 1915; p. 1500
No.11/Nov 27, 1915; p. 1664
No.12/Dec 4, 1915; p. 1853
No.13/Dec 11, 1915; p. 2032
No.14/Dec 18, 1915; p. 2203
No.15/Dec 25, 1915; p. 2389
KELLY, U.S.A. (At)/Feb 25, 1911; p. 431
KELLY FROM THE EMERALD ISLE
(Sol)/May 31, 1913; p. 925
KELLY ON A TIGHT ROPE
(Mil)/Nov 23, 1912; p. 769
KELLY'S GHOST (Cry)/Mar 14,1914; p.1386
KELP INDUSTRY, THE
(Key)/Sep 6, 1913; p. 1069
KENO BATES, LIAR
(KB)/Sep 4, 1915; p. 1644
KENTISH COAST, THE
(UE)/Apr 26, 1913; p. 379
KENTON'S HEIR (Pa)/Dec 6, 1913; p. 1151
KENTUCKIAN, THE (Bio)/Jul 11, 1908; p.32
KENTUCKY DERBY AT CHURCHILL
DOWNS, THE (Sel)/Jul 5, 1913; p. 48
KENTUCKY EPISODE, A
(Bio)/Oct 9, 1915; p. 252
KENTUCKY FEUD, A
(Rex)/Nov 2, 1912; p. 451
KENTUCKY FOES (Re)/Aug 15, 1913; p.745
KENTUCKY GIRL (Ka)/Aug 31, 1912; p.880
KENTUCKY GIRL, A
(Ya)/May 13, 1911; p. 1083
KENTUCKY IDYL, A
(Vic)/Oct 16, 1915; p. 442
KENTUCKY PIONEER, A
(Sel)/Oct 15, 1910; p. 874
KENTUCKY PLANTER, A
(NYM)/Oct 2, 1909; p. 451
KENTUCKY ROMANCE, A
(KB)/Jan 10, 1914; p. 173
KER-CHOO (SA)/May 2, 1908; p. 400
KERKA FALLS (Cin)/Mar 2, 1912; p. 781
KERRY GOW, THE (Ka)/Nov 9, 1912;
p. 530/Nov 30, 1912; p. 877

KNAVES AND THE KNIGHT, THE
(Ka)/Nov 6, 1915; p. 1139
KNIFE OF FIRE, A (Ed)/Aug 9,1913; p.635
KNIGHT AND THE FRIAR, THE
(Maj)/Jul 6, 1912; p. 44
KNIGHT BEFORE CHRISTMAS, THE
(Vi)/Jan 9, 1915; p. 220
KNIGHT ERRANT, A
(Re)/Oct 25, 1913; p. 381
KNIGHT ERRANT, THE
(Sel)/Aug 12, 1911; p. 376
KNIGHT FOR A NIGHT, A
(Ed)/Oct 9, 1909; p. 491
KNIGHT OF CYCLONE GULCH, THE
(Ka)/Jul 12, 1913; p. 204
KNIGHT OF HER DREAMS, THE
(Ne)/Jun 7, 1913; p. 1033
KNIGHT OF THE BLACK ART
(Me)/Jan 18, 1908; p. 45
KNIGHT OF THE GARTER, A
(Ne)/Apr 26, 1913; p. 382
KNIGHT OF THE ROAD, A
(Bio)/May 6, 1911; p. 1019
KNIGHT OF THE TRAILS, THE
(KB)/Aug 21, 1915; p. 1317
KNIGHT OF TROUBLE, A
(Sel)/May 16, 1914; p. 968
KNIGHTS AND LADIES
(Cry)/Mar 15, 1913; p. 1105
KNIGHTS OF RHODES, THE
(Amb)/Mar 8, 1913; p. 977
KNOCK-OUT, THE (Key)/Jul 4, 1914; p. 65
KNOCK WOOD (It)/Jan 18, 1913; p. 265
KNOCKABOUT KELLY, MAGICIAN
(Me)/May 9, 1914; p. 820
KNOCKOUT, THE (Cub)/Sep 18, 1915; p. 1996
KNOCKOUT WALLOP, THE
(St)/Mar 13, 1915; p. 1608
KNOT IN THE HANDKERCHIEF, THE
(It)/Jun 11, 1910; p. 999
KNOT IN THE PLOT, A
(Bio)/Jun 11, 1910; p. 995
KNOTTY KNOT, A (Ch)/Apr 12, 1913; p.165
KNOWING BIRDS, THE
(Pa)/Aug 8, 1908; p. 109
KNOWS ALL, ANTHROPOLOGICAL
DOCTOR (It)/Jun 17, 1911; p. 1388
KODAC CONTEST, THE
(Ec)/Mar 23, 1912; pp 1063-64
KOREA (Pa)/Jul 18, 1908;
p. 51/Oct 30, 1908; p. 338
KREUTZER SONATA, THE
(Fox)/Mar 27, 1915; p. 1934
KRIMMEL WATERFALLS
(Gau)/Feb 18, 1911; p. 370
KRITERION COMIC CARTOONS
(Pyr)/Mar 20, 1915; p. 1764
KRONSTADT (Gau)/Jun 27, 1914; p. 1838

LA GRANDE BRETECHE
(Pa)/Dec 11, 1909; p. 835
LA TOSCA
(Pa)/Jun 5, 1909; p. 752/Jun 19, 1909; p. 832
(UnF)/Oct 19, 1912; pp 230-31
LABOR DEMONSTRATION IN HYDE
PARK, LONDON (Ka)/Jul 11, 1914; p. 255
LABYRINTH, THE
(Rex)/Feb 8, 1913; p. 574
(Eq)/Dec 11, 1915; p. 2029
LACEMAKER'S DREAM, THE
(Lux)/Jun 4, 1910; p. 943
LACKEY, THE (Maj)/Jan 31, 1914; p. 545
LAD FROM OLD IRELAND, THE (Ka)/
Dec 3, 1910; p. 1296/Aug 15, 1914; p. 959
LADDER OF FORTUNE, THE (Rex)/Apr 10,
1915; p. 242/Apr 24, 1915; p. 558
LADDER OF LIFE, THE
(Th)/Nov 16, 1912; p. 660
LADDER OF LOVE, THE
(Pa)/May 8, 1915; p. 922
LADDIE (Ed)/Oct 16, 1909; p. 530
(Ed)/Aug 8, 1914; p. 837
LADIES' COMPANION, THE
(Pa)/Dec 18, 1909; p. 880
LADIES' WAR, THE (Vi)/Jul 4, 1914; p. 64
LADY AND HER MAID, A
(Vi)/Jun 7, 1913; p. 1030
LADY AND THE BURGLAR, THE
(Ed)/Aug 27, 1910; p. 462
(BFF)/Feb 27, 1915; p. 1291
LADY AND THE GLOVE, THE
(Vi)/Aug 30, 1913; p. 960
LADY AND THE MOUSE, THE
(Bio)/May 10, 1913; p. 596
LADY ATHLETE DOWNS THE FOOT-PADS,
THE/Feb 27, 1909; p.237
LADY AUDLEY'S JEWELS
(SA)/Mar 15, 1913; p. 1103
LADY AUDLEY'S SECRET
(Imp)/May 18, 1912; pp 613-14/
Jun 1, 1912; p. 831
(Sup)/Jan 23, 1915; p. 517
LADY BABBIE (Ec)/Nov 15, 1913; p. 738
LADY BAFFLES AND DETECTIVE
DUCK (Uni)
No.1/May 29, 1915; p. 1433
No.2/Jun 12, 1915; p. 1778
No.3/Jun 26, 1915; p. 2097
No.4/Jul 10, 1915; p. 309
No.5/Jul 24, 1915; p. 651
No.6/Aug 7, 1915; p. 998
No.7/Aug 21, 1915; p. 1318
No.10/Oct 2, 1915; p. 80
No.11/Oct 16, 1915; p. 441
11-25/Nov 20, 1915; p. 1501
LADY BARBER OF ROARING GULCH, THE
(Ne)/Nov 2, 1912; p. 452

LAND OF PROMISE, THE
(Imp)/May 18, 1912; p. 630
LAND OF THE PHARAOHS
(He)/Jun 26, 1909; p. 873
LAND SALESMAN, THE
(Key)/Apr 5, 1913; p. 50
LAND SHARKS vs SEA DOGS
(Sel)/Sep 7, 1912; p. 975
LAND SWINDLERS, THE
(Ka)/Feb 22, 1913; p. 759
LAND THIEVES, THE
(Am)/Oct 21, 1911; p. 211
LANDING OF THE PILGRIMS, THE
(Ed)/May 1, 1915; p. 727
LANDING THE HOSE REEL
(Sel)/Oct 23, 1915; p. 625
LANDLADY RENTS THE ROOM, THE
(Re)/Oct 25, 1913; p. 381
LANDLADY'S PORTRAIT, THE
(Ed)/Feb 27, 1909; p. 237
LANDLORD'S TROUBLES, A
(Key)/Jan 25, 1913; p. 365
LANDLUBBER, THE
(Ka)/Nov 30, 1912; p. 877
LANDMARKS OF AVIGNON, FRANCE
(Gau)/Feb 25, 1911; p. 431
LANDON'S LEGACY
(Uni)/Dec 18, 1915; p. 2200
LANGUAGE OF THE DUMB, THE
(Lu)/Feb 13, 1915; p. 984
LAPLANDERS, THE
(Gem)/Apr 26, 1913; p. 382
LARGE LAKES OF ITALY, THE
(Po)/Oct 21, 1911; p. 211
LARGEST BOAT EVER LAUNCHED
SIDEWAYS (Key)/Jul 5, 1913; p. 50
LARGEST DUCK FARM IN THE WORLD,
THE (Ka)/Oct 11, 1913; p. 155
L'ARLESIENNE (Pa)/Nov 28,
1908; pp 423, 433/Dec 5, 1908; p. 448
LARRY O'NEIL, GENTLEMAN
(Imp)/Jun 26, 1915; p. 2098
L'ARTICLE 47 (Maj)/Nov 29, 1913; p. 1009
LASCA (101)/Nov 15, 1913; p. 738
LASH OF FATE, THE
(Rex)/Aug 17, 1912; p. 674
(Fl)/Jan 2, 1915; p. 78
LASS OF GLOUCESTER, THE
(Pa)/Nov 2, 1912; p. 449
LASS OF KILLKRANKIE, THE
(Vic)/Oct 31, 1914; pp 642-43
LASS OF THE LIGHT, THE
(Imp)/Dec 21, 1912; p. 1186
LASS WHO COULDN'T FORGET, THE
(Ka)/Apr 15,1911;p.843
LASS WHO LOVES A SAILOR, THE
(UE)/Feb 12, 1910; p. 216
LASSIE, FRA ABERDEEN, THE

(Lux)/May 18, 1912; p. 630
LASSIE'S BIRTHDAY, A
(Ed)/Nov 19, 1910; p. 1178
LASSOING A LION (Sel)/Jan 16,1915; p.368
LAST ACT, THE (Rex)/Jun 19, 1915; p. 1941
LAST APPEAL, THE
(Imp)/Jun 17, 1911; p. 1388
(Sel)/Aug 1, 1914; p. 705
LAST BATTLE, THE
(WF)/Aug 22, 1914; p. 1102
LAST BLOCKHOUSE, THE (Ka)/Jan 18,
1913; p. 267/Feb 22, 1913; p. 780
LAST CALL, THE (Lu)/Mar 13, 1909; p. 305
LAST CHANCE, THE
(Ec)/Sep 17, 1910; p. 633
LAST CHAPTER, THE
(FP)/Jan 23, 1915; p. 523
LAST CONFESSION, THE
(Gau)/Jul 31, 1909; p. 162
LAST CURTAIN, THE
(Gau)/Feb 11, 1911; p. 316
LAST CURTAIN CALL, THE
(Sav)/Nov 28, 1914; p. 1233
LAST DANCE, THE
(Sel)/Jun 29, 1912; pp 1216-17/
Jul 20, 1912; p. 244
(PP)/Dec 5, 1914; p. 1392
LAST DAYS OF HENRY III OF FRANCE
(UE)/Oct 7, 1911; p. 22
LAST DAYS OF POMPEII, THE
(RR)/May 1, 1909; p. 555
(Amb)/Oct 11,1913; p.135/Oct 25,1913;p.363
LAST DEAL, THE (Bio)/Feb 12, 1910; p. 216
LAST DRINK OF WHISKEY, THE
(Ko)/Jun 20, 1914; p. 1689
LAST DROP OF WATER, THE (Bio)/Jul 29,
1911; p. 1934/Jun 26, 1915; p. 2110/
Aug 28, 1915; p. 1479
LAST EGYPTIAN, THE
(Oz)/Dec 19, 1914; p. 1686
LAST FRIEND, THE
(Amb)/Oct 1, 1910; p. 749
LAST G.A.R. PARADE AT ROCHESTER,
N.Y., THE (Imp)/Oct 21, 1911; p. 211
LAST GUEST, THE
(Po)/Dec 21, 1912; p. 1186
LAST LAUGH, THE
(Re)/Feb 11, 1911; p. 318
(SA)/Nov 29, 1913; p. 1007
LAST MAN'S CLUB, THE
(Sel)/May 9, 1914; p. 820
LAST MINUTE, THE (UE)/Oct 4, 1913;
p. 28/Oct 25, 1913; p. 380
LAST NOTCH, THE
(Am)/Dec 30, 1911; p. 1073
LAST OF THE HARGROVES, THE
(Ed)/Dec 12, 1914; p. 1523
LAST OF THE LINE

LENA RIVERS
(Th)/Aug 27, 1910; p. 464
(Cos)/Oct 31, 1914; p. 656
LEND ME YOUR WIFE
(Sol)/Mar 9, 1912; p. 867
LEO, THE INDIAN (Imp)/Jul 12,1913; p.205
LEO MAKES GOOD
(Imp)/May 17, 1913; p. 705
LEON OF THE TABLE d'HOTE
(Th)/Oct 15, 1910; p. 878
LEONCE AND POUPETTE
(Gau)/Nov 22, 1913; p. 869
LEONCE AND THE MILK MAID
(Gau)/Nov 22, 1913; p. 869
LEONIE (Ed)/Feb 1, 1913; p. 464
LEOPARD, THE (Pa)/Sep 2, 1911; p. 626
LEOPARD HUNTING IN ABYSSINIA
(Amb)/Dec 18, 1909; p. 882
LEOPARD QUEEN, THE
(Sel)/Aug 21, 1909; p. 253
LEOPARD TAMER, THE
(Sel)/Jun 7, 1913; p. 1031
LEOPARD'S FOUNDLING, THE (Sel)/
Jun 13, 1914; pp 1516-17/Jul 11, 1914; p.256
LEOPARD'S LAIR, THE
(Sel)/Feb 20, 1915; p. 1139
LEOPOLD AND THE LEOPARD
(Lux)/Feb 22, 1913; p. 781
LEO'S GREAT CURE (Imp)/Jul 5, 1913; p. 49
LEO'S LAST RESORT
(Imp)/Jun 28, 1913; p. 1360
LEO'S LOVE LETTER
(Imp)/Mar 29, 1913; p. 1337
LEO'S WATERLOO
(Imp)/Apr 19, 1913; p. 281
LEPER'S COAT, THE
(Rex)/Jan 24, 1914; p. 414
LEPRECHAWN, THE (Ed)/Sep 26, 1908;
p. 241/Oct 10, 1908; p. 279
**LERIN'S ABBEY ON ST. HONORAT'S
ISLAND** (Gau)/Jun 25, 1910; p. 1100
LES MISERABLES
(Ecl)/Apr 26, 1913; pp 362-63
LES RICOCHETS (Pa)/Feb 13, 1909; p. 172
LESSER EVIL, THE
(Bio)/May 11, 1912; p. 527
LESSON, THE
(Bio)/Dec 31, 1910; p. 1538
(Me)/Aug 3, 1912; p. 445
(Sel)/Feb 15, 1913; p. 679
(Am)/Mar 15, 1913; pp 1084-85/
Mar 22, 1913; p. 1222
(Po)/Apr 19, 1913; p. 281
LESSON BY THE SEA, THE
(Vi)/Mar 12, 1910; p. 382
LESSON FROM THE FAR EAST, A
(Rex)/Apr 10, 1915; pp 237-38
LESSON FROM THE PAST, A (Cin)/Jan 18,

1913; p. 245/Feb 22, 1913; p. 779
LESSON IN DOMESTIC ECONOMY, A
(Vi)/Dec 18, 1909;p.881
LESSON IN JEALOUSY, A
(Vi)/Dec 20, 1913; p. 1412
LESSON IN LIQUID AIR, A
(CGP)/Jun 8, 1912; p. 944
LESSON IN MECHANICS, A
(Maj)/Sep 5, 1914; p. 1372
LESSON IN ROMANCE, A
(SA)/Jun 5, 1915; p. 1605
LESSON LEARNED, THE
(Ed)/Jun 24, 1911; p. 1453
LESSON OF THE NARROW STREET, THE
(Vi)/Oct 9, 1915; p. 252
LESSON THE CHILDREN TAUGHT, THE
(Po)/Nov 15, 1913; p. 737
LESSON TO HUSBANDS, A
(Imp)/Jan 6, 1912; p. 42
LESSON TO MASHERS, A
(Bio)/Apr 26, 1913; p. 379
LESSONS IN JIU JITSU
(KO)/Jul 11, 1908; p. 36
LESSONS IN LOVE (Ria)/Dec 4,1915; p.1853
LEST WE FORGET (Maj)/Aug 1,1914; p.705
LET 'EM QUARREL (Vi)/Apr 19,1913;p.280
LET KATY DO IT (FiA)/Dec 11, 1915;
p. 2028/Dec 18, 1915; p. 2204
LET NO MAN ESCAPE (SA)/Feb 28, 1914;
p. 1067/Mar 14, 1914; p. 1385
LET NO MAN PUT ASUNDER
(Imp)/Jun 22, 1912; p. 1128
(SA)/Jun 14, 1913; p. 1136
LET NOT MAN PUT ASUNDER
(Sol)/Aug 26, 1911; p. 545
LET THERE BE LIGHT
(Am)/Oct 16, 1915; p. 441
LET US GIVE THANKS
(Ch)/Dec 3, 1910; p. 1299
LET US HAVE PEACE
(Rex)/Nov 7, 1914; p. 789
LET US SMOOTH THE WAY
(Ne)/Oct 21, 1911; p. 210
LET WILLIE DO IT
(Imp)/May 25, 1912; p. 730
LETTER FROM HOME, A
(SA)/Aug 8, 1914; p. 837
LETTER IN THE SAND, A
Dec 7, 1907; pp 651-52
LETTER THAT NEVER CAME OUT, THE
(Ed)/Oct 31, 1914; p. 640
LETTER TO DADDY, A
(Bio)/Aug 14, 1915; p. 1160
LETTER TO THE STORK, A
(At)/Jan 21, 1911; p. 145
LETTER TO UNCLE SAM, A
(Ed)/Mar 22, 1913; p. 1219
LETTER WITH THE RED SEAL, THE

LIGHT THAT CAME, THE
(Bio)/Nov 27, 1909; p. 757
LIGHT THAT FAILED, THE
(Vi)/Jun 29, 1912; p. 1226
(Pa)/Nov 30, 1912; p. 876
LIGHT WOMAN, THE
(Rex)/Sep 6, 1913; p. 1069
LIGHTHOUSE BY THE SEA, THE
(SA)/Nov 13, 1915; pp 1311-12
LIGHTHOUSE KEEPER, THE
(Imp)/Jun 3, 1911; p. 1260
LIGHTHOUSE KEEPER'S DAUGHTER, THE
(Lu)/Dec 12, 1908; p. 485
(Ed)/Mar 2, 1912; p. 769/Apr 6, 1912; p. 42
LIGHTHOUSE KEEPER'S SON, THE
(Dom)/Aug 21, 1915; p. 1317
LIGHTING OF LOVE'S WAY, THE
(Gem)/Nov 23, 1912; p. 768
LIGHTNING CONDUCTOR, THE
(Hef)/May 23, 1914; p. 1094
LIGHTNING PAPER HANGER, THE
(CGP)/Aug 17, 1912; p. 669
LIGHTS AND SHADOWS
(Po)/Oct 24, 1914; p. 493
LIGHTS AND SHADOWS OF CHINATOWN
(Sel)/Oct 30, 1908; p. 347
LIGHTS O'LONDON, THE
(Wor)/Jul 18, 1914; p. 437
LIKE DARBY AND JOAN
(Rex)/Oct 4, 1913; p. 49
LIKE FATHER LIKE SON
(Am)/Apr 4, 1914; p.39/Apr 11, 1914; p.214
(Me)/Jun 6, 1914; p. 1408
LIKE KNIGHTS OF OLD
(Ed)/Nov 2, 1912; p. 449
LIKE THE CAT, THEY CAME BACK
(Bio)/Nov 2, 1912; p. 449
LIL' NOR'WESTER, THE
(Vic)/Nov 13, 1915; p. 1314
LILLIAN'S DILEMNA
(Vi)/Jul 25, 1914; p. 572
LILLIAN'S HUSBANDS
(Vi)/Oct 30, 1915; p. 792
LILLIAN'S NIGHTMARE
(Pa)/Oct 18, 1913; p. 263
LILLIPUTIAN COURTSHIP, THE
(Nov)/Oct 9, 1915; p. 253
LILT OF LOVE, THE
(Lae)/Sep 4, 1915; p. 1645
LILY AND THE ROSE, THE
(FiA)/Nov 13, 1915; pp 1313, 1322
LILY AS A LITTLE MOTHER
(Ec)/Jul 18, 1914; p. 433
LILY IN BOHEMIA, A
(Vi)/May 22, 1915; p. 1259
LILY OF POVERTY FLAT, THE
(Wor)/May 1, 1915; pp 739-40
LILY OF THE RANCH, THE

(Ne)/Jun 11, 1910; p. 999
LILY OF THE TENEMENTS, THE
(Bio)/Mar 11, 1911; p. 542
LILY OF THE VALLEY
(Vi)/Sep 5, 1914; p. 1372
LILY OF THE VALLEY, THE
(Sel)/May 9, 1914; p. 803
LILY'S LOVERS (Bio)/Feb 17, 1912; p. 581
LIMBERGER'S VICTORY
(Lu)/Dec 4, 1915; p. 1852
LIMBURGER AND LOVE
(Po)/Jun 25, 1910; p. 1102
LIMITED DIVORCE, A
(Bio)/Nov 2, 1912; p. 449
LIMPING TO HAPPINESS
(Be)/Dec 19, 1914; p. 1680
LINCOLN FOR THE DEFENSE
(Pi)/Mar 22, 1913; p. 1221
LINCOLN THE LOVER (Vi)/Jan 31, 1914;
p. 523/Feb 21, 1914; p. 946
LINCOLN'S GETTYSBURG ADDRESS
(Vi)/Jun 15, 1912; pp 1017-18/
Jul 20, 1912; p. 244
LINE AT HOGAN'S, THE
(Bio)/Oct 19, 1912; p. 242
LINE RIDER'S SISTER, THE
(Fr)/Jul 19, 1913; p. 321
LINEMAN, THE (Imp)/Aug 19, 1911; p. 465
LINEMAN AND THE GIRL, THE
(Po)/Dec 9, 1911; p. 818
LINES OF THE HAND
(RR)/Nov 20, 1909; p. 721
LINES OF WHITE ON A SULLEN SEA
(Bio)/Nov 6, 1909; pp 644-45/
Nov 13, 1909; p. 684
LINE-UP, THE (Vi)/Sep 6, 1913; p. 1068
LINK IN THE CHAIN, THE
(Ec)/May 30, 1914; p. 1261
LINK THAT BINDS, THE
(Rex)/Nov 28, 1914; p. 1233
LINK THAT HELD, THE
(Ed)/Feb 4, 1911; p. 243
LINKED BY FATE (Me)/Dec 14,1912;p.1080
LINKED TOGETHER
(Ed)/Nov 23, 1912; p. 767
LION, THE (Vic)/Apr 25, 1914; p. 518
LION, THE LAMB AND THE MAN, THE
(Rex)/Dec 12, 1914; p. 1525
LION AND THE MOUSE, THE
(Lu)/Feb 7, 1914; p. 659
LION HUNTER, THE
(Sel)/Dec 19, 1914; p. 1679
LION HUNTERS (Gau)/Sep 20,1913; p.1286
LION-HUNTING (GN)/Apr 11, 1908; p. 325
LION OF VENICE, THE
(GK)/Sep 19, 1914; pp 1619-20
LION TAMER, THE (Sel)/Jul 10, 1909; p. 51
LION TAMER'S REVENGE, THE (Cin)/Oct

LITTLE DECEIVER, THE
(SA)/Jun 19, 1915; pp 1945-46
LITTLE DELICATESSEN STORE, THE
(Ed)/Mar 2, 1912; p. 781
LITTLE DETECTIVE, THE
(Vi)/Aug 8,1908; p.111/Dec 12,1908; p.476
(Pa)/Jul 17, 1909; p. 89
(Lu)/Mar 6, 1915; p. 1447
(Cub)/Oct 23, 1915; p. 620
LITTLE DICK'S FIRST CASE
(Maj)/Jun 5, 1915; p. 1605
LITTLE DOCTOR OF THE FOOTHILLS,
THE (SA)/Jun 4, 1910; p. 941
LITTLE DOLL'S DRESSMAKER, THE
(Vi)/Jul 3, 1915; p. 65
LITTLE DOROTHY (Po)/Feb 4, 1911; p. 251
LITTLE DORRIT (Th)/Aug 9,1913;pp616,638
LITTLE DOVE'S ROMANCE
(Bi)/Sep 9, 1911; p. 692
LITTLE DRUDGE, THE
(SA)/Mar 18, 1911; p. 603
LITTLE DRUMMER BOY, THE
(GN)/Sep 17, 1910; p. 632
LITTLE DRUMMER OF 1792, A
(Gau)/Aug 28, 1909; p. 282
LITTLE DUKE, THE
(Amb)/Dec 9, 1911; p. 818
LITTLE DUTCH GIRL, THE
(Wor)/Aug 28, 1915; p. 1491
LITTLE EASTER FAIRY, THE
(Lu)/Apr 18, 1908; p. 351
LITTLE EGYPT MALONE
(Ne)/Aug 7, 1915; p. 998
LITTLE EM'LY AND DAVID COPPERFIELD
(Th)/Nov 11, 1911; p. 471
LITTLE ENCHANTRESS, THE
(Maj)/Jan 11, 1913; p. 159
LITTLE FAMILY AFFAIR, A
(Lu)/Sep 21, 1912; p. 1175
LITTLE FATHER, THE
(Vi)/Sep 25, 1909; pp 415-16
LITTLE FIDDLER, THE
(Ed)/Jul 9, 1910; p. 85
LITTLE FLOWER GIRL, THE
(Sol)/Apr 29, 1911; p. 961
LITTLE FREGOLI
(Cin)/Aug 24, 1907; p. 394
LITTLE GERMAN BAND, THE
(Gau)/Jun 11, 1910; p. 997
(At)/Jul 16, 1910; p. 144
LITTLE GIRL (Po)/Aug 5, 1911; p. 296
LITTLE GIRL NEXT DOOR, THE
(Ed)/Oct 5, 1912; p. 42
LITTLE GIRL OF THE ATTIC, THE
(Lae)/May 8, 1915; p. 901
LITTLE GIRL WHO DID NOT BELIEVE IN
SANTA CLAUS, A (Ed)/Dec 21, 1907; p. 692
LITTLE GOATHERD, THE

(Lux)/Oct 7, 1911; p. 43
LITTLE GRAY HOME, THE
(Vic)/Dec 12, 1914; p. 1525
LITTLE GRAY LADY, THE
(FP)/Jul 25, 1914; p. 575
LITTLE GYPSY, THE (Fox)/Oct 23, 1915;
p. 631/Oct 30, 1915; p. 794
LITTLE HANDS (Ec)/Apr 20, 1912; p. 231
LITTLE HE AND SHE, THE
(SA)/Jul 4, 1914; p. 64
LITTLE HELPING HANDS
(Po)/Jul 6, 1912; p. 44
LITTLE HERMAN (Fal)/Jun 26,1915; p.2096
LITTLE HERO, A Jan 16, 1909; pp 69-70
(Key)/May 3, 1913; p. 489
(Sel)/Mar 1, 1913; p. 888
LITTLE HERO, THE
(Cub)/Aug 21, 1915; p. 1317
LITTLE HERO OF HOLLAND, THE
(Th)/Jul 2, 1910; p. 26
LITTLE HOBO, THE (Sel)/Jul 18,1914;p.432
LITTLE HOME IN THE VALLEY, THE
(Am)/Jul 11, 1914; p. 257
LITTLE INDIAN MARTYR, THE
(Sel)/Sep 14, 1912; p. 1074
LITTLE INGIN (Sel)/Nov 11, 1911; p. 470
LITTLE JACK (Box)/Nov 14, 1914; p. 934
LITTLE KAINTUCK (Vi)/Dec 6,1913;p.1151
LITTLE KEEPER OF THE LIGHT, THE
(Ka)/Aug 24, 1912; p. 770
LITTLE LAD IN DIXIE
(Vi)/Apr 8, 1911; p. 782
LITTLE LADY ACROSS THE WAY, THE
(Imp)/Dec 4, 1915; p. 1854
LITTLE LADY NEXT DOOR, THE
(Am)/Oct 2, 1915; p. 79
LITTLE LEADER, THE
(Imp)/Jul 8, 1911; p. 1587
LITTLE LILLIAN TURNS THE TIDE
(Sel)/Mar 21, 1914; p. 1524
LITTLE LORD FAUNTLEROY
(Kio)/Jul 4, 1914; p. 69
LITTLE LOUDER, PLEASE, A
(SA)/Oct 12, 1912; p. 142
LITTLE LUMBER JACK, THE
(Re)/Sep 4, 1915; p. 1644
LITTLE MADAMOISELLE, THE
(Wor)/Oct 2, 1915; pp 93-94
LITTLE MADONNA, THE
(Vi)/May 9, 1914; p. 820
LITTLE MAGICIAN, THE
(Pa)/Aug 1, 1908; p. 91
LITTLE MAIL CARRIER, THE
(Vic)/Apr 18, 1914; p. 362
LITTLE MAJOR, THE
(Rex)/Apr 29, 1911; pp 940-41, 960
LITTLE MARIE (Re)/Jul 17, 1915; p. 486
LITTLE MARY AND HER DOLLY

(Pa)/Jun 4, 1910; p. 942
LITTLE MATCHMAKER, THE
(Maj)/Apr 24, 1915; p. 556
LITTLE MEG AND I
(Vic)/Sep 12, 1914; p. 1513
**LITTLE MEG AND THE WONDERFUL
LAMP** (WBE)/Oct 12, 1907; p. 509
LITTLE MINISTER, THE
(Vi)/Oct 12, 1912; pp 132-33
LITTLE MISCHIEF (Th)/Sep 26,1914;p.1776
LITTLE MISS BROWN
(Wor)/Jun 12, 1915; p. 1790
LITTLE MISS MAKE BELIEVE
(Bio)/Dec 12, 1914; pp 1523, 1530
LITTLE MORITZ AND THE BUTTERFLY
(Pa)/Sep 23, 1911; p. 891
LITTLE MORITZ IS TOO SHORT
(Pa)/Oct 14, 1911; p. 129
LITTLE MOTHER
Feb 27, 1909; p. 236
(Ec)/Nov 12,1910; p.1119
(SA)/Apr 26, 1913; pp 379-80
LITTLE MOTHER, THE
(Ka)/Oct 1, 1910; p. 747
(Th)/Mar 11, 1911; p. 543
(Maj)/Apr 24, 1915; p. 556
**LITTLE MOTHER AT THE BABY SHOW,
THE** (Vi)/Jul 2, 1910; p. 25
LITTLE MOTHER OF BLACK PINE TRAIL
(Ec)/Feb 8, 1913; p. 574
LITTLE MOTHER WANTS A HOME, A
(Imp)/Jan 25, 1913; p. 365
LITTLE MUSIC TEACHER
(Maj)/Oct 19, 1912; p. 244
LITTLE NELL'S TOBACCO
(Imp)/Jan 7, 1911; p. 34
LITTLE NUGGET, THE
(Ne)/May 4, 1912; p. 427
LITTLE OLD MEN OF THE WOODS, THE
(Ka)/Feb 19, 1910; p. 258
LITTLE OLD NEW YORK
(Th)/Jun 24, 1911; p. 1455
(Ch)/Jul 13, 1912; p. 148
**LITTLE ORGAN PLAYER OF SAN JUAN,
THE** (Sel)/Jan 11, 1913; p. 158
LITTLE ORGANIST, THE
(Ed)/Feb 3, 1912; p. 392
LITTLE ORPHAN, THE
(Vi)/Aug 14, 1909; p. 226
(Cin)/Aug 17, 1912; p. 672
LITTLE ORPHANS, THE
(Re)/Aug 21, 1915; p. 1317
LITTLE PAL (FP)/Jul 17, 1915; p. 505
LITTLE PEACEMAKER, THE
(SA)/Jun 26, 1909; p. 872
(Ne)/Feb 22, 1913; p. 781
(Gau)/Dec 13, 1913; p. 1280
LITTLE PEOPLE IN FUR

(Po)/Aug 14, 1915; p. 1162
LITTLE PIRATE, THE
(Re)/Aug 2, 1913; p. 537
LITTLE POET, THE
(SA)/Feb 3, 1912; p. 392
LITTLE PREACHER, THE
(Me)/Jul 23, 1910; p. 192
LITTLE PROSPECTOR, THE
(SA)/Dec 3, 1910; p. 1296
(SA)/Jul 17, 1915; p. 485
LITTLE RANCHER, THE
(Bi)/Aug 3, 1912; p. 446
LITTLE RAVEN'S SWEETHEART
(Pa)/Nov 9, 1912; p. 553
LITTLE REBEL, THE
(Lu)/Jul 15, 1911; p. 39
LITTLE REBELS, THE
(WF)/Dec 5, 1914; p. 1386
LITTLE RED RIDING HOOD
(SA)/Dec 16, 1911; p. 903
LITTLE RUNAWAYS, THE
(Bio)/Jul 31, 1915; p. 816
LITTLE SALESLADY, THE
(Ed)/Oct 30, 1915; p. 791
LITTLE SCAPEGOAT, THE
(Bio)/May 29, 1915; p. 1431
LITTLE SENORITA, THE
(Pr)/Jul 4, 1914; p. 65
LITTLE SHEPHERD OF TUMBLING RUN
(Ed)/May 1, 1909; pp 553, 554
LITTLE SHEPARDESS, THE
(Sel)/Mar 18, 1911; p. 603
LITTLE SHERIFF, THE
(SA)/Aug 24, 1912; p. 770
(Vi)/Apr 25, 1914; p. 516
LITTLE SHIPPER, THE
(Po)/Aug 23, 1913; p. 846
LITTLE SHOE, THE
(Sol)/Dec 16, 1911; p. 906
LITTLE SHUT-IN, THE
(Th)/May 25, 1912; p. 730
LITTLE SINGER, THE
(Ka)/Sep 25, 1915; p. 2176
LITTLE SISTER
(Ed)/Sep 25, 1909; pp 414-15
(Rex)/Sep 26, 1914; p. 1777
LITTLE SISTER, THE
(Sel)/Feb 21, 1914; p. 946
LITTLE SLAVEY, THE
(Bio)/Aug 28, 1915; p. 1479
LITTLE SNOWDROP
(Pa)/Dec 31, 1910; p. 1538
LITTLE SOLDIER, THE
(Sol)/Feb 3, 1912; p. 395
LITTLE SOLDIER MAN, THE
(Maj)/May 8, 1915; p. 900
LITTLE SOLDIER OF '64
(Ka)/Jul 15, 1911; p. 39

LITTLE SOULS (It)/Mar 11, 1911; p. 543
LITTLE SPREEWALD MAIDEN, THE
(Ka)/Dec 31, 1910; p. 1536
LITTLE SPY, THE (Vi)/Dec 2, 1911; p. 725
LITTLE STATION AGENT, THE
(Ed)/Nov 19, 1910; p. 1176
LITTLE STOCKING, THE
(Imp)/Dec 23, 1911; p. 990
LITTLE STORIES FROM REAL LIFE (Vic)
No.1/Nov 27, 1915; p. 1665
No.2/Dec 4, 1915; p. 1854
LITTLE STOWAWAY, THE
(Sel)/Feb 17, 1912; p. 581
LITTLE STRAW WIFE, THE
(SA)/Apr 3, 1915; p. 67
LITTLE STREET SINGER, THE
(Pa)/Sep 11, 1909; p. 345
LITTLE SUBSTITUTE, THE
(SA)/Dec 6, 1913; p. 1151
LITTLE SUNBEAM (Box)/Nov 7,1914; p.790
LITTLE SUNSET (Bos)/Jul 3, 1915; pp 80-81
LITTLE TEACHER (Key)/Jul 3,1915;pp65,79
LITTLE TEACHER, THE
(Bio)/Oct 23, 1909; p. 567
LITTLE TEASE, THE
(Bio)/Apr 26, 1913; p. 380
LITTLE THIEF, THE
(Po)/Dec 16, 1911; p. 905
LITTLE TRIP ALONG THE HUDSON, A
(Pa)/Jul 26, 1913; p. 428
LITTLE TRUANT, THE
(Pa)/May 28, 1910; p. 888
LITTLE VAGRANT, THE
(Gau)/May 21, 1910; p. 833
LITTLE VIXEN, THE
(Pa)/Apr 9, 1910; p. 553
LITTLE WAIF/Nov 7, 1908;p.358
LITTLE WANDERER, THE
(Ka)/Sep 7, 1912; p. 976
LITTLE WAYFARER, THE
(It)/Jul 22, 1911; p. 126
LITTLE WESTERN ROSE, THE
(Ya)/Jun 3, 1911; p. 1261
LITTLE WHITE VIOLET, THE
(Vic)/Jul 10, 1915; p. 309
LITTLE WIDOW, THE
(Sel)/Jan 6, 1912; p. 40
(Bio)/Aug 8, 1914; p. 836
LITTLE WILLIE CHALLENGES JIM
JACKSON (Ec)/Nov 18, 1911; p. 552
LITTLE WILLIE CURES UNCLE
(Ec)/Jan 6, 1912; p. 42
LITTLE WILLIE GOES CYCLING
(Lux)/Feb 11, 1911; p. 316
LITTLE WOODEN SHOE, THE (Ed)/
Apr 13, 1912; p. 123/May 4, 1912; p. 426
LITTLEST REBEL, THE
(Py)/Sep 5, 1914; p. 1381

LIVE, LOVE AND BELIEVE
(SA)/Oct 7, 1911; p. 40
LIVE CORPSE, A (Pa)/Jan 15, 1910; p. 56
LIVE WIRE, THE (Pa)/Sep 14, 1912; p. 1074
LIVES OF THE JUNGLE
(Sel)/Jul 31, 1915; p. 816
LIVELY AFFAIR, A
(Vi)/Jul 27, 1912; p. 344
LIVING CORPSE, THE
(WF)/Oct 4, 1913; p. 50
LIVING DEATH, THE
(Maj)/Jun 19, 1915; p. 1940
LIVING DOLL, THE (Me)/Dec 18, 1909;
p. 879/Dec 25, 1909; pp 921-22
LIVING DOLLS (Pa)/Jul 31, 1909; p. 162
LIVING FEAR, THE
(Lu)/Jul 18, 1914; p. 433
LIVING FLAME, THE
(Sel)/Oct 3, 1914; p. 64
LIVING MEMORY, A (Ec)/Apr 6, 1912;p.43
LIVING PEACH, THE
(Ed)/Nov 25, 1911; p. 638
LIVING POSTERS (Pa)/Jul 25, 1908; p. 71
LIVING WAGE, THE
(Sel)/Jan 24, 1914; p. 412
(Dom)/Sep 4, 1915; p. 1644
LIVING WRECK, THE
(UE)/Feb 6, 1909; p. 144
LIVINGSTON CASE, THE
(Ed)/Feb 19, 1910; p. 258
LIZARD, THE (Pa)/Sep 6, 1913; p. 1068
LIZARDS (Ec)/Mar 22, 1913; p. 1221
LIZARDS OF THE DESERT
(Th)/Oct 24, 1914; p. 492
LIZBETH (Imp)/Aug 16, 1913; p. 745
LIZ'S CAREER (Lu)/Oct 29, 1910; p. 996
LIZZARD LORE (Pa)/Nov 29, 1913; p. 1007
LIZZIE, THE LIFE SAVER
(Ka)/Nov 21, 1914; p. 1075
LIZZIE AND THE BEAUTY CONTEST
(Ne)/Sep 4, 1915; p. 1645
LIZZIE AND THE ICE MAN
(Cry)/Mar 14, 1914; p. 1386
LIZZIE BREAKS INTO THE HAREM
(Ne)/Jul 10, 1915; p. 309
LIZZIE'S DIZZY CAREER
(Ne)/Feb 6, 1915; p. 828
LIZZIE'S ESCAPE (Lko)/Nov 21,1914;p.1077
LIZZIE'S FORTUNE (St)/Dec 19,1914;p.1681
LIZZIE'S SHATTERED DREAMS
(Lko)/Dec 11, 1915; p. 2033
LIZZIE'S WATERY GRAVE
(Lko)/Nov 27, 1915; p. 1665
LO, THE POOR INDIAN
(Ka)/Apr 9, 1910; pp 553-54
(Ed)/May 2, 1914; p. 672
LOADED (Ec)/Dec 20, 1913; p. 1413
LOADED DICE (KB)/Oct 4, 1913; p. 49

(Ka)/Jul 26, 1913; p. 428
LOST DISPATCH, THE
(KB)/Mar 8, 1913; p. 998
LOST DOG, THE (Lu)/May 11, 1912; p. 528
LOST FOR MANY YEARS
(Bi)/May 28, 1910; p. 889
LOST FREIGHT CAR, THE
(Ka)/Nov 11, 1911; p. 468
LOST HAT, THE (Sel)/Jun 8, 1912; p. 944
LOST HEIRESS, THE
(Lu)/Jun 5, 1909; p. 753
LOST HORSE, THE (Lu)/Jul 29, 1911; p.211
LOST HOUSE, THE
(Maj)/Mar 27, 1915; pp 1934-35
LOST ILLUSIONS
(Rex)/Oct 14, 1911; p. 131
LOST IN A HOTEL (Po)/Oct 7, 1911; p. 41
LOST IN A STUDIO
(St)/Aug 29, 1914; p. 1242
LOST IN CAMBODIA
(Me)/Sep 13, 1913; p. 1175
LOST IN MID OCEAN (Vi)/Apr 4,1914; p.58
LOST IN SIBERIA
(Sel)/Oct 23, 1909; p. 569
LOST IN THE ALPS
(Ed)/May 25, 1907; p. 187
LOST IN THE ARCTIC
(Sel)/Sep 30, 1911; p. 972
LOST IN THE JUNGLE (Sel)/Oct 14, 1911;
p. 109/Nov 11, 1911; p. 468
LOST IN THE JUNGLE, and A CLOSE
SHAVE (SA)/Jun 26, 1915; p. 2095
LOST IN THE NIGHT
(Cry)/Sep 6, 1913; p. 1069
LOST IN THE SOUDAN
(Sel)/Aug 27, 1910; p. 463
LOST INVITATION, THE
(Ed)/Jun 26, 1909; p. 870
LOST KERCHIEF, THE
(Ya)/Oct 28, 1911; p. 293
LOST KITTEN, THE (Ed)/Mar 9,1912; p.866
LOST LEDGE, THE
(Bi)/Mar 6, 1915; pp 1449-50
LOST LETTER, THE
(Bi)/Sep 23, 1911; p. 892
LOST LORD LOVELL, THE
(Maj)/Mar 6, 1915; p. 1449
LOST MAIL SACK, THE
(Ka)/Oct 24, 1914; p. 492
LOST MELODY, THE
(Ed)/Nov 14, 1914; p. 931
LOST MEMORY
(GN)/Feb 22, 1913; pp 781, 786
LOST MESSENGER, THE
(Maj)/Jul 20, 1912; p. 245
(Sel)/Nov 13, 1915; p. 1311
LOST MILLIONAIRE, THE (Vi)/Aug 16,
1913; p. 722/Sep 27, 1913; p. 1393

LOST MINE, THE (Ka)/Nov 16, 1907; p. 599
LOST NECKLACE, THE
(Pa)/Dec 9, 1911; p. 817
LOST NOTE, THE (Lu)/Feb 15, 1913; p. 680
LOST PARADISE, THE
(FP)/Sep 12, 1914; p. 1495
LOST POCKETBOOK
(KO)/May 16, 1908; p. 444
LOST RECEIPT, THE
(Re)/Jan 23, 1915; pp 517-18
LOST RIBBON, THE
(Ka)/Mar 4, 1911; p. 482
LOST RING, THE (Gau)/May 25,1912; p.731
LOST SECRET, THE (Bal)/Oct 2, 1915; p.80
LOST SERMON, THE
(Am)/May 30, 1914; p. 1262
LOST SHEEP, THE
(Vi)/May 1, 1909; p. 556
LOST STUD, THE (GN)/Nov 16, 1912; p.660
LOST SWITCH, THE
(Lu)/Dec 6, 1913; p. 1151
LOST TIE, THE (Gau)/Jul 24, 1909; p. 124
LOST TRAIL, THE (Vi)/May 14, 1910; p.784
LOST TREASURE, THE
(Am)/Feb 14, 1914; p. 810
LOST YEARS (Gau)/Apr 29, 1911; p. 960
(SA)/Oct 7, 1911; p. 40
LOTTA COIN'S GHOST
(Ka)/May 8, 1915; p. 899
LOTTERY OF LOVE, THE
(Cin)/May 18, 1912; p. 619
LOTTERY PRIZE, THE
(GN)/Nov 2, 1912; p. 451
LOTTERY TICKET (Pa)/Apr 11, 1908; p.326
LOTTERY TICKET, No. 13
(Ne)/May 4, 1912; p. 428
LOTUS DANCER, THE
(Tru)/Dec 20, 1913; p. 1392
LOUDER, PLEASE (SA)/Feb 8, 1908; p. 102
LOUIE, THE LIFE SAVER
(Th)/Oct 18, 1913; p. 265
LOUISA'S BATTLE WITH CUPID
(Lun)/May 8, 1915; p. 901
LOUISE STROZZI (It)/Mar 5, 1910; p. 339
LOVE (CGP)/Mar 8, 1913; p. 995
LOVE, FIREWORKS AND THE JANITOR
(Jo)/Apr 3, 1915; p. 66
LOVE, LOOT AND LIQUOR
(Bio)/Sep 19, 1914; p. 1645
LOVE, LUCK AND A PAINT BRUSH
(Ne)/Nov 1, 1913; p. 497
LOVE, LUCK AND CANDY
(St)/Dec 12, 1914; p. 1524
LOVE, LUCK AND GASOLINE (Vi)/Dec 10,
1910; p. 1356/Apr 25, 1914; p. 496
LOVE, MUMPS, AND BUMPS
(Be)/Oct 9, 1915; p. 253
LOVE, OIL AND GREASE

(Ka)/Jan 16, 1915; p. 368
LOVE, PEPPER AND SWEETS
(Vim)/Dec 11, 1915; p. 2031
LOVE, SNOW AND ICE
(Vi)/Jun 12, 1915; p. 1787
LOVE, SPEED AND THRILLS (Key)/Jan 30,
1915; p. 683/Feb 13, 1915; p. 985
LOVE, THE CONQUEROR
(UE)/Oct 16, 1909; p. 529
LOVE, THE WINNER
(Sel)/May 10, 1913; p. 595
LOVE, WAR AND A BONNET
(Imp)/Jul 6, 1912; p. 44
LOVE, WHISKERS AND LETTERS
(Sol)/Dec 30, 1911; p.1073
LOVE AFFAIR, A
(Pa)/Oct 17, 1908; pp 304-5
LOVE AFFAIR IN TOYLAND, A (KO)/
Nov 21, 1908; p. 408/Dec 19, 1908; p. 500
LOVE AFFAIR OF THE OLDEN DAYS, A
(KO)/Jul 4, 1908; p. 12
LOVE AMONG THE ROSES
(Bio)/May 21, 1910; p. 833
LOVE AND A LEMON
(Ne)/Oct 19, 1912; p. 244
LOVE AND A LOTTERY TICKET
(Imp)/May 23, 1914; p. 1117
LOVE AND A SAVAGE
(Ne)/Dec 18, 1915; p. 2204
LOVE AND BASEBALL (Uni)/Sep 26, 1914;
p. 1759/Oct 24, 1914; p. 493
LOVE AND BITTERS
(Nov)/Nov 13, 1915; p. 1312
LOVE AND BULLETS
(Key)/Jul 25, 1914; p. 572
LOVE AND BUSINESS
(Ko)/Jan 16, 1915; p. 369
LOVE AND CHINESE
(Pa)/Jul 22, 1911; p. 125
LOVE AND CIRCUMSTANCES
(Amm)/Jan 25, 1913; p. 365
LOVE AND COURAGE
(Key)/Jul 26, 1913; p. 429
LOVE AND DOUGH (St)/Feb 6, 1915; p. 828
LOVE AND DYNAMITE
(Key)/Jan 10, 1914; p. 174
LOVE AND ELECTRICITY
(Jo)/Jun 27, 1914; p. 1830
LOVE AND FLAMES
(Lu)/Aug 22, 1914; p. 1099
LOVE AND FORTUNE
(KO)/Jul 4, 1908; p. 12
LOVE AND GASOLINE
(Key)/Feb 28, 1914; p. 1089
LOVE AND GOLD (Ram)/Apr 26,1913; p.381
LOVE AND GRAFT (Jo)/Sep 19,1914; p.1646
LOVE AND HANDCUFFS
(Po)/Apr 24, 1915; p. 558

LOVE AND HASH (Bio)/Sep 19,1914; p.1644
LOVE AND HATRED
(KO)/Jul 11, 1908; p. 38
(Ed)/Nov 18, 1911; p. 550
LOVE AND HYPNOTISM
(Cin)/Apr 20, 1912; p. 230
LOVE AND INSTALLMENTS
(Fa)/Sep 25, 1915; p. 2178
LOVE AND JEALOUSY
(Bi)/Feb 10, 1912; p. 484
LOVE AND LA VALLIERES
(SA)/Feb 22, 1913; p. 780
LOVE AND LABOR (Be)/Sep 4, 1915; p.1644
LOVE AND LAW
(Th)/Dec 24, 1910; p. 1481
(Jo)/Feb 20, 1915; p. 1140
(Vi)/Dec 4, 1915; p. 1852
LOVE AND LEMONS
(Am)/Feb 10, 1912; p. 482
LOVE AND LIMBO
(MnA)/Mar 20, 1915; p. 1763
LOVE AND LIMBURGER
(Jo)/Nov 15, 1913; p. 737
LOVE AND LUNCH (St)/Jul 25, 1914; p. 573
LOVE AND MARRIAGE IN POSTER
LAND (Ed)/May 21, 1910; p. 832
LOVE AND MONEY
(Bi)/May 21, 1910; p. 834
(Th)/May 22, 1915; p. 1260
LOVE AND PAIN (Key)/Mar 22,1913;p.1222
LOVE AND POLITICS
(Jo)/Feb 7, 1914; pp 677, 678
LOVE AND RUBBISH
(Key)/Jul 19, 1913; p. 321
LOVE AND SACRIFICE
(Cin)/Oct 23, 1909; p. 568
LOVE AND SALT WATER
(Key)/Jul 25, 1914; p. 572
LOVE AND SCIENCE
(Ec)/Oct 12, 1912; p. 144
LOVE AND SILENCE
(Pa)/Aug 26, 1911; p. 541
LOVE AND SKATES (WF)/Jan 16,1915;p.370
LOVE AND SODA (SA)/Sep 12, 1914; p.1512
LOVE AND SOUR NOTES
(Lko)/May 22, 1915; p. 1261
LOVE AND SPIRITS (Jo)/Jan 2, 1915; p. 76
LOVE AND SURGERY
(Lko)/Oct 24, 1914; p. 493
LOVE AND SWORDS
(Lu)/Oct 23, 1915; p. 619
LOVE AND THE LAW
(Ed)/Sep 3, 1910; p. 519
(SA)/Oct 25, 1913; p. 379
LOVE AND THE LEOPARD
(Sel)/Mar 6, 1915; p. 1447
LOVE AND THE STOCK MARKET
(Ed)/Mar 18, 1911; p. 602

LOVE AND THE TELEPHONE
(Maj)/Jan 11, 1913; p. 160
LOVE AND THE WORKMAN
(Vic)/Mar 15, 1913; p. 1105
LOVE AND TEARS (Lu)/Mar 16,1912; p.961
LOVE AND TITLE (Lu)/Nov 14, 1914; p.931
LOVE AND TREACHERY
(Lu)/Dec 7, 1912; p. 975
LOVE AND TROUBLE (SA)/Apr 3,1915;p.63
LOVE AND VENGEANCE
(Uni)/Apr 18, 1914; p. 341
LOVE AND WAR (Ed)/Oct 9, 1909; p. 490
(Maj)/Nov 2, 1912; p. 451
(Bi)/Jun 14, 1913; p. 1137
LOVE AND WAR IN MEXICO
(Lu)/Jun 14, 1913; p. 1135
LOVE AND WATER (St)/Jan 2, 1915; p. 76
LOVE AT FIRST SIGHT
(SA)/Dec 3, 1910; p. 1296
LOVE AT GLOUCESTER PORT
(Vi)/Dec 30, 1911; p. 1072
LOVE BEFORE TEN
(Sel)/Mar 29, 1913; p. 1336
LOVE CHASE, THE (Ec)/Feb 8, 1913;
p. 583/Feb 15, 1913; p. 680
LOVE CLAIRVOYANT
(Vi)/Aug 1, 1914; p. 705
LOVE DECIDES (Lu)/Dec 30, 1911; p. 1071
LOVE DISGUISED (Jo)/Oct 3, 1914; p. 65
LOVE DROPS (Ed)/Mar 26, 1910; p. 466
LOVE EVERLASTING
(Glo)/Jan 17, 1914; p. 277
LOVE FINDS A WAY
(Bio)/Jan 16, 1909; p. 68
(Ec)/Feb 3, 1912; p. 394
(Roy)/Nov 28, 1914; p. 1233
(Sel)/Jun 5, 1915; p. 1604
LOVE FINDS THE WAY
(Vi)/Feb 10, 1912; p. 481
LOVE FOR AN ENEMY
(Ka)/Jan 21, 1911; p. 144
LOVE GERMS (Lu)/Feb 6, 1909; p. 145
LOVE HATH WROUGHT A MIRACLE
(Vi)/Jan 18, 1913; p. 263
LOVE HEEDS NOT SHOWERS
(Maj)/Dec 9, 1911; p. 819
LOVE IN A TEPEE
(Imp)/Sep 2, 1911; p. 630
LOVE IN AN APARTMENT HOTEL (Bio)/
Mar 15, 1913; p. 1103/May 22, 1915;
p. 1273/Jul 3, 1915; p. 64
LOVE IN ARMOR (Key)/Apr 3, 1915; p. 64
LOVE IN MADRID (Pa)/Apr 8, 1911; p. 782
LOVE IN MEXICO (Bi)/Aug 6, 1910; p. 298
LOVE IN THE GHETTO
(Vi)/May 25, 1912; p. 729
(Sel)/May 10, 1913; p. 596
LOVE IN THE HILLS

(SA)/Aug 19, 1911; p. 464
(Bio)/Nov 11, 1911; p. 471
LOVE INCOGNITO (SA)/Oct 11,1913; p.155
LOVE IS BEST (Imp)/Jul 8, 1911; p. 1588
LOVE IS BLIND
(Ed)/Mar 20, 1909; p. 338
(Re)/Apr 13, 1912; pp 137-38
(Am)/Feb 22,1913; p.784/Mar 1,1913; p.889
LOVE IS INGENIOUS
Dec 19, 1908; p. 501
LOVE KNOWS NO LAW
(Be)/Jan 9, 1915; p. 221
LOVE KNOWS NO LAWS
(Re)/Sep 21, 1912; p. 1177
LOVE LAUGHS AT LOCKSMITHS
(Vi)/Aug 1, 1908; pp 91-92
(Pa)/Nov 26, 1910; p. 1238
(Vi)/Apr 12, 1913; p. 163
LOVE LETTER, THE
(Pa)/Aug 16, 1913; p. 744
LOVE LUTE OF ROMANY, THE
(SA)/Nov 8, 1913; p. 612
LOVE ME, LOVE MY ANIMALS
(Gau)/Sep 13, 1913; p. 1177
LOVE ME, LOVE MY DOG
(Lu)/Mar 6, 1909; p. 271
(Re)/Jul 27, 1912; p. 344
(Ap)/Oct 11, 1913; p. 157
LOVE MICROBE (Bio)/Oct 19, 1907; p. 526
LOVE MOULDS LABOR
(Pa)/Nov 18, 1911; p. 549
LOVE OF A GYPSY GIRL, THE
(GN)/Jun 10, 1911; p. 1317
LOVE OF A SAVAGE, THE
(NYM)/Dec 31, 1909; p. 961
LOVE OF AN ISLAND MAID
(Sel)/May 25, 1912; p. 729
LOVE OF BEAUTY, THE
(Lu)/Oct 4, 1913; p. 47
LOVE OF CHRYSANTHEMUM
(Vi)/Jun 11, 1910; p. 995
LOVE OF CONCHITA, THE
(Maj)/Oct 11, 1913; p. 157
LOVE OF JOHN RUSKIN, THE (Vi)/
Feb 10, 1912; p. 472/Mar 2, 1912; p. 780
LOVE OF LADY IRMA, THE
(Bio)/Apr 2, 1910; p. 508
LOVE OF LITTLE FLORA, THE
(It)/Dec 11, 1909; p. 842
LOVE OF LONG AGO, A
(Th)/Apr 20, 1912; p. 231
LOVE OF MARY WEST, THE
(U)/Apr 3, 1915; p. 66
LOVE OF LOTI SAN, THE
(Sel)/Dec 11, 1915; p. 2032
LOVE OF MEN, THE
(Bi)/Sep 13, 1913; p. 1178
LOVE OF ORO SAN, THE

(Lu)/Sep 5, 1914; p. 1371

LOVE OF PIERRE LAROSSE, THE
(Vi)/Oct 17, 1914; p. 1914; p. 335

LOVE OF PRINCESS YOLANDE, THE
(WF)/Dec 5, 1914; p. 1385

LOVE OF '64, A (Lu)/Jan 3, 1914; p. 48

LOVE OF SUMMER MORN
(Ka)/Jun 24, 1911; p. 1452

LOVE OF THE WEST, THE
(Am)/Oct 14, 1911; pp 130-31

LOVE OF TOKIWA, THE
(Vi)/Feb 14, 1914; p. 809

LOVE OF WOMEN, THE
(Lu)/Mar 20, 1915; p. 1764

LOVE ON AN EMPTY STOMACH
(Lko)/Aug 21, 1915; p. 1318

LOVE ON TOUGH LUCK RANCH
(SA)/Oct 19, 1912; p. 243

LOVE OR A THRONE
(Imp)/Jan 10, 1914; p. 174

LOVE PIRATE, THE
(Re)/Feb 13, 1915; pp 985, 992

LOVE POTION, THE (Po)/Jul 22, 1911; p. 125

LOVE PROVES STRONGER THAN DUTY
(Pa)/Jun 10, 1911; p.1316

**LOVE ROMANCE OF SIR FRANCIS
DRAKE, THE** (Kio)/Aug 9, 1913; p. 638

LOVE ROMANCE OF THE GIRL SPY
(Ka)/May 14, 1910; p. 784

LOVE ROUTE, VIA PITTMAN, THE
(SA)/Apr 11, 1914; p. 212

LOVE-SICK BARBER (Pa)/May 1,1909;p.553

LOVE SICK MAIDENS OF CUDDLETOWN
(Vi)/Aug 31, 1912; p. 881

LOVE SICKNESS AT SEA
(Key)/Nov 15, 1913; p. 737

**LOVE STORY OF A GREAT ACTRESS,
THE** (Gau)/Jun 24, 1911; p. 1452

LOVE STORY OF OLD JAPAN, A
(CGP)/Aug 31, 1912; pp 864, 881

LOVE SUBLIME (Mil)/Dec 28, 1912; p.1294

LOVE TEST, THE
(Imp)/Sep 14, 1912; p. 1076
(SA)/Oct 5, 1912; p. 40
(Lu)/Jul 12, 1913; p. 205

LOVE THAT LASTS, THE
(Po)/Apr 17, 1915; p. 394

LOVE THAT NEVER FADES, THE
(Com)/Dec 28, 1912; p. 1293

LOVE THAT NEVER FAILS
(Ch)/Jan 20, 1912; p. 203

LOVE THAT TURNED, THE
(Pa)/Mar 29, 1913; p. 1335

LOVE THEFT, THE (SA)/Sep 6,1913; p.1068

LOVE THIEF, THE (Key)/Oct 31,1914;p.642

LOVE THROUGH A LENS
(SA)/Jan 18, 1913; p. 264

LOVE THY NEIGHBOR

(WF)/Jan 16, 1915; p. 370

LOVE TOKEN, THE
(Pa)/Jan 8, 1910; pp 17-18
(Lu)/Jan 18, 1913; p. 264

LOVE TRAGEDY IN SPAIN, A
(Me)/Oct 30, 1908; p. 345

LOVE TRAIL, THE
(Ne)/Apr 27, 1912; p. 330
(Ne)/Oct 11, 1913; p. 157

LOVE TRANSCENDENT, THE
(Bio)/Apr 10, 1915; p. 235

LOVE TRIUMPHS (Ka)/May 15, 1909; p.637
(Lu)/Nov 21,1914; p.1075

LOVE TYRANT, THE
(Po)/Jul 22, 1911; p. 127

LOVE UNCONQUERED
(CGP)/Jan 18, 1913; p. 265

LOVE UNDER DIFFICULTIES
(Pa)/Jan 21, 1911; p. 144

LOVE UNDER SPANISH SKIES
(Sel)/May 1, 1909; p. 556

LOVE VERSUS CHICKENS
(Ka)/Mar 6, 1915; p. 1447

LOVE vs DUTY (KB)/Apr 25, 1914; p. 518

LOVE vs LAW (Imp)/Dec 6, 1913; p. 1153

LOVE vs PRIDE (Sel)/Aug 15, 1914; p. 959

LOVE vs STRATEGY
(Lu)/Feb 17, 1912; p. 582

LOVE WHIP, THE (Vi)/May 1, 1915; p. 727

LOVE WILL FIND A WAY
(Ed)/Jun 27, 1908; p. 546
(Po)/Sep 14, 1912; p. 1075
(Com)/Oct 12, 1912; p. 144

LOVE WILL OUT (Vi)/Jan 16, 1915; p. 368

LOVE WINS (Cen)/Jun 26, 1909; p. 870

LOVE YE ONE ANOTHER
(Pa)/Jul 16, 1910; p. 143

LOVED BY A MAORI CHIEFTESS
(Me)/Mar 8, 1913; p. 1001

LOVER AND THE COUNT
(Ed)/Feb 11, 1911; p. 315

LOVERS' CHARM, THE
(WBE)/Oct 26, 1907; p. 542

LOVER'S EMBARRASSMENT, THE
(Ec)/Apr 2, 1910; pp 509-10

LOVER'S GIFT, THE
(Maj)/May 30, 1914; p. 1262

LOVER'S GUIDE, THE (Ed)/Oct 10, 1908;
p. 285/Oct 24, 1908; p. 318

LOVER'S ILL LUCK (Pa)/Jan 11, 1908;
pp 28-29/Jun 27, 1908; p. 547

LOVER'S LOST CONTROL, A
(Key)/Aug 14, 1915; p. 1161

LOVERS' LUCK (Key)/Oct 3, 1914; p. 64

LOVER'S LUCKY PREDICAMENT, THE
(Jo)/Jun 5, 1915; p. 1607

LOVERS' MILL, THE
(Gau)/Oct 22, 1910; p. 936

LOVERS' POST-OFFICE
(Key)/Nov 14, 1914; p. 932
LOVER'S RUSE, A
(Vi)/Jun 6, 1914; p. 500
LOVERS' RUSE, THE
(Sol)/Oct 28, 1911; p. 292
LOVER'S SIGNAL, THE
(Imp)/Apr 22, 1911; p. 900
(Lu)/May 4, 1912; p. 425
LOVER'S STRATAGEMS, A
(Vi)/Dec 5, 1908; p. 448
LOVER'S TELEGRAPHIC CODE, THE
(Ed)/Nov 14, 1908; pp 378, 384
LOVERS THREE (Cry)/Mar 29, 1913; p.1337
LOVERS TRIBULATIONS, THE
(KO)/May 9, 1908; p. 423
LOVERS' WELL, THE
(Pa)/Sep 10, 1910; p. 574
LOVES, ADVENTURES AND LIFE OF WILLIAM SHAKESPEARE, THE
(Saw)/Oct 24, 1914; p. 498
LOVE'S ACID TEST
(Sel)/Dec 19, 1914; p. 1679
LOVE'S AWAKENING
(Vi)/Apr 30, 1910; p. 690
(SA)/Dec 17, 1910; p. 1418
LOVE'S C.Q.D. (Me)/Jun 25, 1910; p. 1100
LOVE'S DECEPTION
(Pa)/Nov 15, 1913; p. 735
LOVE'S DIARY (Imp)/Aug 3, 1912; p. 446
LOVE'S EBB AND FLOOD
(Ya)/Apr 8, 1911; p. 783
LOVE'S LABOR LOST
(Lu)/Dec 23, 1911; p. 989
LOVE'S LONG LANE
(Lu)/Jun 6, 1914; p. 1409
LOVE'S LUNACY (StU)/Apr 3, 1915; p. 65
LOVE'S MAGNET (SA)/Oct 10, 1914; p. 187
LOVE'S MELODY (Bio)/Jul 17, 1915; p. 485
LOVE'S MESSENGER
(Bio)/Sep 28, 1912; p. 1276
LOVE'S MIRACLE (Th)/May 18, 1912; p. 630
LOVE'S MONOGRAM
(Ryn)/May 31, 1913; p. 921
LOVE'S OBLIVION
(Me)/Mar 28, 1914; p. 1680
LOVES OF DAVID COPPERFIELD, THE
(Th)/Nov 11, 1911; p. 471
LOVE'S OLD DREAM (Vi)/Feb 7,1914;p.676
LOVE'S OLD SWEET MELODY
(Lu)/Jan 30, 1909; p. 121
LOVE'S OLD SWEET SONG
(Lu)/Oct 8, 1910; p. 813
(Ed)/Jul 5, 1913; p. 48
(Asc)/Oct 30a, 1915; p. 986
LOVE'S PROBATION
(Asc)/Oct 9, 1915; p. 286
LOVE'S QUARANTINE

(Vi)/Jul 19, 1913; p. 320
LOVE'S RENUNCIATION
(Pa)/Nov 25, 1911; p. 637
LOVE'S RESCUE (Bio)/Aug 21, 1915; p.1316
LOVE'S SACRIFICE
(Ed)/Aug 7, 1909; p. 195
(KB)/May 9, 1914; p. 822
LOVE'S SAVAGE HATE
(Lu)/Jan 23, 1915; p. 515
LOVE'S SERENADE
(Gau)/Sep 21, 1912; p. 1176
LOVE'S STRATEGY
(Ufs)/Jun 5, 1915; p. 1626
(Mut)/Oct 9, 1915; p. 253
LOVE'S SUNSET (Vi)/Dec 6, 1913;
p. 1127/Dec 27, 1913; p. 1544
LOVE'S TEST (Sol)/Mar 11, 1911; p. 542
LOVE'S TRIALS (Po)/Jan 28, 1911; p. 197
LOVE'S VICTIM (KO)/Apr 18, 1908; p. 354
LOVE'S VICTORY (Lu)/Nov 11, 1911; p.470
(Vic)/Feb 21, 1914; p.948
LOVE'S WAY (Vi)/Jul 24, 1915; p. 649
LOVE'S WESTERN FLIGHT
(Ne)/Jun 6, 1914; p. 1409
LOVE'S YOUNG DREAM
(Ed)/Mar 14, 1914; p. 1384
LOVING HEARTS (Lu)/Feb 26, 1910; p. 298
LOW CAST BURMESE
(Vi)/Nov 8, 1913; p. 611
LOW FINANCIER, A
(Sel)/Sep 12, 1914; p. 1511
LOWER LAKE GENEVA, SWITZERLAND
(Kin)/Feb 22, 1913; p. 782
LOYAL LOVE (Pa)/Jun 17, 1911; p. 1387
LOYALTY OF DON LUIS VERDUGO, THE
(Ka)/May 27, 1911; p. 1200
LOYALTY OF JUMBO, THE
(Sel)/Oct 17, 1914; p. 335
LUCIA'S BROKEN ROMANCE
(Pa)/May 27, 1911; p. 1201
LUCILE (Th)/Aug 24, 1912; pp 755-56
LUCILLE LOVE, THE GIRL OF MYSTERY (GS)
No.1/Apr 18, 1914; p. 362
No.2/Apr 18, 1914; p. 362
No.3/May 2, 1914; p. 674
No.4/May 16, 1914; p. 970
No.5/May 23, 1914; p. 1117
No.6/May 23, 1914; p. 1118
No.7/May 30, 1914; p. 1262
No.8/Jun 6, 1914; p. 1410
No.9/Jun 13, 1914; p. 1542
No.10/Jun 20, 1914; p. 1690
No.11/Jun 27, 1914; p. 1830
No.12/Jul 4, 1914; p. 66
No.13/Jul 11, 1914; p. 257
No.14/Jul 18, 1914; p. 434
No.15/Jul 25, 1914; p. 573

LUCK IN ODD NUMBERS
(SA)/Apr 4, 1914; p. 57

LUCK OF HOG WALLOW GULCH, THE
(Jo)/Apr 4, 1914; p. 59

LUCK OF RECKLESS REDDY, THE
(Ka)/Nov 25, 1911; p. 636

LUCK OF ROARING CAMP, THE
(Ed)/Feb 5, 1910; p. 168

LUCKLESS BANKER, THE
(UE)/Dec 16, 1911; pp 904-5

LUCKY ACCIDENT (Pa)/May 30, 1908; p. 480

LUCKY BANANA SELLER, THE
(GN)/May 20, 1911; p. 1142

LUCKY BLOW-OUT, A
(Bro)/Jan 23, 1915; p. 517

LUCKY BOB (Bi)/Oct 7, 1911; p. 42

LUCKY CARD, THE
(SA)/Jun 10, 1911; p. 1316

LUCKY CHANCE, A
(Lu)/Mar 22, 1913; p. 1220

LUCKY CHANGE, A
(Ec)/Oct 28, 1911; p. 293

LUCKY CHARM, THE
(Pa)/Jan 7, 1911; p. 32

LUCKY COHEN (Lu)/May 24, 1913; p. 812

LUCKY DEAL, A (Sel)/Sep 4, 1915; p. 1643

LUCKY DECEPTION, A
(Ne)/May 30, 1914; p. 1262

LUCKY DISAPPOINTMENT, A
(Re)/Jan 2, 1915; p. 77

LUCKY DOG (Ed)/Feb 17, 1912; p. 581

LUCKY ELOPEMENT, THE
(Vi)/Feb 14, 1914; p. 808

LUCKY FALL, A (Lu)/Dec 21, 1912; p. 1185

LUCKY HORSESHOE, THE
(Bio)/Sep 30, 1911; p. 970

LUCKY HUSBAND, A
(Pa)/Oct 23, 1909; p. 569

LUCKY JIM (Bio)/May 1, 1909; pp 553, 554
(Ch)/May 18, 1912; p. 630

LUCKY LEAP, A (Key)/Mar 6, 1915; p. 1448

LUCKY LOSER, A (Ed)/Apr 17, 1915; p.392

LUCKY LOSER, THE
(Ec)/Oct 12, 1912; p. 144

LUCKY MAN (Lux)/Oct 9, 1909; p. 490
(Maj)/Feb 10, 1912; p. 483

LUCKY MISTAKE, A
(Sel)/Apr 19, 1913; p. 279

LUCKY MIX-UP, A
(SA)/Apr 20, 1912; p. 229

LUCKY NUGGET, THE
(Amm)/Jan 10, 1914; p. 174

LUCKY NUMBER, THE
(Pa)/Dec 31, 1909; p. 960

LUCKY RUBE, THE
(Lu)/Sep 12, 1914; p. 1511

LUCKY SHOT, THE
(Th)/Jul 30, 1910; p. 245

(Re)/Dec 12, 1914; p. 1525

LUCKY STRIKE, A (Lu)/Jun 5, 1915; p.1604

LUCKY TOOTHACHE, A
(Bio)/Oct 29, 1910; p. 996

LUCKY TRANSFER, THE
(Re)/Mar 20, 1915; p. 1765

LUCKY VEST, THE
(Ed)/May 23, 1914; p. 1116

LUCY AT BOARDING SCHOOL
(Pa)/Sep 24, 1910; p. 688

LUCY CONSULTS THE ORACLE
(Pa)/Jun 18, 1910; p. 1049

LUCY'S ELOPEMENT (Th)/Jan 9,1915;p.222

LUDWIG FROM GERMANY
(Ed)/Nov 25, 1911; p. 636

LUELLA'S LOVE STORY
(Vi)/Nov 1, 1913; p. 496

LULU'S ANARCHIST
(Vi)/Mar 16, 1912; p. 962

LULU'S DOCTOR (Vi)/Jun 22, 1912; p. 1126

LULU'S LOST LOTHARIOS
(Fal)/Nov 6, 1915; p. 1140

LUMBERING IN SWEDEN
(Vi)/Mar 7, 1914; p. 1236

LUNATIC AT LARGE, A
(Vi)/Oct 1, 1910; p. 747

LUNATICS, THE (LP)/Jun 20, 1914; p. 1703

LUNATIC'S CHILD, THE
(Pa)/Feb 14, 1914; p. 809

LUNATICS IN POWER
(Ed)/May 15, 1909; pp 635-36

LUNCH TIME (Lu)/Nov 7, 1908; p. 366

LUPIN, THE GENTLEMAN BURGLAR
(Pas)/Aug 8, 1914; p. 839

LURE OF A WIDOW, THE
(Vi)/Oct 30, 1915; p. 791

LURE OF GOLD, THE
(Bi)/Oct 29, 1910; p. 999

LURE OF MAMMON, THE
(Ka)/Jun 5, 1915; p. 1604

LURE OF MILLIONS, THE
(ISP)/May 9, 1914; p. 799

LURE OF THE CAR WHEELS, THE
(Lu)/Aug 15, 1914; p. 960

LURE OF THE CITY, THE
(Am)/Dec 3, 1910; p. 1298
(Ed)/Dec 9, 1911; p. 817

LURE OF THE FOOTLIGHTS, THE
(Pa)/Jun 22, 1912; p. 1127

LURE OF THE GEISHA, THE
(Bi)/Aug 29, 1914; p. 1242

LURE OF THE GREEN TABLE, THE
(Lu)/Jan 9, 1915; p. 220

LURE OF THE LADIES, THE
(Sel)/Aug 8, 1914; p. 836

LURE OF THE LORELEI, THE
(Gau)/Mar 22, 1913; p. 1222

LURE OF THE MASK, THE

(Am)/May 22, 1915; p. 1261
LURE OF THE PIT, THE
(Lu)/Jun 27, 1914; p. 1829
LURE OF THE ROAD, THE
(Sel)/Jan 3, 1914; p. 49
LURE OF THE SAWDUST, THE
(Am)/Jul 11, 1914; p. 231
LURE OF THE STAGE
(Cry)/Dec 27, 1913; p. 1544
LURE OF THE WEST, THE
(Ec)/Feb 6, 1915; p. 829
LURE OF THE WINDIGO, THE
(Sel)/Dec 26, 1914; p. 1841
LURE OF THE YUKON, THE (PP)/Oct 10,
1914; p. 195/Oct 17, 1914; p. 338
LURE OF VANITY (Vi)/Aug 5, 1911; p. 293
LURED BY A PHANTOM
(Gau)/Dec 17, 1910; p. 1416
LURED FROM SQUASH CENTER
(Po)/Apr 25, 1914; p. 517
LURING LIGHTS, THE
(Ka)/Dec 11, 1915; p. 2031
LUST OF REDMEN, THE
(Alb)/Jun 20, 1914; p. 1691
LUTIE'S LOVERS (Jo)/Apr 25, 1914; p. 518
LUXOR, EGYPT (Ka)/Jun 15, 1912; p. 1027
LUXURIOUS LOU (Bio)/Jul 17, 1915; p. 485
LYDIA PUNKHAM'S LOVE STORY
(CGP)/Dec 14, 1912; p. 1080
LYNBROOK TRAGEDY, THE
(Ka)/Nov 7, 1914; p. 788
LYONS, THE SECOND CITY OF FRANCE
(UE)/Aug 26, 1911; p. 541

MA AND PA PLAY POKER
(Jo)/Feb 28, 1914; p. 1089
MA AND THE BOYS
(Cry)/Mar 15, 1913; p. 1105
MA-IN-LAW MESMERIZED
(KO)/Apr 11, 1908; p. 328
MABEL AT THE WHEEL
(Key)/Apr 25, 1914; p. 518
MABEL LOST AND WON
(Key)/Jun 19, 1915; p. 1940
MABEL'S ADVENTURES
(Key)/Dec 21, 1912; p. 1186
MABEL'S AWFUL MISTAKE
(Key)/May 3, 1913; p. 489
MABEL'S BEAR ESCAPE
(Key)/Feb 7, 1914; p. 678
MABEL'S BEAU (Maj)/Sep 14, 1912; p. 1075
MABEL'S BEAU IN TROUBLE
Jan 16, 1909; p. 69
MABEL'S BLUNDER
(Key)/Sep 19, 1914; p. 1645
MABEL'S BUSY DAY
(Key)/Jun 27, 1914; p. 1829
MABEL'S DRAMATIC CAREER

(Key)/Sep 27, 1913; p. 1393
MABEL'S HEROES (Key)/Feb 15,1913;p.681
MABEL'S LATEST PRANK
(Key)/Sep 19, 1914; p. 1645
MABEL'S LOVERS (Key)/Nov 16,1912;p.660
MABEL'S MARRIED LIFE
(Key)/Jul 4, 1914; p. 65
MABEL'S NERVE (Key)/May 23,1914;p.1117
MABEL'S NEW HERO
(Key)/Sep 6, 1913; p. 1069
MABEL'S NEW JOB
(Key)/Aug 15, 1914; p. 961
MABEL'S STORMY LOVE AFFAIR
(Key)/Jan 17, 1914; p. 290
MABEL'S STRATAGEM
(Key)/Jan 4, 1913; p. 52
MACHISTE MAGNIFICENT
(It)/Aug 28, 1915; p. 1494
MACK AT IT AGAIN
(Key)/Apr 18, 1914; p. 361
MAD DOG (Lu)/Apr 3, 1909; p. 404
(Lux)/Jan 27, 1912; p. 305
MAD DOG SCARE, A
(Sel)/Aug 6, 1910; p. 297
MAD HERMIT, THE
(Th)/Aug 20, 1910; p. 408
MAD LADY OF CHESTER, THE
(Cin)/Oct 29, 1910; p. 998
MAD LOVE, A (Pa)/May 2, 1914; p. 673
MAD LOVERS, THE
(WF)/Oct 31, 1914; p. 642
MAD MAID OF THE DESERT, THE
(Bi)/Jul 24, 1915; p. 651
MAD MARATHON, A
(Sel)/Mar 7, 1914; p. 1236
MAD MOUNTAINEER, THE
(Ka)/Oct 31, 1914; p. 641
MAD MUSICIAN, THE
(Sel)/Mar 7, 1908; p. 195
MAD SCULPTOR, THE
(Pa)/Aug 9, 1913; p. 637
MADAM, WHO IS THAT LETTER FROM?
(Sel)/Aug 26, 1911; p. 542
MADAM COQUETTE
(Lu)/May 30, 1914; p. 1261
**MADAM FLIRT AND HER ADOPTED
UNCLE** (Lu)/Nov 21, 1908; p. 408
MADAM IS CAPRICIOUS
(KO)/May 16, 1908; p. 445
MADAM REX (Bio)/Apr 29, 1911; p. 958
MADAME BLANCHE, BEAUTY DOCTOR
(Fal)/Jul 17, 1915; p. 486
MADAME BUTTERFLY
(FP)/Nov 13, 1915; p. 1323
MADAME DOUBLE X
(SA)/Dec 26, 1914; p. 1841
MADAME ROLAND (Cin)/Mar 16, 1912;
p. 951/Apr 27, 1912; p. 329

MADAME SANS GENE (GN)/Apr 2, 1910;
  p. 517/Apr 16, 1910; p. 599
MADAME SATAN
  (FRA)/Dec 27, 1913; p. 1545
MADAME TALLIEN (Pa)/Sep 30,1911; p.971
MADAM'S FANCIES (Pa)/Dec 21, 1907; p. 693
MADCAP, THE (Bro)/Aug 30, 1913; p. 962
MADCAP ADVENTURE, A
  (Vi)/Mar 6, 1915; p. 1447
MADCAP OF THE HILLS, THE
  (Re)/Jun 14, 1913; p. 1138
MADCAP QUEEN OF GREDSHOFFEN,
  THE (GS)/Jan 30, 1915; p. 673
MADEIRA, PORTUGAL
  (UE)/Nov 4, 1911; p. 378
MADELINE'S CHRISTMAS
  (Lu)/Jan 4, 1913; p. 50
MADELINE'S REBELLION
  (Ed)/Jun 17, 1911; p. 1387
MADEMOISELLE ANDREA
  (Rex)/Aug 29, 1914; p. 1243
MADGE OF THE MOUNTAINS
  (Vi)/Nov 11, 1911; p. 470
MADMAN OF THE CLIFF, THE
  (KO)/Dec 5, 1908; p. 459
MADMAN'S WARD, THE
  (Vic)/Aug 8, 1914; p. 838
MADONNA, THE (Be)/Jul 10, 1915; p. 308
MADONNA OF THE POOR, A
  (Th)/Nov 7, 1914; p. 789
MADONNA OF THE SLUMS, THE
  (Bi)/Nov 15, 1913; p. 738
MADONNA OF THE STORM, THE
  (Bio)/Nov 8, 1913; p. 611
MADURA AND ITS PAGODAS
  (Pa)/Jun 5, 1915; p. 1606
MAELSTROM, THE
  (Imp)/May 7, 1910; p. 738
  (KB)/Nov 29, 1913; p. 1009
MAE'S SUITORS
  (Ed)/Oct 21, 1911; p. 209
MAGAZINE COOKING
  (Lu)/Nov 28, 1914; p. 1231
MAGDALENE (GN)/Aug 20, 1910; p. 408
MAGGIE, THE DOCK RAT
  (Ka)/Dec 5, 1908; pp 450, 459
MAGGIE TRIES SOCIETY LIFE
  (Pa)/Mar 8, 1913; p. 996
MAGGIE'S HONEST LOVER
  (Ne)/Aug 8, 1914; p. 837
MAGGY HOOLIHAN GETS A JOB
  (Pa)/Sep 17, 1910; p. 631
MAGIC ALBUM (Pa)/Nov 7, 1908; p. 366
MAGIC BAG, THE (Nor)/Mar 21,1908;p.243
MAGIC BON-BONS, THE
  (Vic)/Oct 23, 1915; p. 621
MAGIC CARPET, THE
  (UE)/Jun 12, 1909; p. 795

  (Lux)/Feb 8, 1913; p. 573
MAGIC CARTONS (Gau)/Sep 18,1909; p.379
MAGIC DICE
  (KO)/Jun 27, 1908; p. 549
  (Pa)/Sep 26,1908; p.242/Mar 27,1909; p.368
MAGIC FLUTE, THE/Nov 7, 1908; p. 358
MAGIC HANDKERCHIEF, THE (Pa)/Dec 5,
  1908; p. 460/Dec 12, 1908; p. 478
MAGIC MELODY (Lu)/Nov 15, 1913; p. 736
MAGIC MELODY, THE
  (SA)/Oct 16, 1909; p. 529
MAGIC MIRROR, THE
  (Pa)/Oct 10, 1908; p. 287
  (Jo)/Jan 30, 1915; p. 673
MAGIC NICKLE, THE
  (Po)/Jul 26, 1913; p. 430
MAGIC NOTE, THE
  (Amb)/May 16, 1914; p. 950
MAGIC OF MUSIC, THE
  (Gau)/Apr 24, 1909; p. 516
MAGIC PURSE, THE
  (GN)/Apr 17, 1909; p. 476
MAGIC RUBBERS, THE
  (GN)/Sep 26, 1908; pp 241-42
MAGIC SHOES, THE
  (Lu)/Apr 26, 1913; p. 379
MAGIC SKIN, THE
  (Vic)/Jan 3, 1914; p. 50
  (KEd)/Oct 23, 1915; p. 626
MAGIC WAND, THE
  (SA)/Aug 31, 1912; p. 880
MAGICAL SUIT OF ARMOR
  (KO)/Jun 6, 1908; p. 496
MAGICIAN FISHERMAN, THE
  (Sel)/Aug 23, 1913; p. 844
MAGICIAN'S LOVE TEST, THE
  (Cin)/Oct 9, 1909; p. 490
MAGISTRATE'S CONSCIENCE, THE (Pa)/
  Sep 26, 1908; p. 243/Oct 10, 1908; p. 279
MAGISTRATE'S CRIME, A
  (Cin)/Jan 18, 1908; p. 45
MAGISTRATE'S STORY, THE
  (Ed)/Dec 11, 1915; p. 2031
MAGNATE OF PARADISE, THE
  (Ed)/Jan 23, 1915; p. 516
MAGNET, THE (Jo)/Jun 6, 1914; p. 1409
MAGNET OF DESTRUCTION, THE
  (Th)/Apr 3, 1915; p. 65
MAGNETIC EYE, THE (Lu)/Feb 1, 1908;
  p. 83/May 30, 1908; p. 481
MAGNETIC MAID, THE
  (Imp)/Jun 7, 1913; p. 1033
MAGNETIC PERSONALITY, A
  (Lux)/Nov 16, 1912; p. 660
MAGNETIC REMOVAL (Pa)/Jun 27, 1908;
  p. 547/Dec 19, 1908; p. 500
MAGNETIC VAPOR (Lu)/Jun 6, 1908; p. 497
MAGNETISM AND MAGNETS

MAN AT THE KEY, THE
(Dom)/Feb 27, 1915; p. 1290
MAN BEHIND THE CURTAIN, THE
(Po)/Jul 16, 1910; p. 144
MAN BEHIND THE DOOR, THE
(Vi)/Dec 5, 1914; p. 1394
MAN BETWEEN, THE
(Vic)/Mar 7, 1914; p. 1238
MAN EATER, THE (Lux)/Apr 5, 1913; p. 49
MAN FOR A DAY, A
(UE)/Dec 14, 1912; p. 1081
MAN FOR A' THAT, A
(SA)/May 9, 1914; p. 821
MAN FOR ALL THAT, A
(Ed)/Dec 16, 1911; p. 903
(Re)/May 1, 1915; p. 728
MAN FROM ARGENTINE, THE
(Po)/Oct 30a, 1915; p. 969
MAN FROM DRAGON LAND, THE
(Sel)/Aug 24, 1912; p. 771
MAN FROM HOME, THE
(Las)/Nov 21, 1914; p. 1088
MAN FROM MEXICO, THE
(FP)/Nov 14, 1914; p. 941
MAN FROM NOWHERE, THE
(Vic)/Aug 29, 1914; p. 1243
(Dom)/May 8, 1915; p. 900
MAN FROM OREGON, THE
(NYM)/Aug 21, 1915; p. 1326
MAN FROM OUTSIDE, THE (Re)/Mar 1,
1913; p. 889/Mar 8, 1913; p. 976
MAN FROM TEXAS, THE
(Bi)/Apr 2, 1910; p. 510
(Sel)/Mar 20, 1915; p. 1763
MAN FROM THE CITY, THE
(Exc)/May 3, 1913; p. 489
MAN FROM THE DESERT, THE
(Vi)/Jul 3, 1915; p. 80
MAN FROM THE EAST, THE
(Sel)/Apr 29, 1911; p. 957
(Sel)/Jan 2, 1915; p. 75
MAN FROM THE GOLDEN WEST, THE
(WF)/Oct 4, 1913; p. 50
MAN FROM THE PAST, THE
(Bio)/Sep 5, 1914; p. 1372
MAN FROM THE SEA, THE
(Lu)/Dec 26, 1914; p. 1841
MAN FROM THE WEST, THE
(Imp)/Mar 30, 1912; p. 1166
(Ed)/May 3, 1913; p. 488
(Lu)/Feb 7, 1914; p. 677
MAN FROM THE NORTH POLE, THE
(Cry)/Oct 19, 1912; p. 244
MAN FROM TOWN, THE
(Bio)/Dec 4, 1915; p. 1852
MAN-HATER, THE (Sel)/Oct 31,1914; p.640
MAN HE MIGHT HAVE BEEN, THE
(Ed)/Jan 11, 1913; p. 138

MAN HIGHER UP, THE
(Po)/Feb 22, 1913; p. 781
(Vi)/Mar 1, 1913; p. 888
MAN HUNT, THE
(Am)/Dec 23, 1911; p. 990
(CGP)/Sep 14, 1912; pp 1063-64
MAN HUNTERS, THE
(Bio)/Oct 24, 1914; p. 491
MAN IN BLACK, THE
(Sel)/Sep 26, 1914; p. 1775
MAN IN HIDING, THE
(Ka)/Oct 30a, 1915; p. 967
MAN IN MOTLEY, THE
(SA)/Apr 17, 1915; p. 392
MAN IN SKIRTS, THE
(WF)/Dec 19, 1914; p. 1681
MAN IN THE ATTIC, THE
(Fr)/Oct 3, 1914; p. 65
MAN IN THE AUTO, THE
(Lux)/Dec 16, 1911; p. 906
MAN IN THE BOX, THE
(Bio)/Jun 20, 1908; p. 531
MAN IN THE CABIN, THE
(SA)/Sep 6, 1913; p. 1067
MAN IN THE CHAIR, THE
(GS)/Nov 6, 1915; p. 1140
MAN IN THE COUCH, THE
(Ko)/May 30, 1914; p. 1261
MAN IN THE DARK, THE (Ed)/Oct 17,
1914; p. 349/Nov 7, 1914; p. 787
MAN IN THE HAMPER, THE
(Lu)/Nov 8, 1913; p. 612
MAN IN THE HOUSE, A
(Bio)/May 9, 1914; p. 820
MAN IN THE MAKING, A
(Ed)/Jul 6, 1912; p. 42
MAN IN THE MOON, THE
(Gau)/Jul 31, 1909; p. 162
MAN IN THE OVERALLS, THE
(Sel)/Apr 11, 1908; p. 328
MAN IN THE SICK ROOM, THE
(Sol)/Jun 7, 1913; p. 1033
MAN IN THE STREET, THE
(Sel)/Sep 13, 1913; p. 1175
(Ed)/Jun 6,1914; p. 1393/Jul 11,1914; p. 256
MAN IN THE TAXI, THE (Lu)/Nov 18,
1911; p. 554/Dec 9, 1911; p. 817
MAN IN THE VAULT, THE
(Ka)/Nov 21, 1914; p. 1075
MAN IN THE WHITE CLOAK, THE (GN)/
May 31, 1913; p. 907/Jun 14, 1913; p. 1137
MAN IN THE WORLD OF MEN, A
(Po)/Oct 25, 1913; p. 382
MAN IN 23, THE (Ne)/Feb 11, 1911; p. 318
MAN INSIDE, THE (Me)/Jul 20, 1912; p. 244
MAN NEXT DOOR, THE
(Key)/Mar 22, 1913; p. 1222
MAN OF DESTINY, THE

(Ed)/Feb 21, 1914; p. 946

MAN OF GOD, THE (Lu)/Nov 6,1915;p.1139

MAN OF HER CHOICE, THE
(Po)/Aug 8, 1914; p. 837

MAN OF HIM, THE (Lu)/Nov 8, 1913; p.612

MAN OF HONOR, A
(Gau)/Dec 17, 1910; p. 1418

MAN OF IRON, A (Th)/Feb 27, 1915; p. 1289

MAN OF IRON, THE
(Ka)/Nov 28, 1914; p. 1232

MAN OF IT, THE (Re)/Jun 12, 1915; p. 1777

MAN OF SHAME, THE
(Uni)/Sep 25, 1915; p. 2196

MAN OF THE HILLS, A
(Pre)/Apr 3, 1915; p. 65

MAN OF THE HOUR, THE
(Wor)/Oct 24, 1914; p. 496

MAN OF THE PEOPLE, A
(Ne)/Nov 15, 1913; p. 737

MAN OF THE WILDERNESS, A
(Maj)/Oct 11, 1913; p. 157

MAN ON THE BOX, THE
(Las)/Aug 8, 1914; p. 812

MAN OUTSIDE, THE
(Imp)/Feb 15, 1913; p. 681
(SA)/Nov 22, 1913; p. 868

MAN OVERBOARD (Sel)/Apr 24,1915; p.555

MAN SERVANT, THE (Ka)/Oct 2,1915; p.78

MAN SUFFRAGETTE FOR THE
ABOLITION OF WORK FOR WOMEN,
THE (It)/Jul 9, 1910; p.86

MAN THAT MIGHT HAVE BEEN, THE
(Vi)/Dec 19, 1914; p. 1679

MAN THEY SCORNED, THE
(Bro)/Nov 16, 1912; p. 660

MAN TO MAN (Vi)/Sep 2, 1911; p. 626
(Pa)/Jun 19, 1915; p. 1941
(Mus)/Nov 20, 1915; p. 1500

MAN TRAIL, THE (SA)/Sep 25,1915; p.2196

MAN UNDER THE BED, THE
(Ed)/Mar 19, 1910; p. 425
(Re)/Feb 10, 1912; p. 482
(Vi)/Jun 1, 1912; p. 830

MAN UNDERNEATH, THE
(Ya)/Jul 29, 1911; p. 212

MAN WANTED (Lu)/Aug 17, 1912; p. 669

MAN WHO BEAT DAN DOLAN
(Got)/Jun 5, 1915; p. 1626

MAN WHO CAME BACK, THE
(Ya)/Oct 28, 1911; p. 293
(Kio)/Feb 28, 1914; p. 1098
(Ec)/Oct 10, 1914; p. 189

MAN WHO COULD NOT BEAT GOD, THE
(Vi)/Oct 30, 1915; p. 808

MAN WHO COULD NOT LOSE, THE
(FaP)/Nov 28, 1914; p. 1237

MAN WHO COULD NOT SIT DOWN, THE
(Lux)/Feb 26, 1910; p.300

MAN WHO COULD NOT SLEEP, THE
(Ed)/Jun 12, 1915; p. 1776

MAN WHO DARED, THE
(Ec)/Mar 8, 1913; pp 997, 1002

MAN WHO DIED, THE
(Lu)/Sep 17, 1910; p. 630
(KB)/Jan 23, 1915; p. 517

MAN WHO DISAPPEARED, THE (Ed)
No.1/Apr 25, 1914; p. 516
No.2/May 9, 1914; p. 820
No.3/May 23, 1914; p. 1116
No.4/Jun 6, 1914; p. 1408
No.5/Jun 20, 1914; p. 1688
No.6/Jul 4, 1914; p. 64
No.7/Jul 25, 1914; p. 571
No.8/Aug 8, 1914; p. 836
No.9/Aug 22, 1914; p. 1099
No.10/Sep 5, 1914; p. 1371

MAN WHO FAILED, THE
(Sol)/Jun 28, 1913; p. 1361

MAN WHO FOUND HIMSELF, THE
(Wor)/Apr 10, 1915; p. 242

MAN WHO FOUND OUT, THE
(SA)/Jul 10, 1915; p. 307

MAN WHO KNEW, THE
(Vi)/Sep 26, 1914; p. 1776

MAN WHO LEARNED, THE
(Ed)/Sep 17, 1910; p. 630

MAN WHO LIED, THE
(Vic)/Jan 17, 1914; p. 290

MAN WHO LOST, THE
(Ka)/Feb 12, 1910; p. 215

MAN WHO LOST BUT WON, THE
(Imp)/Jun 13, 1914; p. 1542

MAN WHO MADE GOOD, THE
(Ed)/Jun 22, 1912; p. 1126

MAN WHO PAID, THE
(Bio)/Aug 15, 1914; p. 959

MAN WHO TRIED TO FORGET, THE
(Ne)/Jun 7, 1913; p. 1032

MAN WHO VANISHED, THE
(Ka)/Nov 22, 1913; p. 868
(Ed)/Jan 9, 1915; p. 220

MAN WHO WAITED, THE
(Po)/Apr 9, 1910; p. 554

MAN WHO WALKS ON WATER, A
(Pa)/Jan 18, 1908; p. 47

MAN WHO WAS MISUNDERSTOOD, THE
(Imp)/Sep 19, 1914; p. 1646

MAN WHO WAS NEVER CAUGHT, THE
(Bio)/Aug 28, 1915; p. 1493

MAN WHO WAS NEVER KISSED, THE
(Vic)/Oct 10, 1914; p. 189

MAN WHO WENT OUT, THE
(Dom)/Jul 24, 1915; p. 651

MAN WHO WOULDN'T MARRY, THE
(Ed)/Apr 26, 1913; p. 380

MAN WHO SLEPT, THE

(Vic)/Feb 7, 1914; p. 678
MAN WITH A FUTURE, A
  (Lu)/Aug 22, 1914; p. 1100
MAN WITH A RAZOR, A
  (Ko)/Dec 6, 1913; p. 1152
MAN WITH A RECORD, THE
  (Re)/Mar 13, 1915; p. 1608
MAN WITH THE CAMERA, THE
  (Com)/Dec 30, 1911; p. 1073
MAN WITH THE GLOVE, THE
  (Ka)/Aug 15, 1914; p. 959
MAN WITH THE IRON HEART, THE
  (Sel)/Sep 18, 1915; p. 1996
MAN WITH THE PULL, THE
  (Gau)/Jan 4, 1913; p. 52
MAN WITH THE PUPPETS, THE
  (GN)/Feb 10, 1912; p. 483
MAN WITH THE WEAK HEART, THE
  (Ed)/Apr 2, 1910; p.509
MAN WITHIN, THE
  (Ne)/Sep 21, 1912; p. 1178
  (Ne)/May 23, 1914; p. 1117
MAN WITHOUT A COUNTRY, THE
  (Ed)/Jul 3, 1909; p. 14
MAN WITHOUT FEAR, THE
  (Th)/Jun 27, 1914; p. 1830
MAN WORTH WHILE, A
  (Me)/Apr 20, 1912; p. 229
MANCHESTER SHIP CANAL, THE
  (UE)/Feb 8, 1913; p. 571
MANDREL'S FEATS
  (Pa)/May 2, 1908; pp 401-2
MANDY'S CHICKEN DINNER
  (Lu)/Jul 25, 1914; p. 571
MANDY'S SOCIAL WHIRL
  (Lu)/Apr 29, 1911; p. 957
**MANEUVERS OF THE NEW YORK
POLICE** (At)/Jul 16, 1910;p.144
MANFREDONIA, SOUTHERN ITALY
  (Cin)/Dec 7, 1912; p. 975
MANIA OF CARICATURE, THE
  (It)/Jan 27, 1912; p. 305
MANIAC, THE (Lu)/Oct 28, 1911; p. 291
          (Amb)/Jun 29, 1912; p. 1228
MANIAC COOK, THE (Bio)/Jan 9,1909; p.37
MANIACS THREE (Bio)/May 23,1914;p.1116
MANICURE, THE (Gem)/Sep 13,1913;p.1177
MANICURE GIRL, THE
  (Ed)/Dec 20, 1913; p. 1412
  (Lko)/Jan 2, 1915; p. 76
MANICURIST, THE (Ch)/Mar 16,1912;p.963
MANICURIST AND THE MUT, THE
  (Ka)/Jan 25, 1913; p. 363
MANILA NORMAL AND PUBLIC SCHOOLS
  (Sel)/Jun 21, 1913; p. 1253
MANITOWOC, WIS.
  (Gem)/Feb 22, 1913; p. 782
MANLY MAN, A (Imp)/Mar 11, 1911; p. 543

MANNA (GS)/Nov 13, 1915; p. 1314
MANNERS AND CUSTOMS OF AUSTRALIA
  (Pa)/Dec 21, 1907; p. 694
MANNERS AND THE MAN
  (SA)/Jun 5, 1915; p. 1604
**MANNERS AND TRADITIONS OF
PIEDMONT** (Ec)/Dec 16, 1911; p. 905
MANOEVRES OF ARTILLERY
  (KO)/May 9, 1908; p. 423
MANON (Pa)/Jul 30, 1910; p. 245
MANON LESCAUT (Pla)/Jun 27, 1914; p. 1808
MANRESSA, A SPANISH TOWN
  (Gau)/Nov 25, 1911; p. 637
MAN'S A MAN, A
  (Sol)/Jan 27, 1912; p. 304
  (Re)/Dec 27, 1913; p. 1545
MAN'S AWAKENING, A
  (Maj)/Dec 27, 1913; p. 1545
MAN'S BEST FRIEND
  (Ec)/Feb 10, 1912; p. 483
  (Kin)/Feb 8, 1913; p. 574
  (Fr)/Apr 18, 1914; p. 362
MAN'S CALLING (Am)/Nov 23, 1912; p.768
MAN'S DUTY (Rex)/Aug 16, 1913; p. 745
MAN'S DUTY, A (Re)/Jul 6, 1912; p. 44
MAN'S FAITH, A (Lu)/Apr 18, 1914; p. 360
MAN'S GENESIS (Bio)/Jul 27, 1912; p. 343/
  Jun 26, 1915; p. 2110
MAN'S GREED FOR GOLD
  (Ka)/May 31, 1913; p. 920
MAN'S LAW (Sel)/Oct 2, 1915; p. 79
MAN'S LUST FOR GOLD
  (Bio)/Jul 13, 1912; p. 148
MAN'S MAKING, A
  (Lu)/Dec 11, 1915; p. 2022
MAN'S SACRIFICE, A (Vi)/Dec 11, 1915;
  p. 2026/Dec 25, 1915; p. 2389
MAN'S SHADOW, A
  (Ecl)/Feb 7, 1914; p. 654
  (Kip)/Jan 2, 1915; p. 63
MAN'S SOUL, A (Ka)/May 30, 1914; p. 1261
MAN'S TEMPTATION, A
  (Rex)/Jan 9, 1915; p. 222
MAN'S WAY, A (Po)/Aug 20, 1910; p. 408
        (Am)/Aug 1, 1914; p. 706
MAN'S WOMAN, A (Mec)/Feb 8,1913; p.573
MANSION OF MISERY, A
  (Sel)/Aug 16, 1913; p. 744
MANSION OF SOBS, THE
  (Lu)/Apr 18, 1914; p. 361
MANSION OF TRAGEDY, A
  (SA)/Oct 2, 1915; p. 78
MANTLE OF RED EVANS, THE
  (Sel)/Dec 21, 1912; p. 1183
MANUAL OF A PERFECT GENTLEMAN
  (Pa)/Aug 22, 1908;p.143
MANUFACTURE OF BIG GUNS (Ed)/
  Apr 3, 1915; p. 52/Mar 13, 1915; p. 1607

MASTER OF THE BENGALS, THE
(Sel)/Sep 11, 1915; p. 1832
MASTER OF THE GARDEN, THE
(Sel)/Dec 20, 1913; p. 1413
MASTER OF THE HOUSE, THE
(KB)/Nov 21, 1914; p. 1078/
Nov 28, 1914; p. 1237
(Eq)/Oct 16, 1915; p. 461
MASTER OF THE MINE
(Vi)/Feb 28, 1914; p. 1088
MASTER OF THE STRONG
(Bio)/Apr 18, 1914; p. 361
MASTER OF THE SWORD, THE
(Bio)/May 22, 1915; p. 1259
MASTER OF THE VINEYARD, THE
(Am)/Dec 2, 1911; p. 727
MASTER OF THE WORLD, THE
(FRA)/Jun 20, 1914; p. 1691
MASTER PAINTER, THE
(Vi)/Aug 2, 1913; p. 535
MASTER ROGUE, THE (Ka)/Apr 25, 1914;
p. 523/May 16, 1914; p. 969
MASTER ROGUES OF EUROPE, THE
(U)/May 15, 1915; p. 1074
MASTERFUL HIRELING, THE
(Bio)/Dec 18, 1915; p. 2202
MASTERPIECE, THE
(Gau)/Oct 16, 1909; p. 530
MASTER'S MODEL, THE
(Th)/Mar 20, 1915; p. 1766
MATCHES (Am)/Mar 29, 1913; p. 1319/
Apr 5, 1913; p. 50
MATCHMAKER, THE (Lu)/Oct 7,1911; p.40
MATCHMAKING DADS
(Lu)/Feb 7, 1914; p. 676
MATE OF THE JOHN M, THE
(Vi)/Oct 14, 1911; p. 130
MATE OF THE SCHOONER SADIE, THE
(Lu)/Nov 1, 1913; p. 495
MATED BY CHESS (Gau)/Sep 30, 1911; p. 970
MATES AND MISMATES
(Po)/Jul 6, 1912; p. 34
MATILDA CHASED
(Lux)/Mar 11, 1911; p. 542
MATILDA LOVESTRUCK
(Lux)/Mar 4, 1911; p. 484
MATILDA'S FLING (Ed)/Sep 11, 1915; p. 1832
MATILDA'S LEGACY
(Lu)/Jun 12, 1915; p. 1776
MATILDA'S WINNING WAYS
(Lu)/Sep 24, 1910; p. 688
MATINEE IDOL, THE
(Po)/Sep 17, 1910; p. 633
MATINEE MIX-UP, A
(Ne)/Feb 3, 1912; p. 395
MATING (Imp)/Aug 16, 1913; p. 745
MATING, THE (Mut)/Jul 24, 1915; p. 669
MATRIMONIAL ADVERTISEMENT, A

(Me)/Aug 22, 1914; p. 1099
MATRIMONIAL AFFAIR, A
(Ne)/Aug 5, 1911; p. 295
MATRIMONIAL AGENCY OF ROARING
GULCH, THE (Ne)/Dec 7, 1912; p. 978
MATRIMONIAL BLISS
(StP)/Sep 18, 1915; p. 1997
MATRIMONIAL BOOMERANG, A
(Sel)/May 29, 1915; p. 1431
MATRIMONIAL DELUGE, A
(Sel)/Feb 8, 1913; p. 571
MATRIMONIAL EPIDEMIC, A
(Gau)/Mar 11, 1911; p. 542
MATRIMONIAL EXPRESS, THE
(Gau)/Dec 7, 1912; p. 977
MATRIMONIAL FEVER, THE
(Lux)/Jan 25, 1913; p. 365
MATRIMONIAL IDYL, A
(Po)/Oct 14, 1911; p. 130
MATRIMONIAL MANOEUVRES
(Vi)/Nov 1, 1913; p. 495
MATRIMONIAL STAGES
(KO)/Jul 25, 1908; p. 69
MATRIMONIAL SURPRISE, A
(Po)/May 27, 1911; p. 1202
MATRIMONIAL VENTURE OF THE BAR
X HANDS, THE (Ka)/Feb 22, 1913; p. 779
MATRIMONY (TKB)/Oct 30a,1915;pp969,985
MATRIMONY'S SPEED LIMIT
(Sol)/Jun 21, 1913; p. 1255
MATTER OF BUSINESS, A (Lu)/Mar 9,
1912; p. 867/Mar 16, 1912; p. 961
MATTER OF COURT, A
(Bio)/Jan 2, 1915; p. 76
MATTER OF DRESS, A
(SA)/Oct 25, 1913; p. 379
MATTER OF HIGH EXPLOSIVES, A
(Ed)/Dec 26, 1914; p. 1840
MATTER OF MATRIMONY, A
(Vi)/Apr 5, 1913; p. 48
MATTER OF PRIDE, A
(Cin)/Sep 7, 1912; p. 975
MATTER OF RECORD, A
(Lu)/Aug 8, 1914; pp 836-37
MATTERHORN, THE
(Sel)/Nov 29, 1913; p. 1007
MATTRESS, THE (Pa)/Mar 7, 1908; p. 194
MATTY, THE UNIVERSAL BOY (Imp)
No.1/Jul 18, 1914; p. 434
No.2/Aug 1, 1914; p. 706
No.3/Aug 22, 1914; p. 1100
No.4/Aug 29, 1914; p. 1242
No.5/Sep 12, 1914; p. 1513
No.6/Oct 3, 1914; p. 65
No.7/Oct 10, 1914; p. 189
No.8/Oct 24, 1914; p. 493
No.9/Nov 7, 1914; p. 789
No.10/Nov 21, 1914; p. 1077

MATTY'S DECISION (GS)/May 1,1915;p.730
MAUD MULLER (SA)/Nov 6, 1909; p. 644
          (Sel)/Oct 21, 1911; p. 207
          (Ne)/Sep 21, 1912; p. 1177
MAVERICK, THE (Sol)/Nov 2, 1912; p. 450
MAVIS OF THE GLEN
  (Lae)/Apr 24, 1915; p. 558
MAX AND HIS MOTHER-IN-LAW
  (Pa)/Aug 7, 1915; p. 1016
MAX AND MAURICE
  (Ed)/Jan 27, 1912; p. 303
MAX AND THE FAIR M.D.
  (Ecl)/Dec 5, 1914; p. 1386
MAX COMES HOME
  (Pa)/Jul 1, 1911; p. 1520
MAX EMBARRASSED
  (Pa)/Mar 18, 1911; p. 603
MAX FIGHTS A DUEL
  (CGP)/Oct 26, 1912; p. 343
MAX FOILS THE POLICE
  (Pa)/Jul 16, 1910; p. 142
MAX GETS THE REWARD
  (CGP)/Nov 30, 1912; p. 876
MAX GOES SKI-ING
  (Pa)/Dec 31, 1910; p. 1536
MAX HAS THE BOXING FEVER
  (Pa)/Feb 18, 1911; p. 371
MAX HAS TO CHANGE
  (Pa)/Aug 27, 1910; p. 463
MAX HAS TROUBLE WITH HIS EYES
  (Pa)/Nov 12, 1910; p.1116
MAX HITS THE HIGH SPOTS
  (Pun)/Dec 18, 1915; p. 2204
MAX IN A DIFFICULT POSITION
  (Pa)/Nov 14, 1914; p. 933
MAX IN A DILEMNA (Pa)/Oct 8, 1910;
  pp 813-14/Nov 19, 1910; p. 1178
MAX IN THE ALPS
  (Pa)/Nov 12, 1910; p. 1116
MAX IS ABSENT MINDED
  (Pa)/Oct 8, 1910; p. 814
MAX IS ALMOST MARRIED
  (Pa)/Feb 4, 1911; p. 244
MAX IS CONVALESCENT
  (CGP)/May 25, 1912; p. 729
MAX IS FORCED TO WORK
  (Pa)/May 20, 1911; p. 1140
  (Pa)/Feb 27, 1915; p. 1289
MAX IS STUCK UP
  (Pa)/Apr 1, 1911; p. 718
MAX JOINS THE GIANTS
  (CGP)/Feb 8, 1913; p. 572
MAX LEADS THEM A NOVEL CHASE
  (Pa)/Jun 4, 1910; p. 942
MAX MAKES A TOUCH
  (Pa)/Jul 2, 1910; p. 24
MAX MAKES MUSIC
  (Pa)/Mar 11, 1911; p. 542

MAX ON THE BRINY
  (Pa)/May 1, 1915; p. 729
MAX SETS THE FASHION
  (CGP)/Jun 15, 1912; p. 1027
MAX TAKES TONICS
  (CGP)/Jul 27, 1912; p. 343
MAX'S DIVORCE (Pa)/Aug 12, 1911; p. 376
MAX'S FEET ARE PINCHED
  (Pa)/Mar 25, 1911; p. 657
MAX'S FIRST JOB (Pa)/Jun 21, 1913; p.1252
MAX'S MONEY (Roy)/Nov 7, 1914; p. 789/
  Nov 14, 1914; p. 933
MAX'S TRAGEDY (CGP)/Oct 5, 1912; p. 41
MAX'S VACATION (Pa)/Jun 6, 1914; p.1408
MAY AND DECEMBER
  (Bio)/Jul 2, 1910; p. 24
  (Bro)/Sep 6, 1913; p. 1069
MAY BLOSSOM (FP)/May 8, 1915; p. 919
MAYA, JUST AN INDIAN
  (Fr)/Sep 6, 1913; p. 1070
MAYOR FROM IRELAND, THE
  (Ka)/Dec 14, 1912; p. 1081
MAYOR'S CRUSADE, THE
  (Ka)/Jan 4, 1913; p. 50
MAYOR'S MANICURE, THE
  (Po)/Oct 3, 1914; p. 65
MAYOR'S SECRETARY, THE
  (Ka)/Jan 2, 1915; p. 76
MAYOR'S WATERLOO, THE
  (Lu)/Mar 1, 1913; p. 888
MAZE OF FATE, THE
  (Imp)/Apr 22, 1911; p. 901
MAZEPPA (Sel)/Aug 6, 1910; p. 296
MAZIE PUTS ONE OVER
  (Lu)/Mar 27, 1915; p. 1932
McBRIDE'S BRIDE
  (Ka)/May 23, 1914; p. 1116
McCARN PLAYS FATE
  (Th)/Aug 29, 1914; pp 1242-43
McGANN AND HIS OCTETTE
  (Bio)/Nov 1, 1913; p. 495
McGINTY AND THE COUNT
  (Ed)/Jan 30, 1915; p. 671
McGINTY'S SUDDEN RISE
  (Ed)/Jul 31, 1909; p. 162
McGUIRK, SLEUTH
  (Cry)/Oct 26, 1912; p. 345
McKEE RANKIN'S "49"
  (Sel)/Sep 30, 1911; p. 972
McNAB VISITS THE COMET
  (Lux)/Jul 2, 1910; p. 26
McQUADE OF THE TRAFFIC SQUAD
  (Ed)/Jun 26, 1915; p. 2095
McSWEENEY'S MASTERPIECE
  (Cry)/Feb 28, 1914; p. 1089
ME AN' BILL (Sel)/Jul 11, 1914; p. 256
ME AND BILL (Sel)/Apr 6, 1912; p. 24/
  Apr 20, 1912; p. 229/Apr 27, 1912; p. 312

MEADOW LARK, THE
(Ed)/Aug 9, 1913; p. 636
MEAL TICKET, A (Bio)/Aug 15, 1914; p. 960
MEALS BY WEIGHT (Maj)/Jul 6,1912; p.44
MEAN MAN, A (KO)/Jun 6, 1908; p. 496
MEANS AND MORALS
(SA)/May 29, 1915; p. 1431
MEANS AND THE END, THE
(SA)/Dec 5, 1914; p. 1384
MEASURE FOR MEASURE
(Lu)/Sep 4, 1909; p. 314
MEASURE OF A MAN, THE
(Rex)/Dec 16, 1911; p. 906
(Lu)/Feb 28, 1914; p. 1087
(Rex)/Jan 30, 1915; p. 673
MEASURE OF LEON DUBRAY, THE
(GS)/Oct 30a, 1915; p. 969
MECHANICAL MAN, THE
(Jo)/Jul 3, 1915; p. 65
MEDAL OF HONOR, THE
(Lu)/Sep 27, 1913; p. 1391
MEDALLION, THE
(Sel)/Mar 25, 1911; p. 657
(Lux)/Oct 12, 1912; p. 144
MEDDLER, THE (Imp)/Oct 23, 1915; p. 622
MEDDLER WITH FATE, A (Pa)/May 16,
1914; p. 950/May 23, 1914; p. 1117
MEDDLERS, THE (Am)/Aug 17, 1912; p.674
MEDDLESOME DARLING, THE
(Lu)/Dec 4, 1915; p. 1852
MEDDLING PARSON
(Ne)/Oct 14, 1911; p. 131
MEDICINE BAG, THE
(MiR)/Jun 20, 1914; p. 1691
MEDICINE BOTTLE, THE
(Bio)/Apr 3, 1909; p. 403
MEDICINE MAN, THE
(Po)/Dec 24, 1910; p. 1480
MEDICINE MAN'S VENGEANCE, THE
(Ka)/Mar 28, 1914; p. 1681
MEDICINE SHOW AT STONE GULCH, THE
(Ka)/Feb 14, 1914; p. 808
MEDICINE WOMAN, THE
(Pa)/Sep 16, 1911; p. 789
MEDITERRANEAN FLEET, THE
(KO)/Jul 18, 1908; p. 51
MEDITERRANEAN SCENES
(Kin)/Dec 14, 1912; p. 1083
MEDIUM WANTED AS SON-IN-LAW
(Pa)/May 21, 1910; p. 832
MEDIUM'S NEMESIS, THE
(Th)/Aug 30, 1913; p. 962
MEETING HIS MATCH
(Po)/Apr 20, 1912; pp 230-31
MEETING MR. JONES
(Bio)/Oct 31, 1914; p. 640
MEETING OF THE WAYS, THE
(Vi)/Jan 27, 1912; p. 303

MEG O' THE CLIFFS
(Lu)/Dec 4, 1915; p. 1852
MEG O' THE MOUNTAINS
(Ed)/Aug 1, 1914; p. 705
MEG OF THE MINES (Maj)/Oct 3,1914;p.65
MEIN FRIENDT SCHNIEDER
(U)/Jul 31, 1915; p. 818
MEIN LIEBER KATRINA
(Am)/Jun 13, 1914; p. 1541
MELITA'S SACRIFICE
(Lu)/Dec 13, 1913; p. 1279
MELLERDRAMA (Sel)/Aug 29, 1914; p.1240
MELODIOUS MIXUP, A
(Ka)/Mar 6, 1915; pp 1447, 1452
MELODRAMA OF YESTERDAY
(Imp)/May 18, 1912; p. 630
MELODY, THE (Imp)/Jan 28, 1911; p. 197
MELODY AND ART
(Bio)/May 2, 1914; p. 672
MELODY OF DOOM, THE
(Sel)/Aug 21, 1915; p. 1316
MELODY OF LOVE, THE
(SA)/Feb 3, 1912; p. 401
MELODY OF FATE
(Po)/May 13, 1911; p. 1081
MELTING POT, THE
(Cor)/Jun 12, 1915; p. 1786
MEMENTO OF THE PAST
(Pa)/Sep 10, 1910; p. 574
MEMORIES (Am)/Mar 18, 1911; p. 603
(Pa)/Aug 17, 1912; p. 669
(Rex)/Oct 11, 1913; p. 157
(Sel)/Mar 7, 1914; p. 1236
MEMORIES IN MEN'S SOULS, THE
(Vi)/Aug 22, 1914; p. 1100
MEMORIES OF A PIONEER
(101)/Jun 22, 1912; p. 1128
MEMORIES OF '49 (Sol)/Feb 3, 1912; p. 395
MEMORIES OF HIS YOUTH
(Lu)/Apr 12, 1913; p. 163
MEMORIES OF THE PAST
(Pa)/Aug 5, 1911; p. 292
MEMORIES OF YEARS AGO
(Fr)/Aug 22, 1914; p. 1100
MEMORIES THAT HAUNT (Vi)/Apr 11,
1914; p. 191/Apr 25, 1914; p. 517
MEMORY OF HIS MOTHER, THE
(KO)/May 9, 1908; p. 423
MEMORY TREE, THE
(U)/May 29, 1915; p. 1433
MEN AND WOMEN (KO)/May 2,1908; p.401
(KE)/Aug 15,1914;p.969
MEN HATERS' CLUB, THE
(Vi)/Sep 10, 1910; p. 575
MEN OF THE MOUNTAIN
(Lu)/Apr 10, 1915; p. 236
MEN OF THE WEST
(Ch)/Apr 29, 1911; p. 960

MEN WERE DECEIVERS EVER
(Gau)/Jun 7, 1913; p. 1033
MEN WHO DARE (Re)/Nov 2, 1912; p. 452
MENACE OF FATE, THE
(Ka)/Nov 14, 1914; p. 932
MENACE OF THE MUTE, THE
(Pa)/Nov 6, 1915; pp 1140, 1156
MENDED LUTE, THE
(Bio)/Aug 14, 1909; p. 226
MENDER, THE PIPE AND THE VASE,
THE (Ec)/Dec 14, 1912; p. 1082
MENDER OF NETS, THE
(Bio)/Mar 2, 1912; p. 780
MENDER OF WAYS, A
(WF)/Dec 5, 1914; p. 1385
MENDELSSOHN'S SPRING SONG
(Imp)/Nov 12, 1910; p. 1118
MENTAL SCIENCE (Po)/Nov 12,1910;p.1119
MENTAL SUICIDE (Po)/Jul 26,1913; p.430
MEPHISTO AND THE MAIDEN
(Sel)/May 8, 1909; p. 595
MEPHISTO AT A MASQUERADE
(Gau)/Apr 30, 1910; p. 689
MEPHISTOPHILIA (Fl)/Mar 28,1914; p.1686
MEPHISTO'S AFFINITY
(Lu)/Jun 27, 1908; p. 547
MERCHANT MAYOR, THE (Ch)/Feb 24,
1912; p. 670/Mar 2, 1912; p. 781
MERCHANT OF VENICE, THE
(Vi)/Jan 9, 1909; p. 38
(Th)/Jul 20, 1912; pp 226-27
(Uni)/Feb 14, 1914; p. 813
MERCY MERRICK (Ed)/May 24, 1913;
p. 791/Jun 21, 1913; p. 1252
MERCY ON A CRUTCH
(Th)/Jul 24, 1915; p. 650
MERELY A MILLIONHEIR
(Sel)/Feb 3, 1912; p. 393
MERELY MOTHER (Bio)/Oct 3, 1914; p. 64
MERELY PLAYERS (Re)/Oct 9, 1915; p.253
MERMAID, THE (Th)/Aug 13, 1910; p. 351
(Ka)/Jul 26, 1913; p. 428
MERRILL MURDER MYSTERY, THE
(Pa)/Oct 4, 1913; p. 47
MERRY CHASE, A (StP)/Sep 4,1915; p.1645
MERRY CHRISTMAS AND A HAPPY NEW
YEAR, A (Vi)/Dec 25, 1909; p. 921
MERRY MARY'S MARRIAGE
(Lko)/Jan 30, 1915; p. 673
MERRY MEDRANO CIRCUS CLOWNS,
THE (Pa)/May 14, 1910; p. 784
MERRY MODELS, THE
(SA)/Dec 18, 1915; p. 2202
MERRY MOVING MEN, THE
(Ka)/Jul 17, 1915; p. 485
MERRY WIDOW, THE (Sol)/Jul 5,1913;p.49
MERRY WIDOW HAT, THE
(Vi)/Oct 24, 1908; p. 328

MERRY WIDOW HATS, THE
(Lu)/May 9, 1908; p. 423
MERRY WIDOW TAKES ANOTHER
PARTNER, THE (Vi)/Apr 30, 1910; p. 689
MERRY WIDOW WALTZ (Pa)/Nov 28,
1908; p. 434/Dec 5, 1908; p. 448
MERRY WIDOW WALTZ CRAZE, THE
(Ed)/May 2, 1908; p.400
MERRY WIDOWER, THE
(Vi)/Aug 22, 1908; p. 145
MERRY WIVES OF WINDSOR, THE
(Sel)/Dec 10, 1910; p. 1356
MESH OF THE NET, THE
(Imp)/Jul 2, 1910; p. 25
MESMERIST, THE (Pa)/Sep 12, 1908; p. 202
MESMERIZING MOE
(Ya)/Sep 23, 1911; p. 893
MESQUITE PETE'S FORTUNE
(Ec)/Sep 5, 1914; p. 1373
MESQUITE'S GRATITUDE, THE
(Ka)/Nov 4, 1911; p. 379
MESSAGE, THE (Bio)/Jul 10, 1909; p. 51
(Re)/Jan 9, 1915; p. 221
MESSAGE FROM ACROSS THE SEA, A
(Sel)/Jan 31, 1914; p. 543
MESSAGE FROM BEYOND, A
(Vi)/Nov 18, 1911; p. 551
(Sol)/Jun 8, 1912; p. 946
MESSAGE FROM HOME, A
(Sel)/Dec 13, 1913; p. 1279
MESSAGE FROM NIAGARA, A
(Th)/Mar 2, 1912; p. 782
MESSAGE FROM THE MOON, A
(Bio)/Mar 16, 1912; p. 961
MESSAGE FROM THE WEST, THE
(Ne)/Jul 22, 1911; p. 126
MESSAGE IN THE BOTTLE, THE
(Imp)/Mar 25, 1911; p. 658
MESSAGE IN THE COCOANUT, THE
(Maj)/Mar 8, 1913; p. 998
MESSAGE IN THE ROSE, THE
(Ed)/Apr 4, 1914; p. 57
MESSAGE OF THE ARROW, THE
(Bi)/Dec 18, 1909; p. 882
(Pa)/Sep 2, 1911; p. 628
MESSAGE OF THE DEAD, THE
(Ecl)/Nov 1, 1913; p. 482
MESSAGE OF THE FLOWERS, THE
(Maj)/Jun 21, 1913; p. 1254
MESSAGE OF THE PALMS, THE
(Ka)/Mar 15, 1913; p. 1103
MESSAGE OF THE ROSE, THE
(Lu)/Aug 16, 1913; p. 743
MESSAGE OF THE SEA, A
(Bi)/Jul 30, 1910; p. 246
MESSAGE OF THE SUN DIAL, THE (Ed)/
Jan 3, 1914; p. 32/Feb 7, 1914; p. 676
MESSAGE OF THE VIOLIN, THE

MIKE AND JAKE IN MEXICO
(Jo)/Dec 6, 1913; p. 1152

MIKE AND JAKE IN SOCIETY
(Jo)/Dec 27, 1913; p. 1544

MIKE AND JAKE IN THE WILD WEST
(Jo)/Dec 6, 1913; p. 1152

MIKE AND JAKE LIVE CLOSE TO
NATURE (Jo)/Jan 10, 1914; p. 173

MIKE JOINS THE FORCE
(Roy)/May 23, 1914; p. 1117

MIKE SEARCHES FOR HIS LONG-LOST
BROTHER (Jo)/May 23, 1914; p. 1118

MIKE SPLINTER, THE SPRINTER
(Box)/Nov 7, 1914; p. 789

MIKE'S BRAINSTORM
(Sel)/Dec 21, 1912; p. 1183

MIKE'S HERO (Ed)/Nov 4, 1911; p. 378

MILADY'S BOUDOIR
(Bio)/Jan 23, 1915; p. 496

MILDRED'S DOLL
(Dom)/Sep 12, 1914; p. 1513

MILESTONES OF LIFE
(Th)/Jul 31, 1915; p. 834

MILITANT, THE (Imp)/Jan 24, 1914; p. 414

MILITANT SCHOOLMA'AM, A
(Sel)/Jan 23, 1915; p. 515

MILITANT SUFFRAGETTE, A
(Th)/Dec 28, 1912; p. 1294
(Pa)/Apr 25, 1914; p. 494

MILITARY AIR SCOUT, THE
(Vi)/Dec 23, 1911; p. 989

MILITARY CYCLISTS IN BELGIUM
(Pa)/Dec 3, 1910; p. 1296

MILITARY JUDAS, A
(Bro)/Jan 3, 1914; p. 50

MILITARY KITE FLYING AT RHEIMES
(UE)/Sep 17, 1910; p. 632

MILITARY PRISON/Jan 16, 1909; p. 69

MILITARY TATTOO AT ALDERSHOT,
ENGLAND (Ka)/Jul 4, 1914; p. 64

MILITARY TOURNAMENT AT SAUMUR
(Pa)/Jan 11, 1908; p. 28

MILITARY TRAINED DOGS, BELGIUM
(Pa)/Aug 29, 1914; p. 1241

MILK INDUSTRY IN THE ALPS, THE
(Pa)/Jun 4, 1910; p. 941

MILK WE DRINK, THE
(Key)/Nov 8, 1913; p. 613

MILKFED BOY, THE
(Maj)/Sep 12, 1914; p. 1513

MILKMAN'S REVENGE, THE
(Th)/Dec 20, 1913; p. 1413

MILL BUYERS, THE
(Vic)/Aug 17, 1912; p. 676

MILL BY THE ZUYDER ZEE, THE
(Dom)/Mar 20, 1915; p. 1766

MILL OF LIFE, THE
(Vi)/Nov 7, 1914; p. 787

MILL OF THE GODS, THE
(Sol)/Apr 15, 1911; p. 843

MILL ON THE FLOSS, THE
(Th)/Dec 18, 1915; pp 2198, 2203

MILL STREAM, THE (Imp)/Sep 26, 1914;
p. 1761/Dec 19, 1914; p. 1681

MILLER, HIS SON AND THE ASS, THE
(Pa)/Aug 22, 1908; p. 144

MILLER OF BURGUNDY, THE (Sel)/Jul 27,
1912; pp 336-37/Aug 10, 1912; p. 545

MILLINERY BOMB, A
(Vi)/Jul 26, 1913; p. 427

MILLINERY MAN, THE
(Lu)/Mar 20, 1915; p. 1763

MILLINERY MIX-UP, A
(Ed)/Dec 5, 1914; p. 1383

MILLION BID, A (Vi)/Feb 7, 1914; p. 658

MILLION DOLLAR BRIDE, THE
(Ko)/Oct 17, 1914; p. 337

MILLION DOLLAR MYSTERY, THE (Th)
No.6/Aug 8, 1914; p. 838
No.7/Aug 8, 1914; p. 838
No.8/Aug 15, 1914; p. 961
No.9/Aug 22, 1914; p. 1101
No.10/Jul 4, 1914; p. 47
No.11/Sep 19, 1914; p. 1647
No.12/Sep 19, 1914; p. 1647
No.14/Sep 26, 1914; p. 1778
No.15/Oct 24, 1914; p. 494
No.16/Oct 24, 1914; p. 494
No.23/Feb 27, 1915; p. 1289

MILLION DOLLAR ROBBERY, THE
(BFF)/Jun 20, 1914; p. 1691

MILLION DOLLARS, A
(Sol)/Jan 18, 1913; p. 265

MILLION IN JEWELS, A
(Ka)/Feb 28, 1914; p. 1088

MILLION IN PEARLS, A
(Vic)/May 16, 1914; p. 970

MILLIONAIRE AND THE GOOSE, THE
(Ka)/Aug 30, 1913; p. 960

MILLIONAIRE AND THE RANCH GIRL,
THE (SA)/Sep 17, 1910; pp 630-31

MILLIONAIRE AND THE SQUATTER, THE
(SA)/Sep 30, 1911; p. 971

MILLIONAIRE BABY, THE
(Sel)/Jun 5, 1915; p. 1623

MILLIONAIRE BARBER, THE
(SA)/Jan 6, 1912; p. 41

MILLIONAIRE CABBY, THE
(Sel)/Mar 13, 1915; p. 1607

MILLIONAIRE COP, THE
(Imp)/Sep 28, 1912; p. 1278

MILLIONAIRE COWBOY, THE
(Sel)/Jan 25, 1913; pp 344-45

MILLIONAIRE ENGINEER, THE (Imp)/
Jan 16, 1915; p. 382/Jan 30, 1915; p. 673

MILLIONAIRE FOR A DAY, A

(Th)/Oct 9, 1915; p. 253
MIRACLE MARY (Vic)/Jan 10, 1914; p. 174
MIRACLE OF A NECKLACE
(Lux)/Dec 11, 1909; p. 842
MIRACLE OF LIFE, THE (Am)/Oct 9, 1915;
pp 281-82/Oct 16, 1915; p. 441
MIRACLE OF LOVE, A
(Lu)/Nov 22, 1913; p. 868
MIRACLE OF THE ROSES, THE
(Pa)/Jul 12, 1913; p. 205
MIRACULOUS FLOWERS, THE
(KO)/Aug 1, 1908; p. 88
MIRIELLE'S SINCERE LOVE
(Pa)/May 15, 1909; p. 635
MIRROR, THE (Imp)/Feb 25, 1911; p. 432
(Bio)/Aug 9, 1913; p. 635
(Am)/Sep 26, 1914; p. 1777
(Lu)/Sep 11, 1915; p. 1832
MIRROR OF LIFE, THE
(Sav)/May 29, 1915; p. 1441
MIRROR OF THE FUTURE, A
(Pa)/Jun 11, 1910; p. 995
MIRTH AND SORROWS
(Pa)/Nov 5, 1910; p. 1059
MISADVENTURE OF AN EQUILIBRIST, A
(KO)/Apr 18, 1908; p. 354
MISADVENTURES OF A CLAIM AGENT,
THE (Am)/Jan 13, 1912; p.126
MISADVENTURES OF A MIGHTY
MONARCH (Vi)/Jan 17, 1914; p. 288
MISADVENTURES OF A PAIR OF
TROUSERS (Pa)/Nov 20,1909;p.721
MISADVENTURES OF A SHERIFF (Pa)/
Jun 13, 1908; p. 516/Mar 20, 1909; p. 337
MISALLIANCE, A (GN)/May 2, 1908; p. 405
MISAPPROPRIATED TURKEY, A
(Bio)/Feb 8, 1913; p. 572
MISCALCULATION, A
(Pa)/Sep 3, 1910; p. 519
MISCHIEF MAKER, THE
(Vi)/Mar 21, 1914; p. 1525
MISCHIEVOUS DIABOLO
(KO)/Jun 6, 1908; p. 496
MISCHIEVOUS ELF, THE
(Ed)/Dec 31, 1909; p. 961
MISER, THE (Lu)/Feb 22, 1913; p. 779
(KB)/May 17, 1913; p. 706
MISER MINER, THE
(Bio)/Dec 2, 1911; p. 724
MISER MURRAY'S WEDDING PRESENT
(Vi)/May 23, 1914; p. 1116
MISER'S CHILD, THE
(Ka)/Mar 5, 1910; p. 339
MISER'S HEART, THE
(Bio)/Dec 2, 1911; p. 724
MISER'S DAUGHTER, THE
(Imp)/Apr 16, 1910; p. 599
(Re)/May 25, 1912; p. 731

MISER'S LEGACY, THE
(Bio)/Apr 24, 1915; p. 555
MISER'S MILLIONS, THE
(Cin)/Apr 19, 1913; p. 258
MISER'S PUNISHMENT, A
(Pa)/Apr 25, 1908; p. 377
MISER'S REVERSION, THE
(Th)/Apr 4, 1914; p. 59
MISER'S SON, THE
(Imp)/Sep 27, 1913; p. 1393
MISFORTUNES OF MR. AND MRS. MOTT,
THE (Me)/Mar 22, 1913; p. 1220
MISGOTTEN GAINS
(Cin)/Oct 18, 1913; p. 264
MISHAPS OF A BASHFUL MAN
(Sel)/Apr 11, 1908; pp 328-29
MISHAPS OF A POLICEMAN
(Har)/Aug 21, 1909; p. 253
MISHAPS OF BONEHEAD, IN SEARCH OF
AN HEIRESS (Cen)/Jan 22, 1910; p. 93
MISHAPS OF MARCELINE
(Th)/Mar 13, 1915; p. 1608
MISJUDGED MR. HARTLEY, THE
(SA)/Feb 6, 1915; p. 827
MISJUDGING OF MR. HUBBY, THE
(SA)/Mar 29, 1913; p. 1335
MISLAID BABY, A (SA)/Dec 4, 1909; p. 799
MISLEADING EVIDENCE
(Pa)/Nov 2, 1912; p. 450
MISMATED (Imp)/Jun 26, 1915; p. 2097
MISPLACED CONFIDENCE, A
(SA)/Feb 14, 1914; p. 809
MISPLACED FOOT, A
(Key)/Jan 10, 1914; p. 174
MISPLACED JEALOUSY
(Bio)/May 20, 1911; p. 1141
MISPLACED LOVE
(Cry)/Sep 20, 1913; p. 1285
MISPLACED PETTICOAT, THE
(Pa)/Jan 14, 1911; p. 90
MISPLACED TWINS, THE
(Lun)/Apr 10, 1915; p. 237
MISS ARABELLA SNAITH
(Th)/May 11, 1912; p. 529
MISS "ARABIAN NIGHTS"
(SA)/Aug 23, 1913; p. 843
MISS BIFFIN'S DEMISE
(Ya)/Jun 24, 1911; p. 1455
MISS BLUM (Pa)/Jun 24, 1911; p. 1452
MISS CHATTERER'S EXPERIENCE
(SA)/Sep 23, 1911; p.889
MISS CINDERELLA (Ecl)/Oct 17,1914;p.337
MISS FATTY'S SEASIDE LOVERS
(Key)/Jun 5, 1915; p. 1605
MISS FAUST (Pa)/Jun 5, 1909; p. 754
MISS FAIRWEATHER OUT WEST
(Fr)/Oct 25, 1913; p. 381
MISS FRECKLES (SA)/Nov 6, 1915; p. 1139

MISS GALISPYE'S VACATION
(Roy)/Aug 15, 1914; p. 961
MISS HOLD'S PUPPETS
(Pa)/Aug 8, 1908; pp 108-9
MISS JEKYLL AND MADAME HYDE
(Vi)/Jul 3, 1915; p. 65
MISS MASQUERADER
(Ec)/Dec 9, 1911; p. 818
MISS MILLY'S VALENTINE
(SA)/Feb 28, 1914; p. 1087
MISS MISCHIEF (Th)/Jun 14, 1913; p. 1138
MISS MONEYBAGS WISHES TO WED
(Pa)/Jan 22, 1910; p. 92
MISS NOBODY (Ne)/May 10, 1913; p. 597
MISS NOBODY FROM NOWHERE
(Imp)/Apr 25, 1914; p. 518
MISS RAFFLES (Vi)/Jun 13, 1914; p. 1540
MISS ROBINSON CRUSOE
(Th)/Oct 19, 1912; p. 244
MISS SHERLOCK HOLMES (Ed)/Dec 5,
1908; p. 458/Dec 12, 1908; p. 477
MISS SIMKINS' SUMMER BOARDER
(SA)/Nov 9, 1912; p. 553
MISS SIMPTON'S JEWELS
(Lux)/Apr 5, 1913; p. 49
MISS STICKY-MOUFIE-KISS
(Vi)/Oct 23, 1915; p. 619
MISS TAKU OF TOKIO
(Th)/Nov 23, 1912; p. 769
MISS TOMBOY AND FRECKLES
(Vi)/Nov 21, 1914; p. 1076
MISS TRILLIE'S BIG FEET
(Nov)/Oct 23, 1915; p. 620
MIS-SENT LETTER, THE
(SA)/Jun 22, 1912; p. 1127
MISSES FINCH AND THEIR LITTLE
NEPHEW, BILL, THE
(Vi)/Jan 21, 1911; p. 144
MISSING BONDS, THE
(Ka)/Mar 15, 1913; p. 1104
MISSING BRACELET, THE
(Gau)/Oct 21, 1911; p. 207
MISSING BRIDE, A
(Key)/Jun 27, 1914; p. 1830
MISSING BRIDE, THE
(Pa)/Feb 25, 1911; p. 430
MISSING BRIDEGROOM, THE
(Po)/Aug 6, 1910; p. 298
MISSING CLUE, THE
(Vi)/Aug 14, 1915; p. 1160
MISSING DIAMOND, THE
(Lu)/Jan 17, 1914; p. 288
MISSING HEIR, THE
(Th)/Nov 18, 1911; p. 551
MISSING JEWELS, THE
(Lu)/Feb 22, 1913; p. 779
(Ka)/Jul 4, 1914; p. 64
MISSING LINKS, THE (TFA)/Dec 18, 1915;

pp 2200-2201/Dec 25, 1915; p. 2390
MISSING LOCKET (UE)/Nov 2, 1912; p.449
MISSING MAN, THE
(Ka)/Jul 10, 1915; p. 308
MISSING PAGE, THE
(Sel)/Sep 26, 1914; p. 1776
MISSING RING, THE
(Re)/Sep 27, 1913; p. 1394
MISSING RUBY, THE
(Sel)/Mar 20, 1915; p. 1763
MISSING TWENTY-FIVE DOLLARS, THE
(Ed)/Apr 18, 1914; p. 360
MISSING WILL, THE
(Vi)/Oct 21, 1911; p. 209
MISSING WITNESS, THE
(Th)/Aug 23, 1913; p. 844
MISSING WOMAN, THE
(FRA)/Sep 27, 1913; p. 1372
MISSION BELLS (Am)/Aug 2, 1913; p. 537
MISSION CARRIER, THE
(Ka)/Mar 25, 1911; p. 656
MISSION FATHER, THE
(Me)/Jan 6, 1912; p. 40
MISSION IN THE DESERT
(Am)/Feb 18, 1911; p. 372
MISSION OF A BULLET, THE
(Ka)/Jan 18, 1913; p. 263
MISSION OF A FLOWER, THE
(WBE)/May 2, 1908; p. 405
MISSION OF DR. FOO, THE
(Ed)/Mar 27, 1915; p. 1931
MISSION OF MORRISON, THE
(Re)/May 15, 1915; p. 1072
MISSION WAIF, THE (Me)/Aug 26, 1911;
p. 524/Oct 14, 1911; p. 128
MISSION WORKER, THE
(Sel)/Jul 1, 1911; p. 1520
MISSIONARIES IN DARKEST AFRICA
(Ka)/May 18,1912;p.614/Jun 15,1912;p.1026
MISSIONARY, THE/Aug 7, 1909; p. 195
MISSIONARY AND THE ACTRESS, THE
(Sel)/Oct 25, 1913; p. 379
MISSIONARY AND THE MAID, THE
(Ed)/Jul 24, 1909; p.125
MISSIONARY'S GRATITUDE, THE
(Bi)/Sep 30, 1911; p. 974
MISSIONS IN SOUTHERN CALIFORNIA
(Pa)/Jan 30, 1915; p. 673
MISSISSIPPI TRAGEDY, A
(Ka)/Apr 19, 1913; p. 280
MISTAKE, THE (Imp)/Aug 6, 1910; p. 298
(Bio)/Jul 26, 1913; p. 428
MISTAKE IN JUDGMENT, A
(Ed)/Sep 6, 1913; p. 1068
MISTAKE IN SPELLING, A
(Vi)/Nov 2, 1912; p. 450
MISTAKE IN THE DARK, A
(KO)/May 9, 1908; p. 422

MODEL WIFE, A (Ka)/Feb 13, 1915; p. 984
　　　　　(Vi)/Dec 4, 1915; p. 1853
MODEL YOUNG MAN, A
　(Vi)/Apr 4, 1914; p. 57
MODELING EXTRAORDINARY
　(Kin)/Apr 19, 1913; p. 281
MODEL'S ADVENTURE, THE
　(Ka)/Dec 4, 1915; p. 1852
MODEL'S REDEMPTION, THE
　(Imp)/Nov 26, 1910; p. 1238
MODERN ALGERIA
　(UE)/Jun 26, 1909; p. 872
MODERN ANANIAS, A
　(Sel)/Jan 27, 1912; p. 302
MODERN ARCHITECT, A
　(Lux)/Feb 22, 1913; p. 781
MODERN CHILD, THE
　(Lux)/Sep 7, 1912; p. 976
MODERN CINDERELLA, A
　(Vi)/Jun 18, 1910; p. 1049
　(Ed)/Nov 18, 1911; p. 551
MODERN COURTSHIP, A
　(Vi)/Dec 3, 1910; p. 1296
MODERN DIANAS, THE
　(Ed)/Sep 2, 1911; p. 627
MODERN DR. JEKYLL, THE
　(Sel)/Dec 31, 1909; p. 960
MODERN ENOCH ARDEN, A
　(U)/May 8, 1915; p. 919
MODERN FAIRY TALE, A
　(Rex)/Mar 14, 1914; p. 1386
MODERN FREE-LANCE, A
　(Am)/Mar 21, 1914; p. 1526
MODERN GARRICK, A
　(Pa)/Jul 19, 1913; p. 319
MODERN HERCULES AT WORK
　(Pa)/Nov 30, 1907; p. 635
MODERN HORSE, A
　(Ed)/Mar 29, 1913; p. 1335
MODERN HOTEL (KO)/May 2, 1908; p. 401
MODERN JEKYLL AND HYDE, A
　(Ka)/Jan 17, 1914; p. 289
MODERN KNIGHT ERRANT, A
　(Vi)/Oct 8, 1910; p. 814
MODERN LIGHT BATTERY IN ACTION, A
　(Ka)/Feb 4, 1911; p. 243
MODERN LOCHINVAR, A
　(Th)/Jul 5, 1913; p. 50
MODERN MAGDALEN, A
　(LF)/Mar 13, 1915; p. 1614
MODERN MAGIC (Pa)/Dec 12, 1908; p. 477
MODERN MELNOTTE
　(Po)/Sep 19, 1914; p. 1646
MODERN MEPHISTO, A
　(GFP)/Jan 31, 1914; p. 529
MODERN MESSENGER BOY, THE
　(SA)/Feb 5, 1910; p. 169
MODERN NAVAL HERO, A

　(GN)/Apr 25, 1908; p. 375
MODERN NOBLE, A
　(Dom)/Feb 6, 1915; p. 830
MODERN OTHELLO, A
　(Be)/Sep 12, 1914; p. 1513
MODERN PORTIA, A
　(Pa)/Dec 27, 1913; p. 1544
MODERN PRODIGAL, THE
　(Bio)/Sep 10, 1910; p. 574
　(Vi)/Apr 12, 1913; p. 164
MODERN PROGRESS IN SOMALILAND,
　EAST AFRICA (Cin)/Apr 19, 1913 p. 280
MODERN PSYCHE, A
　(Vi)/Jun 21, 1913; p. 1251
MODERN RAILWAY CONSTRUCTION
　(UE)/May 28, 1910; p. 889
MODERN RIP, A (Sel)/Jan 6, 1912; p. 41
MODERN RIP VAN WINKLE, A
　(Am)/Oct 10, 1914; p. 189
MODERN ROMANCE, A
　(Imp)/Aug 9, 1913; p. 638
MODERN SAMPSON, A
　(Ed)/Jul 4, 1914; p. 64
　(WF)/Oct 31, 1914; p. 642
MODERN SAMSON, A
　(Cin)/Sep 14, 1907; pp 441-42
　(Pa)/Mar 28, 1908; pp 269-70/
　　　Mar 6, 1909; pp 269-70
MODERN SCULPTORS
　(Pa)/Apr 11, 1908; p. 327
MODERN SNARE, THE
　(Am)/May 24, 1913; p. 813
MODERN STEEL PLANT, A
　(Am)/Nov 22, 1913; p. 869
MODERN VENDETTA, A
　(Sel)/Feb 14, 1914; p. 809
MODERN WEAPONS FOR FIGHTING
　FIRES (Ed)/Jan 6, 1912; p. 40
MODERN WITNESS, A
　(Vic)/Jul 19, 1913; p. 321
MODERN YOUTH, THE
　(Cin)/Aug 17, 1907; p. 378
MODES AND CUSTOMS OF THE HINDOOS
　(Pa)/Aug 5, 1911;p.293
MODEST HERO, A (Bio)/Sep 20,1913;p.1284
MODEST YOUNG MAN, THE
　(Ed)/Feb 6, 1909; p. 144
MOGG MEGONE (Vi)/Mar 6, 1909; p. 270
MOHAMMEDAN CONSPIRACY, A
　(Th)/May 23, 1914; p. 1118
MOHAMMEDIAN AT HOME, THE (Pa)/
　Dec 12, 1908; p. 487/Dec 19, 1908; p. 501
MOHAWK'S WAY, A
　(Bio)/Sep 24, 1910; p. 688
MOLLIE AND THE OIL KING
　(Maj)/Jan 17, 1914; p. 290
MOLLY, THE DRUMMER BOY (Ed)/
　Jun 20, 1914; p. 1674/Jul 18, 1914; p. 432

MOLLY AT THE REGIMENT
(Amb)/Oct 1, 1910; p. 749
MOLLY MAGUIRES, THE (Ka)/Dec 12,
1908; p. 485/Dec 26, 1908; p. 526
MOLLY OF THE MOUNTAINS
(Bro)/Apr 10, 1915; p. 236
MOLLY PITCHER (Ch)/Jul 1, 1911; p. 1522
(Ka)/Dec 23, 1911; p. 988
MOLLYCODDLE, THE
(Be)/Jun 26, 1915; p. 2096
MOLLY'S MILADY (Ne)/Oct 16, 1915; p.441
MOLLY'S MISTAKE
(Me)/Mar 15, 1913; p. 1103
MOMENT BEFORE DEATH, THE
(Lu)/Dec 25, 1915; p. 2388
MOMENT OF MADNESS, A
(Ed)/Dec 5, 1914; p. 1383
MOMENT OF SACRIFICE, THE
(Th)/Apr 17, 1915; p. 393
MOMENTOUS DECISION, A
(Lu)/Nov 15, 1913; p. 735
MONA, OF THE MODOCS
(Bi)/Feb 15, 1913; p. 680
MONA LISA (Ecl)/Jan 25, 1913; p. 349
MONA LIZA IN DISGUISE
(Cin)/Aug 31, 1912; p. 880
MONASTERY IN THE FOREST, THE
(Gau)/Jun 18, 1910; pp 1048-49
MONDAY MORNING IN A CONEY ISLAND
POLICE COURT (Bio)/Sep 5, 1908; p. 181
MONEY
(Ke)/Aug 1,1914; p.708/Sep 26,1914; p.1780
(Bio)/Jan 23, 1915; p. 516
(Wor)/Feb 6, 1915; p. 833
MONEY?, A (SA)/Nov 23, 1912; p. 766
MONEY! MONEY! MONEY!
(Lu)/Jul 24, 1915; p. 649
MONEY BAG, THE
(Gau)/May 14, 1910; p. 784
MONEY GOD, THE
(Met)/Feb 28, 1914; p. 1097
MONEY GULF, THE
(Ka)/Dec 18, 1915; p. 2202
MONEY IN THE BANK (Ka)/Jul 1, 1911;
p. 1519/Jul 8, 1911; p. 1584
MONEY KING, THE
(Vi)/Jul 13, 1912; pp 134-35
MONEY LEECHES, THE
(Ka)/Jun 26, 1915; p. 2096
MONEY LENDER, THE
(UE)/Apr 8, 1911; p. 780
(Am)/Feb 14, 1914; p. 810
MONEY LENDER'S SON, THE
(Lux)/Jul 23, 1910; p. 193
MONEY MAD (Bio)/Dec 5, 1908; p. 457
MONEY MASTER, THE
(KEd)/Oct 2, 1915; p. 91
MONEY SHARKS, THE

(Cin)/Mar 14, 1914; p. 1385
MONEY TO BURN (Ed)/Aug 19, 1911; p.462
MONGOOSE, THE (Pa)/Jul 24, 1915; p. 651
MONKEY ACCOMPLICE, THE
(Sol)/Feb 22, 1913; p. 781
MONKEY BUSINESS
(Lu)/Apr 17, 1915; p. 392
MONKEY INTELLIGENCE
(Pa)/Apr 3, 1915; p. 65
MONKEY SHINES
(At)/Oct 1, 1910; p. 749
(StP)/Sep 11, 1915; p. 1834
MONKEY SHOWMAN OF DJIBAL, THE
(Ec)/Aug 27, 1910; p.464
MONK'S MOTHER, THE
(Gau)/Jul 31, 1909; pp 161-62
MONOGRAM J.O., THE
(Rex)/Jun 17, 1911; p. 1388
MONOGRAMMED CIGARETTE, THE
(Ya)/Oct 22, 1910; p. 939
(Ka)/Sep 27, 1913; p. 1391
MONOPOLIST, THE
(Vic)/Aug 28, 1915; p. 1481
MONSIEUR (Ed)/Apr 22, 1911; p. 898
MONSIEUR BLUEBEARD
(Bi)/Oct 3, 1914; p. 66
MONSIEUR LECOQ
(Fl)/Sep 19, 1914; p. 1620
(Th)/Aug 28, 1915; p. 1491
MONSIEUR NICKOLA DUPREE
(Th)/May 15, 1915; p. 1072
MONSTER AND GIRL
(Sol)/Apr 25, 1914; p. 518
MONTANA ANNA (Sel)/Jun 17, 1911; p.1387
"MONTANA" BLOUNT'S INCRIMINATION
(Asc)/Oct 16, 1915; p. 465
MONTANA LOVE STORY, A
(Po)/Jan 28, 1911; p. 197
MONTANA MIX-UP, A
(SA)/Mar 22, 1913; p. 1220
MONTANA SCHOOLMARM, THE (Sel)/
Dec 19, 1908; p. 512/Dec 26, 1908; p. 525
MONTANA STATE FAIR
(Vi)/Jan 24, 1914; p. 412
MONTE CARLO, MONACO
(Pa)/Aug 16, 1913; p. 743
MONTE CRISTO
(Po)/Jan 28, 1911; p. 196
(Sel)/Aug 17, 1912; pp 641-43
MONTE CRISTO UP TO DATE
(Me)/Feb 7, 1914; p. 676
MONTREAL, QUEBEC, AND HALIFAX
(Pa)/May 24, 1913; p. 811
MONUMENT, THE (Bio)/Aug 16,1913; p.743
MONUMENTS AND CASCADES IN ROME
(Pa)/Aug 26, 1911; p. 541
(Pa)/Jul 5, 1913; p. 47
MONUMENTS OF PISA

(Pa)/May 8, 1915; p. 901
MONUMENTS OF UPPER EGYPT
(Pa)/Mar 7, 1914; p. 1236
MOON FOR HER LOVE
(Gau)/Dec 4, 1909; p. 798
MOONLIGHT (Ec)/Aug 15, 1914; p. 961
MOON'S GIFT, THE
(KO)/Oct 30, 1908; p. 338
MOONSHINE AND LOVE
(Po)/Nov 19, 1910; p. 1179
MOONSHINE MAID AND THE MAN, THE
(Vi)/Dec 19, 1914; p. 1680
MOONSHINE MOLLY
(Maj)/Aug 15, 1914; p. 961
MOONSHINER, THE
(Fr)/Sep 27, 1913; p. 1394
MOONSHINERS, THE
(Re)/Nov 25, 1911; p. 638
(Ka)/Oct 3, 1914; p. 64
MOONSHINER'S DAUGHTER, THE
(Ka)/Apr 4, 1908; p. 300
(Ne)/Sep 17, 1910; p. 632
(Lu)/Oct 26, 1912; p. 342
(Maj)/Mar 21, 1914; p. 1526
MOONSHINER'S HEART, A
(SA)/Aug 10, 1912; p. 545
MOONSHINER'S LAST STAND, THE
(Pa)/Apr 12, 1913; p. 163
MOONSHINER'S MISTAKE, THE
(Ka)/Aug 9, 1913; p. 637
MOONSHINERS' TASK, THE
(Com)/Sep 7, 1912; p. 977
MOONSHINER'S TRAIL, THE
(Ch)/Nov 18, 1911; pp 551-52
MOONSHINER'S WIFE, A
(Lu)/Apr 5, 1913; p. 48
MOONSHINES (MnA)/Apr 17, 1915; p. 392
MOONSTONE, THE
(Sel)/Jun 19, 1909; p. 834
(Wor)/Jun 26, 1915; p. 2110
MOONSTONE OF FEZ, THE
(Vi)/Jul 25, 1914; p. 572
MOONSTRUCK (Pa)/Apr 17, 1909; p. 477
MOORISH BRIDE, THE (Cin)/Feb 17, 1912;
p. 559/Mar 23, 1912; p. 1063
MOORISH GRANADA
(Pa)/Jul 24, 1915; p. 651
MORAL COWARD, A
(Po)/Jul 29, 1911; p. 213
MORALS OF MARCUS, THE
(FP)/Jan 30, 1915; p. 681
MORE AND MORE (Emp)/Feb 6,1915; p.829
MORE OF BETTY'S PRANKS
(Pa)/Aug 6, 1910; p. 296
MORE THAN FRIENDS
(Bio)/Aug 14, 1915; p. 1160
MORE THAN HIS DUTY
(Ed)/Oct 15, 1910; p. 874

MORE THAN QUEEN
(Pa)/Nov 28, 1914; p. 1245
MORGAN'S TREASURE
(Po)/Jul 5, 1913; p. 50
MORMONS, THE (Am)/Feb 3, 1912; p. 393
MORNING AFTER, THE
(Gau)/Aug 14, 1909; p. 225
MORO FISH DRIVE AT JOLO, A
(Sel)/Aug 2, 1913; p. 536
MOROS, THE (Pa)/Apr 12, 1913; p. 165
MORTGAGE, THE (Me)/Feb 10, 1912; p.482
MORTGAGE ON HIS DAUGHTER, A
(Lko)/Oct 9, 1915; p. 254
MORTMAIN (Vi)/Sep 4, 1915; p. 1665
MOSES SELLS A COLLAR BUTTON
(Lu)/Oct 26, 1907; p. 543
MOSCOW UNDER WATER
(KO)/Aug 15, 1908; p. 127
MOSLEM LADY'S DAY, A
(Ec)/Oct 19, 1912; p. 244
MOSQUITO, THE (CGP)/Aug 3, 1912; p.445
**MOSS COVERED RUINS ON THE ISLE
OF WIGHT** (UE)/Sep 2, 1911; p. 628
MOTH, THE (Th)/Sep 9, 1911; p. 718
(Lu)/Feb 7, 1914; p. 676
MOTH AND THE FLAME, THE
(Me)/Sep 7, 1912; p. 975
(Pa)/Jan 10, 1914; p. 173
MOTHER (Th)/Sep 17, 1910; p. 634
(Re)/Apr 13, 1912; p. 137
(Rex)/Dec 28, 1912; p. 1293
(Pa)/Mar 8, 1913; p. 996
(Po)/Sep 13, 1913; p. 1177
(Wor)/Sep 26, 1914; pp 1778, 1789
MOTHER, THE (Sel)/May 6, 1911; p. 1019
MOTHER AND CHILD
(Imp)/Oct 29, 1910; p. 998
MOTHER AND DAUGHTER
(Po)/Jul 9, 1910; p. 85
MOTHER AND THE GIRLS
(Ed)/Feb 10, 1912; p. 482
MOTHER AND WIFE
(Ed)/May 9, 1914; p. 802
MOTHER GOOSE (Ed)/Jul 31, 1909; p. 162
MOTHER HEART, THE
(Sel)/Aug 15, 1914; p. 960
MOTHER-IN-LAW ARRIVES
(GN)/Nov 26, 1910; p. 1239
MOTHER-IN-LAW AT WHITE CITY
(KO)/Jun 22, 1907; p. 252
**MOTHER-IN-LAW BREAKS ALL
RECORDS** (Pa)/Dec 12, 1908;
pp 486-87/Dec 19, 1908; p. 500
**MOTHER-IN-LAW, SON-IN-LAW, AND
TANGLEFOOT** (It)/Jul 30, 1910; p. 245
**MOTHER-IN-LAW'S DAY IN THE
COUNTRY** (UE)/Mar 13, 1909; p. 304
MOTHER INSTINCT, THE

(Bio)/Jan 17, 1914; p. 288
(Vi)/Nov 27, 1915; p. 1663
MOTORING (Th)/Jun 24, 1911; p. 1455
MOTORING AMONG THE CLIFFS AND
  GORGES OF FRANCE
  (Gau)/Jul 16, 1910; p. 142
MOTORING UNDER DIFFICULTIES
  (Sel)/Oct 19,1907; p.526/Nov 21,1908; p.398
MOULDING, THE (Vi)/Jul 26, 1913; p. 428
MOUNT PILATUS RAILWAY
  (KO)/Sep 7, 1907; p. 428
MOUNT ST. MICKEL
  (Pa)/Aug 23, 1913; p. 843
MOUNTAIN BLIZZARD, A
  (Ed)/Mar 26, 1910; p. 467
MOUNTAIN DAISY, THE
  (Ne)/Jun 15, 1912; p. 1027
MOUNTAIN DEW (Ka)/Nov 16, 1912; p. 659
MOUNTAIN DORE, FRANCE, THE
  (Ecl)/Jan 23, 1915; p. 517
MOUNTAIN FEUD (Sel)/Nov 21, 1908; p.398
MOUNTAIN GIRL, THE
  (Maj)/Jul 24, 1915; p. 650
MOUNTAIN GIRL'S SELF-SACRIFICE,
  THE (Ne)/Dec 28, 1912; p. 1292
MOUNTAIN GOAT, A
  (WF)/Nov 14, 1914; p. 933
MOUNTAIN JUSTICE
  (Rex)/Aug 21, 1915; p. 1318
MOUNTAIN LAKE, THE
  (UE)/Jun 18, 1910; p. 1049
MOUNTAIN LAW (Rex)/Apr 25, 1914; p.518
MOUNTAIN LAW, THE
  (Lu)/Nov 14, 1914; p. 932
MOUNTAIN MAID, A
  (Ed)/Dec 24, 1910; p. 1478
MOUNTAIN MARY (Am)/Jul 17, 1915; p.486
MOUNTAIN MELODY, A
  (Rex)/Jun 26, 1915; p. 2097
MOUNTAIN RAT, THE
  (Re)/May 23, 1914; p. 1123
MOUNTAIN TRAGEDY, A
  (Re)/Jan 27, 1912; p. 304
  (Ka)/Jan 11, 1913; p. 158
MOUNTAIN TRAITOR, THE
  (Ec)/Dec 19, 1914; p. 1681
MOUNTAIN WIFE, A
  (Me)/Nov 26, 1910; p. 1236
MOUNTAIN WITCH, THE
  (Ka)/Mar 8, 1913; p. 996
MOUNTAINEERS, THE
  (Lu)/Apr 4, 1908; p. 298
  (Vi)/Dec 5, 1908; p. 448
  (Ed)/Feb 1, 1913; p. 464
MOUNTAINEER'S HONOR, A
  (Bio)/Dec 4, 1909; pp 799-800
MOUNTAINEER'S REVENGE, THE (Lu)/
  Oct 30,1908; pp 344-45/Dec 12,1908; p. 476

MOUNTAINEER'S SON
  (Pa)/May 16, 1908; p. 445
MOUNTEBANK'S DAUGHTER, THE
  (Lu)/Jan 4, 1913; p. 51
MOUNTEBANK'S SON, THE
  (Pa)/Oct 2, 1909; p. 452
MOUNTEBANK'S WATCHCASE
  (Pa)/Nov 13, 1909; p. 684
MOUNTED OFFICER FLYNN
  (Sel)/Dec 6, 1913; p. 1151
MOUSE AND THE LION, THE
  (Vi)/Mar 29, 1913; p. 1336
MOUSTACHES AND BOMBS
  (SA)/Oct 2, 1915; p. 78
MOVIE FANS (Fal)/May 15, 1915; p. 1072
MOVIE NUT, A (Ba)/Oct 23, 1915; p. 622
MOVIN' PITCHERS
  (Sel)/Nov 22, 1913; p. 868
MOVING PICTURE COWBOY, THE
  (Sel)/Oct 17, 1914; p. 336
MOVING PICTURE GIRL, THE
  (Exc)/Apr 26, 1913; p. 382
MOZART'S LAST REQUIEM
  (Gau)/Sep 25, 1909; p. 416
MR. A. JONAH (Sel)/Apr 30, 1910; p. 689
MR. AND MRS. INNOCENCE ABROAD
  (Imp)/Dec 20, 1913; p. 1413
MR. AND MRS. JOLLYWOOD GO
  TANDEMING (Pa)/Mar 14, 1908; p. 217
MR. AND MRS. SUSPICIOUS
  (Lu)/Dec 23, 1911; p. 989
MR. BARNES OF NEW YORK
  (Vi)/May 2, 1914; p. 651
MR. BAUMGARTEN IS ELECTED DEPUTY
  (Amb)/Aug 19, 1911; p. 465
MR. BEACH GOES CALLING
  (Bio)/Aug 19, 1911; p. 464
MR. BIXBIE'S DILEMNA
  (Vi)/Aug 7, 1915; p. 996
MR. BLINK OF BOHEMIA
  (Vi)/Jun 26, 1915; p. 2095
MR. BOLTER'S INFATUATION
  (Vi)/Apr 6, 1912; pp 40-41
MR. BOOZER GETS A FRIGHT
  (Pa)/Jun 27, 1908; p. 547
MR. BRAGG A FUGITIVE
  (Bio)/Oct 21, 1911; p. 209
MR. BROWN HAS A TILE LOOSE
  (KO)/Jun 27, 1908; p. 549
MR. BUMPTIOUS, DETECTIVE
  (Ed)/Mar 4, 1911; p. 483
MR. BUMPTIOUS ON BIRDS
  (Ed)/Jun 18, 1910; p. 1048
MR. BUTTINSKY (Lu)/Aug 7, 1909; p. 195
MR. BUTTLES (SA)/Mar 13, 1915; p. 1611/
  Mar 27, 1915; p. 1932
MR. CARLSON OF ARIZONA
  (Lu)/Apr 24, 1915; p. 556

MR. DALY'S WEDDING DAY (Ed)/Jan 9,
1915; pp 220-21/Feb 6, 1915; p. 827
MR. DIPPY DIPPED
(SA)/Sep 20, 1913; p. 1283
MR. DRAWEE (GN)/May 30, 1908; p. 479
MR. FADDLEAWAY IS ON STRIKE
(Ec)/Feb 25, 1911; p. 432
MR. FARMAN'S AIRSHIP
(KO)/Jun 6, 1908; p. 496
MR. FATTY IS FURNISHED WITH GOOD
LUNGS (Amb)/Dec 14, 1912; p. 1082
MR. FATTY'S ADVENTURES
(Amb)/Jan 13, 1912; p. 126
MR. FIXER (Key)/Nov 30, 1912; p. 878
MR. FORD'S TEMPER
(Vi)/Mar 8, 1913; p. 996
MR. FOUR FLUSH
(Sel)/Nov 26, 1910; p. 1238
MR. FUZZ (Pa)/Aug 29, 1908; p. 162
MR. GASTON OF PARIS
(Pa)/Dec 6, 1913; p. 1150
MR. GAY AND MRS.
(Bio)/Dec 21, 1907; pp 691-92
MR. GREX OF MONTE CARLO
(Las)/Dec 25, 1915; pp 2381-82
MR. GROUCH AT THE SEASHORE
(Bio)/Sep 14, 1912; p. 1074
MR. HADLEY'S UNCLE
(Ko)/Dec 19, 1914; p. 1680
MR. HORATIO SPARKINS
(Vi)/May 24, 1913; p. 812
MR. HUBBY'S WIFE
(SA)/Dec 14, 1912; p. 1080
MR. INQUISITIVE
(SA)/Aug 24, 1907; pp 394, 397
(Lu)/May 29,1909; p. 713/Jul 29,1911; p. 211
MR. ISAACS AND THE SPORTING MICE
(CM)/Aug 28, 1909; p. 283
MR. JINKS BUYS A DRESS
(Lu)/Apr 5, 1913; p. 47
MR. JONAH GETS A LITTLE DUST IN
HIS EYES (Pa)/Mar 6, 1909; p. 269
MR. JONES' BURGLAR
(Bio)/Aug 21, 1909; p. 255
MR. JONES HAS A CARD PARTY
(Bio)/Feb 20, 1909; p. 203
MR. MEESON'S WILL
(Th)/Oct 30a, 1915; p. 968
MR. MINTERN'S MISADVENTURES
(Vi)/Apr 26, 1913; p. 380
MR. MIX AT THE MARDI GRAS
(Sel)/May 7, 1910; p. 736
MR. MUGGINS HAS HIS SEWING DONE
(GN)/Feb 11, 1911; p. 316
MR. NEARSIGHT'S MARRIAGE
(Ec)/Apr 22, 1911; p. 901
MR. NEWCOMB'S NECKTIE
(Ed)/Jun 14, 1913; p. 1135

MR. NOAD'S ADLESS DAY
(Jo)/Oct 31, 1914; p. 642
MR. NOSY BARKER
(It)/Dec 18, 1909; p. 882
MR. PALLETT GOES LANDSCAPING
(UE)/Mar 27, 1909; p. 368
MR. PEPPERIE TEMPER
(Ka)/Feb 27, 1915; p. 1287
MR. PHYSICAL CULTURE'S SURPRISE
PARTY (Vi)/Jun 26, 1909; p. 873
MR. PICKWICK'S PREDICAMENT
(Ed)/Sep 7, 1912; p. 975
MR. PYNHEAD GOES OUT FOR A GOOD
TIME (Pa)/Jan 23, 1909; p. 94
MR. RYHE REFORMS
(SA)/Aug 23, 1913; p. 843
MR. SADMAN'S CURE
(RR)/Dec 25, 1909; p. 922
MR. SANTA CLAUS (Vi)/Jan 2, 1915; p. 76
MR. SHORTSIGHTED GOES SHRIMPING
(Pa)/Feb 15, 1908; p. 124
MR. "SILENT" HASKINS
(KB)/Feb 20, 1915; p. 1141
MR. SLEEPY HEAD (KO)/Jan 18, 1908;
p. 47/Jan 16, 1909; p. 93
MR. SMITH, BARBER
(Imp)/Apr 20, 1912; p. 231
MR. SMITH, THE NEW RECRUIT
(KO)/Jul 11, 1908; p. 36
MR. SMITH'S DIFFICULTIES IN THE SHOE
STORE (KO)/May 2, 1908; p. 401
MR. SNIFFKINS' WIDOW
(Ed)/Mar 21, 1914; p. 1524
MR. SOAKER AT THE SEASIDE
(Pa)/Jan 2, 1909; p. 10
MR. SOFTHEAD HAS A GOOD TIME
(Pa)/Jul 25, 1908; p. 70
MR. SPRIGS BUYS A DOG
(Bio)/Aug 23, 1913; p. 842
MR. STUBBS' PEN (Lu)/Jan 30, 1915; p. 671
MR. SWELL IN THE COUNTRY
(Cen)/Jun 25, 1910; p. 1102
MR. TIBBS' CINDERELLA
(SA)/Aug 10, 1912; p. 546
MR. TOOT'S TOOTH
(Ed)/Oct 18, 1913; p. 263
MR. UP'S TRIP TRIPPED UP
(SA)/Nov 30, 1912; p. 876
MR. WALLACK'S WALLET
(Ko)/Jul 17, 1915; p. 486
MR. WALLINGFORD'S WALLET
(Re)/Jun 28, 1913; p. 1360
MR. WHOOPS, THE DETECTIVE
(Com)/Jan 20, 1912; p.205
MR. WISE, INVESTIGATOR
(SA)/Aug 5, 1911; p. 293
MR. X AND THE UNFORTUNATE HEIRESS
(Lux)/Aug 3, 1912; p. 446

MUTT AND JEFF JOIN THE OPERA
  (Ne)/Oct 28, 1911; p. 292
**MUTT AND JEFF MAKE THE FEATHERS
  FLY** (Ne)/Dec 23, 1911; p. 990
MUTT AND JEFF SPEND A QUIET DAY
  (Ne)/Oct 21, 1911; p. 209
MUTT AND JEFF'S GREAT SCHEME
  (Ne)/Dec 9, 1911; p. 819
MUTUAL UNDERSTANDING, A
  (Ed)/Sep 6, 1913; p. 1068
MUTUAL MONOGRAPHS (Re)
  No.1/Jan 30, 1915; p. 672
MUTUAL WEEKLY (Mut)
  No.97/Nov 21, 1914; p. 1076
  No.103/Jan 2, 1915; p. 77
  No.104/Jan 9, 1915; p. 221
  No.105/Jan 16, 1915; p. 369
  No.1/Jan 23, 1915; p. 516
  No.2/Jan 30, 1915; p. 672
  No.4/Feb 13, 1915; p. 985
  No.7/Mar 6, 1915; p. 1448
  No.8/Mar 20, 1915; p. 1764
  No.9/Mar 20, 1915; p. 1765
  No.12/Apr 10, 1915; p. 236
  No.15/May 1, 1915; p. 728
  No.16/May 8, 1915; p. 900
  No.17/May 15, 1915; p. 1072
  No.18/May 22, 1915; p. 1260
  No.20/Jun 5, 1915; p. 1605
  No.21/Jun 12, 1915; p. 1777
  No.23/Jun 26, 1915; p. 2096
  No.24/Jul 3, 1915; p. 65
  No.25/Jul 10, 1915; p. 308
  No.26/Jul 17, 1915; p. 486
  No.27/Jul 24, 1915; p. 650
  No.28/Jul 31, 1915; p. 817
  No.30/Aug 14, 1915; p. 1161
  No.31/Aug 21, 1915; p. 1317
  No.33/Sep 4, 1915; p. 1644
  No.34/Sep 11, 1915; p. 1833
  No.35/Sep 18, 1915; p. 1996
  No.37/Oct 2, 1915; p. 79
  No.38/Oct 9, 1915; p. 253
  No.39/Oct 16, 1915; p. 440
  No.41/Oct 30, 1915; p. 792
  No.42/Oct 30a, 1915; p. 968
  No.43/Nov 6, 1915; p. 1139
  No.45/Nov 20, 1915; p. 1500
  No.46/Nov 27, 1915; p. 1604
  No.47/Dec 4, 1915; p. 1853
  No.48/Dec 11, 1915; p. 2032
  No.49/Dec 18, 1915; p. 2203
MY BABY (Bio)/Nov 30, 1912; p. 877
MY BABY'S VOICE (Th)/Apr 6, 1912; p. 43
MY BEST GIRL (Mto)/Jul 3, 1915; pp 76-77
MY BROTHER, AGOSTINO
  (Lu)/Dec 2, 1911; p. 725
MY BRUDDER SYLVEST

  (Cry)/Dec 20, 1913; p. 1413
MY CABBY WIFE (KO)/May 9, 1908; p. 423
MY DAUGHTER (Pa)/May 20, 1911; p. 1141
MY FRIEND, THE DOCTOR
  (Sel)/Oct 15, 1910; p. 876
MY FRIEND, THE DUMMY
  (Lu)/Apr 17, 1909; pp 476-77
MY HERO (Bio)/Dec 28, 1912; p. 1292/
  Nov 20, 1915; p. 1503/Dec 11, 1915; p. 2031
MY LADY HIGH AND MIGHTY (Vic)/
  Jan 2, 1915; p. 81/Jan 16, 1915; p. 370
MY LADY IDLENESS (Vi)/Jul 26,1913;p.429
MY LADY'S BOOT (Maj)/May 17,1913;p.705
MY LIFE REMEMBRANCES OF A DAY
  (Amb)/Apr 16, 1910; p.600
MY LORD IN LIVERY
  (Ed)/Dec 18, 1909; p. 881
MY LOST ONE (Vi)/Aug 7, 1915; p. 1016
MY MADONNA (Pop)/Oct 23, 1915; p. 627
MY MAID IS TOO SLOW (Ec)/May 7, 1910;
  p. 738/May 14, 1910; p. 786
MY MILLINER'S BILL
  (Ed)/Mar 19, 1910; p. 426
MY MOTHER'S IRISH SHAWLS
  (Po)/Feb 21, 1914; p. 948
MY OFFICIAL WIFE (Vi)/Jun 6,1914;p.1390
MY OLD DUTCH
  (Vi)/Aug 19, 1911; pp 446-47
  (Uni)/Nov 13, 1915; p. 1322
MY PRAIRIE FLOWER
  (Me)/Mar 11, 1911; p. 540
MY PRINCESS (Lu)/Mar 23, 1912; p. 1062
MY SON IS GUILTY
  (It)/Feb 11, 1911; p. 316
MY TOMBOY GIRL (Vic)/Aug 7, 1915; p. 998
MY WATCH IS SLOW
  (Pa)/Mar 14, 1908; p. 218
MY WIFE'S AWAY (Ko)/Feb 14,1914; p.810
MY WIFE'S AWAY - HURRAH! (Ec)/
  Sep 21, 1912; p. 1162/Sep 28, 1912; p. 1278
MY WIFE'S BONNET
  (Sel)/Oct 26, 1912; p. 343
MY WIFE'S DOG (FIT)/Oct 3, 1908; p. 263
MY WIFE'S HAT (Ec)/Jan 28, 1911; p. 197
MY WIFE'S GONE TO THE COUNTRY
  (NYM)/Aug 21, 1909; p. 255/
  Sep 11, 1909; p. 345
MYER'S MISTAKE (St)/Oct 17, 1914; p. 337
MYSTERIES OF SOULS, THE
  (GN)/Apr 6, 1912; pp 29-30
**MYSTERIES OF THE GRAND HOTEL,
  THE** (Ka)
  No.1/Aug 7, 1915; p. 996
  No.3/Aug 21, 1915; p. 1317
  No.4/Aug 28, 1915; p. 1480
  No.5/Aug 14, 1915; p. 1174
  No.6/Sep 11, 1915; p. 1833
  No.7/Sep 18, 1915; p. 1995

No.8/Sep 25, 1915; p. 2176
No.10/Oct 9, 1915; p. 253
No.11/Sep 25,1915;p.2194/Oct 16,1915;p.440
No.12/Dec 9, 1915; pp 282-83/
 Oct 23, 1915; p. 620
MYSTERIOUS AIRSHIP, THE
 (FI)/Feb 13, 1915; p. 986
MYSTERIOUS ARMOR, THE
 (Pa)/Nov 9, 1907; pp 583-84
MYSTERIOUS AUTO, THE
 (Mil)/Oct 5, 1912; p. 42
MYSTERIOUS BEAUTY, THE
 (Sel)/Oct 31, 1914; p. 640
MYSTERIOUS BLACK BOX, THE
 (Sel)/Dec 5, 1914; p. 1383
MYSTERIOUS CARD, THE
 (Imp)/Apr 19, 1913; p. 281
MYSTERIOUS CASE, A
 (UE)/Jul 27, 1912; p. 343
MYSTERIOUS CIGARETTE, THE
 (Gau)/May 4, 1912; p. 427
MYSTERIOUS CONTRAGRAO, THE
 (GS)/Apr 10, 1915; p. 238
MYSTERIOUS CORRESPONDENT, THE
 Jan 9, 1909; p. 37
MYSTERIOUS EYES, THE
 (Am)/Sep 6, 1913; p. 1070
MYSTERIOUS FLAMES
 (Pa)/Jun 27, 1908; p. 547
MYSTERIOUS FLOWERS, THE
 (Lux)/Aug 17, 1912; p. 674
MYSTERIOUS GALLANT, THE
 (Sel)/Feb 24, 1912; p. 690
MYSTERIOUS HAND, THE
 (Lu)/Jul 19, 1913; p. 320
 (Bi)/Oct 31, 1914; p. 642
MYSTERIOUS KNIGHT (Pa)/Oct 24, 1908;
 p. 327/Oct 30, 1908; p. 339
MYSTERIOUS LEOPARD LADY, THE
 (GS)/Mar 28, 1914; p. 1682
MYSTERIOUS LODGER, THE
 (Vi)/Sep 12, 1914; p. 1511
MYSTERIOUS LUGGAGE, THE
 (Ec)/Nov 27, 1909; p. 759
MYSTERIOUS MAN, THE
 (Cin)/Aug 30, 1913; p. 940
MYSTERIOUS MR. DAVEY, THE (Vi)/
 Dec 5, 1914; p. 1394/Dec 19, 1914; p. 1679
MYSTERIOUS MYSTERY, THE
 (Vic)/Sep 19, 1914; p. 1646
MYSTERIOUS PACKAGE, THE
 (Ed)/Jul 11, 1914; p. 255
MYSTERIOUS PHONOGRAPH, THE
 (Lu)/May 2, 1908; p. 403
MYSTERIOUS PHOTOGRAPH
 Dec 12, 1908; p. 477
MYSTERIOUS ROSE, THE
 (GS)/Nov 28, 1914; p. 1233

MYSTERIOUS SHOT, THE
 (Re)/Apr 18, 1914; p. 362
MYSTERIOUS STRANGER, THE
 (UE)/Dec 16, 1911; p. 903
 (SA)/Jun 28, 1913; p. 1359
MYSTERIOUS TRACK, THE
 (Amb)/Mar 12, 1910; p. 385
MYSTERIOUS WAY, THE
 (Sel)/Dec 27, 1913; p. 1543
MYSTERY, A (Po)/Mar 16, 1912; p. 963
MYSTERY CAVE, THE
 (Ne)/Feb 22, 1913; p. 781
MYSTERY LADY (Dom)/Feb 14,1914; p.810
MYSTERY OF A TAXICAB, THE
 (Jo)/Jan 17, 1914; p. 290
MYSTERY OF BEAUFORT GRANGE, THE
 (Lux)/Nov 25, 1911; p. 638
MYSTERY OF BRAYTON COURT, THE
 (Vi)/Nov 14, 1914; p. 932
MYSTERY OF BUFFALO GAP, THE
 (Fr)/Mar 14, 1914; p. 1386
MYSTERY OF CARTER BREEN, THE
 (Cen)/Dec 25, 1915; p. 2390
MYSTERY OF DEAD MAN'S ISLE, THE
 (Sel)/Jul 17, 1915; p. 485
MYSTERY OF EAGLE CLIFF, THE
 (Th)/Oct 16, 1915; p. 440
MYSTERY OF EDWIN DROOD, THE
 (Wor)/Oct 24,1914;p.501
MYSTERY OF 15 HILL STREET, THE
 (FRA)/Apr 4, 1914; p. 59
MYSTERY OF GRANDFATHER'S CLOCK,
 THE (Ka)/Nov 23, 1912; p. 766
MYSTERY OF GRAYSON HALL, THE
 (Ec)/Oct 31, 1914; p. 643
MYSTERY OF GREEN PARK, THE
 (UE)/Jul 4, 1914; p. 66
MYSTERY OF HENRI VILLARD, THE
 (Bio)/Aug 21, 1915; p. 1324
MYSTERY OF LONELY GULCH, THE
 (Pa)/Nov 5, 1910; p.1056
MYSTERY OF MARY, THE
 (Vi)/Aug 14, 1915; p. 1161
MYSTERY OF ROOM 17, THE
 (WF)/Aug 1, 1914; p. 706
MYSTERY OF ROOM 643, THE
 (SA)/May 23, 1914; p. 1117
MYSTERY OF ROOM 13, THE (Ed)/Oct 30,
 1915; p. 813/Nov 6, 1915; p. 1139
MYSTERY OF ST. MARTIN'S BRIDGE,
 THE (Fid)/Feb 7, 1914; p.684
MYSTERY OF TEMPLE COURT
 (Vi)/Apr 2, 1910; p. 508
MYSTERY OF THE DOVER EXPRESS,
 THE (Ed)/Jan 17, 1914; p. 289
MYSTERY OF THE EMPTY ROOM, THE
 (Vi)/Dec 11, 1915; p. 2031
MYSTERY OF THE FAST MAIL (UE)/

May 16, 1914; p. 974/Jun 6, 1914; p. 1409
MYSTERY OF THE FATAL PEARL, THE
(Kio)/Feb 14, 1914; p.789
MYSTERY OF THE HAUNTED HOTEL,
THE (Th)/Oct 25, 1913; p. 381
MYSTERY OF THE HINDOO IMAGE, THE
(Maj)/Aug 8, 1914; p. 838
MYSTERY OF THE LAMA CONVENT
(GN)/Feb 12, 1910; p. 215
MYSTERY OF THE LOCKED ROOM,
THE (Rex)/Nov 20, 1915; p. 1501
MYSTERY OF THE LOST CAT, THE
(Sol)/Apr 26, 1913; p. 382
MYSTERY OF THE MAN WHO SLEPT,
THE (Rex)/Feb 27, 1915; p. 1289
MYSTERY OF THE MILK, THE
(Bio)/Jan 17, 1914; p. 289
MYSTERY OF THE MOUNTAINS
(Pa)/Jul 18, 1908; p. 51
MYSTERY OF THE MOUNTAINS, A
(Bio)/Nov 6, 1915; p. 1139
MYSTERY OF THE POISON POOL, THE
(PP)/Sep 5,1914; p.1377/Sep 12 1914; p.1517
MYSTERY OF THE SEAVIEW HOTEL, THE
(Rex)/Dec 5, 1914; p. 1385
MYSTERY OF THE SEVEN CHESTS, THE
(Sel)/Dec 19, 1914; p. 1680
MYSTERY OF THE SILENT DEATH, THE
(SA)/May 8, 1915; p. 899
MYSTERY OF THE SLEEPER TRUNK, THE
(Ka)/Oct 16, 1909; p. 530
MYSTERY OF THE SLEEPING DEATH,
THE (Ka)/Sep 12, 1914; pp 1487-88
MYSTERY OF THE STOLEN CHILD, THE
(Vi)/Apr 26, 1913; p. 380
MYSTERY OF THE STOLEN JEWELS, THE
(Vi)/May 3, 1913; p. 487
MYSTERY OF THE TAPESTRY ROOM,
THE (Uni)/Aug 14, 1915; p. 1178
MYSTERY OF THE TEA DANSANT, THE
(Ka)/Feb 13, 1914; p. 988
MYSTERY OF THE THRONE ROOM, THE
(GS)/Jan 9, 1915; p. 222
MYSTERY OF THE TORN NOTE, THE
(Lu)/Nov 26, 1910; p. 1236
MYSTERY OF THE WHITE CAR, THE
(GS)/Apr 11, 1914; p. 214
MYSTERY OF THE YELLOW ASTER MINE
(Bi)/Aug 30, 1913; p. 961
MYSTERY OF THE YELLOW ROOM, THE
(UF)/Sep 20, 1913;p.1270
MYSTERY OF THE YELLOW SUNBONNET,
THE (Ka)/Dec 26, 1914; p. 1841
MYSTERY OF WALL STREET, A
(Th)/Feb 22, 1913; p. 781
MYSTERY OF WEST SEDGWICK, THE
(Ed)/Aug 9, 1913; p. 619
MYSTERY OF WICKHAM HALL, THE

(Po)/Jul 4, 1914; p. 66
MYSTERY WOMAN, THE
(Bi)/Jan 30, 1915; pp 673-74
MYSTIC BALL, THE
(Sel)/Sep 25, 1915; p. 2176
MYSTIC JEWEL, THE
(Maj)/Jul 31, 1915; p. 817
MYSTIC MANIPULATIONS
(Kin)/Feb 15, 1913; p. 681
MYSTIC WELL, THE
(Ufs)/Jun 12, 1915; p. 1778
MYSTIFIED PIERROT, THE
(CGP)/Jul 6, 1912; p. 43
MYTH OF JAMASHA, THE
(Am)/May 18, 1912; p. 630
MYTHICAL MAID OF JAMASHA PASS,
THE (Am)/Apr 27, 1912; p. 319

NABBED (Bi)/May 1, 1915; p. 730
NAIDRA, THE DREAM WOMAN
(Th)/Dec 12, 1914; p. 1524
NAKED TRUTH, THE
(GK)/Jun 20, 1914; p. 1703
NAMELESS FEAR, THE
(Lu)/Feb 20, 1915; p. 1139
NAMING OF THE RAWHIDE QUEEN,
THE (SA)/Dec 13, 1913; p. 1279
NAMING THE BABY
(Cin)/Apr 13, 1912; p. 136
NAN O' THE BACKWOODS (Lu)/Oct 23,
1915; p. 630/Oct 30, 1915; p. 792
NAN OF THE WOODS
(Sel)/Sep 20, 1913; p. 1283
NANCY'S HUSBAND
(Be)/Jun 20, 1914; p. 1690
NANCY'S WEDDING TRIP
(Gau)/Dec 17, 1910; p. 1416
NAN'S DIPLOMACY
(Lu)/Mar 11, 1911; p. 542
NAN'S VICTORY
(Sel)/Aug 29, 1914; pp 1240-41
NANTES AND ITS SURROUNDINGS
(UE)/Dec 3, 1910; p. 1298
NAPATIA, THE GREEK SINGER
(SA)/May 11, 1912; p. 528
NAPOLEON (Pa)/Jul 9, 1910; p. 85
(Ecl)/Mar 28, 1914; p. 1658
NAPOLEON, THE MAN OF DESTINY
(Vi)/Apr 17, 1909; p. 477
NAPOLEON AND PRINCESS HAZFELD
(It)/Nov 20, 1909; p. 721
NAPOLEON AND THE ENGLISH SAILOR
(KO)/Aug 29,1908; p.160/Jan 16,1909; p.69
NAPOLEON IN 1814
(Gau)/Feb 25, 1911; p. 430
NAPOLEON WHIFFLES, ESQ.
(Pa)/Aug 30, 1913; p. 961
NAPOLEON'S LUCK STONE

NEWLY WEDS, THE
(Bio)/Mar 12, 1910; p. 384
NEWLYWEDS, THE
(Ec)/Mar 22, 1913; p. 1221
NEWLYWEDS' DILEMNA, THE
(Ne)/May 16, 1914; p. 969
NEWLYWEDS' FIRST MEAL
(Sel)/Jan 25, 1908; p. 64
NEWS ITEM, A (Cry)/Sep 20,1913; p.1285
NEWSBOY TENOR, THE
(Sel)/Oct 10, 1914; p. 188
NEWSBOY'S LUCK, A
(Lu)/Dec 2, 1911; p. 724
NEWSPAPER ERROR, A
(Po)/May 7, 1910; p. 738
NEWSPAPER NEMESIS, A
(Th)/Mar 6, 1915; p. 1448
NEXT (Maj)/Jan 27, 1912; p. 305
NEXT GENERATION, THE
(Vi)/Nov 8, 1913; p. 612
NEXT IN COMMAND, THE
(Pas)/Aug 22, 1914; p. 1107
NIAGARA, THE BEAUTIFUL
(Th)/May 25, 1912; p. 730
NIAGARA FALLS (Imp)/Dec 30, 1911;p.1072
(Ed)/Feb 17, 1912; p. 581
(Pa)/Jun 29, 1912; p.1227
(Ch)/Aug 31, 1912; p. 882
(Kin)/Mar 15,1913; p.1106
(Vi)/Feb 28, 1914; p.1087
(Ed)/Nov 13, 1915; p.1311
NIAGARA FALLS IN WINTER
(KO)/Jul 11, 1908; p. 34
NIAGARA HONEYMOON, A
(Th)/Jan 27, 1912; p. 305
NIAGARA IN WINTER DRESS
(Vi)/Sep 11, 1909; p. 347
NICA (Pa)/Jan 3, 1914; p. 48
NICE (KO)/Jul 18, 1908; p. 52
NICE NURSEY (Lu)/Jul 11, 1914; p. 255
NICHOLAS NICKLEBY (Th)/Mar 9, 1912;
p. 858/Apr 6, 1912; p. 42
NICHOLS ON A VACATION, THE
(Imp)/Jun 18, 1910; p. 1049
NICK CARTER (Pa)/Jan 16, 1909; p. 70
NICK CARTER AS AN ACROBAT
(Ec)/Mar 12, 1910; p. 383
NICK CARTER'S DOUBLE
(Pa)/Feb 6, 1909; p. 145
NICK WINTER AND THE LOST PRINCE
(Ecl)/Aug 29, 1914; p. 1243
NICK WINTER AND THE MASKED
THIEVES (Pa)/Jun 19, 1915; p. 1941
NICK WINTER TURNS A TRICK
(Pa)/Sep 9, 1911; p. 716
NICOTINE CONSPIRACY, A
(Lu)/Dec 16, 1911; p. 903
NIECE AND THE CHORUS LADY, THE

(Ed)/Jun 10, 1911; p. 1316
NIEDA (Be)/Oct 17, 1914; p. 337
NIGGARD, THE (Maj)/Nov 21, 1914; p.1076
NIGHT ALARM, THE
(War)/Jan 30, 1909; p. 120
NIGHT AND A DAY, A
(Ka)/May 13, 1911; p. 1080
NIGHT AT THE CLUB, A
(Cry)/Jan 18, 1913; p. 266
NIGHT AT THE INN, A
(Ed)/Jan 31, 1914; p. 543
NIGHT BEFORE CHRISTMAS, THE
(Vi)/Dec 28, 1912; p. 1292
NIGHT BIRDS (Pa)/Jun 7, 1913; p. 1030
NIGHT CAP, THE (Sol)/Jan 21, 1911; p. 144
NIGHT GIVEN OVER TO REVELRY, A
(SA)/May 15, 1915; p. 1071
NIGHT HAWKS (SA)/Jul 25, 1914; p. 572
NIGHT HERDER, THE
(Sel)/Dec 2, 1911; p. 725
NIGHT IN KENTUCKY, A
(SA)/May 1, 1915; p. 727
NIGHT IN NEW JERSEY, A
(Ka)/Feb 6, 1915; p. 827
NIGHT IN OLD SPAIN, A
(Lu)/Nov 20, 1915; p. 1499
NIGHT IN THE JUNGLE, A
(Sel)/Apr 17, 1915; p. 392
NIGHT IN THE SHOW, A
(SA)/Nov 27, 1915; p. 1663
NIGHT IN TOWN, A
(Cry)/Mar 8, 1913; p. 998
NIGHT OF ANGUISH, A
(Ec)/Apr 5, 1913; p. 49
NIGHT OF TERROR
(Ed)/Mar 25, 1911; p. 656
NIGHT OF TERROR, A
(Bio)/May 30, 1908; p. 479
NIGHT OF THE EMBASSY BALL, THE
(Ka)/Nov 27, 1915; p. 1664
NIGHT ON THE ROAD, A
(SA)/Feb 7, 1914; p. 676
NIGHT ON THE COAST, A
(Gau)/Jun 18, 1910; p. 1048
NIGHT OUT, A
(Vi)/Oct 24, 1908; p.328/Oct 30, 1908; p.338
(Sel)/Feb 3, 1912; p. 392
(Ed)/Apr 11, 1914; p. 212
NIGHT RIDERS, THE
(Maj)/Apr 12, 1913; p. 166
NIGHT RUSTLERS, THE
(Bi)/Sep 17, 1910; p. 632
NIGHT SHADOWS OF NEW YORK
(Imp)/Dec 6, 1913; p. 1153
NIGHT WATCHMAN, THE
(Pa)/Nov 9, 1907; p. 584
NIGHT WITH A MILLION, A
(SA)/Jul 25, 1914; p. 571

NIGHT WITH MASQUERADERS IN PARIS,
A (Me)/Apr 4, 1908; p. 300
NIGHTINGALE, THE
(AS)/Oct 10, 1914; p. 192
NIGHTMARE, THE
(UE)/Jun 18, 1910; p. 1049
NIGHTMARE OF A MOVIE FAN, THE
(Vic)/May 29, 1915; p. 1433
NIGHTMARE OF A SINGLE MAN, THE
(Lux)/Sep 4, 1909; p. 314
NIGHT'S ADVENTURE, A
(Ch)/Apr 6, 1912; p. 43
(Re)/Jan 16, 1915; p. 369
(Lu)/Feb 20, 1915; p. 1140
NIGHT'S LODGING, A
(MnA)/Jul 24, 1915; p. 668
NIHILIST VENGEANCE
(Vic)/Jul 26, 1913; p. 429
NIHILIST'S DAUGHTER, THE
(WS)/Dec 6, 1913; p. 1153
NINA OF THE THEATER (Ka)/May 30,
1914; p. 1239/Jun 20, 1914; p. 1689
NINE LIVES OF A CAT, THE
(Ed)/Aug 10, 1907; p. 362
NINE OF DIAMONDS
(Vi)/Nov 26, 1910; p. 1236
NINETY AND NINE, THE (Vi)/Sep 16, 1911;
pp 777-78/Oct 14, 1911; p. 129
NINETY BLACK BOXES, THE
(Bi)/Nov 14, 1914; p. 934
99 IN THE SHADE
(SA)/Oct 12, 1907; p. 505
NINTH COMMANDMENT, THE
(Gem)/Jan 25, 1913; p. 365
NINTH INTERNATIONAL RED CROSS
CONFERENCE, THE
(Ed)/Aug 17, 1912; p. 672
NIOBE (FP)/Apr 17, 1915; p. 400
NIPPED (Dom)/Nov 28, 1914; p. 1234
NIPPED IN THE BUD
(Cin)/Mar 15, 1913; p. 1104
NIPPER'S LULLABY, THE
(Vi)/Jun 29, 1912; p. 1227
NITRATE OF SODA
(Sel)/Jun 17, 1911; p. 1387
NO-ACCOUNT COUNT, THE
(Ka)/Nov 14, 1914; p. 931
"NO-ACCOUNT" SMITH'S BABY
(KB)/Sep 19, 1914; p. 1646
NO APPETITE FOR DINNER
(Gau)/Jul 3, 1909; p. 12
NO BABIES ALLOWED
(Jo)/Oct 23, 1915; p. 621
NO CHILDREN WANTED
(Po)/Jun 29, 1912; p. 1228
NO COOKING ALLOWED
(Ed)/Sep 23, 1911; p. 891
NO GREATER LOVE

(Imp)/Dec 14, 1912; pp 1082-83
(Sel)/Dec 11, 1915; p. 2023
NO MAN'S LAND (Pa)/Aug 20, 1910; p. 406
NO PETTICOATS FOR HIM
(Pa)/Dec 19, 1908; pp 500, 509
NO PLACE FOR FATHER
(Bio)/Nov 22, 1913; p. 867
NO PLACE LIKE HOME
(Sel)/Dec 3, 1910; p. 1296
NO QUARTER (Be)/May 8, 1915; p. 900
NO REST FOR THE WEARY
(Pa)/Aug 20, 1910; p. 406
NO SHOW FOR THE CHAUFFEUR
(Ec)/Sep 5, 1914; p. 1373
NO SOUP (Jo)/May 29, 1915; p. 1433
NO SWEETS (Vi)/Jul 5, 1913; p. 48
NO TICKEE, NO WASHEE
(Vi)/Nov 20, 1915; p. 1499
NO TRESPASSING (Lu)/Oct 5, 1912; p. 40
NO TRIFLING WITH LOVE
(Pa)/Apr 9, 1910; p. 553
NO WEDDING BELLS FOR HER
(Sel)/Nov 21, 1914; p. 1075
NO WEDDING BELLS FOR JONES
(Pun)/Mar 15, 1913; p. 1106
NO WEDDING BELLS FOR ME
(Ec)/Mar 16, 1912; p. 963
NOBILITY (It)/Mar 18, 1911; p. 603
(Pa)/Apr 19, 1913; p. 279
NOBLE ENEMY, A (Lu)/Jan 20, 1912; p. 202
NOBLE HEART, A (Po)/Feb 4, 1911; p. 249
NOBLE JESTER, A (Vi)/Jul 4, 1908; p. 13
NOBLE PROFESSION, A
(Ed)/Nov 30, 1912; p. 877
NOBLE RED MAN, THE
(Bi)/Nov 11, 1911; p. 471
NOBLEMAN'S RIGHTS
(Pa)/May 16, 1908; p. 446
NOBODY LOVES A FAT WOMAN
(Th)/Aug 26, 1911; p. 544
NOBODY WOULD BELIEVE
(Lu)/Jun 12, 1915; p. 1776
NOBODY'S BOY (Sel)/Mar 8, 1913; p. 996
NOBODY'S HOME (Be)/Dec 4, 1915; p.1853
NOBODY'S LOVE STORY
(Ec)/Jan 25, 1913; p. 365
NOCTURNAL THIEVES
(Pa)/Jun 27, 1908; p. 547
NOISE FROM THE DEEP, A
(Key)/Jul 26, 1913; p. 430
NOISE OF BOMBS, THE
(Key)/Nov 28, 1914; p. 1233
NOISY NEIGHBORS
(Pa)/Jul 11, 1908; p. 34/Dec 19, 1908; p. 500
(WF)/Oct 31, 1914; p. 642
NOISY SIX, THE (Sel)/Jun 7, 1913; p. 1030
NOISY SUITORS, THE
(Bio)/Jul 19, 1913; p. 320

O'ER GRIM FIELDS SCARRED
(Re)/Jun 10, 1911; p. 1319
O'ER HILL AND DALE
(Gau)/Apr 23, 1910; p. 641
OF SUCH IS THE KINGDOM
(Re)/Aug 16, 1913; p. 745
OFF AGIN ON AGIN FINNEGAN
(Jo)/Oct 17, 1914; p. 337
OFF FOR A BOAT RIDE
(SA)/Oct 16, 1915; p. 439
OFF THE COAST OF MAINE
(Ed)/Sep 30, 1911; p. 972
OFF THE ROAD (Vi)/Feb 1, 1913; p. 465
OFF TO MOROCCO
(KO)/Jul 25, 1908; pp 67-68
OFF TO THE WEDDING
(LeL)/Dec 18, 1909; p. 882
OFFENDING KISS, THE
(Vi)/Sep 18, 1915; p. 1996
OFFICE BOY'S DREAM, THE
(Com)/Dec 2, 1911; p. 727
OFFICE FAVORITE, THE
(Lu)/Feb 10, 1912; pp 481-82
OFFICE SEEKER, THE
(Gau)/Jun 18, 1910; p. 1048
OFFICER AND A GENTLEMAN, AN
(Sol)/Jun 10, 1911; p. 1319
(Vi)/Mar 28, 1914; p. 1681
OFFICER JOHN DONOVAN
(Vi)/Jan 24, 1914; p. 413
OFFICER KATE (Vi)/Aug 15, 1914; p. 959
OFFICER McCUE (Lu)/May 29, 1909; p. 713
OFFICER MULDOON'S DOUBLE
(Lu)/Jun 18, 1910; p. 1048
OFFICER MURRAY (Sel)/Aug 17,1912;p.669
OFFICER 174 (Imp)/Nov 23, 1912; p. 769
OFFICER 666 (GK)/Jan 2, 1915; p. 53
OFFICIAL APPOINTMENT, AN
(Vi)/Nov 16, 1912; p. 659
OFFICIAL GOAT PROTECTOR, THE
(Th)/Oct 4, 1913; p. 49
OFFICIAL LAPSE, AN
(Pa)/May 22, 1915; p. 1261
OFIA, THE WOMAN SPY
(Kin)/Dec 7, 1912; p. 978
O'FLANAGAN'S LUCK
(Roy)/Sep 19, 1914; p. 1645
OGALLALAH (Po)/Apr 8, 1911; p. 782
O'GARRY OF THE ROYAL MOUNTED
(Vi)/Jan 23, 1915; p. 521
OGRE AND THE GIRL, THE
(Lu)/Dec 18, 1915; p. 2203
OH! BABY (Po)/Aug 5, 1911; pp 296-97
OH, BABY! (Roy)/May 29, 1915; p. 1432
OH, DADDY! (Be)/May 1, 1915; p. 728
OH, DOCTOR (Ka)/Dec 4, 1915; p. 1852
OH, DOCTOR! (SA)/Apr 4, 1914; p. 57
OH, LISTEN TO THE BAND

(Lux)/Apr 6, 1912; p. 42
OH, MY FEET! (Lu)/Apr 25, 1908; p. 376
OH! MY PIPE (Lux)/Nov 9, 1912; p. 554
OH, RATS (Ed)/Apr 3, 1909; p. 403
OH! SUCH A BEAUTIFUL OCEAN
(Th)/Aug 16, 1913; p. 745
OH! SUCH A NIGHT
(Cry)/Nov 16, 1912; p. 660
OH! THOSE EYES (Bio)/Apr 13, 1912; p.137
OH, UNCLE (Bio)/Sep 11, 1909; p. 347
OH, WHAT A BEARD!
(Pa)/Oct 2, 1909; p. 451
OH, WHAT A BOOB
(Bio)/Feb 22, 1913; p. 781
OH, WHAT A DREAM
(Ec)/Nov 15, 1913; p. 737
OH, WHAT A KNIGHT
(Th)/Oct 29, 1910; p. 999
OH, WHAT AN APPETITE
(SA)/Feb 27, 1909; p. 236
OH, WHAT LUNGS (SA)/Mar 20,1909; p.338
OH, YOU CITY GIRL
(WF)/Jan 9, 1915; p. 221
OH, YOU CLUBMAN!
(Pa)/Mar 18, 1911; p. 602
OH, YOU DOGGIE! (Pa)/Jan 15, 1910; p. 56
OH, YOU FEMALE COP
(Lun)/Apr 3, 1915; p. 65
OH, YOU FLIRT! (Imp)/Jul 19, 1913; p. 321
OH, YOU KIDS (Pa)/Apr 1, 1911; p. 718
OH, YOU MOTHER-IN-LAW
(Po)/Apr 22, 1911; p. 901
OH, YOU RUBBER (Ec)/Nov 22, 1913; p.869
OH, YOU SKELETON
(Sel)/Nov 5, 1910; pp 1056, 1058
OH, YOU STENOGRAPHER
(Sol)/Oct 7, 1911; p. 42
OH, YOU SUFFRAGETTE
(Am)/Apr 22, 1911; p. 901
OH, YOU TEACHER
(SA)/Mar 25, 1911; p. 657
OH LOOK WHO'S HERE!
(Sel)/Sep 26, 1914; p. 1775
OH ME! OH MY! (Lu)/Dec 14, 1907; p. 673
OHAMI GROUP OF ACROBATS
(GN)/Dec 17, 1910; p. 1419
O'HARA, SQUATTER AND PHILOSOPHER
(Vi)/Dec 14, 1912; p. 1081
O'HARA AND THE YOUTHFUL PRODIGAL
(Vi)/May 10, 1913; p. 596
O'HARA AS GUARDIAN ANGEL
(Vi)/Jul 26, 1913; p. 428
O'HARA HELPS CUPID
(Vi)/Jan 25, 1913; p. 364
O'HARA OF THE MOUNTED
(Fa)/Oct 30a, 1915; p. 970
O'HARA'S GODCHILD
(Vi)/Mar 15, 1913; p. 1104

OIL (Me)/Mar 16, 1912; p. 961
OIL AND WATER (Bio)/Feb 22, 1913;
    p. 780/Aug 14, 1915; p. 1176
OIL COUNTRY ROMANCE, AN
    (Me)/Dec 9, 1911; p. 816
OIL FIELDS, CALIFORNIA
    (Ne)/Jun 8, 1912; p. 944
OIL ON TROUBLED WATERS
    (Am)/Apr 5, 1913; p. 27
OIL WELL CONSPIRACY, THE
    (Ka)/Sep 19, 1914; p. 1645
O'KALEMS VISIT TO KILLARNEY, THE
    (Ka)/Jan 20, 1912; p. 202
OKLAHOMA (Po)/May 27, 1911; p. 1202
OKLAHOMA CITY, OKLAHOMA
    (Gem)/Jul 12, 1913; p. 206
OLAF - AN ATOM (Bio)/May 31,1913; p.919
OLAF ERICKSON, BOSS
    (Rex)/Oct 24, 1914; p. 493
OLD, OLD SONG, AN
    (SA)/Mar 29, 1913; p. 1335
OLD ACTOR, AN (Sel)/May 17, 1913; p.703
OLD ACTOR, THE
    (KO)/Jun 20, 1908; p. 534
OLD ACTOR'S VISION, THE
    (Cin)/Nov 30, 1912; p. 877
OLD AND NEW TAHITI
    (Me)/Nov 8, 1913; p. 611
OLD AND THE NEW, THE
    (Bio)/Oct 23, 1915; p. 619
OLD APPOINTMENT, AN
    (Ed)/Jan 4, 1913; p. 50
OLD ARMY CHEST, THE
    (Lu)/Jul 10, 1909; p. 50
OLD ARMY COAT, THE
    (Ka)/Aug 15, 1914; p. 945
OLD BELLRINGER, THE
    (Ne)/Oct 3, 1914; p. 65
OLD BILLY (Sel)/Nov 25, 1911; p. 636
OLD BOOKKEEPER, THE
    (Bio)/Feb 3, 1912; pp 392-93
OLD CALIFORNIA (GS)/Apr 25,1914; p.518
OLD CAPTAIN, THE
    (Sel)/Aug 19, 1911; p. 462
OLD CHEMIST, THE
    (Maj)/Apr 10, 1915; p. 236
OLD CHESS PLAYERS, THE
    (Lu)/Nov 9, 1912; p. 553
OLD CLERK, THE (Sel)/Apr 5, 1913; p. 48
OLD CLOCK ON THE STAIRS, THE
    (Ec)/Oct 5, 1912; p. 42
OLD CLOTHES SHOP, THE
    (Re)/Jul 3, 1915; p. 65
OLD COBBLER, THE
    (101)/Jun 27, 1914; p. 1830
OLD CODE, THE (Sel)/Jan 23, 1915; p. 516
OLD COLLEGE CHUMS (Pa)/Nov 21, 1908;
    p.410/Nov 28, 1908;p.423/Dec 5, 1908;p.449

OLD CONFECTIONER'S MISTAKE, THE
    (Bio)/Sep 23, 1911; p. 891
OLD COUPONS (Bio)/Nov 22, 1913; p. 867
OLD CURIOSITY SHOP
    (Bli)/Mar 21, 1914; p. 1533
OLD DELHI AND ITS RUINS
    (Pa)/Oct 7, 1911; p. 39
OLD DERELICT, THE
    (Maj)/Jul 25, 1914; p. 572
OLD DOCTOR'S HUMANITY, THE
    (Ec)/Sep 21, 1912; p. 1177
OLD DOLL, THE (Vi)/Jan 6, 1912; p. 41
OLD DOLLMAKER, THE
    (Gem)/Nov 9, 1912; p. 554
OLD DR. JUDD (Th)/Aug 10, 1912; p. 547
OLD DUTCH (Wor)/Feb 13, 1915; p. 990
OLD ENOUGH TO BE HER GRANDPA
    (Am)/Dec 5, 1914; p. 1384
OLD EXCUSE, THE
    (Sol)/May 6, 1911; p. 1021
OLD EXCUSE THAT WORKED, AN
    (Lu)/Jan 20, 1912; p. 203
OLD FAMILY BIBLE, THE
    (Ed)/Mar 25, 1911; p. 656
OLD-FASHIONED ELOPEMENT, AN
    (Ed)/Dec 7, 1912; pp 958-59
OLD-FASHIONED GIRL, AN
    (Rex)/Aug 31, 1912; p. 881
OLD FASHIONED MOTHER, AN
    (Rex)/Nov 16, 1912; p. 660
OLD FIDELITY (SA)/Dec 9, 1911; p. 816
OLD FIDDLER, THE
    (Ka)/Apr 23, 1910; p. 642
OLD FIRE HORSE, THE
    (Ed)/Sep 5, 1914; p. 1371
OLD FIRE HORSE AND THE NEW FIRE
    CHIEF, THE (Vi)/May 23, 1914; p. 1117
OLD FISHERMAN'S STORY, THE
    (Maj)/Jan 9, 1915; p. 222
OLD FLORIST, THE
    (SA)/Jan 27, 1912; p. 303
OLD FLUTE PLAYER, THE
    (Vi)/Dec 12, 1914; p. 1524
OLD FOGEY, THE
    (Pa)/Oct 31, 1914; p. 650
OLD FOLKS (Gau)/May 13, 1911; p. 1080
OLD FOLKS AT HOME, THE
    (Th)/Nov 1, 1913; p. 497
OLD FOLKS CHRISTMAS, THE
    (Imp)/Jan 4, 1913; p. 52
OLD FOLKS' SACRIFICE, THE
    (Vi)/Jul 22, 1911; p. 125
OLD FOOTLIGHT FAVORITE, THE
    (Me)/Oct 10, 1908; p. 286
OLD FORT DEARBORN
    (UB)/Oct 5, 1912; p. 42
OLD GLORY (Vi)/Jul 16, 1910; p. 142
OLD GOOD-FOR-NOTHIN'

Jan 16, 1909; p. 69
OLD SHOEMAKER, THE
(Re)/May 15, 1915; p. 1073
OLD SILVER MINE IN PERU, AN
(Ed)/Dec 24, 1910; p. 1478
OLD SILVER WATCH, THE
(Vi)/Mar 30, 1912; p. 1165
OLD SIN, THE (SA)/Oct 23, 1915; p. 620
OLD SLEUTH (Ka)/Oct 3, 1908; p. 253
OLD SLIPPER, THE
(Sel)/Feb 27, 1915; p. 1287
OLD SOLDIER'S STORY, THE
(Ka)/Mar 13, 1909; p. 305
OLD SONGS AND MEMORIES
(Sel)/Nov 30, 1912; p. 876
OLD STAGE COACH, THE
(Sel)/Jun 29, 1912; p. 1226
OLD STORY WITH A NEW ENDING, AN
(Bio)/Sep 3, 1910; p. 518
OLD STREETS OF CAIRO
(Pa)/Apr 11, 1914; p. 212
OLD SWEETHEART, THE
(Imp)/Oct 26, 1912; p. 344
OLD SWEETHEART OF MINE, AN
(Ed)/Nov 4, 1911; p. 378
OLD SWEETHEARTS OF MINE
(Vi)/May 29, 1909; p. 713
OLD SWIMMING HOLE, THE
(Re)/Aug 24, 1912; p. 772
OLD-TIME NIGHTMARE, AN (Po)/Sep 16,
1911; p. 778/Oct 7, 1911; p. 41
OLD TOWN, ALBUQUERQUE
(Ne)/Apr 20, 1912; p. 231
OLD TUNE, AN (101)/Sep 21, 1912; p. 1177
OLD TUTOR, THE (U)/Apr 17, 1915; p. 394
OLD vs THE NEW, THE
(Sel)/Feb 14, 1914; p. 808
OLD WATER JAR, THE
(Vi)/Jan 21, 1911; p. 144
OLD WEDDING DRESS, THE
(SA)/Aug 24, 1912; p. 771
OLD WOMEN OF THE STREETS OF NEW
YORK (Ka)/May 17, 1913; p. 704
OLD WYOMING DAYS
(WFF)/Aug 12, 1911; p. 379
OLE BRANDEIS' EYES
(Box)/Aug 8, 1914; p. 838
OLE SWIMMIN' HOLE, THE
(Sel)/Oct 8, 1910; p. 814
OLGA THE ADVENTUROUS
(Gau)/Nov 16, 1912; p. 660
OLIVER TWIST
(Vi)/Jun 5, 1909; p. 753
(Pa)/Aug 27, 1910; p. 462
Jun 1, 1912; p. 813
OLIVER TWIST SADLY TWISTED
(WF)/Jan 16, 1915; p. 370
OLIVE'S HERO (St)/Apr 3, 1915; p. 66

OLIVE'S LOVE AFFAIR
(St)/Jan 9, 1915; p. 222
OLIVE'S OPPORTUNTIES (Ed)
No.1/Dec 12, 1914; p. 1523
No.2/Dec 19, 1914; p. 1679
No.3/Dec 26, 1914; p. 1840
No.4/Jan 2, 1915; p. 75
No.5/Jan 9, 1915; p. 220
No.6/Jan 16, 1915; p. 368
No.7/Jan 23, 1915; p. 513
No.8/Jan 9, 1915; p. 196
No.9/Feb 6, 1915; p. 827
No.10/Feb 13, 1915; p. 984
No.11/Feb 20, 1915; p. 1139
No.12/Feb 27, 1915; p. 1287
OLIVE'S PET (St)/Mar 27, 1915; p. 1933
OLYMPIC GAMES (Pa)/Sep 5,1908;pp182-83
OLYMPIC GAMES, PITTSBURG Y.M.C.A.
(Ed)/Oct 12, 1912; p. 143
OLYMPIC GAMES AT STOCKHOLM, THE
(Pa)/Nov 16, 1912; p. 658
OMENS AND ORACLES
(Vi)/May 17, 1913; p. 703
ON A RACKET (Pa)/Jan 29, 1910; p. 127
ON A TRAMP STEAMER (Vi)/Jul 29, 1911;
p. 194/Aug 5, 1911; p. 293
ON ACCOUNT OF A DOG
(Pr)/Mar 6, 1915; p. 1448
ON ACCOUNT OF A HANDKERCHIEF
(Re)/Oct 26, 1912; p. 345
ON AN ALLIGATOR FARM
(Imp)/Apr 26, 1913; p. 382
ON ANOTHER MAN'S PASS
(SA)/Sep 11, 1909; p. 347
ON BAD TERMS WITH THE JANITOR
(Pa)/Jul 4, 1908; p. 11
ON BITTER CREEK
(Lu)/Jun 12, 1915; p. 1777
ON BOARD THE KAISER WILHELM II
(Vi)/Sep 7, 1912; p. 975
ON BOARD THE STEAMSHIP DUBUQUE
(Am)/Dec 7, 1912; p. 978
ON BURNING SANDS (Po)/Jan 18, 1913;
p. 246/Feb 1, 1913; p. 466
ON CHRISTMAS EVE (Ed)/Jan 2, 1915; p.75
ON CIRCUS DAY (Lu)/Oct 17, 1914; p. 336
ON CUPID'S HIGHWAY
(Ne)/May 31, 1913; p. 922
ON DANGEROUS GROUND
(Imp)/Jan 23, 1915; p. 516
ON DANGEROUS PATHS
(Ed)/Jul 10, 1915; p. 320
ON DONOVAN'S DIVISION
(Ed)/Dec 14, 1912; p. 1081
ON EL MONTE RANCH
(SA)/Jun 22, 1912; p. 1126
ON FORBIDDEN PATHS
(Fr)/Sep 20, 1913; p. 1285

(Ed)/Sep 26, 1914; p. 1753
ON THE JOB (SA)/Jun 14, 1913; p. 1135
        (MnA)/Aug 7, 1915; p. 996
ON THE LAKES OF BAYRISCH, BAVARIA
(Pa)/Aug 30, 1913; p. 960
ON THE LAZY LINE
(Ed)/Jan 17, 1914; p. 275
ON THE LEDGE (Re)/Dec 26, 1914; p. 1842
ON THE LEVEL (GS)/Nov 6, 1915; p. 1140
ON THE LITTLE BIG HORN
(Sel)/Dec 4, 1909; p. 800
(Ne)/Mar 19, 1910; p. 427
ON THE LITTLE MILL TRACE
(SA)/Nov 13, 1915; p. 1312
ON THE MEXICAN BORDER
(Lu)/Dec 17, 1910; pp 1416, 1418
ON THE MINUTE (Sel)/May 23,1914; p.1117
ON THE MOONLIGHT TRAIL
(SA)/Aug 31, 1912; p. 880
ON THE MOUNTAIN RANCH
(Lu)/Mar 15, 1913; p. 1105
ON THE NEBI RIVER, EAST AFRICA
(Cin)/Apr 26, 1913; p. 380
ON THE NIGHT STAGE
(NYM)/Apr 3, 1915; p. 65
ON THE PRIVATE WIRE
(SA)/Dec 11, 1915; p. 2032
ON THE PUPIL OF HIS EYE
(Vi)/Jul 20, 1912; p. 243
ON THE RANGERS' ROLL OF HONOR
(Fr)/Aug 16, 1913; p. 744
ON THE REEF (Bio)/Jan 29, 1910; p. 128
ON THE RIO GRANDE
(Rex)/Jul 4, 1914; p. 66
ON THE ROAD TO RENO
(Lu)/Apr 3, 1915; p. 64
ON THE ROADS OF DAUPHINE
(Pa)/Jul 26, 1913; p. 427
ON THE SHORE
(Imp)/May 18, 1912; pp 629-30
ON THE STEPS (Ed)/Jul 4, 1914; p. 64
ON THE STROKE OF FIVE
(Vi)/Nov 21, 1914; p. 1076
ON THE STROKE OF THREE
(Imp)/Jan 6, 1912; p. 41
ON THE STROKE OF TWELVE
Dec 26, 1908; p. 526
(Ed)/Feb 27, 1915; p. 1294/
    Mar 27, 1915; p. 1932
ON THE TABLE TOP
(Maj)/Jan 30, 1915; p. 672
ON THE THRESHOLD
(Gau)/Jul 16, 1910; p. 142
(Lu)/Feb 15, 1913; p. 678
ON THE TRAIL OF THE GERMS
(Sel)/Aug 3, 1912; p. 445
ON THE TRAIL OF THE SPIDER GANG
(Ape)/Jul 19, 1913; p. 300

ON THE TURN OF A CARD
(Vi)/Oct 30a, 1915; p. 967
ON THE VERGE (Fr)/Jul 4, 1914; p. 65
ON THE VERGE OF WAR
(Bi)/Jun 6, 1914; p. 1410
ON THE WAR PATH
(KO)/Jul 25, 1908; p. 69
(101)/Jul 6, 1912; p. 43
ON THE WARPATH
(Sel)/Feb 27, 1909; p. 239
(Ka)/Sep 23, 1911; p. 889
**ON THE WAY FROM KANDY TO
COLOMBO** (Ec)/May 23, 1914; p. 1118
ON THE WRONG SCENT
(SA)/Dec 4, 1909; p. 800
ON THE WRONG TRACK
(Ed)/Sep 4, 1915; p. 1643
ON THEIR HONEYMOON
(Lux)/Mar 18, 1911; p. 604
ON THEIR WEDDING EVE
(Vi)/Nov 8, 1913; p. 612
ON TIME FOR BUSINESS
(Lu)/May 7, 1910; p. 736
ON WITH THE DANCE
(Vi)/Oct 30, 1915; p. 791
ONAWANDA (Vi)/Oct 9, 1909; pp 489-90
ONCE IS ENOUGH
(MnA)/Jun 12, 1915; p. 1776
ONCE OVER, THE (Be)/Apr 17, 1915; p.393
ONCE UPON A TIME
(Imp)/Aug 20, 1910; p. 408
(Re)/Oct 18, 1913; p. 265
ONCE UPON A TIME THERE WAS--
(Mi)/Sep 14, 1907; p. 442
ONE, TWO, THREE
(Am)/Nov 2, 1912; p. 451
ONE AGAINST ONE
(Re)/Aug 31, 1912; p. 882
ONE BEST BET, THE
(Imp)/Jul 11, 1914; p. 256
ONE BEST BET, THE (Ka)/Oct 4,1913; p.47
ONE BUSY HOUR (Bio)/May 15, 1909; p. 636
ONE CAN'T ALWAYS TELL
(Vi)/Jun 14, 1913; p. 1136
ONE CAN'T BELIEVE ONE'S EYES
(Pa)/Jun 11, 1910; p. 997
ONE-CYLINDER COURTSHIP, A
(Ne)/Oct 23, 1915; p. 621
ONE FLAG AT LAST
(Vi)/Sep 30, 1911; p. 972
ONE FLIGHT UP (Re)/Jan 30, 1915; p. 673
ONE FORGOTTEN, THE
(Bio)/Jul 31, 1915; p. 816
ONE GOOD COOK (Roy)/Jul 10, 1915; p.308
ONE GOOD JOKE DESERVES ANOTHER
(Vi)/Jul 12, 1913; p. 204
ONE GOOD TURN (Cen)/Jul 9, 1910; p. 86
ONE GOOD TURN, THE

(Cry)/Aug 23, 1913; p. 844
ONE WOMAN'S WAY
(Cin)/Jul 4, 1914; p. 65
(Am)/Jun 26, 1915; p. 2096
ONE WONDERFUL NIGHT
(SA)/Aug 8, 1914; pp 810-11
O'NEILL, THE (Ka)/Jan 27, 1912; p. 302
ONES WHO SUFFER, THE
(Sel)/Apr 6, 1912; p. 41
ONION FIEND, THE (Sel)/Aug 3,1907; p.346
ONION PATCH, THE (Sel)/Jul 10,1915;p.307
ONIONS MAKE PEOPLE WEEP
(KO)/Nov 2, 1907; p. 563
ONLY A BUNCH OF FLOWERS
(Lux)/Sep 3, 1910; p. 520
ONLY A COUNTRY GIRL
(Ka)/Dec 11, 1915; p. 2031
ONLY A DREAM (Gau)/Jul 17, 1909; p. 88
ONLY A FADED FLOWER
(Pa)/May 14, 1910; p. 785
ONLY A FATHER'S DAUGHTER
(Key)/Jan 30, 1915; p. 672
ONLY A MESSENGER BOY
(Key)/Sep 18, 1915; p. 1996
ONLY A PRIVATE (Lux)/Sep 28, 1912; p. 1277
ONLY A SISTER (Me)/Feb 18, 1911; p. 370
(Vi)/Jul 4, 1914; p. 64
ONLY A SQUAW (Sol)/Dec 2, 1911; p. 726
ONLY A TRAMP (Re)/Apr 3, 1915; p. 64
ONLY AN ICEMAN (Ne)/Dec 23,1911; p.990
ONLY CHANCE, THE
(Sel)/Jul 26, 1913; p. 428
ONLY CLUE, THE (Maj)/Jul 18,1914; p.433
ONLY FIVE YEARS OLD
(Sel)/Oct 25, 1913; p. 379
ONLY GIRL IN CAMP, THE
(Th)/Jan 21, 1911; p. 145
ONLY IN THE WAY
(Th)/Feb 11, 1911; p. 318
ONLY KIDS (Lu)/Nov 23, 1907; p. 618
ONLY ONE SKIRT (Ka)/Jan 31, 1914; p. 543
ONLY SKIN DEEP (Lu)/Nov 7, 1914; p. 787
ONLY SON, THE (Las)/Jun 27, 1914; p. 1802
ONLY THE MAID (Ed)/Apr 10, 1915; p. 235
ONLY THOUGHTLESSNESS
(Pa)/Mar 7, 1908; p. 193
ONLY VETERAN IN TOWN, THE
(Vi)/Jun 14, 1913; p. 1135
ONLY WAY, THE (Vi)/Aug 2, 1913; p. 537
(Be)/Sep 26, 1914; p.1777
(Lu)/Apr 3, 1915; p. 64
ONLY WOMAN IN TOWN
(Cry)/Nov 2, 1912; p. 451
ONONKO'S VOW (Ed)/Oct 15, 1910; p. 874
OPAL RING, AN (SA)/Apr 24, 1915; p. 556
OPAL RING, THE (Imp)/Mar 14,1914;p.1385
OPAL'S CURSE, THE
(Bio)/Jun 27, 1914; p. 1828

OPEN DOOR, THE
(Bro)/Dec 20, 1913; p. 1414
(Sel)/Jan 10, 1914; p. 173
(Re)/May 8, 1915; p. 900
OPEN GATE, THE
(Bio)/Dec 4, 1909; p. 798
(Ya)/Apr 1, 1911; p. 720
OPEN ROAD, THE
(Ka)/Mar 4, 1911; p. 483
(Imp)/Nov 30, 1912; p. 878
(Re)/Feb 1, 1913; pp 466, 472
OPEN SECRET, THE
(Pa)/Jun 7, 1913; p. 1031
OPEN SWITCH, THE
(Ka)/Mar 22, 1913; p. 1219
OPENED SHUTTERS, THE (GS)/Nov 14,
1914; p. 941/Nov 21, 1914; p. 1077
OPENING AN OYSTER
(Sel)/Jul 2, 1910; p. 24
OPENING BUD, THE
(CGP)/Feb 22, 1913; p. 780
OPENING NIGHT, THE
(U)/Jul 17, 1915; p. 487
OPENING OF THE PANAMA CANAL, THE
(Ha)/Jun 13, 1914; p. 1519
OPENING OF THE SHICHIJIO BRIDGE,
JAPAN (Me)/Nov 8, 1913; p. 611
OPENING OF THE Y.M.C.A.
PLAYGROUND AT LYNCHBURG, VA.
(Ed)/Sep 21, 1912; p. 1175
OPERA SINGER'S TRIUMPH, THE
(It)/Aug 8, 1914; p. 818
OPERA SLINGER'S ROMANCE, THE
(Jo)/Dec 11, 1915; p. 2033
OPERATING ON CUPID
(Ne)/Nov 27, 1915; p. 1665
OPERATOR AND THE SUPERINTENDENT,
THE (Ne)/Jul 26, 1913; p. 429
OPERATOR AT BLACK ROCK, THE
(Ka)/Aug 22, 1914; p. 1100
OPERATOR OF BIG SANDY, THE
(Bro)/May 22, 1915; p. 1260
OPIUM SMUGGLER, THE (Am)/May 13,
1911; p. 1067/May 20, 1911; p. 1143
OPIUM SMUGGLERS, THE
(Sel)/Nov 2, 1912; p. 449
(Gau)/May 16, 1914; p. 970
(Box)/May 30, 1914; p. 1262
OPORTO, PORTUGAL, AND ITS HARBOR
(Ec)/Nov 30, 1912; p. 878
OPPORTUNE BURGLAR, AN
(Re)/Apr 13, 1912; p. 138
OPPORTUNITY AND A MILLION ACRES
(Pa)/Aug 9, 1913; p. 635
OPPORTUNITY AND THE MAN
(Lu)/Apr 22, 1911; p. 900
OPPRESSOR, THE (Gau)/Apr 29,1911; p.958
OPTION, THE (Rex)/Jan 17, 1914; p. 290

OTHER WOMAN'S PICTURE, THE
(SA)/Apr 24, 1915; p. 555
OTHERWISE BILL HARRISON
(SA)/Jun 5, 1915; p. 1605
OTTER, THE (Pa)/Sep 20, 1913; p. 1283
(Pa)/May 22, 1915; p. 1261
OUBLIETTE, THE (101)/Jul 18, 1914;
p. 410/Aug 15, 1914; p. 962
OUCHARD, THE MERCHANT
(Pa)/Mar 12, 1910; p. 383
OUR BABY (Imp)/Apr 6, 1912; p. 42
(Gem)/Oct 11, 1913; p. 157
OUR BELOVED COUNTRY
(Ec)/Nov 28, 1914; p. 1233
OUR CHILDREN (Key)/Nov 29,1913; p.1009
OUR COAST DEFENDERS
(Vi)/Apr 19, 1913; p. 279
OUR COUNTRY COUSINS
(Key)/Jul 4, 1914; p. 65
OUR COUNTRY IN ARMS
(Lu)/Sep 18, 1909; p. 379
OUR DARE-DEVIL CHIEF
(Key)/May 22, 1915; p. 1260
OUR DAUGHTER (Ec)/May 16, 1914; p. 970
OUR DEAR UNCLE FROM AMERICA
(Ec)/Dec 24, 1910; p. 1480
OUR DOG FRIENDS (Pa)/Jun 27,1908; p.547
OUR ENEMY THE WASP
(CGP)/Feb 1, 1913; p. 464
OUR ENEMY'S SPY
(101)/Sep 26, 1914; p. 1777
OUR FAIRY PLAY (Vi)/Jun 27, 1914; p.1829
OUR FEATHERED FRIENDS
(Pa)/May 10, 1913; p. 595
OUR FEATHERED FRIENDS AT DINNER
(Gl)/Nov 20, 1915; p. 1501
OUR FUTURE HEROES
(Dra)/Jul 5, 1913; p. 49
OUR HOME-MADE ARMY
(Bio)/Oct 31, 1914; p. 640
OUR HOUSEMAID (Po)/Aug 6, 1910; p. 298
OUR ICE SUPPLY (Lu)/Mar 27, 1909; p. 368
OUR LADY OF THE SNOWS
(Ed)/Sep 17, 1910; p. 623
OUR LAND OF GOLD (Po)/Oct 3,1914; p.65
OUR LARGEST BIRDS
(Key)/May 30, 1914; p. 1261
OUR MUTUAL GIRL (Re)
No.1/Jan 24, 1914; p. 414
No.2/Feb 7, 1914; p. 678
No.3/Feb 14, 1914; pp 809-10
No.4/Feb 21, 1914; p. 947
No.5/Feb 28, 1914; p. 1089
No.6/Mar 7, 1914; p. 1237
No.7/Mar 14, 1914; p. 1385
No.8/Mar 21, 1914; p. 1525
No.9/Mar 28, 1914; p. 1681
No.10/Apr 4, 1914; p. 58

No.11/Apr 11, 1914; p. 213
No.12/Apr 18, 1914; p. 361
No.13/Apr 25, 1914; p. 517
No.14/May 2, 1914; p. 673
No.15/May 9, 1914; p. 821
No.17/May 23, 1914; p. 1117
No.18/May 30, 1914; p. 1261
No.19/Jun 6, 1914; p. 1409
No.20/Jun 13, 1914; p. 1541
No.21/Jun 20, 1914; p. 1689
No.22/Jun 27, 1914; p. 1829
No.23/Jul 4, 1914; p. 65
No.24/Jul 11, 1914; p. 256
No.25/Jul 18, 1914; p. 433
No.26/Jul 25, 1914; p. 573
No.28/Aug 8, 1914; p. 837
No.29/Aug 15, 1914; p. 960
No.30/Aug 22, 1914; p. 1100
No.31/Aug 29, 1914; p. 1242
No.32/Sep 5, 1914; p. 1373
No.33/Sep 12, 1914; p. 1513
No.34/Sep 26, 1914; p. 1776
No.35/Sep 26, 1914; pp 1776-77
No.36/Oct 3, 1914; p. 65
No.37/Oct 10, 1914; pp 188-89
No.38/Oct 17, 1914; p. 337
No.39/Oct 24, 1914; p. 493
No.40/Oct 31, 1914; p. 641
No.41/Nov 7, 1914; p. 788
No.42/Nov 14, 1914; p. 932
No.43/Nov 21, 1914; p. 1076
No.44/Nov 28, 1914; p. 1232
No.45/Dec 5, 1914; p. 1384
No.47/Dec 19, 1914; p. 1680
No.48/Dec 26, 1914; p. 1841
No.49/Jan 2, 1915; p. 77
No.50/Jan 9, 1915; p. 221
No.51/Jan 16, 1915; p. 369
No.52/Jan 23, 1915; p. 516
OUR NAVY (Vi)/Oct 21, 1911; p. 208
(Ch)/Dec 16, 1911; p. 905
OUR NEIGHBORS (Sel)/Oct 18,1913; p.263
OUR NEW MINISTER
(Sel)/Jul 9, 1910; p. 84
(Ka)/Nov 29, 1913; pp 1007-8
OUR OWN LITTLE FLAT
(Lu)/Mar 28, 1908; p. 272
OUR PARENTS IN LAW
(Cry)/Apr 19, 1913; p. 282
OUR POOR RELATIONS
(Sol)/Jan 13, 1912; p. 127
OUR VILLAGE MARATHON
Dec 5, 1908; p. 449
OUR WIVES (Vi)/Oct 4, 1913; p. 49
OUT AGAIN - IN AGAIN
(Ko)/Nov 28, 1914; p. 1232
OUT AND IN (Key)/Jun 21, 1913; p. 1253
OUT-BLACKED (Bio)/Jan 31, 1914; p. 543

OUT FOR A STROLL
 (Lu)/Jun 12, 1915; p. 1776
OUT FOR MISCHIEF
 (Me)/Oct 29, 1910; p. 996
OUT FOR THE DAY
 (Lu)/Oct 23, 1909; p. 568
OUT IN HAPPY HOLLOW
 (Vi)/Jun 6, 1914; p. 1408
OUT IN THE RAIN
 (Ka)/Feb 28, 1914; p. 1088
OUT OF BONDAGE (Maj)/Jun 5,1915;p.1606
OUT OF DARKNESS
 (Am)/Dec 19, 1914; p. 1682
 (Las)/Sep 25, 1915; p. 2199
OUT OF HIS CLASS
 (Fr)/Dec 13, 1913; p. 1280
OUT OF PATIENCE (KO)/Aug 1, 1908; p.88
OUT OF PETTICOAT LANE
 (Sel)/Dec 5, 1914; p. 1384
OUT OF SIGHT, OUT OF MIND
 (Pa)/Apr 9, 1910; p. 554
 (Bio)/Feb 14, 1914; p. 808
OUT OF THE AIR (Maj)/Oct 17, 1914;
 p. 337/Oct 24, 1914; p. 500
OUT OF THE ASHES
 (Am)/Oct 30a, 1915; p. 968
OUT OF THE BEAST A MAN WAS BORN
 (Lu)/Jun 28, 1913; p. 1360
OUT OF THE DARK
 (Ch)/May 20, 1911; p. 1142
OUT OF THE DARKNESS
 (Re)/Aug 12, 1911; p. 360
 (Kin)/Apr 19, 1913; p. 281
 (Rex)/Jul 11, 1914; p. 257
OUT OF THE DEEP
 (Ed)/May 18, 1912; p. 629
OUT OF THE DEPTHS
 (Sol)/Apr 8, 1911; p. 783
 (SA)/Mar 9, 1912; pp 851-52/
  Mar 30, 1912; p. 1165
 (Lu)/Feb 21, 1914; p. 947
 (Rex)/Sep 5, 1914; p. 1373
OUT OF THE DEPUTY'S HANDS
 (Re)/Oct 31, 1914; p. 641
OUT OF THE FAR EAST
 (Imp)/Apr 11, 1914; p. 214
OUT OF THE FLAMES
 (U)/Aug 7, 1915; p. 998
OUT OF THE FRYING PAN
 (Ne)/Oct 3, 1914; p. 65
OUT OF THE JAWS OF DEATH
 (Ka)/Jul 12, 1913; p. 204
OUT OF THE NIGHT
 (Ed)/Jul 23, 1910; p. 193
 (SA)/Apr 20,1912; p.220/May 25,1912; p.728
 (KB)/May 9, 1914; p. 821
OUT OF THE PAST
 (Vi)/Jun 4, 1910; p. 941

 (Sel)/Jan 21, 1911; p. 142
 (Cry)/Jun 28, 1913; p. 1360
 (Vi)/Jan 2, 1915; p. 76
OUT OF THE RUINS
 (Ed)/Apr 3, 1915; pp 67-68
OUT OF THE SEA (Th)/Sep 18, 1915; p.1996
OUT OF THE SHADOW
 (Bio)/Aug 19, 1911; p. 462
OUT OF THE SHADOWS
 (Th)/Jun 6, 1914; p. 1410
OUT OF THE STORM
 (Vi)/Apr 26, 1913; p. 379
 (Lu)/Jan 30, 1915; p. 671
OUT OF THE VALLEY
 (Vic)/Jul 18, 1914; p. 433
OUT OF TUNE (Cin)/Mar 30, 1912; p. 1166
OUT OF WORK (Ka)/Aug 28, 1909; p. 282
OUTBREAK, THE (Sel)/Mar 18, 1911; p. 602
OUTCAST, THE
 (Dra)/May 24, 1913; p. 813
 (Re)/Apr 3,1915;p.65/Apr 10,1915;pp 240-41
OUTCAST AMONG OUTCASTS, AN
 (Bio)/Jun 15, 1912; p. 1026
OUTCAST AND HEROINE
 (Vi)/Apr 24, 1909; p. 517
OUTCAST HEROINE, THE
 (KO)/May 9, 1908; p. 423
OUTCAST'S CHRISTMAS, THE
 (GN)/Jan 8, 1910; p. 17
OUTLAW'S LOVE, THE
 (Pa)/Jul 5, 1913; p. 48
OUTCASTS OF SOCIETY
 (Th)/Jul 31, 1915; pp 817, 831
OUTCAST'S RETURN, THE
 (GN)/Jun 13, 1914; p. 1521
OUTCAST'S SALVATION, THE
 (At)/Jan 14, 1911; p. 91
OUTER EDGE, THE
 (SA)/Oct 30a, 1915; p. 967
OUTER SHELL, THE (SA)/Jul 26,1913;p.427
OUTGENERALED (Sel)/Oct 28, 1911; p. 290
OUTLAW, THE (Bio)/Jun 27, 1908; p. 546
  (Pa)/May 10, 1913; p. 595
  (Vi)/Nov 1, 1913; p. 496
OUTLAW AND THE BABY, THE
 (Me)/Feb 3, 1912; p. 392
OUTLAW AND THE CHILD, THE
 (SA)/Mar 11, 1911; p. 540
OUTLAW AND THE FEMALE
 DETECTIVE (Bi)/Jun 3, 1911; p. 1260
OUTLAW COLONY, THE
 (Am)/Aug 17, 1912; p. 674
OUTLAW DEPUTY, THE
 (SA)/Nov 18, 1911; p. 550
OUTLAW SAMARITAN, THE
 (SA)/Aug 5, 1911; p. 293
OUTLAWED (FRA)/Dec 6, 1913; p. 1153
OUTLAW'S AWAKENING, THE

(SA)/Apr 10, 1915; p. 235
OUTLAW'S BRIDE, THE
(Sel)/Apr 10, 1915; p. 235
OUTLAW'S DAUGHTER, THE
(Fr)/May 2, 1914; p. 674
OUTLAW'S HONOR, AN
(Ne)/Jan 23, 1915; p. 516
OUTLAW'S NEMESIS, THE
(Th)/Jun 27, 1914; p. 1830
OUTLAW'S REDEMPTION, THE
(At)/Jun 18, 1910; p. 1049
(Ne)/Oct 4, 1913; p. 49
OUTLAW'S REVENGE, THE
(Re)/Apr 24, 1915; p. 557
OUTLAW'S SACRIFICE
(SA)/Feb 12, 1910; p. 215
OUTLAW'S SACRIFICE, THE
(SA)/Nov 2, 1912; p. 450
OUTLAW'S TRAIL, THE
(Am)/Jul 29, 1911; p. 211
OUTSKIRTS OF PARIS, THE
(Gau)/Nov 25, 1911; p. 636
OUTTERSNIPE, THE (Vi)/May 8,1915;p.899
OUTWITTED (UE)/Feb 20, 1909; p. 203
(Pa)/Oct 29, 1910; p. 998
OUTWITTED BY BILLY
(Sel)/Dec 6, 1913; p. 1151
OUTWITTED BY HIS WIFE
(Lu)/Jul 18, 1908; p. 49
OUTWITTED BY HORSE AND LARIAT
(Sol)/Aug 12, 1911; p. 378
OUTWITTING DAD (Lu)/May 9, 1914; p.820
OUTWITTING FATHER
(Ya)/Aug 5, 1911; p. 296
OUTWITTING PAPA
(SA)/Nov 11, 1911; p. 470
OVER A CRACKED BOWL
(Ne)/Apr 6, 1912; p. 42
OVER A CRIB (Lu)/Aug 30, 1913; p. 960
OVER AND BACK (Ko)/Sep 18, 1915; p.1996
OVER LUZERNE, SWITZERLAND, IN AN
AIRSHIP (Pa)/May 20, 1911; p. 1141
OVER MONACO IN A HYDRO-AEROPLANE
(CGP)/Aug 10, 1912; p. 545
OVER MOUNTAIN PASSES
(Ed)/Oct 8, 1910; p. 814
OVER NIAGARA (St)/Jan 3, 1914; p. 55
OVER NIGHT (Bra)/Dec 18, 1915; p. 2201/
Dec 25, 1915; p. 2391
OVER SECRET WIRES
(KB)/Aug 14, 1915; p. 1161
OVER SILENT PATHS
(Bio)/May 28, 1910; pp 888-89
OVER THE APPENNINES IN ITALY
(UE)/Mar 2, 1910; p. 509
OVER THE BACK FENCE
(Ed)/Feb 15, 1913; p. 680
OVER THE BOUNDING WAVES

(Jo)/May 8, 1915; p. 901
OVER THE CHAFING DISH
(Vi)/Oct 7, 1911; p. 39
OVER THE CLIFF
(Pa)/Jul 1, 1911; p. 1520
OVER THE CLIFFS
(Gau)/Jun 4, 1910; p. 942
(Ec)/Dec 6, 1913; p. 1153
OVER THE DIVIDE
(Lu)/Jul 6, 1912; p. 43
OVER THE GARDEN WALL
(Vi)/Jun 25, 1910; p. 1100
(Ka)/Aug 19, 1911; p. 464
OVER THE GREAT DIVIDE IN COLORADO
(Ed)/Jul 19, 1913; p. 320
OVER THE HILLS (Imp)/Dec 9, 1911; p. 818
OVER THE HILLS TO THE POORHOUSE
(Bio)/Jun 27, 1908; p.546
OVER THE LEDGE (Re)/Dec 26,1914;p.1850
OVER THE SHADING EDGE (Re)/May 20,
1911; p. 1143/Jun 3, 1911; pp 1238-39
OVER THE WIRE (Lu)/Jan 22, 1910; p. 92
OVERALL OUTING, THE
(Ko)/Nov 1, 1913; p. 497
OVERFLOWING IN ITALY
(KO)/Aug 1, 1908; p. 90
OVERLAND TO FREMONT
(Sel)/Jan 7, 1911; p. 32
OVERZEALOUS DOMESTIC
(Pa)/Jan 15, 1910; p. 57
OWANA, THE DEVIL WOMAN
(Ne)/Jun 7, 1913; p. 1033
OWANEE'S GREAT LOVE
(Bi)/Mar 18, 1911; p. 604
OWING MORE (Vic)/Dec 28, 1912; p. 1292
OWNER OF THE "L.L." RANCH, THE
(Me)/Jan 28, 1911; p.194
OXFORD & CAMBRIDGE BOAT RACE
(KO)/Jun 6, 1908; p. 497
OXYGEN (Ec)/Oct 4, 1913; p. 49
(Pa)/Oct 18, 1913; p. 264
OYSTER, THE (Maj)/May 24, 1913; p. 813
OYSTER DREDGER, THE
(Vic)/Jun 19, 1915; p. 1941
OYSTER FARMING (KO)/May 9,1908; p.423
OYSTER INDUSTRY, THE
(Lu)/Jun 22, 1907; p. 252
(Lu)/Jan 13, 1912; p. 126
(Imp)/May 17, 1913; p. 705
OYSTERMAN'S GOLD, THE
(Lu)/Jul 3, 1909; p. 12

P. HENRY JENKENS AND MARS
(Fal)/Jul 31, 1915; p. 817
PA AND MA ELOPE
(Bio)/Mar 21, 1914; p. 1524
PA SAYS (Bio)/Aug 2, 1913; p. 537
PA TRUBELL'S TROUBLES

No.15/Apr 20, 1912; p. 230
No.16/Apr 27, 1912; p. 329
No.17/May 4, 1912; p. 426
No.18/May 11, 1912; p. 527
No.20/May 25, 1912; p. 729
No.22/Jun 8, 1912; p. 944
No.24/Jun 22, 1912; p. 1126
No.25/Jun 29, 1912; p. 1227
No.26/Jul 6, 1912; p. 42
No.27/Jul 13, 1912; p. 148
No.28/Jul 20, 1912; p. 244
No.29/Jul 27, 1912; p. 344
No.30/Aug 3, 1912; p. 446
No.31/Aug 10, 1912; p. 545
No.32/Aug 17, 1912; p. 672
No.33/Aug 24, 1912; p. 770
No.34/Aug 31, 1912; p. 881
No.35/Sep 7, 1912; p. 976
No.36/Sep 14, 1912; p. 1075
No.37/Sep 21, 1912; pp 1175-76
No.38/Sep 28, 1912; p. 1276
No.39/Oct 5, 1912; p. 41
No.40/Oct 12, 1912; p. 143
No.41/Oct 19, 1912; p. 242
No.43/Nov 2, 1912; p. 450
No.44/Nov 9, 1912; p. 553
No.45/Nov 16, 1912; p. 659
No.46/Nov 23, 1912; p. 767
No.47/Nov 30, 1912; p. 877
No.48/Dec 7, 1912; p. 975
No.49/Dec 14, 1912; p. 1082
No.50/Dec 21, 1912; p. 1184
No.51/Dec 28, 1912; p. 1292
No.52/Jan 4, 1913; p. 51
No.1/Jan 11, 1913; p. 158
No.2/Jan 18, 1913; p. 264
No.3/Jan 25, 1913; p. 364
No.4/Feb 1, 1913; p. 464
No.5/Feb 8, 1913; p. 572
No.6/Feb 15, 1913; p. 679
No.7/Feb 22, 1913; p. 781
No.8/Mar 1, 1913; p. 887
No.10/Mar 15, 1913; p. 1104
No.11/Mar 22, 1913; p. 1219
No.14/Apr 12, 1913; p. 164
No.15/Apr 19, 1913; p. 281
No.16/Apr 26, 1913; p. 380
No.18/May 10, 1913; p. 596
No.19/May 17, 1913; p. 704
No.20/May 24, 1913; p. 812
No.21/May 31, 1913; p. 919
No.22/Jun 7, 1913; p. 1032
No.23/Jun 14, 1913; p. 1136
No.24/Jun 21, 1913; p. 1252
No.25/Jun 28, 1913; p. 1358
No.26/Jul 5, 1913; p. 48
No.28/Jul 12, 1913; p. 205
No.29/Jul 19, 1913; p. 319

No.30/Jul 19, 1913; p. 320
No.32/Jul 26, 1913; p. 428
No.34/Aug 2, 1913; p. 537
No.35/Aug 9, 1913; p. 635
No.36/Aug 9, 1913; p. 636
No.37/Aug 23, 1913; p. 842
No.38/Aug 16, 1913; p. 743
No.39/Aug 23, 1913; p. 843
No.40/Aug 23, 1913; p. 844
No.41/Aug 30, 1913; p. 960
No.42/Aug 30, 1913; p. 961
No.43/Sep 6, 1913; p. 1067
No.44/Sep 6, 1913; p. 1068
No.45/Sep 13, 1913; p. 1175
No.46/Sep 13, 1913; p. 1176
No.47/Sep 20, 1913; p. 1283
No.48/Sep 20, 1913; p. 1284
No.49/Sep 27, 1913; p. 1391
No.50/Sep 27, 1913; p. 1392
No.51/Oct 4, 1913; p. 48
No.52/Oct 4, 1913; p. 48
No.53/Oct 11, 1913; p. 156
No.56/Oct 18, 1913; p. 264
No.58/Nov 1, 1913; p. 496
No.59/Nov 1, 1913; p. 496
No.60/Nov 1, 1913; p. 496
No.64/Nov 15, 1913; p. 736
No.65/Nov 22, 1913; p. 867
No.66/Nov 22, 1913; p. 867
No.68/Nov 29, 1913; p. 1007
No.69/Dec 6, 1913; p. 1150
No.70/Dec 6, 1913; p. 1151
No.72/Dec 13, 1913; p. 1279
No.73/Dec 20, 1913; p. 1411
No.74/Dec 20, 1913; p. 1412
No.76/Dec 27, 1913; p. 1544
No.78/Jan 10, 1914; p. 172
No.80/Jan 17, 1914; p. 289
No.2/Jan 17, 1914; p. 289
No.4/Jan 24, 1914; p. 413
No.5/Jan 31, 1914; p. 543
No.6/Jan 31, 1914; p. 544
No.8/Feb 7, 1914; p. 677
No.12/Feb 28, 1914; p. 1087
No.14/Feb 28, 1914; p. 1088
No.16/Mar 7, 1914; p. 1237
No.18/Mar 14, 1914; p. 1385
No.20/Mar 21, 1914; p. 1525
No.22/Mar 28, 1914; p. 1681
No.24/Apr 4, 1914; p. 58
No.26/Apr 11, 1914; p. 213
No.28/Apr 18, 1914; p. 361
No.30/Apr 25, 1914; p. 517
No.32/May 2, 1914; p. 673
No.39/Jun 20, 1914; p. 1688
No.47/Aug 15, 1914; p. 959
No.48/Aug 22, 1914; p. 1099
No.50/Aug 29, 1914; p. 1240

No.59/Oct 3, 1914; p. 64
No.60/Oct 10, 1914; p. 187
No.61/Oct 10, 1914; p. 187
No.63/Oct 17, 1914; pp 336-37
No.64/Oct 24, 1914; p. 494
No.18/Mar 27, 1915; p. 1933
No.34/May 22, 1915; p. 1261
No.40/Jun 12, 1915; p. 1778
No.42/Jun 19, 1915; p. 1941
No.49/Jul 10, 1915; p. 309
PATHWAY FROM THE PAST, THE
(KB)/Jun 12, 1915; p. 1777
PATHWAY OF YEARS, THE
(SA)/Apr 5, 1913; p. 47
PATIENCE OF MISS JOB, THE
(Ed)/Sep 11, 1909; p. 346
PATIENT FROM PUNKVILLE, THE
(Pa)/Dec 4, 1909; p. 799
PATRICIA OF THE PLAINS
(SA)/Oct 15, 1910; p. 876
PATRIOT, THE
(Vi)/Jul 4, 1908; p. 14/Dec 19, 1908; p. 501
(Th)/Apr 19, 1913; p. 282
PATRIOT AND THE SPY, THE
(Th)/Jun 12, 1915; p. 1777
PATRIOTIC SONS, THE
(Ec)/Feb 24, 1912; p. 691
PAT'S BREECHES (Ch)/Jul 13, 1912; p. 148
PAT'S BUSY DAY (Lux)/Mar 8, 1913; p. 997
PAT'S DAY OFF (Key)/Dec 14, 1912; p.1082
PAT'S REVENGE (Lu)/Feb 21, 1914; p. 946
PATSY BOLIVAR (Lu)
No.1/Jan 9, 1915; p. 221
No.2/Jan 16, 1915; p. 368
No.3/Jan 23, 1915; p. 516
No.4/Jan 30, 1915; p. 672
No.5/Feb 13, 1915; p. 984
No.6/Feb 20, 1915; p. 1139
No.7/Feb 27, 1915; p. 1287
No.11/Mar 27, 1915; p. 1931
No.12/Apr 3, 1915; p. 63
No.13/Apr 10, 1915; p. 235
No.14/Apr 17, 1915; p. 392
PATSY OF THE CIRCUS
(Bi)/Jun 12, 1915; p. 1779
PATSY'S LUCK (Ne)/Sep 27, 1913; p. 1394
PATSY'S MISTAKE
(Ne)/Oct 26, 1912; p. 344
PAUL AND FRANCESCA (Pa)/Jun 3, 1911;
p. 1258/Jan 10, 1911; p. 1300
PAUL AND VIRGINIA
(Th)/Nov 26, 1910; p. 1239
(Rex)/Dec 7,1912; p.962/Dec 14,1912;p.1083
**PAULA PETERS AND HER TRAINED
ANIMALS** (Pa)/Apr 23, 1910; pp 641-42
PAULINE CUSHMAN, THE FEDERAL SPY
(Sel)/Mar 15, 1913; p. 1085/Mar 22, 1913;
pp 1201-2/Apr 5, 1913; p. 48

PAULINE'S NECKLACE
(Me)/Jun 20, 1914; p. 1689
PAWN OF FORTUNE, THE
(Ecl)/Sep 19, 1914; p. 1626
PAWN TICKET No. 913
(Sel)/Sep 19, 1914; p. 1645
PAWNBROKER, THE
(Lu)/Aug 29, 1908; p. 162
PAWNBROKER'S DAUGHTER, THE
(Ka)/Jun 28, 1913; p. 1359
PAWNED BRACELET, THE
(Lu)/Apr 26, 1913; p. 381
PAWNS OF DESTINY, THE
(Vic)/May 2, 1914; p. 659
PAWNS OF FATE
(Th)/Nov 28, 1914; p. 1234
(Rex)/Jan 16, 1915; p. 370
PAWNS OF MARS
(Vi)/Apr 24, 1915; pp 571-72
PAWNSHOP, THE (Sol)/Jan 7, 1911; p. 34
"PAY-AS-YOU-ENTER" MAN, THE
(SA)/Dec 20, 1913; p. 1412
PAY CAR, THE (Ka)/Sep 4, 1909; p. 313
PAY ROLL, THE (Ch)/Apr 8, 1911; p. 782
PAYING ATTENTION
(Gau)/May 7, 1910; p. 736
PAYING BUSINESS, A
(Gau)/Jul 3, 1909; p. 14
PAYING FOR SILENCE
(Ne)/Apr 19, 1913; p. 282
PAYING THE PRICE
(Lu)/May 11, 1912; p. 528
(Rex)/Sep 27, 1913; p. 1393
PAYMASTER, THE
(NYM)/Sep 25, 1909; p. 416
(Lu)/May 24, 1913; p. 812
PAYMENT IN FULL (Re)/Jun 19,1915;p.1940
PAY-TRAIN ROBBERY, THE
(Lu)/Dec 21, 1907; p. 692
PEACE AGITATOR, A
(Gau)/Nov 20, 1909; p. 722
PEACE COUNCIL, THE
(Pa)/Feb 22, 1913; p. 779
PEACE MAKER, THE
(Sel)/Jan 20, 1912; p. 203
PEACE OF BEAR VALLEY, THE
(Ne)/Sep 27, 1913; p. 1393
PEACE OFFERING, THE
(Vi)/May 13, 1911; p. 1081
(Ka)/Jan 18, 1913; p. 263
PEACEFUL INN, A (Pa)/Apr 18, 1908;
p. 353/Apr 3, 1909; p. 403
PEACEFUL VICTORY, A
(Th)/Oct 25, 1913; p. 381
PEACEMAKER, THE
(Vi)/Jun 11, 1910; p. 997
(Rex)/Mar 29, 1913; p. 1337
(Vi)/Oct 31, 1914; p. 640

(GN)/Dec 9, 1911; p. 818

PENALTY OF HIS CRIME, THE
(Pa)/Nov 7, 1908; p. 366

PENALTY OF INTEMPERANCE, THE
(Ka)/Jul 13, 1912; p. 147

PENALTY OF JEALOUSY, THE
(Lu)/Jun 21, 1913; p. 1253

PENALTY PAID, THE
(Pa)/Sep 21, 1912; p. 1175

PENDULUM OF FATE, THE
(Sel)/Nov 8, 1913; pp 612-13
(Th)/Aug 1, 1914; p. 705

PENITENT, THE (SA)/Dec 7, 1912; p. 975

PENITENT OF FLORENCE, A
(Gau)/Apr 30, 1910; pp 689-90

PENITENTES, THE
(Tri)/Nov 27, 1915; pp 1665, 1679

PENNANT PUZZLE, THE
(Sel)/Jul 27, 1912; p. 344

PENNILESS POET'S LUCK
(KO)/Jun 27, 1908; p. 548

PENNILESS PRINCE, THE
(Imp)/Apr 8, 1911; pp 782-83

PENNINGTON'S CHOICE
(Mto)/Nov 6, 1915; pp 1139, 1156

**PENNSYLVANIA STATE POLICE, TROOP
B** (Ed)/Jul 13, 1912; p. 147

PENNYWORTH OF POTATOES, A
(It)/Jun 18, 1910; p. 1049

PENSIONERS, THE
(Am)/May 11, 1912; p. 529

PEOPLE OF THE ARABIAN DESERT
(Gau)/Apr 8, 1911; p. 780

PEOPLE OF THE PIT, THE
(GS)/Jul 17, 1915; p. 487

PEPITA'S ESCAPADES
(CGP)/Jun 29, 1912; p. 1227

**PEPPER INDUSTRY IN THE MALAY
PENINSULA** (Pa)/Apr 1, 1911; p. 718

PERCIVAL CHUBBS AND THE WIDOW
(Ed)/Mar 9,1912; p.853/Apr 13,1912; p.136

PERCIVAL'S AWAKENING
(Lu)/May 15, 1915; p. 1071

PERCY, THE BANDIT
(Ne)/Oct 5, 1912; p. 42

PERCY, THE LADY KILLER
(Bio)/Jun 6, 1914; p. 1408

PERCY, THE MILLINER
(Roy)/Dec 19, 1914; p. 1681

PERCY AND HIS SQUAW
(Sol)/Nov 4, 1911; p. 381

PERCY GETS TIRED OF THE THEATER
(Ec)/Nov 4, 1911; p. 382

PERCY M. BALDWIN, TRIFLER
(Vic)/Feb 15, 1913; p. 681

PERCY NEEDED A REST
(Imp)/Jan 17, 1914; p. 290

PERCY PIMPERNICKEL, SOUBRETTE

(Ka)/Oct 31, 1914; p. 640

PERCY'S FIRST CAMERA
(UE)/Jun 29, 1912; p. 1227

PERCY'S FIRST HOLIDAY
(Th)/Feb 21, 1914; p. 947

PERCY'S NEW MAMMA
(Cry)/Nov 15, 1913; p. 737

PERCY'S WOOING (Ka)/Jun 21, 1913; p. 1252

PERE GORIOT (Bio)/Feb 27, 1915; p. 1288

PERE MILON (Pa)/May 29, 1909; p. 714

PERFECT NUISANCE, A
(KO)/Jun 8, 1907; pp 219-20

PERFECT THIRTY-SIX, THE
(Pa)/Nov 7, 1914; p. 793

PERFIDY OF MARY, THE
(Bio)/Apr 19, 1913; p. 280

PERFORMING LIONS
(Vi)/Dec 27, 1913; p. 1544

PERFUME CLUE, THE
(Pa)/Aug 5, 1911; p. 292

PERFUMED WRESTLER, THE
(Sel)/Feb 27, 1915; p. 1287

PERIL, THE (Imp)/Jun 8, 1912; p. 946

PERIL OF DIAZ, THE
(Ch)/Jun 10, 1911; p. 1319

PERIL OF THE CLIFFS, THE
(Ka)/Nov 9, 1912; p. 552

PERIL OF THE DANCE HALL, THE
(Ka)/Mar 1, 1913; p. 888

PERIL OF THE PAST, THE
(Gau)/May 24, 1913; p. 813

PERIL OF THE PLAINS
(WF)/Sep 21, 1912; pp 1167-68

PERIL OF THE PLAINS, THE
(Ka)/Nov 11, 1911; pp 469-70

PERILOUS CARGO, A
(Ed)/Feb 15, 1913; p. 679

PERILOUS RIDE, A
(Ed)/Dec 16, 1911; p. 904
(Lu)/Jun 7, 1913; p. 1030
(Maj)/Sep 13, 1913; p. 1176

PERILS OF A WAR MESSENGER
(Ch)/Aug 12, 1911; p. 378

PERILS OF PAULINE, THE (Ecl)
No.1/Apr 4, 1914; p. 38
No.4/May 16, 1914; p. 969
No.5/May 30, 1914; p. 1262
No.6/Jun 13, 1914; pp 1517, 1542
No.7/Jun 27, 1914; p. 1830
No.8/Jul 4, 1914; p. 71
No.11/Aug 22, 1914; p. 1101
No.12/Sep 5, 1914; p. 1347
No.13/Sep 19, 1914; p. 1621
No.14/Oct 3, 1914; p. 43
No.15/Oct 17, 1914; p. 319
No.16/Oct 31, 1914; p. 652
No.18/Nov 14, 1914; p. 940
No.20/Dec 26, 1914; p. 1846

PIONEER'S RECOMPENSE, THE
(Pa)/Mar 15, 1913; p. 1103
PIOUS UNDERTAKING, A
(Ed)/Dec 27, 1913; p. 1544
PIPE, THE (Vi)/Apr 27, 1912; p. 329
PIPE DREAM, A
(Ed)/Mar 27, 1915; p. 1931
(SA)/Jul 31, 1915; p. 816
PIPES O' PAN, THE
(Rex)/Oct 3, 1914; p. 66
PIPPA PASSES (Bio)/Oct 16, 1909;
pp 529-30/Oct 9, 1915; p. 285
PIRATE AIRSHIP
(Gau)/Mar 26, 1910; p. 466
PIRATE GOLD (Bio)/Jan 25, 1913; p. 364
PIRATES, THE
(Pa)/Nov 23, 1907; pp 618, 620/
Dec 12, 1908; p. 476
(Vi)/Nov 1, 1913; p. 497
PIRATES BOLD (Maj)/Jun 26, 1915; p. 2096
PIRATE'S DAUGHTER, THE
(Sel)/Oct 19, 1912; p. 243
PIRATE'S DOWER, THE
(Ya)/Jul 23, 1910; p. 194
PIRATE'S GOLD, THE
(Bio)/Nov 7, 1908; p. 364
PIRATE'S HONOR
(FIT)/Oct 30, 1908; pp 338, 344
PIRATES OF PEACOCK ALLEY, THE
(Sel)/May 16, 1914; p. 968
PIRATES OF THE SEA
(Amb)/Nov 27, 1909; p. 760
PISA (Cin)/Apr 6, 1912; p. 42
PISA, ITALY (Maj)/Apr 19, 1913; p. 281
PIT, THE (Wor)/Jan 2, 1915; p. 86
PIT AND THE PENDULUM, THE
(Sol)/Aug 2, 1913; p. 537
PIT THAT SPEAKS, THE
(Amb)/Oct 22, 1910; p. 939
PITCH O' CHANCE, THE
(Mus)/Dec 25, 1915; pp 2387, 2390
PITCH THAT DEFILES
(Maj)/Nov 29, 1913; p. 1009
PITCHER PLANT, THE
(CGP)/Feb 22, 1913; p. 779
PITFALL, THE
(KB)/Dec 20, 1913; p. 1413
(Ka)/Nov 27, 1915; p. 1663
PITFALL OF THE INSTALLMENT PLAN,
A (Am)/Oct 18, 1913; p. 265
PITFALLS (Po)/Apr 18, 1914; p. 362
PITTSBURG MILLIONAIRE, A
(Am)/Feb 18, 1911; p. 372
PITY OF IT, THE (Sel)/Oct 5,1912; pp 41-42
PIZEN PETE (Lu)/Feb 8, 1913; p. 573
PLACE, THE TIME AND THE MAN, THE
(SA)/Dec 19, 1914; p. 1680
PLACES OF INTEREST IN COLORADO

(Pa)/Jun 28, 1913; p. 1359
PLAGUE SPOT, THE
(Vi)/Oct 16, 1915; p. 439
PLAGUE-STRICKEN CITY, THE
(Gau)/Sep 21, 1912; p. 1178
PLAID COAT, THE
(Ba)/Oct 30a, 1915; p. 970
PLAIN JANE (Imp)/Dec 6, 1913; pp 1152-53
PLAIN MAME (Vi)/May 8, 1909; p. 594
PLAIN MARY (Rex)/Jul 18, 1914; p. 433
PLAIN SONG, A (Bio)/Dec 10, 1910; p. 1356
PLAIN TALE, A (Re)/Mar 11, 1911; p. 543
PLAINS ACROSS, THE
(Ne)/Aug 5, 1911; p. 296
PLAN THAT FAILED, THE
(Ne)/Jul 1, 1911; p. 1521
(Po)/Oct 5, 1912; p. 42
PLANK, THE (Pa)/Nov 23, 1907; p. 620
PLANS OF THE HOUSE
(Sol)/Mar 22, 1913; p. 1221
PLANT WITH NERVES, A
(Pa)/Nov 1, 1913; p. 496
PLANTER'S WIFE, THE
(Bio)/Oct 24, 1908; p. 324
PLANTING THE SPRING GARDEN
(Vi)/Jan 11, 1913; p. 158
PLANTS WHICH EAT
(Pa)/Oct 25, 1913; p. 379
PLAY OF THE SEASON, THE
(KB)/Jul 24, 1915; p. 651
PLAYERS, THE (Lu)/Oct 26, 1912; p. 342
PLAYING AT CHESS
(Pa)/Feb 29, 1908; p. 169
PLAYING AT DIVORCE
(Vi)/Dec 31, 1910; p. 1538
PLAYING DEAD (Vi)/Sep 25, 1915; p. 2197
PLAYING FOR A FORTUNE
(Ka)/Feb 14, 1914; p. 808
PLAYING FOR HIGH STAKES
(Mus)/Nov 6, 1915; p. 1140
PLAYING HORSE (Lu)/Oct 30a, 1915; p. 967
PLAYING IN TOUGH LUCK
(Lu)/Nov 6, 1915; p. 1139
PLAYING INJUN (Sol)/Feb 3, 1912; p. 394
PLAYING THE GAME
(Imp)/Jan 13, 1912; p. 127
(Vi)/Jun 19, 1915; p. 1939
PLAYING THE PIPERS
(Vi)/Sep 6, 1913; p. 1068
PLAYING THE SAME GAME
(Lu)/Dec 18, 1915; p. 2202
PLAYING TRUMPS
(Sol)/Sep 14, 1912; p. 1075
PLAYING WITH FIRE
(Vi)/May 3, 1913; p. 488
(Lu)/Sep 27, 1913; p. 1391
(Me)/Feb 21, 1914; p. 946
(Sel)/Nov 7, 1914; p. 788

(Vic)/Apr 3, 1915; p. 66
PLAYMATES
 (Ed)/Mar 7, 1908; p. 192
 (Vi)/Feb 24, 1912; p. 689
 (Maj)/Sep 27, 1913; p. 1393
 (Po)/Oct 25, 1913; p. 381
 (St)/Apr 17, 1915; p. 394
PLAYMATES, THE/Dec 19, 1908; p. 501
PLAY'S THE THING, THE
 (Dom)/Feb 21, 1914; p. 948
PLAYTHING, THE (Vic)/Jun 7,1913; p.1033
PLAYTHINGS OF FATE
 (Mil)/Aug 24, 1912; p. 771
 (Bio)/Jan 23, 1915; p. 515
PLAYWRIGHT, THE
 (SA)/Sep 16, 1911; p. 789
PLAYWRIGHT'S LOVE, THE
 (Th)/Aug 6, 1910; p. 298
PLEASANT EVENING AT THE THEATER,
 A (KO)/Jul 25, 1908; pp 68-69/
 Aug 29, 1908; p. 161
PLEASANT SIDE OF A SOLDIER'S LIFE,
 THE (Pa)/Jan 23, 1909; p. 93
PLEASE HELP THE PORE
 (Th)/Oct 5, 1912; p. 43
PLEASE REMIT (Ed)/Jan 20, 1912; p. 203
PLEASE TAKE ONE
 (Pa)/Jul 30, 1910; p. 244
PLEASING HER HUSBAND
 (Cry)/Sep 13, 1913; p. 1177
PLEASING UNCLE (Pr)/Jan 30, 1915; p. 672
PLEASURES OF CAMPING, THE
 (Maj)/Sep 14, 1912; p. 1076
PLEASURES ON EARTH
 (Lu)/Feb 14, 1914; p. 809
PLOT, THE (Vi)/Jan 16, 1915; p. 369
PLOT AGAINST BERTIE, THE
 (Ka)/Nov 18, 1911; p. 549
PLOT AGAINST THE GOVERNOR, THE
 (Th)/Oct 18, 1913; p. 266
PLOT AND COUNTERPLOT
 (Be)/Sep 18, 1915; p. 1996
PLOT FOILED, A (UE)/Apr 24, 1909; p. 516
PLOT FOR A MILLION, A
 (Ka)/May 3, 1913; p. 488
PLOT OF INDIA'S HILLMEN, THE
 (Ka)/Dec 13, 1913; p. 1279
PLOT THAT FAILED, THE
 (Vi)/Jun 26, 1909; p. 873
 (Po)/Nov 5, 1910; p. 1061
 (Gau)/Mar 4, 1911; p. 483
 (Ka)/Nov 2, 1912; p. 449
 (Sel)/May 16, 1914; p. 968
PLOUGHSHARE, THE
 (Ed)/Sep 25, 1915; pp 2195-96
PLUCKY AMERICAN GIRL, A
 (Me)/Oct 15, 1910; p. 874
PLUCKY BILL (Lux)/Aug 5, 1911; p. 296

PLUCKY GIRL, A
 (Po)/Jul 9, 1910; p. 86
PLUCKY WESTERN KID, A
 (Po)/Dec 24, 1910; pp 1480-81
PLUCKY YOUNG WOMAN, A
 Dec 19, 1908; pp 501, 509-10
PLUGGED NICKEL, A
 (Fal)/Aug 14, 1915; p. 1161
PLUMBER, THE (Sel)/Dec 23, 1911; p. 988
 (Key)/Dec 19, 1914; p.1680
 (Ufs)/Jan 2, 1915; p. 77
PLUMBER WINS THE GIRL, THE
 (Jo)/Feb 13, 1915; p. 985
PLUMBER'S PICNIC, THE
 (Bio)/Oct 10, 1914; p. 187
PLUNDERER, THE (Fox)/Jun 5, 1915;p.1621
POACHER, THE (LeL)/Nov 27, 1909; p. 760
 (GN)/Dec 24, 1910; p. 1479
 (Th)/Mar 23, 1912; p. 1064
POACHER'S WIFE, THE
 (Pa)/Apr 25, 1908; p. 376
POACHER'S TRUCK, A
 (KO)/Jul 11, 1908; p. 36
POCAHONTAS (Th)/Oct 8, 1910; p. 818/
 Oct 22, 1910; p. 939
POCAHONTAS: A CHILD OF THE FOREST
 (Ed)/Oct 3, 1908; p. 263/Oct 10, 1908; p. 279
POCKET POLICEMEN
 (Gau)/Mar 27, 1909; p. 368
POEMS IN PICTURES
 (Gau)/Oct 1, 1910; p. 747
POET AND HIS BABIES, A
 (WBE)/Jul 20, 1907; p. 315
POET AND PEASANT
 (Vi)/Nov 16, 1912; p. 658
 (Lu)/Mar 13, 1915; p. 1607
POET AND THE MAID AT THE MILL,
 THE/Jan 16, 1909; p. 69
POET AND THE SOLDIER, THE
 (Ka)/May 31, 1913; p. 919
POET LARIAT OF THE FLYING A, THE
 (Am)/Feb 21, 1914; p. 948
POET OF THE PEAKS, THE
 (Am)/Apr 24, 1915; p. 556
POET OF THE PEOPLE, THE
 (Th)/May 6, 1911; p. 1021
POET OF THE REVOLUTION
 (Gau)/Mar 19, 1910; p. 425
POETIC JUSTICE OF OMAR KHAN, THE
 (Sel)/May 1, 1915; p. 728
POETRY OF THE SEA/Jan 16, 1909; p. 69
POETRY OF THE WATERS
 (Gau)/Apr 16, 1910; p. 598
POET'S BID FOR FAME, THE
 Apr 20, 1907; p. 108
POET'S VISION, THE
 (Gau)/Apr 24, 1909; p. 517
POINT OF VIEW, THE

(SA)/Dec 2, 1911; p. 725
POISON (Fr)/Apr 11, 1914; p. 214
    (Ka)/Mar 20, 1915; p. 1772
POISON CUP, THE
    (Re)/Dec 9, 1911; p. 819
    (CGP)/Mar 23, 1912; p. 1062
POISON IVY (Sel)/Feb 1, 1913; p. 464
POISONED (Vi)/Apr 3, 1915; p. 63
POISONED BIT, THE
    (Ed)/Oct 17, 1914; p. 336
POISONED BOUQUET, THE
    (Vi)/Aug 15, 1908; pp 129-30
POISONED BY JEALOUSY
    (Ed)/May 15, 1915; p. 1072
POISONED CHOP, THE
    (Am)/Sep 6, 1913; p. 1070
POISONED DARTS, THE
    (Me)/Aug 2, 1913; p. 535
POISONED FLUME, THE
    (Am)/Aug 26, 1911; p. 544
POISONED POOL, THE
    (Ec)/Dec 21, 1912; p. 1186
POISONED STREAM, THE
    (Pa)/Nov 1, 1913; p. 496
POISONED WATERS, THE
    (Ne)/Sep 13, 1913; p. 1177
POISONS OF SERPENTS, THE
    (Pa)/Jun 20, 1914; p. 1689
POKER PAID (Lu)/Oct 4, 1913; p. 48
POKES AND JABS (St)/May 15,1915; p.1073
POKES AND JABS IN CLOVER
    (Wor)/Sep 18, 1915; p. 1997
**POKES AND JABS in "Mashers and
Smashers"** (Wor)/Aug 7, 1915; p. 998
POLAR BEAR HUNT
    (Mi)/May 25, 1907; p. 187
    (Pa)/Apr 9, 1910; p. 553
POLAR ROMANCE, A
    (Cen)/Nov 20, 1915; p. 1500
POLICE BAND, THE (KO)/Dec 19, 1908;
    p. 500/Jan 16, 1909; p. 69
POLICE DOG, THE (Pa)
    No.1/Nov 28, 1914; p. 1233
    No.2/Feb 13, 1915; p. 986
    No.3/Mar 27, 1915; p. 1933
    No.4/May 1, 1915; p. 729
    No.5/Jun 12, 1915; p. 1778
    No.6/Aug 7, 1915; p. 997
    No.9/Oct 30a, 1915; p. 969
POLICE FORCE OF NEW YORK, THE
    (Ed)/Dec 31, 1910; p.1536
POLICEMAN AND THE BABY, THE
    (Sel)/Oct 11, 1913; p. 155
POLICEMAN AND THE COOK, THE
    (KO)/Aug 1, 1908; pp 89-90
POLICEMAN FOR AN HOUR
    (Lu)/Aug 8, 1908; p. 108
POLICEMAN'S CHRISTMAS, THE

    (Lu)/Dec 31, 1909; p. 961
POLICEMAN'S DREAM, A (Vi)/Jul 25,
    1908; p. 72/Dec 19, 1908; p. 501
POLICEMAN'S REVOLVER, THE
    (SA)/Jan 15, 1910; p. 56
POLICEMAN'S SON, A
    (Imp)/Jul 2, 1910; p. 26
POLICEMAN'S VISION (Pa)/Sep 19, 1908;
    pp 222-23/Mar 6, 1909; p. 270
POLICEMEN IN ACTION
    (Gau)/Apr 17, 1909; p. 476
POLISH AND PIE (Ed)/Jul 11, 1911; p. 123
POLISHED BURGLAR, A
    (SA)/Dec 30, 1911; p. 1071
POLISHING DAY (KO)/Nov 9, 1907; p. 581
POLISHING UP (Vi)/Aug 28, 1914; p. 1240
POLISHING UP POLLY
    (Sel)/Jun 19, 1915; p. 1939
POLITENESS PAYS
    (Pr)/May 23, 1914; p. 1117
POLITICAL BOSS, THE
    (Ka)/Jul 18, 1914; p. 432
POLITICAL DISCUSSION, A
    (Pa)/Jul 30, 1910; p. 244
POLITICAL FEUD, A
    (Dom)/Dec 19, 1914; p. 1682
POLITICAL KIDNAPPING, A
    (Ka)/Aug 10, 1912; p. 545
POLITICAL MESS, A (Jo)/Jan 9, 1915; p.222
POLITICIAN, THE (Gau)/Apr 3, 1909; p.404
    (Maj)/Jul 5, 1913; p. 50
POLITICIAN'S DREAMS, THE (Vi)/Nov 25,
    1911; p. 622/Dec 9, 1911; p. 817
POLITICS (Sel)/Feb 19, 1910; p. 257
POLITICS AND SUFFRAGETTES
    (Bio)/Mar 21, 1914; p. 1524
POLITICS AND THE PRESS
    (Vi)/Oct 3, 1914; p. 63
POLKA ON THE BRAIN
    (UE)/Mar 6, 1909; p. 271
POLLY AT THE RANCH
    (Vi)/Mar 1, 1913; p. 888
POLLY OF THE POTS AND PANS
    (Lu)/Sep 4, 1915; p. 1643
"POLLYWOGS" PICNIC, THE
    (Ka)/May 1, 1915; p. 727
POLO CHAMPIONS, THE
    (Jo)/Jul 25, 1914; p. 573
POLO SUBSTITUTE, THE
    (Sel)/Aug 3, 1912; p. 445
POMPEY'S DREAM (Pa)/Aug 21,1909; p.254
POND SNAIL, THE
    (Pa)/Dec 6, 1913; p. 1151
PONTO'S LITTLE JOKE
    (Lux)/Jul 20, 1912; p. 245
PONY EXPRESS, THE
    (Ka)/Jun 15, 1907; p. 237
    (Ed)/May 22, 1909; p. 676

(Ne)/Jul 29, 1911; p. 212
PONY EXPRESS GIRL, THE
(Ka)/Nov 23, 1912; p. 767
PONY EXPRESS RIDER, THE
(SA)/Oct 1, 1910; p. 747
POOL SHARKS (Cas)/Oct 30, 1915; p. 792
POOLROOM, THE (Po)/Jan 24, 1914; p. 414
POOR, BUT DISHONEST
(Lko)/Oct 30, 1915; p. 793
POOR, BUT PROUD (Pa)/Jul 2, 1910; p. 24
POOR, SICK MEN, THE
(Bio)/Feb 11, 1911; p. 315
POOR AUNT MATILDA
(KO)/May 2, 1908; p. 401
POOR BABY (Ed)/Aug 14, 1915; p. 1160
POOR BOOB (Pun)/Jan 11, 1913; p. 160
POOR FINNY (Pun)/Dec 7, 1912; p. 977
POOR FIXER, THE
(Lar)/May 29, 1915; p. 1433
POOR FOLK'S BOY, THE
(Vi)/Jul 18, 1914; p. 433
POOR JAKE'S DEMISE
(Imp)/Jul 5, 1913; p. 49
POOR JOHN (Ko)/Nov 22, 1913; p. 869
POOR JONES' VACATION
(Ne)/Jan 4, 1913; p. 52
POOR KNIGHT AND THE DUKE'S DAUGHTER, A (KO)/Jun 27,1908;pp 548-49
POOR LITTLE CHAP - HE WAS ONLY DREAMING (Ec)/Apr 26, 1913; p. 381
POOR LITTLE KIDDIES
(Pa)/Jun 26, 1909; p. 873
POOR LITTLE RICH BOY
(Pa)/Nov 7, 1914; p. 789
POOR MAN, THE
(KO)/Aug 15, 1908; pp 127-28
POOR MAN'S ROMANCE, A (Pa)/Apr 25, 1908; p. 377/Feb 6, 1909; p. 144
POOR MUSICIAN, THE
(Vi)/Feb 27, 1909; p. 238
POOR OFFICER, THE
(Pa)/Jul 18, 1908; p. 50
POOR OLD COUPLE, THE
(Pa)/Dec 7, 1907; p. 652
POOR OLD MOTHER
(Re)/Oct 25, 1913; p. 381
POOR POLICY (Lko)/May 1, 1915; p. 729
POOR PUSSY (Pa)/Jun 20, 1908; p. 534
POOR RELATION, A
(Th)/Jan 11, 1913; p. 159
(Bio)/Nov 27, 1915; p. 1676/
Dec 18, 1915; p. 2203
POOR RELATION, THE
(Lu)/Feb 17, 1912; p. 581
POOR SCHMALTZ
(FP)/Sep 4, 1915; pp 1664-65
POOR SCHOOLMISTRESS
(KO)/May 9, 1908; p. 423

POOR SINGER GIRL, THE
(KO)/Dec 19,1908;p.512/Jan 9,1909;p.38
POOR STUDENT, THE
(Imp)/Dec 31, 1910; p. 1540
POOR WIFE'S DEVOTION, A
(Ka)/Jun 5, 1909; p. 754
POPE PIUS X AND THE VATICAN
(UF)/Nov 30, 1912; p. 883
(SHF)/Oct 24, 1914; p. 473
POPULAR BETTY (Vi)/Sep 28, 1912; p.1276
PORCELAINS (Pa)/Jul 26, 1913; p. 427
PORGY'S BOUQUET
(Ed)/Nov 15, 1913; p. 736
PORT OF DOOM, THE
(FP)/Nov 29, 1913; p. 989
PORT OF MISSING MEN, THE
(FP)/May 16, 1914; p. 976
PORT OF MISSING WOMEN, THE
(Sel)/Dec 6, 1913; p. 1150
PORTLAND STONE INDUSTRY
(WBE)/May 2, 1908; p. 405
PORTRAIT, THE
(Vi)/May 14, 1910; p. 784
(Imp)/Jan 6, 1912; p. 42
(Ed)/Mar 29, 1913; p.1337
(Vi)/Mar 7,1914;p.1246/Mar 28,1914;p.1681
PORTRAIT IN THE ATTIC, THE
(Ed)/Mar 20, 1915; p. 1764
PORTRAIT OF ANITA, THE
(Maj)/Feb 14, 1914; p. 810
PORTRAIT OF THE LADY ANNE, THE
(Th)/Aug 3, 1912; p. 446
PORTUGESE ARMY
(Ec)/Jun 22, 1912; p. 1128
PORTUGESE CENTAURS, THE
(Ec)/Dec 2, 1911; p. 727
PORTUGESE JOE (Ya)/Jul 22, 1911; p. 127
POSITIVE PROOF? (SA)/Mar 9, 1912; p.867
POSSIBILITY, A (Imp)/Jul 26, 1913; p. 429
POSSUM HUNT, THE (Ka)/Feb 8,1913;p.572
POSTAL CLERK, THE
(Gau)/Mar 13, 1909; p. 303
POSTAL SUBSTITUTE, A
(Me)/Aug 6, 1910; p. 296
POSTHUMOUS JEALOUSY
(KO)/Jul 11, 1908; p. 36
POST NO BILLS (Ed)/Oct 10, 1914; p. 187
POST-IMPRESSIONISTS, THE
(Sel)/May 24, 1913; p. 812
POSTMAN, THE (Imp)/Oct 26, 1912; p. 345
POSTMAN'S ESCAPADE, THE
(Lux)/Aug 17, 1912; p. 676
POSTMASTER OF PINEAPPLE PLAINS, THE (Fal)/Nov 20, 1915; p. 1500
POSTMISTRESS, THE
(Pa)/Feb 12, 1910; p. 216
(Lux)/Jun 3, 1911; p. 1260
POTS, PANS AND POETRY

(Vi)/Apr 6, 1912; p. 41
(Pa)/Jun 7, 1913; p. 1030
(CK)/Apr 18, 1914; p. 361
(Ka)/Dec 19, 1914; p. 1680
PRICE OF THE FREE, THE
(Sel)/Sep 13, 1913; p. 1175
PRICE OF THE NECKLACE, THE
(Ed)/Mar 28, 1914; p. 1681
PRICE OF THOUGHTLESSNESS, THE
(Vi)/Nov 22, 1913; p. 868
PRICE OF TREACHERY, THE
(Wor)/Apr 11, 1914; p. 190
PRICE OF VANITY, THE
(Re)/Jul 1, 1911; p. 1523
(Vi)/Apr 4, 1914; p. 58
PRICE OF VICTORY, THE
(Ed)/Mar 11, 1911; p. 540
(Lu)/Nov 22, 1913; p. 868
PRICE ON HIS HEAD, A
(He)/Sep 19, 1914; p. 1647
PRICE PAID, THE (Ec)/Aug 15, 1914; p.962
PRICE SHE PAID, THE
(SBa)/Sep 25, 1915; p. 2178
PRIDE OF ANGRY BEAR, THE
(Ka)/Feb 15, 1913; p. 679
PRIDE OF INNOCENCE, THE
(Pa)/May 3, 1913; p. 487
PRIDE OF JENNICO, THE
(FP)/Feb 28, 1914; p. 1071
PRIDE OF LEXINGTON
(Rep)/Jan 6, 1912; p. 42
PRIDE OF LONESOME, THE
(Am)/Jul 5, 1913; p. 49
PRIDE OF THE FORCE, THE
(Maj)/Jan 10, 1914; p. 174
PRIDE OF THE SOUTH, THE (KB)/Mar 15,
1913; p. 1086/Mar 22, 1913; p. 1222
PRIDE OF THE WEST
(Po)/Nov 11, 1911; p. 472
PRIEST AND THE MAN, THE
(Ed)/Mar 22, 1913; p. 1220
PRIESTESS OF CARTHAGE, A
(Gau)/May 13, 1911; p. 1080
PRIEST'S CONSCIENCE, A
(KO)/May 9, 1908; pp 422-23
PRIMA DONNA (Pa)/Sep 4, 1915; p. 1645
PRIMA DONNA, THE
(Vic)/Mar 8, 1913; p. 998
PRIMA DONNA'S CAT, THE
(Maj)/Mar 29, 1913; p. 1337
PRIMA DONNA'S MOTHERS, THE
(Sel)/Sep 4, 1915; p. 1643
PRIMAL CALL, THE
(Bio)/Jul 8, 1911; p. 1584
PRIMEVAL TEST, THE (Rex)/Nov 1, 1913;
p. 497/Nov 8, 1913; p. 594
PRIMITIVE CALL, THE
(Dom)/Jan 24, 1914; p. 414

PRIMITIVE INSTINCT, THE
(Ka)/Sep 5, 1914; p. 1372
PRIMITIVE MAN (Ka)/Dec 6, 1913; p. 1150
PRIMITIVE MODEL, THE
(Bio)/Jul 25, 1914; p. 572
PRIMITIVE SPIRIT, THE
(Re)/Apr 10, 1915; p. 236
PRIMITIVE WAY, THE
(Sel)/Feb 6, 1915; p. 828
PRIMROSE PATH, THE (Br)/Dec 4, 1915;
p. 1849/Dec 11, 1915; p. 2033
PRINCE (KB)/Jan 3, 1914; p. 50
PRINCE AND THE PAUPER, THE
(Ed)/Aug 14, 1909; p. 225
(FP)/Nov 20,1915; p.1511/Dec 4,1915;p.1849
PRINCE CHARMING
Dec 12, 1908; p. 477
(Re)/Apr 27,1912; p.335/May 25,1912; p.731
PRINCE IN DISGUISE, THE
(Vi)/Nov 6, 1915; p. 1139
PRINCE OF BOHEMIA, A
(Am)/Jun 13, 1914; p. 1541
PRINCE OF EVIL, A (Vi)/Aug 9,1913; p.637
PRINCE OF INDIA, A (Ecl)/Oct 3,1914; p.67
PRINCE OF ISRAEL, A
(CGP)/Sep 7, 1912; p. 976
PRINCE OF NORTH, A
(Pa)/Jun 11, 1910; p. 995
PRINCE OF PEACE, A
(Lu)/May 1, 1915; p. 728
PRINCE OF YESTERDAY, A
(Gau)/Dec 25, 1915; p. 2387
PRINCE PARTY, THE
(SA)/Nov 28, 1914; p. 1232
PRINCE WILLY (Ec)/Apr 18, 1914; p. 361
PRINCESS AND THE FISHBONE, THE
(Gau)/Aug 6, 1910; p. 296
PRINCESS AND THE MAN, THE
(Ed)/Feb 15, 1913; p. 678
PRINCESS AND THE PEASANT, THE
(Ed)/May 28, 1910; p. 889
PRINCESS ELENA'S PRISONER
(GN)/Dec 13, 1913; p. 1260
PRINCESS FOR A DAY, A
(Vic)/Jun 6, 1914; p. 1409
PRINCESS IN THE VASE, THE
(Bio)/Feb 22, 1908; p. 145
PRINCESS OF BAGDAD, A
(Hel)/Nov 29, 1913; p. 991
PRINCESS OF THE DESERT, A
(Ed)/May 2, 1914; p. 672
PRINCESS OF THE HILLS
(Ka)/Feb 17, 1912; p. 582
PRINCESS OF THE SEA, THE
(Gau)/Oct 23, 1909; p. 569
PRINCESS OF THE VALLEY, THE
(Ne)/Jun 28, 1913; p. 1360
PRINCESS ROMANOFF

(Bi)/Jul 11, 1914; p. 257
PRUNING THE MOVIES
(Ne)/Jan 2, 1915; p. 77
PRUSSIAN SPY, THE
(Bio)/Mar 6, 1909; p. 269
PSEUDO PRODIGAL, THE
(Re)/Jan 3, 1914; p. 49
PSEUDO SULTAN, THE
(Vi)/Jul 13, 1912; p. 147
PSYCHE (Pa)/Jul 10, 1909; pp 50-51
PSYCHOLOGY OF FEAR, THE
(Th)/Feb 8, 1913; p. 573
PUBLIC PARKS OF PARIS, THE
(Pa)/Jul 10, 1915; p. 309
PUEBLO INDIANS, ALBUQUERQUE, N.M.
(Lu)/Aug 10, 1912; p. 545
PUEBLO LEGEND, A
(Bio)/Sep 14, 1912; p. 1074
PUGILIST AND THE GIRL, THE
(Ka)/Jun 22, 1912; p. 1126
PUGILIST'S CHILD, THE
(Po)/Oct 1, 1910; p. 749
PULL FOR THE SHORE, SAILOR
(Ed)/Dec 16, 1911; pp 903-4
PULLMAN NIGHTMARE, A
(Th)/Jun 7, 1913; p. 1033
PULQUE PETE AND THE OPERA
  TROUPE (Ka)/Jan 4, 1913; p. 50
PULVERIZER, THE (Pa)/Jun 26, 1909; p.874
PUMPS (Vi)/Sep 27, 1913; p. 1392
PUNCH (Ec)/Mar 11, 1911;p.543
PUNCH AND JUDY (Pa)/Dec 25, 1909; p.922
PUNCHER'S LAW, THE
(SA)/Sep 30, 1911; p. 971
PUNCHER'S NEW LOVE, THE
(SA)/May 27, 1911; p. 1200
PUNCTURE-PROOF SOCK MAN, THE
(Lu)/Aug 29, 1914; p. 1241
PUNISHMENT, THE
(Bio)/Apr 20, 1912; pp 217, 229
PUNISHMENT OF AN ATHLETE
(TP)/Dec 4, 1909; p. 800
PUNY SOUL OF PETER RAND, THE
(Sel)/Apr 3, 1915; p. 63
PUPA CHANGES INTO A BUTTERFLY,
THE (GN)/Jun 20, 1908; p. 531
PUPPET CROWN, THE
(Las)/Aug 21, 1915; p. 1325
PUPPET SHOW, THE
(Cin)/Feb 24, 1912; p. 690
PUPPET'S DOWRY, THE
(WF)/Aug 29, 1914; p. 1243
PUPPET'S HOUR, THE
(Lu)/Jun 15, 1912; p. 1027
PUPS ON THE RAMPAGE
(Vi)/Apr 18, 1914; p. 361
PURCHASE PRICE, THE
(Ne)/Feb 22, 1913; p. 782

PURE GOLD (Ka)/Aug 13, 1910; p. 350
  (Vi)/Dec 26, 1914; p. 1840
PURE GOLD AND DROSS
(Rex)/Apr 19, 1913; p. 281
PURE GOLD PARTNER, A
(Po)/Oct 23, 1915; p. 621
PURGATION, THE (Bio)/Jul 16, 1910; p. 142
PURGATORY (SFF)/Apr 6, 1912; p. 30
PURGED BY FIRE (UE)/May 21,1910; p.834
PURITAN, THE (Lu)/Apr 11, 1914; p. 212
PURITAN COURTSHIP, A
(Pa)/Nov 4, 1911; p. 380
PURITAN EPISODE, A
(Ec)/Sep 20, 1913; p. 1285
PURITANS AND INDIANS
(Ka)/Feb 11, 1911; p. 316
PURPLE NIGHT, THE (Kni)/Sep 25, 1915;
  pp 2198-99/Oct 2, 1915; p. 79
PURSE AND THE GIRL, THE
(Pr)/Feb 14, 1914; p. 809
PURSUED BY A LIONESS
(Lux)/Jan 4, 1913; p. 52
PURSUER PURSUED, THE
(Am)/Mar 7, 1914; p. 1238
PURSUING SHADOW, THE
(PP)/Jul 17, 1915; p. 508
PURSUIT ETERNAL, THE
(Imp)/Apr 17, 1915; p. 398
PURSUIT OF A SUIT, THE
(Lu)/Mar 28, 1908; p. 272
PURSUIT OF FATE, THE
(Rex)/Jun 20, 1914; p. 1690
PURSUIT OF JANE, THE
(Imp)/Sep 6, 1913; p. 1069
PURSUIT OF THE SMUGGLERS, THE
(Ka)/Apr 26, 1913; p. 379
PUSH CART RACE (Pa)/Nov 7, 1908;
p. 367/Nov 14, 1908; p. 379
PUSHMOBILE RACE HELD AT
SAVANNAH, GA. (Imp)/Mar 2,1912; p.781
PUSS IN BOOTS
(Pa)/Nov 21, 1908; pp 398, 408-9
PUSS IN THE WELL
(WF)/Dec 19, 1914; p. 1681
PUT ME OFF AT WAYVILLE
(Ka)/Jan 23, 1915; p. 515
PUT OUT (Sol)/Mar 25, 1911; p. 658
PUT TO THE TEST (Sel)/Aug 2,1913; p.535
PUT YOURSELF IN HIS PLACE
(Th)/Oct 19, 1912; pp 226-28/
  Nov 2, 1912; p. 452
(Fr)/Feb 7, 1914; p. 678
PUT YOURSELF IN THEIR PLACE
(Vi)/Mar 22, 1913; p. 1220
PUTTIN' IT OVER ON PAPA
(Pa)/May 24, 1913; p. 812
PUTTING IT OVER
(SA)/Sep 23, 1911; p. 889

(Roy)/Jan 2, 1915; p. 77
PUTTING ONE OVER
(U)/Apr 10, 1915; p. 237
PUTTING ONE OVER ON THE DEACON
(Key)/Jan 25, 1913; p. 365
PUTTING PAPA TO SLEEP
(Nov)/Nov 6, 1915; p. 1140
PUZZLE MAD (Lu)/May 8, 1909; p. 594
PYGMY CIRCUS (Re)/May 4, 1912; p. 427
**PYRAMIDS AND THE SPHINX, EGYPT,
THE** (Ed)/Jul 5, 1913; p. 48
PYTHON ROBBERY, THE
(ISP)/May 2, 1914; p. 658

QUACK, THE (Ne)/May 9, 1914; p. 821
             (Lu)/Nov 28, 1914; p. 1232
**QUACK AND THE WOULD-BE SUICIDE,
A** (Me)/May 2, 1914; p. 672
QUAINT CALCUTTA
(Vi)/Sep 13, 1913; p. 1175
QUAINT SEATS IN SARDINIA
(Cin)/Oct 12, 1912; p. 143
QUAINT SPOTS IN CAIRO
(Ed)/Sep 13, 1913; p. 1175
QUAKER MOTHER, THE
(Vi)/Jul 15, 1911; p. 39
QUAKERESS, THE (Bro)/Aug 16,1913;p.744
QUALIFYING FOR LENA
(Ed)/Jul 25, 1914; p. 572
QUALITY OF FORGIVENESS, THE
(Bal)/Mar 27, 1915; p. 1938
QUALITY OF MERCY, THE
(Sel)/Dec 6, 1913; p. 1152
(Vi)/Mar 6, 1915; p. 1447
QUANTRELL'S SON (Vi)/Jan 31,1914; p.544
QUARREL, THE (Re)/Jan 20, 1912; p. 205
           (Ec)/Oct 17, 1914; p. 337
           (Vi)/Sep 18, 1915; p. 1995
QUARREL ON THE CLIFF, THE
(Ed)/May 27, 1911; p. 1200
QUARRY, THE (Sel)/Jun 12, 1915; p. 1777
QUARRY MAN, THE (Pa)/Dec 12, 1908;
p. 487/Dec 19, 1908; p. 500
QUARTER AFTER TWO, A
(Imp)/Aug 5, 1911; p. 294
QUARTZ MINING IN CALIFORNIA
(Po)/Mar 1, 1913; p. 889
QUEEN AND ADVENTURER
(Ecl)/Jan 23, 1915; p. 518
QUEEN ELIZABETH
(FP)/Aug 3, 1912; pp 428-29
QUEEN ELIZABETH'S RING (Cin)/Apr 6,
1912; p. 25/May 4, 1912; p. 426
QUEEN ELIZABETH'S TOKEN
(Gau)/Sep 21, 1912; p. 1178
QUEEN FOR A DAY
(Ed)/Nov 23, 1912; p. 766
QUEEN FOR A DAY, A

(Vi)/Feb 18, 1911; p. 370
QUEEN FOR AN HOUR, A
(Vi)/Oct 16, 1915; p. 440
QUEEN OF HEARTS
(GS)/Sep 18, 1915; p. 1997
QUEEN OF HEARTS, THE
(Sel)/Dec 10, 1910; p. 1358
QUEEN OF MAY (Rep)/Jul 6, 1912; p. 44
QUEEN OF NINEVEH, THE
(Amb)/Aug 26, 1911; p. 543
QUEEN OF SPADES, THE
(UE)/Oct 5,1912;pp 27-28/Nov 23,1912;p.766
(Cin)/Apr 19, 1913; p. 280
QUEEN OF THE ARENA, THE
(Sel)/Dec 12, 1908; p. 487
QUEEN OF THE BAND, THE
(Re)/Oct 23, 1915; p. 620
QUEEN OF THE BURLESQUE, A
(Ed)/Feb 26, 1910; p. 298
QUEEN OF THE FORTY THIEVES
(Ape)/Apr 25, 1914; p. 490
QUEEN OF THE JUNGLELAND
(Bi)/Oct 9, 1915; p. 254
QUEEN OF THE KITCHEN
(Ka)/Oct 12, 1912; p. 142
QUEEN OF THE PRAIRIES
(Col)/Jan 21, 1911; p. 145
QUEEN OF THE QUARRY, THE
(Ka)/Sep 4, 1909; p. 315
QUEEN OF THE SEA NYMPHS, THE
(Maj)/Jun 14, 1913; p. 1138
QUEEN OF THE SEASON, THE
(GN)/Dec 7, 1912; p. 977
QUEENIE AND THE CANNIBALS
(Imp)/Sep 14, 1912; p. 1075
QUEENIE OF THE NILE (Lu)/Sep 18, 1915;
p. 2006/Sep 25, 1915; p. 2176
QUEEN'S JEWEL, THE
(It)/Nov 1, 1913; p. 480
QUEEN'S LOVE, THE (GN)/Jan 2,1909;p.11
QUEEN'S MESSENGER, THE
(CGP)/May 11, 1912; pp 527-28
QUEEN'S TREACHERY, A
(Gau)/Dec 30, 1911; p. 1072
QUEER ELOPEMENT, A
(Bio)/Mar 15, 1913; p. 1104
QUEER FOLKS (Vi)/Sep 16, 1911; p. 789
QUEER QUARANTINE, A
(SA)/Apr 18, 1914; p. 360
QUEERING CUPID (Ka)/Oct 30, 1915; p.791
QUEST, THE
(Am)/Mar 27, 1915; pp 1935, 1940
(Sel)/Aug 14, 1915; p. 1160
QUEST FOR GOLD, THE
(Vi)/Aug 12, 1911; p. 376
QUEST OF THE SACRED GEM, THE
(Pa)/Nov 21, 1914; p. 1087
QUEST OF THE WIDOW, THE

RANCH GIRL'S LEGACY, THE
(SA)/Mar 19, 1910; p. 425
RANCH GIRL'S LOVE, THE
(Bi)/Feb 10, 1912; p. 484
RANCH GIRL'S MEASUREMENTS, THE
(Fr)/Feb 22, 1913; p. 781
RANCH GIRL'S MISTAKE, THE
(SA)/Mar 16, 1912; p. 962
RANCH GIRLS ON A RAMPAGE
(Ka)/Jun 1, 1912; p. 829
RANCH GIRL'S PARTNER, THE
(SA)/May 24, 1913; p. 812
RANCH IN FLAMES, THE
(Pa)/Sep 16, 1911; p. 788
RANCH KING'S DAUGHTER, THE
(Sel)/Feb 5, 1910; p. 169
RANCH LIFE IN THE GREAT
SOUTHWEST (Sel)/Jul 9, 1910; pp 78-79
RANCH MATES (Lu)/Dec 14, 1912; p. 1081
RANCH OWNER'S LOVE MAKING, THE
(Ed)/Mar 8, 1913; p. 997
RANCH RAIDERS, THE
(Bi)/Oct 15, 1910; p. 878
RANCH ROMANCE, A
(Ne)/Jul 11, 1914; p. 257
RANCH STENOGRAPHER, THE
(Fr)/May 24, 1913; p. 813
RANCH TENOR, THE
(Am)/Jun 10, 1911; p. 1319
RANCH WIDOWER'S DAUGHTERS, THE
(SA)/Mar 23, 1912; p. 1062
RANCH WOMAN, A (Ch)/Jun 8, 1912; p.946
RANCHERO'S REVENGE, THE
(Bio)/Jun 14, 1913; p. 1136
RANCHER'S FAILING, THE
(Sel)/Sep 20, 1913; p. 1284
RANCHERS' LOTTERY
(Ec)/Sep 21, 1912; p. 1177
RANCHMAN AND THE MISER, THE
(Ch)/Nov 26, 1910; p. 1238
RANCHMAN'S ANNIVERSARY, THE
(SA)/Nov 23, 1912; p. 766
RANCHMAN'S AWAKENING, THE
(UB)/Sep 28, 1912; p. 1277
RANCHMAN'S BLUNDER, THE
(SA)/Feb 22, 1913; p. 779
RANCHMAN'S BRIDE, THE
(Ne)/Dec 3, 1910; p. 1298
RANCHMAN'S DAUGHTER, THE
(Lu)/Dec 2, 1911; p. 726
RANCHMAN'S DEBT OF HONOR, THE
(Me)/Jan 13, 1912; p.125
RANCHMAN'S DOUBLE, THE
(Fr)/Sep 20, 1913; p. 1285
RANCHMAN'S FEUD, THE
(SA)/Jun 25, 1910; p. 1100
RANCHMAN'S LOVE, THE (Sel)/Oct 10,
1908; p. 288/Oct 17, 1908; p. 298

RANCHMAN'S MARATHON, THE
(Am)/Apr 20, 1912; p. 231
RANCHMAN'S NERVE, THE
(Am)/Jul 29, 1911; pp 190-91
RANCHMAN'S REMEDY, THE
(Ne)/Jul 27, 1912; p. 344
RANCHMAN'S RIVAL, THE
(SA)/Dec 25, 1909; p. 920
RANCHMAN'S SIMPLE SON, THE
(Bi)/Jul 16, 1910; p. 143
RANCHMAN'S SON, THE (SA)/Aug 26,
1911; p. 541/Sep 2, 1911; p. 628
RANCHMAN'S TRUST, THE
(SA)/Sep 21, 1912; p. 1176
RANCHMAN'S VENGEANCE, THE
(Am)/May 13, 1911; p. 1067
RANCHMAN'S WIFE, THE
(Bi)/Nov 27, 1909; p. 760
RANCHMAN'S WOOING, A
(SA)/Apr 16, 1910; p. 597
RANCHMAN'S WOOING, THE
(Uni)/Dec 14, 1912; p. 1082
RANCH'S NEW BARBER, THE
(Lu)/Sep 30, 1911; p. 970
RANGE GIRL AND THE COWBOY, THE
(Sel)/Oct 9, 1915; p. 252
RANGE LAW, THE (Sel)/Mar 8,1913; p.995
RANGE PALS (Sel)/Jul 1, 1911; p. 1520
RANGE RIDERS, THE
(Sel)/Jun 25, 1910; p. 1100
RANGE ROMANCE, A
(Bi)/Dec 16, 1911; p. 905
RANGER AND HIS HORSE, THE
(Sel)/Dec 28, 1912; p. 1291
RANGER AND THE GIRL, THE
(Lu)/Mar 12, 1910; p. 382
RANGER'S BRIDE, THE
(SA)/Apr 23, 1910; p. 641
RANGER'S REWARD, THE
(Lu)/Aug 3, 1912; p. 446
RANGER'S ROMANCE, THE
(Sel)/Nov 28, 1914; p. 1231
RANGER'S STRATEGEM, THE
(Ka)/Sep 30, 1911; p. 971
RANGOON, INDIA (Pa)/Oct 14, 1911; p. 129
RANSOM, THE (Gau)/Jul 8, 1911; p. 1585
(Po)/Jul 27, 1912; p. 345
RANSOM OF RED CHIEF, THE
(Ed)/Mar 4, 1911; p. 482
RANSOMED (Vi)/Oct 15, 1910; p. 874
RANSON'S FOLLY (Ed)/Mar 12, 1910; p.383
RASCAL'S WOLFISH WAY, A
(Key)/Aug 21, 1915; p. 1317
RASKEY'S ROAD SHOW
(Ka)/Jul 3, 1915; p. 64
RASTUS AMONG THE ZULUS
(Lu)/Aug 9, 1913; p. 637
RASTUS IN ZULULAND

(Vi)/Oct 23, 1909; p. 567
RED WING'S LOYALTY
(Bi)/Apr 23, 1910; p. 642
"RED" WINS (Sel)/Jun 19, 1915; p. 1939
REDBIRD WINS (Am)/Nov 28, 1914; p. 1234
REDDY'S REDEMPTION
(Am)/Apr 22, 1911; p. 901
REDEEMED CLAIM, THE
(SA)/Oct 4, 1913; p. 47
REDEEMED CRIMINAL, THE
(SA)/Jan 14, 1911; p. 90
REDEEMING ANGEL
(Amb)/Mar 4, 1911; p. 484
REDEMPTION (Ec)/Apr 20, 1912; pp 221-22
(Th)/Sep 27, 1913; p. 1393
REDEMPTION, THE
(Re)/Sep 28, 1912; p. 1277
(Ka)/Mar 8, 1913; p. 996
REDEMPTION OF A COWARD, THE
(Ch)/Nov 25, 1911; p. 638
REDEMPTION OF A PAL, THE
(Am)/Oct 3, 1914; p. 65
REDEMPTION OF BEN FARLAND, THE
(Vi)/Jun 8, 1912; p. 942
REDEMPTION OF BRONCHO BILLY, THE
(SA)/Jan 17, 1914; p. 288
REDEMPTION OF DAVID CORSON, THE
(FP)/Apr 25, 1914; p. 518
REDEMPTION OF GREEK JOE, THE
(Sel)/Apr 27, 1912; p. 329
REDEMPTION OF RAWHIDE, THE
(Me)/Jun 3, 1911; p. 1259
REDEMPTION OF RED RUBE, THE
(Vi)/Aug 3, 1912; p. 445
REDEMPTION OF SLIVERS, THE
(SA)/Oct 19, 1912; p. 242
REDEMPTION OF STEVE HARDING, THE
(Amm)/Jan 31, 1914; p. 546
REDEMPTION OF THE JASONS, THE
(Be)/Jun 19, 1915; p. 1940
REDMAN AND THE CHILD, THE
(Bio)/Aug 1, 1908; p. 87
REDMAN'S BURDEN, THE
(Ed)/Jan 18, 1913; p. 264
REDMAN'S DEVOTION, A
(Bi)/Jan 22, 1910; p. 92
REDMAN'S DOG, THE
(Pa)/Sep 23, 1911; p. 890
REDMAN'S LOYALTY, A
(Pa)/Oct 19, 1912; p. 242
REDMAN'S PERSECUTION, THE
(Bi)/Sep 3, 1910; p. 520
REDMAN'S VIEW, THE
(Bio)/Dec 25, 1909; pp 920-21
RED'S CONQUEST (Sel)/Apr 22, 1911; p.898
REDSKIN RAIDERS, THE
(Ka)/Oct 26, 1912; p. 342
REDSKIN RECKONING, A

(Bi)/Oct 31, 1914; p. 643
REDSKINS AND RENEGADES, THE
(Ka)/Jun 6, 1914; p. 1409
REDSKIN'S APPEAL, A
(Pa)/Jun 29, 1912; pp 1226-27
REDSKIN'S MERCY, THE
(Pa)/May 31, 1913; p. 920
REEDHAM'S ORPHANAGE FESTIVAL, 1910
(UE)/Oct 22, 1910; p. 934
REFINING FIRES (Am)/Jan 30, 1915; p. 673
REFLECTIONS FROM THE FIRELIGHT
(Imp)/Feb 24, 1912; p. 691
REFORM CANDIDATE, THE
(Ed)/Sep 30,1911; p.957/Nov 11,1911; p.471'
(Pal)/Dec 25, 1915; pp 2384-85
REFORMATION (Am)/Apr 10, 1915; p. 237
REFORMATION, THE
(KB)/Sep 20, 1913; p. 1285
REFORMATION OF CALLIOPE, THE
(Ec)/Oct 18, 1913; p. 266
REFORMATION OF DAD, THE
(Sel)/Jul 26, 1913; p. 427
REFORMATION OF HAM, THE
(Ka)/Jan 9, 1915; p. 220
REFORMATION OF JACK ROBINS, THE
(Me)/May 13, 1911; p. 1081
REFORMATION OF KID HOGAN, THE
(Lu)/Apr 20, 1912; p. 230
REFORMATION OF PETER AND PAUL,
THE (Th)/May 1, 1915; p. 728
REFORMATION OF SIERRA SMITH, THE
(Am)/Oct 19, 1912; p. 244
REFORMATION OF THE SUFFRAGETTES,
THE (Gau)/Feb 25, 1911; p. 431
REFORMED CANDIDATE, THE
(Maj)/Mar 7, 1904; p. 1238
REFORMED OUTLAW, THE
(Lu)/Sep 6, 1913; p. 1068
REFORMED SANTA CLAUS, A
(Vi)/Jan 6, 1912; p. 40
REFORMED THIEF (TP)/Dec 18,1909; p.882
REFORMER, THE (Cas)/Oct 30a,1915; p.968
REFORMERS, THE (Bio)/Aug 23,1913;p.844
REFORMING A HUSBAND
(Lu)/Mar 20, 1909; p. 337
REFRIGERATOR CAR'S CAPTIVE, THE
(Ka)/Apr 11, 1914; p. 213
REFUGE (Vic)/Aug 21, 1915; p. 1318
REFUGEE, THE (Lux)/Jan 29, 1910; p. 128
(Th)/May 29, 1915; p. 1432
REFUGEES, THE (Jo)/Mar 20, 1915; p. 1765
REFUGEE'S CASKET, THE
(Gau)/Aug 24, 1912; pp 757-58
REFUSING A MANSION
(Gau)/Sep 3, 1910; p. 519
REGAINED REPUTATION, A
(Re)/Mar 29, 1913; p. 1337
REGAN'S DAUGHTER

(Vi)/Oct 17, 1914; p. 336
REGATTA ALONG THE RIVER MEKONG
(Pa)/Mar 25, 1911; p. 656
REGATTAS IN LONDON
(Pa)/Feb 29, 1908; p. 172
REGENERATING LOVE, THE
(Lu)/Feb 20, 1915; p. 1140
REGENERATION (Vi)/Nov 11, 1911; p. 469
REGENERATION, THE
(Ka)/May 23, 1914; p. 1117
(Fox)/Oct 2, 1915; p. 94/Oct 9, 1915; p. 254
REGENERATION OF APACHE KID, THE
(Sel)/Aug 26, 1911; p. 542
REGENERATION OF JOHN STORM, THE
(Imp)/Apr 26, 1913; p. 381
REGENERATION OF WORTHLESS DAN, THE (Ne)/Dec 7, 1912; p. 977
REGGIE, THE SQUAW MAN
(Ka)/Mar 14, 1914; p. 1384
REGGIE'S ENGAGEMENT
(Lu)/Dec 24, 1910; p. 1476
REGIMENT OF TWO, A (Vi)/May 24, 1913; p. 792/Jun 28, 1913; p. 1358
REGIMENTAL BALL, THE
(Th)/May 27, 1911; pp 1201-2
REGIMENTAL PALS (Bi)/Jan 25,1913;p.365
REGINALD'S COURTSHIP
(Ed)/Nov 1, 1913; p. 496
REGINALD'S REVENGE
(Pre)/Jan 2, 1915; p. 77
REGULAR RIP, A (Bio)/Nov 21,1914; p.1075
REHEARSAL, THE
(Po)/Dec 24, 1910; p. 1480
(Bio)/Oct 2, 1915; p. 79
REIGN OF TERROR, THE
(Ecl)/Jul 18, 1914; p. 413
REIGN OF THE SIREN, THE
(Ka)/Apr 3, 1915; p. 68
REINCARNATION (TH)/Sep 11,1914; p.1833
REINCARNATION OF A SOUL, THE
(Po)/Aug 30, 1913; p. 961
REINCARNATION OF KOMAR
(Vi)/Dec 7, 1912; pp 963-64
REJECTED (Gau)/Oct 21, 1911; p. 208
REJECTED LOVER'S LUCK, THE
(Sel)/Oct 4, 1913; p. 47
REJUVENATION (Th)/May 4, 1912; p. 427
REJUVENATION OF FATHER
(Lu)/May 28, 1910; p. 889
REJUVENATION OF 'LISA JANE, THE
(Jo)/Mar 20, 1915; p. 1765
RELENTLESS LAW, THE
(Am)/Jan 27, 1912; p. 304
RELIANCE EDUCTIONAL PICTURE No. 3
(Re)/Feb 17, 1912; p. 583
RELIANCE NATURAL HISTORY SERIES
(Re)/Feb 3, 1912; p. 394
RELIC, THE (Bro)/Mar 7, 1914; p. 1238

RELIC OF OLD JAPAN, A
(Dom)/Jun 13, 1914; p. 1542
RELIC OF OLDEN DAYS, A
(Fr)/Nov 28, 1914; p. 1233
RELIEF OF LUCKNOW, THE
(Ed)/Aug 10, 1912; p. 545
RELIGION AND GUN PRACTICE
(Sel)/Jun 7, 1913; p. 1031
RELIGIOUS FESTIVAL IN INDIA
(Pa)/Apr 10, 1915; p. 237
RELIGIOUS FETES OF TIBET, THE
(Ec)/Nov 19, 1910; p. 1179
RELUCTANT CINDERELLA, A
(Ed)/May 17, 1913; p. 704
RE-MAKING OF A MAN, THE
(Po)/Apr 30, 1910; p. 690
REMEMBER MARY MAGDALEN
(Vic)/Feb 28, 1914; p. 1089
REMITTANCE MAN, THE
(Me)/Apr 13, 1912; p. 136
REMORSE (Th)/Jun 27, 1914; p. 1830
REMORSEFUL SON (KO)/Jun 6, 1908; p.497
REMOVING SUNKEN VESSELS
(Ed)/Nov 2, 1912; p. 449
RENDEZVOUS IN HYDE PARK, A
(GN)/Dec 9, 1911; p. 818
RENE HAGGARD JOURNEYS ON
(Rex)/May 8, 1915; p. 901
RENEGADE, THE
(Ne)/Apr 20, 1912; p. 231
(Am)/Oct 12, 1912; p. 143
(Bro)/Mar 27,1915;p.1939/May 1,1915; p.729
RENEGADE BROTHER, THE
(Pa)/Nov 4, 1911; p. 378
RENEGADES, THE (Lu)/Oct 5, 1912; p. 41
RENEGADE'S HEART, THE
(Am)/Apr 5, 1913; p. 50
RENEGADE'S SISTER, THE
(MiR)/Jun 20, 1914; p. 1691
RENEGADE'S VENGEANCE, THE
(Sel)/Mar 21, 1914; p. 1524
RENO ROMANCE, A
(Imp)/Jun 11, 1910; p. 999
RENT JUMPERS, THE
(Key)/Apr 24, 1915; p. 556
RENUNCIATION (Vi)/Oct 8, 1910; p. 814
RENUNCIATION, THE
(Vi)/Oct 30, 1908; p. 347/Jan 9, 1909; p. 37
(Bio)/Jul 24, 1909; pp 124-25
(Ne)/Aug 30, 1913; p. 962
(Ec)/Jul 25, 1914; p. 573
REPAID (Bro)/Feb 28, 1914; p. 1090
REPARATION (SA)/Oct 21, 1911; p. 208
(Rep)/Jun 15, 1912; p. 1027
(Sel)/Oct 24, 1914; p. 491
REPENTANCE (Th)/Apr 11, 1914; p. 214
REPENTANCE OF DR. BLINN, THE
(Vi)/Aug 21, 1915; p. 1316

(Vi)/Apr 24, 1915; p. 556
RETURN OF RICHARD NEAL, THE
(SA)/May 1, 1915; p. 728
RETURN OF TA-WA-WA
(Me)/Aug 27, 1910; p. 463
RETURN OF THUNDER CLOUD'S SPIRIT,
THE (101)/Mar 29, 1913; p. 1338
RETURN OF TONY, THE
(Imp)/Dec 13, 1913; p. 1280
RETURN OF WIDOW POGSON'S
HUSBAND, THE (Vi)/Aug 12,1911; pp 375-76
RETURN OF WILLIAM MARR, THE
(SA)/Jun 15, 1912; p. 1019
RETURNING GOOD FOR EVIL
(KO)/Oct 12, 1907; p. 507
REUBEN AND THE BOYS
(Cin)/Oct 12, 1912; p. 143
REUBIN'S BUSY DAY
(WF)/Oct 31, 1914; p. 642
REUNION DAYS IN ELI TOWN
(Gau)/Oct 26, 1912; p. 344
REUNION OF THE BLUE AND GRAY AT
GETTYSBURG (SEF)/Jul 19, 1913; p. 322
RE-UNITED (Imp)/Jan 28, 1911; p. 196
REUNITED (Cin)/Apr 6, 1912; p. 42
(Ec)/Jan 16, 1915; p. 370
REUNITED AT GETTYSBURG
(Imp)/Aug 9, 1913; p. 637
REUNITED BY THE SEA
(Imp)/Aug 10, 1912; p. 547
REV. GOODLEIGH'S COURTSHIP
(Imp)/Feb 11, 1911; p.319
REV. JOHN WRIGHT OF MISSOURI
(Ne)/Nov 5, 1910; p. 1061
REV. SALAMANDER, UNATTACHED,
THE (SA)/Jul 31, 1915; p. 816
REVELATION, THE (Ne)/Mar 9,1912; p.876
(KB)/Oct 11,1913;p.157
REVELER, THE (Sel)/Sep 5, 1914; p. 1371
REVENGE IS BLIND
(GN)/Apr 27, 1912; p. 330
REVENGE IS SWEET
(Lu)/Oct 28, 1911; p. 290
(GN)/Mar 9, 1912; p. 867
(Ed)/Aug 3, 1912; p. 445
REVENGE OF THE FAKIR, THE
(Ec)/Dec 14, 1912; p. 1087
REVENGE OF THE SILK MASKS
(Ec)/May 18, 1912; p. 629
REVENGE OF THE STEEPLEJACK, THE
(Th)/Aug 21, 1915; p. 1317
REVENGEFUL WAITER, THE
(FIT)/Oct 24, 1908; p. 326
REVENGING PICTURE, THE
(It)/Feb 11, 1911; p. 318
REVENUE AGENT, THE
(SA)/Jun 5, 1915; p. 1604
REVENUE AND THE GIRL, THE

(Ka)/Jan 6, 1912; p. 41
REVENUE MAN AND THE GIRL, THE
(Bio)/Oct 7, 1911; p. 41
REVENUE OFFICER'S DEPUTY, THE
(Re)/Oct 31, 1914; p. 642
REVENUE OFFICER'S LAST CASE, THE
(Po)/Nov 4, 1911; p. 381
REVIEW OF AUSTRIAN ARMY
(Gau)/Dec 9, 1911; p. 817
REVIEW OF THE FRENCH ARMY
(Pa)/Aug 5, 1911; p. 292
REVIEW OF THE TURIN EXPOSITION
(Amb)/Jun 24, 1911; p. 1455
REVIEW OF UNITED STATES TROOPS AT
FORT LEAVENWORTH
(SA)/Jan 29, 1910; p. 127
REVIEWING FRENCH TROOPS BY
AIRSHIP (UE)/Nov 30, 1912; p. 876
REVOLT, THE (Gau)/Dec 24, 1910; p. 1478
REVOLT OF MR. WIGGS, THE
(Vi)/Jul 24, 1915; p. 649
REVOLT OF THE PEASANTS, THE
(CGP)/Dec 7, 1912; p. 975
REVOLUTION IN THE BACHELOR'S
CLUB, A/Nov 11, 1911; p. 468
REVOLUTIONARY ROMANCE, A
(Sol)/Dec 9, 1911; p. 819
(Sel)/Feb 1, 1913; p. 464
REVOLUTIONIST, THE
(Lu)/Apr 6, 1912; p. 42
(Ape)/Jan 30, 1915; p. 684
REVOLVER IS RETURNED TO ITS
OWNER, THE (It)/Jul 29, 1911; p. 212
REVOLVING DOOR, THE
(Imp)/Dec 10, 1910; p. 1359
REWARD, THE (Lu)/Feb 28, 1914; p. 1088
(Re)/Mar 27, 1915; p. 1933
(KB)/Jun 26,1915; pp 2105-6
(Vi)/Oct 23, 1915; p. 619
(Imp)/Oct 30a, 1915; p. 969
REWARD OF COURAGE, THE
(Am)/Jun 14, 1913; p. 1138
REWARD OF SERVICE, THE
(Lu)/Jun 7, 1913; p. 1032
REWARD OF THRIFT, THE
(Vi)/Oct 3, 1914; p. 64
REWARD OF VALOR, THE
(Am)/Jun 8, 1912; p. 946
RHINE FALLS AT SCHAFFHAUSEN, THE
(Pa)/Apr 16, 1910; p. 599
RHINE FROM COLOGNE TO BINGEN, THE
(Pa)/Jul 16, 1910; p. 143
RHODA'S BURGLAR
(Cen)/Oct 23, 1915; p. 620
RHODES, ASIATIC TURKEY
(Pa)/Jun 28, 1913; p. 1360
RHODESIA RAILROAD IN SOUTH
AFRICA (UE)/Feb 6, 1909; p. 145

(Bio)/Jun 10, 1911; p. 1316
ROMANY WIFE, THE
(Ka)/Sep 3, 1910; p. 520
ROME ON THE TIBER
(Cin)/Jun 15, 1912; p. 1027
ROMEO AND JULIET
(Vi)/Jul 4, 1908; p. 14
(Sel)/Jun 25, 1910; p. 1101
(Th)/Aug 19, 1911; p. 446
(Pa)/Jan 18, 1913; p. 264
(Bio)/Jun 6, 1914; p. 1408
ROMEO TURNS BANDIT
(Pa)/Jun 4, 1910; p. 942
ROOM AND BOARD, $1.50
(Lko)/Oct 23, 1915; p. 621
ROOM BETWEEN, THE
(Emp)/Apr 10, 1915; p. 244
ROOM MATES (Lu)/Jul 10, 1909; p. 51
ROOM OF THE SECRET, THE
(Amb)/Aug 6, 1910; p. 298
ROOMS FOR RENT
(Vic)/Mar 6, 1915; p. 1449
ROONEY, THE BRIDE
(Ed)/Mar 27, 1915; p. 1931
ROONEY'S SAD CASE
(Vi)/Dec 18, 1915; p. 2202
ROOSEVELT IN CAIRO
(UE)/May 21, 1910; p. 834
ROOST, THE KIDDER (Ka)/Oct 5, 1912; p. 41
ROOT OF ALL EVIL, THE
(Maj)/Aug 28, 1915; p. 1480
ROOT OF EVIL, THE
(Bio)/Mar 30,1912; p.1165/Apr 6,1912; p.32
(Lu)/Apr 25, 1914; p. 517
ROPED AND TIED
(Ne)/Aug 26, 1911; pp 544-45
ROPED IN (Me)/Jan 27, 1912; p. 302
(Sel)/Dec 14, 1912; p. 1081
**ROPE-MAKING BY HAND, IN KENT,
ENGLAND** (UE)/Jun 15, 1912; p. 1026
ROPING A BRIDE (Sel)/Feb 27,1915; p.1287
RORKE'S DRIFT (Ed)/Feb 28, 1914; p. 1088
RORY OF THE BOGS
(Vic)/Dec 20, 1913; p. 1414
RORY O'MORE (Ka)/Aug 19, 1911;
pp 445-46/Oct 10, 1914; p. 188
ROSA AND THE AUTHOR
(Bio)/Nov 20, 1915; p. 1499
ROSALIE'S DOWRY
(Lux)/Jan 7, 1911; p. 35
ROSARY, THE (SA)/Jul 29, 1911; p. 209
(Imp)/Apr 23, 1910;pp 642-43
(Rex)/May 10, 1913; p. 597
(Sel)/Jun 26, 1915; p. 2105
ROSE AMONG THE BRIARS, THE
(Bal)/Dec 18, 1915; p. 2204
ROSE AND THE DAGGER, THE
(Rex)/Oct 7, 1911; p. 42

ROSE AND THE THORN, THE
(Vi)/Oct 24, 1914; p. 492
**ROSE AT SIXTEEN AND A CACTUS AT
FORTY-FIVE, A** (Fr)/Jul 12, 1913; p. 206
ROSE CARNIVAL, PORTLAND, ORE.
(Po)/Aug 10, 1912; p. 547
**ROSE CITY, JEYPORE, RAJPUTANA,
INDIA, THE** (Pa)/Jun 12, 1915; p. 1778
ROSE LEAVES (Vi)/Sep 10, 1910; p. 574
(Re)/May 1, 1915; p. 728
ROSE O' MY HEART
(Sel)/Jun 20, 1914; p. 1688
ROSE O' SALEM TOWN
(Bio)/Oct 8, 1910; p. 813
ROSE O' THE SHORE
(Bio)/Mar 20, 1915; p. 1763
ROSE OF CALIFORNIA, THE
(Imp)/Mar 9, 1912; p. 868
ROSE OF KENTUCKY, THE
(Bio)/Sep 9, 1911; p. 716
ROSE OF MAY, A (Sel)/Jun 28,1913; p.1359
ROSE OF OLD ST. AUGUSTINE
(Sel)/Jun 17, 1911; pp 1363, 1386-87
ROSE OF SAN JUAN, THE
(Am)/Jan 3, 1914; p. 49
ROSE OF SHARON, THE
(SA)/Aug 2, 1913; p. 536
ROSE OF THE CIRCUS
(Sol)/Apr 22, 1911; pp 901-2
ROSE OF THE PHILIPPINES
(Imp)/Feb 5, 1910; p. 169
ROSE OF THE RANCH
(Bi)/Mar 26, 1910; p. 467
ROSE OF THE RANCHO, THE (Las)/
Nov 21, 1914; p. 1078/Dec 12, 1914; p. 1531
ROSE OF THE TENDERLOIN, A
(Ed)/Dec 11, 1909; p. 841
ROSE OF YESTERDAY, A
(Fr)/Sep 26, 1914; p. 1777
ROSEBUSH OF MEMORIES, THE
(Re)/Jun 20, 1914; p. 1690
ROSELYN (Vi)/Mar 20, 1915; p. 1764
ROSEMARY (Qua)/Dec 11, 1915; pp 2029-30/
Dec 18, 1915; p. 2203
**ROSEMARY, THAT'S FOR
REMEMBRANCE** (Sel)/Nov 14, 1914; p. 932
ROSEMARY FOR REMEMBRANCE
(Lu)/Jul 30, 1910; pp 244-45
ROSES AND THORNS
(Ec)/May 25, 1912; p. 730
(U)/May 8, 1915; p. 901
ROSES FOR ROSIE (Lu)/Aug 16,1913; p.744
ROSES OF MEMORY
(Ed)/Dec 4, 1915; p. 1852
ROSES OF REMEMBRANCE
(Ne)/Apr 5, 1913; p. 49
ROSES OF THE VIRGIN, THE
(Ka)/Dec 10, 1910; p. 1356

(Sel)/Dec 7, 1912; p. 976
SAINT CLAUDE AND ITS ENVIRONS
(Pa)/Nov 1, 1913; p. 496
SAINTS AND SINNERS
(Rex)/Nov 18, 1911; p. 551
(Am)/Feb 27, 1915; p. 1288
(Vi)/Dec 4, 1915; p. 1852
SALAMANDER, THE
(Ec)/May 10, 1913; p. 597
(Mos)/Dec 25, 1915; p. 2386
SALAMBO (Amb)/Nov 4, 1911; p. 381
SALE OF A HEART, THE
(Vi)/Dec 6, 1913; p. 1150
SALESLADY, THE (Th)/May 18, 1912; p.630
SALLIE CASTLETON, SOUTHERNER
(Ed)/May 29, 1915; p. 1441
SALLIE'S SURE SHOT
(Sel)/Jul 19, 1913; p. 320
SALLY ANN'S STRATEGY
(Ed)/Dec 7, 1912; p. 976
SALLY IN OUR ALLEY
(Sel)/Apr 12, 1913; p. 163
SALLY SCRAGGS, HOUSEMAID
(Rex)/Aug 16, 1913; p. 745
SALLY'S GUARDIAN
(Ka)/Mar 15, 1913; p. 1103
SALLY'S ROMANCE
(Ed)/Feb 22, 1913; p. 780
SALMON FISHING IN CANADA
(Sol)/Jan 21, 1911; p. 144
SALOME (Vi)/Aug 29, 1908; pp 163-64
(Sav)/Feb 1, 1913; p. 467
SALOME AND THE DEVIL TO PAY
Oct 24, 1908; p. 318
SALOMY JANE (Alc)/Nov 7, 1914; p. 768
SALOON DANCE, THE
(Lu)/Oct 10, 1908; p. 286
SALOON-KEEPER'S NIGHTMARE, THE
(KO)/Jun 27, 1908; p. 548
SALOON NEXT DOOR, THE
(Imp)/Jul 30, 1910; p. 245
SALT DID IT, THE
(Vi)/Jun 6, 1908; p. 500
SALT INDUSTRY IN SICILY
(UE)/Dec 16, 1911; p. 903
**SALT LAKE CITY, UTAH, AND ITS
SURROUNDINGS** (Ed)/Nov 23, 1912; p. 768
SALT MACKEREL MINE, A
(Ka)/May 9, 1914; p. 820
SALT ON THE BIRD'S TRAIL, THE
(Me)/Oct 8, 1910; p. 813
SALTED MINE, THE
(Lu)/May 25, 1912; p. 729
SALUTORY LESSON, A
(Bio)/Aug 27, 1910; p. 463
**SALVAGE OPERATIONS OF S.S.
OCEANA** (Kin)/Dec 14, 1912; p. 1083
SALVATION ARMY LASS, THE

(Bio)/Mar 20, 1909; p. 336
SALVATION NELL
(Cal)/Aug 28, 1915; p. 1493
**SALVATION OF NANCE
O'SHAUGHNESSY, THE**
(Sel)/Mar 21, 1914; p. 1507
SALVATION SAL (Vi)/Oct 18, 1913; p. 263
"SALVATION" SMITH
(Po)/May 21, 1910; pp 834-35
SALVATION SUE (Ch)/Apr 20, 1912; p. 230
SALVATIONIST, THE
(Pa)/May 18, 1912; p. 629
SAM AND THE BULLY
(Lu)/Dec 26, 1914; p. 1840
SAM NOT WANTED IN THE FAMILY
(Pa)/Sep 18, 1909; p. 379
SAM SIMPKINS, SLEUTH
(SA)/May 4, 1912; p. 425
SAM SLAMEM SLAMMED
(Imp)/Jan 3, 1914; p. 49
**SAMARITAN OF COOGAN'S TENEMENT,
THE** (Lu)/Dec 14, 1912; p. 1081
SAME OLD STORY, THE
(SA)/May 31, 1913; p. 920
SAMMY, THE LITTLE BOOT BOY
(Amb)/Feb 10, 1912; p. 483
SAMMY CELEBRATES
(Pa)/Jan 30, 1909; p. 120
SAMMY ORPHEUS (Sel)/Dec 21, 1912;
p. 1168/Jan 4, 1913; p. 50
SAMMY'S DILEMNA
(Me)/May 30, 1914; p. 1260
SAMMY'S IDEA (KO)/Jul 18, 1908; p. 52
SAMMY'S SUCKER (KO)/Jun 6, 1908; p. 496
SAMMY'S VACATION
(Cry)/Dec 5, 1914; p. 1384
SAMOURAI'S EXPIATION, THE
(Pa)/May 27, 1911; p. 1200
SAM'S ARTISTIC BEARD
(Pa)/Nov 27, 1909; p. 759
SAM'S SWEETHEART
(Vi)/Dec 18, 1915; p. 2202
SAMSON
(Uni)/Apr 4, 1914; p. 59/Apr 25, 1914; p. 504
(Box)/Jan 16, 1915; p. 383
SAMSON AND DELILAH (Pa)/Sep 5, 1908;
p. 182/Oct 3, 1908; p. 253
SAMSON'S BETRAYAL
(Gau)/Dec 10, 1910; p. 1356
SAMUEL OF POSEN
(Sel)/Mar 19, 1910; p. 425
SAMURAI SCHOOL, THE
(CGP)/May 25, 1912; p. 729
SAN FRANCISCO, THE DAUNTLESS CITY
(Am)/Jul 12, 1913; p. 206
SAN FRANCISCO CELEBRATION, THE
(Key)/Dec 6, 1913; p. 1152
SAN XAVIER MISSION

(Lu)/Jan 25, 1913; p. 364
SAND HILL LOVERS, THE
(Vic)/Jun 20, 1914; p. 1690
SAND HOPPERS (CGP)/Jan 18, 1913; p. 264
SAND RAT, THE (Kri)/Mar 20, 1915; p.1766
SAND STORM, THE (Lu)/Aug 24, 1912; p. 770
SANDS OF DEE, THE (Bio)/Aug 3, 1912; p.
446/May 22,1915; p.1273/Jul 17,1915; p.485
SANDS OF FATE (Maj)/Oct 24, 1914; p. 493
SANDS OF LIFE, THE
(Bal)/Jul 11, 1914; p. 257
SANDS OF TIME (Sel)/Jul 10, 1915; p. 308
SANDS OF TIME, THE
(Sel)/Mar 29, 1913; p. 1336
SANDWICH WOMAN (Pa)/Feb 8, 1908; p. 104
SANDY, THE POACHER
(Lu)/Oct 23, 1909; p. 569
SANDY, THE SUBSTITUTE
(Ed)/Apr 23, 1910; p. 641
SANDY AND SHORTY
(Vi)/Aug 2, 1913; p. 535
SANDY AND SHORTY START SOMETHING
(Vi)/May 23, 1914; p. 1116
SANDY GETS SHORTY A JOB
(Vi)/Sep 27, 1913; p. 1392
SANDY McPHERSON'S QUIET FISHING
TRIP (Ed)/Oct 3, 1908; p. 263
SANE ASYLUM, A (Rex)/Feb 3, 1912; p. 394
SANE FOURTH, A (Ed)/Jun 17,1911; p.1386
SANITARIUM, THE (Sel)/Oct 22,1910; p.936
SANTA CATALINA (Key)/Oct 24,1914;p.493
SANTA CATALINA, THE MAGIC ISLE OF
THE PACIFIC (Am)/Dec 23,1911;pp973,990
SANTA CLAUS AND THE CLUBMAN
(Ed)/Dec 30, 1911; p. 1072
SANTA CLAUS VERSUS CUPID
(Ed)/Dec 25, 1915; p. 2388
SANTA FE, NEW MEXICO
(Ne)/Apr 6, 1912; p. 42
SANTA MONICA AUTO ROAD RACE
(Ne)/Jun 8, 1912; p. 944
SAPHEAD'S REVENGE, A
(Lko)/Dec 4, 1915; p. 1854
SAPHO (Ec)/Oct 4, 1913; p. 30
SAPHO UP-TO-DATE
(WF)/Jan 9, 1915; p. 222
SARABAND DANCE, THE
(Gau)/Mar 26, 1910; p. 467
SARAGOSSA (Pa)/May 31, 1913; p. 920
SARAH BERNHARDT AT HOME
(PyR)/Jul 31, 1915; p. 836
SARDINE INDUSTRY, THE
(Lu)/Jun 17, 1911; p. 1387
SARGEANT HOFMEYER
(St)/May 9, 1914; p. 821
SARGENT JIM'S HORSE
(KB)/Jan 23, 1915; p. 517
SATAN (Amb)/Jan 18, 1912; pp 243-44

SATAN AT PLAY/Nov 28, 1908; p. 423
SATAN DEFEATED (Pa)/Mar 18,1911; p.602
SATAN McALLISTER'S HEIR
(Dom)/Mar 13, 1915; p. 1609
SATAN ON A RAMPAGE
(UE)/Aug 5, 1911; p. 294
SATAN'S CASTLE
(Amb)/Dec 27, 1913; p. 1522
SATAN'S RHAPSODY
(GK)/Jul 25, 1914; p. 588
SATAN'S RIVAL (Pa)/Sep 2, 1911; p. 628
SATCHEL GAME, THE
(Imp)/Mar 22, 1913; p. 1221
SATIN AND GINGHAM
(Lu)/Dec 14, 1912; p. 1081
SATURDAY HOLIDAY, A
(Bio)/Oct 11, 1913; p. 156
SATYR AND THE LADY, THE
(Th)/Oct 28, 1911; p. 293
SAUCE FOR THE GOOSE
(Vi)/Sep 27, 1913; p. 1392
SAUCY SUE (Lu)/Jun 26, 1909; p. 874
SAUL AND DAVID
(Gau)/Mar 4, 1911; p.482
(CGP)/Apr 6,1912; p.40/Apr 13,1912; p.118
SAVAGE, THE (Ne)/Jun 17, 1911; p. 1388
SAVED BY A DOG (Ec)/Nov 5, 1910; p.1060
SAVED BY A DREAM
(Vic)/Apr 17, 1915; p. 394
SAVED BY A SHOWER
(Jo)/Feb 27, 1915; p. 1289
SAVED BY A SKIRT
(Ne)/Nov 20, 1915; p. 1501
SAVED BY A VISION (At)/Dec 10, 1910;
p. 1360/Dec 17, 1910; p. 1418
SAVED BY A WATCH
(Sel)/Dec 26, 1914; p. 1840
SAVED BY AIRSHIP
(Re)/Feb 8, 1913; p. 573
SAVED BY AN AUTO
(Am)/Aug 17, 1912; p. 674
SAVED BY BOSCO (GN)/Oct 29, 1910; p. 998
SAVED BY DIVINE PROVIDENCE
(Pa)/Dec 31, 1910; pp 1536, 1540
SAVED BY FIRE (Sel)/Nov 23, 1912; p. 767
SAVED BY HER CHEE-ILD
(Bio)/Dec 12, 1914; p. 1530
SAVED BY HER HORSE
(Sel)/Jun 26, 1915; p. 2095
SAVED BY HIS CHILD
(Gau)/Sep 6, 1913; p. 1069
SAVED BY HIS HORSE
(Pa)/Feb 15, 1913; p. 679
SAVED BY LOVE (Ed)/Nov 7,
1908; pp 358, 364/Nov 14, 1908; p. 379
SAVED BY PARCELS POST
(Imp)/Mar 29, 1913; p. 1337
SAVED BY TELEPATHY

(Sel)/Aug 21, 1915; p. 1317
SCARLET LETTER, THE
  (Ka)/Mar 28, 1908; pp 271-72
  (Imp)/Apr 22, 1911; pp 881-82/
    May 13, 1911; p. 1082
  (Kin)/May 10, 1913; p. 599
SCARLET SIN, THE
  (UnF)/Aug 7, 1915; p. 998
SCARS (Sel)/Mar 13, 1915; p. 1607
SCARS OF POSSESSION
  (SA)/Dec 12, 1914; p. 1524
SCENARIO WRITER, THE
  (Maj)/Nov 15, 1913; p. 737
SCENARIO WRITER'S DREAM, A
  (Imp)/Nov 21, 1914; p. 1077
SCENE OF HIS CRIME, THE
  (Ko)/May 23, 1914; p. 1117
**SCENES ALONG THE CANVERY RIVER,
INDIA** (Pa)/Feb 28, 1914; p. 1087
SCENES ALONG THE MEKONG RIVER
  (Pa)/May 13, 1911; p. 1081
SCENES ALONG THE PESCARA RIVER
  (Cin)/Apr 19, 1913; p. 281
SCENES ALONG THE SALERNO COAST
  (Cin)/Sep 28, 1912; p. 1276
**SCENES AND INCIDENTS - PANAMA
CANAL** (Ed)/Jun 1, 1907; pp 203-4
**SCENES AT THE FLOWER CARNIVAL,
PARIS** (Pa)/Aug 26, 1911; p. 542
SCENES FROM OTHER DAYS
  (Ed)/Jul 19, 1913; p. 320
SCENES FROM THEATRICAL LIFE
  (Ec)/Mar 30, 1912; p. 1167
SCENES IN BRITISH INDIA
  (UE)/Dec 24, 1910; p. 1478
SCENES IN COLUMBO, CEYLON
  (UE)/May 13, 1911; p. 1080
SCENES IN CUBA (Sel)/May 25, 1912; p. 729
SCENES IN DELHI (Kin)/Nov 23, 1912; p. 769
SCENES IN JAPAN (Vi)/Apr 12, 1913; p. 163
SCENES IN JERSEY (UE)/Feb 11, 1911; p. 315
SCENES IN KENT, ENGLAND
  (UE)/Jun 1, 1912; p. 829
SCENES IN KOREA
  (Sel)/May 11, 1912; p. 527
SCENES IN MANILA
  (Sel)/Jun 14, 1913; p. 1135
SCENES IN MONSONE, NORTH AFRICA
  (Cin)/Mar 22, 1913; p. 1220
SCENES IN NORWAY (Pa)/Sep 3, 1910; p. 520
SCENES IN OUR NAVY
  (Sel)/Jul 8, 1911; p. 1585
SCENES IN PADUA, ITALY
  (Cin)/Jun 1, 1912; p. 830
SCENES IN SAIGON, COCHIN CHINA
  (Me)/Nov 1, 1913; p. 495
SCENES IN SOMERSET
  (UE)/Jul 20, 1912; p. 244

SCENES IN THE CELESTIAL EMPIRE
  (UE)/Oct 1, 1910; p. 748
SCENES IN THE TURKISH-ITALIAN WAR
  (Cin)/Jun 22, 1912; p. 1126
**SCENES FROM THE BATTLEFIELD OF
GETTYSBURG** (Lu)/Aug 22, 1908; p. 143
SCENES OF IRISH LIFE
  (Vi)/Nov 9, 1912; p. 553
SCENES OF THE ITALIAN-TURKISH WAR
  (Cin)/Jun 1, 1912; p. 818
**SCENES ON THE COAST OF NORTH
AFRICA** (Gau)/Jan 6, 1912; p. 41
SCENTING A TERRIBLE CRIME
  (Bio)/Oct 25, 1913; p. 379
SCHEME OF SHIFTLESS SAM SMITH, THE
  (Ka)/Jun 21, 1913; p. 1252
SCHEME THAT FAILED, THE
  (Sol)/Apr 29,1911; p.960/ May 6,1911;p.1021
  (Lu)/Sep 30, 1911; p. 971
SCHEMERS, THE (Po)/May 18, 1912; p. 629
    (Imp)/Jun 29, 1912;p.1228
    (Vi)/Dec 6, 1913; p. 1151
SCHEMERS OF SQUEEDUNK, THE
  (Imp)/Mar 21, 1914; p. 1526
SCHEMING WOMAN, THE
  (Sol)/Feb 8, 1913; p. 574
SCHNEIDER'S ANTI-NOISE CRUSADE
  (Bio)/Apr 17, 1909; p. 477
SCHNITZ THE TAILOR
  (Key)/Oct 18, 1913; p. 265
SCHOOL DAYS (Pi)/Jun 14, 1913; p. 1137
SCHOOL FOR SCANDAL, THE
  (Ka)/Dec 19, 1914; p. 1663
SCHOOL IN NEW GUINEA, A
  (Pa)/Sep 3, 1910; p. 519
SCHOOL KID'S PICNIC, THE
  (Maj)/Aug 9, 1913; p. 637
SCHOOL MA'AM, THE
  (Pa)/Jul 26, 1913; p. 427
SCHOOL MA'AM COURAGE, THE
  (Re)/Feb 25, 1911; p. 431
**SCHOOL MARM OF COYOTE COUNTY,
THE** (Me)/Apr 29, 1911; p. 957
SCHOOL MASTER'S OVERCOAT, THE
  (Amb)/Aug 5, 1911; p. 294
SCHOOL OF NEW GUINEA, A
  (Pa)/Jun 12, 1915; p. 1778
SCHOOL PRINCIPAL, THE
  (Lu)/May 10, 1913; p. 596
SCHOOL TEACHER AND THE WAIF, THE
  (Bio)/Jul 13, 1912; p. 147
SCHOOLBOY'S JOKE
  (KO)/Jun 6, 1908; pp 496-97
SCHOOLBOY'S REVENGE, THE
  (Pa)/Apr 10, 1909; p. 443
SCHOOLING OF MARY ANN, THE
  (Sel)/May 16, 1914; p. 968
SCHOOLMA'AM OF SNAKE, THE

(Gau)/Feb 19, 1910; p. 257
SEASIDE FLIRT, A
(Cry)/Sep 5, 1914; p. 1373
SEASIDE FLIRTATION
(Pa)/Mar 26, 1910; p. 466
SEASIDE GIRL, A
(WBE)/Oct 19, 1907; pp 526-27
SEASIDE SAMARITAN, A
(Po)/Nov 29, 1913; p. 1009
SEAT IN THE BALCONY, A
(Gau)/Jan 22, 1910; p. 92
SEATS OF THE MIGHTY, THE
(Wor)/Dec 12, 1914; p. 1539
SECOND BEGINNING, THE
(U)/Jun 19, 1915; p. 1941
SECOND-CHILDHOOD
(Sel)/Jun 13, 1914; p. 1540
SECOND CLUE, THE
(Am)/Apr 11, 1914; p. 214
SECOND COMMANDMENT, THE
(Ka)/Apr 24, 1915; p. 555
SECOND DOOR LEFT, THE
(Ecl)/Oct 10, 1914; p. 189
SECOND GENERATION, THE
(Pa)/Mar 21, 1914; p. 1524
SECOND-HAND CAMERA, A
(KO)/Jul 11, 1908; pp 36, 38
SECOND HOME-COMING, THE
(Ne)/Aug 9, 1913; p. 638
SECOND HONEYMOON, A
(Vi)/Sep 16, 1911; p. 788
SECOND MRS. ROEBUCK, THE
(Maj)/Sep 5, 1914; p. 1373
SECOND MRS. TANQUERAY, THE
(WF)/Nov 14, 1914; p. 938
SECOND SHOT, THE
(Pa)/Jul 12, 1913; p. 204
(Lu)/Sep 4, 1915; p. 1643
SECOND SIGHT (Imp)/May 13, 1911; p.1083
(Vi)/Aug 22, 1914; p. 1099
SECOND SON, THE
(SA)/Nov 20, 1915; p. 1500
SECOND WIFE, THE
(Sel)/May 9, 1914; p. 820
SECRET, A (Lu)/Mar 6, 1909; p. 270
SECRET, THE (Lu)/Sep 16, 1911; pp 788-89
SECRET CHAMBER, THE
(UE)/Dec 18, 1909; p. 881
SECRET CRIME, A (Ka)/May 16, 1914; p. 968
SECRET FORMULA, THE
(Pa)/Aug 2, 1913; p. 535
(Ka)/May 2, 1914; p. 673
SECRET LODE, THE (KB)/Feb 7, 1914; p. 677
SECRET MARRIAGE, THE
(Ka)/May 10, 1913; p. 595
(Lu)/Apr 4, 1914; p. 58
SECRET NEST, THE
(Bio)/Sep 26, 1914; p. 1775

SECRET OF ADRIANOPLE, THE
(FRA)/Dec 6, 1913; p. 1154
SECRET OF BALANCED ROCK, THE
(Fr)/Nov 29, 1913; p. 1008
SECRET OF HYPNOTISM
(KO)/Aug 1, 1908; p. 89
SECRET OF LOST RIVER, THE
(KB)/Jun 19, 1915; p. 1940
SECRET OF PADRE ANTONIO, THE
(Fr)/Jul 12, 1913; p. 206
SECRET OF THE BULB, THE
(Vi)/Jan 17, 1914; p. 288
SECRET OF THE CELLAR
(UE)/Nov 26, 1910; p. 1236
SECRET OF THE CELLAR, THE
(Ed)/Aug 7, 1915; p. 996
SECRET OF THE DEAD, THE
(Dom)/Feb 20, 1915; p. 1141
SECRET OF THE FOREST, THE
(Gau)/Apr 15, 1911; p. 843
SECRET OF THE IRON MASK, THE
(Pa)/Aug 1, 1908; p. 90
SECRET OF THE LAKE, THE
(Amb)/May 21, 1910; p. 835
SECRET OF THE LOCKET, THE
(Ed)/Jul 17, 1909; p. 88
SECRET OF THE MISER'S CAVE, THE
(Ka)/Apr 27, 1912; p. 328
SECRET OF THE MOUNTAIN, THE
(Ecl)/Jan 9, 1915; p. 222
SECRET OF THE OLD CABINET
(GN)/Nov 1, 1913; p. 498
SECRET OF THE OPAL MINE
(Ya)/Apr 22, 1911; p. 901
SECRET OF THE PALM, THE
(Imp)/Mar 25, 1911; p. 658
SECRET OF THE SEA, A
(Mil)/Jan 18, 1913; p. 266
SECRET OF THE STILL, THE
(Ka)/Feb 11, 1911; p. 315
SECRET OF THE WILL, THE
(Ka)/Mar 21, 1914; p. 1525
SECRET ORCHARD, THE
(Las)/Aug 21, 1915; p. 1327
SECRET ORDER OF HORNS, THE
(Po)/Dec 16, 1911; p. 906
SECRET ROOM, THE
(Ka)/Feb 20, 1915; p. 1146
(Lu)/Nov 10, 1915; p. 1500
SECRET SERVICE (Lux)/Jul 22, 1911; p. 126
SECRET SERVICE MAN, THE
(Re)/Sep 7, 1912; p. 977
SECRET SERVICE SAM
(Imp)/Jun 7, 1913; p. 1032
SECRET SERVICE SNITZ
(St)/Oct 31, 1914; p. 642
SECRET SIN, THE (Las)/Oct 30a, 1915; p. 983
SECRET TREASURE, THE

SENORITA'S REPENTANCE, THE
(Sel)/Aug 2, 1913; p. 536
SENORITA'S SACRIFICE, THE
(Ya)/Mar 25, 1911; p. 658
SENSATIONAL DUEL (KO)/Aug 1,1908;p.88
SENSATIONAL LODGING
(SA)/Feb 19, 1910; p. 257
SENSATIONAL SHEATH GOWN, THE
(Lu)/Aug 8, 1908; p. 108
SENSE OF HUMOR, A
(Ed)/Dec 13, 1913; p. 1279
SENTIMENTAL BURGLAR, A
(Vi)/Jun 13, 1914; p. 1540
SENTIMENTAL BURGLAR, THE
(Pa)/Jul 3, 1909; p. 13
SENTIMENTAL LADY, THE
(KEd)/Nov 6, 1915; p. 1156
SENTIMENTAL SAM
(Lu)/Feb 19, 1910; p. 257
SENTIMENTAL SISTER, THE
(Bio)/Feb 7, 1914; p. 676
SENTIMENTAL SOPHIE
(SA)/Feb 6, 1915; p. 827
SENTINELS ASLEEP, THE
(Imp)/Oct 21, 1911; p. 211
SENTRY ON GUARD, THE
(UE)/Apr 6, 1912; p. 40
SEPOY'S WIFE, THE
(Vi)/Sep 24, 1910; p. 689
SEPTEMBER MORN
(Pa)/Mar 14, 1914; p. 1384
SEPTEMBER MOURNING
(Lko)/Nov 13, 1915; p. 1319
SERAPHINA'S LOVE AFFAIR
(Ed)/Jun 6, 1914; p. 1408
SERENADE BY PROXY, A
(Ed)/Feb 15, 1913; p. 678
SERGE PANINE (Bio)/Oct 2, 1915;
p. 90/Oct 30, 1915; p. 792
SERGEANT, THE (Sel)/Oct 8, 1910; p. 813
SERGEANT BYRNE
(Sel)/Sep 21, 1912; p. 1175
SERGEANT DILLON'S BRAVERY
(Sol)/Aug 5, 1911; p. 295
SERGEANT WHITE'S PERIL
(Lu)/Jan 6, 1912; p. 40
SERGEANT'S BOY, THE
(101)/Oct 26, 1912; p. 344
SERGEANT'S DAUGHTER, THE
(Sol)/Nov 12, 1910; p. 1119
(Dra)/May 24, 1913; p. 813
SERGEANT'S SECRET, THE
(KB)/Apr 26, 1913; p. 382
SERGEANT'S STRIPES, THE
(Pa)/Jan 23, 1909; p. 94
SERIES OF TULLULAH FALLS,
GEORGIA, A (Ed)/Sep 20, 1913; p. 1283
SERINGAPATAM (Pa)/Mar 27, 1915; p.1933

SERINGAPATAM, SOUTHERN INDIA
(Pa)/Feb 14, 1914; p. 809
SERIOUS ERROR, A
(TP)/Nov 27, 1909; p. 760
SERIOUS SIXTEEN (Bio)/Aug 6, 1910; p.296
SERPENT, THE (Rep)/Jun 29, 1912; p. 1228
SERPENTS, THE (Vi)/Apr 27, 1912; p. 316/
May 25, 1912; p. 728
SERPENT'S FANG, THE
(GN)/Sep 20, 1913; p. 1286
SERPENT'S TOOTH, THE
(Vi)/Aug 21, 1915; p. 1316
SERVANT AND THE TUTOR, THE
(It)/Apr 16, 1910; p. 599
SERVANT FROM THE COUNTRY
(Gau)/Feb 19, 1910; p. 258
SERVANT GIRL'S LEGACY, THE
(Lu)/Dec 12, 1914; p. 1523
SERVANT OF THE ACTRESS, THE
(It)/Dec 18, 1909; p. 882
SERVANT OF THE RICH, A
(Lu)/Jan 31, 1914; p. 544
SERVANT PROBLEM, THE
(Ko)/Jan 31, 1914; p. 545
SERVANT QUESTION, THE
(SA)/Dec 5, 1914; p. 1383
SERVANT QUESTION OUT WEST, THE
(Sel)/Jul 11, 1914; p. 255
SERVANT'S GOOD JOKE
(Pa)/Oct 9, 1909; p. 491
SERVICE UNDER JOHNSON AND LEE
(Ch)/Jun 17, 1911; p. 1389
SERVING A SUMMONS
(WBE)/Oct 12, 1907; p. 505
SET OF TEETH, A (Gau)/Nov 27,1909;p.759
SETH'S SWEETHEART
(Ed)/Oct 24, 1914; p. 491
SETH'S TEMPTATION
(Ka)/Dec 24, 1910; p. 1478
SETH'S WOODPILE (Ed)/Nov 22,1913;p.868
SETTING THE STYLE
(Vi)/May 16, 1914; p. 968
SETTLED OUT OF COURT
(Gau)/Feb 19, 1910; p. 258
(Sel)/Nov 12, 1910; p. 1118
(Ne)/Mar 2, 1912; p. 781
SETTLEMENT WORKERS, THE
(Sel)/Mar 27, 1909; p. 368
SETTLER'S WIFE, THE
(Ne)/Aug 12, 1911; p. 377
SETTLING A BOUNDARY DISPUTE
(At)/Jun 25, 1910; p. 1102
SEVEN AGES OF THE ALLIGATOR
(Th)/Feb 15, 1913; p. 681
SEVEN AND SEVENTY
(U)/Feb 6, 1915; p. 828
SEVEN BARS OF GOLD
(Me)/Mar 23, 1912; p. 1062

SEVEN DAYS (Sel)/May 21, 1910; p. 833
SEVEN SEALED ORDERS
(SA)/Sep 12, 1914; p. 1512
SEVEN SISTERS (FP)/Aug 7, 1915; p. 1013
SEVEN YEARS BAD LUCK
(Ed)/May 3, 1913; p. 488
SEVENTEEN MILE DRIVE, THE
(Pa)/Jan 31, 1914; p. 543
1776 - HESSIAN RENEGADES
(Bio)/Sep 18, 1909; p. 379
SEVENTH COMMANDMENT, THE
(Ka)/Jul 24, 1915; p. 649
SEVENTH DAY, THE
(Bio)/Sep 11, 1909; p. 347
(Ed)/Oct 9, 1915; pp 286-87
SEVENTH NOON, THE
(Mut)/Oct 30a, 1915; p. 968
SEVENTH PRELUDE, THE
(SA)/Aug 15, 1914; p. 960
SEVENTH SON, THE (Vi)/Mar 30, 1912;
p. 1150/Apr 20, 1912; p. 229
SEVERED FROM THE WORLD
(It)/Jan 27, 1912; p. 305
SEVERED HAND, THE
(Po)/Jul 18, 1914; p. 434
SEVERED THRONG, THE
(Maj)/Jul 4, 1914; p. 66
SEVILLE, THE ANCIENT CAPITAL OF
ANDALUSIA (Pa)/May 1, 1915; p. 729
SEVILLE AND ITS GARDENS
(Ec)/Nov 30, 1912; p. 878
SEVRES PORCELAIN
(Gau)/Sep 11, 1909; p. 347
SEWER, THE (Sol)/Mar 30, 1912; p. 1142/
Apr 20, 1912; p. 215/May 4, 1912; p. 427
SEWING GIRL, THE
(Po)/Sep 3, 1910; p. 521
SEXTON OF LONGWYN, THE
(Lu)/Nov 28, 1908; p. 432
SEYMOUR HOUSE PARTY, THE
(Bio)/Oct 16, 1915; p. 439
SH! DON'T WAKE THE BABY!
(Rex)/Sep 11, 1915; p. 1834
SHABBIES, THE (Vi)/Nov 13, 1915; p. 1312
SHABBY DOLL, THE
(Th)/Mar 15, 1913; p. 1105
SHACK NEXT DOOR, THE
(UI)/Oct 10, 1914; p. 189
SHADE OF AUTUMN, THE
(Gau)/May 11, 1912; p. 529
SHADOW, THE (Rex)/Jun 7, 1913; p. 1033
(Ka)/Mar 7, 1914; p. 1237
SHADOW AND THE SHADE, THE
(Sel)/Aug 7, 1915; p. 996
SHADOW OF A CRIME, THE
(Cry)/Jan 24, 1914; p. 414
SHADOW OF DOUBT, THE
(Pa)/Mar 20, 1915; p. 1767

SHADOW OF FEAR, THE
(Vi)/Oct 2, 1915; p. 78
SHADOW OF GUILT, THE
(Ka)/Feb 7, 1914; p. 677
SHADOW OF SHAME, THE
(Pa)/Dec 6, 1913; p. 1151
SHADOW OF THE CROSS, THE
(SA)/Dec 21, 1912; p. 1185
SHADOW OF THE PAST
(KB)/Dec 28, 1912; p. 1277
(Vi)/May 30, 1914; p. 1236
SHADOW OF THE PAST, A
(Pa)/Nov 26, 1910; p. 1238
(Rep)/Jun 29, 1912; p. 1228
SHADOW OF THE PAST, THE
(Maj)/Jul 19, 1913; p. 321
SHADOW ON THE BLIND, THE
(Ed)/Jun 22, 1912; p. 1126
SHADOW OF TRAGEDY, THE
(Lu)/Jul 18, 1914; p. 433
SHADOWED (Cry)/Jan 3, 1914; p. 49
SHADOWGRAPH MESSAGE, THE
(SA)/Jun 21, 1913; p. 1253
(Bro)/Jun 26, 1915; p. 2097
SHADOWS (Lu)/Dec 6, 1913; p. 1150
(SA)/Apr 4, 1914; p. 58
(Imp)/Oct 10, 1914; p. 189
SHADOWS AND SUNSHINE
(Pr)/Jan 2, 1915; p. 77
SHADOWS OF THE HARBOR
(Id)/Apr 3, 1915; p. 71
SHADOWS OF THE MOULIN ROUGE, THE
(Sol)/Jan 24, 1914; p. 417
SHADOWS OF THE PAST
(Ed)/Aug 7, 1915; p. 1015
SHADOWS OF YESTERDAY
(Amm)/Apr 4, 1914; p. 59
SHALL CURFEW RING TO-NIGHT?
(Lu)/Jan 2, 1915; p. 75
SHALL NEVER HUNGER
(Lu)/Apr 20, 1912; p. 229
SHAM BEGGARS/Dec 12, 1908; p. 477
SHAM SWORD SWALLOWER, THE
(WBE)/Oct 12, 1907; p. 509
SHAMUS O'BRIEN
(Sel)/Mar 21, 1908; p. 246
(Imp)/Mar 23, 1912; p. 1064
SHANGHAI, CHINA
(Pa)/Apr 11, 1908; p. 326
(Sel)/Apr 12, 1913; p. 164
SHANGHAI OF TO-DAY
(UE)/Jan 15, 1910; p. 57
SHANGHAIED (De)/Sep 3, 1910; p. 520
(Sel)/Nov 30, 1912; p. 877
(Ch)/Apr 19, 1913; p. 282
(SA)/Oct 23, 1915; p. 792
SHANGHAIED BABY, THE
(Lu)/Feb 6, 1915; p. 828

SHANGHAIED COWBOYS, THE
(Ne)/Nov 30, 1912; p. 878
SHANNON OF THE SIXTH
(Ka)/Jul 11, 1914; p. 233
SHANTY AT TREMBLING HILL, THE
(SA)/Jan 16, 1915; p. 369
SHARK GOD, THE (Ch)/May 17,1913; p.705
SHARPS AND CHAPS
(Ne)/Nov 16, 1912; p. 660
SHARPS WANT A FLAT, THE
(Jo)/Apr 25, 1914; p. 518
SHARPSHOOTERS, THE
(KB)/Feb 15, 1913; p. 681
SHATTERED DREAM, A
(Me)/Sep 30, 1911; pp 970-71
SHATTERED MEMORIES
(GS)/Jun 5, 1915; p. 1607
SHATTERED ROMANCE, A
(Da)/Sep 25, 1915; p. 2178
SHATTERED TREE, THE
(Ed)/Jul 18, 1914; p. 433
SHAUGHRAUN, THE
(Ka)/Dec 14, 1912; p. 1065
SHAVED IN MEXICO
(Lko)/May 1, 1915; p. 729
SHE (Ed)/Nov 14, 1908; p. 384
(Th)/Dec 23, 1911; pp 976-78
SHE CAME, SHE SAW, SHE CONQUERED
(Vi)/Jul 29, 1911; p. 194/Aug 19, 1911; p. 463
SHE COULD BE HAPPY WITH EITHER
(KO)/Nov 28, 1908; p.432/Dec 5,1908; p.449
SHE COULDN'T GET AWAY FROM IT
(Lun)/May 29, 1915; p. 1433
SHE CRIED (Vi)/Oct 19, 1912; p. 242
SHE GAVE HIM A ROSE
(Lu)/Aug 15, 1914; p. 959
SHE GOT THE MONEY
(SA)/Jul 8, 1911; p. 1584
SHE IS A PIPPIN
(Bio)/Dec 21, 1912; p. 1184
SHE LANDED A BIG ONE
(SA)/Oct 31, 1914; p. 641
SHE MADE HERSELF BEAUTIFUL
(Lu)/Oct 3, 1914; p. 63
SHE MARRIED FOR LOVE
(Lu)/Nov 14, 1914; p. 931
SHE MUST BE UGLY
(Lu)/May 24, 1913; p. 811
SHE MUST ELOPE (Lu)/Feb 15,1913; p.679
SHE NEVER KNEW
(Vi)/Apr 13, 1912; p. 137
(Imp)/May 31, 1913; p. 921
(Am)/Mar 20, 1915; p. 1764
SHE REQUIRED STRENGTH AND GOT IT
(Lux)/Nov 12, 1910; p. 1119
SHE SHALL NOT KNOW
(Cin)/Feb 8, 1913; p. 571
SHE SHOULD WORRY

(Jo)/Dec 27, 1913; p. 1544
SHE SLEPT THROUGH IT ALL
(Imp)/Jan 18, 1913; p. 265
SHE STOOPS TO CONQUER
(Th)/Sep 3, 1910; p. 520
(Co)/Jul 11, 1914; p. 283
SHE SURVEYS HER SON-IN-LAW
(Ec)/Aug 13, 1910; p. 352
SHE TOOK A CHANCE
(Vi)/Sep 4, 1915; p. 1643
SHE TOOK MOTHER'S ADVICE
(Lu)/Dec 18, 1909; p. 880
SHE WALKETH ALONE
(Am)/May 1, 1915; p. 728
SHE WANTED A BOARDER
(Vi)/Sep 21, 1912; p. 1175
SHE WANTED A BOW-WOW
(SA)/Apr 30, 1910; p. 690
SHE WANTED A COUNT
(Lu)/Mar 28, 1914; p. 1681
SHE WANTED A MAN WITH BRAINS
(Ch)/May 13, 1911; pp 1081-82
SHE WANTED TO BE A WIDOW
(Sel)/Feb 13, 1915; p. 984
SHE WANTED TO BE AN ACTRESS
(Vi)/May 9, 1908; p. 426
SHE WANTED TO KNOW
(Lu)/Aug 1, 1914; p. 704
SHE WANTED TO MARRY A HERO
(Th)/May 14, 1910; p. 786
SHE WAS A PEACH
(Lu)/Apr 18, 1914; p. 360
SHE WAS HIS MOTHER
(Imp)/Jan 9, 1915; p. 223
SHE WAS ONLY A WORKING GIRL
(Ne)/Feb 28, 1914; p. 1090
SHE WAS THE OTHER
(Lu)/Dec 5, 1914; p. 1383
SHE WOLF, THE
(Re)/May 3, 1913; pp 489-90
(Bi)/Oct 18, 1913; p. 266
SHE WON'T PAY HER RENT
(KO)/Jun 22, 1907; p. 253
SHE WOULD BE A BUSINESS MAN
(Cen)/Jul 16, 1910; p. 144
SHE WOULD BE A COWBOY
(Ka)/Mar 13, 1915; p. 1607
SHE WOULD BE AN ACTRESS
(Lu)/Aug 14, 1909; p. 226
SHE WROTE A PLAY
(Ec)/Jan 17, 1914; p. 290
SHED AND THE HARVEST
(Ka)/Oct 31, 1914; p. 641
SHEEP HERDER, THE
(Vic)/May 30, 1914; p. 1262
SHEEP RUNNERS, THE
(Sel)/Jun 20, 1914; p. 1688
SHEEP SHEARING IN NEW MEXICO

SHERIFF'S REWARD, THE
(UB)/Oct 5, 1912; p. 42
(Pa)/Apr 12, 1913; p. 163
SHERIFF'S RIVAL, THE
(Fr)/May 17, 1913; p. 705
SHERIFF'S ROUND-UP, THE
(Ne)/May 25, 1912; p. 730
SHERIFF'S SACRIFICE, THE
(SA)/May 21, 1910; p. 832
SHERIFF'S SISTER, THE
(Ka)/Feb 18, 1911; p. 370
SHERIFF'S SISTERS, THE (Am)/Nov 25,
1911; pp 619-20/Dec 9, 1911; p. 818
SHERIFF'S SON, THE
(SA)/Apr 12, 1913; p. 165
SHERIFF'S STORY, THE
(SA)/Feb 15, 1913; p. 679
(Fr)/May 23, 1914; p. 1118
(Bio)/May 29, 1915; p. 1431
SHERIFF'S STREAK OF YELLOW, THE
(KB)/Feb 27, 1915; p. 1290
SHERIFF'S SWEETHEART
(Am)/Mar 11, 1911; p. 543
SHERIFF'S TRAP, THE
(Bio)/Nov 13, 1915; p. 1311
SHERIFF'S WARNING, THE
(Ne)/Apr 26, 1913; p. 382
SHERIFF'S WIFE, THE
(SA)/Apr 26, 1913; p. 379
SHERLOCK BONEHEAD
(Ka)/Sep 5, 1914; p. 1371
SHERLOCK HOLMES (GN)
No.1/Dec 5, 1908; p. 450
No.2/Feb 27, 1909; pp 239-40/
Mar 6, 1909; pp 268-69
No.3/Mar 13, 1909; p. 302
SHERLOCK HOLMES AND THE SIGN OF
THE FOUR (Th)/Mar 8, 1913; p. 998
SHERLOCK HOLMES GIRL, THE
(Ed)/Jan 24, 1914; p. 412
SHERLOCK HOLMES IN THE GREAT
MURDER MYSTERY
(Cre)/Nov 28, 1908; pp 434-35
SHERLOCK HOLMES JR.
(Rex)/Aug 5, 1911; pp 291, 295
SHERLOCKO AND WATSO
(Ch)/Mar 9, 1912; p. 868
SHERMAN WAS RIGHT
(Roy)/Dec 26, 1914; p. 1841
SHE'S A PIPPIN (StP)/Jul 10, 1915; p. 309
SHE'S DONE IT AGAIN
(Th)/Apr 9, 1910; p. 554
SHIELD OF INNOCENCE, THE
(Me)/Aug 22, 1914; p. 1100
SHIP BOY'S GRIT, A
(CGP)/Oct 19, 1912; p. 243
SHIP OF HORROR, THE
(Uni)/May 15, 1915; p. 1074

SHIP OWNER'S DAUGHTER, THE
(Pa)/Jan 18, 1908; p. 47
SHIP WITH THE LIONS, THE
(Amb)/Oct 26, 1912; p. 323
SHIPBUILDING IN TOULSON, FRANCE
(UE)/Sep 3, 1910; p. 520
SHIPPING A CLOCK
(Lu)/Apr 12, 1913; p. 165
SHIP'S HUSBAND, THE
(Ed)/Nov 26, 1910; p. 1236
SHIPWRECKED (Sel)/Oct 7, 1911; p. 40
(Ka)/Aug 23, 1913; p. 843
SHIPWRECKED MAN, A
(Amb)/Jun 18, 1910; p. 1049
SHIRTS AND SHOCKS
(Maj)/Mar 8, 1913; p. 998
SHOAL LIGHT, THE
(Dom)/May 15, 1915; p. 1072
SHOCKING HER FUTURE MOTHER-IN-
LAW (Maj)/Dec 7, 1912; p. 977
SHOCKING STOCKINGS
(Ko)/Sep 11, 1915; p. 1833
SHODDY, THE TAILOR
(Lu)/Feb 6, 1915; p. 828
SHOEING THE MAIL CARRIER
(KO)/Jun 22, 1907; p. 253
SHOEMAKER AND THE DOLL, THE
(Maj)/Oct 4, 1913; p. 49
SHOEMAKER OF COEPENICK, THE (Vi)/
Nov 28, 1908; p. 423/Dec 5, 1908; p. 449
SHOEMAKER'S ELEVENTH, THE
(Vic)/Nov 21, 1914; p. 1077
SHON, THE PIPER (Bi)/Sep 27,1913; p.1394
SHOOING THE WOOER
(Gau)/Aug 23, 1913; p. 845
SHOOTING AN OIL WELL
(Sel)/Feb 12, 1910; p. 215
SHOOTING IN THE HAUNTED WOODS
(Gau)/Jan 22, 1910; p. 92
SHOOTING JACK RABBITS
(Pa)/Nov 6, 1909; p. 642
SHOOTING MATCH, THE
(St)/Oct 3, 1914; p. 65
SHOOTING OF DAN McGREW, THE
(Mto)/May 22, 1915; p. 1271
SHOOTING PARTY (KO)/May 2,1908; p.401
SHOOTING THE FAMOUS HAZU RAPIDS
(Me)/Dec 6, 1913; p. 1150
SHOOTING THE RAPIDS
(Gau)/Jun 3, 1911; p. 1259
SHOOTING THE RAPIDS IN JAPAN
(Pa)/Jun 3, 1911; p. 1259
SHOOTING THE RAPIDS OF THE
PAGSANJAN RIVER IN THE
PHILIPPINES (Sel)/Jun 28, 1913; p. 1358
SHOP GIRL'S BIG DAY, THE
(Fr)/Oct 4, 1913; p. 49
SHOP NUN, THE (Emp)/May 8, 1915; p. 901

SHOPLIFTER, THE (Th)/Feb 13,1915; p.985
SHORE ACRES (AS)/Nov 7, 1914; p. 792
SHORES OF THE OCLOWAHA RIVER AND EVERGLADES OF FLORIDA
(Ka)/Aug 24, 1912; p. 771
SHORT LIFE AND A MERRY ONE, A
(Ed)/Oct 18, 1913; p. 264
SHORT LIVED HAPPINESS
(Pa)/May 20, 1911; p. 1141
SHORT LIVED TRIUMPH, A
(Pa)/Sep 3, 1910; p. 518
SHORTSIGHTED MISS PRIM
(Lux)/Jul 15, 1911; p. 40
SHORTSTOP'S DOUBLE, THE
(Sel)/Aug 2, 1913; p. 536
SHORTY (Ed)/Nov 21, 1914; p. 1075
SHORTY AMONG THE CANNIBALS (Bro)/
Feb 27, 1915; p. 1298/Apr 3, 1915; p. 65
SHORTY AND SHERLOCK HOLMES
(Bro)/Oct 24, 1914; p. 493
SHORTY AND THE ARIDVILLE TERROR
(Bro)/Aug 8, 1914; p. 838
SHORTY AND THE FORTUNE TELLER
(Bro)/Aug 15, 1914; p. 962
SHORTY AT THE SHORE
(Lu)/Sep 3, 1910; p. 518
SHORTY FALLS INTO A TITLE
(Bro)/Nov 21, 1914; p. 1077
SHORTY GETS INTO TROUBLE
(Bro)/Jul 4, 1914; p. 66
SHORTY INHERITS A HAREM
(Bro)/Aug 14, 1915; p. 1161
SHORTY MAKES A BET
(Bio)/Mar 28, 1914; p. 1680
SHORTY TURNS ACTOR
(Bro)/Apr 17, 1915; p. 393
SHORTY TURNS JUDGE
(Bro)/Jul 18, 1914; p. 434
SHORTY'S ADVENTURES IN THE CITY
(Bro)/Feb 13, 1915; p. 986
SHORTY'S ESCAPE FROM MATRIMONY
(Bro)/May 2, 1914; p. 674
SHORTY'S RANCH
(Bro)/Sep 18, 1915; p. 1996
SHORTY'S SACRIFICE
(Bro)/Apr 11, 1914; p. 214
SHORTY'S SECRET
(Bro)/Feb 20, 1915; p. 1141
SHORTY'S STRATEGY
(Bro)/May 9, 1914; p. 822
SHORTY'S TRIP TO MEXICO
(Bro)/Jun 6, 1914; p. 1410
SHORTY'S TROUBLE SLEEP
(Bro)/May 29, 1915; p. 1432
SHOT, THE (Po)/Sep 4, 1915; p. 1645
SHOT AT SUNRISE (Ma)/Oct 30a, 1915;
p. 970/Nov 6, 1915; p. 1141
SHOT FROM THE BRUSH, A

(Gau)/Aug 5, 1911; p. 292
SHOT IN A BAR-ROOM
(Lko)/Aug 14, 1915; p. 1162
SHOT IN THE DARK, A
(Rex)/May 15, 1915; p. 1073
SHOT IN THE EXCITEMENT
(Key)/Oct 31, 1914; p. 642
SHOT IN THE FRACAS
(WF)/Dec 5, 1914; p. 1385
SHOT IN THE NIGHT, A
(Ka)/Jan 17, 1914; p. 290
SHOT IN TIME, A
(Bi)/Apr 16, 1910; p. 600
SHOT THAT FAILED, THE
(101)/Aug 24, 1912; p. 772
SHOTGUN CUPID, A
(Pr)/Dec 6, 1913; p. 1152
SHOTGUN JONES (Sel)/May 9, 1914; p. 821
SHOTGUN MAN AND THE STAGE DRIVER, THE (Sel)/Apr 26, 1913; p. 379
SHOTGUN RANCHMAN, THE
(SA)/Oct 26, 1912; pp 342-43
SHOTGUN ROMANCE, A
(Cub)/Dec 4, 1915; p. 1853
SHOTGUNS THAT KICK
(Key)/Dec 19, 1914; p. 1680
SHOULD A MOTHER TELL?
(Fox)/Jul 17, 1915; pp 506-7
SHOULD A WOMAN DIVORCE
(Iv)/Dec 19, 1914; p. 1693
SHOULD A WOMAN FORGIVE?
(Eq)/Nov 6, 1915; pp 1141, 1155
SHOULD A WOMAN TELL?
(Ape)/Apr 25, 1914; p. 490
SHOW BUSTERS, THE
(Bio)/Aug 8, 1914; p. 836
SHOW GIRL, THE
(Vi)/Jun 3, 1911; pp 1238, 1258
SHOW GIRL'S GLOVE, THE
(Ka)/Jul 11, 1914; p. 256
SHOW GIRL'S STRATAGEM, THE
(Lu)/Feb 25, 1911; p. 431
SHOW YOUR LICENSE
(Pa)/Sep 18, 1909; p. 378
SHOWDOWN, THE (Re)/Jul 10, 1915; p. 308
SHOWER OF SLIPPERS, A
(Ed)/Apr 19, 1913; p. 281
SHOWING UNCLE
(SA)/Nov 25, 1911; p. 636
SHRIEK IN THE NIGHT, A
(Vic)/Oct 23, 1915; p. 621
SHRIMPER, THE (Pa)/Jan 4, 1908; p. 11
SHRIMPS (Sel)/Aug 13, 1910; p. 351
SHRINER'S DAUGHTER, THE
(Am)/Jan 3, 1914; p. 50
SHRINER'S PARADE
(Ec)/Mar 23, 1912; p. 1064
SHRINER'S PARADE AT LOS ANGELES,

SILENT MESSENGER, THE
(Dom)/Mar 28, 1914; p. 1682
SILENT PERIL, THE
(Bi)/Nov 21, 1914; p. 1077
SILENT PIANO, THE
(Amb)/Feb 26, 1910; p. 300
SILENT PLEA, A (Vi)/Jan 2, 1915; p. 52/
Mar 20, 1915; p. 1764
SILENT SANDY (Re)/Jun 13, 1914; p. 1542
SILENT SIGNAL, THE
(Sol)/Jul 22, 1911; p. 126
(Lu)/Dec 7, 1912; p. 975
SILENT TONGUE, THE
(Ed)/Sep 16, 1911; p. 789
(Ed)/Oct 2, 1915; p. 78
SILENT VALLEY (Imp)/Sep 5, 1914; p. 1374
SILENT VOICE, THE
(Qua)/Sep 4, 1915; p. 1662
SILENT W, THE (Vi)/Jul 10, 1915; p. 308
SILENT WARNING, THE
(Ka)/Nov 22, 1913; p. 867
SILENT WAY, THE
(Am)/Dec 26, 1914; p. 1841
SILENT WITNESS, THE
(Th)/Feb 24, 1912; p. 690
(Vic)/Jun 27, 1914; p. 1830
(Pa)/Dec 12, 1914; p. 1534
SILK HATS IRONED (KO)/Jul 11,1908; p.36
SILK HOSE AND HIGH PRESSURE
(Lko)/Sep 11, 1915; p. 1834
SILLY SEX, THE (Re)/Aug 16, 1913; p. 745
SILVER BELL, THE
(Dom)/Sep 5, 1914; p. 1373
SILVER CANDLESTICKS, THE
(KB)/Sep 12, 1914; p. 1513
SILVER CIGARETTE CASE
(Vi)/Jun 28, 1913; p. 1358
SILVER CLOUD'S SACRIFICE
(Ka)/Nov 19, 1910; p. 1176
SILVER CROSS, THE
(Sol)/May 10, 1913; p. 598
SILVER DOLLAR, THE
(Lu)/Feb 20, 1909; p. 202
SILVER KING, THE (Lu)/Jan 4, 1908;
pp 12-13/Jan 18, 1908; p. 46
SILVER LEAF'S HEART
(Pa)/Feb 25, 1911; p. 430
SILVER LINING, THE
(Bal)/Aug 15, 1914; p. 962
(Am)/Nov 27, 1915; pp 1665, 1677-78
SILVER LOVING CUP, THE
(Imp)/Mar 21, 1914; pp 1526, 1535
SILVER SKULL, THE (Vi)/Sep 6, 1913;
p. 1046/Oct 18, 1913; p. 264
SILVER SNUFF BOX, THE
(Vi)/Apr 11, 1914; p. 213
SILVER TAIL AND HIS SQUAW
(Po)/Sep 16, 1911; p. 790

SILVER THREADS
(Gem)/Jun 14, 1913; p. 1137
SILVER THREADS AMONG THE GOLD
(Ed)/Apr 29, 1911; p. 957
(KR)/May 1, 1915; p. 743
SILVER-TONGUED ORATOR, THE
(Th)/Nov 15, 1913; p. 737
SILVER WING'S DREAM
(Bi)/Aug 5, 1911; p. 297
SILVER WING'S TWO SUITORS
(Pa)/Aug 31, 1912; p. 881
SILVERSMITH TO KING LOUIS XI, THE
(Ec)/Aug 6, 1910; p. 298
SIMLA (Ed)/Sep 14, 1912; p. 1074
SIMON, THE JESTER (GR)/Sep 25, 1915;
p. 2198/Oct 2, 1915; p. 80
SIMONE (Pa)/Apr 30, 1910; p. 689
SIMON'S SWIMMING SOULMATE
(Fal)/Sep 25, 1915; p. 2177
SIMP AND THE SOPHOMORES, THE
(Ed)/Sep 18, 1915; p. 1995
SIMP SIMPSON AND THE SPIRITS
(Sel)/Jun 13, 1914; p. 1540
SIMPLE CHARITY
(Bio)/Nov 26, 1910; p. 1236
SIMPLE FAITH (Vic)/Aug 15, 1914; p. 961
SIMPLE HOUSE DINNER, A
(Ed)/Aug 28, 1909; pp 281-82
SIMPLE IKE DECIDES TO MARRY
(Ka)/Sep 9, 1911; p. 715
SIMPLE LIFE, THE
(Pa)/Nov 9, 1912; p. 553
(Rex)/Sep 6, 1913; p. 1069
(Ne)/Oct 11, 1913; p. 157
SIMPLE MISTAKE, A
(Pa)/Oct 8, 1910; p. 814
SIMPLE RUSTIC TALE, A
(Gau)/Jan 28, 1911; p. 194
SIMPLE SIMON SUFFERS SORELY
(Gau)/Mar 8, 1913; p. 998
SIMPLER LIFE, THE
(Maj)/Oct 26, 1912; p. 343
SIMPLETON, THE
(KO)/Jul 18, 1908; pp 52-53
SIMPSON'S SKATE
(Po)/Oct 22, 1910; p. 939
SIN (Fox)/Oct 16, 1915; p. 465/
Oct 23, 1915; p. 622
SIN OF OLGA BRANDT, THE
(Rex)/Jan 9, 1915; p. 221
SIN ON THE SABBATH
(Lko)/Dec 4, 1915; p. 1854
SIN UNPARDONABLE, A
(SA)/Feb 4, 1911; p. 244
SINCERITY (Vic)/Jun 21, 1913; p. 1253
SINEWS OF THE DEAD
(Me)/Aug 29, 1914; p. 1240
SINEWS OF WAR, THE

(Bro)/Apr 5, 1913; p. 50
SINGER'S SACRIFICE, A
(Bio)/Feb 20, 1909; p. 203
SINGLE ACT, THE (Lu)/Jan 9, 1915; p. 221
SINGLE HANDED (SA)/Apr 4, 1914; p. 57
SINGLE-HANDED JIM
(Am)/Aug 2, 1913; p. 537
SINGULAR CYNIC, A
(Vic)/Jun 27, 1914; p. 1830
SINNER, THE (Th)/May 20, 1911; p. 1142
SINNER MUST PAY, THE
(Rex)/Jul 3, 1915; p. 66
SINNER'S SACRIFICE, A
(Bi)/Jul 16, 1910; p. 144
SINS OF THE FATHER
(Lu)/Dec 16, 1911; p. 905
SINS OF THE FATHER, THE
(Pa)/Apr 20, 1912; p. 230
(Ch)/Jan 25, 1913; p. 365
SINS OF THE FATHERS
(Vi)/Dec 4, 1909; p. 798
(Bro)/Mar 15, 1913; p. 1106
SINS OF THE MOTHERS, THE
(Vi)/Jan 9, 1915; p. 195
SINS OF THE PARENTS
(Iv)/Aug 29, 1914; p. 1250
SIOUX LOVER'S STRATEGY, A
(Pa)/Nov 18, 1911; p. 549
SIOUX SPY, A (Bi)/Sep 2, 1911; pp 630-31
SIOUX'S REWARD, A
(Bi)/Dec 24, 1910; p. 1480
SIR GALAHAD OF TWILIGHT
(Am)/Nov 7, 1914; p. 789
SIR JOHN FALSTAFF
(UE)/Jun 24, 1911; p. 1454
SIR PERCY AND THE PUNCHERS
(Me)/Apr 8, 1911; p. 780
SIR THOMAS LIPTON OUT WEST
(Key)/Jan 11, 1913; p. 159
SIREN, THE (Ne)/May 23, 1914; p. 1117
(Ec)/Aug 15, 1914; p. 940
(Vi)/Sep 25, 1915; p. 2176
SIREN OF CORSICA, A
(Lu)/Mar 27, 1915; pp 1932-33
SIREN OF IMPULSE, THE
(Bio)/Mar 16, 1912; p. 962
SIREN OF THE DESERT, A
(Lu)/Aug 22, 1914; p. 1099
SIREN'S CALL TO DUTY, THE
(Amb)/Nov 23, 1912; p. 769
SIRENS' NECKLACE, THE
(Vi)/Oct 9, 1909; p. 494
SIREN'S SONG, THE (Wor)/Dec 11, 1915;
p. 2027/Dec 18, 1915; p. 2205
SIS (Pr)/Sep 26, 1914; p. 1776
(Vi)/Nov 20, 1915; p. 1499
SIS DOBBINS, OIL MAGNATE
(Po)/Nov 14, 1914; p. 933

SI'S WONDERFUL MINERAL SPRING
(Ka)/Oct 31, 1914; p. 640
SISSYBELLE (Sel)/Oct 4, 1913; p. 48
SISTAL INDUSTRY IN THE BAHAMAS,
THE (Lu)/Jun 11, 1910; p. 995
SISTER, THE (Ka)/Feb 25, 1911; p. 430
SISTER ANGELICA
(Pa)/Oct 23, 1909; p. 568
SISTERS (Ed)/Jun 4, 1910; p. 941
(Ch)/Jun 29, 1912; p. 1228
(Vic)/Nov 16, 1912; p. 659
(Po)/May 30, 1914; p. 1261
(Vi)/Nov 28, 1914; p. 1232
SISTERS, THE
(Imp)/Mar 1, 1913; p. 889
(Maj)/Dec 12, 1914; pp 1525, 1532
SISTERS ALL (Vi)/Mar 29, 1913; pp 1335-36
SISTER'S BURDEN, A
(Ka)/May 8, 1915; pp 916-17
SISTER'S DEVOTION, A
(Bi)/May 14, 1910; p. 786
(CGP)/May 18, 1912; p. 629
(Am)/Oct 19, 1912; p. 244
SISTER'S LOVE, A
(Bio)/Feb 24, 1912; p. 689
SISTER'S SACRIFICE, A
(Vi)/Jan 29, 1910; p. 128
(Imp)/Sep 24, 1910; p. 690
SISTER'S SOLACE, THE
(Bio)/Apr 17, 1915; p. 392
SISTER'S STRATAGEM, A
(Cin)/Mar 16, 1912; p. 961
SIX CENT LOAF, THE
(Th)/Jun 12, 1915; p. 1777
SIX CYLINDER ELOPEMENT, A
(Th)/Oct 12, 1912; p. 144
SIX-FOOT ROMANCE, A
(Lu)/Oct 10, 1914; p. 187
SIX LEGGED SHEEP, THE
(Ec)/May 7, 1910; p. 738
SIX MONTHS TO LIVE
(Rex)/Jan 23, 1915; p. 517
SIX OR NINE (Rex)/Mar 13, 1915; p. 1608
SIXES AND NINES
(Lu)/Mar 29, 1913; p. 1335
SIXFOLD DUEL OF FOOLSHEAD, THE
(It)/Jan 27, 1912; p. 305
SIXTH COMMANDMENT, THE
(Vi)/Aug 23, 1913; p. 842
SIXTUS THE FIFTH
(Amb)/Jul 8, 1911; p. 1588
SIXTY YEARS A QUEEN/Jan 3, 1914; p. 51
SKATING BUG, THE
(Imp)/Aug 12, 1911; p. 378
SKATING MASTER, THE
(Th)/Feb 28, 1914; p. 1089
SKATING RINK, THE
(Bio)/Dec 25, 1915; p. 2380

SKELETON, THE (Vi)/Feb 12, 1910; p. 216
    (Po)/Nov 2, 1912; p. 451
    (Ne)/Jun 13, 1914; p. 1543
SKELETON IN THE CLOSET, THE
  (Ka)/Aug 30, 1913; p. 960
SKELLY AND THE TURKEY
  (Bio)/Mar 7, 1914; p. 1236
SKELLY BUYS A HOTEL
  (Bio)/Feb 28, 1914; p. 1087
SKELLY'S BIRTHDAY
  (Bio)/Apr 18, 1914; p. 360
SKELLY'S SKELETON
  (Bio)/Jan 17, 1914; p. 288
SKETCH WITH THE THUMB PRINT, THE
  (Ed)/Aug 3, 1912; pp 445-46
SKETCHES FROM LIFE
  (Imp)/Jul 12, 1913; p. 205
SKIER TRAINING, A
  (Gau)/Oct 22, 1910; p. 936
SKI-ING AT ISPHEMING, MICHIGAN
  (Vi)/Jul 17, 1909; p. 88
SKI-ING MANIAC, THE
  (KO)/Apr 18, 1908; p. 354
SKINFLINT, THE (Ka)/Nov 16, 1912; p. 659
    (Pr)/Mar 27, 1915; p.1933
SKINNY'S FINISH (Ed)/May 30, 1908; p.479
SKIPPER SIMPSON'S DAUGHTER
  (Jo)/Apr 17, 1915; p. 394
SKIPPER'S DAUGHTERS, THE
  (Sel)/Mar 6, 1909; p. 268
SKIPPER'S YARN, THE
  (Ed)/Feb 12, 1910; p. 215
SKIVVY AND THE MAT
  (Lux)/Feb 10, 1912; p. 483
SKIVVY'S GHOST, THE
  (Lux)/Mar 9, 1912; p. 867
SKULL, THE (Vi)/Feb 22, 1913; p. 780
    (Imp)/Jul 4, 1914; p. 66
SKULL AND THE CROWN, THE
  (Sel)/Aug 22, 1914; p. 1099
SKY HUNTERS, THE (SA)/Aug 7,1915;p.997
SKY IS THE LIMIT, THE
  (StP)/Aug 21, 1915; p. 1318
SKY MONSTER, THE
  (Uni)/Mar 14, 1914; p. 1365
SKY PILOT (Vi)/Aug 12, 1911; p. 376
SKY PILOT'S INTEMPERANCE, THE
  (Am)/Jul 8, 1911; p. 1587
SLABSIDES (Ka)/May 13, 1911; p. 1081
SLANDER'S TONGUE
  (Ed)/Sep 20, 1913; p. 1284
SLATE INDUSTRY, THE
  (Lu)/Nov 30, 1912; p. 876
  (Pa)/Nov 29, 1913; p. 1007
SLAVE, THE (Bio)/Aug 7, 1909; p. 194
SLAVE GIRL, THE (Re)/Apr 3, 1915; p. 65
SLAVE OF SATAN, A
  (Pa)/Nov 29, 1913; p. 1008

SLAVE TO DRINK, A
  (Ka)/Jan 15, 1910; p. 56
SLAVERY DAYS (Rex)/May 17, 1913; p.705
SLAVERY OF CHILDREN
  (Cin)/Aug 31, 1907; p. 410
SLAVERY OF FOXICUS, THE
  (Ka)/Oct 17, 1914; p. 335
SLAVE'S HATE (Pa)/Jan 25, 1908; p. 65
SLAVES' REVOLT, THE
  (Pa)/Feb 18, 1911; p. 370
SLAVEY STUDENT, THE
  (Ed)/Sep 11, 1915; p. 1833
SLAVEY'S AFFINITY, THE
  (Lu)/Oct 21, 1911; p. 209
SLAVEY'S ROMANCE, THE
  (Vic)/Aug 22, 1914; p. 1101
SLEEP, BEAUTIFUL SLEEP
  (Ed)/May 8, 1915; p. 899
SLEEP, GENTLE SLEEP
  (Ed)/Jan 14, 1911; p. 90
SLEEP WALKER, THE
  (Vi)/Jul 8, 1911; p. 1585
SLEEP WALKING CURE, A
  (Sel)/Aug 6, 1910; p. 197
SLEEPER, THE (Pa)/Dec 11, 1909; p. 842
    (Lu)/Sep 28,1912;pp 1276-77
SLEEPING BEAUTY (Pa)/Apr 4, 1908; p.299
SLEEPING BEAUTY, THE
  (VF)/Jul 26, 1913; p. 430
SLEEPING BURGLAR, THE
  (Com)/Dec 7, 1912; p. 977
SLEEPING SENTINEL, THE
  (Lu)/Feb 28, 1914; p. 1088
SLEEPING TONIC, THE
  (SA)/Jun 12, 1909; p. 795
SLEEPY HEAD, THE
  (Ko)/Feb 14, 1914; p. 810
SLEEPY HOLLOW (Ne)/Feb 11, 1911; p.318
SLEEPY JONES (Po)/Oct 29, 1910; p. 999
SLEEPY ROMANCE (Lu)/Nov 1,1913; p.496
SLEEPY TRAMPS, THE
  (Lu)/Jul 8, 1911; p. 1586
SLEUFOOT'S SEVENTH SUICIDE
  (Pa)/Sep 20, 1913; p. 1284
SLEUTH, THE (UE)/Jun 10, 1911; p. 1316
SLEUTH AND THE WIG, THE
  (Gau)/Oct 23, 1909; p. 568
SLEUTHING (Vi)/May 3, 1913; p. 488
SLEUTHS AT THE FLORAL PARADE, THE
  (Key)/Mar 8, 1913; p. 997
SLEUTH'S LAST STAND, THE
  (Key)/Mar 8, 1913; p. 998
SLEUTHS UNAWARES
  (Vi)/Nov 8, 1913; p. 611
SLICE OF LIFE, A
  (Am)/Nov 14, 1914; p. 933
SLICK'S ROMANCE
  (Sel)/Aug 19, 1911; p. 464

SLIGHT MISTAKE, A
(Vi)/Dec 16, 1911; p. 904
(Lu)/May 3, 1913; p. 487
(Me)/Sep 5, 1914; p. 1371
SLIGHT MISUNDERSTANDING, A
(Maj)/Oct 11, 1913; p. 157
SLIGHTLY MISTAKEN
(Jo)/Dec 11, 1915; p. 2033
SLIGHTLY WORN GOWN, THE
(Vi)/Feb 13, 1915; p. 984
SLIM, FAT OR MEDIUM
(Imp)/Dec 4, 1915; p. 1854
SLIM AND THE DYNAMITERS
(Fr)/Jan 31, 1914; p. 545
SLIM AND THE MONEY POT
(Fr)/Jan 24, 1914; p. 413
SLIM AND THE MUMMY
(WF)/Nov 7, 1914; p. 789
SLIM AND THE OUTLAW
(Fr)/Dec 27, 1913; p. 1545
SLIM AND THE PETTICOATS
(Fr)/Dec 20, 1913; p. 1413
SLIM BECOMES A COOK
(Fr)/Feb 28, 1914; p. 1089
SLIM BECOMES A DETECTIVE
(Fr)/Nov 22, 1913; p. 869
SLIM BECOMES AN EDITOR
(Fr)/Feb 7, 1914; p. 678
SLIM DRISCOLL, SAMARITAN
(Vi)/Aug 30, 1913; p. 961
SLIM GETS THE REWARD
(Fr)/Nov 15, 1913; p. 737
SLIM HIGGINS (Sel)/Mar 13, 1915; p. 1607
SLIM JIM'S LAST CHANCE
(Ka)/Apr 29, 1911; p. 958
SLIM JOINS THE ARMY
(Fr)/Feb 21, 1914; p. 948
SLIM PRINCESS, THE
(SA)/May 29, 1915; p. 1443
SLIM PROPOSES, BUT --
(Fr)/Nov 29, 1913; p. 1008
SLIM THE BRAVE AND SOPHIE THE FAIR (SA)/Feb 27, 1915; p. 1287
SLIM TO THE RESCUE
(Fr)/Feb 14, 1914; p. 810
SLIM'S LAST TRICK
(Fr)/Jan 10, 1914; p. 173
SLIM'S STRATEGY (Fr)/Jan 10, 1914; p.174
SLIP, THE (Sel)/Apr 6, 1912; p. 40
SLIPPERY DAY, A (Lu)/Jan 29, 1910; p. 128
SLIPPERY JIM (Pa)/Oct 22, 1910; p. 934
SLIPPERY JIM, THE BURGLAR
(WBE)/Apr 6, 1907; p. 74
SLIPPERY JIM'S REPENTANCE (Vi)/
Dec 12, 1908; p. 488/Dec 19, 1908; p. 500
SLIPPERY SADIE (WF)/Dec 5, 1914; p.1386
SLIPPERY SLIM - DIPLOMAT
(SA)/Jul 25, 1914; p. 571

SLIPPERY SLIM, THE MORTGAGE AND SOPHIE (SA)/Nov 7, 1914; p. 787
SLIPPERY SLIM AND HIS TOMBSTONE
(SA)/Aug 29, 1914; p. 1240
SLIPPERY SLIM AND THE CLAIM AGENT (SA)/Sep 5, 1914; p. 1371
SLIPPERY SLIM AND THE FORTUNE TELLER (SA)/Sep 12, 1914; p. 1511
SLIPPERY SLIM AND THE GREEN-EYED MONSTER (SA)/Oct 10, 1914; p. 187
SLIPPERY SLIM AND THE IMPERSONATOR (SA)/Nov 21, 1914; p.1075
SLIPPERY SLIM AND THE STORK
(SA)/May 9, 1914; p. 820
SLIPPERY SLIM GETS CURED
(SA)/Oct 17, 1914; p. 335
SLIPPERY SLIM REPENTS
(Bio)/Jun 21, 1913; p. 1251
SLIPPERY SLIM'S DILEMNA
(SA)/Aug 22, 1914; p. 1099
SLIPPERY SLIM'S INHERITANCE
(SA)/Aug 8, 1914; p. 836
SLIPPERY SLIM'S STRATEGEM
(SA)/May 30, 1914; p. 1260
SLIPPERY SLIM'S WEDDING DAY
(SA)/Mar 20, 1915; p. 1763
SLIPPERY SPY, THE
(Ec)/May 9, 1914; p. 821
SLIPPERY TOM (UE)/Jun 15, 1912; p. 1026
SLIPPING FINGERS
(Sel)/Nov 15, 1913; p. 736
SLOW BUT SURE (SA)/Aug 10, 1907; p. 362
(Rex)/Dec 5, 1914; p.1384
SLUMBERLAND (Vi)/Dec 19, 1908; pp 510-11
SLUMBERVILLE'S SCARE
(Lu)/Mar 28, 1914; p. 1680
SLY SERVANT, A (GN)/Oct 5, 1912; p. 42
SMALL DENIZENS OF THE SEASHORE
(Pa)/Jul 10, 1915; p. 309
SMALL TIME ACT, THE
(Key)/Nov 8, 1913; p. 613
SMALL TOWN GIRL, A (101)/Jan 9, 1915;
p. 197/Jan 23, 1915; p. 517
SMALL TRADES IN HAVANA
(Pa)/Mar 23, 1912; p. 1063
SMALLPOX ON THE CIRCLE U
(Ec)/Oct 24, 1914; p. 493
SMALLPOX SCARE AT GULCH HOLLOW, THE (Fr)/Jul 26, 1913; p. 430
SMART CAPTURE, A
(WBE)/Apr 27, 1907; p. 124
SMART TRICK, A (Ec)/Sep 4, 1909; p. 314
SMASHING TIME (Lu)/Sep 6, 1913; p. 1068
SMILE OF A CHILD, A
(Bio)/Jun 17, 1911; p. 1387
SMILES OF FORTUNE
(Lu)/Jan 24, 1914; p. 413
SMILING BOB (Me)/Mar 2, 1912; p. 780

(SA)/Dec 12, 1914; p. 1523
SNAKEVILLE'S RISING SONS
(SA)/Jan 16, 1915; p. 368
SNAKEVILLE'S TWINS
(SA)/Aug 14, 1915; p. 1160
SNAKEVILLE'S WEAK WOMEN
(SA)/Oct 23, 1915; p. 619
SNAP SHOTS (Ed)/Apr 24, 1915; p. 555
SNAPSHOTS (Th)/Aug 28, 1915; p. 1480
SNAPSHOTS OF JAVA
(Me)/Aug 23, 1913; p. 843
SNARE, THE (SA)/Nov 2, 1912; p. 450
SNARE OF FATE, THE
(Vi)/Jun 14, 1913; p. 1113
(Th)/Jun 21, 1913; pp 1233, 1254
SNARE OF SOCIETY, THE (Lu)/Jul 29,
1911; p. 209/Oct 7, 1911; p. 35
SNARE OF THE CITY, THE
(SA)/May 20, 1911; p. 1140
SNARED IN THE ALPS
(UF)/Dec 20, 1913; p. 1391
SNATCHED FROM A BURNING DEATH
(Vi)/Mar 13, 1915; p. 1618
SNATCHED FROM THE ALTAR
(Ne)/Oct 2, 1915; p. 80
SNEAK, THE (Ka)/May 3, 1913; p. 487
SNEAKTHIEF, THE (Pa)/Jan 17, 1914; p.289
SNITZ JOINS THE FORCE
(St)/Jun 6, 1914; p. 1410
SNOBBERY (Ne)/Jan 24, 1914; p. 414
SNOBS (Las)/Apr 24, 1915; p. 570
SNOOKEE'S DAY OFF
(St)/Oct 31, 1914; p. 642
SNOOKEE'S DISGUISE
(St)/Sep 5, 1914; p. 1373
SNOOKEE'S FLIRTATION
(St)/Jul 18, 1914; p. 433
SNOOKEM'S LAST RACKET
(Cry)/Mar 28, 1914; p. 1681
SNOOKUM'S BIRTHDAY
(Roy)/May 16, 1914; p. 969
SNORER, THE (At)/Sep 17, 1910; p. 632
SNOW BURNER, THE
(SA)/Apr 17, 1915; p. 395
SNOW EFFECTS IN AUSTRIA
(Pa)/Jan 24, 1914; p. 412
SNOW GIRL, THE (Lae)/Jun 19,1915; p.1941
SNOW MAIDEN, THE
(Amb)/Jun 3, 1911; p. 1260
SNOW WHITE (Po)/Feb 8, 1913; p. 582
SNOWBALL PETE (Ko)/Mar 28, 1914; p. 1681
SNOWBOUND WITH A WOMAN HATER
(Vi)/Jul 29, 1911; p. 209
SNOWDRIFT (Ec)/Jul 4, 1914; pp 66, 79
SNOW-MAN, THE (Bio)/Feb 15, 1908; p.121
SNOWMAN, THE (Sol)/Mar 9, 1912; p. 867
SNOWY EGRET AND ITS
 EXTERMINATION, THE

(Pa)/Jul 12, 1913; p. 184
SO LONG COUNT (Lu)/Apr 4, 1914; p. 57
SO NEAR, BUT NOT QUITE
(Pa)/Feb 4, 1911; p. 244
SO NEAR, YET SO FAR
(Bio)/Oct 12, 1912; p. 143
SO RUNS THE WAY (Bio)/Oct 25,1913;p.380
SO SHALL YE REAP
(Imp)/Apr 15, 1911; p. 844
(Fr)/Feb 28, 1914; p. 1089
SO SHINES A GOOD DEED
(Re)/Aug 22, 1914; p. 1100
SOAKING THE CLOTHES
(Phu)/Aug 21, 1915; p. 1318
SOAP IN HIS EYES
(Pa)/Dec 24, 1910; p. 1476
SOAP-SUDS STAR, THE
(Fal)/Oct 30, 1915; p. 792
SOB SISTER, THE (Rex)/Jul 18, 1914; p. 434
SOCIAL LAW, THE (GK)/Sep 18, 1915;
p. 2009/Oct 2, 1915; pp 78-79
SOCIAL SECRETARY, THE
(Lu)/Apr 13, 1912; p. 137
(Re)/Sep 6, 1913; p. 1069
SOCIALLY AMBITIOUS
(Lu)/Mar 20, 1915; p. 1764
SOCIETY AND CHAPS
(Am)/Mar 2, 1912; p. 782
SOCIETY AND THE MAN
(Vi)/Feb 18, 1911; p. 370
SOCIETY AT SIMPSON CENTER
(Ec)/Jun 13, 1914; p. 1543
SOCIETY FOR YOUNG WOMEN'S
 PROTECTION (GN)/Apr 6, 1912; p. 43
SOCIETY GIRL AND THE GYPSY, THE
(Pa)/Jul 1, 1911; p. 1520
SOCIETY HOBOES (Ya)/Oct 21, 1911; p.211
SOCIETY MOTHER, A (Gau)/Aug 5, 1911;
p. 294/Sep 23, 1911; pp 890-91
SOCIETY RACES AT PIPING ROCK
(Imp)/Jan 18, 1913; p. 266
SOCIETY SINNER, A
(GN)/Sep 10, 1910; p. 576
SOLD (FP)/Aug 21, 1915; p. 1326
SOLD BY HIS PARENTS
(KO)/Nov 14, 1908; p. 379
SOLDIER, A (Pa)/Mar 4, 1911; p. 482
SOLDIER BOY, A (Bio)/Oct 31, 1914; p. 641
SOLDIER BROTHERS OF SUSANNAH, THE
(Ka)/Jul 27, 1912; p. 349/Aug 17, 1912; p. 669
SOLDIER MUST OBEY RULES, A
(CR)/Dec 7, 1907; p. 652
SOLDIER OF PEACE, A
(Lu)/Jan 9, 1915; p. 221
SOLDIER OF THE C.S.A., A
(Sel)/Feb 28, 1914; p. 1087
SOLDIER OF THE CROSS, A
(It)/Dec 24, 1910; p. 1479

(Lu)/Sep 5, 1914; p. 1372
SOMNAMBULIST, THE
  (SA)/Nov 28,1908; p.431/Dec 5,1908; p.449
  (GN)/May 21, 1910; p. 834
  (Me)/Jan 24, 1914; p. 412
  (Th)/May 23, 1914; p. 1118
SOMNAMBULISTIC HERO, A
  (Ed)/May 29, 1909; pp 713-14
SOMNAMBULISTS, THE
  (Bio)/Dec 13, 1913; p. 1279
SON (Ec)/Sep 26, 1914; p. 1777
SON, THE (Lu)/Oct 23, 1915; p. 619
SON OF HIS FATHER, THE
  (Lu)/Jan 3, 1914; p. 49
SON OF OLD GLORY, A
  (Ya)/Feb 11, 1911; p. 318
SON OF "THE DOG"
  (Re)/May 22, 1915; p. 1260
SON OF THE EXECUTIONER, THE (GN)/
  Feb 4, 1911; p. 248/Mar 25, 1911; p. 658
SON OF THE SEA, A
  (Cin)/Apr 25, 1914; p. 517
SON OF THE SHUNAMMITE, THE
  (Gau)/Sep 2, 1911; pp 627-28
SON OF THE WILDERNESS, A
  (Amb)/Jan 29, 1910; pp 127-28
SON OF THOMAS GRAY, THE
  (Am)/Jan 24, 1914; p. 414
SONATA OF SOULS
  (Re)/Jun 3, 1911; p. 1260
SONG IN THE DARK, THE
  (SA)/Jun 27, 1914; p. 1829
SONG OF SOLOMON, THE (Ed)/Apr 18,
  1914; p. 346/May 23, 1914; p. 1117
SONG OF SUNNY ITALY, A
  (Bio)/Jul 11, 1914; p. 255
SONG OF THE CRADLE, THE
  (Gau)/Nov 13, 1909; p. 684
SONG OF THE GHETTO, THE
  (Vi)/Aug 1, 1914; p. 705
SONG OF THE GYPSY, THE
  (UE)/Mar 9, 1912; pp 850-51
SONG OF THE HEART, THE
  (Th)/May 15, 1915; p. 1073
SONG OF THE SEA, A
  (Da)/Oct 16, 1915; p. 442
SONG OF THE SEA SHELL, THE
  (Am)/Sep 12, 1914; p. 1512
SONG OF THE SHIRT, THE
  (Bio)/Nov 28, 1908; p. 423
SONG OF THE SHORE, THE
  (Maj)/Jun 6, 1914; p. 1409
SONG OF THE SOUP, THE
  (Am)/Jul 12, 1913; p. 206
SONG OF THE TELEGRAPH, THE
  (101)/Feb 22, 1913; p. 782
SONG OF THE WAGE-SLAVE, THE
  (Mto)/Oct 2, 1915; p. 93

SONG OF THE WILDWOOD FLUTE
  (Bio)/Dec 3, 1910; p. 1296
**SONG THAT REACHED HER HEART,
  THE** (RR)/Dec 18, 1909;p.882
SONG THAT REACHED HIS HEART
  (Ed)/Oct 22, 1910; p. 936
SONG-BIRD OF THE NORTH, THE
  (Vi)/Jul 19, 1913; p. 319
SONGS OF TRUCE (Sel)/Jul 12, 1913; p.205
**SONNY JIM AND THE AMUSEMENT CO.,
  LTD.** (Vi)/Oct 2, 1915; p. 78
SONNY JIM AND THE FAMILY PARTY
  (Vi)/Dec 4, 1915; p. 1852
**SONNY JIM AND THE GREAT AMERICAN
  GAME** (Vi)/Nov 27, 1915; p. 1663
SONNY JIM AND THE VALENTINE
  (Vi)/May 8, 1915; p. 899
SONNY JIM AT THE MARDI GRAS
  (Vi)/Jun 19, 1915; p. 1939
SONNY JIM AT THE NORTH POLE
  (Vi)/May 2, 1914; p. 673
SONNY JIM IN SEARCH OF A MOTHER
  (Vi)/Feb 28, 1914; p. 1087
SONNY JIM'S FIRST LOVE AFFAIR
  (Vi)/Dec 18, 1915; p. 2202
SON'S DEVOTION, A
  (Lu)/May 18, 1912; p. 628
  (Ec)/Nov 29, 1913; p. 1009
SON'S EXAMPLE, A (Me)/Nov 9,1912;p.552
SON'S INGRATITUDE, A
  (Ec)/Apr 27, 1912; p. 330
SONS OF A SOLDIER
  (Ec)/May 17, 1913; p. 705
SONS OF THE MINISTER, THE
  (GN)/Jul 16, 1910; p. 144
SONS OF THE NORTH WOODS
  (Sel)/Apr 6, 1912; p. 41
SONS OF THE WEST
  (Ne)/Aug 20, 1910; p. 408
SONS OF TOIL, THE
  (Dom)/Apr 17, 1915; p. 393
SON'S RETURN, THE
  (Bio)/Jun 19, 1909; p. 834
SOPHIA'S IMAGINARY VISITORS
  (Ed)/Mar 7, 1914; p. 1236
SOPHIE AND THE FAKIR
  (SA)/Jun 19, 1915; p. 1939
SOPHIE AND THE MAN OF HER CHOICE
  (SA)/Nov 28, 1914; p. 1231
SOPHIE CHANGES HER MIND
  (SA)/Mar 13, 1915; p. 1607
SOPHIE OF THE FILMS (Ne)
  No.1/Jun 6, 1914; p. 1410
  No.2/Jun 13, 1914; p. 1542
  No.3/Jun 20, 1914; p. 1690
  No.4/Jun 27, 1914; p. 1830
SOPHIE PICKS A DEAD ONE
  (SA)/Feb 28, 1914; p. 1088

(CGP)/Nov 23, 1912; p. 767
SPAIN'S LOYALTY
(Gau)/Dec 3, 1910; p. 1296
SPANISH ARMY, THE (Pa)/Jul 10, 1909; p. 50
SPANISH BLOOD (Pa)/Jan 16, 1909; p. 68
SPANISH CAVALIER, THE
(Ed)/Apr 27, 1912; p. 328
SPANISH DILEMNA, A
(Bio)/Mar 23, 1912; p. 1063
SPANISH FRONTIER, THE
(Gau)/Jul 2, 1910; p. 24
SPANISH GIRL, THE
(SA)/Dec 31, 1909; p. 960
SPANISH GIRL'S REVENGE, THE
(Pho)/Aug 21, 1909; p. 253
SPANISH GYPSY, THE
(Bio)/Apr 15, 1911; p. 842
SPANISH JADE, THE
(Fic)/Mar 20, 1915; p. 1768
SPANISH LOVE SONG, A
(Me)/Sep 9, 1911; p. 716
SPANISH MARRIAGE
(Pa)/Dec 11, 1909; p. 841
SPANISH OMELET, A
(Bio)/Jul 11, 1914; p. 255
SPANISH PARROT GIRL, THE
(Sel)/Mar 22, 1913; p. 1220
SPANISH REVOLT OF 1836, THE
(Ka)/Apr 20, 1912; p. 229
SPANISH ROMANCE, A
(Vi)/Oct 17, 1908; p. 307
SPANISH WIFE (Lu)/Apr 9, 1910; p. 553
SPANISH WOOING, A
(Sel)/Dec 2, 1911; p. 725
SPARE THE ROD (Maj)/Feb 3, 1912; p. 394
SPARK AND THE FLAME, THE
(Lu)/Sep 11, 1915; p. 1832
SPARK ETERNAL, THE
(KB)/Oct 24, 1914; p. 493
SPARK IN THE EMBERS, THE
(Bro)/May 8, 1915; p. 900
SPARKS OF FATE (SA)/Oct 3, 1914; p. 64
SPARROW, THE (LP)/Apr 11, 1914; p. 193
SPARROW OF THE CIRCUS
(Am)/Jun 20, 1914; p. 1690
SPARTACUS (Pas)/Jun 6, 1914; pp 1388-89
SPARTAN FATHER, A
(Th)/Aug 30, 1913; p. 962
SPARTAN GIRL, THE
(Pas)/Mar 21, 1914; p. 1536
SPARTAN MOTHER, A (Ka)/Mar 2, 1912;
pp 770-71/Mar 23, 1912; p. 1062
SPEAK NO EVIL (SA)/Feb 28, 1914; p. 1087
SPEC ON THE WALL, A
(Sel)/Aug 29, 1914; p. 1241
SPECIAL AGENT, THE
(Vi)/May 28, 1910; p. 888
SPECIAL MESSENGER (Ka)/Aug 12, 1911;

p. 359/Sep 2, 1911; p. 627
SPECIAL OFFICER, THE
(Lu)/Oct 18, 1913; p. 264
SPECIES OF A MEXICAN MAN, A (Lu)/
Sep 4, 1915; p. 1666/Sep 11, 1915; p. 1833
SPECIMENS OF LIZARDS AND FROGS
(UE)/Nov 30, 1912; p. 876
SPECKLED BAND, THE
(UF)/Nov 23, 1912; p. 779
SPECTER, THE (Pa)/Jul 4, 1908; p. 12/
Apr 17, 1909; p. 478
SPECTRE BRIDEGROOM, THE (Ec)/
Jan 25, 1913; p. 349/Feb 1, 1913; p. 466
SPECULATION (Po)/Aug 12, 1911; p. 378
SPEED BEAR, THE (Ap)/Oct 11, 1913; p.157
SPEED DEMON, THE
(Bio)/Jul 27, 1912; p. 344
SPEED KING, THE
(Th)/Jan 23, 1915; p. 518
SPEED KINGS, THE
(Key)/Nov 15, 1913; p. 738
SPEED LIMIT, THE
(Ka)/Nov 15, 1913; p. 735
SPEED QUEEN, THE
(Key)/Jun 14, 1913; p. 1138
SPEEDERS' REVENGE, THE
(Vi)/Mar 21, 1914; p. 1524
SPEEDWAY OF DESPAIR, THE
(Sel)/Mar 28, 1914; p. 1680
SPELL, THE (Po)/Jun 21, 1913; p. 1255
(Vi)/Aug 9, 1913; p. 636
SPELL OF THE POPPY, THE
(Maj)/May 22, 1915; p. 1260
SPELL OF THE PRIMEVAL
(Sel)/Oct 11, 1913; p. 155
SPENDER, THE (Vic)/Nov 1, 1913; p. 498
(Emp)/May 1, 1915; p. 742
(Pa)/Oct 2, 1915; p. 92
SPENDER FAMILY, THE
(SA)/Aug 12, 1911; p. 377
SPENDING IT QUICK
(Bio)/Sep 12, 1914; p. 1512
SPENDTHRIFT, THE (GK)/Jul 3, 1915; p. 78
SPENDTHRIFT'S REFORM, THE (Pa)/
Dec 7, 1912; p.966/Dec 21, 1912; p.1184
SPHINX, THE (Vic)/May 29, 1915; p. 1444
SPICY TIME, A (Imp)/Feb 15, 1913; p. 680
SPIDER, THE (Ec)/Jun 14, 1913; p. 1137
(Gra)/Jun 12, 1915; p. 1778
(SA)/Oct 30a, 1915; p. 968
SPIDER AND HER WEB, THE
(Rex)/Mar 28, 1914; p. 1682
SPIDER BARLOW CUTS IN
(Am)/Nov 27, 1915; pp 1664, 1677
SPIDER BARLOW'S SOFT SPOT
(Am)/Dec 18, 1915; p. 2203
SPIDER IN THE BRAIN, A
(It)/Dec 7, 1912; p. 977

STATUE DOG, THE
(Vi)/Dec 10, 1910; p. 1356
STATUE OF FRIGHT, THE
(UE)/Jul 26, 1913; p. 427
STATUE ON A SPREE, A
(Pa)/Mar 7, 1908; pp 193-94
STAY-AT-HOMES, THE
(Be)/Jun 5, 1915; p. 1605
STEADFAST, THE (Lu)/Oct 30, 1915; p. 791
STEADY COMPANY (Rex)/Jul 10,1915;p.309
STEALING A RIDE
(Th)/Feb 11, 1911; p. 318
STEAM (Kin)/Apr 19, 1913; p. 281/
Jun 21, 1913; p. 1239
STEAMSHIP MAURETANIA, THE
(At)/Oct 22, 1910; p. 939
STEEL (Ec)/Sep 6, 1913; p. 1069
STEEL INDUSTRY (KO)/Jun 6, 1908; p. 497
STENOGRAPHER, THE
(Ed)/Dec 26, 1914; p. 1840
STENOGRAPHER TROUBLES
(Vi)/Feb 22, 1913; p. 780
STENOGRAPHER WANTED
(Ka)/Nov 23, 1912; p. 767
STENOGRAPHERS WANTED
(Vi)/Mar 9, 1912; p. 867
STEP SON, THE (Ne)/Sep 20, 1913; p. 1285
STEP-BROTHERS, THE
(Am)/Nov 1, 1913; p. 498
STEPDAUGHTER, THE
(Lu)/Aug 6, 1910; p. 297
(Ya)/Aug 5, 1911; p. 296
STEPMOTHER, THE
(GN)/Jan 2, 1909; pp 10-11
(Pa)/Jan 30, 1909; p. 120
(Ka)/Feb 12, 1910; p. 216
(Sel)/Dec 24, 1910; p. 1476
(Vic)/Feb 28, 1914; p. 1090
STEPPING WESTWARD
(Id)/Jun 12, 1915; p. 1778
STEPSISTERS, THE (Pa)/Jul 15, 1911; p. 38
STERN DESTINY, A
(Pa)/Jun 22, 1912; p. 1127
STERN PAPA (Bio)/Sep 28, 1912; p. 1276
STEVE HILL'S AWAKENING
(NyC)/Oct 17, 1914; p. 350
STEVE O'GRADY'S CHANCE
(Vi)/Oct 3, 1914; p. 64
STICK IT JOHN (Lux)/Nov 2, 1912; p. 451
STICKLEBACK, THE
(CGP)/Mar 22, 1913; p. 1220
(Pa)/Apr 10, 1915; p. 237
STICKY BICYCLE, THE
(WBE)/Dec 7, 1907; p. 651
STIGMA, THE (Pa)/Oct 22, 1910; p. 936
(Ne)/Dec 28, 1912; p. 1293
(SA)/Jan 3, 1914; p. 49
(KB)/Aug 15, 1914; p. 962

STILETTO, THE (Re)/May 2, 1914; p. 674
STILL, SMALL VOICE, THE
(Vi)/Mar 13, 1915; p. 1607
STILL ALARM
(Sel)/Jun 3, 1911; pp 1238, 1258
STILL ON SUNSET MOUNTAIN, THE
(Dom)/Jan 23, 1915; p. 517
STILL VOICE, THE (Vi)/Jun 7, 1913; p.1031
STILL WATERS (FP)/Nov 13, 1915; p. 1321
STING OF IT, THE (Am)/Oct 16,1915; p.440
STINGAREE (Ka)
No.1/Nov 6,1915; p.1154/Dec 4,1915; p.1852
No.2/Nov 13, 1915; p. 1320u
No.3/Nov 20, 1915; p. 1506
No.5/Nov 27, 1915; p. 1674
No.6/Dec 4,1915;p.1847/Dec 11,1915;p.2027
STINGERS STUNG, or JAKE AND MIKE IN
THE OIL FIELDS (Jo)/Nov 22, 1913; p. 869
STIRRUP BROTHER, THE
(Ec)/Jun 20, 1914; p. 1690
STOCK FARMING IN SOUTH AMERICA
(Pa)/Jun 5, 1915; p. 1606
STOCKHOLM (Pa)/Jul 18, 1908; p. 51
STOCKINGS (WF)/Dec 5, 1914; pp 1385-86
STOLEN ANTHURIUM, THE
(Fal)/Jun 26, 1915; p. 2096
STOLEN BIRTHRIGHT, THE
(Pa)/Dec 5, 1914; p. 1392
STOLEN BRIDE, THE
(Bio)/Apr 19, 1913; p. 281
STOLEN BY AN EAGLE
(LeL)/Jun 26, 1909; p. 873
STOLEN BY THE INDIANS
(Ch)/Oct 29, 1910; p. 999
STOLEN CASE, THE
(MnA)/Jul 10, 1915; p. 307
STOLEN CHICKEN
(Cin)/Oct 19, 1907; pp 527-28
STOLEN CLAIM, THE
(Ed)/Dec 3, 1910; p. 1296
(Me)/Jun 28, 1913; p. 1359
STOLEN CODE, THE (Re)/Jul 4, 1914; p. 66
STOLEN DAGGER, THE
(KO)/May 2, 1908; p. 401
STOLEN DIAMOND, THE
(Lux)/Sep 30, 1911; p. 974
STOLEN DOG, THE (Ed)/Aug 26,1911;p.541
STOLEN ENGINE, THE
(Ka)/Nov 28, 1914; p0. 1243
STOLEN FACE, THE
(Sel)/Aug 9, 1913; p. 636
STOLEN FATHER, THE
(Ed)/Oct 29, 1910; p. 994
STOLEN FORTUNE, THE
(SA)/May 21, 1910; p. 834
(SA)/Aug 1, 1914; p. 705
STOLEN GOODS (Las)/Jun 5, 1915; p. 1624
STOLEN GRAY, THE

STUDY IN SOCIOLOGY, A
(Maj)/Apr 12, 1913; p. 165
STUDY IN TRAMPS, A
(Vi)/Mar 27, 1915; p. 1931
STUDY OF BIRD LIFE, A
(Pa)/Aug 16, 1913; p. 743
STUDY OF THE FLY
(Ec)/Dec 14, 1912; p. 1082
STUFF HEROES ARE MADE OF, THE
(Bio)/Sep 23, 1911; p. 890
STUFF THAT AMERICANS ARE MADE OF
(Ed)/May 21, 1910; p. 833
STUFF THAT DREAMS ARE MADE OF
(Ed)/Jan 6, 1912; p. 41
STUFF THAT DREAMS ARE MADE OF,
THE (Ed)/Jul 11, 1914; p. 265/
Aug 15, 1914; p. 960
STUNG (SA)/Mar 6, 1909; p. 269
(Imp)/Apr 2, 1910; p. 510
(Pa)/Sep 6, 1913; p. 1067
(Ec)/Sep 13, 1913; p. 1177
(Ka)/May 16, 1914; p. 968
STUNG! (StU)/Apr 10, 1915; p. 237
STUNG BY A BEE (Gau)/Jul 3,1909; p.14
STUNG BY THE BEE
(WF)/Dec 5, 1914; p. 1386
STUNTS ON SKATES BY EDWARD LAMY
(Imp)/Apr 9, 1910; p. 554
STURDY SAILOR'S HONOR
(KO)/Jul 25, 1908; p. 69
SUBDUING MRS. NAG
(Vi)/Jul 29, 1911; p. 210
SUBLIME DECEPTION, A
(Me)/Aug 1, 1914; p. 705
SUBLIME PARDON, THE
(Pa)/Jul 8, 1911; p. 1585
SUBMARINE MYSTERIES
(Pa)/Feb 7, 1914; p. 676
SUBMARINE PIRATE, A (TK)/Nov 20,
1915; p. 1501/Nov 27, 1915; p. 1681
SUBSTITUTE, THE
(Pa)/Nov 28, 1908; p. 434
(RR)/Nov 27, 1909; p. 759
(Lu)/Dec 30, 1911; p. 1071
(Cin)/May 25, 1912; p. 729
(Lu)/May 29, 1915; p. 1431
SUBSTITUTE DRUG CLERK, THE
(KO)/Jun 8, 1907; p. 220
SUBSTITUTE ENGINEER, THE
(Ka)/Aug 30, 1913; p. 961
SUBSTITUTE FOR PANTS, A
(Ka)/Aug 29, 1914; p. 1240
SUBSTITUTE HEIR, THE
(Sel)/Aug 8, 1914; p. 836
SUBSTITUTE HEIRESS, THE
(Lu)/Nov 23, 1912; p. 766
SUBSTITUTE MINISTER, THE
(Am)/Nov 13, 1915; p. 1312

SUBSTITUTE MODEL, THE
(Sel)/Sep 28, 1912; p. 1277
SUBSTITUTE STENOGRAPHER, THE
(Ed)/Aug 16, 1913; p. 744
SUBSTITUTE WIDOW, THE
(Imp)/Aug 21, 1915; p. 1318
SUBSTITUTION, A
(Lu)/Sep 14, 1912; p. 1075
SUBTERFUGE (Sel)/Nov 2, 1912; p. 450
SUBTERFUGE, THE (Pa)/May 14,1910;p.784
SUBTERRANEAN CITY, THE
(UE)/Nov 15, 1913; p. 717
SUBURBAN, THE (Imp)/Oct 2, 1915; p. 80
SUBURBANITE'S INGENIOUS ALARM,
THE (Ed)/Jan 18, 1908; p. 47
SUCCESS (Re)/Aug 23, 1913; p. 845
SUCCESS OF SELFISHNESS, THE
(Th)/Feb 21, 1914; p. 947
SUCCESSFUL FAILURE, A
(SA)/Oct 18, 1913; p. 263
SUCH A BUSINESS
(Roy)/Jul 4, 1914; p. 65
(Lun)/Jan 23, 1915; p. 517
SUCH A GOOD JOKE, BUT WHY DON'T
HE LAUGH? (Lu)/Jan 18, 1908; p. 46
SUCH A HUNTER (Vi)/Sep 12,1914; p.1511
SUCH A LITTLE QUEEN
(FP)/Oct 3, 1914; p. 45
SUCH A MESS (Lu)/Nov 7, 1914; p. 787
SUCH A MISTAKE
(Cry)/Dec 19, 1914; p. 1681
SUCH A PICNIC (Sup)/Jan 23, 1915; p. 517
SUCH A PRINCESS (Rex)/Nov 6,1915;p.1140
SUCH A VILLAIN (Ne)/Apr 4, 1914; p. 59
SUCH AN APPETITE (Lu)/Apr 5, 1913; p.49
SUCH IS LIFE (SA)/Aug 16, 1913; p. 743
(Rex)/Mar 6, 1915; p. 1449
SUCH IS THE KINGDOM
(Re)/May 20, 1911; p. 1142
SUDDEN TELEPHONE CALL, A
(Amb)/Apr 9, 1910; p. 554
SUE (Ch)/Nov 9, 1912; p. 554
(SA)/May 22, 1915; p. 1259
SUE SIMPKINS' AMBITION
(Vi)/Jan 11, 1913; p. 158
SUFFER LITTLE CHILDREN
(Ed)/Sep 11, 1909; p. 347
(Vi)/Nov 25, 1911; pp 636-37
SUFFERER FROM INSOMNIA, THE
(It)/Nov 19, 1910; p. 1179
SUFFERIN' BABY, THE
(Ed)/Dec 11, 1915; p. 2031
SUFFERING OF SUSAN, THE
(Bio)/Jan 9, 1915; p. 220
SUFFRAGETTE, THE (Sel)/Feb 8,1913;p.572
SUFFRAGETTE BATTLE OF NUTTYVILLE,
THE (Maj)/Jul 25, 1914; p. 572
SUFFRAGETTE IN SPITE OF HIMSELF, A

SWAMP FOX, THE (Ka)/May 2, 1914; p.646
SWAN GIRL, THE (Vi)/Dec 20,1913; p.1411
SWAN LIFE (St)/Feb 27, 1915; p. 1289
SWANS (Gau)/Jun 3, 1911; p. 1259
SWASH-BUCKLER (Sel)/Mar 28,1908; p.271
SWASTICA, THE (Me)/Jun 1, 1912; p. 829
SWAT THE FLY (SA)/Jul 22, 1911; p. 123
          (Po)/Oct 5, 1912; p. 42
SWEAT BOX, THE (Bio)/Aug 2,1913; p.535
SWEDE LARSON (Rex)/Jun 6, 1914; p. 1410
SWEDEN (Pa)/May 2, 1908; p. 402
SWEDISH DANCES (Pa)/Mar 28, 1908;
  p. 270/Apr 3, 1909; p. 404
SWEDISH SPORTS (Pa)/Nov 9,1907; p.584
SWEDISH SUBMARINE MANOUVERS, THE
  (CGP)/Feb 22, 1913; p. 779
SWEEDIE AND HER DOG
  (SA)/Jan 30, 1915; p. 672
SWEEDIE AND THE DOUBLE EXPOSURE
  (SA)/Aug 29, 1914; p. 1241
SWEEDIE AND THE HYPNOTIST
  (SA)/Dec 19, 1914; p. 1680
SWEEDIE AND THE SULTAN'S PRESENT
  (SA)/Jan 16, 1915; pp 368-69
SWEEDIE AT THE FAIR
  (SA)/Dec 5, 1914; p. 1384
SWEEDIE COLLECTS FOR CHARITY
  (SA)/Jan 9, 1915; p. 221
SWEEDIE GOES TO COLLEGE
  (SA)/Feb 27, 1915; p. 1287
SWEEDIE IN VAUDEVILLE
  (SA)/May 29, 1915; p. 1431
SWEEDIE LEARNS TO RIDE
  (SA)/Apr 10, 1915; p. 235
SWEEDIE LEARNS TO SWIM
  (SA)/Oct 24, 1914; p. 492
SWEEDIE SPRINGS A SURPRISE
  (SA)/Sep 5, 1914; p. 1372
SWEEDIE THE SWATTER
  (SA)/Aug 1, 1914; p. 704
SWEEDIE THE TROUBLE MAKER
  (SA)/Nov 21, 1914; p. 1076
SWEEDIE'S CLEAN-UP
  (SA)/Oct 10, 1914; p. 188
SWEEDIE'S FINISH
  (SA)/Jun 26, 1915; p. 2095
SWEEDIE'S HERO (SA)/Jun 5, 1915; p.1604
SWEEDIE'S SKATE (SA)/Oct 3, 1914; p. 64
SWEEDIE'S SUICIDE
  (SA)/Jan 23, 1915; p. 516
SWEENEY AND THE MILLION
  (Sel)/Feb 22, 1913; p. 779
SWEENEY'S CHRISTMAS BIRD
  (Vi)/Jan 9, 1915; p. 220
SWEENEY'S DREAM (Sel)/Aug 2,1913;p.535
SWEENY AND THE FAIRY
  (Sel)/Jun 21, 1913; p. 1252
SWEET ALICE, BEN BOLT

(Imp)/Sep 28, 1912; p. 1277
SWEET ALYSSUM (Sel)/Nov 13,1915;p.1321
SWEET AND LOW (Am)/Nov 7, 1914; p.788
SWEET AND TWENTY
  (Bio)/Jul 31, 1909; p. 161
SWEET DECEPTION
  (Vi)/Jul 19, 1913; p. 319
SWEET FAMILIAR FACES
  (Gau)/Mar 8, 1913; p. 998
SWEET LAND OF LIBERTY
  (Be)/Apr 11, 1914; p. 213
SWEET MEMORIES (Imp)/Apr 8,1911;p.782
SWEET REVENGE (Bio)/Dec 4, 1909; p. 799
          (SA)/Oct 4, 1913; p. 47
SWEET TOOTHED DOGS
  (Pa)/Jul 31, 1909; p. 161
SWEETER THAN REVENGE
  (Lu)/Dec 25, 1915; p. 2388
SWIMMING AND LIFE-SAVING
  (Lu)/Oct 5, 1912; p. 41
SWIMMING LESSON, THE (KO)/Nov 21,
  1908; p. 408/Nov 28, 1908; p. 423
SWIMMING PARTY, THE
  (Ka)/Feb 24, 1912; pp 689-90
SWINDLER, THE (Ka)/Feb 13, 1915; p. 985
SWINDLERS, THE
  (Maj)/May 30, 1914; p. 1261
SWINGING DOORS, THE
  (U)/Jun 12, 1915; p. 1779
SWISS ALPS (KO)/Jul 11, 1908; p. 36
SWISS GUARD, THE
  (Ed)/Nov 12, 1910; p. 1116
SWITCH TOWER, THE
  (Bio)/Jun 28, 1913; p. 1358
SWITCHMAN'S TOWER, THE
  (Ed)/Aug 19, 1911; p. 462
SWITZERLAND: CONQUERING THE ALPS
  (UE)/Dec 25, 1909; p. 921
SWORD AND THE CROSS, THE
  (Gau)/Mar 25, 1911; p. 657
SWORD OF DAMOCLES, A
  (Pa)/Feb 7, 1914; p. 677
SWORDS AND HEARTS
  (Bio)/Aug 26, 1911; pp 523-24
SYDNEY AND ITS HARBOR
  (Me)/Nov 22, 1913; p. 867
SYLVERE SISTERS ON THE DOUBLE
  TRAPEZE, THE (CGP)/Jun 8, 1912; p. 944
SYMPATHY SAL (Re)/Apr 17, 1915; p. 393
SYMPHONY, THE (Rex)/Feb 1, 1913; p. 466
SYMPHONY IN BLACK AND WHITE, A
  (Ec)/Mar 30, 1912; p. 1167
SYMPHONY OF SOULS
  (Rex)/Aug 8, 1914; p. 837

TABARIN'S WIFE
  (Pa)/Jul 8, 1911; p. 1585
TABLES ARE TURNED, THE

(Ne)/Aug 24, 1912; p. 772

TALE OF THE HAT, THE
(Ka)/Apr 10, 1915; p. 235

TALE OF THE HOT DOG, THE
(At)/Sep 3, 1910; p. 521

TALE OF THE NORTHWEST MOUNTED, A
(Bro)/Sep 19, 1914; p. 1646

TALE OF THE SEA, A
(Sel)/Dec 24, 1910; p. 1478

TALE OF THE SNOW, A
(Ch)/Jan 27, 1912; p. 305

TALE OF THE TICKER, THE
(Am)/Nov 22, 1913; p. 869

TALE OF THE WEST
(SA)/Apr 10, 1909; p. 442

TALE OF THE WEST, A
(Ne)/Dec 27, 1913; p. 1545

TALE OF THE WILDERNESS, A
(Bio)/Jan 20, 1912; p. 203

TALE OF TWO CITIES, A (Vi)
Pt.1/Mar 4, 1911; p. 483
Pt.2/Mar 11, 1911; p. 540
Pt.3/Mar 11, 1911; p. 540

TALE OF TWO COATS, THE
(Ed)/Jul 16, 1910; p. 143

TALE THE AUTUMN LEAVES TOLD
(Ed)/Apr 11, 1908; p. 325

TALE THE MIRROR TOLD, THE
(Pa)/Dec 17, 1910; p. 1416

TALE THE SEARCHLIGHT TOLD
(Ed)/Aug 8, 1908; p. 108

TALE THE TICKER TOLD, THE
(Ed)/Dec 12, 1908; p. 476

TALESMAN, THE (Am)/Apr 8, 1911; p. 782

TALISMAN, THE (Pa)/Jan 4, 1908; p. 12

TALKATIVE TESS (Pa)/Oct 25, 1913; p. 380

TALKER, THE (Lu)/Aug 10, 1912; p. 546

TAM O'SHANTER (U)/Sep 4, 1915; p. 1645

TAMANDRA, THE GYPSY
(Lu)/Apr 5, 1913; p. 48

TAMER: ALFRED SCHNEIDER AND HIS LIONS, THE (Amb)/Jul 23, 1910; p. 194

TAMING A BACHELOR
(Com)/Oct 26, 1912; p. 343

TAMING A COWBOY
(Am)/Oct 18, 1913; p. 265

TAMING A GROUCH
(Nov)/Nov 27, 1915; p. 1664

TAMING A HUSBAND
(Ec)/May 22, 1909; p. 676
(Bio)/Mar 12, 1910; p. 383
(Maj)/Dec 23, 1911; p. 993

TAMING A TENDERFOOT
(Sel)/Jun 28, 1913; p. 1360

TAMING A TYRANT
(SA)/Mar 11, 1911; p. 542

TAMING OF BETTY, THE
(Vi)/Aug 2, 1913; p. 536

TAMING OF BUCK, THE
(Po)/Oct 8, 1910; p. 816

TAMING OF JANE (Imp)/Sep 3, 1910; p. 521

TAMING OF MARY (Th)/Apr 6, 1912; p. 42

TAMING OF MARY, THE
(Vic)/Aug 21, 1915; p. 1318

TAMING OF RITA, THE
(Vi)/May 8, 1915; p. 899

TAMING OF SUNNYBROOK NELL, THE
(Am)/Oct 3, 1912; p. 65

TAMING OF TEXAS PETE, THE
(Sel)/Aug 23, 1913; p. 842

TAMING OF THE SHREW
(UE)/Jul 8, 1911; p. 1586

TAMING OF THE SHREW, THE (Bio)/
Nov 21, 1908; p. 398/Nov 28, 1908; p. 423

TAMING OF WILD BILL, THE
(Lu)/Nov 19, 1910; p. 1178

TAMING TERRIBLE TED
(Lu)/Feb 28, 1914; p. 1087

TAMING THE TERROR
(Bi)/Jan 14, 1911; p. 91

TAMING THEIR GRAND CHILDREN
(Th)/Sep 13, 1913; p. 1176

TAMING WILD HORSES FOR USE IN "FLYING A" PICTURES
(Am)/Jan 13, 1912; p. 127

TAMMANY BOARDER, A (Ec)/Jan 4, 1913;
p. 58/Jan 11, 1913; p. 159

TANANARIVE (Pa)/Jun 21, 1913; p. 1252

TANDJONG PRIOK, THE HARBOR OF JAVA'S CAPITAL, BATAVIA
(Me)/Jun 14, 1913; p. 1135

TANGLE, THE (Po)/Aug 1, 1914; p. 706

TANGLE IN HEARTS, A
(Cas)/Dec 4, 1915; p. 1853

TANGLED (Po)/Jul 20, 1912; p. 245

TANGLED CAT, THE
(Pr)/Feb 28, 1914; p. 1089

TANGLED HEARTSTRINGS
(Ya)/Sep 23, 1911; p. 892

TANGLED LINES (Re)/Mar 18, 1911; p. 603

TANGLED LIVES (Th)/Sep 24, 1910; p. 690
(Ka)/Jun 10, 1911; p. 1313

TANGLED MARRIAGE, A
(Cry)/Dec 14, 1912; p. 1083

TANGLED PATHS (Maj)/Aug 7, 1915; p.997

TANGLED SKEIN, A
(Rep)/Mar 9, 1912; p. 868

TANGLED TANGOISTS
(Vi)/May 9, 1914; p. 820

TANGLED WIRES (Vi)/Nov 29,1913; p.1007

TANGLED WEB, THE (Re)/Jul 5, 1913; p.49

TANGO CRAZE, THE
(Pa)/May 9, 1914; p. 821

TANGO FLAT, THE
(Bio)/May 9, 1914; p. 820

TANGO IN TUCKERVILLE (Ed)/May 16,

TENDER HEARTED MIKE
(Po)/Apr 6, 1912; p. 42
TENDER-HEARTED SHERIFF, THE
(Jo)/Feb 21, 1914; p. 948
TENDERFOOT, THE
(Ka)/Jul 27, 1907; p. 331
Jan 16, 1909; p. 69
(Ne)/Apr 2, 1910; p. 509
TENDERFOOT BOB'S REGENERATION
(Sel)/Apr 13, 1912; p. 136
TENDERFOOT FOREMAN, THE
(SA)/Jan 27, 1912; p. 303
TENDERFOOT MESSENGER, A
(SA)/Dec 31, 1910; p. 1536
TENDERFOOT SHERIFF, THE
(SA)/Aug 16, 1913; p. 743
TENDERFOOT'S CLAIM, THE
(Ka)/Jul 29, 1911; p. 210
TENDERFOOT'S LUCK, THE
(Ka)/Aug 9, 1913; p. 635
TENDERFOOT'S MONEY, THE
(Bio)/May 17, 1913; p. 703
TENDERFOOT'S REVENGE, A
(Bi)/Feb 17, 1912; p. 583
TENDERFOOT'S ROUNDUP, THE
(Am)/Jan 28, 1911; p. 196
TENDERFOOT'S SACRIFICE, THE
(Ne)/Jan 13, 1912; p. 127
TENDERFOOT'S TRIUMPH, THE
(Bio)/May 7, 1910; p. 737
(Sel)/Nov 27, 1915; p. 1663
TENDERFOOT'S TROUBLES, A
(Ka)/Mar 16, 1912; p. 961
TENDERFOOT'S TURN, THE
(Fr)/Apr 5, 1913; p. 49
TENDERLOIN TRAGEDY, THE
(Bio)/May 11, 1907; p. 158
TENERIFFE, THE GEM OF THE CANARIES
(Gau)/Aug 20, 1910; p. 407
TENNESSEE (KB)/Jun 6, 1914; p. 1410
TENNESSEE GUARDS (Pa)/Sep 4,1909;p.316
TENNESSEE LOVE STORY, A
(Sel)/Sep 23, 1911; p. 890
TENOR, THE (GS)/Sep 25, 1915; p. 2177
TENT VILLAGE (Lu)/Aug 26, 1911; p. 541
TENTH COMMANDMENT, THE (Imp)/
Sep 26, 1914; p. 1755/Oct 3, 1914; p. 66
TERMITE, THE INSECT ARCHITECT, THE
(Pa)/Apr 25, 1914; p. 516
TERMS OF THE WILL, THE
(Pa)/Nov 25, 1911; p. 636
TERRIBLE ALTERNATIVE, THE
(Me)/Jun 13, 1914; p. 1541
TERRIBLE CATASTROPHE, A
(Sol)/Jul 15, 1911; p. 40
TERRIBLE DAUGHTER, THE
(Ec)/Feb 22, 1913; p. 782
TERRIBLE DISCOVERY, A

(Bio)/Jan 6, 1912; p. 40
TERRIBLE LESSON, A
(Sol)/Feb 10, 1912; p. 491
TERRIBLE LESSON, THE
(Bio)/Sep 12, 1914; p. 1511
TERRIBLE NIGHT, A
(Ec)/Mar 2, 1912; p. 781
(Sol)/Sep 6, 1913; p. 1069
TERRIBLE ONE, THE
(Lu)/May 8, 1915; p. 900
TERRIBLE OUTLAW, THE
(Ec)/Oct 25, 1913; p. 381
TERRIBLE TED (Bio)/Sep 21, 1907;
p. 456/Sep 28, 1907; p. 472
TERRIBLE TEDDY (SA)/Oct 19, 1912; p.243
TERRIBLE TRAGEDY, A
(Krp)/Mar 27, 1915; p. 1933
TERRIBLY STUCK UP
(Phu)/Aug 28, 1915; p. 1481
TERRITORIAL ON THE BRAIN
Aug 7, 1909; p. 195
TERROR (Ec)/Feb 13, 1915; p. 986
TERROR OF ANGER, THE
(Th)/Nov 21, 1914; p. 1077
TERROR OF CONSCIENCE, THE
(Ka)/Jun 21, 1913; p. 1253
TERROR OF THE MOUNTAINS, THE
(Re)/Jan 23, 1915; p. 516
TERROR OF TWIN MOUNTAINS, THE
(Am)/Oct 9, 1915; p. 253
TERRORS OF A GREAT CITY, THE
(WF)/Nov 14, 1914; p. 934
TERRORS OF RUSSIA, THE
(IA)/Nov 29, 1913; p. 1013
TERRORS OF THE JUNGLE, THE
(Sel)/Nov 8, 1913; p. 590
(Bi)/Feb 13, 1915; p. 986
TESS OF THE d'URBERVILLES
(FP)/Sep 13, 1913; p. 1155
TESS OF THE STORM COUNTRY
(FP)/Apr 4, 1914; pp 40-41
TEST, THE (Bio)/Jan 8, 1910; p. 16
(Lu)/Mar 4, 1911; p. 483
(Vi)/Oct 25, 1913; p. 380
(Vic)/Jan 31, 1914; p. 545
(Ne)/Apr 18, 1914; p. 362
(Sel)/Jan 2, 1915; p. 75
(Ed)/May 22, 1915; p. 1273
TEST OF A MAN, THE
(Re)/Nov 4, 1911; p. 381
(Bi)/Jun 26, 1915; p. 2098
TEST OF COURAGE, THE
(Lu)/Jun 13, 1914; p. 1540
TEST OF FRIENDSHIP, A
Dec 19, 1908; pp 501, 507
TEST OF FRIENDSHIP, THE
(Ed)/Jan 21, 1911; p. 144
TEST OF LOVE, THE

(Ya)/Mar 25, 1911; p. 658
TEST OF MANHOOD, THE
(Box)/Nov 14, 1914; p. 942
TEST OF SINCERITY, THE
(Bio)/May 1, 1915; p. 727
TEST OF THE FLAME, THE
(Dom)/Sep 26, 1914; p. 1778
TESTED BY FIRE (Sel)/Mar 14,1914; p.1384
TESTED BY THE FLAG
(Vi)/Jul 22, 1911; p. 124
TESTER TESTED, THE
(Ec)/Mar 15, 1913; p. 1105
TESTING OF A LIFEBOAT (WBE)/Nov 16,
1907; pp 599-600/Jan 18, 1908; p.45
TEXAN TWINS, THE
(Pa)/Jun 22, 1912; p. 1127
TEXAS BILL'S LAST RIDE
(Maj)/Apr 18, 1914; p. 362
TEXAS FEUD, A (Re)/May 24, 1913; p. 813
TEXAS KELLY AT BAY
(KB)/Mar 29, 1913; p. 1338
TEXAS STEER, A (Sel)/Jul 24, 1915; p. 665
TEXAS TEX (GN)/Jun 27, 1908; p. 546
THAIS (Saw)/Dec 12,1914; p. 1536
**THAMES FROM OXFORD TO RICHMOND,
THE** (UE)/Apr 1, 1911; p.718
THAMES IN WINTER, THE
(Hep)/Dec 25, 1909; p. 922
THANKS FOR THE LOBSTER
(Vi)/Nov 21, 1914; p. 1075
THANKSGIVING (Re)/Dec 7, 1912; p. 978
THANKSGIVING SURPRISE, A
(Th)/Dec 10, 1910; p. 1359
THAT AWFUL BROTHER
(Lu)/May 20, 1911; p. 1141
THAT AWFUL MAID
(Cry)/Dec 6, 1913; p. 1152
THAT BOY FROM MISSOURI
(Vic)/Mar 22, 1913; p. 1221
THAT BOY FROM THE EAST
(Ec)/Jun 28, 1913; p. 1361
THAT BOY FROM THE POORHOUSE
(Bio)/Jul 25, 1914; p. 572
THAT CATCHY RAGTIME DANCE
(Pun)/Jan 18, 1913; p. 265
THAT CHICKEN DINNER
(Lu)/Apr 27, 1912; p. 329
THAT COLLEGE LIFE
(Vi)/Mar 22, 1913; p. 1220
THAT COUNTRY GIRL
(Be)/Dec 25, 1915; p. 2389
THAT DAREDEVIL (Bio)/Aug 26,1911;p.541
THAT DOG GONE SERENADE
(Roy)/May 8, 1915; p. 900
THAT DOGGONE DOG
(At)/Dec 3, 1910; p. 1298
THAT EXPENSIVE RIDE
(Maj)/Feb 3, 1912; p. 394

THAT FATAL SNEEZE
(WBE)/Aug 3, 1907; p. 346
THAT GENTLEMAN HAS WON A MILLION
(It)/May 28, 1910; p. 891
THAT GIRL OF DIXON'S
(Ed)/Mar 12, 1910; p. 382
THAT HEAVENLY COOK
(Ed)/Mar 20, 1915; p. 1763
THAT HOUN' DAWG
(Pa)/May 11, 1912; p. 528
THAT HOUSE THAT JACK BUILT
(Kin)/Feb 8, 1913; p. 574
THAT INFERNAL MACHINE
(Cry)/Feb 28, 1914; p. 1089
THAT IS MY NAME
(Lux)/Feb 4, 1911; p. 251
THAT JUNE BUG (Sol)/Jul 22, 1911; p. 127
THAT LETTER FROM TEDDY
(De)/Sep 17, 1910; p. 632
THAT LITTLE BAND OF GOLD
(Key)/Mar 20, 1915; p. 1766
THAT LOVING MAN (Ec)/Jul 27,1912;p.344
THAT MAIL ORDER SUIT
(Sel)/May 3, 1913; p. 488
THAT MAN FROM THE FOOTHILLS
(Ne)/Feb 10, 1912; p. 484
THAT MINSTREL MAN
(Key)/Aug 29, 1914; p. 1242
THAT MOTHER-IN-LAW IS A BORE
(Pa)/Mar 7, 1908; pp 192-93
THAT OTHER GIRL (Cry)/Mar 1,1913;p.889
THAT POOR DAMP COW
(Fal)/Sep 4, 1915; p. 1644
THAT POPULAR TUNE
(SA)/Dec 10, 1910; p. 1356
THAT RAGTIME BAND
(Key)/May 3, 1913; p. 489
THAT SPRINGTIME FEELING
(Key)/Mar 20, 1915; p. 1764
THAT SUIT AT TEN
(Vi)/Dec 27, 1913; p. 1544
THAT TERRIBLE KID
(Lu)/Mar 21, 1914; p. 1524
THAT TYPIST AGAIN
(Lux)/Sep 3, 1910; p. 520
THAT WINSOME WINNIE SMILE
(Ed)/Sep 23, 1911; p. 891
THAT WOMAN LAWYER
(Po)/Nov 26, 1910; pp 1238-39
THAT'S FAIR ENOUGH
(Jo)/Aug 8, 1914; p. 837
THAT'S HAPPINESS
(Th)/Jul 29, 1911; p. 213
THEATER OF PHENOMENONS, THE
(Ec)/Apr 16, 1910; p. 599
THEFT IN THE DARK, A
(Ed)/Mar 27, 1915; p. 1937
THEFT OF DIAMONDS, THE

THEIR SOCIAL SPLASH
(Key)/May 22, 1915; p. 1260
THEIR STEPMOTHER
(Sel)/May 17, 1913; p. 704
THEIR TINY BABIES
(SA)/Nov 4, 1911; p. 378
THEIR TWO KIDS (Ne)/Oct 25, 1913; p. 381
THEIR UPS AND DOWNS
(Key)/Oct 10, 1914; p. 189
(Ne)/Dec 12, 1914; p. 1524
THEIR VACATION (Jo)/May 23,1914;p.1117
THEIR WATERLOO (SA)/Nov 1,1913; p.495
THEIR WEDDING GIFTS
(SA)/Mar 4, 1911; p. 483
THEIR WIVES' INDISCRETION
(SA)/Nov 22, 1913; p. 867
THEIR WORLDLY GOODS
(Am)/Aug 29, 1914; p. 1242
THELLYS' HEART (Pa)/Aug 14, 1909; p.226
THELMA (Th)/Jun 18, 1910; p. 1045/
Jul 2, 1910; p. 26
THEM OL' LETTERS (Po)/Jan 3, 1914; p.49
THEN YOU'LL REMEMBER ME
(Ed)/Sep 9, 1911; p. 714
THEODORA (WF)/Jul 12, 1913; pp 183-84
THEODORE ROOSEVELT
(Pa)/Oct 19, 1912; p. 242
THERE, LITTLE GIRL, DON'T CRY
(Sel)/May 28, 1910; p. 888
THERE FELL A FLOWER
(Ec)/Dec 16, 1911; p. 905
THERE IS A DESTINY
(Vic)/Aug 29, 1914; p. 1242
THERE IS A GOD (Kin)/Mar 8, 1913; p. 997
THERE SHE GOES (Pa)/Apr 19, 1913; p.279
THERE WERE HOBOES THREE
(Bio)/Mar 8, 1913; p. 995
THERE'S A WOMAN IN TOWN
(Pa)/Jul 1, 1911; p. 1519
THERE'S GOOD IN THE WORST OF US
(Mus)/Dec 11, 1915; p. 2032
THERE'S MANY A SLIP
(Re)/Jun 3, 1911; p. 1260
(SA)/Mar 2, 1912; p. 780
(Po)/Jun 15, 1912; p. 1028
(Ne)/Jul 24, 1915; p. 651
THERE'S MUSIC IN THE HAIR
(Vi)/May 10, 1913; p. 595
THERE'S SOMETHING WRONG
(Ne)/Jan 27, 1912; p. 304
THESPIAN BANDITS, THE
(Ne)/May 18, 1912; p. 630
THEY BOUGHT A BOAT
(Lu)/Aug 29, 1914; p. 1241
THEY CALL IT "BABY"
(Bio)/Nov 7, 1914; p. 787
THEY DID NOT BUDGE
(Lux)/Apr 29, 1911; p. 961

THEY DIDN'T KNOW
(Cry)/Nov 7, 1914; p. 788
THEY HAVE VANISHED MY WIFE
(Amb)/Mar 26, 1910; p. 467
THEY LOOKED ALIKE
(Lu)/Jan 23, 1915; p. 515
THEY LOVED HIM SO
(Vi)/Apr 24, 1915; p. 555
THEY NEVER KNEW
(Re)/Dec 5, 1914; p. 1384
THEY RAN FOR MAYOR
(Roy)/Jul 17, 1915; p. 486
THEY WANT A DIVORCE
(KO)/Jul 4, 1908; p. 13
THEY WERE COLLEGE BOYS
(Bio)/Oct 24, 1914; p. 491
THEY WERE HEROES
(Ne)/May 22, 1915; p. 1261
THEY WERE ON THEIR HONEYMOON
(Sel)/Sep 6, 1913; p. 1068
(Ne)/Mar 27, 1915; p. 1933
THEY WHO DIG PITS
(Maj)/Apr 4, 1914; p. 58
THEY WOULD BANDITS BE
(Bio)/Aug 22, 1914; p. 1099
THEY WOULD ELOPE
(Bio)/Aug 21, 1909; pp 255-56
THEY WOULD ROLLER SKATE
(Lux)/May 21, 1910; p. 834
THIEF, THE (SA)/Jul 30, 1910; p. 245
(Ka)/Aug 3, 1912; p. 446
(Box)/Dec 19, 1914; p. 1698
THIEF AND THE BOOK, THE
(Maj)/Jan 31, 1914; p. 546
THIEF AND THE CHIEF, THE
(Ec)/Feb 6, 1915; p. 828
THIEF AND THE GIRL, THE
(Bio)/Jul 15, 1911; p. 39
THIEF AT THE CASINO, THE
(WBE)/Oct 3, 1908; p. 268
THIEF IN THE DARK, A
(Ed)/Mar 27, 1915; p. 1937
THIEF IN THE NIGHT, A
(Vi)/Jan 6, 1912; p. 41
(Ka)/Aug 2, 1913; p. 535
THIEF IN THE NIGHT, THE
(Lu)/Apr 10, 1915; p. 235
(Lu)/Dec 25, 1915; p. 2389
THIEF OF HEARTS, A
(Pa)/Jan 31, 1914; p. 544
THIEF'S WIFE, THE
(Am)/Nov 23, 1912; p. 768
THIEVES (Vi)/Nov 22, 1913; p. 868
(Dom)/Apr 25, 1914; p. 518
THIEVES AND THE CROSS
(Rex)/Dec 6, 1913; p. 1153
THIEVES AS QUICK CHANGE ARTISTS
(It)/Dec 31, 1910; p. 1539

THIEVING UMBRELLA, THE
(KO)/Nov 9, 1907; pp 581-82
THINGS ARE SELDOM WHAT THEY SEEM
(Ka)/Feb 3, 1912; p. 392
THINGS IN THE BOTTOM DRAWER, THE
(Lae)/Apr 24, 1915; p. 557
THINGS JAPANESE (Me)/Oct 18,1913;p.264
THINK MOTHERS (Lu)/Oct 23, 1915; p. 619
THINK OF THE MONEY
(Lu)/Oct 23, 1915; p. 619
THIRD ACT, THE (Bio)/Jan 23, 1915; p. 672
THIRD COMMANDMENT, THE
(Ka)/Apr 10, 1915; p. 239
THIRD DEGREE, THE (Lu)/Nov 29, 1913;
p. 992/Jan 3, 1914; p. 30
THIRD HAND HIGH
(SA)/Feb 20, 1915; p. 1140
THIRD PARTY, THE (Jo)/Aug 8,1914; p.837
THIRD STRING, THE
(Co)/Aug 15, 1914; p. 937
THIRD THANKSGIVING, THE (Ed)/
Nov 16, 1912; p. 638/Dec 7, 1912; p. 975
THIRD THIEF, THE (Ec)/Aug 2,1913; p.538
THIRST FOR GOLD (Ec)/Aug 23,1913;p.842
THIRSTY MOVING MEN
(Pa)/Apr 18, 1908; pp 351-52
THIRTEEN AT TABLE
Dec 26, 1908; p. 526
(Ec)/Aug 30, 1913; p. 961
THIRTEEN DOWN (SA)/Feb 27,1915; p.1288
THIRTEENTH MAN, THE
(SA)/Feb 8, 1913; p. 571
THIRTY (SA)/May 22, 1915; p. 1260
THIRTY DAYS (Com)/Jan 27, 1912; p. 304
THIRTY DAYS AT HARD LABOR
(Ed)/Jan 20, 1912; p. 202
THIRTY YEARS AFTER
(KO)/May 16, 1908; pp 444-45
THIRTY YEARS OF A GAMBLER'S LIFE
(Pa)/Dec 12, 1914; p. 1525
THIS IS LIFE (SA)/Jun 27, 1914; p. 1828
(Ram)/Jul 25, 1914; p. 574
THIS IS TH' LIFE
(Am)/Sep 5, 1914; p. 1373
THIS IS THE LIFE
(Po)/Sep 5, 1914; p. 1373
THIS IS THE LIFE (Mus)
No.3/Nov 20, 1915; p. 1504
THIS ISN'T JOHN (Lu)/Oct 4, 1913; p. 48
THOMAS CHATTERTON
(Amb)/Mar 23, 1912; p. 1064
THOMPSON'S NIGHT OUT
(Bio)/Jun 6, 1908; p. 496
THOMPSON'S NIGHT WITH THE
POLICE (KO)/Nov 28, 1908; p. 432/
Dec 5, 1908; p. 448
THOR, LORD OF THE JUNGLE
(Sel)/Dec 6, 1913; p. 1126

THORN AMONG ROSES, A
(Ed)/Feb 20, 1915; p. 1139
THORNS OF SUCCESS
(Maj)/Sep 21, 1912; p. 1177
THOROUGHBRED, A
(Ed)/Jul 1, 1911; pp 1520-21
THOSE AWFUL HATS
(Bio)/Jan 30, 1909; p. 121
THOSE BITTER SWEETS
(Key)/Jun 26, 1915; p. 2096
THOSE BOYS (Bio)/Jan 23, 1909; p. 94
THOSE COLLEGE DAYS
(Ne)/Jun 13, 1914; p. 1542
THOSE COLLEGE GIRLS
(Key)/Jun 12, 1915; p. 1777
THOSE COUNTRY KIDS
(Key)/Aug 29, 1914; p. 1242
THOSE EYES (GN)/Apr 27, 1912; p. 329
THOSE GERMAN BOWLERS
(St)/Jan 16, 1915; p. 370
THOSE GOOD OLD DAYS
(Key)/Apr 19, 1913; p. 282
THOSE HAPPY DAYS
(Key)/Aug 15, 1914; p. 960
THOSE HICKSVILLE BOYS
(Bio)/Apr 13, 1912; p. 137
THOSE JERSEY COWPUNCHERS
(Ne)/Oct 14, 1911; p. 131
THOSE KIDS AND CUPID
(Ne)/Nov 6, 1915; p. 1140
THOSE LITTLE FLOWERS
(Bio)/Aug 23, 1913; p. 842
THOSE LOVE PANGS
(Key)/Oct 17, 1914; p. 337
THOSE LOVESICK COWBOYS
(Ne)/Sep 21, 1912; p. 1177
THOSE MARRIED MEN
(GN)/Mar 9, 1912; p. 867
THOSE PERSISTENT OLD MAIDS
(Ne)/Mar 21, 1914; p. 1526
THOSE TROUBLESOME TRESSES
(Vi)/Aug 30, 1913; p. 961
THOSE WERE THE HAPPY DAYS
(Po)/Jun 22, 1912; p. 1128
(Ne)/Nov 14, 1914; p. 933
THOU SHALT NOT
(Bio)/Apr 30, 1910; p. 689
(Ram)/May 30, 1914; p. 1265
THOU SHALT NOT?
(Ch)/Apr 6, 1912; pp 42-43
THOU SHALT NOT COVET
(Vi)/May 25, 1912; p. 728
THOU SHALT NOT FLIRT
(Lko)/Jan 16, 1915; p. 369
THOU SHALT NOT KILL
(Po)/Dec 3, 1910; p. 1299/
Dec 10, 1910; pp 1358-59
(Vi)/Feb 1, 1913; p. 464

(Sel)/Mar 7, 1914; p. 1236
THOU SHALT NOT LIE
(Re)/Jul 22, 1911; p. 127
(Imp)/Jul 24, 1915; p. 651
THOU SHALT NOT LOVE
(KO)/Nov 7, 1908; p. 364
THOU SHALT NOT RUBBER
(Imp)/Oct 11, 1913; p. 157
THOU SHALT NOT STEAL
(Re)/Aug 12, 1911; p. 378
(Po)/Oct 21, 1911; p. 210
(Rex)/Mar 15, 1913; p. 1105
THOU SHALT PAY (Ya)/Jun 24,1911; p.1455
THOUGH THE SEAS DIVIDE
(Vi)/Apr 1, 1911; p. 720
THOUGH YOUR SINS BE AS SCARLET
(Vi)/Apr 29, 1911; p. 958
THOUGHTLESS BEAUTY, A
(He)/May 1, 1909; p. 555
THOUSAND DOLLAR BILL, THE
(Dom)/Aug 14, 1915; p. 1161
THREAD OF DESTINY, THE
(Bio)/Mar 19, 1910; p. 425
THREAD OF LIFE, THE
(Am)/Jun 1, 1912; p. 831
THREADS OF FATE, THE
(Rex)/Feb 27, 1915; p. 1289
THREE BAD MEN AND A GIRL
(Bi)/Feb 20, 1915; p. 1141
THREE BEARS, THE (SA)/Dec 9, 1911;
p. 823/Dec 30, 1911; p. 1072
THREE BLACK TRAMPS, THE
(PP)/Jan 30, 1915; p. 687
THREE BOILED DOWN FABLES
(SA)/Nov 28, 1914; p. 1231
THREE BROTHERS (Vi)/Sep 16,1911; p.789
THREE BROTHERS, THE
(It)/Apr 30, 1910; p. 690
THREE CALLS (Ch)/Aug 26, 1911; p. 544
**THREE CELEBRATED MOUNTAIN
CLIMBERS** (UE)/Mar 20, 1909; p. 338
THREE CHERRY PITS, THE
(Vi)/Sep 3, 1910; pp 519-20
THREE CHILDREN (Po)/Dec 27,1913;p.1544
THREE CHRISTMAS DINNERS
(Lu)/Dec 31, 1909; p. 960
THREE COMRADES, THE
(GN)/May 31, 1913; pp 920-21
THREE DAUGHTERS OF THE WEST
(Am)/Oct 28, 1911; p. 292
THREE-FINGERED JACK
(Lu)/Jan 15, 1910; p. 56
THREE FRIENDS (Bio)/Jan 18, 1913; p. 263
THREE FRIENDS, THE
(Gau)/Oct 22, 1910; p. 936
THREE GEESE, THE
(Me)/Apr 25, 1914; p. 517
THREE GIRLS AND A MAN

(Vi)/Dec 14, 1912; p. 1080
THREE HATS (Bio)/Feb 20, 1915; p. 1140
THREE HEARTS (Lu)/Aug 13, 1910; p. 351
THREE KISSES, THE
(Ed)/Nov 13, 1909; p. 683
**THREE KNAVES AND A HEATHEN
CHINEE** (Ed)/Jun 6, 1914; p. 1408
THREE LITTLE POWDERS
(SA)/May 30, 1914; p. 1260
THREE MEN (Re)/Mar 4, 1911; pp 483-84
THREE MEN AND A GIRL
(Ec)/Jul 6, 1912; p. 44
(Cry)/Apr 18, 1914; p. 362
THREE MEN AND A MAID
(Vi)/Jan 28, 1911; p. 196
THREE MEN AND A WOMAN
(Lu)/Aug 15, 1914; p. 960
THREE MEN WHO KNEW, THE
(Imp)/Dec 12, 1914; p. 1525
THREE MILLION DOLLARS
(Am)/Sep 23, 1911; p. 892
THREE MUSKETEERS, THE
(Ed)/Sep 23, 1911; p. 890
(AA)/Mar 14, 1914; p. 1369
THREE NEIGHBORS, THE
(Pa)/Dec 18, 1909; p. 880
THREE OF A KIND
(Gau)/May 20, 1911; p. 1141
(Imp)/Jun 10, 1911; p. 1317
(Ne)/May 4, 1912; p. 428
(Roy)/Jun 6, 1914; p. 1409
**THREE OF A KIND, A TRIP THROUGH
THE GARDEN OF THE GODS, COLO.**
(Ed)/Nov 4, 1911; p.378
THREE OF THEM, THE
(Vi)/Sep 24, 1910; p. 689
THREE OF US, THE (LF)/Jan 2, 1915; p. 79
THREE PAIRS AND A CAT
(Pa)/Feb 7, 1914; p. 676
THREE PROPOSALS, THE
(Ch)/Mar 4, 1911; p. 483
THREE QUEENS, THE
(SA)/Mar 1, 1913; p. 887
THREE QUEENS AND A JACK
(Pa)/Mar 5, 1910; pp 338, 340
THREE ROGUES OUTWITTED
(UE)/Jan 4, 1913; p. 50
THREE ROSES (Th)/Jun 5, 1915; p. 1605
THREE SCRAPS OF PAPER
(SA)/Oct 25, 1913; p. 380
THREE SCRATCH CLUE, THE
(SA)/Apr 11, 1914; p. 213
THREE SHADOWS, THE
(Gau)/Mar 28, 1914; p. 1660
THREE SHELL GAME, THE
(Am)/Nov 18, 1911; p. 552
THREE SISTERS (Bio)/Feb 18, 1911; p. 370
THREE SPORTSMEN AND A HAT

(KO)/Jun 27, 1908; p. 549

THREE SUITORS AND A DOG
(Ka)/Feb 22, 1913; p. 779

THREE THANKSGIVINGS
(Ed)/Dec 4, 1909; p. 798

THREE TIMES AND OUT
(Imp)/Jan 9, 1915; p. 222

THREE TO ONE (SA)/Sep 14, 1912; p. 1074
(Vi)/Jun 21, 1913; p. 1251

THREE VALISES, THE
(Sel)/Aug 10, 1912; p. 545

THREE WHIFFLES, THE
(Pa)/Apr 22, 1911; pp 898, 900

THREE WISE MEN, THE
(Sel)/Feb 22, 1913; p. 780

THREE WISHES, THE
(Vi)/May 21, 1910; p. 833
(WF)/Jan 16, 1915; p. 370

THRIFTY JANITOR, THE
(Ed)/Dec 20, 1913; p. 1411

THRIFTY PARSON, THE
(SA)/Nov 9, 1912; p. 552

THRILLING LEAP, A
(Rex)/Aug 12, 1911; p. 381

THRILLING POWERS FIRE, THE
(Po)/Aug 5, 1911; p. 297

THRILLING RESCUE BY UNCLE MUN, A
(Ed)/Nov 30, 1912; p. 876

THROUGH A KNOT HOLE
(Lko)/Jan 16, 1915; p. 369

THROUGH AN ORANGE GROVE
(Lu)/Nov 21, 1908; p. 408

THROUGH ANOTHER MAN'S EYES
(Sel)/Aug 16, 1913; p. 743

THROUGH BARRIERS OF FIRE
(Bi)/Oct 11, 1913; p. 158

THROUGH BOSNIA AND DALMATIA
(Pa)/Aug 1, 1914; p. 704

THROUGH CHINA (Ec)/Oct 5, 1912; p. 42

THROUGH DANTE'S FLAMES
(Ram)/May 9, 1914; p. 801

THROUGH DARKENED VEILS
(Bio)/Dec 2, 1911; p. 724

THROUGH DARKNESS TO LIGHT
(Lu)/Jan 4, 1908; p. 11

THROUGH DERBYSHIRE DALES
(UE)/Oct 26, 1912; p. 342

THROUGH DUMB LUCK
(Bio)/Sep 14, 1912; p. 1074

THROUGH EDITH'S LOOKING GLASS
(Th)/Jun 19, 1915; p. 1940

THROUGH EYES OF LOVE
(SA)/Oct 31, 1914; p. 640

THROUGH FIRE AND FLAMES
(LeP)/Apr 11, 1914; p. 214

THROUGH FIRE AND SMOKE
(Sel)/Sep 16, 1911; p. 788

THROUGH FIRE AND WATER

(Box)/Nov 14, 1914; p. 934

THROUGH FIRE TO FORTUNE
(Lu)/Mar 7, 1914; pp 1240-41

THROUGH FLAMING GATES
(Rex)/Mar 9, 1912; p. 868

THROUGH FLAMING PATHS
(Lu)/Jan 10, 1914; p. 172

THROUGH HIS WIFE'S PICTURE
(Bio)/Nov 4, 1911; p. 380

THROUGH JEALOUS EYES (Lu)/Aug 12,
1911; p. 380/Sep 2, 1911; p. 628

THROUGH JEALOUSY
(Lu)/Jun 19, 1909; p. 835

THROUGH LIFE'S WINDOW
(Vi)/Aug 22, 1914; p. 1100

THROUGH MOUNTAINS MAJESTIC
(Gau)/Jul 26, 1913; p. 429

THROUGH SHADOWED VALES
(Imp)/Dec 14, 1912; p. 1082

THROUGH SHADOWS TO SUNSHINE
(WF)/Dec 12, 1914; p. 1525

THROUGH STRIFE (Rex)/Jul 26,1913; p.429

THROUGH THE AGONY COLUMNS
(Lux)/Jan 13, 1912; p. 127

THROUGH THE AIR
(Imp)/Oct 14, 1911; p. 131

THROUGH THE BREAKERS
(Bio)/Dec 18, 1909; p. 881

THROUGH THE CENTURIES
(Sel)/Mar 7, 1914; p. 1236

THROUGH THE CLOUDS
(Ed)/Dec 3, 1910; p. 1296
(Ape)/Dec 27, 1913; p. 1530

**THROUGH THE CUMBERLAND
MOUNTAINS** (SA)/Aug 23, 1913; p. 842

THROUGH THE DARK
(Re)/Sep 12, 1914; p. 1513

THROUGH THE DARKNESS
(Vi)/May 7, 1910; p. 736

**THROUGH THE DELLS OF WISCONSIN IN
A MOTOR BOAT** (Imp)/Oct 7, 1911; p. 43

THROUGH THE DRIFTS
(Lu)/Feb 17, 1912; p. 582

THROUGH THE ENEMY'S LINE
(UE)/Jul 30, 1910; p. 245

THROUGH THE ENEMY'S LINES
(Gau)/Dec 30, 1911; pp 1071-72
(GN)/Feb 27, 1915; p. 1300

THROUGH THE EYES OF THE BLIND
(Imp)/May 2, 1914; p. 674

THROUGH THE FLAMES
(Imp)/Feb 24, 1912; p. 691
(Th)/Nov 16, 1912; p. 660
(Ka)/Jul 11, 1914; p. 256

**THROUGH THE HOOD RIVER VALLEY
AND ALONG THE COLUMBIA RIVER,
IN OREGON** (Sel)/Dec 31, 1909; p. 960

THROUGH THE KEYHOLE

(Lae)/Mar 27, 1915; p. 1934
TO RENO AND BACK
(Imp)/Apr 5, 1913; pp 49-50
TO RENT, FURNISHED
(Am)/Nov 20, 1915; p. 1500
TO SAVE HER BROTHER
(Ed)/Feb 3, 1912; p. 392
TO SAVE HER SOUL (Bio)/Jan 8, 1910; p.16
TO SAVE HIM FOR HIS WIFE
(Vi)/May 29, 1915; p. 1431
TO THE AID OF STONEWALL JACKSON
(Ka)/Jul 22, 1911; p. 124
TO THE BRAVE BELONG THE FAIR
(Ne)/Jun 28, 1913; p. 1361
TO THE CITY (Rex)/Dec 28, 1912; p. 1292
TO THE DEATH (Vi)/Jul 3, 1915; p. 64
TOAD TRAITS (Pa)/Oct 4, 1913; p. 48
TOAST OF DEATH, THE
(Mut)/Aug 7, 1915; p. 1013
TOBACCO CULTURE
(Pa)/Mar 26, 1910; p. 467
TOBACCO CULTURE IN CUBA, THE
(Pa)/Apr 12, 1913; p. 163
TOBACCO EDICT, THE
(Ed)/Aug 21, 1909; p. 254-55
TOBACCO INDUSTRY
(Lu)/Jan 24, 1914; p. 413
TOBACCO INDUSTRY, THE
(Lu)/Nov 4, 1911; p. 378
TOBACCO MANIA (Ed)/Jan 8, 1910; p. 17
TOBIAS TURNS THE TABLES
(Sel)/Aug 30, 1913; p. 961
TOBIAS WINS OUT (Sel)/Oct 4, 1913; p. 47
TOGETHER (Lu)/Aug 3, 1912; p. 445
TOILERS, THE (Ka)/Aug 14, 1915; p. 1160
TOILERS OF THE SEA
(Vic)/May 16, 1914; p. 969
TOILERS OF THE SEA, THE
(Bal)/Sep 25, 1915; p. 2177
TOILET OF AN OCEAN GREYHOUND, THE
(KO)/Jun 22, 1907; p. 254
TOILS OF DECEPTION, THE
(Sel)/Sep 27, 1913; p. 1392
TOLD IN COLORADO
(Sel)/Oct 21, 1911; p. 209
TOLD IN CONFIDENCE
(GN)/May 3, 1913; p. 489
TOLD IN THE FUTURE
(Maj)/Aug 16, 1913; p. 745
TOLD IN THE GOLDEN WEST
(Sel)/Mar 19, 1910; p. 426
TOLD IN THE ROCKIES
(Lar)/May 8, 1915; p. 901
TOLD IN THE SIERRAS
(Sel)/Jul 8, 1911; p. 1584
TOLEDO, SPAIN (Pa)/Apr 24, 1915;p. 557
TOLL, THE (Vi)/Jul 18, 1914; p. 433
TOLL GATE RAIDERS

(Ka)/Dec 28, 1912; p. 1291
TOLL OF FEAR, THE (Lu)/Apr 5, 1913;
p. 28/Apr 26, 1913; p. 379
TOLL OF MAMMON, THE
(Exc)/Jul 4, 1914; p. 46
TOLL OF THE DESERT, THE
(Fr)/Aug 2, 1913; p. 538
TOLL OF THE MARSHES, THE
(SA)/Nov 15, 1913; p. 736
TOLL OF THE SEA, THE
(Gem)/Dec 7, 1912; p. 978
(Bi)/Jul 17, 1915; p. 487
TOLL OF THE WAR-PATH, THE
(WF)/Aug 8, 1914; p. 838
TOLL OF WAR, THE
(Bi)/May 17, 1913; p. 706
TOLL OF YOUTH, THE
(Lae)/May 15, 1915; p. 1073
TOM, DICK AND HARRY
(Pun)/Jan 18, 1913; p. 265
TOM, DICK AND HARRY ON THE JOB
(Pun)/Feb 15, 1913; p. 681
TOM AND JERRY (Ya)/Apr 8, 1911; p. 782
TOM TELLING'S BABY
(Vi)/Feb 3, 1912; p. 392
TOM THUMB (Pa)/Sep 25, 1909; p. 416
(CGP)/Nov 9, 1912; p. 553
TOMBOY, THE (Ka)/Jul 31, 1909; p. 161
(Th)/Dec 30, 1911; p. 1073
(Bal)/Jul 3, 1915; p. 65
TOMBOY BESSIE (Bio)/Jun 15, 1912; p.1026
TOMBOYS (Ka)/Mar 13, 1915; p. 1607
TOMBOY'S RACE, THE
(Maj)/Nov 29, 1913; p. 1009
**TOMBS OF THE ANCIENT JAPANESE
EMPERORS, ANNAM, THE**
(Pa)/Aug 1, 1914; p. 704
TOMMY AT THE DENTIST
(Ec)/Jun 17, 1911; p. 1389
TOMMY BECOMES A TOREADOR
(Gau)/Jun 1, 1912; p. 831
TOMMY GETS A TRUMPET
(Ec)/Jul 1, 1911; p. 1522
TOMMY GETS HIS SISTER MARRIED
(Pa)/Aug 13, 1910; p. 350
TOMMY HAS THE SPLEEN
(KO)/May 9, 1908; p. 423
TOMMY SAVES HIS LITTLE SISTER
(Lux)/Aug 31, 1912; p. 882
TOMMY WANTS TO BE AN ACTOR
(Ec)/Jul 15, 1911; p. 41
TOMMY'S ADVENTURES IN DREAMLAND
(UE)/Feb 5, 1910; p. 169
TOMMY'S ATONEMENT
(Sel)/Apr 26, 1913; p. 379
TOMMY'S CAMERA
(Lux)/Nov 11, 1911; p. 472
TOMMY'S GEOGRAPHY LESSON

(Ed)/Apr 6, 1912; p. 41
TOMMY'S PLAYMATE
(Lux)/Sep 28, 1912; p. 1277
TOMMY'S ROCKING HORSE
(Me)/Oct 28, 1911; p. 291
TOMMY'S STRATAGEM
(Ed)/Nov 15, 1913; p. 736
TOMMY'S TRAMP (Vi)/Apr 18,1914; p.360
TO-MORROW IS PAY DAY
(Ec)/Jul 30, 1910; p. 246
TONGUE MARK, THE
(Maj)/Jun 21, 1913; p. 1255
TONGUE OF SCANDAL, THE (Vi)/Apr 16,
1910; p. 599/Apr 23, 1910; p. 642
TONGUELESS MAN, THE
(Gem)/Nov 30, 1912; p. 878
TONSORIAL LEOPARD TAMER, A
(Sel)/Nov 7, 1914; p. 787
TONY (Imp)/May 8, 1915; p. 901
TONY, THE FIDDLER
(SA)/Oct 18, 1913; p. 264
TONY, THE GREASER
(Vi)/May 16, 1914; p. 968
TONY, THE TENOR (Pi)/May 31,1913;p.920
TONY, THE WOP (Ne)/Aug 21,1915; p.1318
TONY AND MALONEY
(Sel)/Feb 21, 1914; p. 946
TONY AND MARIE (Lu)/Oct 16, 1915; p.439
TONY AND THE STORK
(Imp)/Dec 16, 1911; p. 905
TONY HAS EATEN GARLIC
(KO)/Apr 18, 1908; p. 354
TONY WOULD BE A COWBOY
(Ch)/Jul 29, 1911; p. 211
TONY'S OATH OF VENGEANCE
(Ed)/Mar 16, 1912; p. 961
TONY'S SACRIFICE
(Re)/Dec 13, 1913; p. 1280
TONTILINI IS IN LOVE
(Cin)/Nov 12, 1910; p. 1119
TOO-DEVOTED WIFE, A
(WBE)/Oct 12, 1907; p. 509
TOO GENTLEMANLY
(Gau)/Sep 4, 1909; p. 316
TOO HUNGRY TO EAT
(KO)/Aug 1, 1908; p. 88
TOO LATE (Sel)/Jan 31, 1914; p. 544
TOO MANY AUNTS (Lu)/Sep 26,1914;p.1776
TOO MANY BACHELORS
(Lko)/Mar 27, 1915; p. 1933
TOO MANY BEAUX (Pa)/Mar 6,1915;p.1448
TOO MANY BRIDES
(Key)/Jan 24, 1914; p. 414
TOO MANY BURGLARS
(Bio)/Oct 14, 1911; p. 128
TOO MANY CASEYS
(Vi)/Dec 21, 1912; p. 1184
TOO MANY COOKS (Po)/Jan 17,1914; p.290

TOO MANY COPS (Ka)/Sep 27,1913; p.1392
TOO MANY CROOKS
(Ne)/Jun 5, 1915; p. 1606
TOO MANY ENGAGEMENTS
(SA)/Nov 11, 1911; p. 468
TOO MANY GIRLS (De)/Jul 9, 1910; p. 86
TOO MANY HUSBANDS
(Vi)/Jun 20, 1914; p. 1689
TOO MANY JOHNNIES
(Ka)/Mar 7, 1914; p. 1236
TOO MANY SMITHS
(Ne)/Sep 18, 1915; p. 1997
TOO MANY SWEETHEARTS
(Cin)/Aug 10, 1912; p. 546
TOO MANY TENANTS
(Pa)/Nov 15, 1913; p. 735
TOO MANY WIVES (Lun)/Jan 2, 1915; p. 77
TOO MUCH AUNT (Am)/Feb 25,1911; p.432
TOO MUCH BEAUTY
(It)/Dec 7, 1912; p. 977
TOO MUCH BULL (Pa)/Apr 3, 1915; p. 65
TOO MUCH BURGLAR
(Vi)/Dec 5, 1914; p. 1383
TOO MUCH CHAMPAGNE
(Vi)/Feb 22, 1908; p. 147
TOO MUCH ELIXIR OF LIFE
(Aa)/Oct 23, 1915; p. 622
TOO MUCH INDIAN (Po)/Dec 9,1911; p.818
TOO MUCH MARRIED
(Po)/Mar 28, 1914; p. 1682
TOO MUCH MOTHER-IN-LAW
(Lu)/Jun 15, 1907; p. 238
(Com)/Dec 14, 1912; p. 1082
TOO MUCH PARCELS POST
(Pa)/Apr 26, 1913; p. 379
TOO MUCH REALISM
(Ka)/Dec 23, 1911; p. 988
TOO MUCH SNUFF
(Pa)/Dec 26, 1908; p. 525
TOO MUCH SWEDISH DRILL
(Ec)/Aug 19, 1911; p. 465
TOO MUCH TURKEY
(SA)/Dec 2, 1911; p. 725
(Pr)/Apr 25, 1914; p. 517
(SA)/Nov 27, 1915; p. 1663
TOO MUCH UNCLE
(Vi)/Sep 19, 1914; p. 1645
TOO MUCH WATER
(Gau)/Oct 8, 1910; p. 814
TOO MUCH WOOING OF HANDSOME DAN
(Vi)/Aug 17, 1912; p. 672
TOO POLITE (KO)/Jul 25, 1908; p. 69
TOO PROUD TO BEG
(Re)/Feb 7, 1914; p. 678
TOODLES (Maj)/Aug 24, 1912; p. 773
TOODLES, TOM AND TROUBLE
(Fal)/Dec 25, 1915; p. 2389
TOODLEUMS (Cry)/May 31, 1913; p. 922

TOOLS OF PROVIDENCE
(Bro)/Jul 10, 1915; p. 309
TOOTHACHE (Ka)/May 24, 1913; p. 811
TOP HEAVY MARY
(Gau)/Dec 18, 1909; p. 881
TOP OF NEW YORK, THE
(Th)/Aug 2, 1913; p. 537
TOPLITSKY & COMPANY
(Key)/May 31, 1913; p. 921
TOPSY TURVY (Pa)/Mar 6, 1909; p. 269
TOPSY-TURVY (SA)/Aug 22, 1914; p. 1100
TOPSY TURVY LOVE AFFAIR, A
(Re)/Dec 14, 1912; p. 1082
TOREADOR'S OATH, THE
(Pa)/Nov 28, 1914; p. 1234
TOREADOR'S ROMANCE, THE
(Cin)/May 30, 1914; p. 1261
TORMENTED BY HIS MOTHER-IN-LAW
(Pa)/Jun 6, 1908; p. 498
TORN LETTER, THE
(Ne)/Apr 20, 1912; p. 231
TORN NOTE, THE (Pa)/Apr 27, 1912; p. 328
TORN SCARF, THE (Rex)/Sep 9,1911; p.717
TORPEDO PRACTICE IN U.S. NAVY
(Vi)/Mar 16, 1912; p. 961
TORRENT, THE (KO)/Jul 25, 1908; p. 68
(GS)/May 1, 1915; p. 738
TORTOISES AT CLOSE RANGE
(Pa)/Nov 22, 1913; p. 867
TOSS OF A COIN, THE
(Imp)/Sep 16, 1911; p. 790
TOTEM MARK, THE
(Sel)/Sep 23, 1911; p. 890
TOTO, A DOOR-KEEPER
(It)/Feb 17, 1912; p. 583
TOTO AN ENTHUSIAST FOR A NEW
FASHION (It)/Jul 29, 1911; p.212
TOTO AND THE DUMMY
(It)/Nov 11, 1911; p. 471
TOTO AND THE FLAG
(It)/Mar 18, 1911; p. 604
TOTO IS IN LOVE
(It)/Feb 3, 1912; p. 394
TOTO ON THE STAGE
(It)/Apr 1, 1911; p. 720
TOTO WANTS TO GET THINNER
(It)/Apr 8, 1911; p. 782
TOTO WITHOUT WATER
(It)/Aug 12, 1911; p. 378
TOTO'S LITTLE CART
(It)/Aug 26, 1911; p. 545
TOTVILLE EYE, THE
(Ed)/Dec 14, 1912; pp 1080-81
TOUAREGS IN THEIR COUNTRY
(Pa)/Feb 15, 1908; p. 124
TOUCH OF A CHILD, THE
(Sel)/Dec 6, 1913; p. 1150
(Imp)/Feb 28, 1914; pp 1089-90

TOUCH OF A CHILD'S HAND, THE (Ka)/
Dec 10, 1910; p. 1358/Dec 17, 1910; p. 1416
TOUCH OF A LITTLE HAND, THE
(Pr)/Oct 31, 1914; p. 641
TOUCH OF LOVE, A
(Am)/Apr 17, 1915; p. 393
TOUCHING AFFAIR, A
(Am)/Dec 24, 1910; p. 1479
TOUCHING MYSTERY, A
(At)/Nov 5, 1910; p. 1061
TOUGH GUY, LEVI
(Lu)/Mar 23, 1912; p. 1063
TOUGH LUCK (Lu)/Aug 1, 1914; p. 704
(StU)/May 15, 1915; p. 1073
TOUGH LUCK SMITH
(Ka)/Dec 12, 1914; p. 1523
TOUGH TENDERFOOT, A
(Bi)/Feb 11, 1911; p. 318
TOULA'S DREAM (Pa)/Mar 14, 1908; p. 217
TOUR IN THE ALPS, A
(Pa)/Mar 29, 1913; p. 1335
TOUR THROUGH TOURAINE, A
(Pa)/Jun 28, 1913; p. 1360
TOURING ATHENS (Po)/Apr 22,1911; p.901
TOURING BRUSSELS
(Po)/Dec 30, 1911; p. 1073
TOURING ITALY - VENICE
(Po)/Jan 20, 1912; p. 204
TOURING THE CANARY ISLANDS
(Gau)/Apr 30, 1910; p. 689
TOURING WITH TILLIE
(Be)/Oct 30, 1915; p. 792
TOURIST AND THE FLOWER GIRL, THE
(Imp)/May 24, 1913; p. 813
TOURISTS, THE (Bio)/Aug 17, 1912; p. 669
TOURNAMENT OF ROSES, PASADENA
(Ne)/Feb 22, 1913; p. 782
TOUT'S REMEMBRANCE, A
(SA)/Oct 8, 1910; p. 814
TOWER OF NESLE, THE (Pa)/Sep 25,
1909; pp 416-17/Oct 9, 1909; p. 491
TOWN MARSHALL, THE
(Ne)/Oct 28, 1911; p. 293
TOWN OF COGNAC, FRANCE, AND ITS
BRANDY INDUSTRY
(UE)/Nov 30, 1912; p. 876
TOWN OF NAZARETH, THE
(Am)/Apr 4, 1914; p. 59
TOWN THAT LOOKS ON BISCAY BAY,
THE (Pa)/May 16, 1914; p. 968
TOWN TRAVELER'S REVENGE
(It)/Mar 19, 1910; p. 427
TOWNHALL TONIGHT
(SA)/Oct 21, 1911; p. 207
TOWSER'S NEW JOB
(Gau)/Jan 22, 1910; p. 92
TOY, THE (Maj)/Aug 9, 1913; p. 637
TOY SHOP, THE (Pr)/Jun 27, 1914; p. 1829

(Th)/Dec 7, 1912; p. 977
TRUE BELIEVER, A
  (KB)/Jun 7, 1913; pp 1032-33
TRUE CHIVALRY (Cry)/Jul 12, 1913; p. 205
TRUE COUNTRY HEART, A
  (Bi)/Aug 20, 1910; p. 408
TRUE HEARTED MINER
  (Bi)/Aug 12, 1911; p. 378
TRUE HEARTS (Vi)/Apr 25, 1908; p. 377
           (Sol)/Jul 12, 1913; p. 206
TRUE INDIAN BRAVE, A
  (Bi)/Sep 24, 1910; p. 689
TRUE IRISH HEARTS
  (Dom)/Dec 27, 1913; p. 1545
TRUE LOVE (Pa)/Jul 13, 1912; p. 147
TRUE LOVE, THE (Re)/Aug 3, 1912; p. 446
TRUE LOVE NEVER DIES
  (GN)/Jun 24, 1911; p. 1455
TRUE LOVE NEVER RUNS SMOOTHLY
  (Ed)/Oct 9, 1909; p. 491
TRUE PAL, A (Ne)/Aug 6, 1910; p. 298
TRUE PATRIOT, A
  (Lu)/Oct 2, 1909; p. 450
TRUE TILL DEATH (Me)/Apr 13, 1912;
  p. 143/May 11, 1912; p. 527
TRUE TO HIS MASTER
  (Gau)/Jul 31, 1909; p. 162
TRUE TO HIS OATH
  (UE)/Jan 22, 1910; p. 93
TRUE TO HIS TRUST
  (Ka)/Sep 3, 1910; pp 518-19
TRUE TO LIFE
  (Go)/Oct 26, 1907; pp 542-43
TRUE TO THEIR TRUST
  (UE)/Jan 13, 1912; p. 126
TRUE UNTIL DEATH
  (Mi)/May 25, 1907; p. 187
TRUE WESTERN HEARTS
  (Am)/Feb 14, 1914; p. 810
TRUE WESTERN HONOR
  (Bi)/Dec 10, 1910; p. 1359
TRUE WESTERNER, A
  (Ne)/Nov 18, 1911; p. 551
TRUER LOVE, THE
  (Vi)/Jun 12, 1909; p. 795
TRULY RURAL TYPES
  (Fal)/Jun 12, 1915; p. 1777
TRUNK MYSTERY, THE
  (GN)/Feb 4, 1911; p. 249
  (Lu)/Jun 13, 1914; p. 1541
  (Sup)/May 8, 1915; p. 901
TRUST, THE (Vic)/Jul 17, 1915; p. 487
TRUST BEGETS TRUST
  (Po)/Jan 17, 1914; p. 290
TRUSTEE OF THE LAW, A
  (Lu)/Sep 28, 1912; p. 1276
TRUTH, THE (Ne)/Apr 8, 1911; p. 782/
  Apr 15, 1911; p. 843

TRUTH ABOUT DAN DEERING, THE
  (U)/Mar 13, 1915; p. 1609
TRUTH ABOUT HELEN, THE (Ed)/Nov 13,
  1915; pp 1322-23/Nov 20, 1915; p. 1500
TRUTH IN THE WILDERNESS (Am)/Jul 12,
  1913; p. 185/Jul 19, 1913; p. 321
TRUTH OF FICTION, THE
  (Am)/Mar 20, 1915; p. 1766
TRUTH REVEALED, THE
  (Lux)/Nov 26, 1910; pp 1238-39
TRUTH SHALL PREVAIL
  (Ya)/Aug 19, 1911; p. 466
TRUTH STRANGER THAN FICTION
  (Bio)/Jun 12, 1915; p. 1776
TRUTH WAGON, THE
  (MFC)/Jan 16, 1915; p. 383
TRYING OUT 707 (Sel)/Nov 29,1913; p.1007
TRYING TO FOOL UNCLE
  (Bio)/Jul 27, 1912; p. 343
TRYING TO GET RID OF A BAD DOLLAR
  (KO)/Jul 18, 1908; p. 52
TRYING TO KEEP BEDELIA
  (Re)/Jan 11, 1913; p. 160
TRYOUT, THE (Ed)/Feb 11, 1911; p. 316
TRYSTING TREE, THE
  (Ch)/Sep 21, 1912; p. 1177
TSING, THE YELLOW DEVIL
  (GN)/Apr 16, 1910; p. 599
TUDOR PRINCESS, A
  (Ed)/Jan 10, 1914; p. 173
TULIP, THE (Pa)/Jan 4, 1908;p.11
TULIP STUDY (Kin)/Nov 23, 1912; p. 769
TULIPS (Gau)/Dec 4, 1909;p.800
TUMULTUOUS ELOPEMENT, A
  (Me)/Nov 20, 1909; p. 722
TUNIS, AFRICA (Gau)/May 20,1911; p. 1140
TUNISIAN FISHERIES
  (Ec)/Apr 20, 1912; p. 231
TUNISIAN INDUSTRIES
  (Pa)/Jul 10, 1909; p. 49
TUNN MILITARY TOURNAMENT
  (It)/Jul 22, 1911; p. 127
TUNNELING THE ENGLISH CHANNEL
  (Me)/Jul 27, 1907; pp 331-32
TUNNY FISHERIES IN SICILY
  (Pa)/Nov 9, 1907; p. 583
TUNNY FISHING (Pa)/Aug 26, 1911; p. 541
TUNNY FISHING OFF PALERMO, ITALY
  (UE)/Oct 29, 1910; p. 998
TURKEY TROT TOWN
  (Th)/Jan 31, 1914; p. 545
TURKISH BATH, THE
  (Maj)/Sep 13, 1913; p. 1176
TURKISH CIGARETTE, A
  (Sel)/Aug 26, 1911; p. 542
TURKISH POLICE, THE
  (Ec)/Feb 3, 1912; p. 394
TURKISH RUG, THE

(Cry)/Oct 11, 1913; p. 157
TURN HIM OUT (Sel)/Mar 29, 1913; p. 1337
TURN OF FATE, A
  (Gem)/Sep 21, 1912; p. 1177
TURN OF THE BALANCE, THE
  (Vi)/Aug 27, 1910; p. 462
TURN OF THE CARDS, A
  (Maj)/Feb 21, 1914; p. 947
TURN OF THE DICE, THE
  (Imp)/May 28, 1910; pp 889, 891
TURN OF THE ROAD, THE
  (Vi)/Nov 6, 1915; pp 1141, 1153
TURN OF THE TIDE, THE
  (Rex)/May 10, 1913; p. 598
  (Imp)/Nov 7, 1914; p. 789
TURN OF THE WHEEL, THE
  (SA)/May 1, 1915; p. 728
TURNED BACK (Re)/Sep 12, 1914; p. 1513
TURNED TO THE WALL
  (Ed)/May 6, 1911; p. 1019
TURNING OF THE ROAD, THE
  (Th)/Nov 14, 1914; pp 933, 942
TURNING OF THE WORM, THE
  (At)/Nov 12, 1910; p. 1119
TURNING OVER A NEW LEAF
  (Ed)/Dec 19, 1908; p. 508
TURNING POINT, THE
  (UE)/Aug 14, 1909; p. 225
  (Re)/Jul 29, 1911; p. 211
  (Po)/Feb 24, 1912; p. 691
  (SA)/Mar 16, 1912; p. 962
  (Sel)/May 25, 1912; p. 729
  (Pa)/Sep 6, 1913; p. 1067
  (Fr)/Jan 31, 1914; p. 545
  (Am)/Mar 28, 1914; p. 1682
  (Emp)/Jun 19, 1915; p. 1941
  (Re)/Sep 11, 1915; p. 1833
TURNING THE TABLES
  (Bio)/Dec 24, 1910; p. 1476
  (Ed)/Oct 14, 1911; p. 129
  (Vi)/Dec 28, 1912; p. 1292
  (Lu)/Dec 20, 1913; p. 1411
TURPENTINE INDUSTRY, THE
  (Lu)/Oct 5, 1912; p. 40
TURTLE INDUSTRY, THE
  (Lu)/May 18, 1912; p. 629
TURTLE TRAITS (UI)/Sep 5, 1914; p. 1373
'TWAS EVER THUS
  (SA)/Dec 16, 1911; p. 903
  (Bos)/Oct 9,1915; p.283/Oct 16,1915; p.441
'TWAS THE NIGHT BEFORE CHRISTMAS
  (Ed)/Jan 9, 1915; p. 220
TWEEDLE DUM INSURES HIS LIFE
  (Imp)/Sep 20, 1913; p. 1285
TWEEDLEDUM - AVIATOR
  (Amb)/Mar 18, 1911; p. 603
TWEEDLEDUM AND HIS RESCUERS
  (Amb)/Jul 1, 1911; p. 1523

TWEEDLEDUM AND HIS TRICKS
  (Amb)/Oct 21, 1911; p. 210
TWEEDLEDUM AND THE ADVENTURESS
  (Amb)/Aug 26, 1911; p. 545
TWEEDLEDUM AS A RIDING SCHOOL
  MASTER (Amb)/Feb 17, 1912; p. 583
TWEEDLEDUM IN A CASE
  (Amb)/Feb 11, 1911; p. 318
TWEEDLEDUM IN FINANCIAL DISTRESS
  (Amb)/Jan 27, 1912; p. 304
TWEEDLEDUM IS IN LOVE WITH A
  SINGER (Amb)/Jan 6, 1912; p. 42
TWEEDLEDUM IS LATE
  (Amb)/May 27, 1911; p. 1201
TWEEDLEDUM IS SHY
  (Amb)/Mar 4, 1911; p. 484
TWEEDLEDUM LEARNS A TRAGICAL
  PART (Amb)/Dec 24, 1910; p. 1480
TWEEDLEDUM MARRIES AN AMERICAN
  GIRL (Amb)/Dec 30, 1911; p. 1074
TWEEDLEDUM ON HIS FIRST BICYCLE
  (Amb)/Oct 22, 1910; p. 939
TWEEDLEDUM WANTS TO BE A JOCKEY
  (Amb)/Nov 5, 1910; p. 1061
TWEEDLEDUM'S APRIL FOOL JOKE
  (Amb)/Apr 8, 1911; p. 782
TWEEDLEDUM'S CORPORATION DUTY
  (Amb)/Dec 3, 1910; p. 1298
TWEEDLEDUM'S DREAM
  (Amb)/Jun 10, 1911; p. 1319
TWEEDLEDUM'S DUEL
  (Amb)/Oct 22, 1910; p. 939
TWEEDLEDUM'S EVASION
  (Amb)/Mar 9, 1912; p. 867
TWEEDLEDUM'S FATHER AND HIS
  WORTHY SON (Amb)/Feb 10, 1912; p. 483
TWEEDLEDUM'S FORGED BANK NOTE
  (Amb)/Sep 10, 1910; p. 576
TWEEDLEDUM'S MONKEY
  (Amb)/Oct 21, 1911; p. 210
TWEEDLEDUM'S MOTOR CAR
  (Amb)/Nov 18, 1911; p. 552
TWEEDLEDUM'S NEW YEAR'S GIFT
  (Amb)/Mar 9, 1912; p. 867
TWEEDLEDUM'S RIDING BOOTS
  (Amb)/Sep 30, 1911; p. 976
TWEEDLEDUM'S SLEEPING SICKNESS
  (Amb)/Oct 29, 1910; p. 999
TWEEDLEDUM'S WHITE SUIT
  (Amb)/Sep 16, 1911; p. 790
'TWEEN TWO LOVES (Imp)/Sep 16, 1911;
  pp 776-77/Oct 7, 1911; p. 43
TWELFTH JUROR, THE
  (Ed)/May 3, 1913; p. 487
TWELFTH NIGHT (Vi)/Feb 19, 1910; p. 257
TWENTIETH CENTURY FARMER, A
  (Th)/Nov 8, 1913; p. 613
TWENTIETH CENTURY PIRATE, A

(Vic)/Jul 4, 1914; p. 65
TWENTIETH CENTURY SUSIE
(Jo)/Nov 6, 1915; p. 1140
$20,000 COROT, THE
(Ka)/Mar 29, 1913; p. 1336
**TWENTY-FOUR HOUR AUTOMOBILE
RACE** (Pa)/Jun 25, 1910; p. 1100
20 MILLION DOLLAR MYSTERY, THE (Th)
No.12/Feb 13, 1915; p. 986
No.13/Feb 20, 1915; p. 1141
No.14/Mar 6, 1915; p. 1449
No.15/Mar 13, 1915; p. 1608
No.16/Mar 20, 1915; p. 1766
No.17/Mar 27, 1915; p. 1915
No.20/Apr 17, 1915; p. 393
29-CENT ROBBERY, A
(Th)/Apr 30, 1910; p. 690
TWICE INTO THE LIGHT
(SA)/Nov 20, 1915; p. 1499
TWICE RESCUED (Ed)/Nov 1, 1913; p. 496
(Vi)/Mar 6, 1915; p. 1448
TWICE WON (Bio)/Sep 11, 1915; p. 1832
TWICKENHAM FERRY (Re)/Sep 13, 1913;
p. 1157/Sep 20, 1913; p. 1285
TWILIGHT (SA)/Sep 21, 1912; p. 1175
TWILIGHT OF A SOLDIER'S LIFE
(Gau)/Feb 4, 1911; p. 244
TWILIGHT SLEEP
(MES)/Apr 17, 1915; p. 396
TWIN AND SHOSHONE FALLS, THE
(Gem)/Mar 22, 1913; p. 1221
TWIN BROTHERS, THE
(Bio)/May 1, 1909; p. 554
(Ed)/Jun 28, 1913; p. 1360
TWIN BROTHERS VAN ZANDT, THE
(Lu)/Oct 3, 1914; p. 64
TWIN CINDERELLAS, THE
(Pa)/Jan 21, 1911; p. 144
TWIN SISTER, THE
(Lu)/May 22, 1915; p. 1259
TWIN SQUAWS, THE
(Po)/Sep 23, 1911; p. 893
TWIN TOWERS, THE
(Ed)/May 13, 1911; p. 1080
TWINS (SA)/Aug 10, 1912; p. 545
TWINS, THE (Rex)/Jul 1, 1911; p. 1522
(GN)/Dec 30, 1911; p. 1072
(Imp)/May 31, 1913; p. 922
TWINS AND A STEPMOTHER
(Th)/Feb 14, 1914; p. 810
TWINS AND THE OTHER GIRL, THE
(Th)/Oct 11, 1913; p. 157
TWINS AND TROUBLE
(Ed)/Oct 10, 1914; p. 188
TWINS' DOUBLE, THE (GS)/Apr 4, 1914;
p. 59/Jun 13, 1914; p. 1543
TWINS OF DOUBLE X RANCH, THE
(Fr)/Jun 21, 1913; p. 1254

TWINS OF G. L. RANCH, THE
(Th)/Sep 25, 1915; p. 2177
TWISTED TRAIL, THE
(Bio)/Apr 9, 1910; p. 553
'TWIXT HEAVEN AND EARTH
(Tru)/Sep 27, 1913; p. 1381
'TWIXT LOVE AND AMBITION
(Lu)/Dec 21, 1912; p. 1183
'TWIXT LOVE AND DUTY
(WBE)/Mar 21, 1908; p. 246
'TWIXT LOVE AND FIRE
(Key)/Feb 28, 1914; p. 1089
'TWIXT LOVE AND FLOUR
(Ne)/Feb 7, 1914; p. 677
'TWIXT LOVE AND LOYALTY
(Imp)/Dec 24, 1910; p. 1479
'TWIXT LOVE AND WAR
(Cin)/May 11, 1912; p. 528
TWO AFFINITIES, THE
(Vi)/Nov 14, 1908; p. 379
TWO AFFLICTED HEARTS
(Cin)/Dec 7, 1912; p. 975
TWO AND TWO (Vi)/Mar 20, 1915; p. 1763
**TWO ARTISTS AND ONE SUIT OF
CLOTHES** (Sel)/Aug 9, 1913; p. 635
TWO BANDBOXES (Pa)/Feb 6, 1909; p. 144
TWO BATTLES (Vi)/Aug 31, 1912; p. 880
TWO BEARS, THE (It)/Aug 13, 1910; p. 351
TWO BOLD, BAD MEN
(SA)/Apr 10, 1915; p. 235
TWO BOYS (Lu)/Jan 11, 1913; p. 158
TWO BRAVE LITTLE HEARTS
(Ec)/Sep 14, 1912; p. 1076
TWO BROKEN HEARTS
(Vi)/Oct 17, 1908; p. 308
TWO BROTHERS, THE
(Pa)/Apr 4, 1908; pp 298-99
(KO)/Jul 18, 1908; p. 52
(SA)/Oct 9, 1909; p. 489
(Lux)/Mar 26, 1910; p. 467
(Bio)/May 28, 1910; p. 888
(Vi)/Apr 12, 1913; p. 164
TWO BROTHERS AND A GIRL
(Sel)/Jun 12, 1915; p. 1776
TWO BROTHERS OF THE G.A.R.
(Lu)/Jun 6, 1908; p. 497
TWO BROWNS, THE (Ch)/Dec 9,1911;p.819
TWO BOYS IN BLUE
(Sel)/Nov 5, 1910; p. 1058
TWO CASTAWAYS, THE
(Vi)/Jan 23, 1909; p. 93
TWO CHEFS, THE (Pun)/Dec 7, 1912; p.977
TWO CHUMS LOOKING FOR WIVES
(Pa)/Nov 27, 1909; p. 759
TWO CINDERS (Vi)/Sep 14, 1912; p. 1074
TWO CLEVER DETECTIVES
(Pa)/Sep 12, 1908; pp 201-2
TWO COCKADES, THE

(Lu)/Dec 5, 1914; p. 1383
UNKNOWN HAND, THE
  (Me)/Jul 4, 1914; p. 65
UNKNOWN MODEL, THE
  (Ne)/Mar 23, 1912; p. 1064
UNKNOWN MONSTER, THE
  (UF)/Feb 28, 1914; p. 1070
UNKNOWN TRAVELER, THE
  (UE)/May 4, 1912; p. 425
UNKNOWN VIOLINIST, THE
  (Vi)/Apr 20, 1912; p. 229
UNLAWFUL TRADE, THE
  (Rex)/May 16, 1914; p. 969
UNLIKE OTHER GIRLS
  (Rex)/May 1, 1915; p. 730
UNLIMITED TRAIN, THE
  (Gau)/Jul 9, 1910; p. 85
UNLUCKY ACQUISITION, AN
  (Ec)/Dec 4, 1909; p. 800
UNLUCKY ARTIST
  (Pa)/Jun 20, 1908; pp 533-34
UNLUCKY FISHERMAN
  (Pa)/Feb 5, 1910; p. 169
UNLUCKY HORSESHOE
  (Lu)/Feb 20, 1909; p. 202
UNLUCKY HORSESHOE, THE
  (Ki)/Nov 30, 1912; p. 883
UNLUCKY INTERFERENCE
  (KO)/Jul 20, 1907; p. 314
UNLUCKY LOUEY (Vi)/Sep 25,1915; p.2176
UNLUCKY LUCK (KO)/Jun 6, 1908; p. 496
UNLUCKY MIKE (GN)/Mar 30,1912; p.1166
UNLUCKY OLD FLIRT
  (KO)/Mar 7, 1908; p. 194
UNLUCKY PRESENT, AN
  (Ne)/Jan 13, 1912; p. 127
UNLUCKY SUITOR, AN
  (Roy)/Jun 12, 1915; p. 1777
UNLUCKY THIEF, THE
  Sep 25, 1909; p. 416
UNMAILED LETTER, THE
  (Sel)/Jun 4, 1910; p. 942
UNMARRIED HUSBAND, THE
  (Lu)/Apr 17, 1915; pp 392-93
UNMASKED (It)/Jul 26, 1913; p. 435
UNMASKED BY A KANAKA
  (Me)/Mar 1, 1913; p. 888
UNMASKING, THE
  (Am)/Jun 27, 1914; p. 1829
  (U)/Jan 30, 1915; p. 673
UNNECESSARY SEX, THE
  (Imp)/Oct 9, 1915; p. 254
UNOPENED LETTER, THE (Ed)/Apr 4,
  1914; p. 44/May 9, 1914; p. 821
UNPAID RANSOM, AN
  (Ed)/Apr 24, 1915; p. 555
UNPAINTED PORTRAIT, THE
  (Maj)/Oct 24, 1914; p. 492

UNPLANNED ELOPEMENT, THE
  (SA)/Nov 14, 1914; p. 931
UNPLEASANT DREAM, AN
  (Amb)/Apr 16, 1910; p. 600
UNPROFITABLE BOARDER, THE
  (Ed)/Apr 12, 1913; p. 163
UNPROFITABLE CALL, A
  (KO)/Jan 9, 1909; p. 38
UNREASONABLE JEALOUSY
  (Imp)/Jan 14, 1911; p. 91
UNREDEEMED PLEDGE, THE
  (Maj)/May 2, 1914; p. 673
UNREQUITED LOVE
  (KO)/Jul 4, 1908; p. 12
UNREST (Sel)/Dec 12, 1914; p. 1524
UNROMANTIC MAIDEN, AN
  (Th)/Aug 30, 1913; p. 962
UNSEEN DEFENSE, THE
  (Sel)/Aug 9, 1913; p. 635
UNSEEN ENEMY, AN (Bio)/Sep 21, 1912;
  p. 1176/Oct 9, 1915; p. 252
UNSEEN INFLUENCE, THE
  (Vic)/May 17, 1913; p. 705
UNSEEN METAMORPHOSIS
  (Ec)/Nov 15, 1913; p. 737
UNSEEN TERROR, AN
  (Ka)/Jan 3, 1914; pp 31-32
UNSEEN VENGEANCE, THE
  (Am)/Jan 9, 1915; p. 221
UNSELFISH LOVE, AN
  (Ed)/Oct 1, 1910; pp 747-48
UNSELFISH QUEST, AN (Pa)/Oct 17, 1908;
  p. 306/Jan 2, 1909; p. 11
UNSIGNED AGREEMENT, THE
  (GS)/Jan 24, 1914; p. 414
UNSPOKEN GOOD-BYE, THE
  (Vi)/Oct 2, 1909; p. 451
UNSUCCESSFUL FLIRTATION, AN
  (GN)/Nov 2, 1912; p. 451
UNSUCCESSFUL FLIRTS
  (Pa)/Jul 11, 1908; p. 33
UNSUCCESSFUL SUBSTITUTION, AN
  (Ed)/May 8, 1909; p. 594
UNSULLIED SHIELD, AN (Ed)/Dec 28,
  1912; pp 1278-79/Jan 18, 1913; p. 265
UNSUSPECTED ISLES, THE (Ria)
  No.1/Sep 18, 1915; pp 1996, 2007/
  Sep 25, 1915; p. 2177
UNTIL DEATH (Rex)/Apr 19, 1913; p. 282
UNTIL THE SEA (Sel)/Jan 3, 1914; p. 48
UNTO THE THIRD AND FOURTH
  GENERATION (Sel)/Jan 17, 1914; p. 290
UNTO THE THIRD GENERATION
  (Vic)/Nov 29, 1913; p. 1008
UNTO THE WEAK (Am)/Jan 31, 1914; p.544
UNTO US A CHILD IS BORN
  (Sel)/May 6, 1911; p. 1020
UNUSUAL COOKING

URCHIN, THE (Lu)/Nov 13, 1915; p. 1311
URIAGE AND VICINITY
  (Pa)/Aug 29, 1914; p. 1241
URIEL ACOSTA (GP)/Jul 11, 1914; p. 284
URSULA, THE WORLD'S FASTEST
  MOTOR BOAT (UE)/Nov 20, 1909; p. 722
USE OF DYNAMITE BY UNITED STATES
  ENGINEERING CORPS
  (Vi)/May 17, 1913; p. 704
USEFUL BEARD, A (Pa)/May 2, 1908; p.401
USEFUL PRESENT FOR A CHILD
  (Pa)/Apr 18, 1908; p. 352
USEFUL SHEEP (Key)/Dec 21, 1912; p. 1186
USEFULNESS AT AN END
  (KO)/Jun 27, 1908; p. 548
USELESS ONE, THE (U)/Jan 16, 1915; p.369
USELESS SACRIFICE, A
  (Ec)/May 25, 1912; p. 730
USUAL WAY, THE (SA)/Dec 6,1913; p.1150
USURER, THE (Bio)/Aug 27, 1910; p. 462
USURER'S GRIP, THE (Ed)/Oct 5, 1912;
  pp 22-25/Oct 19, 1912; p. 243
USURER'S SON, THE
  (GN)/Jun 21, 1913; p. 1254
USURPER, THE (Lu)/Feb 5, 1910; p. 168

VACANT CHAIR, THE
  (Pr)/Feb 7, 1914; p. 678
VACATION IN HAVANA, A
  (Ed)/Jul 30, 1910; p. 244
VACCINATING THE VILLAGE
  (Ka)/Feb 21, 1914; p. 946
VACCINATION AGAINST INJURIES
  (Lux)/May 29, 1909; p. 713
VACUUM CLEANER, THE
  (Pa)/Aug 1, 1908; p. 91
VACUUM TEST, THE
  (Imp)/Dec 11, 1915; p. 2033
VAGABOND, THE
  (SA)/Oct 26, 1907; p. 542
  (Pa)/Nov 28, 1908; p. 434/Dec 5, 1908;
      p. 448/Dec 12, 1908; p. 478
  (Rex)/Jul 29, 1911; p. 212
  (Gau)/Nov 18, 1911; p. 550
  (Rex)/Oct 31, 1914; p. 643
VAGABOND CUPID, A
  (SA)/Jan 10, 1914; p. 172
VAGABOND LOVE (Vic)/Sep 11,1915;p.1834
VAGABOND SOLDIER, THE
  (Bi)/Feb 7, 1914; p. 678
VAGABONDS, THE (Ka)/Feb 24,1912; p.689
               (Sel)/Jun 1, 1912; p. 829
               (Th)/Sep 4, 1915; p.1644
VAGARIES OF FATE, THE
  (Lu)/Feb 21, 1914; p. 946
VAGARIES OF LOVE, THE
  (Vi)/Oct 1, 1910; p. 747
VAIN JUSTICE (SA)/Jul 3, 1915; p. 65

VALE OF AUDE, THE
  (Gau)/Mar 12, 1910; p. 383
VALET'S VINDICATION, THE
  (Ed)/Sep 10, 1910; p. 574
VALET'S WIFE, THE
  (Bio)/Dec 5, 1908; pp 449, 457
VALKYRIE, THE
  (Th)/Nov 20, 1915; pp 1500-1501
VALLEY FEUD, THE
  (Mus)/Nov 27, 1915; p. 1665
VALLEY FOLKS (Ne)/Dec 10,
  1910; p. 1360/Dec 17, 1910; p. 1418
VALLEY OF CHEVREUSE, THE
  (CGP)/Oct 26, 1912; p. 343
VALLEY OF HATE, THE
  (KB)/May 1, 1915; p. 729
VALLEY OF HUMILIATION, THE
  (Vi)/May 29, 1915; p. 1432
VALLEY OF LA VIERGE, THE
  (It)/Sep 9, 1911; p. 717
VALLEY OF LOST HOPE, THE
  (Lu)/Dec 26, 1914; p. 1853
VALLEY OF REGENERATION, THE
  (U)/Sep 4, 1915; p. 1645
VALLEY OF REGRETS, THE
  (SA)/Jan 20, 1912; p. 202
VALLEY OF SILENT MEN, THE
  (Rex)/Jun 12, 1915; p. 1779
VALLEY OF THE BOURNE
  (Pa)/Dec 26, 1914; p. 1842
VALLEY OF THE BOURNE, FRANCE,
  THE (Pa)/Sep 13, 1913; p. 1175
VALLEY OF THE LAUTERBRUNNEN,
  THE (CGP)/Mar 22, 1913; p. 1219
VALLEY OF THE MOON, THE
  (Bos)/Aug 22, 1914; p. 1079
VALLEY OF THE UMBRIA, THE
  (Cin)/Mar 2, 1912; p. 780
VALOR'S REWARD
  (Ec)/Mar 13, 1915; p. 1609
VALUABLE HAT, THE
  (It)/Apr 23, 1910; p. 642
VALUE BEYOND PRICE
  (Th)/Dec 10, 1910; pp 1359-60
VALUE OF MOTHERS-IN-LAW, THE
  (SA)/Jun 21, 1913; p. 1251
VALUE RECEIVED (Me)/Nov 30,1912;p.876
VAMPIRE, THE (Sel)/Nov 26, 1910; p. 1236
              (Ka)/Nov 1, 1913; p. 496
VAMPIRE OF THE DESERT, A
  (Vi)/May 31, 1913; p. 920
VAMPIRES OF THE NIGHT
  (GFP)/Mar 21, 1914; p. 1513
VAMPIRE'S TRAIL, THE (Ka)/Jul 25, 1914;
  p. 580/Aug 15, 1914; p. 960
VAN BIBBER'S EXPERIMENT
  (Ed)/Jul 1, 1911; p. 1520
VAN NOSTRAND TIARA, THE

(Bio)/Nov 1, 1913; p. 496
VAN THORNTON DIAMONDS, THE
(Sel)/Feb 27, 1915; p. 1288
VAN WARDEN RUBIES, THE
(Maj)/Oct 25, 1913; p. 382
**VANDERBILT CUP RACE, SANTA
MONICA, CAL., THE**
(Ko)/Apr 11, 1914; p. 213
VANDERHOFF AFFAIR, THE
(Ka)/Aug 28, 1915; p. 1490
VANISHED CRACKSMAN, THE
(Ed)/Dec 6, 1913; p. 1151
VANISHED DREAM, A
(Cin)/Apr 29, 1911; p. 961
VANISHING CINDERELLA
(Pa)/Jun 12, 1915; p. 1778
VANISHING TRIBE, THE
(Ka)/Oct 10, 1914; p. 188
VANISHING VASES, THE
(Ka)/Jul 3, 1915; p. 65
VANISHING VAULT, THE
(Vi)/May 22, 1915; p. 1259
VANITY AND ITS CURE
(Lu)/Mar 18, 1911; p. 603
VANITY CASE, THE (Vi)/May 2, 1914; p. 673
VANITY FAIR
(Vi)/Dec 16, 1911; pp 886-87
(Ed)/Oct 9, 1915; p. 281/Oct 16, 1915; p. 440
VAPOR BATH, THE
(Ko)/Jan 31, 1914; p. 545
VAQUERO'S VOW, THE
(Bio)/Oct 17, 1908; p. 304
VARSITY RACE, THE (Th)/Sep 26, 1914;
p. 1758/Oct 3, 1914; p. 65
VASCO, THE VAMPIRE
(Imp)/May 16, 1914; p. 969
VASES OF HYMEN, THE
(Vi)/Jul 25, 1914; p. 571
VAUDEVILLE STAR'S VACATION, THE
(Pa)/Nov 15, 1913; p. 736
VAUDRY JEWELS, THE
(U)/Feb 13, 1915; p. 736
VAVASOUR BALL, THE (Vi)/Jan 10, 1914;
p. 176/Feb 7, 1914; p. 677
VEGETARIANS, THE
(WF)/Oct 31, 1914; p. 642
VEIL OF HAPPINESS, THE
(Pa)/Jul 15, 1911; pp 19-20
VEIL OF SLEEP, THE
(Lu)/May 17, 1913; p. 704
VEILED LADY, THE
(Cry)/Apr 19, 1913; p. 282
VEIN OF GOLD, A
(SA)/May 14, 1910; p. 785
VELVET AND RAGS
(Th)/Apr 29, 1911; p. 960
VENDETTA (Pa)/Oct 16, 1909; p. 530
(Ecl)/Oct 4, 1913; p. 29

(GK)/Aug 29, 1914; pp 1214-15
VENDETTA, THE/Nov 28, 1908; p. 423
(CGP)/Nov 25, 1911; p. 638
VENETIAN ISLES (UE)/Feb 19, 1910; p. 258
VENETIAN NIGHT, A
(Mas)/Apr 25, 1914; p. 495
VENETIAN ROMANCE, A
(KB)/Oct 11, 1913; pp 157-58
VENETIAN TRAGEDY, A
Nov 28, 1908; p. 422
VENGEANCE (Imp)/Dec 7, 1912; pp 976-77
(Maj)/Nov 1, 1913; p. 498
(SA)/Jun 12, 1915; p. 1777
VENGEANCE BEQUEATHED
(FRA)/Jan 10, 1914; p. 174
VENGEANCE HATH BEEN HAD
(Re)/May 13, 1911; p. 1082
VENGEANCE IS MINE
(Sel)/Apr 19, 1913; pp 280-81
(Lu)/May 23, 1914; p. 1116
(Maj)/Jan 16, 1915; p. 371
VENGEANCE OF DURAND, THE
(Vi)/Feb 8, 1913; p. 571
VENGEANCE OF EGYPT, THE
(Gau)/Oct 19, 1912; p. 251
VENGEANCE OF GALORA, THE
(Bio)/Aug 9, 1913; p. 637
VENGEANCE OF GOLD, THE
(Re)/Jul 25, 1914; p. 573
VENGEANCE OF GUIDO, THE
(Po)/Oct 23, 1915; p. 621
VENGEANCE OF HEAVEN, THE
(Re)/Apr 5, 1913; p. 49
VENGEANCE OF NAJERRA, THE
(Maj)/Feb 14, 1914; p. 809
VENGEANCE OF RANNAH, THE
(Sel)/Nov 27, 1915; p. 1663
VENGEANCE OF THE KABYLE, THE
(Pa)/Mar 29, 1913; p. 1337
VENGEANCE OF THE LION TAMER, THE
(Har)/Aug 21, 1909; p. 253
VENGEANCE OF THE SKYSTONE, THE
(Bi)/May 10, 1913; p. 597
VENGEANCE OF THE VAQUERO, THE
(Ka)/Jun 6, 1914; p. 1408
VENGEANCE OF THE WILD
(Ray)/Jun 5, 1915; p. 1624
VENGEANCE OF WINONA, THE
(Ka)/Nov 14, 1914; p. 931
VENICE (Pa)/May 7, 1910; p. 736
VENICE, CALIFORNIA
(Kin)/Mar 15, 1913; p. 1106
VENICE AND THE LAGOON
(KO)/Jul 25, 1908; p. 69
VENOM AND THE POPPY, THE
(Ed)/Sep 9, 1911; p. 716
VENOMOUS SERPENTS
(Pa)/Jul 18, 1914; p. 432

WANDERERS, THE
(Ka)/Jul 2, 1910; p. 25
(Vi)/Dec 25, 1915; pp 2385-86
WANDERER'S PLEDGE, THE
(Bio)/Aug 14, 1915; p. 1160
WANDERER'S RETURN, THE
(Po)/Dec 9, 1911; p. 818
WANDERING GYPSY, THE
(Am)/Jun 1, 1912; p. 831
WANDERING MINSTREL, THE
(Cin)/Jul 13, 1912; p. 148
WANDERING MUSICIAN
(KO)/Jul 18, 1908; pp 51-52
WANDERING MUSICIAN, THE
(Ka)/Aug 24, 1912; p. 771
WANDERING WILLIE'S APRIL FOOL'S
DAY (Ka)/Apr 16, 1910; p. 598
WANTED - A BABY
(Lu)/May 25, 1912; p. 729
WANTED: A BABY
(Po)/Dec 10, 1910; p. 1359
WANTED, A BURGLAR
(Ed)/Dec 13, 1913; p. 1279
WANTED - A CHAPERON
(Ne)/May 15, 1915; p. 1074
WANTED, A CHILD
(Bio)/Oct 16, 1909; p. 529
WANTED: A COLORED SERVANT
(KO)/Jul 11, 1908; p. 36
WANTED, A GOVERNESS
(Ec)/Feb 3, 1912; p. 394
WANTED, A GRANDMOTHER
(Vi)/Aug 24, 1912; p. 770
WANTED - A HOUSE
(Vi)/Jun 20, 1914; p. 1688
WANTED - A HUSBAND
(Cin)/Mar 15, 1913; p. 1105
WANTED, A HUSBAND
(Pun)/Dec 14, 1912; p. 1083
WANTED, A LEADING LADY
(Ne)/Nov 13, 1915; p. 1314
WANTED, A MAID (Pa)/Apr 11, 1908; p.326
WANTED: A MILITARY MAN
(Lu)/Oct 3, 1908; p 264
WANTED, A NURSE (Vi)/Feb 6, 1915; p.827
WANTED - A PLUMBER
(Ka)/Sep 27, 1913; p. 1392
WANTED, A PRACTICE
(Po)/Aug 24, 1912; p. 772
WANTED, A SISTER (Vi)/Aug 3,1912; p.446
WANTED - A SON-IN-LAW ON TRIAL
(Pa)/Aug 1, 1908; p. 90
WANTED - A STRONG HAND
(Vi)/Apr 26, 1913; p. 380
WANTED - A WIFE (Me)/Apr 27,1912;p.328
WANTED, A WIFE (Re)/Feb 24, 1912; p.691
WANTED, A WIFE IN A HURRY
(Ec)/Aug 31, 1912; p. 882

WANTED: AN ARTIST'S MODEL
(Lu)/Aug 15, 1908; p. 127
WANTED: AN HEIR (Ka)/Aug 1,1914; p.704
WAR (Po)/Oct 15, 1910; p. 876
(Vi)/Dec 9, 1911; p. 800
(Bi)/Apr 26, 1913; p. 382
(Vi)/Sep 27, 1913; p. 1370
(Vi)/Feb 6, 1915; p. 828
WAR AND THE WIDOW
(Ch)/Jul 8, 1911; p. 1587
WAR AT HOME (Gra)/May 29, 1915; p.1433
WAR AT TRIPOLI, THE
(Amb)/Dec 30, 1911; p. 1073
WAR BABY, A (Lu)/Jan 23, 1915; p. 516
WAR BONNET, THE
(Ka)/May 30, 1914; p. 1260
WAR CORRESPONDENT, THE
(Ka)/Mar 22, 1913; p. 1220
(Bro)/Nov 22, 1913; p. 870
WAR CORRESPONDENTS
(It)/Aug 30, 1913; p. 942
WAR DOG, THE (WF)/Feb 21, 1914; p. 948
WAR EPISODE (KO)/Aug 1, 1908; p. 90
WAR IS HELL (Ecl)/May 9, 1914; p. 800
WAR O' DREAMS, THE
(Sel)/Jul 17, 1915; p. 486
WAR OF THE BEETLES, THE
(Imp)/Jun 21, 1913; p. 1253
WAR OF THE CATTLE RANGE, THE
(Bi)/Nov 29, 1913; p. 1009
WAR OF THE LILLIPUTIANS
(Pa)/Jun 6, 1914; p. 1409
WAR OF THE WILD, THE
(Bi)/Apr 24, 1915; p. 558
WAR ON THE MOSQUITO, THE
(Ed)/Sep 7, 1912; p. 975
WAR ON THE PLAINS
(101)/Mar 2, 1912; p. 781
WAR SCENES FROM GERMANY
(Eik)/Jun 5, 1915; p. 1624
WAR STRICKEN LOUVAIN
(Ecl)/Sep 26, 1914; p. 1790
WAR TIME ESCAPE, A
(Ka)/Apr 1, 1911; p. 718
WAR TIME MOTHER'S SACRIFICE, A
(Bro)/Aug 2, 1913; p. 537
WAR TIME PALS (Po)/Mar 26, 1910; p. 468
WAR TIME ROMANCE, A
(Sel)/Aug 10, 1912; p. 546
WAR-TIME SIREN, A
(Ka)/Apr 12, 1913; p. 164
WAR TIME SWEETHEART, A
(Sel)/Jun 5, 1909; pp 754-55
WAR TIME TALE, A
(Pa)/Apr 24, 1909; p. 516
WAR TIME WOOING
(Th)/Jun 17, 1911; p. 1363
WAR WITH HUERTA

(Mag)/Jun 6, 1914; p. 1417
WARD OF THE KING, THE
(Th)/Aug 30, 1913; p. 962
WARD OF THE MISSION, THE
(Bio)/Mar 20, 1915; p. 1763
WARD OF THE SENIOR CLASS, THE
(Maj)/Nov 15, 1913; p. 737
WARD OF UNCLE SAM, A
(Ya)/Dec 31, 1910; p. 1539
WARDEN'S NIGHTMARE, THE
(Pa)/Apr 3, 1909; p. 403
WARDROBE LADY, THE
(SA)/Apr 19, 1913; p. 280
WARDROBE WOMAN, THE
(Vi)/Sep 11, 1915; p. 1832
WARD'S CLAIM (Vi)/Sep 5, 1914; p. 1372
WARDS OF SOCIETY, THE (Pa)/Nov 29,
1913; p. 988/Jan 24, 1914; p. 413
WARFARE IN THE SKIES
(Vi)/Aug 22, 1914; p. 1100
WARM WELCOME, A
(Maj)/Dec 6, 1913; p. 1152
WARMAKERS, THE (Vi)/Nov 15,1913;p.736
WARNER'S WAXWORKS
(Th)/Aug 24, 1912; p. 773
WARNING, THE
(Th)/Oct 12, 1912; p. 144
(SA)/Nov 2, 1912; pp 449-50
(SA)/Mar 28, 1914; p. 1680
(Ecl)/Oct 17, 1914; p. 344
(Maj)/Oct 24, 1914; p. 493
(Tiu)/Dec 4,1915;p.1847/Dec 11,1915;p.2033
WARNING CRY, THE
(Maj)/Apr 11, 1914; p. 213
WARNING FROM THE PAST, A
(Ed)/Jun 27, 1914; p. 1829
WARRANT, THE (Sel)/Jul 29, 1911; p. 211
WARRANT FOR RED RUBE, THE
(Me)/Apr 15, 1911; p. 842
WARRENS OF VIRGINIA, THE (Las)/
Jan 30, 1915; p. 674/Feb 27, 1915; p. 1268
WARRIOR BOLD, A
(Ed)/Jan 29, 1910; p. 127
WARRIOR'S FAITH, A
(Bi)/Mar 11, 1911; p. 543
WARRIOR'S SACRIFICE, THE
(Gau)/Nov 20, 1909; p. 722
WARRIOR'S SQUAW, A (Bi)/Mar 4, 1911;
p. 484/Mar 11, 1911; p. 543
WARRIOR'S TREACHERY, A
(Bi)/Oct 28, 1911; p. 293
WAR'S HAVOC (Ka)/Apr 27, 1912; p. 329
WARSMEN AT PLAY
(KO)/Jun 6, 1908; p. 496
WARTIME REFORMATION, A
(GS)/Jan 10, 1914; p. 174
WARTIME WOOING, A
(Th)/Jun 10, 1911; p. 1319

WAS HE A COWARD?
(Bio)/Apr 29, 1911; p. 957
(ISP)/Feb 6, 1915; p. 842
WAS HE A SUFFRAGETTE?
(Rep)/Jun 22, 1912; p. 1128
WAS HE A HERO?
(Cry)/Sep 12, 1914; p. 1513
WAS HIS DECISION RIGHT
(Lu)/Dec 12, 1914; p. 1524
WAS IT HER DUTY
(Ed)/Jul 17, 1915; p. 485
WAS IT WORTH WHILE? (Ne)/Mar 25,
1911; p. 658/Apr 29, 1911; p. 960
WAS MABEL CURED?
(Vic)/Nov 30, 1912; p. 878
WAS SHE JUSTIFIED?
(Ya)/Feb 25, 1911; p. 432
WAS SHE RIGHT IN FORGIVING HIM?
(Th)/Jun 6, 1914; p. 1410
WAS SHE TO BLAME?
(Rex)/Mar 22, 1913; p. 1221
WASHED ASHORE
(Lux)/Apr 23, 1910; p. 643
(UE)/Jan 21, 1911; p. 144
WASHERWOMEN'S REVENGE, THE
(Lu)/Sep 12, 1908; p. 201
WASHINGTON AT VALLEY FORGE
(GS)/Jun 13, 1914; p. 1542
WASHINGTON IN DANGER
(Th)/Mar 2, 1912; p. 782
WASHINGTON RELICS
(Pa)/Jul 15, 1911; p. 39
(Pa)/Mar 20, 1915; p. 1765
WASP, THE (Sel)/Nov 14, 1914; p. 931
(Am)/Nov 6, 1915; p. 1140
WASTED LIVES (Vi)/Dec 18, 1915; p. 2203
WASTED SACRIFICE, A
(Vi)/Sep 21, 1912; p. 1175
WASTED YEARS, THE
(Pa)/Apr 4, 1914; p. 58
WATCH DOG OF THE DEEP
(Imp)/Jan 17, 1914; p. 290
WATCHMAKER'S HAT, THE
(Ec)/Jun 11, 1910; p. 999
WATER BABIES (Kin)/Apr 26, 1913; p. 381
WATER BEETLE AND ITS YOUNG, THE
(Pa)/Jul 15, 1911; p. 38
WATER CARRIER OF SAN JUAN, THE
(Am)/Dec 11, 1915; p. 2032
WATER CLUE, THE
(Lae)/Dec 25, 1915; p. 2390
WATER CONTEST, A
(Gau)/Feb 4, 1911; p. 243
WATER CURE (Pa)/Aug 1, 1908; p. 91
WATER CURE, THE
(Gau)/Aug 20, 1910; p. 407
(Th)/Nov 15, 1913; p. 737
WATER DOG, A (Key)/May 30,1914; p.1261

WEST WIND (Vi)/Oct 2, 1915; p. 79
WESTERN BORDER, THE
  (KrM)/Mar 6, 1915; p. 1449
WESTERN BRIDE, A
  (Bi)/Oct 28, 1911; p. 293
WESTERN CHILD'S HEROISM, A
  (Ch)/Jun 29, 1912; p. 1228
WESTERN CHIVALRY
  (SA)/Feb 26, 1910; p. 299
  (Lu)/Dec 16, 1911; p. 904
WESTERN COURTSHIP
  (Vi)/Sep 5, 1908; p. 184
WESTERN COURTSHIP, A
  (Pa)/Mar 4, 1911; p. 482
  (Lu)/Aug 3, 1912; p. 446
WESTERN DOCTOR'S PERIL, THE
  (Am)/Sep 9, 1911; pp 717-18
WESTERN FEUD, A (Ne)/Dec 9, 1911; p.819
WESTERN GIRLS (SA)/Dec 14,1912; p.1082
WESTERN GIRL'S CHOICE, A
  (Ch)/Mar 18, 1911; p. 603
WESTERN GIRL'S DREAM, A
  (Bi)/Aug 17, 1912; p. 674
WESTERN GIRL'S LOVE, A
  (Ne)/Jan 6, 1912; pp 42-43
WESTERN GIRL'S SACRIFICE, A
  (Ch)/Oct 22, 1910; p. 938
  (SA)/Sep 23, 1911; p. 889
WESTERN GOVERNOR'S HUMANITY, A
  (Lu)/Nov 13, 1915; p. 1317
WESTERN HEARTS
  (Sel)/Nov 18, 1911; p. 551
  (SA)/Jun 29, 1912; p. 1226
WESTERN HERO, A (Pa)/Jul 3, 1909; p. 12
WESTERN HEROINE, A
  (Vi)/Oct 14, 1911; pp 128-29
WESTERN JUSTICE
  (Sel)/Jun 29, 1907; p. 268
  (Bi)/Sep 17, 1910; p. 633
WESTERN KIMONO, A
  (SA)/Mar 16, 1912; p. 961
WESTERN LAW THAT FAILED, THE
  (SA)/Mar 8, 1913; pp 996-97
WESTERN LEGACY, A
  (SA)/Jun 1, 1912; p. 830
WESTERN LOVE (Sol)/Oct 4, 1913; p. 49
WESTERN MAID, A
  (SA)/Jan 15, 1910; p. 56
WESTERN MEMORY, A
  (Pa)/Sep 30, 1911; p. 971
WESTERN NIGHT, A
  (Ed)/Jan 21, 1911; p. 142
WESTERN ONE-NIGHT STAND, A
  (Bi)/Dec 9, 1911; p. 818
WESTERN POSTMISTRESS, A
  (Pa)/Dec 2, 1911; p. 724
WESTERN PRINCE CHARMING, A
  (Ed)/Jun 8, 1912; pp 942-43

WESTERN REDEMPTION, A
  (SA)/Nov 4, 1911; p. 379
WESTERN ROMANCE, A
  (Ed)/Apr 2, 1910; p. 509
  (Sel)/Jul 12, 1913; p. 204
WESTERN RUSE, A
  (Po)/Apr 15, 1911; p. 844
WESTERN SISTER'S DEVOTION, A
  (SA)/Sep 13, 1913; pp 1175-76
WESTERN TRAMP, A
  (Bi)/Sep 23, 1911; p. 893
WESTERN TRIANGLE, A
  (Rep)/Jun 22, 1912; p. 1128
WESTERN VACATION, A
  (Ne)/Sep 28, 1912; p. 1277
WESTERN WAIF, A (Am)/Jul 15, 1911; p.40
WESTERN WAY, THE
  (SA)/Nov 19, 1910; p. 1176
  (SA)/Apr 3, 1915; p. 64
WESTERN WELCOME, A
  (Me)/Jan 7, 1911; p. 32
WESTERN WOMAN'S WAY, A
  (SA)/Dec 10, 1910; p. 1356
WESTERNER AND THE EARL, THE
  (Th)/Feb 18, 1911; p. 371
WESTMINSTER KENNEL CLUB DOG
  SHOW, THE (Ed)/Jun 15, 1912; p. 1027
WHALE FISHING IN SOUTHERN WATERS
  (Pa)/Apr 3, 1909; p. 402
WHARF RATS, THE
  (St)/May 30, 1914; p. 1262
WHAT A BABY DID
  (Ne)/Mar 14, 1914; p. 1386
WHAT A CHANGE OF CLOTHES DID
  (Vi)/Feb 1, 1913; p. 464
WHAT A CINCH (Lu)/Jul 31, 1915; p. 816
WHAT A DINNER! (Pa)/Dec 17,1910; p.1416
WHAT A PENNYWORTH DID
  (Lux)/Sep 9, 1911; p. 717
WHAT A RAZOR CAN DO
  (Pa)/Feb 29, 1908; p. 169
WHAT A UNIFORM WILL DO
  (Pa)/Mar 6, 1909; p. 270
WHAT A WOMAN WILL DO
  (Ch)/Aug 17, 1912; p. 674
  (Co)/Aug 29, 1914; p. 1215
WHAT BECAME OF JANE?
  (Sel)/Sep 5, 1914; p. 1371
WHAT CAME TO BAR "Q"
  (SA)/Feb 14, 1914; p. 808
WHAT COULD SHE DO?
  (Ed)/Nov 7, 1914; p. 766
WHAT CUPID DID (SA)/Sep 13,1913; p.1175
WHAT DID HE WHISPER?
  (Vi)/Aug 28, 1915; p. 1479
WHAT DRINK DID (Bio)/Jun 5, 1909; p. 753
WHAT FATHER DID
  (Ec)/Nov 16, 1912; p. 659

WHAT GEORGE DID (SA)/Feb 1,1913;p.464
WHAT GIRLS WILL DO
(Gem)/Aug 30, 1913; p. 961
WHAT GOD HATH JOINED TOGETHER
(Vi)/Jun 14, 1913; p. 1136
WHAT GREAT BEAR LEARNED
(Me)/Dec 24, 1910; p. 1476
WHAT HAPPENED ON THE BARBUDA
(Ed)/Sep 25, 1915; p. 2176
WHAT HAPPENED TO AUNTY
(SA)/Apr 29, 1911; p. 958
WHAT HAPPENED TO FATHER
(Vi)/Dec 11, 1915; p. 2026
WHAT HAPPENED TO FRECKLES
(Po)/Dec 20, 1913; p. 1413
WHAT HAPPENED TO JONES
(Wor)/Mar 27, 1915; p. 1914g
WHAT HAPPENED TO MARY (Ed)
No.1/Aug 10, 1912; pp 545-46
No.2/Sep 7, 1912; p. 976
No.3/Oct 12, 1912; p. 143
No.4/Nov 9, 1912; p. 552
No.5/Dec 7, 1912; p. 975
No.6/Jan 11, 1913; p. 158
No.7/Feb 8, 1913; p. 572
No.8/Mar 15, 1913; p. 1104
No.9/Apr 12, 1913; p. 163
No.10/May 10, 1913; p. 595
No.11/Jun 7, 1913; p. 1031
No.12/Jul 12, 1913; p. 204
WHAT HAPPENED TO SCHULTZ
(Jo)/Aug 15, 1914; p. 961
WHAT HE FORGOT (Lu)/Jan 16,1915; p.368
WHAT HER DIARY TOLD
(Am)/Nov 8, 1913; p. 613
WHAT IS IN A NAME (Gau)/Jan 2,1915;p.77
WHAT IS SAUCE FOR THE GOOSE
(Me)/May 3, 1913; p. 488
WHAT IS THE USE OF REPINING
(Bio)/Feb 15, 1913; p. 679
WHAT IS TO BE WILL BE
(Sol)/Dec 17, 1910; p. 1418
WHAT IT MIGHT HAVE BEEN
(KO)/Oct 30, 1908; p. 338
WHAT IT WILL BE
(Lux)/Dec 24, 1910; p. 1479
WHAT KATIE DID (Ed)/Jan 4, 1913; p. 51
WHAT MIGHT HAVE BEEN
(Ch)/May 25, 1912; p. 730
(Th)/Dec 13, 1913; p. 1280
(Maj)/Jan 30, 1915; p. 685
(Imp)/Jul 24, 1915; p. 651
WHAT MONEY WILL DO
(Lu)/May 29, 1915; p. 1431
WHAT NEW YORK IS DOING FOR ITS
DEAF, DUMB AND BLIND
(Ka)/Mar 15, 1913; p. 1103
WHAT ONE SMALL BOY CAN DO

(Vi)/May 2, 1908; pp 404-5
WHAT PAPA GOT (Cry)/Aug 2, 1913; p.538
WHAT PEARL'S PEARLS DID
(Cry)/Jul 18, 1914; p. 433
WHAT POVERTY LEADS TO
(Cre)/Oct 10, 1908; p. 286
WHAT SHALL IT PROFIT A MAN?
(Ed)/Dec 20, 1913; p. 1412
WHAT SHALL WE DO WITH OUR OLD?
(Bio)/Feb 25, 1911; p. 431
WHAT THE BELL TOLD
(Gem)/Oct 26, 1912; p. 345
WHAT THE CARDS FORETOLD
(Ed)/Dec 18, 1909; p. 881
WHAT THE CRYSTAL TOLD
(Maj)/Jan 31, 1914; p. 545
WHAT THE DAISY SAID
(Bio)/Jul 23, 1910; p. 192
WHAT THE DOCTOR ORDERED
(Bio)/Aug 17, 1912; p. 669
(Ka)/Aug 2, 1913; p. 536
WHAT THE DRIVER SAW
(Lu)/Jul 13, 1912; p. 148
WHAT THE GODS DECREE
(WS)/Nov 29, 1913; p. 1009
WHAT THE GOOD BOOK TAUGHT
(Pa)/Jun 21, 1913; p. 1251
WHAT THE INDIANS DID
(Ch)/Oct 21, 1911; p. 210
WHAT THE MILK DID
(Po)/Sep 7, 1912; p. 976
WHAT THE RIVER FORETOLD
(Bi)/Nov 6, 1915; p. 1141
WHAT THE TIDE TOLD
(Re)/Jul 8, 1911; p. 1587
WHAT THE WILD WAVES DID
(Ne)/Oct 25, 1913; p. 381
WHAT THREE TOTS SAW IN THE LAND
OF NOD (Pa)/Apr 3, 1909; p. 403
WHAT WILL BE, WILL BE
(Lu)/Oct 21, 1911; p. 208
WHAT WOULD YOU DO?
(Po)/Mar 4, 1911; p. 484
(Cob)/Oct 24, 1914; p. 491
WHAT'S HIS NAME
(Las)/Nov 7, 1914; p. 792
WHAT'S IN A NAME?
(Lu)/Feb 15, 1913; p. 679
(Be)/Sep 11, 1915; p. 1833
WHAT'S OURS (Vi)/Jul 10, 1915; p. 307
WHAT'S THE MATTER WITH FATHER?
(SA)/Jul 19, 1913; p. 320
WHAT'S THE USE? (Po)/Apr 27,1912; p.330
WHATSOEVER A WOMAN SOWETH
(SA)/Nov 14, 1914; p. 932
WHEAT AND THE TARES, THE
(Vi)/Aug 29, 1914; p. 1241
WHEEL OF DEATH, THE

(Ka)/Jun 28, 1913; p. 1358
WHEEL OF DESTINY, THE
(Rex)/Dec 14, 1912; p. 1083
WHEEL OF DESTRUCTION, THE (Ecl)/
Aug 16, 1913; p. 727/Sep 20, 1913; p. 1286
WHEEL OF LIFE, THE
(Ne)/Jan 31, 1914; p. 545
WHEEL OF THE GODS, THE
(Bio)/Sep 18, 1915; p. 1995
WHEELED INTO MATRIMONY
(Lun)/Feb 13, 1915; p. 986
WHEELS OF DESTINY, THE
(KB)/Feb 1, 1913; pp 444, 465
WHEELS OF FATE, THE (Sel)/Sep 6, 1913;
pp 1045-46/Sep 20, 1913; pp 1284-85
WHEELS OF JUSTICE (Sel)/Oct 7,1911;p.39
WHEELS OF JUSTICE, THE
(Cin)/Nov 1, 1913; p. 497
(Vi)/Feb 27, 1915; p. 1299
WHEELS WITHIN WHEELS
(U)/Mar 6, 1915; p. 1449
WHEN A COUNT COUNTED
(Th)/Sep 7, 1912; p. 977
**WHEN A FELLER'S NOSE IS OUT OF
JOINT** (Vi)/May 29, 1915; p. 1431
WHEN A GIRL LOVES
(Pi)/Jun 28, 1913; p. 1361
WHEN A MAN FEARS
(Th)/Jul 22, 1911; p. 127
WHEN A MAN LOVES
(Bio)/Jan 28, 1911; p. 194
WHEN A MAN MARRIES
(Ne)/Feb 22, 1913; p. 782
WHEN A MAN'S FICKLE
(Ne)/Oct 9, 1915; p. 254
WHEN A MAN'S MARRIED
(Vi)/May 27, 1911; p. 1201
WHEN A MAN'S SINGLE
(Am)/Feb 4, 1911; p. 251
WHEN A WOMAN GUIDES
(Bio)/Apr 25, 1914; p. 516
WHEN A WOMAN LOVES
(Cin)/Jun 14, 1913; p. 1136
WHEN A WOMAN WAITS
(Am)/Jan 9, 1915; p. 222
WHEN A WOMAN WASTES
(Pa)/Aug 23, 1913; p. 843
WHEN A WOMAN WILLS
(Cin)/Dec 13, 1913; p. 1258
WHEN A WOMAN WON'T
(Am)/Mar 22, 1913; p. 1222
WHEN A WOMAN'S FORTY
(Sel)/Sep 5, 1914; p. 1372
WHEN ALGY FROZE UP
(Th)/May 2, 1914; p. 673
WHEN AMBROSE DARES WALRUS
(Key)/Jul 24, 1915; pp 650, 668
WHEN AMERICA WAS YOUNG

(Bro)/Sep 5, 1914; p. 1373
WHEN AN OLD MAID GETS BUSY
(Ec)/Dec 28, 1912; p. 1294
WHEN AVARICE RULES
(Cen)/Nov 6, 1915; p. 1140
WHEN BEAUTY BUTTS IN
(Imp)/Oct 30a, 1915; p. 969
WHEN BEAUTY CAME TO KOSKOB
(Roy)/May 22, 1915; p. 1260
WHEN BESS GOT IN WRONG
(Ne)/Oct 31, 1914; p. 642
WHEN BILLY PROPOSED
(Ne)/Jan 31, 1914; p. 545
WHEN BOBBY FORGOT
(Vi)/Feb 8, 1913; p. 572
WHEN BROADWAY WAS A TRAIL
(Wor)/Oct 31, 1914; p. 656
WHEN CALIFORNIA WAS WILD
(Sel)/Nov 13, 1915; p. 1311
WHEN CALIFORNIA WAS WON
(Ka)/Nov 25, 1911; p. 636
WHEN CALIFORNIA WAS YOUNG
(Vi)/Oct 26, 1912; p. 343
WHEN CAMERON PASSED BY
(Re)/May 29, 1915; p. 1432
WHEN CASEY JOINED THE LODGE
(Vi)/Jul 4, 1908; pp 13-14
WHEN CHARLIE WAS A CHILD
(Pa)/Jul 3, 1915; p. 65
WHEN CHERRIES ARE RIPE
(CR)/Dec 7, 1907; p. 652
WHEN CHILDHOOD WINS
(Pa)/Nov 15, 1913; p. 735
WHEN CIDERVILLE WENT DRY
(Pa)/Feb 27, 1915; p. 1289
WHEN CONSCIENCE CALLS
(Lu)/May 23, 1914; p. 1117
WHEN CONSCIENCE SLEEPS
(Ed)/Oct 9, 1915; p. 252
WHEN COURAGE FLED
(Lu)/Dec 25, 1909; p. 921
WHEN CUPID CAUGHT A THIEF
(Ne)/Jan 23, 1915; p. 517
WHEN CUPID CROSSED THE BAY
(Ne)/May 22, 1915; p. 1261
WHEN CUPID RUNS WILD
(Imp)/Nov 23, 1912; p. 768
WHEN CUPID SLEEPS
(At)/Oct 22, 1910; p. 939
WHEN CUPID WON (Ne)/Aug 23,1913;p.845
WHEN DADDY WAS WISE
(Vi)/May 25, 1912; p. 728
WHEN DARKNESS CAME
(Th)/Aug 2, 1913; p. 537
WHEN DEATH RODE THE ENGINE
(Ec)/Aug 1, 1914; pp 705-6
WHEN DOLLY DIED
(Po)/Apr 26, 1913; p. 381

WHEN DOOLEY PASSED AWAY
(Lu)/Mar 21, 1914; p. 1524
WHEN DREAMS COME TRUE
(Th)/Mar 8, 1913; p. 998
(Key)/Oct 4, 1913; p. 49
WHEN DUMBLEIGH SAW THE JOKE
(Vi)/Apr 17, 1915; p. 392
WHEN DUTY CALLS
(Pa)/Mar 30, 1912; p. 1165
(Cry)/Nov 1, 1913; p. 497
WHEN EAST COMES WEST
(Am)/Aug 5, 1911; p. 295
WHEN EAST MEETS WEST
(Th)/Dec 26, 1914; p. 1841
WHEN EAST MET WEST IN BOSTON
(Ed)/May 9, 1914; p. 820
WHEN EDDIE TOOK A BATH
(Ne)/Jan 30, 1915; p. 673
WHEN EDDIE WENT TO THE FRONT
(Ne)/Jul 18, 1914; p. 434
WHEN EDITH PLAYED JUDGE AND JURY
(Sel)/Oct 26, 1912; p. 342
WHEN FATE DECREES
(Ka)/Jun 21, 1913; p. 1251
WHEN FATE FROWNED
(Re)/Mar 14, 1914; p. 1386
WHEN FATE LEADS TRUMP
(Exc)/Nov 28, 1914; p. 1239
WHEN FATE REBELLED
(Pr)/Jan 16, 1915; p. 369
WHEN FATE WAS KIND
(Ecl)/Dec 5, 1914; p. 1386
WHEN FATHER GOES TO CHURCH
(Fr)/Oct 11, 1913; p. 157
WHEN FATHER HAD HIS WAY
(Lu)/Oct 5, 1912; p. 40
WHEN FATHER HAD THE GOUT
(Ne)/Jul 17, 1915; p. 487
WHEN FATHER INTERFERED
(Lu)/Feb 27, 1915; pp 1287-88
WHEN FATHER WAS KIDNAPPED
(Ne)/May 3, 1913; p. 490
WHEN FATHER WAS THE GOAT
(Ne)/Nov 20, 1915; p. 1501
WHEN FIRST WE MET
(Po)/Nov 25, 1911; p. 639
WHEN FRIENDSHIP CEASES
(Vi)/Oct 25, 1913; p. 379
WHEN GLASSES ARE NOT GLASSES
(Vi)/Sep 6, 1913; p. 1068
WHEN GOD WILLS
(Ec)/Feb 28, 1914; p. 1090
WHEN GRATITUDE IS LOVE
(Ed)/Apr 17, 1915; p. 392
WHEN GREEK MEETS GREEK
(Ed)/May 17, 1913; p. 703
(Vi)/Feb 27, 1915; p. 1287
WHEN HE DIED (SA)/Oct 14, 1911; p. 129

WHEN HE FORGAVE
(Ufs)/Feb 6, 1915; p. 829
WHEN HE JUMPED AT CONCLUSIONS
(Ne)/Mar 8, 1913; p. 997
WHEN HE LOST TO WIN
(Ne)/Nov 29, 1913; p. 1008
WHEN HE PROPOSED
(Ne)/Mar 6, 1915; p. 1449
WHEN HE SEES (Lu)/Jan 3, 1914; p. 48
WHEN HE WORE THE BLUE
(Ne)/Jul 19, 1913; p. 321
WHEN HEARTS ARE TRUMPS
(Ne)/Jul 13, 1912; p. 148
WHEN HEARTS ARE YOUNG
(Bio)/Apr 17, 1915; p. 397
WHEN HEARTS WERE TRUMPS
(Po)/Jul 17, 1915; p. 487
WHEN HELEN WAS ELECTED
(Sel)/Dec 21, 1912; p. 1184
WHEN HER IDOL FELL
(Ne)/May 29, 1915; p. 1433
WHEN HIRAM WENT TO THE CITY
(Jo)/Sep 11, 1915; p. 1834
WHEN HIS COURAGE FAILED
(Ne)/Jul 19, 1913; p. 321
WHEN HIS DOUGH WAS CAKE
(Be)/Sep 18, 1915; p. 1996
WHEN HIS LORDSHIP PROPOSED
(Ne)/Jan 9, 1915; p. 222
WHEN HIS SHIP CAME IN
(Sel)/Nov 21, 1914; p. 1076
WHEN HONOR CALLS
(Ecl)/Sep 26, 1914; p. 1780
WHEN HONOR WAKES
(Lu)/Jan 30, 1915; p. 672
WHEN HUBBY ENTERTAINED
(Ne)/Mar 15, 1913; p. 1105
WHEN HUBBY GREW JEALOUS
(Ne)/Jul 3, 1915; pp 65-66
WHEN HUBBY WENT TO COLLEGE
(Po)/Jan 20, 1912; p. 204
WHEN HUNGRY HAMLET FLED
(Th)/Aug 21, 1915; p. 1317
WHEN HUSBANDS GO TO WAR
(MnA)/Oct 9, 1915; p. 252
WHEN IT STRIKES HOME
(Wor)/May 22, 1915; p. 1274
WHEN IT'S ONE OF YOUR OWN
(Ne)/Jan 2, 1915; p. 76
WHEN JIM RETURNED
(Am)/Apr 26, 1913; p. 382
WHEN JOE WENT WEST
(Ne)/Nov 15, 1913; p. 738
WHEN JOEY WAS ON TIME
(Ed)/Jan 4, 1913; p. 50
WHEN JOHN BROUGHT HOME HIS WIFE
(Lu)/Mar 29, 1913; p. 1335
WHEN KELLEY WENT TO WAR

(Pun)/Aug 7, 1915; p. 998
WHIFFLE'S BALCONY BUDS
(Pa)/Mar 7, 1914; p. 1236
WHIFFLE'S BUSTED ALIBI
(Pa)/Jun 26, 1915; p. 2097
WHIFFLE'S COURTSHIP
(Pa)/Mar 25, 1911; p. 657
WHIFFLES DECIDES TO BE BOSS
(Pa)/Sep 13, 1913; p. 1176
WHIFFLE'S DOUBLE
(Pa)/Mar 4, 1911; p. 482
(Ecl)/Sep 12, 1914; p. 1513
WHIFFLE'S HARD LUCK STORIES
(Pa)/Oct 7, 1911; p. 40
WHIFFLES HAS THE GOUT
(Pa)/Jun 5, 1915; p. 1606
WHIFFLES HAS THE TOOTHACHE
(Pa)/Nov 7, 1914; p. 789
WHIFFLE'S HOME TROUBLES
(Pa)/Apr 29, 1911; p. 958
WHIFFLES HUNTS THE SWAG
(Pa)/May 9, 1914; p. 820
WHIFFLES MISSES MRS. WHIFFLES
(Pa)/Dec 26, 1914; p. 1842
WHIFFLES MOURNS HIS TWIN
(CGP)/Aug 3, 1912; p. 445
WHIFFLES' NEW PROFESSION
(Pa)/Apr 11, 1914; p. 212
WHIFFLE'S NEW SLEEVE
(Pa)/Feb 11, 1911; p. 315
WHIFFLE'S NIGHT OUT
(Pa)/Apr 25, 1914; p. 516
WHIFFLE'S NIGHTMARE
(CGP)/Nov 30, 1912; p. 877
(Pa)/Nov 14, 1914; p. 933
WHIFFLES PICKS A PARTNER
(Pa)/Apr 18, 1914; p. 360
WHIFFLES WINS THE WINSOME
(Pa)/Nov 28, 1914; p. 1233
WHIFFLES WOOS AND TROUBLE BREWS
(Phc)/Oct 30a, 1915; p. 969
WHILE AUNTIE BOUNCED
(Lu)/Jul 25, 1914; p. 571
WHILE BABY SLEPT
(Th)/Jun 21, 1913; p. 1253
WHILE FATHER TELEPHONES
(Ka)/Dec 20, 1913; p. 1412
WHILE FIRE RAGED
(Ecl)/Sep 12, 1914; p. 1494
WHILE JOHN BOLT SLEPT (Ed)/May 17,
1913; p. 685/Jun 21, 1913; p. 1252
WHILE SHE PONDERED HER NOSE
(Vi)/Jan 4, 1913; p. 51
WHILE THE BAND PLAYED
(Bio)/May 30, 1914; p. 1260
WHILE THE CHILDREN SLEPT
(Po)/Aug 2, 1913; p. 538
WHILE THE COUNT GOES BATHING

(Bio)/Aug 2, 1913; p. 537
WHILE THE STARLIGHT TRAVELS
(SA)/Sep 20, 1913; p. 1284
WHILE THE TIDE WAS RISING
(Ed)/Aug 29, 1914; p. 1240
WHILE THERE'S LIFE
(Am)/Sep 6, 1913; p. 1069
WHILE THERE'S LIFE, THERE'S HOPE
(Imp)/May 6, 1911; p. 1020
WHILE WIFIE IS AWAY
(Sel)/Apr 11, 1914; p. 212
WHIM OF DESTINY, THE
(Maj)/May 10, 1913; pp 597-98
WHIMSICAL PEOPLE
(Pa)/Mar 21, 1908; p. 243
WHIMSICAL THREADS OF DESTINY, THE
(Vi)/Nov 8, 1913; p. 593/Dec 6, 1913; p. 1152
WHIP HAND, THE (SA)/Aug 30, 1913; p.961
WHIRL OF DESTINY, THE
(Sav)/Jan 31, 1914; p. 552
WHIRLPOOL, THE (SA)/Sep 4, 1915;
pp 1663-64/Sep 18, 1915; p. 1996
**WHIRLWIND COURTSHIP ON BRADON'S
RANCH, A** (Pa)/Jun 15, 1912; p. 1027
WHIRR OF THE SPINNING WHEEL, THE
(He)/Jul 18, 1914; p. 407
WHISKEY RUNNERS, THE
(Sel)/Sep 7, 1912; p. 976
(Dom)/Oct 3, 1914; p. 66
WHISPERED WORD, THE
(Vi)/Feb 22, 1913; p. 780
WHIST (SA)/Oct 1, 1910; p. 747
WHISTLING HIRAM
(Fr)/May 9, 1914; p. 821
WHITE AND BLACK SNOWBALL, THE
(Vi)/Jul 24, 1915; p. 649
WHITE APRONS, THE
(Ec)/Apr 13, 1912; p. 138
WHITE BONNET, THE
(Ec)/Oct 26, 1912; p. 344
WHITE BRAVE'S HERITAGE
(Ka)/Nov 25, 1911; p. 637
WHITE BROTHER'S TEXT, THE
(Po)/Jun 8, 1912; p. 946
WHITE CAPTIVE OF THE SIOUX, THE
(Ka)/Jul 2, 1910; p. 24
WHITE CHIEF, THE
(Lu)/Jul 25, 1908; p. 72
(Po)/Sep 9, 1911; p. 718
WHITE CLOUD'S SECRET
(Ne)/Feb 17, 1912; p. 583
WHITE DOE'S LOVERS
(Me)/Jul 9, 1910; p. 84
WHITE DOVE'S SACRIFICE
(Gem)/Aug 31, 1912; p. 882
WHITE FAWN'S DEVOTION
(Pa)/Jul 2, 1910; p. 24
WHITE FAWN'S ESCAPE

(Bi)/Dec 2, 1911; p. 726

WHITE FAWN'S PERIL
(Bi)/Oct 7, 1911; p. 42

WHITE FEATHER, THE
(Vi)/Nov 1, 1913; p. 496
(Lae)/Oct 30a, 1915; p. 969

WHITE GHOST, THE (GN)/Jan 17, 1914;
p. 276/Jan 31, 1914; p. 546

WHITE GLOVED BAND, THE (Gau)/Jan 11,
1913; p. 160/Jan 18, 1913; p. 266

WHITE GODDESS, THE
(Ka)/Mar 27, 1915; p. 1932

WHITE HAND SOCIETY, THE
(Bio)/Oct 10, 1914; p. 188

WHITE HERON, THE
(Ch)/Jan 11, 1913; p. 160

WHITE INDIAN, A
(UB)/Sep 21, 1912; p. 1177

WHITE KING OF THE ZARAS, THE
(Cen)/Oct 30a, 1915; p. 968

WHITE LIE, A
(Cen)/Oct 2, 1909; pp 451-52
(It)/Jul 9, 1910; p. 86
(Ne)/Nov 23, 1912; p. 768
(Box)/May 30, 1914; p. 1235

WHITE LIES (Pa)/Jun 14, 1913; p. 1135
(SA)/Oct 17, 1914; p. 335

WHITE LIGHT OF PUBLICITY, THE
(Sel)/Nov 20, 1915; p. 1499

WHITE MAN'S FIRE WATER
(Ne)/Feb 8, 1913; p. 573

**WHITE MAN'S MONEY, THE RED MAN'S
CURSE** (Ka)/Sep 17, 1910; p. 630

WHITE MASK, THE (Lu)/Jan 23,1915; p.493

WHITE MEDICINE MAN, THE
(Sel)/Jul 22, 1911; p. 123
(Ne)/Nov 25, 1911; p. 638

WHITE MOUSE, THE
(Sel)/Sep 5, 1914; p. 1372

WHITE PEARL, THE
(FP)/Oct 23, 1915; p. 630

WHITE PIRATE, THE
(WF)/Dec 19, 1914; p. 1681

WHITE PRINCESS OF THE TRIBE, THE
(Ch)/Oct 1, 1910; pp 749-50

WHITE RED MAN, THE
(Rex)/Aug 26, 1911; p. 543

WHITE ROSE, A (Pa)/Feb 22, 1913; p. 780

WHITE ROSE OF THE WILDS, THE
(Bio)/Jun 10, 1911; p. 1313

WHITE ROSES (Bio)/Jan 7, 1911; p. 32
(Rex)/Oct 31, 1914; p. 642

WHITE SCAR, THE (Uni)/Nov 27, 1915;
p. 1678/Dec 4, 1915; p. 1854

WHITE SLAVE CATCHERS, THE
(Ko)/Jul 11, 1914; p. 256

WHITE SQUAW, THE
(Ya)/Oct 1, 1910; p. 750

(Pa)/Apr 22, 1911; p. 900
(Bi)/Dec 6, 1913; p. 1153

WHITE TERROR, THE
(Uni)/May 22, 1915; p. 1275

WHITE TRAIL, THE
(Pik)/Feb 6, 1915; p. 830

WHITE TULIP, THE
(GN)/Oct 14, 1911; p. 131

WHITE VAQUERO, THE
(Bi)/Nov 29, 1913; p. 1009

WHITEWASHING WILLIAM
(Ka)/Oct 23, 1915; p. 619

WHO BEARS MALICE
(Lu)/May 29, 1915; p. 1432

WHO HAS MY SKY PIECE?
(SA)/Mar 13, 1909; p. 305

WHO DISCOVERED THE NORTH POLE?
(Lu)/Oct 16,1909;p.530

WHO GETS THE ORDER
(Ed)/Apr 8, 1911; p. 780

WHO GOES THERE
(Ed)/Dec 19, 1914; p. 1680

WHO GOT STUNG (Sel)/Oct 10, 1914; p.187

WHO GOT STUNG? (Pr)/Feb 27,1915;p.1288

WHO GOT THE REWARD?
(Bio)/Jan 20, 1912; p. 202

WHO IS BOSS (Pa)/Sep 17, 1910; p. 631

WHO IS GUILTY? (Pa)/Nov 6, 1915; p. 1111

WHO IS IN THE BOX (Cry)/Jul 5,1913; p.49

WHO IS MOST TO BLAME
(GN)/Mar 8, 1913; p. 997

WHO IS NELLIE? (Pa)/Dec 10, 1910;
p. 1358/Dec 17, 1910; p. 1416

WHO IS SHE? (GN)/Nov 12, 1910; p. 1118

WHO IS SMOKING THAT ROPE?
(SA)/Dec 19, 1908; p.508/Jan 9, 1909; p.36

WHO IS THE BOSS
(Po)/Dec 28, 1912; p. 1293

WHO IS THE SAVAGE?
(Lu)/Feb 8, 1913; p. 571

WHO KILLED GEORGE GRAVES?
(Sel)/Sep 12, 1914; p. 1512

WHO KILLED GEORGE LAMBERT
(Gau)/Sep 20, 1913; p. 1286

WHO KILLED HER?
(Amb)/May 28, 1910; p. 891

WHO KILLED JOE MERRION
(Vi)/Dec 25, 1915; p. 2385

WHO KILLED JOHN DARE?
(Ya)/Sep 10, 1910; p. 575

WHO KILLED MAX?
(Pa)/Mar 11, 1911; p. 542

WHO KILLED OLGA CAREW
(Imp)/Nov 22, 1913; p. 870

WHO NEEDED THE DOUGH? (Vi)/Apr 11,
1908; p. 329/Apr 17, 1909; p. 476

WHO OWNS THE BABY?
(Lu)/Nov 25, 1911; p. 637

WHO OWNS THE BASKET?
(KO)/Jul 11, 1908; p. 36
WHO OWNS THE RUG?
(Pa)/Oct 15, 1910; p. 876
WHO PAYS? (Pa)
No.1/May 8, 1915; p. 916
No.2/Apr 24,1915; p.557/May 8,1915; p.916
No.3/May 22, 1915; p. 1261
No.4/May 22, 1915; p. 1261
No.5/May 8, 1915; p. 916
No.6/May 22, 1915; p. 1275
No.7/Jun 5, 1915; p. 1625
No.8/Jun 12, 1915; p. 1790
No.9/Jun 26, 1915; p. 2097
No.10/Jul 3, 1915; p. 65
No.11/Jul 3, 1915; p. 82
WHO SEEKS REVENGE
(Lu)/Aug 8, 1914; p. 837
WHO SHOT BUD WALTON
(Re)/Dec 19, 1914; p. 1681
WHO STOLE BUNNY'S UMBRELLA?
(Vi)/Jan 4, 1913; p. 50
WHO STOLE CASEY'S WOOD
(Lu)/Jan 30, 1909; p. 121
WHO STOLE THE DOGGIES
(Lu)/May 29, 1915; p. 1431
WHO WANTS A HERO?
(Sel)/Feb 6, 1915; p. 827
WHO WAS GUILTY?
(Cin)/Feb 7, 1914; p. 677
WHO WAS THE CULPRIT?
(It)/Jan 7, 1911; p. 34
WHO WAS THE GOAT?
(Cry)/Mar 22, 1913; p. 1221
WHO WILL MARRY MARY? (Ed)
No.1/Aug 9, 1913; p. 636
No.4/Nov 8, 1913; p. 611
No.5/Dec 6, 1913; p. 1150
No.6/Jan 10, 1914; p. 173
WHO WINS THE WIDOW?
(Po)/Dec 10, 1910; p. 1359
WHOLE WORLD KIN, THE
(Ed)/Jul 3, 1909; p. 13
WHOLE TRUTH, THE
(Imp)/May 10, 1913; p. 598
WHO'LL WIN MY HEART?
(Pa)/May 28, 1910; p. 889
WHOM GOD HATH JOINED
(Th)/Jun 15, 1912; p. 1028
(Pa)/Jan 24, 1914; p. 412
WHOM THE GODS DESTROY
(Fl)/Jun 6, 1914; pp 1391-92
WHOM THE GODS WOULD DESTROY
(Lu)/Jul 24, 1915; p. 650
WHOOF, WATCH WHIFFLES!
(Pa)/Jun 20, 1914; p. 1689
WHO'S BOSS OF THE HOUSE?
(Lu)/Oct 12, 1907; p. 509

WHO'S CHAMPION NOW?
(Cin)/Mar 29, 1913; p. 1337
WHO'S TO WIN? (Vi)/Jun 15, 1912; p. 1027
WHO'S WHO (SA)/Sep 10, 1910; p. 575
(Vi)/Nov 25, 1911; p. 637
(Lu)/Jul 11, 1914; p. 255
(Lu)/Jan 2, 1915; p. 75
(Cub)/Oct 30a, 1915; p. 968
WHO'S WHO? (Po)/Apr 6, 1912; p. 42
(Vic)/May 9, 1914; p. 821
WHO'S WHO IN HOGG'S HOLLOW
(Vi)/Jan 2, 1915; p. 75
WHO'S WHO IN SOCIETY
(GK)/Apr 24, 1915; p. 567
WHOSE BABY? (Cry)/Dec 12, 1914; p. 1524
WHOSE HAT IS IT?
(KO)/Jun 15, 1907; pp 237-38
WHOSE HUSBAND? (Vi)/May 8,1915; p.899
WHOSE IS IT? (Lu)/Nov 29, 1913; p. 1007
WHOSE WAS THE SHAME?
(SA)/Jul 3, 1915; p. 64
WHOSO DIGGETH A PIT
(Po)/Jan 10, 1914; p. 173
WHY? (Ec)/May 31, 1913; p. 923/
Jun 14, 1913; p. 1138
WHY AUNT JANE NEVER MARRIED
(Ec)/Sep 27, 1913; p. 1393
WHY "BABE" LEFT HOME
(Th)/May 31, 1913; p. 922
WHY BILLINGS WAS LATE
(Sel)/Apr 3, 1915; p. 63
WHY BRONCHO BILLY LEFT BEAR
COUNTY (SA)/Sep 27, 1913; p. 1371/
Oct 11, 1913; p. 155
WHY GIRLS LEAVE HOME
(Ed)/Oct 18, 1913; p. 264
WHY HE DID NOT WIN OUT
(SA)/Jan 15, 1910; p. 56
WHY HE GAVE UP
(Bio)/Dec 16, 1911; p. 904
WHY HE SIGNED THE PLEDGE
(Lu)/May 30, 1908; p. 481
WHY HE WENT WEST
(Ch)/Feb 4, 1911; p. 249
WHY I AM HERE (Vi)/Dec 6, 1913; p. 1150
WHY JIM REFORMED
(Sel)/Oct 12, 1912; p. 142
WHY JONES REFORMED
(Po)/Jul 9, 1910; p. 86
WHY KENTUCKY WENT DRY
(Fr)/Apr 4, 1914; p. 59
WHY PREACHERS LEAVE HOME
(Me)/Aug 8, 1914; p. 837
WHY RAGS LEFT HOME
(Po)/Jul 26, 1913; p. 430
WHY REGINALD REFORMED
(Th)/Feb 14, 1914; p. 809
WHY THE BOARDERS LEFT

(Ch)/Mar 2, 1912; p. 781
WIFE'S LOVE, A (Po)/Feb 4, 1911; p. 251
WIFE'S ORDEAL, A (Ed)/Jun 12,1909; p.794
WIFE'S STRATAGEM, THE
(Bio)/Nov 14, 1914; p. 931
WIFEY'S CHARMS (Pun)/Apr 11,1914;p.214
WIFEY'S MA COMES BACK
(Lu)/Mar 23, 1912; p. 1063
WIFEY'S NEW HAT
(Lu)/Aug 12, 1911; p. 376
WIFEY'S VISIT HOME
(Bio)/Apr 11, 1914; p. 212
WIFIE'S ATHLETIC MAMMA
(Lu)/Oct 24, 1914; p. 491
WIFIE'S BUSY DAY
(Jo)/Aug 1, 1914; p. 706
WIFIE'S MA COMES BACK
(Lu)/Jul 31, 1915; p. 816
WIFIE'S MAMMA (Lu)/Aug 13, 1910; p. 350
WIG WAG (Vi)/Nov 4, 1911; p.380
WIGGS TAKES THE REST CURE
(Sel)/Aug 1, 1914; p. 704
WILBUR WRIGHT AND H.M. KING
EDWARD VII (UE)/May 15, 1909; p. 634
WILBUR WRIGHT'S AEROPLANE (Pa)/
Apr 17, 1909; p. 473/May 1, 1909;
p. 553/May 8, 1909; p. 593
WILD AND WOOLLY WEST, THE
(Pr)/Dec 12, 1914; p. 1524
WILD BILL'S DEFEAT
(De)/Oct 22, 1910; p. 938
WILD BIRD LIFE (Po)/Dec 18, 1915; p.2204
WILD BIRDS (Pa)/Mar 6, 1915; pp 1448-49
WILD BIRDS AT HOME (CGP)/Apr 27,
1912; p. 311/Jul 20, 1912; p. 243
WILD BIRDS' HAUNTS
(Pa)/Apr 2, 1910; p. 508
WILD BLOOD (Imp)/Apr 24, 1915; p. 557
WILD CAT WELL, THE
(Vi)/Mar 18, 1911; p. 603
WILD COAST OF BELLE ISLE, THE
(Gau)/Apr 2, 1910; p. 509
WILD DUCK HUNTING ON REEL FOOT
LAKE (Lu)/Jan 29, 1910; p. 127
WILD FLOWER AND THE ROSE, THE
(Th)/Dec 10, 1910; p.1358
WILD FLOWER OF PINO MOUNTAIN,
THE (Fr)/Feb 8, 1913; p. 574
WILD GOOSE CHASE, A
(Ch)/Oct 1, 1910; p. 749
WILD GOOSE CHASE, THE
(Las)/Jun 12, 1915; p. 1789
WILD IRISH ROSE, A
(GS)/Apr 17, 1915; p. 394
WILD LIFE IN FILMS
Mar 6, 1915; pp 1462-63
WILD MAN FOR A DAY
(Lu)/Mar 1, 1913; p. 887

WILD MAN OF BORNEO, THE
(Lu)/Jun 25, 1910; p. 1101
WILD OLIVE, THE (Mor)/Jul 3, 1915; p. 77
WILD PAT (Vi)/Dec 7, 1912; p. 975
WILD RIDE, A
(Sel)/Jul 5,1913; pp 28-29/Jul 26,1913; p.428
(St)/Aug 8, 1914; p. 837
WILD WALES (Ed)/Nov 15, 1913; p. 736
(Pa)/Mar 13, 1915; p. 1608
WILD WAVES AT ST. JEAN-de-LUX
(Gau)/Feb 12, 1910; p. 215
WILD WEST COMES TO TOWN, THE
(Maj)/Aug 9, 1913; p. 637
WILD WEST LOVE (Key)/Jan 2, 1915; p. 77
WILDCAT, THE (Lu)/Sep 18, 1915; p. 1995
WILDERNESS MAIL, THE
(Sel)/Jul 25, 1914; p. 572
WILDFIRE (Wor)/Jan 30, 1915; p. 681
WILDFLOWER (FP)/Oct 17, 1914; p. 478
WILDMAN, THE (SA)/Sep 21,1912; p.1175
WILES OF A SIREN, THE
(Ka)/Apr 25, 1914; p. 517
WILES OF CUPID, THE
(Lu)/Aug 2, 1913; p. 535
WILFUL DAME, A (Pa)/Apr 2, 1910; p. 508
WILFUL WALLOPS FOR HEALTH
(StP)/Oct 23, 1915; p. 621
WILL, THE (GN)/May 30, 1908; p. 479
(Ec)/Sep 7, 1912; p. 977
WILL AND A WAY, A
(Th)/Dec 14, 1912; p. 1083
WILL-BE WEDS, THE
(SA)/Apr 19, 1913; p. 279
WILL BLOOD TELL (Lu)/May 9,1914; p.820
WILL GRANDFATHER FORGIVE?
(Pa)/Apr 11, 1908; p. 326
WILL HE OVERTAKE THEM?
(Pa)/Jan 2, 1909; p. 10
WILL IT EVER COME TO THIS?
(Lu)/Jan 28, 1911; p. 196
WILL O' THE WISP
(KB)/Apr 19, 1913; p. 282
WILL O' THE WISP, THE
(Bal)/Jul 4, 1914; p. 77
WILL OF DESTINY, THE
(Me)/Aug 17, 1912; p. 669
WILL OF JOHN WALDRON, THE
(Am)/Aug 31, 1912; p. 881
WILL OF PROVIDENCE, THE
(Sol)/Dec 2, 1911; p. 726
WILL OF THE PEOPLE, THE
(Ed)/Mar 8, 1913; p. 995
WILL POWER (Cry)/Jun 28, 1913; p. 1360
WILL THEY EVER GET TO TOWN?
(Pa)/Nov 14,1908; p.387/Nov 21,1908; p.398
WILL WILLIE WIN?
(Lu)/Mar 22, 1913; p. 1220
WILL YOU MARRY ME?

(Maj)/Jan 6, 1912; p. 42
WILLFUL COLLEEN'S WAY, A
(Ed)/Oct 25, 1913; p. 379
WILLIAM HENRY JONES' COURTSHIP
(Vi)/Nov 14, 1914; p. 931
WILLIAM TELL
(GN)/Apr 3, 1909; p.402/Apr 17, 1909; p.483
(GFP)/May 2, 1914; p. 652
WILLIE (Sel)/Sep 3, 1910; p. 518
(Imp)/Nov 19, 1910; p. 1178
(Sel)/Aug 22, 1914; p. 1100
WILLIE, THE HUNTER
(Lu)/Mar 9, 1912; p. 866
WILLIE, THE WILD MAN
(Th)/Aug 9, 1913; p. 638
WILLIE AND THE MUSE
(Ec)/Apr 25, 1914; p. 518
WILLIE BECOMES AN ARTIST
(Bio)/Aug 10, 1912; p. 546
WILLIE GOES TO SEA
(Sel)/Jun 26, 1915; p. 2095
WILLIE PLAYS TRUANT
(Ec)/Feb 10, 1912; p. 483
WILLIE RUNS THE PARK
(RoU)/Feb 6, 1915; p. 829
WILLIE STAYED SINGLE
(Vi)/Oct 9, 1915; p. 252
**WILLIE VISITS A MOVING PICTURE
SHOW** (GN)/Oct 29, 1910; p. 998
WILLIE WALRUS, DETECTIVE
(Jo)/Jun 27, 1914; p. 1830
**WILLIE WALRUS AND THE AWFUL
CONFESSION** (Jo)/Jul 18, 1914; p. 434
WILLIE WALRUS AND THE BABY
(Jo)/Jun 6, 1914; p. 1409
WILLIE WANTS TO CURE HIS FATHER
(Ec)/Mar 1, 1913; pp 889-90
WILLIE WISE AND HIS MOTOR BOAT
(Ed)/Nov 25, 1911; p. 637
WILLIE'S CONSCIENCE
(Lu)/Nov 4, 1911; p. 379
WILLIE'S DISGUISE
(Cry)/Aug 15, 1914; p. 961
WILLIE'S DOG (Maj)/Sep 14,1912; p.1076
WILLIE'S FALL FROM GRACE (Vi)/
Sep 19, 1908; p. 224/Apr 3, 1909; p. 403
WILLIE'S GREAT SCHEME
(Cry)/Oct 11, 1913; p. 157
WILLIE'S HAIRCUT
(Sel)/Jun 20, 1914; p. 1688
WILLIE'S MAGIC WAND
(KO)/Mar 21, 1908; pp 244, 246
WILLIE'S PARTY (Lu)/Apr 25, 1908; p. 376
WILLIE'S SISTER (Vi)/Jan 27, 1912; p. 302
WILLIE'S TICKER (Lux)/Nov 30,1912;p.878
WILLIE'S WINNING WAYS
(Ya)/Apr 29, 1911; p. 961
WILLING TO BE COURTEOUS

Dec 19, 1908; p. 501
WILLING TO OBLIGE
(UE)/Feb 27, 1909; p. 237
WILLOW TREE, THE
(Vi)/Sep 23, 1911; p. 890
WILLY, KING OF THE JANITORS
(Ec)/Jan 18, 1913; p. 265
WILLY AND THE PARISIANS
(Ec)/Jul 18, 1914; p. 433
WILLY WANTS A FREE LUNCH
(Ec)/Jul 6, 1912; p. 44
WILLYBOY GETS HIS
(Pa)/Dec 25, 1909; p. 920
WILLY'S FIRST CIGAR
(Ec)/Mar 23, 1912; p. 1064
WILSON'S WIFE'S COUNTENANCE
(Vi)/Jul 16, 1910; p. 142
WINDOW ON WASHINGTON PARK, A
(Vi)/May 17, 1913; p. 704
WINDS OF FATE, THE (Ed)/Aug 26, 1911;
p. 540/Sep 2, 1911; p. 610
WINDY DAY, A (It)/Dec 10, 1910; p. 1359
(Lu)/Jun 22, 1912; p. 1126
WINE (Key)/Nov 29, 1913; p. 1009
WINE, WOMAN AND SONG
(SA)/Nov 20, 1915; p. 1499
WINE HARVEST, THE
(Po)/Apr 29, 1911; p. 961
WINE OF MADNESS, THE
(Lu)/Jun 28, 1913; p. 1358
WINGED IDOL, THE
(KB)/Nov 20, 1915; pp 1501, 1507-8
WINGED MESSENGER, THE
(Gau)/Jan 20, 1912; p. 202
(Dom)/Apr 10, 1915; p. 236
WINGS OF A MOTH, THE
(Vi)/Jan 18, 1913; p. 265
WINGS OF LOVE, THE
(Vi)/Jun 4, 1910; p. 941
WINKING PARSON, THE
(Ed)/Dec 21, 1912; p. 1183
WINKING ZULU, THE
(Ka)/Sep 19, 1914; p. 1644
**WINKY WILLIE AND THE TELEPHONE
CRIME** (Me)/Mar 21, 1914; p. 1524
WINKY WILLIE'S ARITHMETIC
(Me)/Mar 14, 1914; p. 1384
WINKY WILLIE'S BIRTHDAY GIFTS
(Me)/Feb 28, 1914; p. 1087
WINKY WILLY AND THE FISHERMAN
(Me)/Feb 14, 1914; p. 808
WINKY WILLY'S DISAPPEARING STUNT
(Me)/Feb 21, 1914; p. 946
WINKY WILLY'S MAXIMS
(Me)/May 23, 1914; p. 1116
WINKY WILLY'S PRIVATE SHOW
(Me)/Apr 4, 1914; p. 57
WINNER, THE (Vic)/Oct 11, 1913; p. 158

(SA)/May 2, 1914; p. 673
WINNER AND THE SPOILS, THE
(Maj)/Oct 19, 1912; p. 244
WINNER LOSES, THE
(Maj)/Feb 22, 1913; p. 781
WINNER WINS, THE
(Vi)/Feb 28, 1914; p. 1087
WINNIE'S DANCE (Ed)/Apr 27, 1912; p. 329
WINNING A PRINCESS
(UE)/Jul 3, 1909; p. 14
WINNING A PRIZE
(GN)/Jul 19, 1913; p. 322
(Imp)/Jan 2, 1915; p. 76
WINNING A WIDOW
(Ka)/Jul 20, 1912; p. 243
WINNING A WINDOW
(Sel)/Sep 18, 1909; p. 380
WINNING AN HEIRESS
(SA)/Jan 6, 1912; p. 40
WINNING BACK (Bro)/Feb 6, 1915; p. 839
WINNING BACK HIS LOVE
(Bio)/Jan 7, 1911; p. 34
WINNING BOAT, THE
(Ka)/Oct 9, 1909; p. 490
WINNING COAT, THE
(Bio)/Apr 17, 1909; p. 476
WINNING HAND, THE
(Vi)/Feb 1, 1913; p. 465
(Pa)/Mar 14, 1914; p. 1384
(Re)/Apr 17, 1915; p. 393
WINNING HIS FIRST CASE
(PD)/Mar 14, 1914; p. 1386
WINNING IS LOSING
(Vi)/Feb 24, 1912; p. 690
WINNING LOSER, A
(Maj)/Sep 27, 1913; p. 1393
WINNING LOSER, THE
(Emp)/Apr 3, 1915; p. 66
WINNING MISS, THE
(Imp)/Jan 20, 1912; p. 204
WINNING MISTAKE, A
(Lu)/Mar 7, 1914; p. 1236
WINNING NUMBER, THE
(KO)/May 16, 1908; p. 444
WINNING OF DENISE, THE
(KB)/Aug 29, 1914; p. 1243
WINNING OF FATHER, THE
(SA)/Mar 5, 1910; p. 339
WINNING OF HELEN, THE
(Maj)/Dec 21, 1912; p. 1185
WINNING OF JESS, THE
(Cen)/Dec 25, 1915; p. 2390
WINNING OF LA MESA, THE
(Am)/Jan 20, 1912; p. 205
WINNING OF MISS LANGDON, THE
(Ed)/Dec 17, 1910; p. 1418
WINNING OF WONEGA, THE
(Bi)/Nov 25, 1911; p. 639

WINNING PAPA'S CONSENT
(Re)/Oct 14, 1911; p. 131
WINNING PUNCH, THE
(Imp)/Jan 8,1910; p.18/Jan 22,1910; pp 91,92
(Vic)/Sep 7, 1912; p. 976
(Bio)/Nov 8, 1913; p. 611
WINNING RUSE, A (Imp)/Feb 8, 1913; p.573
WINNING SMILES
(Cin)/Mar 29, 1913; p. 1336
WINNING STROKE, THE
(Fr)/Jan 10, 1914; p. 173
WINNING THE LATONIA DERBY
(Imp)/Jul 27, 1912; p. 244
WINNING THE OLD MAN OVER
(Bio)/Feb 20, 1915; p. 1139
WINNING THE WIDOW
(Bio)/Oct 16, 1915; p. 439
WINNING TRICK, THE
(Vi)/Aug 8, 1914; p. 836
WINNING WASH, THE
(Ka)/Aug 28, 1915; p. 1479
WINNING WHISKERS, THE
(Ka)/Jan 9, 1915; p. 220
WINNING WINSOME WINNIE
(Lu)/Mar 27, 1915; p. 1931
WINNINGS OF SILAS PEGG, THE
(Rex)/Oct 19, 1912; p. 243
WINONA (Ka)/Sep 24, 1910; p. 696
WINSOME WINNIE (Be)/Oct 24,1914; p.493
WINSOME WINNIE'S WAY
(Ed)/Jul 19, 1913; p. 320
WINSOR McCAY (Vi)/Apr 22, 1911; p. 900
WINTER BATHING IN THE WEST INDIES
(Lu)/Jun 4, 1910; p. 942
WINTER FLOWERS
(Gau)/Aug 19, 1911; p. 463
WINTER HOLIDAY IN BERNES,
SWITZERLAND, A (Ed)/Apr 4, 1914; p. 57
WINTER IN SWITZERLAND
(GN)/Dec 16, 1911; p. 906
WINTER IN UPPER ENGADINE,
SWITZERLAND (Pa)/May 17, 1913; p. 704
WINTER LOGGING IN MAINE
(Ed)/May 11, 1912; p. 528
WINTER MANOEUVRES OF THE
NORWEGIAN ARMY
(GN)/May 23, 1908; p. 463
WINTER SCENES IN THE VALLEY OF
CHAMOUNI, FRANCE
(Pa)/Jan 16, 1915; p. 370
WINTER SPORTS AND PASTIMES AT
CORONADO BEACH (Am)/Apr 6, 1912; p.43
WINTER SPORTS AT BODELE, AUSTRIA
(Pa)/May 3, 1913; p. 487
WINTER SPORTS AT LUCERNE,
SWITZERLAND (Pa)/May 27, 1911;
p. 1200/Jul 1, 1911; p. 1520
WINTER SPORTS IN SWITZERLAND

WRONG ROAD, THE
(Pa)/May 28, 1910; p. 888
(Rex)/Jul 5, 1913; p. 49
WRONG ROAD TO HAPPINESS, THE
(Pa)/May 3, 1913; p. 487
WRONG TELEPHONE CALL, THE
(Amb)/Jul 22, 1911; p. 127
WRONG TRAIL, THE
(Bi)/Nov 5, 1910; p. 1060
WRONG VALISE, THE (Lu)/Aug 22, 1908;
pp 142-43/Nov 14, 1908; p. 379
WRONG WOMAN, THE
(Ed)/May 8, 1915; p. 917
WRONGFULLY ACCUSED
(SA)/Oct 24, 1908; pp 325-26
WRONGLY ACCUSED
(Ch)/Mar 9, 1912; p. 868
(Me)/Nov 16, 1912; p. 658
(UE)/Dec 21, 1912; p. 1183
WRONGLY CHARGED
(KO)/May 2, 1908; p. 401
WUN LUNG'S STRATEGY
(Am)/Sep 21, 1912; p. 1178
WYNONA'S VENGEANCE
(101)/Nov 22, 1913; p. 870

X-RAY GLASSES (Gau)/Dec 18, 1909; p. 881
XENOPHON, A STORY OF THE CIRCUS
(Vi)/Mar 23, 1912; p. 1062

YACHTING OFF COWES
(UE)/Oct 16, 1909; p. 528
YALE LAUNDRY (Bio)/Nov 2, 1907; p. 562
YANKEE DOODLE (Ch)/Dec 16, 1911; p.905
YANKEE DOODLE DIXIE
(Sel)/Mar 15, 1913; p. 1103
YANKEE FROM THE WEST, A
(Majj)/Sep 11, 1915; p. 1845
YANKEE GIRL, THE
(Mor)/Oct 30a, 1915; pp 968-69, 984
YANKEE GIRL'S REWARD, THE
(Ya)/Oct 8, 1910; p. 816
YANKEE IN MEXICO, A
(Pa)/Oct 25, 1913; p. 380
YANKEE MAN 'O WARSMAN'S FIGHT
FOR LOVE (Ed)/Feb 1, 1908; p. 82
YANKEEANNA (Imp)/Aug 20, 1910; p. 408
YAQUI CUR, THE (Bio)/May 31,1913; p.919
YAQUI GIRL, THE (Pa)/Jan 14, 1911; p. 90
YAQUI'S REVENGE, THE
(101)/Mar 14, 1914; p. 1386
YARN A-TANGLE (SA)/May 16, 1914; p.968
YARN OF A BABY'S SHIRT, THE
(Po)/Oct 28, 1911; p. 293
YARN OF THE NANCY BELL, THE
(Ed)/Feb 17, 1912; p. 564
YARN OF THE NANCY BELLE, THE
(Lu)/Jun 14, 1913; p. 1137

YE GODS! WHAT A CAST
(Lun)/Feb 6, 1915; p. 829
YE OLDEN GRAFTER
(Key)/Mar 6, 1915; p. 1448
YE VENGEFUL VAGABONDS
(Sel)/Sep 26, 1914; p. 1776
YEGGMAN, THE (Re)/Mar 16, 1912; p. 963
YELLOW BIRD (Vi)/Jun 29, 1912; p. 1226
YELLOW FLAME (Bro)/Feb 21, 1914; p.948
YELLOW JACKET MINE
(Sel)/Sep 4, 1909; p. 314
YELLOW PERIL, THE (Bio)/Feb 29, 1908;
p. 168/Mar 7, 1908; p. 192
YELLOW SLAVE, THE
(Mel)/Nov 29, 1913; p. 995
YELLOW STAR, THE
(Bi)/Oct 16, 1915; p. 442
YELLOW STREAK, A
(Pa)/Nov 22, 1913; p. 867
(Mto)/Dec 4, 1915; pp 1849-50, 1853
YELLOW STREAK, THE
(Vi)/Aug 2, 1913; p. 536
(Ec)/Nov 14, 1914; p. 933
YELLOWSTONE (Ka)/Apr 3, 1909; p. 403
YELLOWSTONE NATIONAL PARK
(Ed)/Nov 23, 1912; p. 766
YENS YENSEN (Vi)/Nov 14, 1908; p. 379
YES OR NO? (Am)/Dec 25, 1915; p. 2389
YIDDISHER COWBOY, THE
(Am)/Jul 1, 1911; p. 1520
Y.M.C.A. SCHOOL, SILVER BAY, LAKE
GEORGE, N.Y., AUGUST 1911, THE
(Ed)/Nov 25, 1911; p. 638
YOGI, THE (Imp)/Jul 26, 1913; p. 430
YOKOHAMA FIRE DEPARTMENT
(Vi)/Jul 5, 1913; p. 47
YORKSHIRE SCHOOL, A
(Ed)/May 14, 1910; p. 784
YOSEMITE, THE (Key)/Aug 29,1914; p.1242
YOSEMITE NATIONAL PARK
(Ed)/Jan 18, 1913; p. 263
YOSEMITE VALLEY IN WINTER
(Sel)/Mar 8, 1913; p. 996
YOU CAN NEVER TELL
(Sel)/Oct 10, 1914; p. 187
YOU CAN'T BEAT IT
(Nov)/Oct 30, 1915; p. 792
YOU CAN'T BEAT THEM
(Lu)/Dec 12, 1914; p. 1523
YOU NEED A DOCTOR
(StU)/Apr 24, 1915; p. 557
YOU NEVER CAN TELL
(Ba)/Oct 30, 1915; pp 793-94
YOU REMEMBER ELLEN
(Ka)/Mar 16, 1912; p. 962
YOU STOLE MY PURSE
(SA)/Sep 10, 1910; p. 575
YOU'LL FIND OUT (Ka)/Mar 6,1915; p.1447

No.8/Jan 16, 1915; pp 371, 378
No.9/Jan 16, 1915; p. 378
No.10/Jan 30, 1915; p. 673
No.11/Feb 6, 1915; p. 829
ZULU KING, THE
(Lu)/Jul 5, 1913; p. 48
ZULU'S HEART, THE

(Bio)/Oct 10, 1908; p. 285
ZULULAND (Sel)/Apr 29, 1911; p. 957
ZUMA, THE GYPSY
(Cin)/Oct 18, 1913; p. 244
ZUZU THE BAND LEADER (Key)/Dec 13,
1913; p. 1262/Jan 10, 1914; p. 174
ZYLRAS, THE (Pa)/Aug 19, 1911; p. 464

About the Author

ANNETTE M. D'AGOSTINO is Adjunct Professor of Speech Arts at Hofstra University. She is the author of *Harold Lloyd: A Bio-Bibliography* (Greenwood, 1994) as well as numerous articles on Lloyd and the silent film era.

Recent Titles in
Bibliographies and Indexes in the Performing Arts

ISBN 0-313-29381-3

90000>

EAN

9 780313 293818

HARDCOVER BAR CODE